Language Policy and the New Speaker Challenge

'New speakers' is a term used to describe those who have learned a minority language not within their home or community settings but through bilingual education, immersion or migration. Looking specifically at the impact of new speakers on language policy, this book provides an authoritative and detailed examination of minority language policy in Wales, Scotland, Ireland, the Basque Autonomous Community, Navarre, Catalonia and Galicia. Based on interviews with politicians, senior civil servants, academics and civil society activists, it assesses the extent to which interventions derived from a new speakers' perspective have been incorporated into official language practice. It describes several challenges faced by new speakers, before proposing specific recommendations on how to integrate them into established minority language communities. Shedding new light on the deeper issues faced by minority language communities, it is essential reading for students and researchers in sociolinguistics, language policy and planning, language education and bi- and multilingualism.

COLIN H. WILLIAMS is Senior Research Associate at the Von Hügel Institute, University of Cambridge, and Honorary Professor at Cardiff University. He has been a policy adviser to governments in the UK, Ireland and Canada. Notable publications include *Linguistic Minorities in Democratic Context* (2013) and *Minority Language Promotion, Protection and Regulation* (2013).

Language Policy and the New Speaker Challenge
Hiding in Plain Sight

Colin H. Williams
Cardiff University
University of Cambridge

Shaftesbury Road, Cambridge CB2 8EA, United Kingdom

One Liberty Plaza, 20th Floor, New York, NY 10006, USA

477 Williamstown Road, Port Melbourne, VIC 3207, Australia

314–321, 3rd Floor, Plot 3, Splendor Forum, Jasola District Centre, New Delhi – 110025, India

103 Penang Road, #05–06/07, Visioncrest Commercial, Singapore 238467

Cambridge University Press is part of Cambridge University Press & Assessment, a department of the University of Cambridge.

We share the University's mission to contribute to society through the pursuit of education, learning and research at the highest international levels of excellence.

www.cambridge.org
Information on this title: www.cambridge.org/9781009048392

DOI: 10.1017/9781009047326

© Colin H. Williams 2023

This publication is in copyright. Subject to statutory exception and to the provisions of relevant collective licensing agreements, no reproduction of any part may take place without the written permission of Cambridge University Press & Assessment.

First published 2023
First paperback edition 2025

A catalogue record for this publication is available from the British Library

ISBN 978-1-316-51775-8 Hardback
ISBN 978-1-009-04839-2 Paperback

Cambridge University Press & Assessment has no responsibility for the persistence or accuracy of URLs for external or third-party internet websites referred to in this publication and does not guarantee that any content on such websites is, or will remain, accurate or appropriate.

Contents

List of Figures		*page* vi
List of Tables		vii
Acknowledgements		viii
1	The Emergence of the New Speaker Phenomenon	1
2	Popinjays, Pragmatism and Policy: A New Speaker Triptych	31
3	Wales: Normalised Expectations	53
4	Scotland: Cautious Consideration	110
5	Ireland: Tempered Acceptance	154
6	The Basque Autonomous Community and Navarre: Enthusiastic Endorsement	212
7	Catalonia and Galicia: Unalloyed Support?	254
8	The Policy Community and Recommendations on New Speakers	306
9	Conclusion: Contemporary Challenges	336
Appendices		345
Bibliography		348
Index		376

Figures

3.1	Proportion of people (aged three and over) able to speak Welsh, by LSOA, 2011 (Source: 2011 Census)	*page* 56
3.2	Number able to speak Welsh by community, 2011 (By permission of the Welsh Government)	57
4.1	Number of Gaelic speakers in 2011 by local administrative units (By permission of Bòrd na Gaidhlig)	113
4.2	Local authority areas with indigenous Gaelic (By permission of Bòrd na Gàidhlig)	115
5.1	Gaeltacht areas in 2016 (By permission of Ordnance Survey Ireland)	179
5.2	Gaeltacht Language Planning Districts and Service Towns (By permission of John Walsh, University of Galway)	191
6.1	Numerical representation of Basque speakers in BAC, 2016	221
6.2	Proportional representation of Basque speakers in BAC, 2016	222
6.3	Evolution of Basque speakers in BAC, 1986–2016	228
7.1	Place of birth of population, 1981–2020	262
7.2	Students of foreign origin within statutory education, 2009–20	263
7.3	Registrations on CPNL courses, 2017–20	273

Tables

3.1	Schools where Welsh is the sole or main medium of instruction, 2020–1	*page* 67
3.2	Overview of sabbatical course provision, 2021	101
5.1	Lead Organisations by thematic responsibilities	176
6.1	Proportionate change in school attendance by type	224
7.1	First language, language of identification and usual language, percentages 2013–18	260
7.2	Those who declare that they can speak Catalan in 2018	260
7.3	Total and foreign population series, 2000–11, Catalonia	261

Acknowledgements

I have accumulated many debts of gratitude while working on this book, which grew out of my involvement with the EU COST New Speakers Network. Three determined colleagues, Bernie O' Rourke, Maite Puigdevall i Serralvo and Kathryn Jones, inveigled me to be involved with the project and having finally succumbed I offered to focus on the issues which face new speakers and policy makers in formulating new strategies to cope with the demands of language learners, migrants and refugees, three very different categories posing quite distinct challenges.

The volume's immediate origins were two invitations I received in 2017 and 2018. The first was to deliver the plenary opening address to the COST New Speakers Network, Final Action Conference, University of Coimbra, 14 September 2017, which was graciously presented by Dr K. Jones in my enforced absence as a result of recent surgery. The second was the plenary address to the Annual Meeting of the Canadian Federal and Provincial Ministers Responsible for Francophone Affairs, Montreal, 7 November 2018, entitled 'Three Conundrums for Language Policy'. In these presentations I developed variants on a critique of the new speaker phenomenon. My underlying message was that in too many cases policy makers were not dealing with the issues raised by new speakers in a systematic and inclusive manner. I sought to increase their awareness, hence the arguments of this book.

I should like to express my gratitude to St Edmund's College, Cambridge University for inviting me in 2015 to become a Visiting Fellow and continue as a Senior Research Associate of the Von Hügel Institute under its directors Dr Philip McCosker and Dr Vittorio Montemaggi. The first drafts of the volume were written in Cambridge in a most stimulating and fascinating environment. I am happy to acknowledge the support of Dr Dylan Foster Evans, head of school, School of Welsh, Cardiff University where I remain an Honorary Professor.

I am also very grateful to the following individuals and organisations who furnished data, copies of official documents and criticisms of earlier drafts of this volume and without whose detailed insights about their own language planning processes I would not have been able to understand the nuances of policy formulation and implementation. They are Liam Andrews, Jasone Aldekoa Arana, Julia Barnes, Albert Bastardas Boada, Daibhidh Boag, N. O. Bretón, Emili Boix-Fuster, Jasone Cenoz, Ane Crespo, Michael Cronin, Xabier Erize, Xose Gregerio Ferreiro Fente, Mireya Folch-Serra, Pierre Foucher, Jone Goirigolzarri Garaizar, Durk Gorter, Michael Hornsby, Meirion P. Jones, Xavier Lamuela, Joe Le Bianco, Joe Mac Donnacha, Liam Mac Mathúna, Bláthnaid ní Ghréacháin, Pádraig Ó hAoláin, Pádraig Ó Ceithearnaigh, Seán Ó Cuirreáin, Pádraig Ó Duibhir, the late Peadar Ó Flatharta, Tadhg Ó hIfearnáin, Eamonn Ó Neachtain, Fernando Ramallo, Dónall Ó Riagáin, Itxaso Rodríguez-Ordóñez, the late Miquel Strubell i Trueta, Huw Thomas.

Institutional representatives who deserve especial mention include Graham Fraser, former OCOL Commissioner, together with Commissioner Raymond Théberge and his colleagues at the Office of the Commissioner of Official Languages, Canada; Seán Ó Cuirreáin and Rónán Ó Domhnaill and their colleagues at the Coimisinéir Teanga, Ireland; Meri Huws, Aled Roberts and Eleri James and their colleagues at the Welsh Language Commissioner's Office; David F. Vila, Marta Xirinachs i Codina and Vicent Climent-Ferrando of the Secretaria de Política Lingüística Catalonia; Joxean Amundarain, Estitxu Alkorta and Beñat Egues Cuesta of the Gipuzkoa Provincial Council, the Basque Autonomous Community; Seán Ó Coinn and his colleagues at Foras na Gaeilge. Bláthnaid ní Ghréacháin, Ciara Ni Bhroin and Clare Spáinneach of Gaeloideachas; members and staff of Bòrd na Gàidhlig; Douglas Andsell and his colleagues at the Scottish Government; members of Soillse, particularly Iain Campbell and Conchúr Ó Giollagáin; and the Welsh Government, particularly Bethan Webb, Iwan Evans, Llŷr Jones, Catrin Redknapp, Jeremy Evas and Hywel Befan Owen.

I acknowledge with real thanks the small grant funding received from the EU COST New Speakers Network, Soillse, the Welsh Government and IAITH, which enabled me to undertake fieldwork over the period 2013–21. I interviewed four categories of informants, namely: ministers and politicians; senior public servants responsible for language and education policy; civil society agents and activists; academic scholars and think tank researchers.[1] In most cases those interviewed were happy to be identified, given their particular roles within their organisations, and I am grateful to them for their perspectives and insights. Others who were interviewed wished to remain anonymous.

---

[1] Owing to Covid-19 restrictions, some of the proposed face-to-face interviews planned for 2020–1 were conducted either by Zoom or as an exchange of emails, hence the disproportionate references to named individuals followed by 2021, pers. comm.

Whilst working on this book, I have benefitted from stimulating conversations with Bernie O' Rourke, Maite Puigdevall i Serralvo, Joan Pujolar, Kathryn Jones, John Walsh, Jeroen Darquennes, Josep Soler Carbonell, Steve Morris, Gwennan Higham, Wilson McLeod and Stuart Dunmore, all members of the COST Network. In addition, Robert Dunbar, Carsten Quell, Richard Bourhis and Linda Cardinal have been generous with supplying information and observations.

My deep appreciation goes to my dear friend Mireya Folch-Serra of Western University, London, Ontario, Canada who graciously granted permission for me to use her painting *Hidden in Plain Sight* as the cover illustration as it captures the essence of new speakers who, though so often present, go unrecognised.

Finally, I am very grateful for the invaluable professional support offered by Rachel Goodyear, Helen Baron, Isobel Collins and their colleagues at Cambridge University Press.

1 The Emergence of the New Speaker Phenomenon

Introduction

This volume is an exercise in interrogation which attempts to answer the question of whether there is a genuine and sustainable sociolinguistic policy dimension to the new speaker phenomenon. The question would seem to be open to empirical verification by the mustering of observational facts. So many specialists discuss new speakers as part of their repertoire that it must be a significant element in our evolving societal landscape. Be that as it may, does it necessarily follow that such discussions and analyses feed into our official language policies, especially those concerned with minority language communities? That is the question I seek to answer.

Let us start with a preliminary definition of the new speaker concept. Most interpreters identify new speakers as those who relate to and make regular use of a language that is not their first language or the predominant language used within the household as they matured. This is meant to relate to a language they acquired outside of the home, often through the statutory education system or as adult learners. O'Rourke and Walsh (2020) urge us to remember the difference between a 'learner', someone only learning a target language in an educational setting, and a 'new speaker', someone who makes social and economic use of it in other non-institutional settings.

It is immediately evident that such a broad definition can mask a multitude of grades of identification, association and cognitive affiliation. In short it would seem at first sight to be a complex phenomenon and one not easily able to be categorised or manipulated in a consistent manner. The broad range of experiences covered by the new speaker phenomenon will thus be an intriguing subject to dissect and interpret.

In the absence of a single precise definition, together with other emerging debates, such as those on racial linguistics, translanguaging and the impact of the global pandemic, the emergence of the new speaker phenomenon is something of an enigma, a conundrum, almost a paradox. On the one hand there are signs that something unprecedented in scale and volume is happening as more people take on additional identities as a result of linguistic transitioning.

Whether this movement is described in terms of producing super-diversity, hybridity, a melding or a melange of cultures, there is undoubtedly an increase in the range of identities with which we interact in daily life.

On the other hand, to call new speakers a fresh sociolinguistic category is to downplay the many immigration waves in history which peopled settler communities in the USA, Canada, Australia and Argentina, whose progeny matured to become new speakers of English, French or Spanish and who by the third generation had generally shifted their linguistic repertoire from their historic familial language to the language of their native soil. It also ignores the thousands of individuals who, as a result of betterment, economic deprivation or fears of genocide, were forced to quit their homeland, some of whom became stellar representatives of their adopted countries and whose origins could scarcely be detected, such was their mastery of the new language and culture to which they contributed. One need only think of personalities such as Isaiah Berlin, born in Riga in 1909 before moving to the UK in 1921, or André Previn (Andreas Ludwig Priwin), born in Berlin in 1929, whose family settled in Los Angeles in 1938.

It is said that history is a common ground, but it is also a battleground for language contact and conflict. The roots of current difficulties reach back centuries, as is the case in the conquest of Wales and Ireland by the proto-English state and the imposition of the English language and laws by force. The same may be said of Basque and Catalan as these languages and their associated social orders struggled with the imposition of rule from Madrid. Their leading role in Spanish industrialisation and wealth creation did not save them from a more authoritarian impress, made all the more unbearable by defeat in the Spanish Civil War (17 July 1936–1 April 1939) and the subsequent acts of suppression under the dictatorship of General Franco which lasted until his death on 20 November 1975. The transition to democracy, the establishment of seventeen Autonomous Communities under the 1978 Constitution together with the Statutes of Autonomy of the bilingual communities, heralded a new dawn. This new political framework has allowed for a remarkable recovery of self-worth, involving political divergence and the search for economic autarchy, if not always harmony.

However, the long shadow of history still falls on the not forgotten cleavages which are recast in contemporary times in the struggle for linguistic authority and national self-determination. Structural strains and animosities are fuelled by each new discovery of an atrocity unearthed in the archaeology of grievances!

For some, the recruitment and retainment of new speakers into their language rather than a rival one is a driving force that sustains extraordinary efforts which go way beyond rational thought and practice. It is part of the collective struggle for survival. The fact that most new speakers of a minority language also by default have to learn the state's hegemonic language does not deter such enthusiasts, so long as an additional tongue and soul is added to the ledger sheet of the linguistic balance.

Yet describing new speakers as a single, unproblematic category also underplays the inherent complexity of the range of experiences summed together as the new phenomenon. Thus, the experiences of new speakers represent a continuum rather than a single category. The difficulty is in establishing the parameters of this spectrum, for the truth is that many new speakers are hiding in plain sight.

More disturbing still is the realisation that once an attempt is made to translate the needs, interests and aspirations of new speakers into an organised body of fact and action, the resultant policy recommendations can appear fatuous and incapable of being incorporated into mainstream language and educational strategies. Accordingly, the discerning person would abandon the category and seek more tangible, manageable issues. And yet, there is a challenge wrapped up in the phenomenon to be unpicked, rearticulated and refined into realisable policy proposals. My intention in writing this volume is to contribute to this process of understanding the parameters of this new phenomenon without judging in advance its pertinence to decision makers and policy formulation. In that sense it is a study in exploration. Despite the increased energies being expended in the development of new speaker studies, it is surely wise to be cautious, if not overly critical, of the potential which this paradigm holds, lest we promise too much and deliver too little.

We recognise that the new speaker is not a singular identity conferred by naming but rather a plural reality, spearheaded by a language not originally one's own. The academic use of the term refers to those who are fluent regular speakers of languages which were not the dominant language of their rearing in early childhood. The popular use may be less specific and is often used as a synonym for a learner because it would appear to have a less pejorative and more encouraging meaning.[1] This simple distinction in use makes it hard to interpret what precisely is being referred to in official documents and political statements. Does it refer to those who have made some sort of linguistic transition or simply learners who are seeking to gain an improved competence in a chosen language?

An abiding concern of those who work on the issue of new speakers is to construct a satisfactory working definition of the concept and the phenomena it seeks to describe. The definition adopted here refers to individuals who identify with and make regular use of a language that is not their first language. This is

---

[1] See for example its use in Wales, where the term 'siaradwr newydd' is a popular term replacing 'dysgwr' as discussed by Dafydd Iwan on BBC Radio Cymru, Rhaglen Ifan Evans, 15 October 2020; www.bbc.co.uk/sounds/play/live:bbc_radio_cymru (accessed 15 October 2020).

meant to relate to a language they acquired outside of the home, often through the education system or as adult learners. This interpretation may not satisfy all, but it is a good approximation to cover the range of scenarios and situations within which the concepts and paradigms which undergird new speaker discussions may lie.

Rather than be preoccupied with precise definitions, some of the leading scholars in the field aver that despite the lack of definitional precision the concept itself has captured a momentum and a trajectory which is significant both in terms of the specific cases analysed and as an added value approach to language policy analysis.[2]

Soler and Darquennes (2019b) have demonstrated how the new speaker research feeds into a revised approach to language policy, especially in relation to the contribution of more discursive and ethnographically oriented perspectives (Barakos and Unger, 2016; Hornberger and Johnson, 2007; Johnson and Ricento, 2013). A distinction is made between the experience of new speakers in three settings: minority languages, migrant and transnational settings (O'Rourke and Pujolar, 2013). At one level, it is quite legitimate to include all these experiences as relevant to new speakers, but for policymakers such a general categorisation can appear daunting and in consequence may limit their scope of action, for it is hard to know where best to intervene in the many domains which pertain to their initiatives and programmes.

The cynic may reasonably ask why if the new speaker paradigm is little more than a nuanced extension of long-established descriptors, such as advanced language learners, L2 speakers and the like, there should be calls for a fresh appreciation of this phenomenon. Surely enough is known about language learning and socialisation! Accordingly, can we not simply transfer the narratives and pedagogical techniques from the experience of majoritarian languages, such as happens in the learning of Spanish, French and English, to minority language situations? Cannot the great weight of research and practice which has been accumulated in acquiring world languages be applied as best practice to inform developments in the minority new speaker work? Yes and no. There is undoubtedly a great deal of similarity, of common process, whether cognitive or socio-cultural, involved in the acquisition of any additional language. For curriculum development, techniques of instruction, classroom practice, the application of online teaching, terminological development, AI and digital advances and a host of other features of gaining competence in a language, the experience of hegemonic languages is most valuable to minority language development.

---

[2] In interview at Universitat Oberta de Catalunya (UOC), Barcelona, 20 March 2018, both Joan Pujolar and Maite Puigdevall believed that the current emphasis on new speakers had opened up new avenues of enquiry and enriched the methodological and epistemological approaches used in their fieldwork and analysis.

However, certain factors make the automatic transfer into a minority language situation somewhat problematic. Whether by design or convention, the whole apparatus of the state, the economy, the media and social and cultural activities reinforce the utility, legitimacy, prevalence and pressure exerted by a hegemonic language. There is hardly any need for conscious interventionist language planning for English in the UK or the USA as everyday society performs this function most effectively in both conscious and subliminal ways. The most obvious consideration is scale and numbers. The acquisition of English by newcomers or migrants to the UK or the USA boosts the hegemonic position of a well-established dominant language. The acquisition and use of English in Europe or South Asia undoubtedly contribute to the development of New Englishes or new varieties of English which may have a legitimacy all of their own. In both cases the political, communicative power of English is enhanced and becomes a cumulative force for its wider diffusion and relevance.

In contrast, given the smaller numbers of new speakers involved in minority language settings, their net worth as a contributing factor, while valued, is not necessarily going to change the dynamics and diffusion of the language in question, either geographically or in terms of domain and functional usage. In addition, for most newcomers, migrants or refugees, their way into the formal acquisition of the minority language is normally through instruction in the state's hegemonic language. Thus, such learners are often involved in a double language learning process, elements of which may not be completely understood, let alone mastered, for quite some time. Thirdly, the resources available to help learn a minority language will undoubtedly be fewer and presumably less widely used within society. Fourthly, when a new speaker of French or Spanish wishes to engage in a conversation or purchase an item, they have only to step outside their door in Toulon or Seville and conduct an everyday transaction in the default language of the local context, in which they may also earn their living in society. Mutual daily reinforcement and meaningful interaction is the best teacher. By contrast a new speaker of Gaelic or Welsh may find it very difficult to locate another speaker in many domains and even then there is no guarantee that the interaction will be satisfying, regular or sustained. Most people struggle to live full and fulfilling lives entirely through their minority language without constant reference to the ubiquitous majority language. So many basic socio-economic needs may not necessarily be fulfilled within the minority language and thus it is always in competition with the dominant language in the public realm and often with a different mother tongue within the home environment. For all these reasons and others, the stability and reassurance of the minority new speaker experience are assumed to be more fragile than for a learner of a majoritarian language.

A further difficulty in assessing the salience of the new speaker concept is determining what exactly is being discussed in official reports and documents. It is evident that for some their use of the term merely means an additional learner in the classroom or community, whereas for others it denotes an active desire to become fluent in the target language and be accepted as a fully functional interlocutor. Often official pronouncements contain a fair degree of lip service and equivocation, as if by intoning the term new speaker, alongside other elements, the government or official agency is both conscious of, and committed to, the needs of such distinct segments within the population. At other times no such distinction is entertained, and the crude use of the term is merely an apologia, an expedience and a lightly considered appendage to more mainstream considerations. However, it is only by reviewing the evidence over time and by seeking to understand what policy formulators had in mind when drafting official documents for their political masters that one can come to a judgement about the salience of the new speaker concept within official discourse.

By focussing on policy implications this volume has less to say about ethnographic explorations into what it feels like to be a new speaker of a particular language. Rather my aim is to establish what considerations are being made in the provision of policy programmes and interventions to encourage the social integration of new speakers into host communities.

The New Speaker Enquiry

In previous work I suggested that there was little explicit reference to the needs of new speakers in several European government strategies for official language policy.[3] This is a justifiable tendency given the recent nature of interdisciplinary work on new speakers.[4] However, what is missing from the cogent and well-researched evidence undertaken by both the COST New Speakers Network members and others is the perspective of the policy community we seek to influence. It is my contention that, without knowing the predisposition of key decision makers to act so as to strengthen the needs and likely requirements of new speakers in context, well-formulated recommendations will not gain much purchase and would be seen as being one step removed from the

---

[3] In preparation for my plenary address at the Coimbra New Speakers conference in September 2017, I investigated the degree to which the needs of, and considerations related to, new speakers of selected minority languages in Europe were reflected within a variety of official language strategies and policy documents. Based on this search, the plenary address identified some of the current trends and possible challenges faced by those who sought to influence key decision makers and senior civil servants but argued that the emphasis within the New Speakers Network had been mainly on describing and evaluating the needs of new speakers within a variety of domains and contexts.

[4] I am grateful to the Chair of the COST New Speakers Network, Professor Bernadette O'Rourke for encouraging me to undertake this set of interviews and fieldwork as part of the COST impact and engagement mission.

policy landscape they seek to influence.[5] Thus in order to exercise any degree of influence I will argue that we need to address some of the issues, uncertainties and prejudices which decision makers may hold regarding their approach to, and responsibilities for, meeting the needs of new speakers in their communities and networks. Current hegemonic state language policies are often at odds with or slightly removed from the constituent official minority languages within their jurisdiction. How much more so, then, might the interests of new speakers of minority languages be marginalised and in need of being foregrounded within the administrative cultures of senior civil servants and their political masters?

Accordingly, I sought to interview and interact with decision makers, senior civil servants and specialists in several jurisdictions to ascertain how they thought about the issue of incorporating the needs of new speakers into their policy formulation processes. The eight themes I selected for investigation are reproduced below and the full interview questions and permission form template are reproduced in the Appendices.

Key Research Questions
- How can the new speaker concept inform language policy scholarship?
- How do different jurisdictions interpret the role and potential contribution of new speakers to the vitality of the target language population(s)?
- How do decision makers, senior civil servants and politicians interpret the contribution of new speakers to their policy portfolios?
- What have been their responses to date?
- What policy outcomes can be identified in terms of inequalities and social stratification affecting new speakers more directly?
- What are the ideas and beliefs of different sorts of actors about new speakers in a given setting?
- What particular aspect does the new speaker concept illuminate more clearly than other related concepts?
- What are the theoretical and methodological challenges encountered when trying to capture the link between horizontal and vertical layers of governmentality and regimentation?

Approach and Methodology

The salient feature of new speakers is their dynamism for, as a Summary Report of the COST New Speakers Network suggested: 'new speakers are multilingual citizens who, by engaging with languages other than their "native" or

---

[5] The COST Action focussed on the dynamics involved in becoming a 'new speaker' of a language in a multilingual Europe. The Action (2013–17) was part of an intergovernmental framework for European Cooperation in Science and Technology (COST).

"national" language(s), cross existing social boundaries, re-evaluate their own levels of linguistic competence and creatively (re)structure their social practices to adapt to new and overlapping linguistic spaces' (COST, 2018).

The New Speakers Network has produced fascinating data on issues such as the adjustment process undertaken by speakers of additional, non-mother tongue languages; the role of immigration and mobility in inducing someone to become a new speaker; the underlying and trigger factors which conduce to the transition towards being competent and confident in an additional language; the emotional and psychological factors involved with the *mudes* transition;[6] the melding of several disciplines so as to produce a syncretic overview of the new speaker process; the reinforcement of linguistic anthropological methodology as a suitable means of garnering data and evidence; the introduction of the new speaker concept into the public discourse on language, education, the health services, mobility and immigration. I would add that one of the more intriguing characteristics of the experience of becoming a new speaker is its liminal quality for in too many cases the transition is accompanied by ambiguity, confusion, a degree of emotional upheaval and doubt as to whether, even having achieved a high level of confidence, one may fit in to the host community.

In welcoming these fresh insights there is a need to translate the descriptive and ethnographic results into realisable policy recommendations so that the interests of the new speakers may be incorporated into mainstream public policy. This is easier said than done in a crowded policy environment. One of the key determining factors in navigating this busy scene is the attitude, predisposition and value judgement of senior policy advisers and decision makers regarding the necessity and pragmatism of foregrounding new speakers as a policy item. To that end the research investigation sought to interrogate the opinions of decision makers from significant agencies together with senior public servants in several jurisdictions and to report on their views prior to presenting a series of domain-specific policy recommendations which may be of value in the formulation of future policy objectives and best practice actions. These findings were calibrated by discussions with a range of leading actors in the field from academia, politics and civil society so as to contextualise the interpretation.

The investigation sought to undertake a preliminary analysis in respect of three mutually reinforcing areas of work, specifically:

1. To conduct face-to-face interviews and follow-up requests for additional material and opinion from within a select group of senior public servants

---

[6] The *muda* framework 'invites us to rethink the assumed purposes of minority language sociolinguistics and to formulate more general questions of what it means to be a legitimate speaker' (Pujolar and Puigdevall, 2015, p. 170).

and policy advisers. These enquiries were conducted within the following jurisdictions: the Basque Autonomous Community (BAC) and Navarre, Catalonia, Finland, Galicia, Ireland, Scotland and Wales, with supplementary material gathered through interviews in Canada.[7]

2. To explore the potential policy implications of the data and evidence generated from within the New Speakers Network, specifically Work Group 8 and Work Group 9 during their lifespan (2015–17). My active participation within the WG9 and early sight of the final reports of selected Work Groups have allowed me to harvest good ideas and experiences at a variety of levels of interaction and to gauge the tendencies reported within the network as to the relevance or not of the new speaker phenomenon.

3. To extend a long-running interpretation of the official language strategies discussed below and to undertake further work to harness the latest material and insights so as to ascertain how integral (or not) any reference to new speakers is to several of the revised language strategy and policy reforms currently being undertaken.

The resultant interpretation does not offer a systematic comparison of all the jurisdictions, despite using a common interview frame. Rather the focus has been on those agencies most conducive to the promotion of the needs of new speakers and will vary from investigating, for example, the community enterprise organisations in Wales, the Gaelic parental support agency in Scotland and the work of the Consorci and Voluntariat per la Llengua in Catalonia. Whilst not claiming that such agencies are fully representative of each country, they do at least offer valuable insights into how localised, ground-up interventions manage the challenge of offering additional opportunities for the integration of new speakers into the community and its networks. Each case study is prefaced by contextualised data on demographic trends, educational overviews and idiosyncratic features not necessarily replicated elsewhere.

I am conscious that this analysis concentrates on a small sample of minority language jurisdictions, but in principle several of the recommendations and examples of good practice should be transferable to other contexts, either in terms of raising awareness or in relation to broad policy developments in education, local administration, community engagement and civil–government interactions.[8] Of course, the long-term aim is to influence outcome-related behaviour through such policy interventions. I am also conscious that there may be an element of composition or confirmatory bias in some of the answers and discourses, as some of the proponents of a new speaker perspective may

---

[7] Advice from members of the COST NS network was sought to identify key interviewees in Catalonia, Finland and Ireland.
[8] Cornwall, the Isle of Man and the Channel Islands do not figure in this analysis.

seek to exaggerate the impact which this new awareness has either on their work or on those organisations with which they have dealings.

One feature of the New Speakers Network interaction was the production of a wide array of publications describing the situation in many jurisdictions and the related aspects of the transformative processes by which new speakers were produced.[9] A second feature was the attempt to engage and empower local communities in discussing a range of issues and aspects of how new speakers were welcomed and treated.[10] A third was the production of a set of guidelines to stakeholders. However, to date there is little evidence on whether the guidelines have been adopted or have had a positive effect.[11] It could be argued that it is too early to expect such an impact and a better gauge would be to test to what extent the concepts discussed within the network appear in the next round of official language strategies being prepared currently. Nevertheless, the interviews which were conducted sought to find material related to changed attitudes, more inclusive behaviour and plans for the future.

Official Language Strategies

In order to gauge the future impact of a new speaker perspective on language policy it is necessary to outline the embedded context of thought and action represented within and by official language strategies. This is intended as a framework to gauge how reactive they may be to including aspects of new speaker considerations and to offer an overview as to how formulators of strategies conceive and manage the needs of the diverse population groups which constitute their audience. A subsidiary justification is to enable those who wish to advance the cause of new speakers to know how and where to influence official strategies in the name of civil society.[12]

---

[9] However, there is one ironic feature of an Action designed to analyse 'New Speakers in a Changing Multilingual Europe', namely the hegemonic position of written English as most of the network's outputs are in English. This may be the nature of the academic publishing beast, but to mitigate this somewhat it would be good to anticipate a range of future publications in Polish, Catalan, Irish and Galician (even if some of these are national reports to a 'local' readership).

[10] Many of the meetings held under the auspices of this Action were in fact at least bilingual if not more generally multilingual, so that the contributors practise what they preach about the value of linguistic diversity.

[11] Many of the Action activities took place in a wide variety of contexts – academic, stakeholder, lobby group meetings – resulting in a very good geographical spread, both large and small polities and jurisdictions and with the co-operation of many institutions.

[12] Earlier work on comparing official language strategies may be found in Williams (2013; 2015). My original interest was prompted by an invitation to contribute to the thinking of the NPLD and its preparation of a European Language Roadmap.

The following strategies were subjected to a detailed analysis in terms of aims, content, methodology and implementation:

> Criterios para la normalización del uso del euskera en las administraciones públicas (Eusko Jaurlaritza, 2007)
> Plan general de promoción del uso del euskera (Eusko Jaurlaritza, 2003)
> Iaith Pawb (Welsh Government, 2003)
> A Living Language: A Language for Living (Welsh Government, 2011)
> 20-Year Strategy for the Irish Language (Government of Ireland, 2010)
> Plan general de normalización lingüística (Xunta de Galicia, 2004)
> Plan general de normalización lingüística del catalán en las Islas Baleares (Comunidad Autónoma de las Islas Baleares, 2009)
> The Roadmap for Canada's Linguistic Duality 2008–2013 (Government of Canada, 2008)
> Pla general de normalització lingüística (Generalitat de Catalunya, 1995)
> First National Plan for Gaelic 2007–12 (Scotland, 2006)
> National Gaelic Language Plan II (Scotland, 2011)
> Plan xeral de normalización da lingua galega (Xunta de Galicia 2008)
> Development Plan of the Estonian Language, 2011–2017 (Estonian Language Foundation, 2011).

Additional detailed investigation was carried out for their successor strategies in the decade 2011–21. None of the strategies which held sway for the period 2000–17 includes a specific section on new speakers per se, and where there is any mention at all it is usually in a commonplace reference to additional or new speakers of Basque/Catalan/Irish/Welsh being welcomed and not to any transitional identity process as encapsulated in the *muda* concept. However, the latest iterations of the Gaelic and the Basque strategy in Navarre do include sections on and reference to the relevance of new speakers and this might act as a precedent for additional references in future language strategy revisions elsewhere.

The desire to influence behaviour so as to promote the target official language(s) certainly informs this current analysis as it is the logical corollary of advancing best practice language policy. At one level this is the stock-in-trade of all public policy, namely, to identify and then action realistic targets so as to fulfil the legal or political obligations of the state or local state. But at another level behavioural modification is also part of the evolving science of 'nudge theory' whereby those in authority seek to modify behaviour, usually in an indirect manner.

While official regional and minority languages are our focus, the discussion relates consciously and explicitly to a broader language continuum including, by definition, official state languages with a global reach, such as Spanish and English, for they are the default operative languages of authority, officialdom and citizen–state interaction in many cases. Regardless of whether or not we typify the relationship between the prevailing state language and a localised language as the interaction between dominant and subordinate, hegemonic and non-hegemonic or majoritarian and minoritised languages, the key issue is that this interactive relationship is at the heart of the manner in which we manage the myriad needs of speakers in tandem. In consequence, the tone adopted in this volume is one of inclusion not exclusion, of multiplicity not uniqueness and of the often flexible, hybrid and idiosyncratic nature of sociolinguistic change rather than adherence to some notion of linguistic purity or conservation. Ultimately, the fundamental question is whether or not language strategies are effective and if so which elements of good practice and new recommendations can be identified so as to inform future policy and debate in this field.

Turning to notable absences in most strategies it is evident that hardly any of them discuss issues of added economic value, finance, setting budgets or identifying target thresholds by which progress may be measured.[13] Canada has been the pioneer in inculcating within its strategies strong elements of fiscal evaluation and justifications for its linguistic duality approach in terms of value added, which is linked strongly to the view that the language skills of its citizens and public servants are an economic asset, a resource to be nurtured by the system. Indeed, the very essence of the current Action Plan 2018–2023 is encapsulated in its title 'Investing in Our Future' and each of the three pillars of involvement is accompanied by detailed targeted budgets. Appendix 1 of the Action Plan summarises the cumulative expenditure over the first five years of the long-term strategy totalling 2,653.91 ($m) between 2018 and 2023. Clearly this level of detail is meant to reassure citizens that the current government is fully committed to official languages. But it is also intended as an indictment of the relative lack of funding expended by the earlier Conservative Governments led by Prime Minister Harper between 2008 and 2015.

A second lacuna is the relative absence of discussion on outcomes as opposed to outputs. Behaviour-changing strategies derived from social psychology, behavioural science, applied economics and public administration are ripe for inclusion in the current round of strategies being prepared as so much of the justification for moving things forward is to increase the actual use of the target languages in as many domains as possible. In several other government strategies, nudge theory and other intellectual frameworks derived from behavioural economics have already established themselves as proven instruments informing policy. Thus, one can expect to see a far greater reference to key concepts such as the design of choices and encouraging positive helpful

---

[13] This lacuna has much to do with the broader culture of the public service within a state or region.

decisions, together with more subtle indirect techniques of persuasion and behaviour-changing impulses.

Many universities now have institutes which are devoted to analysing and influencing policy options, such as the Bennett Institute of Cambridge University[14] which seeks to focus upon: 'the promise of digital government; the growing imperative to bring a place-based perspective into the understanding and practice of policymaking; the imbalanced and unpredictable character of the emerging digital economy; the need to interrogate and reconfigure the relationship between science and democracy' (Bennett Institute, 2020). An intriguing feature of this Institute's commitment is to harness local knowledge as stated: 'We will go further still and explore the limitations of the state's understanding of its peoples – despite the stocks of knowledge it holds about them – and explore how policymaking might better engage and harness local, situated forms of knowledge and identity' (Bennett Institute, 2020). Such think tanks, if they could also be persuaded to focus on the plight of lesser-used languages and the manner in which policies designed to address their needs are actually implemented, would go a long way to answering several of the questions raised in this volume.

However, the best-known instigator within the UK policy sector is the work of Nesta: The Innovation Foundation which seeks to provide robust answers to several challenges, such as boosting economic performance, translating innovative designs into manufacturing production, innovation mapping and testing innovation in the real world, whilst their Innovation in International Development programme is organised around four interconnected themes: 1. How to fund innovation, 2. How to organise for innovation, 3. How to harness new partnerships and collaborations, 4. How to scale innovations and change systems.[15]

These elements are important for they seek to track the whole process of innovation from the design stage to the change-inducing triggers required. Too often in my survey of official language strategies and interviews with their formulators, other senior civil servants and academic specialists, all were content to itemise issues of funding, or partnership and co-creation, but were silent as regards how to bring about the most fundamental outcome, namely behavioural change in language interaction. Put starkly, how to change language regimes and language systems did not figure often. Now, one can be sympathetic to the framers of documents if they refrain from claiming too much for their programme aims, but to abrogate responsibility for charting and guiding change is not advisable especially as the whole aim of the strategy is

---

[14] www.bennettinstitute.cam.ac.uk/blog/new-public-policy-institute-age-disruption/.
[15] Formerly Nesta, National Endowment for Science, Technology and the Arts, which was established in 1998 with an £250 million endowment from the UK National Lottery and in 2012 became an independent charity.

to intervene so as to change the status quo ante! I am confident that as developments in other spheres of policymaking will filter across, we shall see much more reference to, and action plans for, behavioural modification in boosting language use.

A further area ripe for improvement is the capacity of the authorities to gather time-series data so as to construct evidence-based policy. There is a general concern about the range and quality of data associated with the preparation and evaluation of language strategies. Whilst calling for core sociolinguistic and economic data regarding language, I am acutely conscious that in so many jurisdictions even the most fundamental source of population data, the decennial census count, is undergoing widespread change. This change threatens to no longer include language-related questions, either because they are better garnered from more frequent sample surveys which can ask a range of questions and then be aggregated to cover the whole of the population, or because those in authority wish to ask questions about more recent societal trends, such as the availability and use of digital technologies in the household or access to the Internet for online shopping in a post-Covid environment. Even when robust evidence is available it is often subject to challenge, such is the contested nature of the public space in these trying times.

Official language strategies offer an insight into how governments view their responsibilities and statutory obligations towards designated languages. The practice for many is barely one generation old, whereas Canada's language policy has been over fifty years in the making.[16] The rich inheritance, despite new challenges, offers strong evidence that official bilingualism will remain a cornerstone of Canadian public life, and in so many ways is capable of reacting to the increasing demands of a multicultural polity where the position and proportion of Francophones continue to decline (Clément and Foucher, 2014).

In Europe revised language strategies are being prepared and they will be dealing with the demands of new legislation, reacting to the increased recognition of linguistic human rights, the reform of school organisation and the introduction of new curricula, harnessing the pressures of fiscal reform either as a result of the long-term effects of the 2008 banking crisis or the Covid-19 pandemic, seeking to ameliorate the continued concern with losing speakers and the atrophying of territories and heartlands, all within the context set by the challenges of globalisation, increased immigration or emigration and the consequent emergence of the phenomenon of new speakers.

---

[16] I recognise that so much of the infrastructure and framework of the Canadian language planning experience predates the Action Plan of 2003. In turn the Action Plan would not have come about in its specific form were it not for the claims of language groups and the type of language planning in place since the late 1980s.

Notwithstanding that many strategies achieve a large proportion of their stated aims the process is not as proficient as many believe. I have previously identified inherent contradictions, tensions between the promotional and regulatory arms of language management, structural barriers, such as the lack of interdepartmental co-ordination, political about-turns and programme cancellations, court challenges and judicial reviews (Williams, 2013a; 2021a). For at the heart of official language strategies lies political expedience.[17] The survival of many lesser-used languages requires long-term strategic thinking and support. However, so much of political life is short-to-medium term and as a consequence few governments are really committed to levels of investment and intervention which carry over into decades rather than the life of a single or two-term administration. There are exceptions of course, the most notable being the Welsh Government's Well-Being of Future Generations (Wales) Act 2015. The Act makes it clear that the listed public bodies must work to achieve all seven of its goals, not just one or two, and to ensure compliance there is a Future Generations Commissioner for Wales.[18] It is likely that under the influence of the Climate Change initiatives, such as the commitment to net zero carbon, more long-term programmes will be put in place across many departments of government and thus both the strategic and financial models will be adjusted to take account of such paradigmatic shifts. The science of well-being is an important source of fresh ideas and justifications which can penetrate so many concerns and reconfigure a debate on what we value and how we account for things in the marketplace. Support for lesser-used languages, as an expression of ecological and linguistic diversity and social well-being, may yet climb up the hierarchy of collective values, although there can be no certainty given past trajectories.

Even so the focus of policy success must be emotional intelligence and a commitment to policy implementation, else not only will the target population cry foul but so also will opposition political parties, ever willing to cite failings in government programmes. Procedural damage limitation is an important feature of government practices but tends not to be as readily applied when it comes to minority issues as opposed to mainstream programmes and the fulfilment of majoritarian democratic mandates.

A more incontrovertible conclusion is the assertion that if language policies are to be successful, they have to be redesigned so as to include people's linguistic resources, registers and repertoires and their uses in the everyday

---

[17] I acknowledge the idiosyncratic and unusual workings of government and administration. Many of the successful elements have been the result of the enthusiastic and committed efforts of parents and activists as interpreted by key political actors, senior public servants and organisational managers in tandem with members, agencies and organisations from within the target community itself.

[18] www.futuregenerations.wales/about-us/future-generations-act/.

complex through the 'ordered' reality of languaging. Part of this reconceptualisation involves foregrounding the agency of language practitioners in deciding on language policies. However, it is quite another matter as to who among the contending interest groups of a linguistically diverse citizenship will be selected to be representatives and whether their participation is by invitation or because, being motivated, they push themselves to act as informants and stakeholders. The outcome has more to do with political projection and expedience than any demonstrable sociolinguistic theory or evidence-based need. Uncertainty, fragmentation and a certain creative ambiguity will doubtless characterise the formulation of language strategy from the European level down to that of the sub-state and the evidence suggests that in this hybrid, super-diverse context, it is the abstract, flexible, catch-all rhetoric of political pronouncements and official strategy which will prevail, rather than any detailed assessment of the needs of new speakers.

The Policy Community

The policy community itself is a diverse array of interests, resource allocation imperatives and competing political ideologies. For agencies and departments concerned with language promotion, regulation and revitalisation there is a clear understanding that the contribution of 'native or indigenous speakers' is vital as a source of legitimacy, authenticity and creativity in reproducing both language and its associated culture(s).[19] However, policymakers are less certain as to how to categorise or operationalise programmes which also seek to acknowledge the salience and contribution of new speakers as opposed to early-stage L2 learners. Given this, there is no prior expectation that there will be a comprehensive interpretation of the requirements and roles of new speakers in language policy development expressed by those official representatives interviewed in this research exercise. Rather some critical detective work and creative trajectories are needed to tease out some of the salient features of official responses to the questions posed.

Joan Pujolar and Bernadette O'Rourke, two of the leaders of the New Speakers Network, have traced how their theoretical lens has moved from a native speaker/new speaker perspective to one which incorporates all speakers by focussing on research which seeks to dissect the political economy of speaker categorisation in specific contexts, thereby illuminating how language participates in struggles over access to resources (Pujolar and O'Rourke, 2019).[20] The concern with resources gets to the heart of the relevance of the

---

[19] The interpretation is concerned with instances of language revitalisation although Catalan and Canadian data relates to localised majorities.

[20] The authors argue that 'this "speaker" perspective will allow researchers to further illuminate who has access to which codes, how and where they are able to deploy them, and with what

new speaker paradigm within the political economy of most states. Indeed, it could be argued that the new speaker lens opens up new possibilities for interpreting long-established discussions on language pedagogy, in-group and out-group membership, migration and adjustment, open and closed boundaries and the like. Ultimately how new speaker policies are framed is a reflection of underlying political cultures covering the entire spectrum of European (and other) jurisdictions from Conservative through Liberal and Social Democratic to Socialist/Communist precepts. Ministerial decisions are crucial but so also is the context of the respective public administrative and governmental departments acting as a key influence on the predisposition of public servants to consider integrating new speaker requirements into their programmes.

Given the complex nature of decision-making, evidence gathering and policy formulation, one would not expect to see a tailor-made, stand-alone new speaker policy, even if one were considered feasible. Rather it was anticipated that green shoots, fragments of an argument, elements within a policy agenda would be identified. This is because I assumed that, as the new speaker phenomenon was recent, civil servants would only now be beginning to consider extending their established language policies to reflect a changing environment. Neither was it assumed that the responses derived from civil service experience would fit neatly into any linear conception of policymaking. Indeed, the opposite was assumed, and thus I sought to focus on the degree to which understanding, awareness and conviction would influence the agenda-setting stage.

A clear demarcation of the successive stages of policymaking has been constructed by Cairney (2012; 2016) whose six stages are: 1. Agenda setting; 2. Policy formulation; 3. Legitimation; 4. Implementation; 5. Evaluation; 6. Policy maintenance, succession or termination. However, this apparently rational process of policy delivery is compounded by a number of inherent difficulties which relate to the gathering of data, the separation of fact and value, and the downward pressures exerted by ministers who often want relatively quick, expedient solutions to the issues of the day. Cairney (2016) alerts us to several features we should consider, such as problems with the supply of evidence, problems with the demand for evidence, the competition or policymakers' attention, overcoming the evidence-policy gap and the psychology of policymaking.

Managing our expectations as to how much interest and evidence one would find in relation to the new speaker awareness among policymakers, let alone concrete policy implementation, is thus a necessary precondition to our enquiries. Reality has a coercive force and even when policymakers have sincere

social and economic consequences, across a wide range of settings in today's multilingual, globalised Europe' (Pujolar and O'Rourke, 2019).

intentions to focus more on advanced learner provision and new speaker needs, the expedient pressure of governance can dent such fine ambitions. The policy environment is a competitive one. Getting ideas on the agenda is a tough process, especially for 'minority' interest issues.

Gathering the Evidence: Case Study Findings

Between 2015 and 2021 a series of interviews were conducted with key agencies, senior civil servants, politicians and academics in several jurisdictions.[21] These were supplemented by an analysis of official documents, significant statements and the core messages and programmes of relevant organisations. It may be asked, what precisely is under investigation? If I ask questions on new speakers in an interview or consultation, does it necessarily follow that my interlocutors will perceive the concept and phenomenon in the same manner? This is especially tricky in those jurisdictions, such as Finland or Canada, which have not been exposed to the level of activity that characterises, for example, Galicia in relation to the *neofalantes* as an active minority pressure group.

Returning to the matter of definition, participants in the New Speakers Network have proposed relatively similar definitions of the term and descriptions of the people targeted. Here I commend the interpretation offered by McLeod and O'Rourke (2017) who suggest that the term 'new speaker of Gaelic' is used to refer to:

people who did not acquire Gaelic in the home when growing up but have nevertheless acquired Gaelic to a significant degree of competence and are now making active use of the language in their lives. This is itself a fairly expansive definition and there are significant divergences in the learning trajectories and language use patterns of the participants in this study. (McLeod and O' Rourke, 2017, p. 1)

I embrace this definition because, in almost all of the jurisdictions, the main avenue of learning the target language was the statutory education system which produced active speakers of the 'new' language not initially acquired within the home. Thus, in rank order we would expect our interviewees to be concerned with new speakers produced through the education system and the community, followed by migrants and then refugees who have gained competence in the language. The overwhelming majority of new speakers are the

---

[21] Given that key decision makers and policy formulators spoke in confidence, while they granted permission for me to record the interviews and to use the material which they shared, I have adopted a policy of rarely using direct quotations and attribution by name. Interviews, discussions and commentary by academics have been treated in a more direct manner, using significant direct quotes as and when appropriate. In all cases I have sought to weave the answers to my interview questions into a holistic narrative so as to provide a more consolidated interpretation of the issues under discussion.

product of the statutory and adult education system and in consequence it may be difficult for decision makers to discern any special need for new speakers as distinct from the general population who attend minority immersion or bilingual educational establishments. We shall see!

However, first we need to give some consideration to the characteristics and experiences of new speakers before we embark on our policy-oriented analysis. For those who wish to trace the experiential nature of such linguistic transformations there are many excellent interpretive case studies, as what we know about the experiences of new speakers comes from studies in education and ethnography (Higham, 2020; Puigdevall, 2014; Walsh and Ní Dhúda, 2015; O'Rourke and Walsh, 2020).

Selected Features of New Speaker Profiles

Let me preface this section by stating that, in most cases, new speakers are made very welcome by the host community of speakers. The majority of new speakers produced by the statutory education system are hardly distinguishable from their neighbours who have not become competent in the chosen language as happens within Ireland, Wales or Scotland.

Yet such is the fragility of host speaker numbers in several contexts that new speakers may be seen as the salvation of the language and are thus treated with great respect and 'loved into the community'. The more so if they are identifiably very different in their country of origin or socio-cultural background. This could range from Irish speakers from Poland, Welsh speakers from among the Bengali or Somali population, Basque speakers from among the Mapuche or Catalan speakers born in China. This new diversity not only reflects globalising trends but also bespeaks a welcome, open and hospitable stance which minorities are very keen to advance, for it distances them from majoritarian, hegemonic tendencies and practices. In a more symbolic form, it may also echo and resonate generations of minority support for the struggle of peoples to become independent from former colonial masters; for many autochthonous minorities in Europe would claim to have been internal colonies of powerful 'foreign' overlords who were central to the process of state formation they now endure. This expresses solidarity with the call to liberty which was so prominent in the 1960s and 1970s and also seeks to absolve certain minorities who would claim not only to have suffered from similar forms of internal colonialism but also to have been forced to serve as unwilling participants in the colonial struggle for European mastery in such places as Colombia, Sri Lanka, Egypt or the Congo. This revisionist narrative faces difficulties in accounting for the activities of Scottish, Irish and Welsh slave-traders, plantation owners, administrators, merchants and soldiers in the colonial impress, while proponents are keen to celebrate the contribution of seafarers, farmers, commercial agents, politicians and the professions to the settlement of North America, Southern Africa, Australia and New Zealand, all of which reflect a distinctive Celtic influence on the landscape and structure of settler societies. However, we should be careful not to accept uncritically all the elements of a grievance narrative which characterises so many of the minorities we are considering.

Identification, empathy and solidarity have become the watchwords of the new speaker's path of acceptance. Accordingly, in most minority situations they are celebrated and valued as a net addition to the community. However, their demographic weight and significance for policy formulation vary. In Galicia, the *neofalantes* are a small but highly visible proportion of all Galician speakers. In Scotland they are critical to the survival of Gaelic as total speakers constitute only 1 per cent of the nation's population while in Wales they are the product of a statutory education system and tend to blend into the mainstream Welsh-speaking populace. Consequently, identifying distinctive policy initiatives for new speakers as a subset of more holistic policies remains a challenge and we should not therefore anticipate too many well-developed programmes at this stage. Green shoots rather than fully mature policies are the order of the day.

Why is it significant that we search for these green shoots? With the atrophying of traditional homelands and communities and the demise of so many indigenous minority language networks, it is logical to expect that the new speakers produced through the statutory and adult education systems will comprise a greater proportion of minority language speakers in the future. Accordingly, it is imperative that we seek to learn as much as possible about their profiles, their motivations, their ability to integrate and the manner in which cumulatively they are influencing the speech community.

Learner Development

The rich literature on language learning offers insights into how language is acquired, internalised, reproduced and communicated. What is not so clear is at what stage an individual chooses to take on additional identities through becoming competent in an additional language. Work on second language acquisition, such as the learning of Italian or German by a British student, does not pretend to suggest that such endeavours lead to an identity transition or that by such means students wish to be accepted as a new member of an Italian or German community. By contrast most new speaker research to date is ultimately concerned with social cohesion as individuals seek to be incorporated into their local host environment. What are the mechanisms by which such transitions operate and with what consequences?

Mudes

Catalan researchers have coined the term *mudes* to describe key turning points or specific biographical junctures in the transition from habitually using one language to another, seeking thereby to integrate into a new speech community (Pujolar and Puigdevall, 2015). *Mudes* is the Catalan term for variations in social performance, such as dressing up for an event or changing one's appearance generally (Pujolar and Gonzalez, 2013). This concept has been adapted in contexts such as Ireland, the BAC and Galicia (Walsh and O'Rourke, 2014; Puigdevall et al., 2018; Lourido and Evans, 2019). An important element of this approach is the assertion that by tracking changes in language behaviour, demonstrating how linguistic practices may evolve and change throughout the life cycle of individuals, ethnographers are able to provide a more nuanced view of the linguistic ideologies that underpin linguistic practices. These insights may be applied to improve the teaching of a target language, to ease the acceptance of new speakers into a host community or to raise awareness among native speakers of the significance of welcoming a more diverse and dynamic set of fellow speakers. A particular concern is to counter the view that seeks to reduce these practices to their base instincts so as to construct a defence for ethnolinguistic belonging, reinforcing the 'we' against the 'other' in society.

Role Models and Authenticity

Who counts and who is accepted? How are the rules of incorporation framed? Is it essentially a matter of linguistic skills and competence or are there deeper cultural norms that have to be imbibed and demonstrated as testimony to one's new identity? New speakers can struggle with their own authenticity. They often describe the range of their language skills, registers and usages as being different from those of the native speakers they seek to emulate. This is not necessarily an unalloyed deficiency, for although their language may not be as idiomatic, rich, intuitive or colourful as that of native speakers, they do possess 'skills associated with more modern functions and new terminology required in these new contexts which many native speakers are seen to be lacking' (McLeod and O'Rourke, 2015, p. 157).

On the other hand, a young new speaker seeking to emulate or pattern their speech on an older native speaker will experience a time lag, for older speakers often derive their linguistic behaviour and repertoire from an earlier socialisation period when the community norms and style were quite different from those which the new speaker would encounter today. This is also true of the cultural material, songs, dances, Scripture-based stories and general experiences gained in a more limited face-to-face age as opposed to a digital context. Many new speakers report being at a loss when several cultural clues, memorised poems and songs of childhood are shared in gatherings and as a consequence they feel inadequate because such elements of one's identity do not intuitively resonate with them. This in turn leads to concerns over imposter syndrome and a fear that they will never fully fit in or be accepted. Emotional and psychological elements constitute an essential part in the confidence levels of new speakers as they hone their new identities in challenging environments.

An earlier concern with authenticity has been expressed by Kathryn Woolard and Alexandra Jaffe. Woolard has commented that

If local linguistic varieties index authentic local identities, by the same logic they are off-limits to outsiders. Lack of control of such a variety can indicate that one does not share an essential identity. To learn such a language secondarily through study is a contradiction in terms, marking the learner as inauthentic. Heritage language learners and what are now often called 'new speakers' in settings around the world have been reported to experience this contradiction. (Woolard, 2016, p. 24)

Jaffe reports that heritage Corsican learners fear making inauthenticating errors, and that having to learn one's 'own' language in school was in itself 'viewed by people as a contaminating, deauthenticating, act'. The requirement to teach it in order to ensure its survival 'could be seen as collectively deauthenticating' for the linguistic community. (quoted in Woolard, 2016, p. 24). Generalising is difficult but one prescient insight which is useful for the arguments of the new speaker proponents is that 'anonymous languages supposedly can be learned by anyone, but authentic language can be learned by no one; speakers are supposed to come by them "naturally" rather than working to acquire them' (Woolard, 2016, p. 24).

Issues of identity, authenticity and belonging suffuse the new speaker experience. Charles Taylor (1991) has identified the importance of recognition and acceptance for identity construction. He argues that 'on the intimate level, we can see how much an original identity needs and is vulnerable to the recognition given or withheld by significant others. It is now surprising that in the culture of authenticity, relationships are seen as the key loci of self-discovery and self-confirmation' (Taylor, 1991, p. 49). Equal recognition and fair treatment of the other become the hallmarks of a just society. Their denial is a form of oppression. But such discrimination and hurt can be manifested also by sincere and well-meaning individuals in the manner in which they continually remind new speakers of their origins and of their differences when compared with indigenous speakers. What is meant as a sincere compliment can appear patronising and a ready reminder of being not quite fully accepted by the host community.

There is an assumption that many learners, and most new speakers, aspire to gain native speaker competence. While this may be achieved, especially if the person starts learning the target language at a young age, the majority of learners and new speakers will still portray their individual characteristics, whether it be because of the influence of their native tongue, their accent or their idiosyncratic patterning and distinctive use of language. Many teachers and their students are under the impression that the most authentic and justifiable manner of gaining an acceptable standard of speech performance is to imitate a native speaker, even if this may at times conflict with the student's self-perception and identity. The truth is that some new speakers may struggle to attain a native speaker level of performance, leading specialists to argue that the ideal native speaker model is something of a myth and certainly can lead to difficulties if people feel that they are underperforming or falling short of the mark. Davies (2007) and Crystal (2003; 2019) point to the inherent tension between the need to be intelligible and the need to assert or protect one's identity when learning languages. They argue that just as there is no absolute native speaker model to which one may aspire so there is no absolute learner model or by extension absolute new speaker model to emulate. Rather there are multiple role models which contain an enormous amount of variation in form, accent, dialect and overall speech pattern. To add to this difficulty, one must take note of the listener's reaction to the conversation and ascertain to what extent the new speaker feels comfortable or well received by the host community. In strong ethnolinguistic communities such as Catalonia, the host population is willing to accept a wide variety of speech behaviour on the part of the new speakers, whereas in more linguistically fragile communities, such as Gaelic-speaking networks in Scotland, the degree of accommodation may be much less. It all depends on how far the host community feels any sustained threat to the integrity of their language and culture by the emergence of a new speaker cohort.

Geolinguistic and Territorial Perspectives

Geography also matters. All the cases dealt with here are characterised by a set of territorial spaces we may call homelands, places which are or have been until recently a redoubt for the languages, offering both a core area for cultural reproduction and a bastion against the atrophying pressures of modernisation. In the recent past newer, non-territorial, non-contiguous spaces have been produced enabling new communities of interest to be established – what geographers and urban planners have termed 'community without propinquity' (Webber, 1963). And yet in so many cases new speakers and learners are socialised into believing that periods spent in historical homelands will strengthen their appreciation of the language, add meaning to their existence and help them identify with native speakers in some version of communal solidarity. Intuitively one would expect new speakers who are socialised within heartland regions to have a more complete grasp of the language and its associated cultures, as opposed to new speakers who gain meaning only from non-territorial social network interaction. But is this necessarily true? If so with what consequences for policy and for intervention? If it does not necessarily hold, can one sustain a viable, robust language network without recourse to spatial and geographical referents, by using digital opportunities and resources within an epoch of deterritorialisation?

This might seem a tall order. Is it the case, as Robert Ardrey postulated in 1966, that the territorial imperative governs human no less than animal behaviour? It is claimed that it serves a psychological need, and the possession of a territory serves the purposes of security, stimulation and identity, which W. D. Davies explores so exquisitely in his analysis of the territorial dimension of Judaism (Davies, 1982). And yet, given that the overwhelming majority of new speakers of Basque, Irish and Welsh live cheek by jowl in contentment with neighbours who do not have any compunction to return to the heartland or sojourn for a few weeks in the summer in heartland communities, is the return to the land a necessary feature of their experience? I think not. What is distinctive is their yearning for safe spaces, for pockets of security within the multilingual metropolis or city region where they can feel secure, where their language is respected and nourished by a wide range of social and performative activities. Perhaps this is the post-modern expression of the territorial imperative, where the same virtues of security, stimulation and identity can be enjoyed. It may also be the physical representation of the *muda* concept, wherein entering safe spaces can encourage steps in the transition process and allow someone to feel comfortable, confident and stimulated in such milieux. However it is described, it is certain that new geographies of communities of practice are being shaped.

Opportunities and Legitimacy

A common complaint made by new speakers is the relative lack of opportunity to use their language except in dedicated centres or 'safe places' where almost everyone else is using their language and they thus would feel more comfortable participating. It is as if such spaces draw them out and offer them a genuine set of places to be heard and be counted.

For some, having located routine safe places, such as conversation classes, choirs, social activities, bars and cafes, sporting clubs, they are still disconcerted by native speakers' attitudes and behaviours towards them. This may take the form of having to justify their membership of the community or group, to identify where they are from, when and where they learned the language, for how long and by whom were they taught, which regional dialect and accent did their tutors impart to them, do their partners and children also speak the language, if not why? Several of these enquiries can appear to be aggressive intrusions or almost accusations by less sensitive interlocutors, the more so when individuals are constantly reminded that 'we do not say it like that' or 'you need to mutate there if you want to speak correctly', 'the language has its own words for these loan words, you know'. For some native speakers the emergence of a large number of new speakers may be unsettling. They may complain that the quality and purity of their language is being diluted, grammatical forms being overturned, mutations being mangled and far too many loan words being used so that the resultant admixture of majoritarian and minority language use renders the new speaker a poor representative of the speech community.

Other more discriminating stances can remind the new speaker that although they may have learned the language, they are still not members of the host community by virtue of several other cultural markers, such as appearance, skin colour, faith or food habits. Still others are downright hostile and reject attempts by new speakers to fit in.

Agents or Supplicants?

There is a tendency by commentators to speak on behalf of new speakers as if they are pliant supplicants in this process of recognition and empowerment. What evidence can we muster of new speakers being active agents in their own interests, constructing arguments, lobbying power brokers and formulating elements of policy? We have plenty of evidence of learner societies and associations throughout Europe, annual prizes being granted for the best speaker of language *x*, role models and actors who appear on television or within official promotional campaigns, sporting figures and rock stars used to appeal to young people. But we have very few examples of organised lobby groups persuading and cajoling those in authority to attend to their needs and interests qua new speakers.

It might be expected that migrant and refugee interest groups would be more active in this process than those who have gained an additional language through the statutory education system. Even so it would be of interest to know how the latter view their educational experiences and discern what factors triggered their transition to being active new speakers as opposed to episodic learners. It would also be of interest to discover how long-established speakers of a language might react to being characterised by others as a new speaker. If the reaction is consistently negative, might this support the abandoning of the term?

These are some of the characteristics and experiences of new speakers which will form the backdrop to the more focussed attention being paid to policy, planning and official intervention strategies. Let us turn now to the structure of the volume and identify its key aims.

The Structure of the Volume

Chapter 2 offers a series of reflections on the key issues of the new speaker debate. It sets forth the opportunities and challenges for those who wish to develop the relevance of the new speaker phenomenon in selected disciplines, such as sociolinguistics and ethnography, together with observations on how evidence-based policy recommendations may be formulated. Policy is always the product and the servant of political will and there is a certain logic in the argument that says innovative policy is a reaction to, and reflection of, a modest degree of crisis management. In our investigation it is the migrant and refugee element of the new speaker continuum which is most urgent, but it is also the least developed area of explicit policy discourse to date.

Chapter 3 reports on the evidence gathering I undertook in Wales. By interviewing selected politicians and a range of senior civil servants charged with the formulation and implementation of language policy, I arrive at an evaluation of current thinking on the relevance of the new speaker phenomenon within official language policy. These enquiries are supplemented by interviews with civil society policy formulators, decision makers from national organisations and academic specialists who have studied the phenomenon. But the neat division between governmental and civil society policy formulators is misleading. Neither category is impervious to the ideas of the other, for in so many minority language communities there is a close relationship between them. In the most promising contexts this interaction is mutually stimulating, if not necessarily co-dependent, as together they fight for the survival of their threatened languages.

In Chapter 4 I repeat the exercise for Scotland which has a much lower number of Gaelic speakers and as a consequence the addition of new speakers to the total mix of interlocutors is far more significant. However, the Gaelic language figures far less prominently as an element of both Scottish identity and public investment. Accordingly, with far fewer agencies and actors involved it may be easier to discern the role which the new speaker concept plays in policy discourse and resultant interventions. One complicating factor is the lack of a shared perspective on which elements should be prioritised in Gaelic language promotion and policy. On the one hand there are proponents who argue that as the Gaelic communities are in crisis all efforts should be prioritised into stabilising and sustaining language transmission within these atrophying communities. Others acknowledge the perilous state of traditional communities but argue that support is needed wherever Gaelic is present and elements such as Gaelic medium education, the media and opportunities for new speakers to flourish also deserve attention. Both perspectives are reflective of what may be called the beleaguered self and contain a fair number of non-cognitive emotional predispositions which colour the rational debate on what is to be done. Consequently tension, disagreement, anger, grief and recrimination can come to shape the various discourses surrounding language policy. In a large-scale language community such fears can be absorbed as part of the general cut and thrust and may not presage any lack of mutual respect and constructive dialogue. But in a small, marginal context such tensions can lead to institutional polarisation between contending agencies and render the central thrust of language promotion less effective.

In Chapter 5 I reflect on the Irish experience and report on the documentary and interview evidence gathered. By contrast to Scotland and Wales, Ireland should be more fertile ground for the promotion of new speaker interests. This is because Ireland is an independent state and as Irish is the first language according to the constitution it has been used within the education system for far longer than has Welsh or Gaelic. Moreover, the statutory education system features the teaching of Irish as a core subject which has created a social mass of 1,761,420 people – 39.8 per cent of the population – who can speak Irish according to the 2016 Census. The overwhelming majority of these would be learners and a significant proportion would be assumed to be new speakers. However, the 2016 Census also shows that, of these, only 73,803 – 4.2 per cent of the population – use Irish daily outside of the education system. This is down 3,382 since 2011.[22] Thus it will be an interesting proposition to see how the formal policy of language promotion and the actual usage of Irish conduce to the production and maintenance of new speakers within the system.

In Chapter 6 the same approach to evidence gathering is adopted in the context of the Spanish polity by focussing on two of the seventeen Autonomous Communities, namely the Basque Country and Navarre. It is here that the new speaker concept has been most readily welcomed and has entered into official discourse. Accordingly, we may expect to find examples of good practice which should be applicable in other jurisdictions. Detailed consideration of excellent initiatives is given to the Euskaraldia: 11 days in Euskera campaign in the Basque Autonomous Community and in the next chapter to the Voluntariat per la Llengua programme in Catalonia. Here civil society activists and local agencies were far more inclined to argue that the needs of new speakers should be an integral element of official language policy than were those charged with the formulation and implementation of such policies at the national level. We explore to what extent this official reticence is a result of ideological stances, caution as to the costs involved or a conviction that current policies already

---

[22] www.irishpost.com/news/new-figures-show-many-people-ireland-actually-speak-irish-daily-141399.

cater very well for the needs of new speakers, even if they are not described in those terms.

Chapter 7 investigates the reception of, and approach to, new speakers in Catalonia and Galicia. There is considerable evidence of a buy-in to the need to integrate new speakers and thus not only boost the profile of the respective language but also add to social cohesion in an increasingly multicultural and multilingual context.

Chapter 8 is concerned with the policy community and with making recommendations at international, state, regional and local levels. The first task is to refine the results of the study, the second is to determine a set of generic observations, the third is to present country-specific recommendations. Defining a recommendation and distinguishing it from mere wish fulfilment are by no means simple tasks and some recommendations available in the literature are so general that it is difficult to interpret their meaning with any degree of precision. That is why the recommendations should be realisable. Where the recommendation is unclear its implementation will often depend upon political goodwill and more often on political expedience so as to ascertain whether or not it fits into the broad parameters of language and educational policy. Its adoption also depends on who is required to finance the intervention and whether the powers that be can safely transfer the responsibility and costs to a partner agency, preferably without requiring long-term financial commitments. Such is the stuff of normal politics. Some local authorities will choose the safe option and say that the needs of new speakers are already incorporated within their comprehensive language-related provisions, even if we know that they are not. This is particularly the case for international migrants, refugees and what are sometimes called translational workers as local authorities will determine that their obligation is to provide instruction in each state's dominant language so as to enable the residents to function within the 'normal' parameters of the educational, health and social services. Additional instruction in a minority language may be considered a step too far, even if local regulations allow for this.

We know that for managers of public services there are two types of imperatives which they face when a fresh challenge is presented. First are the key performance indicators, usually measurable by tried and tested formulae, on which their careers and advancement may depend. Achieving these essential KPIs is a priority, and the current best example would be the attracting of more Black and Asian and Minority Ethnic (BAME) personnel in all sorts of positions in an organisation. Then there are the softer targets, which may be considered nice things to do, such as satisfying the interests of new speakers of language y: useful if it could be achieved, but not essential, and certainly not likely to damage the career of a middle manager if agreed targets were not met in the medium term. Accordingly, while the focus of the investigation is on the reception and adoption of the new speaker concept as an element in policy formulation, the narrative also seeks to strengthen the interpretation by providing additional information on the various contexts within which the investigation was undertaken.

Chapter 9 offers an opportunity for reflection and conclusion. Where has our investigation led us and with what profit? Looking forwards, there is clearly much of relevance which remains to be resolved in a set of new speaker developments that are currently uncharted, fragmented and difficult to pin down.

What is remarkable in all the jurisdictions studied is the degree of variation that was found in the empirical fieldwork. The responses are highly variable from jurisdiction to jurisdiction. In reflecting on the answers given to the questions presented in the light of the evidence set forth here, a plea for further regular research suggests itself; not only to improve on the insufficiencies of this interpretation but also to allow for the passage of time within which it is assumed that greater attention will have been paid to the new speaker phenomenon by policymakers over the coming decade. In that sense this is a preliminary investigation to set the scene for more authoritative interpretations in the future.

What is not in doubt is that the human spirit continues to demonstrate its creativity and innovative approaches to social interaction. Charles Taylor (2016) has reminded us that language is at the heart of this generative process. It is far more than a tool for encoding and communicating information and symbols, as those in the rational empiricist tradition, such as Hobbes, Locke, Condillac and their followers, assert. Rather it is a deeply meaning-seeking enterprise, capable of shaping the thoughts and idioms it aims to explain and share. The articulation of meaning and the creative force of discourse are wholly integral to being human. Through language we shape our human experience and in turn are shaped by social interactions, which teaches us how to articulate language and thoughts in context, as a shared social enterprise. Thus by tracking both structural and sociolinguistic change over time we can gain additional insights into issues such as identity formation, group mobilisation, the vicissitudes of demographic transitions, economic interdependence and networking and the effects of government policies on social cohesion and fragmentation.

The substantive aim of this volume is to use the new speaker conceit as a means of exploring much wider and deeper issues faced by selected minority language communities. The focus will not always be exclusively on new speaker characteristics, needs, contributions and engagement, but it will always seek to relate the broader contextual discussion to the environment within which such needs can be fulfilled. The new speaker approach offers a different entrée into multilingualism, as it relies less on linguistic science and more on the people themselves. This relatively early, incomplete and varied excursion into the field of new speaker studies means that the core normative appeal of the phenomenon, qua conceptual advance, retains its promise. Whether this promise is fulfilled or whether it is destined to reside in the charnel house of ambition and desire will be determined by events in the next generation. For the present we shall see below to what extent any of this promise has been transferred into the contemporary policy community at both governmental and civil society agency level.

2 Popinjays, Pragmatism and Policy: A New Speaker Triptych*

As researchers we are deeply involved with language and with words. In that sense each of us could be described as a popinjay. A pop·in·jay (pŏp'ĭn-jā') is a vain, talkative person. The *Dictionary of the English Language* defines the term as being based on a Middle English word, *parrot*, 'derived from Anglo-Norman and Old North French papejai, alteration (influenced by jai, *jaybird*) of earlier papegai, ultimately (possibly via Old Provençal papagai, with influence from Old French and Old Provençal gai, *joyous, merry*) from Arabic babġā', babbaġā'; akin to Persian bapġā and probably ultimately of imitative origin' (Harcourt, 2016).

Popinjays Bear Repetition!

Just like parrots, we talk about new speakers often in our work and repeat others' findings, statements and convictions as we seek to describe and delineate this apparently new phenomenon. Accordingly, the overwhelming majority of research prompted by the New Speakers Network has been detailed ethnographic accounts of the interaction between so-called native and new speakers of a particular language. Repetition of our concerns, findings and recommendations needs to be continued so that the messages we have about the contribution and experiences of new speakers can filter through into the mainstream discourse and therefore not be seen as exceptional, marginal or partisan but as part of the response to the new needs presented by growing linguistic diversity. We are, after all, seeking to interpret the lives of real people, many of whom have been marginalised in the academic and policy literature. Thus, at the very least the new speakers phenomenon is a useful corrective, and we need to keep pursuing its implications. By asking questions we create a narrative![1]

---

* This is a revised version of the plenary address to the COST New Speakers Network, Final Action Conference, University of Coimbra, 14 September 2017, which was kindly presented by Dr K. Jones on my behalf as I was recovering from surgery. The presentation contained several messages coded within famous triptychs reproduced with kind permission from the Fitzwilliam Museum, Cambridge University, which are not included here.

[1] Here I adopt a normative and advocacy approach as the address was designed both to critique and to inspire the efforts of my colleagues within the New Speakers Network.

In seeking to advance a relatively new subject I argue that we should take heed of some preliminaries which may guide our attempts to place the new speaker perspective on the policy agenda. First, I suggest that our discourse must be honest, edifying, evidence-based and relevant. Where power is transacted, facts would appear to be sacred and indisputable. But in truth there are many facts, all contending for attention and action. Thus, in our discourse as we seek to uncover a reality beyond words and speak truth to power, we need to ascertain to what extent our discourse has lasting meaning and a resonance beyond our special interest. I would contend that paying attention to the new speaker phenomenon not only approaches multilingualism from a new perspective but also adds real value to social cohesion and integration. Secondly, we need to remember that each new speaker is a soul, not just a number or a category. Human dignity and respect for the other is a principal component of most world faiths, even if so often our responsibilities to uphold such values are abrogated in reality. Thus, in our collective efforts we need to bear in mind that each new speaker can also represent simultaneously an added value, a contribution to diversity, an individual who can also pose a set of challenges, an unknown commodity, a resource, a cost. An enigma indeed to try policymakers' minds! However, on a more disturbing note, taken together new speakers are as subject to political and policy manipulation as any other category of humanity. Thus, we need to be wary of not being either naive or too simplistic in our interpretations and policy recommendations.

Second-Hand Philosophies: Proven Methodologies

Almost by definition, the philosophies we use in our new speaker enquiries are largely derivative and our theories are not well developed. By contrast, several of the methodologies employed are well proven and come largely from ethnographic, educational and policy management traditions. Accordingly, we know a great deal in descriptive terms about critical junctures in the lives of new speakers, about *mudes* and the search for acceptance and contributions to social cohesion. But it may be asked whether what we have collectively produced to date is a representation and not a critique.

So who are our new speakers and where are they located? Conventionally they fall into four types: those who have learned the target language as young pupils; those who have learned the language as adults, often as a result of parenthood or moving to a new area; those who have come as refugees and asylum seekers; and an idiosyncratic admixture of others who have learned it for sporting, leisure, musical or special interest reasons.

Each type contains a number of inconsistencies and paradoxes which make it hard to generalise, let alone predict behaviour. Let us use school pupils as an illustration. Can such pupils be counted as new speakers if they do not consider themselves to be anything other than standard speakers of a language? Take the case of young people educated entirely through the *ikastolas* system in the Basque Autonomous Community or the *Ysgolion Cymraeg* in Wales, but whose parents are not speakers of Basque or Welsh. When they attain adulthood how will such speakers react to being defined, perhaps for the first time, as new speakers of Basque or Welsh? Rather than exhibit pride, they may baulk at any implied suggestion that they are less proficient or competent than their 'native speaker' referents. A concept like new speaker, if misapplied, can cut like a double-edged sword of truth and belonging!

Given our concern with relevance, scale and intimacy, we may ask if the new speaker concept is more useful for minority than hegemonic language contexts. It is undoubtedly true that a significant number of researchers working in the field are concerned with the health, vitality and survival of selected minority languages, such as Frisian, Gaelic or Sorb; another cohort is engaged in tracking the vicissitudes of slightly larger language groups such as Basque and Galician speakers while a further cohort is interested in the experience of migrants and refugees as they seek to meld into the host state language such as English, Spanish or French.

One thorny structural issue is the tendency to over-exaggerate the relevance of new speakers to the vitality of smaller language groups, precisely because such groups are vulnerable and in more need of additional 'types' of speakers than are larger communities. This is doubly appealing for largely homogenous, autochthonous minorities who welcome new speakers of an Asian, African or Latin American heritage as it both demonstrates the minority's attraction to a global audience and demonstrates the increasing diversity of group members and possible ways of extending their associated culture. Thus, Welsh-medium primary schools in historically immigrant areas, such as Ysgol Hamadryad in Cardiff, are recognised for the promotion of equality and diversity and the celebration of multiculturalism in and through the Welsh language, a feature one would not have anticipated a generation ago.[2]

One can also readily understand the intellectual and emotional urge to seek palliative solutions to atrophying language communities but, precisely because it is a relatively novel concept, there is a tendency to make new speakers the answer of the day, just as in each successive decade since the 1960s we have in turn seen bilingual education, public administration, the mass media, the judicial system and legislation all lauded as the essential element which would secure the survival of the language. So is the new speaker phenomenon more than a passing fad?

---

[2] Visit www.ysgolhamadryad.cymru/.

Language Is Not an End in Itself!

Language is a necessary, but not a sufficient, requirement for social and spatial interaction. It provides opportunities for new interests. It stretches the realm of language use from intimate face-to-face relations, community engagement, digital space and interaction, producing new networks which are not necessarily physically rooted. 'Community without propinquity' was a recognition that place-centred urban design, that is the physical, concrete foundation of city life, was being supplemented by non-place interest group interaction, which focussed on movement, reducing the friction of distance and the barriers of conventional time-space thinking (Webber, 1963; 1964).[3]

Thus, whether we are concerned with urban design, the development of radical forms of architecture or the reach of urbanisation to the outer periphery of the modern state, communication is vital to sustain a whole host of socio-economic activities. The hypermobility of society demands new forms of identity formation and means of belonging. This in turn requires a well-crafted definition of community with which new speakers are meant to identify. Clearly there cannot be a single definition but, given the myriad possibilities for interaction within and between speech communities, settlement types, neighbourhood groups, school catchment areas and the like no longer adequately describe the ambit of social interaction, even if they remain the primary means of securing some degree of identification for new members. Therefore we need to be ambitious and imaginative in the supplementary ways in which we seek to recruit and retain new speakers within our spaces.

Artificial intelligence promises to connect a complex physical network using a highly articulated organisational logic. But who has access to such developments? Ever-expanding entry points which are sustainable and vitiating require a more rigorous evaluation of the channels of socio-economic empowerment through which new speakers may be integrated, else they are destined to be passive participants in their own life trajectories.

How are such tendencies to be avoided and which sets of domains will best reward a concentration of our energy and resources? The obvious answer is the public sector, for it above all others is a reflection of our collective values and common purpose. Thus, when a language choice is offered in statutory or higher education, the health system, local government, housing and social services, this choice deserves scrutiny as to how the delivery of the services they offer is perceived and used by new speakers (Cardinal and Williams, 2020). We also need to enquire into and emphasise the role of the private and voluntary sectors and seek to provide examples of good initiatives – especially if they are evaluated

---

[3] Network communication is a relatively new phenomenon as conventional infrastructures were dependent on physical distance and the energy required to overcome space for the delivery of post, newspapers, military commands and information.

in terms of their intended outcomes. This effort is dependent on the gathering of time-series data and evidence, of behavioural changes, of new trajectories and of old path dependency in institutional planning and decision-making. Yet precisely when we need new sources of data, we are faced with the reality that the conventional means of collecting data in terms of the decennial census is being scaled down in the name of fiscal probity. The substitution of small-scale sampling, so as to ask more fine-grained questions about language and other behaviour, offers some ameliorative hope and mitigation against complete abandonment but too often it is deemed unwise to aggregate the findings of small samples to give definitive representations of the traits of the whole population. Accordingly, we know less than we should about the actual language-related behaviour of our fellow citizens. This in turn makes it far more problematic for decision makers to make assumptions about the reception and outcome of their policies.

Sources of Evidence

A priority would be to assess the current awareness of policymakers about the interests of new speakers. One way is to analyse the extent to which there is direct reference to new speakers within official language strategies and related policies. This would determine to what extent the concept is operative and already established in some jurisdictions and not in others. Another would be to search for indirect references to new speakers in official language strategies and policies. While the former is self-evident, the latter is a little trickier. Accordingly, we need to identify what this might look like and how adequate this might be in relation to promoting the interests of new speakers. A further means of garnering evidence about current orthodoxies is to evaluate the interpretation of discourses about new speakers and ask why these narratives were prepared, with what purpose and for what effect. Having undertaken such surveys it may be that there is far more material about such issues than we imagine; it is just that it is not presented as relating to new speakers per se. Alternatively, it could be that policymakers assume that they are covering the interests of new speakers when they discuss the categories of second language learners, of migrants, of refugees without specifying that any significant change has been undertaken akin to the linguistic *mudes* identified by Pujolar and Puigdevall (2015). If this is the case, we may wonder if such assumptions are fine-grained enough to inform programmes and policies. Similarly we need to caution against exaggerating the impact of new speakers in policy formulation. None of this is to argue that policymakers are not acutely aware of the demolinguistic changes that are happening in their respective societies; it is just that the political and policy reaction has not deemed new speakers to be sufficiently critical an issue to require separate and detailed treatment to date.

What Are the Integrative Threads We Need to Emphasise?

In terms of our evolving framework of thought and action we need to ask fundamental questions which may be applied to all the cases currently under investigation by scholars and policymakers regarding new speakers. Accordingly:

Does the concept of new speaker travel equally well across cultures and polities, with a similar impact and set of implications?

Are there fundamental differences in what counts as a new speaker by state and language regime?

What is it about the institutional and administrative culture of the respective states that gives rise to such differences?

Does it make a significant difference to our interpretation if we aggregate the cumulative experiences of a particular sub-set of new speakers in a locality, regardless of their individual life trajectories?

Are the transitions made by tracking life trajectories across linguistic boundaries of equal predictive value in calculating who might sustain their additional language and who might become a recidivist?

Would some new speakers who appear as having been 'nativised' resent being categorised as new speakers?

For many, the term 'new speaker' was coined to avoid stigmatisation, thus how do we avoid it becoming a mark of differentiation as opposed to inclusion?

How do we deal with the inherent bias that exists within the New Speakers Network of focussing on the context of new speakers in minority language situations?

Does this inevitably skew the scholarship and the deductions made about new speaker behaviour in such contexts?

Does it also limit the transferability of their experience to majoritarian contexts?

What lessons can be learned from analysing the experiences of new speakers within hegemonic languages such as English, French, Spanish and German?

What lessons can be learned from analysing the experiences of new speakers who are simultaneously getting to grips with both a majority and a minority culture, as happens for many migrants, refugees and displaced persons?

Is the hegemonic-subordinate continuum a useful axis for analysing the comparative contexts of new speakers?

Clearly many other questions could be raised, as it is the whole person and their relation to others within a social context which is under scrutiny. Once we have a range of answers to such questions, we should be in a position to unpack the complexity of the new speaker phenomenon and might even discover that it is a far more widespread condition than we were initially led to understand by scrutiny of official documents and ethnographic interviews only.

Scale and Hierarchy

The principle of representation suggests that we seek to use the new speaker discourse to influence language policy and planning. Presumably, this attempt will be made at the level of state or sub-state authorities so as to reach the widest possible audience. This is commendable but there may be some mileage in emphasising the smaller scales of language policy, especially in relation to localised bilingual education and community development. It may also be worth emphasising the role of professional training bodies, of language testing and evaluation and of commercial and private sector interests, as each of these domains will have a role to play in the interpretation and implementation of actions designed to enhance the new speaker involvement. Accordingly, I believe that localised or very specific language policies could be developed so as to allow new speakers to navigate into the mainstream of the economic life of both individuals and organisations. One barrier which may hinder these normative arguments is the presumption that minoritised languages such as Basque or Irish are accessed primarily through the relevant hegemonic language, such as Spanish or English. In the early stages many speakers do not have the linguistic skills to cope simultaneously with learning a minority language through the dominant language which may also be their own third, fourth or fifth language. So how, if at all, is the curriculum and assessment regime designed to accommodate diversity? One resolution is to imitate best practice principles and programmes from within hegemonic language teaching circles, where there is a huge amount of experience which takes account of diverse linguistic backgrounds. The transfer of good practice would strengthen the argument for sound policy and interventions and lead to a more convincing basis on which to counter the claims of detractors that 'there is nothing to see here', 'we have seen it all before', 'why waste money on minority language promotion when they would all be better off speaking English/French/Spanish/German anyway?'

Safe Spaces, Opportunities and Challenges

Once new speakers have gained more than a threshold amount of capacity in the target language, they naturally will want to extend their range of vocabulary, interaction and confidence levels. Thus, in answering the 'so what?' and 'what next?' questions for new speakers, we need to consider how they apply their language skills in a meaningful way. One solution is to make available opportunities which promise not to threaten or dislocate the upward trajectory of new speaker progress. Many new speakers crave a 'safe' environment within which they can demonstrate their skills without the ridicule of mockers or the scorn of language purists. One approach is to identify and construct a set of physical spaces within which they may feel comfortable and nurtured by fellow travellers on this linguistic trajectory. Such spaces, where the target language is 'normalised', would allow participants to cross the competence and confidence threshold and thereby reinforce domain use and participation. Long before the *muda* concept was developed in Catalonia, throughout Latinate Europe the *muda* name was used for the designation of a physical space, a portal or gate, to denote a transition from one jurisdiction to another, a transition of authority through space. A striking example today is the Muda Gate set within the walled compound of the port of Koper (Capodistria) in Slovenia. It is entirely feasible that the *muda* paradigm can be extended from its current behavioural transitional use to also encompass physical spaces, contact areas and boundaries. Once within the confines of such spaces the new speaker and advanced learners could feel safe and nurtured as they communicate and enjoy the company of fellow speakers.

The Canolfannau Cymraeg in Wales represent just such an example. They combine the opportunities to extend the social networks of new speakers of Welsh with simultaneously providing a wide range of activities for all who speak the language, be that in conversation, sports activities, choirs and drama groups or occasionally more unusual specialist activities. The significant feature I want to emphasise is that these centres act as local hubs, which do not cater exclusively for new speaker needs only and thus provide a more reassuring, 'normal' social environment for all.[4]

An influential report outlining the advantages of such centres was presented to the Welsh Assembly in 2012 by H. Gruffudd and S. Morris of Swansea University and on the basis of their recommendations a further seven Canolfannau were established in Wales with an investment of £2 million during the period 2014–16. Such centres tend to be in non-Welsh-speaking areas with the aim of transforming adult learners into new speakers of Welsh. In essence these centres are the physical representation of *mudes* and often provide the only structured opportunity for new speakers to socialise, integrate and develop confidence in their communication skills. Another feature of these initiatives is that they derive from local community activism and as such constitute a self-help instrument for language revival efforts. However, as with so many community bottom-up initiatives, their flexibility and room for further innovation can be emasculated somewhat as they become part of a government-directed, target-oriented and prescriptive set of intervention edicts, the price to be paid perhaps for recognition, funding and mainstreaming.

---

[4] The best example is Canolfan Cymraeg Abertawe, Tŷ Tawe in Swansea.

Migrants, Costs and Benefits

Turning to one sub-category of new speakers, namely migrants, some might argue that most of the costs of their integration are borne by the host community. Typically, they would cite access to housing, employment and social and health services and conclude that the additional costs incurred by society are part of the social contract by which migrants become settled residents. The public conscience, let alone the strictures of the marketplace, would determine that such additional costs be considered as the exercise of a public good, namely the application of equal and fair treatment of all in a democratic society. However, in advocating a raft of measures to improve the lot of new speaker migrants, we need to be mindful of the collective costs involved. Thus, in our narratives we need to emphasise that there are public costs for the private gains of the new speakers, such as offering a subsidy for educational courses in selected languages or providing social welfare services with a language component.

But to rest content with such an account is to rob the migrant of their autonomy, volition, and the possibility of having to face a set of often harsh choices. This would need a recognition, if not always a full assessment, of the social-psychological costs for migrants of not fully adjusting to the new language context. Concern and confusion over identity reconstruction, degrees of acceptance and belonging and the apprehension involved in adjusting to a new moral code or set of fundamental values can each induce anxiety and additional coping pressures. This focus on norms, ethical, political and legal, as explanatory variables in a process of adjustment should alert us to the fact that so little of our enquiry to date has been on the internal, often poorly articulated concerns of the subject. It is my conviction that far more rigorous work on the experiences of migrants transitioning through the various stages of identification will create a robust body of evidence which can be used in a variety of fields, not just language and education but also housing policy, employment prospects, social networking and the steps required to attain full citizenship.

There are also the unintended consequences of well-intentioned policies to be considered. If we limit ourselves only to the formal setting of adult language classes, we will need to recognise that for many migrants in bilingual contexts the local authority policy to require instruction in language x, be it Basque, Welsh or Frisian, could also be seen as a permanent barrier to integration, as for many migrants their primary goal is to master the hegemonic language, such as Spanish, English or Dutch. In bilingual regions of hegemonic states, the parallel learning process, in which Basque and Spanish, for example, are learned simultaneously, could represent a double weighting of pressure whereby the lesser-used language often falls by the wayside. Thus, we may need to enquire whether some courses represent a merely symbolic function rather than act as a means to migrants becoming fully integrated.

Inhabitants, Residents and Citizens

Further along the linguistic trajectory we could ask how the process of becoming a 'successful' new speaker might add value and quality to both the individual's life and that of the community. Do we have sufficient diagnostic tools by which we can measure the influence of those factors which encourage or inhibit the transition from being an inhabitant of a country to being a full citizen with all that implies? It ill behoves us to advocate new policy programmes unless we also recognise that policy expert and general taxpayer alike would wish to know how each successive intervention contributes to the overall outcome of improving the new speaker's chances of being both accepted and fully functional in their chosen domains. Clearly much of this adjustment is driven by the individual concerned but we also need to know, how does the possession of an additional language take shape and to what extent do other new speakers and the host society representatives 'allow' new speakers to fully participate? In this linguistic *mudes* drama who writes the script and who predetermines the respective roles of the participants? What happens to those who do not follow the script, but in the eyes of some presume too much – how are they treated and how is their linguistic performance evaluated, reinforced or knocked back?

In seeking to become part of a community of communities is there necessarily a strong territorial or place identification in the motivation of new speakers to fit in, or are we concerned essentially with social networks and particularistic associations rather than with communal solidarity? This is an important consideration as so many of the interventionist strategies one could envisage would perforce have to deal with the dialectical relationship between hardware and software, whereby the design of a service could easily be rendered in a non-territorial fashion and still fulfil the statutory obligations of service delivery requirements. I have in mind the minority language empathetic platforms and geospatial analysis described in Cunliffe (2019a; 2019b) or the use of ICT to deliver information involving robotic processes, software support for digital language developments and the adoption of repeatable reactions so as to speed up flows of communication. Of course, there may be some dangers inherent in the unchecked spread of such developments. Recent concerns in, for example, the BAC and Canada, have suggested that the increased automation of online bilingual services reduces the necessity for front-line service personnel to be fully bilingual as services are shifted from face-to-face interactions to automatic consumer choice options. While the legal requirements of service delivery systems are not being flouted, indeed they may be enhanced in terms of range and consistency, the capacity of the public service to operate in a bilingual manner could be severely reduced thereby.

In a climate of reduced funding, the production of ICT applications can be both edifying and politically useful as governmental authorities can argue that the provision of ICT resources can make up for reduced expenditure. But, as the Tilburg case study material of Spotti, Kroon and Li (2019) suggests, there is a double bind for new speakers in having to familiarise themselves with both the new language(s) and a command or fluency in ICT; the one may suffer as a result of lack of proficiency in the latter. Yet in a neoliberal environment, such ICT provision puts the onus on the individual to succeed or fail, and the wider question of encouraging positive outcomes becomes much more difficult to predict, assess and modify through policy and practice improvements.

The Salience of Values, Motivations and Emotions

Above and beyond the technical, managerial solutions offered by ICT there remains the ethical consideration of the respect for individual dignity. In short this is the operation of civility and related virtues such as justice, mutual co-existence, tolerance and public engagement. Recognition or non-recognition of the legitimacy of new speaker attempts to transition into fully fledged members of a speech community is a powerful, if at times delicate, variable and the conditions of possibility which determine the outcomes are ill defined at present. Neither the structural preconditions nor the triggering factors are well understood despite the detailed ethnographic descriptions we have. At times it could be that issues related to race and origin act as a deterrent to full transition or it may be that the host community objects to the new speaker on grounds of faith and religion; that is, that speakers who come from a certain religious background can never become 'one of us'. At other times it could be their social status which represents a barrier, as is often the case with refugees and asylum seekers. Abstract notions of mutual respect, human dignity and the worth of each and every individual can fall by the wayside when the scale of the integrative efforts to absorb newcomers threatens to overwhelm small, apparently fragile communities.[5] And yet for every single well-publicised act of protest or intolerance, there are scores of unreported, persistent and constructive attempts to socialise strangers in our midst, with the hope that fledgling learners of our language become in time new speakers, treated with equal dignity and worth. The continued success of the Voluntariat per la Llengua throughout Catalonia is ample evidence of the power of human friendship and commitment to the well-being of others.

---

[5] Witness the standoff between protestors and asylum seekers at Penally Camp, Wales. 'An unusual battle rages in a tourist town riven by the arrival of an asylum seeker camp', www.walesonline.co.uk/news/wales-news/tenby-penally-asylum-seeker-camp-19121558.

In order to tease out the experiential side of transitioning to become a new speaker, attention should be paid to the powerful effect of conscious and subliminal reactions to a continuous set of new speaker experiences and contact situations. For every celebrated individual who crosses the threshold from learner to new speaker there is a back story involving issues of ambition, self-worth, relationships, frustration, confusion, lack of dignity, fear of failure, shame and exposure to ridicule which can result in 'adaptation among the resisters' and 'resistance among the adapters'. These are complex issues for personality and identity construction and maintenance, and few in-depth studies have emerged to date to inform us how to handle them. It would also be significant to understand the experience of those who, while wishing to become fully fledged new speaker members of a community, have failed to do so for whatever reason. We should not be so preoccupied with the novelty of the phenomenon not to report the many instances of relative failure and rejection.

Experience and Evaluations

Ethnographic research has identified various strategies which can be adopted by all the interlocutors in an exchange so as to implement skills and make the most of the potential within each individual. But we should not under-estimate the huge effort involved in learning and interacting, and paradoxically this effort often does not get recognised by either the individual involved or the wider host community. Accordingly, it goes without saying that managing in a new language is not the same as coping with a new culture!

Thus, there is considerable potential to enquire into the lived experience of new speakers, especially the significant personal relationships they establish. This could take the form of linear tracking whereby the evolution of a relationship is recorded and monitored, identifying the strains and the successes. Non-linear trajectories could also be employed using ethnographic methods to track key stages in the learning process and the subsequent greater use of the language within the wider society. If this were to be done in a systematic manner across many societies, we could identify which trigger factors induce some people to try harder, to become mentors to others or alternatively to give up, to be demotivated and to become linguistic recidivists, so to speak. We could also identify a range of factors which have to do with formal curriculum design, the construction and deployment of resources, the medium and quality of teaching materials and methods. Then we could identify other factors which have to do with time, expenditure, convenience, isolationism and pressures. Taken together these are the considerations that condition regulated interaction, from which we can learn and distil into our interventionist behavioural strategies. The complexity of trigger factors operating within structural boundaries can also lead them to be misunderstood as the single most important variable in this process of adaptation. One does not have to be an unbiased supporter of new speaker rights and interests to recognise that the most empowering feature is to give everyone an equal say in the process. But we cannot appeal to equality in the outcome because there is too much that is unknown about what a just outcome looks like. So, in order to arrive at an equality of outcome we must perforce constrict policy choices which address these issues in a non-linguistic and largely societal sense. The primacy of outcomes, not just outputs, is a key message of this argument but, as we shall see in this volume, one of the difficulties is that outcomes are not necessarily perceived as being a constituent part of the policymakers' aims and armoury.

Searching for Evidence

In time one could imagine a whole series of evidence profiles capturing data during the transition process of learners becoming new speakers and formulating recommendations for policy. Useful broad precedents for this approach in other fields exist, for example, in clinical medical trials, such as the evaluation of breast cancer treatments or alternatively in the adoption of very specific procedures, such as the management of critical illness-related corticosteroid insufficiency (CIRCI) in critically ill patients (Djillali et al., 2017). One could readily adopt the broad outlines of such approaches particularly in relation to evidence profiling. This would require a patterned approach involving a narrative summary, outcome data, a measure of intervention effect, the significance of the outcome and a summary of the evidence for each outcome. Having undertaken such profiling, it would then be possible to formulate actionable recommendations. This requires a great deal of teamwork and collaborative interchange. In the case of corticosteroid insufficiency, the following factors were considered before constructing recommendations: 'the quality of the evidence, the balance of desirable and undesirable consequences of compared management options, the assumptions about the patient's values and preferences associated with the decision, the implications for resource use and health equity, the acceptability of intervention to stakeholders, and the feasibility of implementation' (Djillali et al., 2017).

Clearly, I am not suggesting that such detail be required for all our purposes, but a scaled-down version could prove useful for two reasons. First, because it relies on a process of evidence-based policymaking. Secondly, because the resultant recommendations would be arrived at in a collective fashion and would thereby seek to minimise any unintended bias or limited experiential judgement on behalf of the author(s) of such recommendations.

While most analyses of global migration focus on the economic push and pull factors, there is a growing literature on the forced migration patterns and processes of refugees and asylum seekers and their attempts to come to terms with the host language in their resettlement location. Spotti, Kroon and Li (2019) ask what role institutionalised language policies can have in the life of those displaced human beings that recently have been theorised as 'new speakers' (McLeod et al., 2014).

Drawing on the innovative ICT-led Virtual Neighbourhood integration classes for learning Dutch as a second language, Kurvers and Spotti (2015) critique the adequacy of these methods and conclude that students are often confused and frustrated by such machine-driven methods which eschew books, rules and 'a good dose of grammar'. Having completed the course the new speakers were unsure what they should do with their language in the ICT-based 'real life' situations, a register-bound language learning, and whether what they did with a given register was right. The lack of e-literacy that these new speakers experience when dealing with ICT-led language learning compounds their learning trajectory, especially in relation to communication skills and pronunciation.

A second intriguing issue raised by Spotti, Kroon and Li (2019) is how speakers of three languages simultaneously acquire their languages. They cite the case of youngsters of Chinese origin in the Netherlands who perforce use their Dutch at the same time as they are learning Chinese and English. For this group the very notion of learning a conventional language together with its associated cultural norms and mores is a contested reality. The central message of Spotti, Kroon and Li's analysis is that the students' bottom-up language practices and metalinguistic perspectives, in the Chinese school and on the Internet, combine to challenge the top-down family language policies of their parents who want them to learn 'Chinese' as well as learning Chinese values. The new speakers of Dutch and Chinese in the Netherlands 'seek and manage to acquire their own voice offline as well as online. In doing so they represent global youth in a superdiverse society that eclectically opts for the language and identity resources that come in handy for achieving their communicative goals irrespective of the policies set for them' (Spotti, Kroon and Li, 2019).

The authors argue that the chasm between top-down policies and bottom-up practices may yet jeopardise the very stability and harmony which national language policies seek to achieve. Not everyone would agree with the statement that 'the actual language practices and the underlying attitudes that can be observed in times of globalization led mobility are no longer a valid reflection of institutionally supported language policies, understood as "an attempt by someone to modify the linguistic behaviour of some community for some reason"', as Kaplan and Baldauf (1997, p. 3) wrote more than twenty-five years ago. But there is great merit in interrogating the ambition and progress of conventional language policies as interpreted by both refugees and long-established migrant communities.

The Impact of the Regulatory State

We recognise that just as we have had a legislative turn in relation to minority language normative ambition and rights, so we have had a regulatory turn in the interventionist stance of the state. In most cases there has been an undoubted effect of increased regulation on the lives of residents, migrants and refugees. This has included more robust language-testing regimes for applicants seeking to settle in various countries. When conducted according to the standards laid down by the Council of Europe's European Language Portfolio and linked to the categories of language use and levels of proficiency outlined in the Common European Framework of Reference for Languages (CEFR), four advantages are advanced for adult language tests, namely:

- results are standardised and reliable, which means that it is easy to compare candidates across the same or different administrations
- candidates are assessed with a high degree of independence and objectivity
- large numbers may be tested in a short space of time
- test validity helps to ensure fairness. (Council of Europe, 2020)

However, we also know that changes in immigration policy (Kurvers and Spotti, 2015) are made more acute by language tests that can be used in a variety of ways, such as for newcomers in the Netherlands, as described in Extra and Spotti (2009), or settled residents in the UK when on 18 January 2016 the Prime Minister announced a new English language requirement for family route migrants seeking to extend their stay in the UK.[6]

Such measures imply a move to greater strictures on international mobility and resettlement, and thus it would be significant to ascertain how and when many of the identifiable new speakers we investigate came either as migrants or as refugees. Is there a path dependency we can measure as to their success? What does this regulatory trend tell us about the prospects of many new speakers, especially those who came as migrants or refugees to their current home?

In contradistinction to the regulatory state, we have the rise of civil society agencies concerned with the welfare of refugees, many of which were started by former refugees themselves. A good illustration is the work of Mosaic in Vancouver. This organisation offers the following services to support the resettlement of refugees:[7]

- Welcoming privately sponsored refugees at the airport
- Providing orientation to community and to life in Canada

---

[6] Non-EEA national partners and parents on the family route would need to pass a speaking and listening test at level A2 in order to qualify. Since October 2013, adult migrants applying for settlement (indefinite leave to remain) have been required to meet level B1 in speaking and listening skills and pass the Life in the UK Test (www.gov.uk/government/news/new-a2-english-requirement-in-the-family-route).

[7] See www.mosaicbc.org/services/settlement/refugees/our-work-with-refugees/.

- Providing refurbished computers to refugee families, in partnership with BC Technology for Learning Society
- Assistance to apply for government benefits and services
- Providing training to private sponsors
- Organizing networking sessions for private sponsors and individuals interested in working/supporting refugees
- Providing language support to private sponsors
- Assisting refugees overseas who are identified by Private Sponsorship Group by completing applications and forms. (Mosaic, 2017)

Assisting such refugees to become competent in either official language is a necessary first step in their journey to becoming fluent in either/both English and French.

Once we have identified such patterns of behaviour, we can speculate further on what is the role of the law, the legislative environment, in influencing the discourse on new speakers. It would be interesting to know if there are examples of any prohibitions facing new speakers accessing the full services of the local state and, if so, what the ideological and practical justification is for such prohibition. Further we need to ask if there is an identifiable persistent negative effect being uncovered in our collective work which we should tackle if we are to be honest in our interpretation.

Engagement and Impact on Policy

The difficulties addressed in summarising the myriad strands of new speaker research force us to ask whether or not our collective work demonstrates that the new speaker phenomenon is a sufficiently robust concept and consideration to be of use in policy formulation.

In formulating realisable objectives, should policy pronouncements and recommendations be focussed explicitly on new speakers, with all the concomitant implications that it is either a very fuzzy field or an easily neglected element in the big scheme of policies devoted to education, language, workplace and integration? Or is it more advisable to include recommendations on new speakers within a continuum of policy needs and remedial actions? A stealth-like inclusion of such needs into the policy cycle may upset advocates but may win over policymakers, as it suggests a more nuanced, balanced approach until such time as a well-defined field of action can be determined.

While acknowledging their importance it is perhaps not advisable to restrict our recommendations to governments and local authorities. Rather we should recognise the salience of multi-level policy implementation, including institutional, health-care agency and organisational/business policy stratagems. Each of these will have their own internal administrative cultures, interpreting factors such as social capital, modes of governance and the management of expectations in line with their own norms and mandates. Accordingly, the recommendations advanced must take account of such variations as these institutions would need to be convinced of the origin and authority of any proposals which are directed towards their programmes of action and interventions. I doubt very much that they are minded to acknowledge the veracity of scholarly injunctions alone, thus we need partner agencies through which we can reach decision makers and have an impact.

Translating any of these recommendations into programmes requires policy conviction. In terms of normative reach, we need to ascertain whether any specific or implied reference to new speakers is a notional assent or real assent (cf. Newman, 1852) both to the concept and the working out of an action plan. From our point of view as scholar/activists we need to determine if it is mere signification or conviction policymaking that we are aiming to advance. If the latter, what best practice approaches can we supply to policymakers?

We recognise that a supportive context is essential if an adequate infrastructure is to flow from policy intervention; thus, we need to ask in what ways can we create a legitimisation of positive feelings toward new speakers as well as evidence of their needs. The hegemonic majority is key to the overall process and their views should be factored into policy formulation, as they will ultimately be the wielders of power.

We should not assume that any emergent new speaker policy will be necessarily popular or politically acceptable. It has to be fought for, and over, just like any other intrusive/additional policy. We should expect a lack of agreement on several policy suggestions, even if the evidence is sound. Then fledgling policies have to be mainstreamed and enriched as a result of on-going analysis and treated as a public good, especially in those jurisdictions where new speakers form a growing proportion of the target population, such as Catalonia, Ireland and the Basque Autonomous Community.

The Case against New Speaker Initiatives

We could provide a signal service to those who wish to advance the cause of new speakers by identifying the barriers to further development among opponents. Knowing which arguments to contend with is half the battle if a strategy of cumulative pressure is to be effective.

Perhaps the most deep-seated objections to actioning new speaker initiatives are ideological. It is far too simplistic to assume that this is a manifestation of a majority–minority, zero-sum contestation. Such binary divides are not helpful in interpreting a very complex situation. We know that within majoritarian societies there are strong advocates of language diversity and language justice and within minority communities there are very conservative ideologues who would rather see their languages atrophy than be rendered a 'bastardised tongue' by the infusion of so many loan words, non-native forms of sentence construction, mangled mutations and the like.

One way forward would be to seek insights into the ideological origins of opposition from among the established theories of language contact and conflict and political ethics. Yael Peled and Matteo Bonotti (2019) argue that 'How we think about language tends to significantly influence, if not shape, how we think about the political ethics of language, namely how we theorize language when considering the empirical and normative dimensions of political life. In the history of ideas, approaches to language, and, consequently, to linguistic agency, generally fall under either the "designative" or "constitutive" category (Taylor, 2016).' They explain that Taylor's designative view sees language as a logos-based system of labels that are detached from the life and experience of the speaker, and which are employed to represent, order and understand a reality that pre-exists and is independent from them. The constitutive viewpoint identifies language as a socially embedded dialogic and interactive process and is normally premised on the idea of linguistic holism:

This is the view that different languages provide a distinctly comprehensive system of meaning through which co-linguals jointly perceive and experience the world. But the holistic label can also be extended to the designative category in certain cases, especially when it is grounded in a perception that considers ontological monolingualism (Schmidt, 2014) to be a natural state of individuals and societies. (Peled and Bonotti, 2019).

Peled and Bonotti argue that the premise of ontological monolingualism, and the epistemic holism it presupposes, are no longer an adequate basis for theorising moral and political agency in language. So many of the fundamental tenets of political theorising about language, including opposition to recognising the co-equality of languages in the linguistic justice debate, are based on a monolingual experience of the world; reminding us of the old Marxian principle that the theories not only describe to us what the reality of the situation is but also how it should be! And yet for an increasing number of individuals, their daily lives as members of a bi- or multilingual network run counter to such assumptions.[8]

Accordingly, long-standing assumptions about the sufficiency and normalcy of state hegemonic languages need to be challenged if linguistic pluralism is to flourish. This is as true for citizens who have a range of powerful languages in their repertoire, such as English, French or German, as it is for those who speak an admixture of powerful and lesser-used languages such as Spanish, French and Basque. Linguistic justice and linguistic equality, together with

---

[8] http://blogs.cardiff.ac.uk/openfordebate/2017/09/11/the-ethics-of-linguistic-plurality/.

ecolinguistics and the embedding of traditional ecological knowledge in local languages, are promising attempts to counter the pervasive influence of monolingual normative and ideological currents in social and political thought. Demonstrating how linguistic ethics and linguistic ecology can raise awareness regarding human diversity is challenging enough; harnessing linguistics so as to address key ecological issues, from climate change and biodiversity loss to environmental justice is a much bigger task. And yet if an alliance can be formed between advocates of lesser-used languages, ecologists, proponents of subsidiarity[9] and regionalists, it might be possible to embed more radical streams of justice within official discourses relating to minority language communities.

Civil Society Policymakers and Stakeholders

Over and above the advice offered to governmental policymakers there are many other layers of influence we should seek to inform. The most logical and immediate for us are the academic networks and scholarly publications, which are our stock-in-trade. Then there are the professional bodies in language and education, concerned with curriculum development, pedagogical techniques and assessment frameworks. Thirdly, there are the civil society organisations and institutions which are the bedrock of minority communities, including social development agencies, student and teachers' associations, arts and cultural venues, museums, leisure and sporting clubs, local media and most third sector activities. Finally, there are the specialist agencies concerned with refugee processing and migrant adjustment. Whilst not yet ready to formulate programmes for new speakers in toto, such agencies do offer a vital first step on the road to competence in a target language and are thus part of the purview of new speaker concerns.

Diffusing information, detailing specific case studies and making robust arguments regarding the pertinence of new speakers for interpreting a changing reality within multicultural societies may be sufficient for the majority of researchers. The fascination for them is to identify and track new identities, new processes of sociolinguistic transformation, to detail how varieties of speech and the construction of linguistic forms are being impacted by the presence of different speakers. Is this sufficient? It may be argued that this is the norm for scholarship, and it is the responsibility of others outside academia to make of such studies what they will for social and political purposes.

---

[9] Jean-Pierre Danthine, 'Subsidiarity: The forgotten concept at the core of Europe's existential crisis'. *Vox EU* 12, April 2017. https://voxeu.org/article/subsidiarity-still-key-europe-s-institutional-problems.

This objection does not hold, for in so many fields of human thought and action the application of scholarly enquiry to the improvement of the quality of life has been the desiderata. I contend it is the same for the new speaker phenomenon. Accordingly, one of our pressing collective considerations should be to write policy briefing papers on a variety of related topics; to prepare articles on our findings for the media and social network channels so as to raise awareness and influence public discourse; to ally ourselves with relevant lobbying groups and contribute the data and evidence they need to articulate their messages. In time it may be that some are invited to present evidence in submissions to parliamentary committees and reviews or to other governmental agencies through access to decision makers/civil servants who are seeking to construct a narrative discourse on the changing nature of our multicultural societies. Underpinning all these efforts there remains the constant opportunity to pepper our private conversations with colleagues, friends and neighbours so that supportive insights can feed into the popular discourse concerning the wider variety of speakers in our midst.

Artificial Intelligence and Communication

We should not under-estimate the powerful advantages which can accrue through the embedding of AI within lesser-used language communication networks. Deep machine learning can assist knowledge and its application through many dimensions in so many fields of human endeavour and experience. Well-placed language communities can benefit by piggybacking on developments within larger language groupings if the infrastructure is in place in fields such as public administration, education, health sciences and the like. However, as a consequence of digital developments, such as machine learning and commercial communication strategies, hegemonic languages are likely to increase their power and influence, posing fresh challenges for lesser-used languages. Three issues command our attention. First, which type of agency, if not government, will seek to secure some degree of engagement in such developments on behalf of lesser-used language speakers? Digital exclusion from the mainstream is a real possibility for many unless there are interventionist and prescient political authorities willing to invest and anticipate future developments. Secondly, were lesser-used language speakers to be able to benefit from access to these digital developments, who controls, regulates and proctors continued access? Newer forms of dependency will ensue as much of our behaviour will be influenced by sophisticated algorithms and consequently choice may be severely limited, thereby reducing the vitality of such languages in significant domains. Thirdly, there is the question of liability. If there is an interruption in digital developments leading to digital tension, which agency will resolve resultant issues and at what cost to whom?

Conclusion: The Glimpsed and the Possible

What will happen to our collective work once the organising framework of the New Speakers Network is removed? Let me conclude with some salient challenges yet to be faced in all the societies represented within the COST Network. The first is that given the sterling efforts to construct such a rich and productive network, measures should be put in place to encourage the sustainable development of the efforts made to date so that fruitful co-operation can be maintained. More intriguing suggestions for sustained innovative work could be entertained, especially as we widen our sphere of influence to other disciplines and agencies. We should identify and mobilise our involvement with stakeholders and organisations that would most likely benefit from learning from and adopting some of our ideas and findings. Let us be honest with ourselves and ask, do our ideas and contributions have sufficient merit to infuse the policy communities we seek to influence? If so, how will we seek to track the efficacy of our interventions? Will best practice transfer be recorded, evaluated and improved? Above all, perhaps, we need to determine how we might engage new speakers themselves to take increased ownership of the policy-influencing process itself rather than speak on their behalf.

Learning is at the heart of the process of paradigmatic change. The normative advocacy approach we are tempted to adopt should not blind us to our own analytical weaknesses or the methodological mistakes in our work. Accordingly, we should acknowledge errors and identify those parts of initiatives which do not work, so that best practice principles and processes do not become suspect as a result of an over-exaggeration of the effects of intervention. Fundamentally, as researchers on new speakers we constitute a community of learners ourselves and it behoves us to share that knowledge with a range of stakeholders in society.

Towards a New Speaker Consciousness

New speaker consciousness is controversial because it does not constitute an established body of knowledge undergirded by a long pedigree. There is little doubt that there are very promising strands to celebrate. Perhaps the most hopeful sign is a recognition that the oft-predicted ineluctable decline of selected minority languages can be mitigated by the production of new generations of speakers through the statutory education system. The change of attitude towards bilingualism and multilingualism by so many parents and responsible governments at both national and local level is encouraging. However, we should not take such gains for granted, as there are so many examples of countervailing pressures, most notably within the contemporary

Spanish state, that vigilance and resistance remain the watchwords of the open society.

My task in the remainder of the volume is to sift the evidence, dissect the arguments and ascertain to what extent the contours of a shared consciousness can be mapped and measured so as to offer a pathway to more holistic and focussed analyses in the future.

3 Wales: Normalised Expectations

The salient feature regarding Welsh language vitality is not that it has experienced an epiphenomenal trajectory but that it survives at all, given the country's steady incorporation into the burgeoning English/British state over many centuries. Following its conquest in 1277–83, Wales was formally incorporated into the English realm by the Henrician Acts of Union 1536 and 1542 and one of the provisions was the banning of Welsh from public life. However, under Elizabeth I in 1567 a translation of the New Testament into Welsh was prepared by William Salesbury and his colleagues Richard Davies and Thomas Huet. By 1588 the whole of the Bible had been translated by William Morgan and accordingly the Welsh language not only became a medium for religious observance, sealing the populace in its Protestant faith, but also its elegant and standardised linguistic forms provided a rich foundation upon which a whole range of literary and scholarly activity could be produced.

As a result of continued political assimilation, anglicisation and industrialisation, the Welsh language was weakened further and during the twentieth century lost a great deal of ground (Williams, 1980; Morgan, 1995). In reaction to this, revitalisation efforts have been marked by increasing sophistication, specialisation and breadth of approach.[1]

Wales has historically been more closely bound to England than has Scotland, whether in terms of legal, economic or political domains. Geographic interaction along a common, open boundary has resulted in several Welsh social and economic networks being focussed on English urban cores such as Liverpool, Manchester, Chester, Stoke on Trent, Birmingham, Bristol and especially London. This pattern of core–hinterland physical and social communication has resulted in a close integration of the Welsh populace into UK space while its coastal strips have also served as a road and rail transit corridor linking Ireland with the primate English cities of the expanding British economy. Anglicisation was promoted through the passage of prohibitive

---

[1] The concern with devising an official policy for Welsh language education within the Welsh Department of the Education Board may be traced to 1907; thereafter a small number of highly influential central government reports drew attention to the desirability of increasing the provision of Welsh language teaching.

measures against the use of Welsh in public life and when in the nineteenth century early patterns of popular education were established, Welsh had no official place on the curriculum. Consequently, the dominant language is English while Welsh is spoken by around a quarter of the population.

So much of the vitality of Welsh language and culture happens organically through communal activities such as the Young Farmers Clubs, *eisteddfodau*, a vibrant musical scene, sport and drama groups. To which one may add the opportunities for the development of friendship and talent within the Urdd movement and the many competitive aspects of the National Eisteddfod. These opportunities to socialise and enjoy aspects of life in and through Welsh provide the everyday background to this analysis, whereas the prime focus is to investigate the contribution of government, organisations and agencies to the construction of a supportive infrastructure for the promotion of Welsh. Then the chapter describes the responses of officials, civil society agencies and academic specialists to my enquiries concerning language policy and new speaker interests.[2]

The general understanding seems to be that new speakers have long been a feature of Welsh life, as a result of the intermingling of families, community socialisation and work practices associated with the industrialisation and urbanisation processes of the mid-eighteenth century and particularly the nineteenth century which attracted thousands of immigrants from the rest of the UK and Europe. At its apogee in 1911 the Census recorded the highest number of Welsh speakers – 977,366, constituting 43.5 per cent of the population. The twentieth century witnessed a decline such that by 1991 there were only 508,000 speakers, constituting 18.7 per cent of the population. At the 2001 Census the number of Welsh speakers increased for the first time in over 100 years, with 575,744 or 20.8 per cent of a population of over 2.9 million claiming fluency in Welsh. A further 28 per cent of the population of Wales claimed to understand Welsh. By 2011 some 562,000, 19 per cent of the population, were recorded as being able to speak Welsh.

Conventionally the hearth and the community were the prime sites of language production but since the 1950s the expansion of Welsh immersion education has produced at least three generations of speakers. Accordingly, many whom I interviewed thought the process, if not always the term new speaker, was an integral part of the social history of the language and some did

---

[2] These include interviews and discussions with Cefin Campbell, AS Gwenllian Lansdown Davis, Lowri Davies, Paula Evans, Cathryn Griffith, Ifor Gruffydd, Gwennan Higham, Meri Huws, Eleri James, Carol Jenkins, Hywel Charles Jones, Kathryn Jones, Meirion Prys Jones, Steve Morris, Hywel B. Owen, Helen Prosser, Ruth Richards, the late Aled Roberts and Dafydd Trystan. Bethan Webb and her team within the Welsh Language Division of the Welsh Government have been generous with their time and information during our regular meetings since 2015. Other public servants and politicians also contributed but wished to remain anonymous.

not want to make a fetish of the process by singling out new speakers as a distinct category, hence the title of this chapter. A representative view is that of M. P. Jones, the former Chief Executive of the Welsh Language Board who observed that 'New speakers is not a term practised / used in the Welsh speaking community. All who speak / show a desire to speak Welsh are welcome. There is great respect for people who have learned' (Jones, pers. comm., 2021; author's translation).

The general presumption is that there is something specific, but not unique, about Welsh-medium culture that predisposes people to welcome all who have learned the language and seek to 'fit in' to the local and national community. We shall see to what extent this is a generic feature of all the minoritised communities examined in this volume, or whether some cases are more reticent to welcome entrants as new speakers.

But first let us examine the latest data on Welsh speakers to set the scene. While the 2011 Census reported that 562,016 people (19 per cent) were able to speak Welsh, intervening Annual Population Surveys (APS) have reported higher figures. For the year ending 31 June 2022 the APS reported that 29.7 per cent of people aged three or over were able to speak Welsh, which equates to 899,500 people. This is 0.5 percentage points higher than the previous year, equating to around 13,700 more people.

Figure 3.1 reveals how the number of speakers has been gradually increasing since March 2010 (25.2 per cent, at 731,000), after gradually declining from 2001 to 2007. The number of people able to speak Welsh decreased from December 2018 to March 2020, before increasing again in the most recent four quarters.[3] The Chief Statistician advises that such results highlight the issues around the subjective nature of self-assessment of language ability. There is a positive trend in the numbers reporting that they speak Welsh in surveys: both in the APS and for those reporting to have 'some Welsh language ability' in the National Survey.[4] However, it is the Census which informs long-term strategy regarding the health of the language

As Figure 3.2 demonstrates, the highest numbers of Welsh speakers continue to be found in Carmarthenshire (94,600) and Gwynedd (90,700). The lowest numbers of Welsh speakers are in Blaenau Gwent (10,900) and Merthyr Tydfil (11,600). The highest percentages of Welsh speakers are in Gwynedd (76 per cent) and the Isle of Anglesey (68 per cent). The lowest percentages of Welsh speakers are in Blaenau Gwent (16 per cent), Monmouthshire (16 per cent) and Bridgend (18 per cent).

---

[3] Government data analysts advise that this increase should be treated with caution due to the change of survey mode since mid-March 2020 because of the Covid-19 pandemic. Source: https://gov.wales/welsh-language-data-annual-population-survey.

[4] https://digitalanddata.blog.gov.wales/2019/03/27/chief-statisticians-update-a-discussion-about-the-welsh-language-data-from-the-annual-population-survey/.

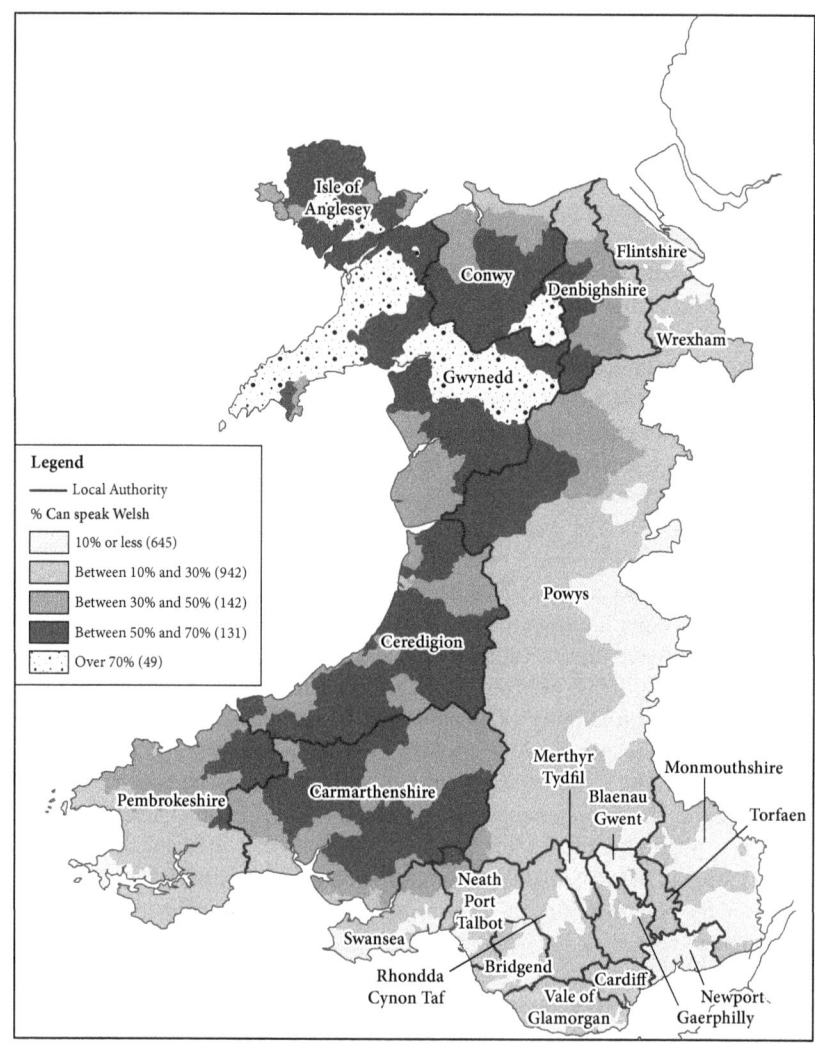

Figure 3.1 Proportion of people (aged three and over) able to speak Welsh, by LSOA, 2011 (Source: 2011 Census)

Government strategy seeks to emphasise regular language use and thus it is revealing that 14.8 per cent 449,900 of people aged three or over reported that they spoke Welsh daily, 5.6 per cent 169,700 weekly and 7.6 per cent 229,500 less often. Around 1.7 per cent 50.300 reported that they never used Welsh

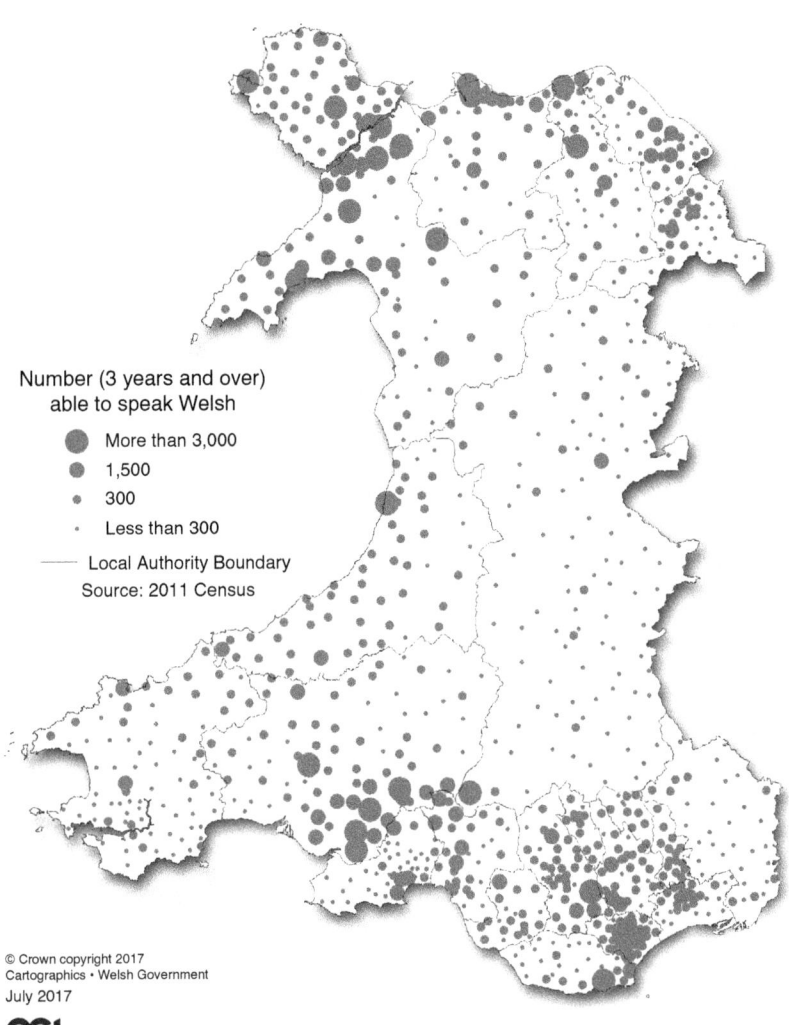

Figure 3.2 Number able to speak Welsh by community, 2011 (By permission of the Welsh Government)

despite being able to speak it, with the remaining 70.3 per cent not able to speak Welsh. Some 33.4 per cent 1,013,000 reported that they could understand spoken Welsh, 26.0 per cent 789,700 could read and 24 per cent 726,200 could write Welsh. These figures are generally more encouraging than those provided by the decennial census results as the last Census in 2011 reported that 562,016 people were able to speak Welsh. The Chief Statistician warns that the APS results are indicative and should be used to monitor trends between Censuses, while the Census should be taken as a more reliable measure of linguistic vitality as the results of the 2021 Census do provide insighs into the progress towards the current government target of producing a million Welsh speakers by 2050.

The Institutional and Socio-economic Context of Language Revitalisation

Three distinct phases of language revitalisation may be identified. In the period 1912–62, the concern was with gaining public recognition for the language and with establishing a designated Welsh language education system The second stage, c.1962–1980s, witnessed a period of mobilisation linked to a wider sustained protest at the perceived discriminatory treatment of Welsh in civic life.[5] Mobilisation efforts sought to promote the growth of Welsh-medium education, to ensure bilingual public services and to secure the establishment of a Welsh-medium television channel, S4C. The third, current, stage is preoccupied with two different sets of challenges. The first is the spatial and geolinguistic impact of differential migration on predominantly Welsh-speaking communities and the attempts to 'normalise' Welsh through expanding the demolinguistic base of pupils who attend Welsh-medium schools. The challenge is to construct a sociolinguistic context which reinforces Welsh language skills and regular usage outside the school-based socialisation experience. A second political, administrative and legal challenge has to do with constructing a national infrastructure which embeds the current opportunities to use Welsh more deeply within society. The focus here has been on the articulation of language policy, citizen services and rights and the passage of new language legislation, the role of IT in accessing virtual and digital space and the need to secure a greater presence for Welsh language skills within the economy.

The government's current long-term strategy, *Cymraeg 2050*, seeks to both increase the numbers capable of speaking Welsh and significantly improve the opportunities to use the language across most domains. This is part of an evolutionary approach to improving the position of Welsh in legislative,

---

[5] 1962 was the date of the BBC radio lecture by Saunders Lewis, *Tynged yr Iaith*, which acted as a catalyst for the formation of influential actors such as Cymdeithas yr Iaith Gymraeg (The Welsh Language Society), and subsequently Cefn, RHAG (a parents' association promoting Welsh-medium education), CYDAG (a national association representing Welsh-medium schools) and more episodically Cymuned (a community-based action group established in 2001).

administrative and socio-economic terms. Significant reforms have included the Welsh Language (Wales) Measure of 2011, which made Welsh an official language and established a Welsh Language Commissioner while introducing Welsh Language Standards (No. 5) Regulations 2016, which helped normalise the use of Welsh both in honouring the official status of the languages and in raising expectations through imposing standards on service delivery.[6] The immediate impact was to embed more Welsh-designated positions in the workforce and to increase the internal use of Welsh in many organisations.

The Welsh Language Commissioner contends that:

> The development that has had the most far-reaching impact on the position of the Welsh language in the public domain in recent years must be the introduction of the Welsh language standards. To date, 123 public organisations have specific legal duties relating to the Welsh language. These may relate to communicating with or delivering services to the public, formulating policies or using Welsh internally in the workplace. (Welsh Language Commission, 2021, p. 303)

The most important advance was that the language standards imposed a statutory obligation on local authorities to prepare a Welsh language promotional strategy every five years, thus enabling consistency and cumulative growth to characterise the system (James, pers. comm., 2021). However, it is recognised that 'there is also no requirement for those organisations that are subject to standards to monitor the use made of the Welsh language.' (Welsh Language Commission, 2021, p. 303). Further,

> the second target of *Cymraeg 2050* is to double the daily use of the language and therefore careful, but urgent, consideration needs to be given as to how to measure that progress in a meaningful way. In order to see real progress, one of our consistent findings is that more needs to be done to promote the Welsh language services available. Even in the absence of robust data, it can be said with certainty that the number of people currently choosing to use Welsh language services does not match the number who can speak the language. (Welsh Language Commission, 2021, p. 304)

Commentators often credit Plaid Cymru with championing the Welsh language and culture. Whilst this is true, Plaid does not have a monopoly on language intervention, relying as much on influence as on real power to effect action. At the UK level it has been successive Conservative governments which

---

[6] 'WLWM 2011 was made under Part 3 of the Government of Wales Act 2006 (GOWA 2006). This meant that it had to relate to the specific matters (and could not relate to any of the exceptions) set out in Schedule 5 to that Act. The National Assembly for Wales now makes Acts under Part 4 of GOWA 2006, and the limitations on the National Assembly's competence are now those set out in Schedule 7A and 7B. However, both WLWM 2011 and any orders or regulations (including regulations specifying the standards) made under WLWM 2011 must comply with the limitations in Schedule 5 because WLWM was made under Part 3' (https://law.gov.wales/culture/welsh-language/welsh-language-wales-measure-2011/?lang=en#/culture/welsh-language/welsh-language-wales-measure-2011/?tab=overview&lang=en).

have introduced significant elements, such as the enlargement of the Welsh Office and the establishment of S4C on 1 November 1982, following the campaign led by the Plaid Cymru president Gwynfor Evans (Evans, 2008).

Similarly, it was the Labour administration of Harold Wilson which introduced the 1967 Welsh Language Act, and Labour local authorities in Wales who pioneered Welsh-medium education. Following the Government of Wales Act 1998 which established a devolved National Assembly, the Labour-led administrations have been active in promoting and regulating aspects of the use of Welsh, particularly in public administration.

Since its establishment on 4 August 1962 the lightning rod of Welsh language activism has been Cymdeithas yr Iaith Gymraeg, which operates in three spheres. The first is its non-violent direct action campaigning programme highlighting issues such as community development, bilingual education, housing and legislative reforms. The second is its preparation of detailed policy papers, often drawing on acknowledged experts within specialist fields. The third is its role as a social events organiser, gigs and festivals adding an element of enjoyment and frisson to living and being in and through Welsh.[7] Whilst Cymdeithas does not have a long history of interpreting the role of new speakers, it has produced a number of papers and statements relating to the development of the educational curriculum, particularly the debate over second language status and provision for learners. It has a learner's development officer and committee and organises regular learner weekends and events.[8] It also makes representation to national and local authorities on issues relating to the national curriculum, the threatened closure or reorganisation of Welsh-medium schools and the rights of parents to enable their children to receive a Welsh-medium education.

The Education System and the Production of New Speakers

Cymdeithas, together with other actors, has long recognised that the education system is central to language revitalisation and promotional efforts. The statutory education system and the Welsh for Adults (now termed Dysgu Cymraeg / Learn Welsh) framework provides the essential taught element of competence and skills which new speakers apprehend as part of their learning process.[9] In 2021 there were 420 designated primary schools delivering Welsh-medium education to almost 65,380 learners across Wales (c.24 per cent), and 49 secondary schools delivering Welsh-medium education to 44,762 learners (22.7 per cent). Within the dominant English-medium school system, Welsh is taught up to the age of sixteen and an attempt has been made to introduce

---

[7] https://cymdeithas.cymru/news/archive?page=1.
[8] https://cymdeithas.cymru/search/node/pwyllgor%20dysgwyr.   [9] https://dysgucymraeg.cymru.

a stronger bilingual ethos into some schools by establishing Welsh-medium streams and emphasising Welsh-content elements within the revised national curriculum. The key developments in the evolution of Welsh-medium education may be found in Thomas and Williams (2013), while this chapter will focus on the current debate surrounding educational reform to ascertain to what extent any of the thinking regarding the new speaker concept has informed debates and decisions.

The core of the debate has been the issue of skill development and the categorisation of whole schools and pupils according to Welsh linguistic criteria. The performance of, and division between, first and second language learners has been a concern of practitioners and commentators for some time, so much so that the government announced significant reviews of both the education system writ large and of the role of Welsh within it. An important contribution was 'One Language For All – Review of Welsh Second Language at Key Stages 3 and 4' (Welsh Government, 2013b). The report highlighted a number of issues in Welsh second language provision as follows.

- Pupils do not continue to develop their Welsh skills well enough on transition to Key Stages 2 and 3;
- The time allocated to teaching the subject is not sufficient, and in some schools, the allocation is as little as one hour a fortnight;
- Many teachers in primary schools lack confidence and ability to teach Welsh second language;
- Too many pupils who follow the GSCE Welsh second language short course are entered for the foundation tier though they are capable of gaining A*- B grades which cannot be achieved in the foundation tier;
- In most schools there are not enough opportunities for pupils to hear and practise using the language beyond formal Welsh lessons; and
- In too many secondary schools, the subject is taught by non-specialist teachers who lack a thorough understanding of second language teaching methodology. (Welsh Government, 2013b)

The report identified:

- The need to embed processes for planning Welsh-medium provision: strengthening strategic planning processes for all phases of education and training continues to be a priority;
- The need for improved workforce planning and support for practitioners: ensuring a sufficient workforce for Welsh-medium education and training is vital; and
- The need to ensure that young people have the confidence to use their Welsh language skills in all walks of life: education and training alone cannot guarantee that speakers become fluent in Welsh or choose to use the language in their everyday lives. (Welsh Government, 2013b).

It recommended that the Welsh Government should 'ensure that Welsh second language continues to be a statutory subject within the National Curriculum and continues to be a compulsory subject for all pupils in Wales until the end of Key Stage 4' (Welsh Government, 2013b).

Welsh was considered within the broader educational framework and was influenced by the Welsh Government's decision to recast its curriculum design following the recommendations of the Donaldson Report (Welsh Government, 2015a) which argued that all children and young people should be:

> ambitious, capable learners, ready to learn throughout their lives
> enterprising, creative contributors, ready to play a full part in life and work
> ethical, informed citizens of Wales and the world
> healthy, confident individuals, ready to lead fulfilling lives as valued members of society. (Welsh Government 2015a)

Different Categories of Bilingual Schools

As a category, bilingual high schools may be divided into four non-statutory subdivisions according to the percentage of subjects taught through the medium of Welsh, and whether there is parallel provision in English. In Type A schools at least 80 per cent of subjects, apart from Welsh and English, are taught only through the medium of Welsh to all pupils. One or two subjects are taught to some pupils in English or in both languages. In Type B at least 80 per cent of subjects, excluding Welsh and English, are taught through the medium of Welsh, but are also taught through the medium of English. In Type C 50–79 per cent of subjects, excluding Welsh and English, are taught through the medium of Welsh, but are also taught through the medium of English. In Type D all subjects, except Welsh and English, are taught to all pupils using both languages. Clearly with such a variety of actual practice there is a need for a more robust definition of what counts as a Welsh-medium or bilingual school and the government is currently seeking to generalise or standardise the type of education received within this broad sectoral category so as to conform with the new Cynlluniau Strategol y Gymraeg mewn Addysg (CSGA; Welsh in Education Strategic Plans).[10]

Currently there is an ongoing debate on the adequacy of curriculum development, the sufficiency of teacher training, the role of Welsh as a subject and Welsh as a medium of teaching and most critically a definition of what counts as a Welsh-medium or bilingual school. These issues figure prominently in the various political party statements on the need for new Welsh education legislation. In more broad terms there is a debate on the whole issue of second

---

[10] https://gov.wales/school-categories-according-welsh-medium-provision.

language acquisition and a separate but equally pressing issue regarding the attitude of some who demonstrate resistance to bilingualism and express fears and suspicions of the bilingual agenda. Part of this has to do with identity politics and part with a perception that too much attention has been focussed on the Welsh language, which threatens to increase the distinctiveness of Wales within the UK. This is a long-standing issue, as in other jurisdictions such as Ireland or the Basque Country, and has little to do with the recent Brexit divisions in the UK.

Both government spokespeople and specialists acknowledge that despite the spectacular growth there remain weaknesses in the bilingual education provision. The most salient are the inconsistency in the nature of the educational experience provided; the confusion elicited by the four identifiable 'types' of bilingual schools; the poor succession rates at each stage in education, primary (26 per cent) secondary (17 per cent) and tertiary (4 per cent); and the general perception that there is too much fragmentation in sector.

In January 2022 the Welsh Government advised that following a review of international trends in stimulating minority language education, particularly the Basque experience, it was minded to establish a tripartite categorisation of both primary and secondary schools:

Categori 1: Ysgol Cyfrwng Saesneg/English-medium School
Categori 2: Ysgol Dwy Iaith/Dual Language School
Categori 3: Ysgol Cyfrwng Cymraeg/Welsh-medium School.

The details and implications as set out in the government report (Welsh Government, 2022) were partially implemented in September 2022 when a fuller consideration was given to the supportive infrastructure necessary to realise these educational and political ambitions, including a statutory basis for the definition and justification for the new categorisation.

In welcoming this initiative on which he acted as adviser, M. P. Jones stated that, 'I hope that the Government will now insert the new categorization system in the Bill for Welsh Medium Education that they intend to publish in the next couple of years. This would significantly strengthen the position of Welsh Medium Education' (Jones, pers. comm., 2022). While it is anticipated that there will be challenges in operationalising this new system, the fundamental aim is to provide more opportunities for pupils currently in English-medium schools to engage with Welsh to a far greater degree than hitherto. It is recognised that these reforms may also impact on the salience of Welsh-medium schools as an option for some pupils, especially at the secondary level, but my view is that such reforms offer a clearer and more systematic way of planning for the greater institutionalisation of Welsh within the education system, so that the twin pressures of parental demand and numerical growth may be satisfied.

If these are generally well-understood structural weaknesses, why they have not been addressed until now? Part of the answer pertains to where power lies in the system. The Department of Education and Skills had a crucial role to play, but the relationship with local authorities was often tense when it came to sanctioning or disallowing the establishment of Welsh-medium schools. There have been struggles (at times very acrimonious) surrounding school reorganisation in several areas past, such as at Cardiff (Morgan, 2013), Caerphilly, Carmarthenshire and at Sandfields Neath Port Talbot. Until its abolition in 2012 the Welsh Language Board had a statutory duty to provide strategic oversight of this sector, but in truth it had little real power to direct. Its former Chief Executive M. P. Jones observes that 'it was only in 2010 with the publication of the Strategy for Welsh-medium Education that the Welsh Government first assumed strategic responsibility for Welsh-medium/bilingual education in Wales. That process is still developing and government expertise in the field is growing slowly. They also missed all targets set out in the 2010 strategic document!' (Jones, pers. comm., 2021).

Direct oversight now rests with the Welsh Government which has devised a system of Welsh in Education Strategic Plans (WESPs) to regulate provision which has made important contributions to improvements within the sector. The Welsh-Medium Education Strategy (WMES) in April 2010 was included as a statutory duty in the School Standards and Organization (Wales) Act 2013. The strategy sets out six strategic aims and a number of objectives within them:

- To improve the planning of Welsh-medium provision in the pre-statutory and statutory phases of education, based on informed parental demand;
- To improve the planning of Welsh-medium provision in the post-14 phases of education and training, taking account of linguistic progression and continuing development of skills;
- To ensure that all learners develop their Welsh language skills to their full potential, and encourage sound linguistic progression from one phase of education and training to the next;
- To ensure a Welsh-medium education workforce that provides sufficient numbers of practitioners for all phases of education and training, with high-quality Welsh language skills and competence in teaching methodologies;
- To improve the central support mechanisms for Welsh-medium education and training; and
- To contribute to the acquisition and reinforcement of Welsh language skills in families and in the community. (Welsh Government, 2010)

The government's aims for this sector are set out in the Cymraeg 2050 declarations and more particularly the Welsh in Education Action Plan 2017–2021.[11] This states that:

- It is the Welsh Government's policy that all pupils should study Welsh from ages 3–16, either first or second language.

---

[11] https://beta.gov.wales/welsh-education-action-plan-2017-2021.

- Approximately 16% of pupils attend Welsh-medium schools and study Welsh as a first language. A further 10% attend bilingual, dual-medium, or English with significant Welsh provision.
- Welsh Government statistics show that in 2014, 22.2% of 7-year-old learners were assessed through the medium of Welsh first language and 17.1% of 14-year-olds were assessed in Welsh first language. (Welsh Government, 2017f)

Debates Concerning the Welsh Language in Education

A significant issue for educational practitioners and for achieving government targets in relation to second language learning is the consistently low-level standard of teaching and linguistic progress as reported by Estyn, the Education and Training Inspectorate for Wales.[12] The Annual Report of Her Majesty's Chief Inspector of Education and Training in Wales 2016–2017 had this to say about the principal shortcomings:

> Two-thirds of English-medium secondary schools do not plan well enough to develop pupils' Welsh language skills. As a result, most pupils do not practise their Welsh often enough outside Welsh lessons and lack confidence in speaking the language. Planning for progression at important transition points between key stages is weak. This is an important shortcoming in the majority of schools across Wales. (Estyn, 2017, p. 70).

Two earlier reports had focussed on the review of teacher education (Welsh Government, 2014b) and on the teaching of Welsh as a Second Language (Welsh Government, 2014c). The latter was a final version of the 'One Language for All' (2013) analysis which drew attention to the weaknesses in the manner in which Welsh was taught and advocated the abolition of the curriculum and the qualification divide between first and second language learners. Drawing on these three reports the Welsh Government announced far-reaching changes to the manner in which Welsh and other languages were to be taught within the statutory education sector as part of a new curriculum for Wales. The former Education and Skills Minister Kirsty Williams declared, 'We want all our learners to be citizens of both Wales and the world and that means ensuring that all young people from all backgrounds have an opportunity to develop their language skills – whether that's in Welsh, English or international languages.'[13]

The new national curriculum will be taught to those up to Year 6 from September 2022. Years 7 and 8 will all be taught with it from 2023 and it will then roll out year by year until it includes Year 11 by 2026. It will see Welsh remain compulsory for all learners aged three to sixteen alongside English, but no longer separated into first and second language programmes of study. All

---

[12] For details on Estyn visit www.estyn.gov.wales/.
[13] www.walesonline.co.uk/news/education/subject-second-language-welsh-being-15693728.

learners will follow the same curriculum and there will be more of an emphasis on improving their skills and use of the language.

The four regional school improvement consortia are planning ways to ensure teachers can deliver the changes through professional learning including the recruitment and retention of teachers and the augmentation of a sabbatical scheme of intensive Welsh language training for teachers and teaching assistants. Currently a continuum, a sliding scale of performance and assessment and a recasting of the primacy of teaching Welsh as a first language constitute the elements of the new approach to promoting Welsh within the education system. This reform has sparked controversy by both supporters and detractors of Welsh. It is argued that in-service teacher training and the sabbatical scheme, while doubtless efficient in improving skills and creating new speakers, both represent remedial action which would be mitigated were the teacher education programme for relevant teachers to include a year of intensive Welsh courses (Gruffydd, pers. comm., 2021).

Cymwysterau Cymru, the regulatory body for educational qualifications in Wales, advocates the development of separate qualifications for first and second language learners and the latter is likely to create a space for a new descriptor of non-native speakers. But in truth how sustainable is the idea of a continuum and with what effect for the teaching of Welsh as a first language? Opposing such reforms Simon Brooks has pointed to the fact that:

A 'language continuum' will destroy the principle of Welsh-medium education, replacing it with an emphasis on 'bilingual' schools. English of course will remain a proper language, taught not on a continuum but as a first language. Welsh instead becomes a second language for all. It a nonsense that children who cannot hold a conversation in a language be on a continuum with those who speak Welsh as a first language all day, every day. This is a damaging idea which will harm the education of children all over Wales. (Brooks, 2019)

Others such as Ifor Gruffydd argue that:

consideration should be given to using a communicative methodology for new speakers in schools up to year 11. Young people need to use the Welsh language and feel that they can assimilate (at least to some degree). The formal register taught in the curriculum militates against using their Welsh naturally orally (as they will sound different). Language is a communication tool, and the method used in schools does not facilitate that. The more formal and literary elements could be introduced whilst studying Advanced level Welsh. (Gruffydd, pers. comm., 2021)

The new speaker paradigm has promised a way of easing this tension and of providing a new social category of competent speakers who were not mother tongue Welsh but rather have learned the language either through the education system or as a result of social immersion. The difficulty is that there is no universal definition of who qualifies as a new speaker and as a consequence it is that much harder for decision makers to target their needs in a structured manner. Consequently, there is no certainty among policymakers as to how the new speaker concept could be operationalised.

This raises the question as to what descriptor will be used for the many who do not become new speakers despite an increased exposure to formal instruction in and through the language. Are they to be referred to as Welsh speakers, L2 students or advanced learners? These are important questions, not only for teachers and school managers but also for curriculum designers, assessors, students and their families. It is probable that this category of student will grow as a proportion of all students and speakers because the conventional L1 category appears not to be growing within a fairly stable system. Recent data suggests the number of Welsh-medium schools and pupils has not grown substantially, and Table 3.1 reveals the difficulty with succession, as twice as many pupils are registered in primary as opposed to secondary schools. Were this succession rate to be improved significantly then the investment in skills and confidence imparted by the primary school experience would strengthen the progressive development of more students and could lead to a greater use of Welsh in adulthood in socio-economic domains. Skill development is one thing, actual increased usage of a minority language is quite a different challenge. Thus, Gruffydd observes that 'in more Welsh speaking areas, most/many of the primary schools produce confident new speakers. However, in the same areas, there is a significant loss of ground in the secondary sector, and for a variety of reasons a large number of second language pupils leave secondary schools lacking confidence, unwilling or unable to speak Welsh' (Gruffydd, pers. comm., 2021).

Table 3.1 *Schools where Welsh is the sole or main medium of instruction, 2020–1*

School level	No. of schools	No. of pupils
Primary	404	60,770
Middle	8	7,905
High	47	22,715
TOTAL	**459**	**89,390**

Source: StatsWales, 2021.

The New Curriculum for Wales

The new curriculum for Wales is the first complete reform of the statutory education system in thirty years. Six areas of learning and experience have been identified, as follows:[14]

- 1. **Expressive arts** incorporating art, dance, drama, film and digital media, and music. It will encourage creativity and critical thinking and include performance.
- 2. **Humanities** incorporating geography, history, RE, business studies and social studies. It will be based on human experiences and will also cover Welsh culture.
- 3. **Health and wellbeing:** this covers the physical, psychological, emotional and social aspects of life, helping students make informed decisions about their health and wellbeing and learn how to manage social influences. It will include PE.
- 4. **Science and technology** incorporating biology, chemistry, physics, computer science, and design and technology.
- 5. **Mathematics and numeracy:** in the early years, this will involve learning through play. In later stages, it will include working both independently and collaboratively with others.
- 6. **Languages, literacy and communication:** this will include Welsh and English, literature and international languages. Welsh language teaching will still be compulsory (as an additional language for children who don't use Welsh as their first language.
- In addition, literacy, numeracy and digital skills will be embedded throughout all curriculum areas.[15]

On 14 October 2021 it was announced that English Language and Literature GCSEs would be combined into one qualification, while new GCSEs in Engineering and Manufacturing and Film and Digital Media will be taught from 2025 (BBC News, 2021). However, such was the uncertainty surrounding the Welsh language qualification that a final decision was postponed.

Given the growing concern with economic and racial disparities in the UK, made more acute by heightened awareness of the issue of slavery and exploitation during British imperialism, and the reaction of various groups to the Covid-19 pandemic, it will be mandatory for the histories of BAME communities to be taught. Additional non-core themes include Relationships and Sexuality Education and Religious Education. The curriculum aims to produce individuals who are (a) ambitious, capable learners; (b) healthy, confident individuals; (c) enterprising, creative contributors; (d) ethical, informed citizens.

Recent policy reforms and legislation have focussed on creating a bilingual society. The six significant policy innovations are A Curriculum for Wales: A Curriculum for Life, 2015; New Deal for Education Workforce, 2015; Welsh

---

[14] A late addition to the details was the insistence that lifesaving skills and first aid be taught.
[15] www.theschoolrun.com/curriculum-for-wales.

Medium Education Strategy, 2016; Well-Being of Future Generations Act (Wales) 2015; Successful Futures, 2016; Cymraeg 2050: A Million Welsh Speakers, 2016.[16] The Well-Being of Future Generations Act (Wales) 2015 and Cymraeg 2050: A Million Welsh Speakers, 2016 are particularly significant for they set the strategic framework and are sufficiently flexible to enable future policy reforms to be dovetailed into a strong, mainstreamed approach to shaping the contours of society with all the resonance that promoting Welsh within an increasingly multicultural context can sustain. Running in parallel are a series of promotional campaigns such as Iaith Gwaith (Working Welsh), initiated in 2005, and an annual Welsh Language Rights Day held each December since 2019 (Welsh Language Commission, 2021, pp. 149–50).

A cabinet reshuffle following the Senedd elections of May 2021 saw Jeremy Miles, AS appointed as the Minister for Education and the Welsh Language, a pairing of responsibilities which should facilitate the further integration of Welsh language priorities into the educational domain, especially if and when proposed new legislation on Welsh-medium education comes into force. This coupling is more of a natural fit as it is through the statutory educational system that the projected numbers of additional speakers will be produced.

One critical intervention has been the decision to offer free Welsh language lessons to 16–25-year-olds, teachers and teaching assistants from September 2022 whose fee to register for a one-year course with the National Centre for Learning Welsh will be covered by the government. Together with other interventions related to nudge theory, the design of choice theory and the greater encouragement to use Welsh in the workplace, government plans reflect a serious intent to secure the aim of growing the numbers able to speak Welsh and increase the opportunities for its greater use.

Intergenerational Language Transmission

In 'default' language situations such as Sweden, Portugal or Chile intergenerational language transmission is the norm and citizens do not necessarily worry about the survival of Swedish, Portuguese or Spanish. However, in minority language situations the survival of the language is a constant concern. A significant feature of the language acquisition process is intergenerational language transmission. Decisions prior to the birth of the child regarding the

---

[16] There is a cluster of important strategies and acts which when combined offer a more robust framework for the promotion and regulation of Welsh, viz. Taking Wales Forward 2016–2021 (2016); A Living Language: A Language for Living – Welsh Language Strategy 2012–17 (2012); A Living Language: A Language for Living – Moving Forward (2014); Welsh Language (Wales) Measure 2011; Welsh-Medium Education Strategy (2010). All can be accessed at https://gov.wales/?lang=en.

language to be used in the home and in early childhood thus become critical and serious attempts have been made by parental pressure groups and agencies to inform and influence the linguistic choices of parents or guardians. This is an important trigger point for the linguistic trajectory both of the individual and of the household unit. Early work has identified the role which grandparents, caregivers, medical and other professional advice given to expectant mothers can have on the decision-making process and the language development of children (Harrison et al., 1981; Bellin, 1994; Bellin and Thomas, 1996; Gathercole et al., 2007).

The Welsh Government produces statistical bulletins on language transmission for one-family households with children aged 3–4, which in 2011 represented 92 per cent of 3–4-year-olds (Welsh Government, 2013a).[17] The transmission rate is defined as the proportion of 3–4-year-olds within a family type able to speak Welsh. Previous statistical bulletins had noted that the number of 3–4-year-olds able to speak Welsh increased from 13,329 in 2001 to 16,495 in 2011 (an increase from 18.8 per cent to 23.3 per cent).[18] The transmission rate for couple households where two adults could speak Welsh remained stable between 2001 and 2011 at around 82 per cent.[19] The transmission rate for couple households where one adult could speak Welsh increased from 40 per cent in 2001 to 45 per cent in 2011. The transmission rate for lone parent households, where one adult could speak Welsh was 53 per cent, as compared with 55 per cent in 2001. The transmission rate for couple households with one adult able to speak Welsh was higher in cases where the Welsh-speaking adult was a female rather than a male (49 and 40 per cent respectively). The transmission rate for lone parent households with one adult able to speak Welsh was higher in cases where the Welsh-speaking adult was a female rather than a male (54 and 42 per cent respectively).

Turning to Welsh speakers by household size in 2011, there was a decrease in the proportion of households containing at least one person who could speak Welsh, from 28 per cent in 2001 to 26 per cent in 2011. Of the over 555,000 people who could speak Welsh who lived in households, nearly 230,000 (41 per cent) lived either by themselves or in households where everyone could speak Welsh. In 2001, the equivalent figure was 45 per cent. The proportion of households that were entirely Welsh speaking decreased from 11.1 per cent in 2001 to 9.4 per cent in 2011 (Welsh Government, 2013a).

---

[17] Please visit https://gov.wales/sites/default/files/statistics-and-research/2019-03/130628-welsh-language-households-transmission-en.pdf.

[18] The 2011 Census question in Wales asked, 'Can you understand, speak, read or write Welsh?' – answered by ticking one or more of five boxes in any combination. The Census did not collect information on fluency levels or on frequency of use (Welsh Government, 2013a).

[19] 2011 figures include children living in households where more than two adults were able to speak Welsh (e.g. two parents and older non-dependent sibling).

These facts are an important source of time-series analysis, but do not drill down into the social usage patterns or motivation for language transmission rates. The government commissioned a report from Cardiff University which made recommendations about transmission and usage The three principal findings were that:

Intergenerational language transmission tended to be an unconscious behaviour except in couples where one respondent spoke Welsh (and came from a Welsh-speaking family) and their partner did not.

Intergenerational language *donation* was considered both prior to birth and/or during early years by most of the respondents who had acquired Welsh through Welsh-medium education.

Social factors (e.g., linguistic background) seem to be more influential than psychological factors (e.g., attitudes towards Welsh). (Evas, Morris and Whitmarsh, 2017)

The government response, as set out in *National Policy on Welsh Language Transmission and Use in Families* (Welsh Government, 2020a) was to identify four aims for their policy, namely to:

1. Inspire today's generation of children and young people to speak Welsh to their children in the future. 2. Reignite the Welsh language skills of those who may not have used Welsh since their school days, or who aren't confident in their language skills, to speak Welsh with their own children. 3 Support and encourage use of Welsh within families where not everybody speaks Welsh. 4. Support Welsh-speaking families to speak Welsh with their children.

The principles on which this policy is based reflect a holistic perspective on language transmission.

1. Children are individuals and have their own sense of agency. They aren't just passive recipients of a language from parents/carers. Children may express language preferences themselves regarding what language they use, and therefore attempt to influence which language their parents/carers use with them, as well as which language they use with their siblings and friends.
2. We'll listen to the child's voice and consider their perspective in designing and implementing everything we do.
3. Messaging is an important element of any intervention in any field, but it's not necessarily the intervention itself.
4. Where we do use messaging, we'll make sure that we speak with one voice across all our work and that this is based on a common verbal strategy.
5. Technology and the internet have revolutionised how we communicate. It's also had a significant impact on children's play. Our work in the field of Welsh language transmission in families will examine how technology could contribute to children's play in Welsh.
6. Much of the work in family language policy has taken place in two parent, heterosexual families. When we plan and implement our work, we'll take into account that family types are more diverse, e.g., many children reside in one parent families and/or in families where parents/carers belong to LGBTQI groups.

7. We'll consider how to use the contribution of wider family networks beyond parents/carers in supporting Welsh language transmission in families.
8. We will consider the balance between the influence of the home, the wider family, community and external social influences and life changes on language transmission. This could for example include times of transition in our lives such as childbirth, starting, changing or leaving school and so on. Some language planning literature calls these life changes linguistic 'mudes'. (Welsh Government, 2020a)[20]

I believe this is the first mention of linguistic *mudes* in Welsh Government documentation and together with the emphasis on behavioural science reflects the expertise of specialist language planners in the Welsh Language Division.

Mudiad Meithrin

If language transmission is to be reinforced for the low percentage of households who are Welsh-speaking families, how much more crucial is it to introduce the language to the general population of child-bearing age? A key trigger factor in encouraging a new generation of Welsh speakers is the initial entry point into the nursery school system, provided by Mudiad Meithrin (Mudiad Ysgolion Meithrin before 2011) which since 1971 has been socialising successive generations of children to become bilingual. In 2021 the MM was comprised of 452 Cylch Meithrin, 301 Cylch Ti a Fi, 50 nurseries, 74 Cymraeg for Kids groups and 58–80 Clwb Cwtsh groups. In 2017 there were 11,000 children attending Cylch Meithrin, 80 per cent of whom came from homes where English was the main language and 86 per cent of whom transferred to Welsh-medium primary education. The annual budget is about £5 million, 80 per cent of which is derived from the Welsh Government.[21] By 2019 nineteen new Cylchoedd Meithrin had opened since 2017 and forty-three new Cylch Ti a Fi; 12,773 children were in Cylchoedd Meithrin and nurseries and 33,564 individual Cymraeg for Kids sessions (comprising baby massage and baby yoga for example) had been attended by a parent and child all over Wales.

Mudiad Meithrin has the dual role of offering parental advice and of stimulating demand for Welsh-medium education, through the provision and enabling of registered childcare, which together with other organisations such as Rhieni dros Addysg Gymraeg (RhAG)[22] and Dyfodol i'r Iaith, feeds into the public awareness and policy formulation considerations through regular lobbying and exchanges with the Welsh Government.[23]

---

[20] The 2020 report has this reference on page 15: 'See, amongst others, Pujolar, J. & Puigdevall, M. (2014) "Linguistic mudes: how to become a new speaker in Catalonia"; *International Journal of the Sociology of Language*, 231.'
[21] Information from Gwenllian Lansdown Davies, MM, 8 September 2017.
[22] www.rhag.net/RhAG Parents for Welsh-medium Education.
[23] www.dyfodol.net/ A Future for Welsh. This pluralist network of organisations makes authoritative statements on public policy such as the press release of 19 September 2018 where it

The main aims of MM are:

Supporting, advising and assisting provisions (Cylchoedd Meithrin and Cylchoedd Ti a Fi) to remain open as community facilities, to strengthen their sustainability, and to expand every aspect of their services (by ensuring coordination with relevant agencies such as Estyn, CIW, County Councils, and by providing them with professional advice and guidance.)

Promoting Welsh-medium childcare and education in order to meet the requirements of the 'Cymraeg 2050' strategy, and doing this through Cymraeg for Kids, Cylchoedd Ti a Fi and Cylchoedd Meithrin, and also by establishing new combined Cylchoedd in line with our 'Set up and Succeed' scheme.

Identifying gaps in childcare provision and identifying opportunities to expand services through the 'Childcare Offer' (30 hours) by opening new provisions. Stimulate the demand for Welsh-medium childcare and education (Cylchoedd Ti a Fi and Cylchoedd Meithrin) by collecting and analysing data.

Responding proactively to consultations and participate in policy-making processes and language forums at a local, regional and national level (such as the WESPs, Childcare Sufficiency Assessments, Welsh Promotion Group etc.).

Influencing civic discourse and the research agenda to promote Welsh-medium childcare and education. Conducting events to promote, market and normalise Welsh-medium care and education, by working in partnership and promoting a 'light-hearted strategy' e.g., Parti Pyjamas, Gŵyl Dewin a Doti (the nursery festival), 'Dau Gi Bach' events, and by attending local and national shows and events.

Offering the Mudiad Meithrin community a range of CPD (Continuous Professional Development) through the 'Academi' department, ensuring that all aspects of life in the Cylch Meithrin are covered.

Working with partners in the National Centre for Learning Welsh in order to identify opportunities to introduce 'Cymraeg i'r Teulu' courses, to run the 'Erfyn Diagnostig Iaith' (EDI) scheme and and 'Camau' (Professional Welsh) scheme for early years workers, to promote the 'Cymraeg Gwaith' course and to run the innovative 'Clwb Cwtsh' scheme.[24]

Providing advice and guidance to the sector on matters relating to the Foundation Phase, and every aspect of good management, robust governance and quality provision (through robust management plans, and the 'Safonau Serennog' s quality assurance scheme) within the Cylchoedd.[25]

Despite its undoubted success in introducing new speakers into the system there remain severe challenges to the well-being of the population. The lack of

---

welcomed the Government's decision to spend £51m on promoting Welsh language education. It also raises awareness and hosts evidence-based documents to inform language and education policy.

[24] Gruffydd observes that 'my experience suggests that they are successful and popular as a medium in their own right, but I do not know what influence they have on language choice in the home, and from my experience, the progression from Learning Welsh via *Clwb Cwtsh* to mainstream courses is extremely limited' (Gruffydd, pers. comm., 2021; author's translation).

[25] MM Annual Report, 2018–19, www.meithrin.cymru/creo_files/upload/downloads/terfynol_sa es_adroddiad_blynyddol_18-19_llai.pdf, together with details provided by Dr Davies, 18 March 2021.

childcare provision in Welsh and the ongoing empowerment of females are related challenges to language policy and planning as is the incidence of relative poverty, which the Chwarae Teg scheme is addressing.[26]

Given their national remit Dr Gwenllian Lansdown Davies, MM's Chief Executive, her staff and the Board of Directors[27] are acutely aware of the needs of very young Welsh learners, the majority of whom come from non-Welsh-speaking homes, and as a consequence MM are fully appraised of the significance of their activities in anchoring good habits of language learning and usage from the earliest years onwards. Innovative features include the promotion of active offer of service and the Academi Mudiad Meithrin which offers support in transferring good ideas and best practice from one Cylch Meithrin to another, as detailed in their Winter 2020 Newsletter:

> It's the start of a new term, and once again Academi offers new and exciting courses for our members. This term's programme includes courses on subjects such as: Using the outdoor environment as a learning space. How to introduce simple Science into the Early Years Understanding GDPR and its new regulations. (Mudiad Meithrin, 2020)

The Newsletter also reminds staff and volunteers about the operational nature of the active offer principle (Cardinal and Williams, 2020), thus:

> In accordance with the Welsh Language Measure (Wales) 2011, Welsh speakers have the right to communicate in Welsh face to face, electronically, over the phone and in writing. As part of the new inspection framework, CIW will be considering and reporting on whether the service offered by the Cylch Meithrin or nursery provides the 'active offer' in Welsh. Providing the 'active offer' means that the service is provided through the medium of Welsh without it being specifically requested – remember that this is also required by Mudiad Meithrin's language policy! (Mudiad Meithrin, 2020)

Asked to summarise her perception of the term 'new speaker', the Chief Executive responded thus:

> The term 'new speakers' conveys a sense of an inclusive and welcoming community without using the 'learner' label. However, the question is worth asking at what point does someone become a 'new speaker' and is everyone – regardless of their confidence in Welsh – considered new speakers? Does this risk undermining a language use strategy, meaning that people's understanding of the Welsh language is only passive? Of course, Mudiad Meithrin's job is to facilitate and create new speakers as every toddler acquires one or more languages from birth. It is also difficult to separate the labels we use to describe ourselves as users of the Welsh language (I learn, I understand, I speak Welsh) from broader questions about identity and Welshness. Although I speak French and Spanish and learn Arabic and Italian (for example) I don't worry about being corrected while learning. Speakers of a minority or lesser-used language may

---

[26] www.cteg.org.uk/.
[27] The Directors are volunteers who represent different regions and specialisms of the Mudiad.

nevertheless be more aware of the interrelationship between language and identity and the 'learner' label may suggest that someone does not really belong. It's complicated! (Davies, pers. comm., 2021)

Conscious that the family and educational domains do not necessarily satisfy the desire for greater usage of the language in everyday life, successive governments, initially through the Welsh Language Board (1994–2012) and now through the Government's Welsh Language Division, introduced a range of initiatives whereby Welsh speakers can interact and receive services. These are intended for the general populace, but by definition once new speakers become confident and desirous of engaging in meaningful activities, they seek out opportunities where they may fulfil their desire to participate in and through the Welsh language. The key to language proficiency is regular usage and thus outcome-oriented interventions seek to widen the range of opportunities and activities available in and through Welsh.[28]

I have selected two initiatives to identify whether or not the concerns of new speakers are reflected in the core or supplementary aims of the Mentrau Iaith (Language Enterprise Initiatives) and Canolfannau Cymraeg (Welsh Language Centres). These and other agencies will then be contextualised to see to what extent they can illustrate the challenges faced by the aims and ambitions set out within the Cymraeg 2050 strategy.

Mentrau Iaith

In the eighties and nineties, the Menter Iaith (Language Enterprise Initiative) was developed as an innovative and much-needed local instrument for community language planning. Today there are twenty-two Mentrau Iaith in Wales and one in Patagonia, and their cumulative work is integral to the implementation of language policy. They have grown organically, in varying geolinguistic contexts, primarily on a county or part-county basis. Typically, just as with the volunteers of MM, some of the Mentrau staff are former learners who have become new speakers and seek to share their linguistic journey with others. Their strength is the fact that the Mentrau Iaith are rooted in their communities and offer an impressive range of opportunities for Welsh-medium activities for all ages (Williams, 2000; Campbell, 2000). In the anglicised south-east and north-east, they provide much-needed support for new speakers to interact, as

---

[28] Peled has observed that 'an intervention in a person's linguistic freedoms isn't seen as equivalent as intervening in their freedoms e.g., to drink before the legal age or drive without wearing a seatbelt. In some ways, language-related behaviour modification is a much more politically charged topic than supposedly clear "life or death" issues. Although there is a fair bit of language policy that is very much a "life or death" issue, again from my specific healthcare-specific vantage point. I do think that there is a way to build language policy on the basis of safeguarding a set of basic social functionings'; (Y. Peled, pers. comm., 2019).

a significant proportion of their clientele are the products of the Welsh-medium school system, which enrols the majority of its students from non-Welsh-speaking homes (Thomas and Williams, 2013). Here there is an emphasis on providing opportunities for engagement, thus Menter Iaith Caerffili, Urdd Gobaith Cymru and Caerphilly C.B. Council have co-funded and co-led a Welsh language youth project. A full-time youth worker, based in Ysgol Gyfun Cwm Rhymni (the Welsh-medium comprehensive school in the area), is responsible for developing opportunities and Welsh-medium activities for young people across the county outside school hours and during school holidays. These activities include trips, sporting competitions as well as weekly clubs devoted to drama, animation, sport, outdoor pursuits and visits to local sites.[29] Menter Merthyr Tudful sponsors folk festivals, a global village festival, regular concerts, holiday clubs and adult learner classes.[30] Menter Caerdydd offers similar services, whose highlight is a summer festival, Tafwyl, which attracts many to the capital. The national co-ordinating body, Mentrau Iaith Cymru (MIC), offers training courses in child protection, management and leadership, language planning and community development. It hosts innovative projects such as Marchnad Lafur Cymraeg (the Welsh Labour Market) led by Four Cymru, which relates the Welsh language to economic activities and creates a connection between sectors and businesses with the potential to develop services that build on Welsh language skills.[31]

Despite their valuable contribution in creating and sustaining innovative Welsh language networks, it was never really feasible to expect the Mentrau to perform all the functions they are generally expected to achieve. Accordingly in March 2013, Cardiff University was commissioned by the government to conduct an independent review of the Mentrau Iaith as part of the Iaith Fyw: Iaith Byw Strategaeth y Gymraeg 2012–17.[32] The review was to report on:

- the methods used by the organisations to promote and facilitate the use of Welsh
- identifying the whole range of activities conducted by the organisations
- assessing to what extent they reflect local needs
- evaluating to what extent the organisations collect data effectively in order to assess the impact of activities
- whether the organisations' structures ensure effective working, partnership working and sharing of good practice

---

[29] Menter Caerffili, 2020, www.mentercaerffili.cymru/en/obl-ifanc/.
[30] www.merthyrtudful.com/?lang=en.
[31] Mentrau Iaith Cymru, 2020, www.mentrauiaith.cymru/amdanom-ni/?lang=en.
[32] Iaith fyw: iaith byw Strategaeth y Gymraeg 2012–17/Welsh Language Strategy: A Living Language: A Language for Living's Commitment to Strengthen the Welsh Language in the Community (Welsh Government, 2012), https://llyw.cymru/sites/default/files/publications/2018-12/strategaeth-y-gymraeg-2012-i-2017-iaith-fyw-iaith-byw.pdf.

- the potential to further develop the role of the Mentrau
- whether the Mentrau are doing work that should be done by others, such as local authorities
- if the level of funding provided by the Welsh Government is appropriate

The review judged that the Mentrau Iaith were effective organisations but faced operational difficulties which had not been overcome during the previous seventeen or so years.[33] The Mentrau made solid efforts to promote the Welsh language considering the budgets available to them and the structural barriers they faced. The more successful Mentrau had plans that met local requirements in terms of language planning and community development and had administrative and management systems that demonstrated a high level of professionalism. Others, meanwhile, operated in an ad hoc, fragmented way and went beyond their remit in order to provide services neglected by others or to generate income so as to retain their staff. This trend exemplifies Marquand's (2004) analysis of the hollowing out of the state, for with the decline of the public sector the Mentrau were aggregating to themselves functions and duties formerly sustained by other bodies, such as local authorities and the social care system, so that the Welsh language element could be preserved or promoted within the system.

One significant finding was the need for examples of language-planning good practice that took public policy into consideration alongside micro-level language planning and community development. A lack of good practice exemplars hindered the Mentrau's imaginative and practical work, while a lack of holistic planning rendered them less able to engage with policymakers within local authorities.

The review's conclusion was that too much attention was given to processes and activities, without sufficiently addressing the means of providing evidence of the impact and difference made by organisations to the language at grassroots level. There was little evidence of working in an integrated manner to address language-planning needs at micro level, i.e., through comprehensive discussion and joint planning with relevant organisations in other domains. The priority was achieving operational targets and managing regular administrative tasks rather than engaging in outcome-based behavioural change.

The evidence identified a consensus in favour of establishing a national co-ordinating body, Mentrau Iaith Cymru, which would improve the management and operational methods as well as increasing investment in staff training and development so as to produce strategic leadership. A real difficulty is that the short-term expenditure cycles for the government Grants to Promote the Welsh Language (from year to year) prevents organisations from recruiting

---

[33] The review and the government's response may be accessed at http://gov.wales/topics/welsh language/publications/review-of-mentrau-iaith/?lang=en and http://gov.wales/topics/welshlan guage/publications/response-to-the-review-of-mentrau-iaith-and-aman-tawereport/?lang=en.

sufficiently and from planning on a medium to long-term basis. The respondents argued that the level of funding allocated to the organisations was inconsistent, which was the cause of great frustration at grassroots level. As a result, some organisations have felt the need – understandably – to find funding through alternative means, and this could constitute a risk of compromising their original language mission. The review identified the need to strengthen better training and systematic methods to identify language priorities (based on research, data analysis, focus group views etc.), turning need into action plans, implementing more effective monitoring processes and appropriate methods of measuring outcomes and impact since this did not generally happen. Attention was required so as to maintain the supply of volunteers who constitute the backbone of the organisations and from whose local committees most of the key initiatives and programmes are derived.

The nature of the government's leadership was a concern for a number of the organisations. Specifically, they explained that they are driven by targets set by government officials which do not necessarily arise from analyses of local needs. The Mentrau's targets are set independently of the targets of other language organisations and are not agreed collaboratively in a specific geographic area. This can lead to duplication of work, with Mentrau encroaching on the remits of other organisations.

In general, the government agreed with the results of the review and implemented many of its recommendations, especially in relation to the role of Mentrau Iaith Cymru.[34] While in 2013 the Mentrau were conscious of the needs of advanced learners, by October 2018, my discussions with Mentrau staff indicated a strong recognition that a significant portion of their activities were now devoted to satisfying the needs of new speakers also.[35] Two themes emerged in our discussions: one was an increasing emphasis on partnerships within the community, partly to reduce overlap with other agencies such as the Urdd and sporting bodies; the other was the continuous need for financial support as government grants did not sustain all their committed activities. There thus was a tendency to take on other services, such as social care and community help, funded by local authorities but not directly connected in principle to the promotion of Welsh; although it could be argued that in some areas in west and north Wales, a large proportion of social services clients are Welsh speakers. There was also a tendency to compete for other contracts, such as teaching programmes. Dr Ifor Gruffydd's judgement is that:

In the field of Welsh for Adults, this was seen as a problem as there were cases where the Mentrau Iaith duplicated the Work of Welsh for Adults providers (led by the

---

[34] Their response may be seen at http://gov.wales/topics/welshlanguage/publications/response-to-the-review-of-mentrau-iaith-and-aman-tawereport/?lang=en.

[35] Mentrau Iaith Annual Conference, Newtown, 2 October 2018.

National Centre) and even competed against the providers. This has been raised more than once with the Welsh Government and the National Centre and subsequently the situation has improved. I now think that there is a consensus in both sectors that the Mentrau should provide opportunities for new speakers to practise their Welsh and assimilate into the Welsh community and that language training takes place through the Centre and its providers. (Gruffydd, pers. comm., 2021; author's translation)

When asked about future developments the Mentrau representatives expressed a strong desire to increase their involvement with supporting learners and new speakers from within refugee and migrant communities. This was prompted by the various experiences reported to Mentrau Iaith Cymru by its members and was also a reaction to the widespread media reporting of success stories of migrants and others identifying with their new locales. Thus, as far as the Mentrau leadership is concerned, they are fully aware of the contribution which new speakers of whatever background can make to their collective aims and are actively seeking innovative ways of engaging with a more diverse clientele.

However, the case study reveals how difficult it is to transpose general aims and ideals into a diverse programme of support for community action which influences real behaviour in the anticipated manner. How much more difficult might it be for such organisations to implement new speaker recommendations if they are not framed within the administrative culture of each organisation? Accordingly, policy entrenchment should include an explicit recognition that the new speaker perspective is integral to mainstream language policy else it could become marginalised and dismissed as an addendum to normal policy imperatives.

Canolfannau Cymraeg

While the Mentrau Iaith activities have been integral to increasing the visibility of Welsh language provision, space and vitality, they have not catered sufficiently for adult learners and the needs of new speakers. Several studies have demonstrated that while the Welsh for Adults sector had been successful in imparting Welsh language skills, many of the former adult students were frustrated at their lack of integration into Welsh language networks (Newcombe, 2002; 2016). Part of this is due to the attitude of native Welsh speakers, part to the nature of the conventional networks and part to the lack of targeted spaces within which new speakers would feel comfortable. Such empirical observations run counter to the popular narrative that Welsh speakers embrace new speakers; they may do so but not in an uncritical manner. In consequence several working in the field of Welsh for Adults have lobbied for the development of Canolfannau Cymraeg.

Although the concept of Canolfannau Cymraeg can be traced back to the 1960s (e.g. Clwb y Bont in Pontypridd)[36] the variety of those that now exist is testimony to the different models which have evolved to respond to local needs and aspirations. The overriding motivation is a desire to promote the teaching of Welsh, often but not uniquely in the context of communities which are not majority Welsh speaking, and aligning this with developing the potential to use the language in a social context.

The guidelines for how such centres should operate are contained in the commissioned report prepared by Gruffudd and Morris (2012).[37] The prime justification for Canolfannau Cymraeg[38] has been to enhance the experience and networks of learners of Welsh. Initially, nearly all of the Canolfannau Cymraeg could be described as community enterprises which were forged by local efforts and fund-raising with little governmental financial support. They were a classic example of the bottom-up language initiatives which have been so characteristic of language revitalisation, as was seen in relation to the development of Welsh-medium education (Thomas and Williams, 2013) and community language planning (Williams, 2000).

From the point of view of policy, no mention was made of the Canolfannau Cymraeg in the final annual review of the Welsh Language Board in 2010 and similarly there was no reference to them in the government's language strategy for 2012–17, A Living Language: A Language for Living (Welsh Government, 2011).[39] However, following the acceptance of the commissioned report the government acknowledged that Canolfannau Cymraeg could facilitate the aim of creating more users of Welsh as articulated in their policy document for 2012–17, *Moving Forward* (Welsh Government, 2014a).

At the Carmarthenshire National Eisteddfod (August 2014) First Minister Carwyn Jones, announced that four Canolfannau Cymraeg would be established in 2015 through the strategic capital investment fund. This amounted to £1.25 million for 2014–15 and £1 million for 2015–16. Local authorities, colleges and universities were invited to bid to develop Canolfannau Cymraeg to facilitate the process of learning or using Welsh in centres which would act as focal points for the language within their communities.

Many of the Canolfannau Cymraeg combine their role as centres for learning the language with other Welsh language promotional work. Several now

---

[36] www.81170.mrsite.com/page5.htm.
[37] I am grateful to S. Morris for sharing his expertise on the Canolfannau Cymraeg.
[38] Early examples include: Clwb y Bont – Pontypridd (established in 1960s); Nant Gwrtheyrn – Llŷn Peninsula (1978); Clwb Ifor Bach – Cardiff (1983); Yr Hen Lyfrgell – Cardiff (2016–21); Clwb Brynmenyn – Bridgend (1987–2003); Canolfan Merthyr (1987); Popeth Cymraeg – Clwyd (1988); Tŷ Tawe – Swansea (1987).
[39] For details on how this strategy was to be evaluated please see http://dera.ioe.ac.uk/18421/1/130321-welsh-language-strategy-measuring-indicators-en.pdf.

incorporate their local Menter Iaith, Welsh language bookshops, performance spaces where gigs or live events can be held and social spaces such as cafés, bars or coffee mornings. Given the demise of established Welsh language domains, the Canolfannau Cymraeg provide one of the few community foci for speakers of Welsh to use their language, especially in the more anglicised parts of the country. Their co-location with many of the Mentrau Iaith means that they are able to offer a unique space for learners of Welsh as well as the many young people who have received all their education through the medium of Welsh but face a challenge on where to use the language outside the school. Such centres also meet the needs of advanced learners/new speakers who are seeking safe spaces within which they can use their language in an unchallenged or non-threatening environment, which is so essential to the development of self-confidence, let alone their language repertoire and social satisfaction.

In August 2016 the government launched a consultation on their official language strategy to create a million Welsh speakers by the year 2050 (Welsh Government, 2017d). A proposal in development area 4 of the consultation includes the objective to 'Ensure that more places exist where it is completely obvious that Welsh is the natural language, so that it feels completely normal and safe to use Welsh as the default language.' The existence of Canolfannau Cymraeg – and their location in visible, multi-purpose buildings at the heart of their communities – is likely to continue to be a contributory policy instrument for the realisation of this goal. The lobby group Dyfodol i'r Iaith continue to press for the establishment of more Canolfannau as they represent a powerhouse driving forward local developments.[40] Steve Morris endorses the local ground-up element of such centres and argues that it was the lack of such momentum and local ownership which led to the failure of the Yr Hen Lyfrgell, the Cardiff Canolfan Cymraeg (Morris, pers. comm., 2021) while Eleri James speculates on what impact the post-Covid recovery might have on the sustainability of such centres (James, pers. comm., 2021). A dissenting view containing strategic criticism is that offered by M. P. Jones who argues that 'the fundamental problem of the centres is that they do not derive from the community and consequently are too closely tied to the educational system and to higher education in particular. What happens when government capital funding ends? They are likely to disappear, witness the current difficulties of the Carmarthen Centre which is struggling to survive' (Jones, pers. comm., 2021; author's translation). In sum, the breathing space which Canolfannau provide is a major feature of the new speaker research literature and is likely to figure prominently in future policy proposals. However, they have yet to

---

[40] Dyfodol i'r Iaith (www.dyfodol.net/wp-content/uploads/2020/11/Troi_dyhead_yn_realiti.pdf), p. 6.

overcome the two limitations identified herein, namely a lack of sustainable community and volunteer engagement and a reluctance on the part of government to provide long-term financial support. Both elements will test the adequacy of current post-welfare governance and partnership arrangements and if they are found wanting could scupper the whole idea of a one-stop shop for Welsh language activities in many locations, thereby reducing the synergies so vital for the nurturing of new speakers.

The Revision of the Welsh Language Strategy

Wales has adopted a number of language strategies since the establishment of the National Assembly in May 1999. Section 78(1) of the Government of Wales Act 2006 requires Welsh ministers to adopt a strategy stating how they propose to promote and facilitate the use of the Welsh language. Section 78(4) requires the Welsh ministers to keep the strategy under review and enables them to periodically adopt a new strategy. Accordingly an Executive Summary for the Cymraeg 2050: A Million Welsh Speakers strategy was prepared for public consultation during the autumn of 2016 which declared that in order to reach the target of a million speakers there was a need for 'more children in Welsh-medium education, better planning in relation to how people learn the language, more easy-to-access opportunities for people to use the language, a stronger infrastructure and a revolution to improve digital provision in Welsh, and a sea change in the way we speak about it' (Welsh Government, 2017d).

Strong evidence of the government's thinking and priorities may be gleaned from the consultative draft of Cymraeg 2050: A Million Welsh Speakers (Welsh Government, 2017d) which offered an ambitious programme of action as outlined in the Executive Summary which is reproduced below:

Section 1 – Executive summary

The year 2050

The Welsh language is thriving, and the number of speakers has risen to a million. It is natural to use it in every aspect of life, and among those who do not speak it there is goodwill towards it and an appreciation of its contribution to the culture and economy of Wales.

2016 – now and next

Our vision is clear – to have a million Welsh speakers by 2050. For us to achieve that, we believe that several things need to happen: more children in Welsh-medium education, better planning in relation to how people learn the language, more easy-to-access opportunities for people to use the language, a stronger infrastructure and a revolution to improve digital provision in Welsh, and a sea change in the way we speak about it.

The Revision of the Welsh Language Strategy 83

This document sets out our strategic priorities on how to reach a million speakers and describes the key things that need to happen if we are to achieve the necessary changes.

Our priorities

The Welsh language is one of Wales's treasures. It is part of that which defines us as a people, and an integral part of our everyday lives. According to the most recent Census in 2011 there were 562,000 Welsh speakers in Wales. On that basis, the aim of this strategy will be to almost double the number of Welsh speakers by the middle of the century. In order for that to happen, we believe we need to prioritise 6 key areas for action.

1 – Planning and Language Policy: For all the other elements of this strategy to be effective, we need to plan sensibly and deliberately to put the appropriate programmes in place at the appropriate time. For instance, if we are to increase the number of Welsh speakers on the scale needed, the first step in any strategy must be to create enough teachers to teach children through the medium of Welsh.
2 – Normalisation: By fostering a willingness to use Welsh among people who speak it, and goodwill towards it among those who don't, we want the language to be a normal part of everyday life. This means that people feel comfortable beginning a conversation in Welsh, that they can expect to receive services in Welsh, and that people are used to hearing it and seeing it.
3 – Education: We need to see a significant increase in the number of people receiving Welsh-medium education and who have Welsh language skills, as it is only through enabling more people to learn Welsh that we will reach a million speakers. Early years provision is also essential, as the earlier a child comes into contact with the language, the more opportunity he or she has to become fluent.
4 – People: As well as education, it will be essential to increase the number of people who transmit the language to their children. We also need more opportunities for people to use it in a variety of settings and encourage more of them to take up those opportunities. These include opportunities as individuals, for the family, by taking part in local activities, or as members of networks or wider communities of interest that may be scattered throughout the world.
5 – Support: It is essential to develop a robust and modern infrastructure to support the language in order to increase the number of speakers, improve their confidence, and make it easier to use in a wide variety of settings. Digital resources, a healthy and diverse media, a responsive and modern translation profession, and a corpus which reflects and maintains the status of Welsh as a living language, are essential for Welsh speakers whatever their ability.
6 – Rights: Legislation provides an unequivocal basis for organisations to act in support of the language and for Welsh speakers to use it. We need to encourage individuals to take up the opportunities that come with these rights. The long-term aim is to move to a situation where these rights are embedded as a natural part of services.

We propose these six development areas as a basis for deliberate action over the long term to realise the ambition of a million speakers (Welsh Government, 2017d).

Following consultation and reflection the six priority areas were reduced to three strategic themes, namely (1) increasing the number of Welsh speakers; (2)

increasing the use of Welsh; (3) creating favourable conditions: infrastructure and context (Welsh Government, 2017e).[41] While the elements of both the draft and final strategy are broadly similar, the Minister for the Welsh Language Alun Davies and civil servants were desirous that clear supportive messages would characterise the strategy going forward and consequently the published version includes a greater emphasis on facilitating the use of Welsh in many spheres. There is also greater synergy in the discourse with an emphasis on how the Welsh language and other features of social and economic life can be interrelated. One prominent reference is to the protection and well-being of Welsh speakers and communities, and this resonates with the broader Welsh Government commitment to quality of life as laid out in the Well-Being of Future Generations Act (Wales) 2015 and its follow-up programme.

Consequently rather than being seen as a sectoral interest of government and of civil society, the underlying message of the Cymraeg 2050 strategy is to normalise the use of the language. The strategic document is replete with well-articulated interventions and proposed actions together with a description on how the success of these reforms are to be measured (Welsh Government, 2017e).

Clearly the scope of any official language strategy is influenced by the parameters of the political context. One challenge for formulators of language strategy is how to balance the need to be faithful to the remit given by political or legislative enactment, while also striving to be creative; to be responsive to a professional vision of how a language strategy can be an enabling policy document together with its programmes and actions. Undoubtedly the Welsh Language Board had contributed a great deal to the discourse and practice of corpus, status and acquisition language planning and had emphasised the need to use the language in every conceivable situation. Following the board's demise in 2012, the Welsh Government shouldered full responsibility for language policy and planning, a development which articulated a powerful set of messages that the government was committed to strengthening a bilingual society. In interview, government policy formulators admitted that Cymraeg 2050 required a radical rethink both of the strategy and of their need to engage far more intensively with major government departments and civil society so as to deliver its declared aim.[42] Whereas they had been considering planning for some 750,000 speakers by 2050 they were now committed to securing a target of over a million speakers.[43] Above all, they argued that a new set of justifications were needed to mainstream Welsh as a public good, one

---

[41] https://gov.wales/sites/default/files/publications/2018-12/cymraeg-2050-welsh-language-strategy.pdf.
[42] Interview with Welsh Language Division staff, Cardiff, 7 September 2016.
[43] I say over a million because in order to achieve a target of one million speakers by 2050, many more have to be produced by the system as a significant proportion of speakers would have

which would feed into a more relevant narrative and discourse surrounding the creation of a bilingual society.

However, questions may be raised about both the intent and the operational implementation of the strategy, such as:

1. How feasible is the target of achieving a million Welsh speakers by 2050?
2. Will the speakers be those who reside in Wales or those who reside anywhere and have been produced by the system so as to constitute a virtual network of speakers/users, for who knows how people will be able to communicate in effective ways by 2050?
3. Where did the figure originate? Is it based on solid evidence or on political propaganda and wish fulfilment by both government and language activists?
4. If the target is not met, does it really matter? For what really matters is the actual usage of Welsh in a wide range of domains in daily life, not a putative set of skills.
5. How will progress towards the implementation of the strategy be evaluated?
6. There is a change of emphasis in this iteration of the strategy as opposed to the two previous versions; less detail, fewer instrumental outputs to be measured, more discourse and a clearer relationships between elements of the strategy.
7. But the strategy, although belonging to the government and devised by its Welsh Language Division, is heavily dependent on all government departments contributing – and the largest of such contributors, namely the Welsh education system from the cradle to the grave, is key; but not necessarily a co-sponsor of the strategy. How does this impact on the effectiveness of the implementation?
8. Concern with rights, regulation of Welsh-medium services and language standards now rests with the Welsh Language Commissioner. How will this agenda serve the interests of the strategy as it plays out and as the Commissioner's Office develops (Williams, 2017b)?

An initial opportunity to comment on these developments was the stakeholder meeting entitled 'Supporting "New Speakers": Building Irish Language Networks and Communities outside the Gaeltacht' held at Trinity College, Dublin on 14 October 2016. As recorded in the official report, my opening remarks argued that good ideas about language planning arise from committed individuals, not just from governments or funders. But I also recognised that government support is essential for larger issues such as institution building, legitimisation and training (Walsh and O'Rourke, 2018b). An abiding challenge is to adapt good ideas and robust practice within language management and to fashion them in such a way that they can appeal to public servants and

---

migrated to other parts of the UK and Europe, or lost interest in the habitual use of the language. Thus, they would be a net loss to the overall total required.

decision makers. I further argued that a priority of the New Speakers Network should be to influence decision makers who can release resources and legitimise projects, which include a language-related element, but can also be justified as contributing to the mainstream of government thinking and programme development in a wide variety of policy fields. In so doing we would be adding value to the quality of life. Accordingly, we need the support of civil servants and politicians to turn what is often seen as a private 'minority' interest into a generic public good. Language revitalisation is in the public interest; it is not about excluding a section of the population but improving the quality of life of many in society based on something that is already there. In the case of the Irish language, it is engrained in this island and nowhere else.

I then turned to the case of Wales and suggested that, although there was a common perception that large numbers of new speakers had reached a high level of proficiency, many of them subsequently did not continue to engage in Welsh-medium activities and networks. This was because many new speakers were not interested in conventional native speaker activities or cultural networks whether these be music, sport or poetry competitions; they simply wanted to live some of their life through Welsh. The Welsh Government had backed the idea that multi-purpose safe spaces could help promote the social use of Welsh through its support for Canolfannau Cymraeg, an initiative which I commended to my Irish hosts.

With regard to the government aim of creating one million speakers of Welsh by 2050, I suggested that the figure was an ambitious target if it referred only to residents of Wales and not to all Welsh speakers wherever they lived in the UK. Logic and statistical modelling suggested that if the threshold target were to apply to Welsh residents, something like 1.3 million speakers would need to be produced by the education system so as to compensate for the large number of people who move away or who through marriage patterns do not necessarily reproduce the language within their families. Something approaching 3,000 Welsh speakers are lost each year. I explained how language activists had prompted the government into setting the target, a reminder of why such organisations are vital. But I also suggested that the target was less important than the actual embodied use of the language. It was evident that better ideas and convincing arguments which appeal to the majority were needed, for after all they constitute a large part of the electorate, the tax-paying base population and most critically of all they are the parents of those children who might attend Welsh-medium education. The majority need to be convinced that the language promotion efforts derive from a concern for the public good of society.[44]

---

[44] These sections are derived from the Walsh and O'Rourke Report (2018b) for reasons of objectivity and triangulation.

An additional matter raised in my Dublin contribution was the balance between the role of public servants and civil society. The creative energy is more likely to come from community activists/intellectuals, while it is public servants who fashion some of these ideas into government programmes. As a consequence, formal language planning is too often content with changing attitudes, not behaviour. The complex process of producing speakers and new speakers is not just about attitudes and values but also about the manner in which daily reality, expectations and behaviour interact with meaningful experiences, some of which it is acknowledged can be detrimental as well as encouraging (Walsh and O'Rourke, 2018b).

Thus, we may ask, how do civil servants react to these new developments and how do they perceive the role of new speakers in their thinking and planning?

The Welsh Government

The most telling point about the devolved administration in Wales is that in comparison with pre-devolution arrangements the fortunes of the Welsh language are now a salient political issue. Indeed, the health of Welsh and the promotion of bilingualism is one of the central cross-cutting features of government programmes and policy. Equally significant is the fact that each successive First Minister has been a Welsh speaker and thus intuitively understands the role of the language both in the national psyche and within the national political culture.[45] Between 1999 and March 2012 responsibility for Welsh language strategy and promotion was undertaken by the Welsh Language Board (WLB). One abiding source of discussion within the interviews conducted for this project was the government's decision to abolish the WLB, to strengthen the capacity of the Welsh Language Division (WLD) and establish the office of a Welsh Language Commissioner. I have previously interpreted the official reasoning for these decisions Williams (2013b; 2021a), as have Mac Giolla Chríost (2016) and Dunbar (2019). While the creation of a Language Commissioner followed developing international norms in official language regulation as represented by the members of the International Association of Language Commissioners, the unease remains, even for supporters of a Commissioner such as myself, as to why could not both the WLB and a Commissioner's office be supported side by side. A great deal of expertise, creativity and community trust and involvement with the WLB was lost with the abolition of this pioneering body.

Since 2014 I have been engaged with regular meetings with Bethan Webb, the head of the WLD, and her senior colleagues and have taken the opportunity to enquire and learn about their attitudes to the role of new

---

[45] H. B. Owen has suggested that the practice of the first minister in answering Covid-19 briefing questions in both English and Welsh has raised the profile of Welsh (Owen, pers. comm., 2021).

speakers.[46] The underlying position was that, given that most speakers created by the education system would be new speakers, then in a sense almost all of the government's language-related programmes include the needs and interests of new speakers. Consequently, new speakers are treated as regular speakers and thus there is no need to fetishise what may turn out to be an unhelpful concept. This strikes at the heart of the debate on the relevance of the new speaker phenomenon and leads us to enquire which is the more important feature, references to the phenomenon in official documentation and intellectual justifications of changed priorities or actual programmes which deliver the necessary support, space and resources required to promote a robust speech community.

The ideology, framework and discourse of the current language strategy, together with the regular policy briefings, statistical bulletins and commissioned reports, all take as read the necessary assumption that many language learners will become new speakers, whether or not they have attended Welsh-medium schools. Given that all students now undertake a statutory number of hours of Welsh as part of the core curriculum, then it is the considered view of senior civil servants that there is little merit in drawing attention to a subcategory, defined as new speakers, as the overwhelming proportion of students of Welsh already constitute such a category. Thus, 'students of Welsh' is a sufficient term and this explains why so few specific references to new speakers may be gleaned in official documents.

Data and evidence were seen as crucial to the understanding of the behaviour of new speakers, especially in their social activities outside the formal educational environment. At interview in 2015 government language policy formulators argued that the Welsh Government should adopt an integrated approach to garnering data to support its language policy by focussing on both statistical and social analyses. Regular evidence-based policy formulation is undertaken within the Code of Practice as required by the Statistics and Registration Service Act 2007. An annual Welsh Language Evidence Plan is drawn up and that for the period 2015–16 identified the following goals:

- to develop a robust evidence base to inform policy and practice in Welsh-medium education
- to support language planning policy through an informed balance of quantitative and qualitative analysis of language vitality
- to strengthen the Welsh Government's capacity to mainstream the Welsh language in research activity across Welsh Government portfolios.[47]

---

[46] The ready co-operation of the Welsh Language Division, Welsh Government throughout this research investigation is acknowledged with gratitude.
[47] Interview with Bethan Webb and the Welsh Language Division team, Cardiff, 27 November 2015.

One significant change identified at interview was to build on the earlier statements related to linguistic behavioural change.[48] The 6 August 2014 Policy Statement on the Welsh Language, A Living Language: A Language for Living – Moving Forward had identified behavioural change as one of the four key strands together with the need to strengthen the links between the economy and the Welsh language; the need for better strategic planning for the Welsh language; and the use of Welsh in the community:[49]

> A number of factors influence our behaviour and the impetus behind the use of language can be complex. We learn norms of behaviour from a very early age and choosing which language to use in a given situation is an integral part of these norms. Throughout our lives, we take subconscious and more prominent 'cues' from others about where, when and how we should use the Welsh language. We assess each language situation in an instant, according to a multitude of inter-related factors. For example, this simple model illustrates what factors an individual might consider when deciding whether or not to ask for a Welsh service.
>
> - Are the signs and general 'feel' of the organisation Welsh or bilingual?
> - Can 'Working Welsh' material be found throughout the organisation?
> - Do I feel confident enough in my own Welsh in this field?
> - Will the person behind the counter be offended if I speak Welsh first?
> - What is the person's name on his or her badge?
> - What is my perception of people who ask for services in Welsh?
>
> Influencing language behaviour is more complex than an individual's personal preference. At a cash machine or on a website, for example, evidence shows that changing the first language a user sees increases the use of that language. We need to ascertain in what situations these simple examples could be used to promote greater use of Welsh. We will begin by developing a series of campaigns aimed at changing linguistic behaviour that will utilise social marketing expertise, beginning with the 'Pethau Bychain' campaign.[50] The campaign will highlight how simple, everyday actions can have a cumulative impact on the use of Welsh and aims to motivate individuals to become more confident in using Welsh in their own lives. (Welsh Government, 2014a)

A supplementary feature emphasised at interview was that it was First Minister Carwyn Jones, who hosted Y Gynhadledd Fawr in Aberystwyth on

---

[48] Interview with Welsh Language Division and other officials in government offices, Cardiff, 27 November 2015.
[49] https://gov.wales/sites/default/files/publications/2018-12/welsh-language-strategy-2012-to-2017-moving-forward.pdf
[50] The Little Things campaign encouraged small incremental steps to increase the use of Welsh in everyday tasks. For illustration see www.mentrauiaith.cymru/ymgyrch-pethau-bychain-llywodraeth-cymru/?lang=en.

4 July 2014.[51] and fronted the new campaigns while endorsing official statements, such as the 17 June 2014 draft policy statement on the Welsh language, the 6 August 2014 policy statement (Welsh Government, 2014a) and most importantly Cymraeg 2050 (Welsh Government, 2017e).[52] The involvement of the First Minister had three advantages. First it suggested to the general population that this was an important issue for government and accordingly they could expect active leadership in this policy area. Secondly, it signalled to cabinet ministers and heads of government departments that, as this was a personal commitment by the First Minister, they would do well to facilitate the aims of the strategy. Thirdly, it was a boost to the confidence and appreciation shown to staff of the WLD, who believed they could now use the authority of the First Minister's Office to good effect when dealing with recalcitrant colleagues across government.

Hitherto the emphasis had been on providing opportunities and building confidence to use the new services on offer. However, the government were increasingly aware that so many people who had learned Welsh through the education system and in the community were not necessarily choosing to use Welsh when confronted with formal documents or when making decisions in official contexts. By employing social marketing techniques and wider UK government practices related to nudge theory, the WLD hoped to boost the practical use of the language as a means of transacting business and accessing services. This trajectory was confirmed as the WLD now sought to diffuse a discourse which emphasised principles of normalisation of the language throughout the government system and beyond. It was critical, according to the head of the WLD, that this discourse should also impact on the attitudes and choices of the majority so as to create new speakers. In consequence a more robust approach to the creation, diffusion and evaluation of discourses and narratives which explained both the advantages of bilingualism and the salience of new speakers would be developed. This is a change in emphasis from that which was first enunciated in 2015 and by 2018 was confirmed as being part and parcel of current programmes.[53] It was also evident that this was an exercise not only in capacity building but also in increasing trust in government actions to deliver their stated policy aims.

Given that the government sponsors so many of the organisations involved in the promotion of Welsh, then clearly those which do have a special focus on new speakers would be well known to the civil service team, who in turn would offer advice, enable the co-ordination of efforts and encourage the involvement of other government departments in appropriate initiatives. Initially such co-ordination

---

[51] Y Gynhadledd Fawr was the culmination of a period of national consultation regarding the future of the language which had previously involved twenty local focus groups and the participation of 2,300 in an online survey. https://gov.wales/written-statement-y-gynhadledd-fawr.
[52] https://gov.wales/written-statement-publication-policy-statement-welsh-language-living-language-language-living.
[53] Discussions with Welsh Language Division, Cardiff, 27 April 2018.

was difficult to achieve and at interview government policy formulators suggested that a more systematic approach to language policy implementation had reduced these concerns but acknowledged that a major stumbling block was the ability of the WLD to influence much larger departments of government, such as Education and Skills, to both contribute fully to the formulation of the language strategy and seek to the uttermost to implement its recommendations.[54]

A member of the WLD observed that the current reformulation of the 2050 strategy has the singular advantage of having a clear message, namely securing a million Welsh speakers. The disadvantage of Iaith Fyw: Iaith Byw (Welsh Government, 2011) was that it was dense, and people did not know what the real message was. 'Now we have a story, a narrative and a discourse.'[55] For all its difficulty in implementation the current strategy has been welcomed for offering a bold set of targets and reflecting the government's commitment to growing the numbers of speakers within a generation.

However, one criticism levied at this ambitious target of achieving one million speakers by 2050 was that it might tend to undersell other aspects of Welsh, such as the quality of the language, the proportion of first as opposed to second language speakers, the tendency to treat all speakers as new speakers and the need to preserve the richness of the dialect forms which tend to be eroded by the teaching of standard Welsh. The public servants were well aware of such issues but argued that it was hard to incorporate such concerns within a strategy document. I suggested that one way of capturing these concerns was by making reference to the preservation and enhancement of the richness of the varieties of Welsh. This was acknowledged and would be considered in the redrafting process. The other aspect relative to the strategy is the suggestion that the government has gone native in incorporating the Welsh Language Society's declared aim of creating a million speakers. This was acknowledged as the conceptual source, and it was observed that such shared ambitions emerged from time to time for government tends to be good at appropriating and adopting original ideas as its own.

In the case of Welsh-medium education and language policy Wales does have a rather intimate and well-connected civil service operation which regularly engages with civil society and activist groups. This does not, however, stifle criticism; indeed in such a small country it could even encourage intelligence sharing and a ready acknowledgement of perceived inadequacies.

One such criticism is the manner in which the then current language policy review was carried out, as some have claimed that it is yet another meaningless exercise, despite there being a statutory obligation to consult. A related theme was how to reach the non-mainstream speakers so as to ascertain their views.

---

[54] Interview with Welsh Language Division, Cardiff, 7 September 2016.
[55] Interview with Welsh Language Division, Cardiff, 7 September 2016.

These included recent migrants and some refugees, but above all those from among the majority who have yet to decide on whether or not to place their children in Welsh-medium education.

However, the public servants were confident that a solid programme of action would be implemented as the Minister, Alun Davies, was very committed and provided a strong steer to his staff. The Minister was considered to be direct, well versed in the brief and keen on the WLD getting some simple messages across. The Minister's robust defence of the rights and interests of Welsh speakers characterised his period in office which included the formulation of Cymraeg 2050, the preparation of a Welsh Language Bill and the expansion of standards regulations for new domains, particularly the health sector (Welsh Government, 2017a; 2017b). His personal commitment and strong steer to civil servants can also be seen in the emphasis placed on restructuring the language regime to make it more efficient and effective. This is reflected in the consultation document Striking the Right Balance: Proposals for a Welsh Language Bill which sought to reconfigure the promotion and regulation aspects of language planning, including the radical proposal to abolish the office of Welsh Language Commissioner and gather together many of the various elements of the whole system within a single body to be named the Welsh Language Commission (Welsh Government, 2017c). The balance he sought to strike was reserving to the government the powers to make and impose standards on bodies whilst making the Commission responsible for the monitoring and compliance of such standards.[56] He also was keen to emphasise the necessity for assessing the impact of the proposals for a Welsh Language Bill. While the civil servants I interviewed recognised that this is a statutory obligation, they were also conscious that, rather than adopt a minimum set of requirements, the Minister sought to develop a framework incorporating a Welsh Language Impact Assessment, a Children's Rights Impact Assessment, an Equality Impact Assessment and a Regulatory Impact Assessment.

Getting the balance right for both the proposed Welsh Language Bill and the Cymraeg 2050 strategy was a challenge as the consultation process for the former produced a great deal of support in favour of retaining an independent Language Commissioner. The consultative round for the new strategy had revealed a constant criticism that the target of one million was threatening to overshadow the dynamic use of Welsh in different contexts. Consequently, the revised strategy drafting team determined that there would need to be more in the document about increasing the daily use of Welsh among different sectors of the population. This was less a matter of fine detail and more a matter of

---

[56] Since 1 April 2018 the Reserved Powers Model allows the Assembly to make laws on matters that are not reserved to the UK parliament: www.assembly.wales/en/abthome/role-of-assembly-how-it-works/Pages/Powers.aspx.

getting the narrative right and prioritising the core messages of government programmes. For the drafters it was hard to stand back from the detail and see the overarching scheme, especially one that would remain relevant for a considerable period.[57] In particular they were preoccupied by how to construct a post-Brexit narrative on the assumption that the UK would leave the EU before 2020. For example, would civil servants seek to persuade the political decision makers that it was worth arguing that the Welsh Government had different aims and expectations regarding Europe than did the UK government? Given the often declared aims and statements of leading ministers of the Welsh Government this was not a particularly large risk, but considerations were debated as to whether or not a post-Brexit discussion should be foregrounded. A second consideration was the maintenance of the previously strong connections with other EU minorities in the new dispensation. Wales has a strong record of international co-operation, from the local authority-led involvement with the European Bureau for Lesser Used Languages to being one of the co-founders and subsequent host of the Network for the Promotion of Linguistic Diversity (NPLD). In neither organisation did the government figure prominently but, with the demise of the WLB, the Welsh Government is now an active player in the NPLD and provides the secretariat for the language stream of the British-Irish Council. Thus, in no way could it be said that either the head or the staff of the WLD is unaware of developments either at home or abroad. Indeed, Bethan Webb is the vice chair of the NPLD and consequently is involved in the promotion and dissemination of projects across Europe concerned with new speakers.[58] A third consideration was that if the UK withdrew from the Erasmus scheme should the Welsh Government initiate its own more limited version? We now know that a replacement scheme, entitled Taith, will operate as a five-year programme (2022–6) with Welsh Government funding of up to £65 million. It is designed to offer life-changing opportunities to travel and learn for all learners and staff in every part of Wales, related to adult education, further and vocational education, higher education, schools and youth work. It will also sponsor students and educators from across the world to study in Wales.[59]

In November 2017 Eluned Morgan, AM was appointed Minister for Welsh Language and Lifelong Learning, a policy area which she had developed in her fifteen years as an MEP (1994–2009), during which she served as president of

---

[57] One side effect of operating within a bilingual administration is that when drafts of the strategy in English have been shared, they sound very different in tone and impact than their Welsh version. They sound harsher and more unremitting in English – for example, the Welsh word *cymhathu* has been translated as 'assimilate', which sends negative tones, whereas I would favour 'integrate', which is perceived as being a more positive and inclusive term.

[58] www.npld.eu/about-us/structure/.

[59] https://gov.wales/taith-international-learning-exchange-programme.

the European Parliament Cross Party Committee on Regional and Minority Languages. She represented lesser-used languages across Europe and secured the inclusion of minority languages in the European Charter of Fundamental Rights. In addition to her ministerial roles Baroness Morgan of Ely was the Labour Shadow Minister in the Lords for Foreign Affairs and also Shadow Minister for Wales.

On 13 December 2018 she was appointed Minister for International Relations and the Welsh Language. The list of her responsibilities was extensive and confirms one of the underlying themes of this volume that it is senior civil servants who are core to successive language strategies, because politicians tend to be exercised by the issue of the day.[60] Her expanded mandate sought to present the Welsh language as one among many of the world's lesser-used languages and accordingly civil servants developed associations with groups that had hitherto been less central to their work. The Action Plan 2021–2 rehearses the domains which need to be influenced, chief of which are education, increasing the use of Welsh, developing a linguistic infrastructure and making common cause with other endangered languages.[61]

So, we are left with a strong set of messages including a numerical target of one million speakers, an ambition to double the use of Welsh and a set of educational measures designed to reach the target through placing a greater emphasis on the teaching of Welsh both as a subject and as a medium within all types of schools.

Some politicians and commentators feel that the Welsh model has shifted too far towards the regulation of language standards and services and has neglected preservation and promotion. The former Minister, Alun Davies, has proposed that an expert body be established to advise the government on how it may better encourage the use of Welsh in as many domains as is possible. His fear is that by focussing on the operation of some 174 new language standards in a time of austerity the language-planning process becomes sterile and formulaic. Accordingly, the richness and creativity which characterised the interventions championed by the Welsh Language Board have been lost.[62] Emphasising the social use of Welsh would also provide additional opportunities for new speakers to engage with others in meaningful interactions.

---

[60] Her initial responsibilities focussed on International Relations and the Welsh Language and during the Covid-19 pandemic her responsibilities were directed to well-being and her title in March 2021 was Minister for Mental Health, Wellbeing and Welsh Language. https://gov.wales/eluned-morgan-am.
In the May 2021 Cabinet reshuffle, she was made Minister for Health and Social Services and Jeremy Miles, MS was appointed Minister for Education and the Welsh Language.

[61] https://gov.wales/sites/default/files/publications/2021-03/cymraeg-2050-action-plan-2021-2022.pdf and https://gov.wales/national-policy-welsh-linguistic-infrastructure.

[62] Alun Davies, MS for Blaenau Gwent, observations at Gwlad, Gwlad meeting in the Senedd, Cardiff, 29 September 2019.

This is a theme which has been central to the advice offered by Heini Gruffudd and the networked think tank Dyfodol i'r Iaith (Future for the Language). In his 2014 Learned Society of Wales lecture he argued that 'while Welsh heartland communities have been disintegrating, the main government thrust has been in ensuring language status and rights' (Gruffudd, 2014, p. 10). He voiced what many believed: that the demise of the WLB and the creation of a Welsh Language Commissioner had created a language-planning intelligence vacuum at the heart of government. Soon after abolishing the WLB the government signalled its change of direction by refusing to maintain Local Language Action Plans, in part following the recommendations of the Cardiff University report on the Mentrau Iaith and Local Action Plans. Some, such as Jones (2021) would argue that this represented a lack of real-world understanding by the government of what was needed and what had worked in relation to community language planning. Indeed, he lamented that so many of the WLB initiatives had been abandoned and as a consequence a lack of forethought in the redistribution of WLB public servant expertise has weakened the language-planning potential of the government.[63] Similarly, Gruffudd has argued that:

> There is little evidence at present of holistic thinking on the language. An example is a recent decision to cut the funding available to the Welsh for Adults programme. If the Welsh for Adult provision had been viewed as a crucial part of renewing the language in communities, and as an essential element in establishing a Welsh speaking workforce, and also pivotal for promoting new Welsh speaking families, the decision would have been vastly different. This would have meant that the Ministers responsible for Welsh, Education, the Economy and Community Development and Local Authorities would have come together to discuss funding possibilities, but it is clear that this never happened. (Gruffudd, 2014, p. 12)

He advocates the establishment of two key agencies to mitigate this apparent lack of attention by government. The first would be the opening of many more Welsh language and cultural centres.

> Once learned, Welsh needs to be practised. We have witnessed the breakdown of Welsh language networks in anglicised Wales. One creative and productive solution that has emerged over recent years is the establishment of Welsh language and cultural centres – *Canolfannau Cymraeg* – which could, for example, house Welsh for Adults, Mentrau Iaith and yr Urdd, and which could provide social and cultural events. Such network enhancing centres exist in Swansea, Merthyr, Pontypridd and Wrexham, with learning centres in Denbigh and Flint and some other places. There are around 200 such centres in the Basque Country and we need to emulate their practice. This local level, under the auspices of the proposed Centre for Welsh for Adults, with the support of local volunteers and local authorities. (Gruffudd, 2014, p. 15)

---

[63] M. P. Jones, interview 24 May 2021.

The second innovation would be the establishment of a Welsh Language Authority which would:

provide leadership at the strategic planning stage, rather than as an afterthought in consultation. It will have an overarching role across ministries and advise and formulate government policies holistically. Its priority will be to ensure that Welsh can thrive in viable language communities and domains, whether in the Welsh heartland or in the comparatively less Welsh-speaking parts of Wales. Regulation and legislation, essential as they are, must now take second place to an innovative language use and promotion programme, aimed at expanding and enhancing the domains, social and work networks available to Welsh speakers. (Gruffudd, 2014, p. 16)

The call for a language authority was repeated in Dyfodol's 2020 manifesto prior to the May 2021 Senedd elections (Dyfodol i'r Iaith, 2020a; 2020b).

Such a development was endorsed by many who were interviewed as part of this project. A typical reaction by Ifor Gruffydd carries a warning about impact and capacity.

As you know, there have been a series of strategies such as *Iaith Pawb*, and *Iaith Fyw: Iaith Byw* (Living Language: A Living Language) over the past 20 years, and as you wrote about regarding *Iaith Pawb* we need to ask what comes out of them and what difference have they made? What difference will Cymraeg 2050 make? This is why we need some kind of Authority like this, from competent language planners, to lead the government. (Gruffydd, pers. comm., 2021)

He doubted that the appointment of a handful of experienced personnel within the WLD would make a sufficient difference! However, James (pers. comm., 2021) would remind us that there have been significant investments, such as the establishment of the National Centre for Learning Welsh and the Cymraeg Gwaith (Work Welsh) programme.[64] What most of those interviewed regretted was that there was not a sustained national discussion regarding the role and advantages of Welsh in an increasingly multicultural society.

During the intervening years 2014–21 the WLD has addressed several of these lacunae and has strengthened its language-planning expertise. The government does not wish to establish a Welsh Language Authority although several alternative arrangement by which specialists can be brought into the policy arena have been discussed both within government and between government and other agencies such as the Welsh Language Commissioner, Welsh Universities and civil society. At each stage the stumbling block appears to be the definition of which responsibilities will be shared and who ultimately decides on the contours of language policy. This was a major bone of contention between the government and the direction of the Welsh Language

---

[64] https://learnwelsh.cymru/work-welsh/introducing-work-welsh/.

Commission under its former head Meri Huws, who insisted on exercising her statutory mandate to promote as well as regulate language affairs.

For a significant period up until late 2018 the government were minded to abolish the office of the Welsh Language Commissioner and take into government several of its more pertinent responsibilities (Williams, 2021a). On 6 December 2018 Mark Drakeford replaced Carwyn Jones as leader of the Welsh Labour Party and First Minister. In February 2019 the government took the decision to leave arrangements as they were. Both the First Minister and Eluned Morgan, Minister for the Welsh Language, were reticent to open 'another front' on the language issue and create more social unrest by abolishing the role of the Commissioner.[65] This decision was compounded by the uncertainty surrounding how well the language standards were embedding and functioning and this in turn was another theme addressed by the Culture, Welsh Language and Communications Committee which made the following two recommendations:

Recommendation 4. We recommend that the Welsh Government explore options to adapt Welsh language standards, within the current legislative framework. This could be done by streamlining or combining multiple standards that have the same aim or outcome. Any changes made should not have a detrimental impact on the provision of services for Welsh speakers. Recommendation 5. Any potential changes to standards should only be made for sectors which are not currently implementing the Welsh language standards under the 2011 Measure, such as housing associations, utilities and transport bodies. (National Assembly for Wales, 2019, p. 7)

Clarification of government roles and responsibilities was another recommendation made by the Culture, Welsh Language and Communications Committee in its 2019 report on Supporting and Promoting the Welsh Language: 'Recommendation 10. The Welsh Government should set out clear demarcation of roles and responsibility between itself and the Welsh Language Commissioner, and that is communicated clearly with stakeholders and the public' (National Assembly for Wales, 2019, p. 35). This was implemented when the government and the Language Commissioner signed a New Memorandum of Collaboration in August 2019 which set out a comprehensive list of promotional areas and initiatives.

One of the key decisions taken by the government was to invest more in the capacity of the civil service to deliver the Cymraeg 2050 strategy. Recommendation 11 suggests that 'the Welsh Government should move to enhance the status and role of the Welsh Language Unit. The Unit, in addition to its current responsibilities, would be responsible for drawing together external knowledge and expertise that will provide a strategic overview of language planning nationally. The Unit should also have an increased

---

[65] Bethan Webb, Cardiff, 15 February 2019.

cross-governmental role, ensuring internal arrangements for effective implementation of *Cymraeg 2050* is undertaken across government departments.' A further recommendation is that 'the Welsh Government must ensure adequate funding for promotional activities undertaken by Government, the Commissioner or external agencies if it is to succeed in its aim for a million Welsh speakers by 2050'. A final recommendation is that 'the Welsh Government should work closely with those conducting research in academia to identify gaps in knowledge and develop programmes of research to support the *Cymraeg 2050* Strategy' (National Assembly for Wales, 2019, pp. 5–7).

The WLD has responded by appointing an experienced language planner as head of the Cymraeg 2050 strategy together with other appointments in the field and has launched a series of new initiatives which integrate academic research, behavioural language planning, particularly nudge theory, and IT, AI and organisational experience in seeking to strengthen the position of Welsh in social, economic and governance affairs.[66] Accordingly, there is more confidence now in the ability of the government to deliver on its Cymraeg 2050 strategy.

'Dysgu Cymraeg / Learn Welsh'

Now that the broad parameters of the Welsh language strategy are known and largely endorsed within civil society, I asked a range of agencies and interest groups how they reacted to the use of the term new speakers and what implications they envisioned for the quality and use of Welsh being produced within the new framework.

Welsh for Adults has long been a mainstay of educational provision and a key source for the production of new speakers although it must be admitted that relatively few students attain full fluency. Dr Ifor Gruffydd, the Director of Learn Welsh North West, Bangor University, was asked if the Welsh for Adults sector used the term new speaker.[67] He replied that the concept has now been accepted by the sector and was used mainly in relation to specific students when they felt that the term learner was either patronising or did not do justice to their individual competence in mastering Welsh. In such contexts new speaker was a more pertinent description of a skill set and levels of attainment. However, Learn Welsh North Wales had not formally adopted the term, whose application remained inconsistent. Nor was there any great desire to see new speaker displace learner as a term and in consequence the National Centre for

---

[66] https://cymru-wales.tal.net/vx/mobile-0/appcentre-1/brand-2/candidate/so/pm/1/pl/6/opp/6719-Head-of-Prosiect-2050/en-GB.
[67] Author's translation of answers given on the 15 March 2021.

Learning Welsh stance remains pretty neutral. Formal opportunities for new speakers to converse were obviously centred on classroom instruction, but other opportunities were also provided, which include:
- *Sadyrnau Siarad* Conversation Saturdays
- *Panad neu Beint a Sgwrs* A cup of tea or a pint and a chat
- *Cynllun 'Siarad' sydd yn paru dysgwr gyda siardwr rhugl er mwyn rhoi cyfle i'r siaradwyr newydd ymarfer eu sgiliau men cyd-destun anffurfiol* The 'Siarad scheme' which pairs new speakers with fluent speakers so that language skills can be honed in informal settings
- *Pwyslais ar integreiddio dysgwyr mewn digwyddiadau lleol* An emphasis on integrating learners in local events
- *Teithiau amrywiol e.e. cerdded, amgueddfa, hanes etc* Various activites, such as walking, visits to museums, history, etc.
- *Cyrsiau pynciol fel Hanes Cymru, Archaeoleg nad ydynt yn gyrsiau iaith ond yn gyrsiau sy'n addas i ddysgwyr a siaradwyr rhugl fel ei gilydd* Subject specific courses such as the History of Wales, Archaelology, which while not being specific language classes are appropriate for both learners and new speakers
- *Cwisiau* Quizzes

When asked what he thought were the strengths and weaknesses of the term new speaker in comparison with learner or advanced learner, Dr Gruffydd advised that on occasion the term learner could convey a rather negative image. This is particularly the case for advanced learners who have a good command of Welsh as opposed to those who are at an earlier entry or foundation stage. The idea that someone who can converse well in different contexts or using different registers should still be called a learner could be interpreted as belittling or insulting. 'We are conscious that we are always improving the languages that we speak but we would not call ourselves learners', he said. Accordingly, one of the strengths of employing the term new speaker is that it places the 'learner' on an equal footing with a regular speaker. In general terms the new speaker concept is to be welcomed for it is an affirmative term. Also, the new speaker term does not differentiate between a pure learner and one who can converse well, and this to be commended for it is not a divisive concept, as the term learner might be.

Dr Gruffydd welcomed the government's 2050 language strategy as signalling a strong reinforcement of the language's position. However, he was not fully convinced that there would be a substantial increase in speakers unless a range of structural issues was overcome. These include the lack of transmission within the family, the educational standards and nature of the reforms in first and second language teaching and the lack of government commitment to do more, for example in legislative terms, to guarantee an abundant supply of bilingual workers within the public sector.

One serious issue in terms of teaching within the Welsh for Adults sector, particularly within the workplace, is the lack of pressure exerted by managers to upskill their workforce in regard to language considerations. The impact of the Welsh Language (Wales) Measure 2011 has not been sufficient to see a 'revolutionary' turnaround in the world of work, particularly within the public sector. However, guideline advice and evaluations by Estyn and the government's actions to develop its own workforce augur well for some improvement in this regard.[68]

If we consider growth in relation to the production of new speakers through the Learn Welsh network/organisation the current numbers are insufficient to have a real impact on future prospects. For example, the losses identified previously through failures in language transmission are far greater than the annual rate of 13,000 adult learners, which is not the total of fluent speakers but the total number of all learners within the system. Some have argued that even this number cannot compensate for the annual rate of outmigration of fluent Welsh speakers, which may not be entirely accurate but is certainly a consideration in the popular consciousness.

Ifor Gruffydd believes that:

Currently, the Welsh for Adults sector provides language training for approximately 2 per cent of the non-Welsh speaking population throughout Wales. Various surveys conducted over recent years e.g., Welsh Government (2018) demonstrate that the aspiration to learn Welsh is consistently relatively high amongst the non-Welsh speaking population at c. 62 per cent. This huge reality-aspirational gap is there due to a variety of complex social, economic and political factors, but there is an argument that nothing will change unless radical changes are made by the Welsh Government so that learning Welsh becomes a requirement in certain areas of Welsh work and life rather than a desirable skill. (Gruffydd, pers. comm., 2021)

When asked whether the anticipated growth would change the nature and character of Welsh, Dr Gruffydd viewed this issue as one which would require complex and multi-layered solutions. Clearly many factors influenced language over time, such as the natural phenomenon of language change, the impact of the hegemonic position of English and the development of Welsh-medium education for children from non-Welsh-speaking homes. A common trope is to suggest that, as second language speakers will become more numerous than first language speakers, the nature and standard of Welsh will inevitably decline. This may be true to some extent. However, his conviction is that the natural imbibing of Welsh at home is the most effective way to uphold the standard and character of the language. Alongside this, effective education

---

[68] www.gov.uk/guidance/january-2021-further-education-and-skills-providers. https://gov.wales/cymraeg-it-belongs-to-us-all-html (July 2020).

is of the upmost importance and a 'revolutionary' effort is required in this sector just as much as within the world of work. Far too many individuals have experienced twelve years of Welsh-medium education, either as second language learners, who often lack confidence to speak Welsh once they have left school, or as first language students, whose written Welsh is all too often non-standard. Such consequences undermine both the spoken and written standards of Welsh and are reflective of a fundamental problem which he argues deserves to be tackled forthwith.

I identified teacher training as a key issue above and remarked that the fragmented nature of planning the supply of future teachers was a strategic weakness. However, one successful scheme since 2005 has been the National Sabbatical Scheme for Welsh Language Training hosted by Bangor University, Cardiff University and Trinity St David's University. The courses are free for participants and are underwritten by the government which is responsible for the costs of the training, including paying supplies, travel and accommodation. The Sabbatical Scheme is a language course for teachers, lecturers, instructors and classroom assistants who wish to improve their Welsh and gain more confidence in using the language. The course is available at three levels: Higher (first language Welsh speakers and fluent learners), Entry (learners) and Foundation (learners), as demonstrated in Table 3.2.

Table 3.2 *Overview of sabbatical course provision, 2021*

Level/Course	Target audience	Nos.	Notes
Higher Level for Teachers	Primary/secondary teachers in Welsh/English primary/secondary schools	599	
Higher Level for Teaching Assistants	Assistants in Welsh-medium schools	216	
Intermediate	Teachers in English or bilingual primary schools	13	Piloted in April 2019. Courses scheduled in 2020 postponed due to Covid-19
Foundation	Teachers in English-medium primary schools	611	
Entry	Teaching assistants in English-medium primary schools	652	
Welsh in a Year	Teachers in English-medium primary schools	232	Includes 55 teachers attending current course
		2323	

Source: Education Directorate, Welsh Government, 2021.

Canolfan Bedwyr at Bangor suggest that after having been on this course, you should:

- feel more confident using oral and written Welsh while teaching, assessing, and doing administrative work;
- be more confident in finding the terminology of your subject and using it effectively;
- be aware of the methodology of teaching through the medium of Welsh and bilingually;
- be more confident in using and developing these methodologies in Welsh-medium / bilingual situation.[69]

The Cardiff University Sabbatical Scheme manager, Lowri Davies, was asked about her perception of the utility of the term new speaker in her work of training teachers.[70] Her response was that whilst they do not use the term new speaker in their publicity or documentation, consideration of the term has been discussed at a national level in response to evaluations of the scheme and more recently there has been some discussion as to whether or not the term should be adopted. Many of the teachers who attended would identify as new speakers. Accordingly, a great deal of the formal teaching and the informal conversation sessions acknowledge this fact in the delivery and material presented. The sessions would range from formal training workshops, conversation classes, creative workshops and observational sessions in the Welsh-medium sector. When asked about the perceived strengths and weaknesses of the new speaker concept in contrast to the designation of learner or advanced learner, Lowri Davies considered it to be a positive term as it neither points to a specific level nor suggests a point on the Welsh learner trajectory. However, the difficulty rises when one asks at what point does one cease being a new speaker and become a Welsh speaker.

The questioning turned to her reaction to the anticipated increase in the numbers being able to speak Welsh should current plans come to pass. Her fear was that a shortage of sufficiently qualified staff within the English-medium primary and secondary sector would inhibit the chances of students in the English-medium sector from becoming bilingual. Such teachers are essential if the government targets are to be achieved. The Cwricwlwm i Gymru was moving in the right direction and the sabbatical courses certainly contribute to ensuring that the teachers can react effectively to the requirements of the Curriculum for Wales.[71] However, it is doubtful whether the majority of such teachers will be able to so contribute. For this to happen it is essential that the heads of schools allow their staff to take advantage of the necessary training.

---

[69] www.bangor.ac.uk/canolfanbedwyr/sabothol.php.en.
[70] Material translated by the author from answers given by Lowri Davies on 11 March 2021 and follow-up correspondence on 17 March 2021.
[71] https://hwb.gov.wales/curriculum-for-wales.

This is the only realistic way in which one can increase the number of students able to speak Welsh within the English-medium sector. Even greater investment in this workforce is needed as the aim of creating confident speakers within this sector is essential.

One of the concerns expressed regarding both the proposed increase in Welsh speakers and the adoption of the term new speakers has been the impact on the structure of the language and the changes in the character and quality of Welsh used. Lowri Davies acknowledges that the nature of the language will change. In many cases pupils in Welsh-mediums schools who speak Welsh at home converse with their friends in English and this inevitably has an impact on the nature of their Welsh. However, despite some linguistic flaws it is far better to encourage pupils to use their language rather than inhibit them through too much criticism. She would rather hear people using their Welsh, even with mistakes, than not use their Welsh.[72] If the numbers are to increase, then so must the proportion of confident speakers and as a consequence it is inevitable that there will be changes both in the nature of the language and the disposition of native speakers to learners and new speakers.[73] In June 2021 Dysgu Cymraeg began using *siaradwyr newydd* (new speakers) within its official documentation and internal discussions.[74]

Since 2017 the Cymraeg Mewn Blwyddyn/Welsh in a Year for those working within English-medium education has proven to be successful. The course pays a great deal of attention to methodology which is vital as it seeks to train teachers to discharge their lessons in and through Welsh with a great deal of confidence. The course enables teachers to meet the requirements of the Cwricwlwm i Gymru. Lowri Davies is convinced that cumulatively these courses will contribute to the goal of producing a million Welsh speakers by 2050.

Others are not so sanguine. Gruffydd argues that the 2050 Strategy could be criticised from a language-planning perspective by asking how SMART are the objectives? He queries

whether the objects are stacking up e.g., is it possible to train enough teachers in the period under review? How do we achieve everything within the period under review, and more importantly perhaps – how to get language planners who are central in the

---

[72] S. Morris has added 'Gwell Cymraeg Slac na Saesneg Slic!' (Better Slack Welsh than Slick English)! (Morris, pers. comm., 2021).

[73] Gruffydd advises that 'I did a small study in 2019 with National Centre funding looking at changing the behaviour of reluctant Welsh speakers (mainly due to lack of confidence). One of the main reasons for not using their Welsh language was the experience of criticism from other Welsh speakers (probably first language) for the standard of their Welsh. This is an important social factor that is going to affect the use of the Welsh language' (Gruffydd, pers. comm., 2021).

[74] Helen Prosser, Director of Teaching and Learning, Dysgu Cymraeg (Prosser, pers. comm., 2021).

process to address the different elements? For Welsh for Adults, for example, this has not happened. What drives Welsh for Adults is funding, and that is also one of the factors holding it back. Since the publication of a Million Speakers strategy, the Welsh for Adults budget has been reduced! (Gruffydd, pers. comm., 2021; author's translation)

In March 2021, the government published its review and continued support for the Sabbatical Scheme and made nine key recommendations. In addition to securing that the teachers from the scheme go on to share their newly honed skills, the report emphasised the acute need to gather time-series evidence as detailed below:

Recommendation 8: Welsh Government should consider undertaking quantitative research to gather information from beneficiaries of the Scheme, practitioners and schools alike, to contribute to a fuller picture of the Scheme's impact.

The evidence gathered through the evaluation process suggests that the theory of change offers an accurate reflection of the logic flow between the Scheme's inputs, outputs and outcomes and its contribution to longer-term outcomes. The process of analysing the theory has revealed certain gaps in data: the evidence on which the evaluation findings are based is, on the whole, limited to observations and examples provided during interviews. The conclusions could have been strengthened had documentary evidence been available, including data against the indicators of practitioners' use of skills after returning to school (see Recommendation 3 above).

Recommendation 9: Welsh Government should address refining the theory of change for the Sabbatical Scheme by (i) including more stakeholder input; (ii) making the widest possible use of data already available in terms of workforce skills capacity (ability in Welsh and to teach through the medium of Welsh) and (iii) dealing with the gaps in data and evidence that have been highlighted in this evaluation to ensure a fuller understanding of the Scheme's contribution to longer-term outcomes. (Welsh Government, 2021)

A significant development is the emulation of the Catalan Voluntariat per la Llengua (VxL) initiative termed Siarad which was launched in 2018 and relaunched in a virtual format during the Covid-19 pandemic.[75]

- The scheme brings Welsh speakers and learners together for 10 hours of informal conversations in social settings.
- The aim is to increase learners' confidence and introduce them to opportunities to use their Welsh locally.
- The scheme is available to learners at Intermediate (*Canolradd*), Advanced (*Uwch*) or Proficient (*Hyfedredd*) levels.

Evidence of the success of the Catalan scheme features in Chapter 7, but one of the strategic directions in Wales would be to target part of the Siarad scheme towards the needs of migrants as discussed below.

---

[75] https://learnwelsh.cymru/news/plenty-of-opportunity-to-talk-online-with-the-relaunch-of-the-siarad-scheme/.

Migrants, Refugees and Asylum Seekers

Within the COST New Speakers Network's purview, new speakers include both those who have adopted a language not initially learned at home but through formal education and also those who having arrived as migrants have chosen to participate in society through their local language of choice. How the latter do so is a matter of great interest, especially in those sub-state polities whose statutory educational systems involve the acquisition of an indigenous lesser-used language, such as the Basque Autonomous Community and Wales.

Augustyniak and Higham (2019) demonstrate the manner in which integration policies impact differentially on types of migrants, depending on whether the policies are developed by state or sub-state political authorities. Yet despite the official rhetoric, it is clear that many migrants do not recognise the claim that the sub-state language is an integral element of their integration. In contrast those migrants who are enthusiastic learners of the target language are seen as a useful boost to the language revitalisation efforts, while recalcitrant migrants are deemed to undermine such efforts. In that respect the differential positions of migrants reflect the dominant hegemonic position of the host majority. The multiplicity of messages relayed by the Spanish and British states, together with those in circulation within civil society, threaten to occlude the official discourse as represented in sub-state language and educational policies. This feature is compounded by the inconsistency and fragmentation which characterises such policies.

Augustyniak and Higham (2019) point to the difficulty which new speakers face when they seek to evaluate the role of each language in the process of their own integration. This is made far more complex in cases such as Wales, Euskadi and Catalonia when they are confronted by the demands of both state-wide language and educational policies and those which derive from the sub-state authorities. A worthy follow-up study could scrutinise the daily choices, experiences and uncertainties faced by migrants and new speakers alike occasioned by this multiple set of competing demands. This would illumine the crux of the argument which revolves around the gap between the official rhetoric and the various delivery systems employed to secure a degree of integration in and through the lesser-used language. The authors conclude that they have shown that while

Basque is promoted as the language of integration, suggesting that it is the (main) pathway to belonging and 'Basqueness', while in Wales, more ambiguously, policies promote the cultural assets of the Welsh language, but deliver language learning strategies for migrants solely in English. While language policies promote bilingualism, interculturality and bidirectional cultural exchange between migrants and host communities, a one-dimensional role of language in integration is nevertheless put forward. (Augustyniak and Higham, 2019)

Again, one is struck by the irony of such apparently laudable and logical policy practices, and in Wales it would seem that the default use of English as the 'natural' language of migrant instruction not only reflects British mores and values, but perhaps global ones also.

In March 2020, the Welsh Language Society and the Welsh Refugee Council piloted a scheme where 300 adult asylum seekers and refugees would get the chance to learn Welsh for free both in online sessions and with mentors. The *Guardian* reports that

> there is frustration from some language campaigners at what they see as a lack of provision in Wales for refugees to learn the country's language. The Welsh government funds free English classes for asylum seekers and refugees. It does offer Welsh lessons for asylum seekers, but not for refugees. Refugees who want to learn have to seek out free classes given by volunteers, which can be hard to find, or pay for them.[76]

The question of new speakers has received additional impetus with the programmes developed by Cardiff and Swansea Universities to teach Welsh to recent migrants and refugees. In June 2021 Dysgu Cymraeg launched a new course Croeso i Bawb which is aimed at participants who do not speak English as their first language. No English is used within the course teaching and conversations reflect the multicultural character of the programme (Prosser, pers. comm., 2021).

However, I have raised concerns as to how one would identify new speakers, how programmes which sought to satisfy their needs would be evaluated, measured and funded and most critically whether identifying new speakers as a priority may run counter to current reforms which seek to avoid distinctions within and between Welsh speakers (Williams, 2019a). One way of reducing this fragmentation is to empower some within the migrant community to become more active stakeholders in shaping language policy. There are practical difficulties in co-opting migrant representatives as by continuing to view them as supplicants rather than as actors in the process, their agency is weakened. Another practical difficulty is to gauge how representative any migrant delegate(s) might be of the whole migrant experience of learning a lesser-used language, whose constituents could range from birth origins in Latin America, North Africa or Asia. But even if this were to be achieved there would remain the issue of influencing the predominant approach adopted by civil servants as framers of language and educational policies as to what such

---

[76] A spokesman for the Welsh Government said: 'Through work with the National Centre for Learning Welsh, we provide support for learners from all backgrounds to learn Welsh, with the centre offering free courses for asylum seekers. We fully support efforts such as the partnership in examining all possibilities to help refugees and asylum seekers to learn the language of their choice' (www .theguardian.com/uk-news/2020/mar/06/i-was-lucky-the-asylum-seeker-campaigning-for-others-to-learn-welsh). Helen Prosser advises that all *blasu* tasting courses are now free (Prosser, pers. comm., 2021).

policies are meant to achieve and their implicit assumptions regarding both the role and the salience of migrant new speakers in the civic integration ideologies and practice.

Cymdeithas yr Iaith

This pivotal movement has long been at the forefront of organising classes and events for Welsh learners and has developed a suite of policies designed to aid their integration into Welsh-speaking communities. In the spring of 2021, they moved towards the adoption of the term new speaker to describe some of their engagement as it suggested a more positive tone than learner. The society's general secretary, Carol Jenkins, summarised their deliberations as follows:

> We have recently established a Learner Committee (now the New Speakers Support Committee) to support the work of the Learner Officer (we have not changed the title of this post as this is currently in the Constitution); it includes Welsh speakers and those who have learned the language. We are currently organizing an event in late May to discuss how we can better support new speakers. We will have another event at the end of September – again under the 'Supporting New Speakers' brand. This will replace the Learner Weekends that we would normally hold about three times a year (and are currently unable to because of the Pandemic) and something more social (yet aiming to draw in new and experienced speakers together). The ultimate aim is to update the Living Communities Toolkit produced some years ago. At last week's Committee meeting, there was extensive discussion on what to call these events and the general feeling was that the term 'new speakers' suited better – and that was when it was decided to change the name of the committee as well. I notice that the www.paned.cymru website produces three types of badges – Learner, New Speaker, Welsh – so I wonder if this suggests some kind of development along the Welsh learning path! But I think the feeling at the meeting was that a 'new speaker' conveys something more positive than a 'learner'. This is not an 'official' decision of the Society. (Jenkins, pers. comm., 2021).

A comprehensive analysis of the initiatives required to reach the government's target of creating a million Welsh speakers by 2050 was produced in the WLS strategy document Mwy na Miliwn (More than a Million) in June 2020.

> We have a chapter on 'creating speakers' in our 'More than a Million' vision document where we say: 'Creating speakers is the only way to reach a million speakers and more.' There are only four ways to increase numbers the speakers: in the family, at school, adults learning, and attracting speakers back to Wales. The Welsh Government and indeed any national government, has more direct control over education than any other major area the process of creating new speakers. The term 'learners' does not appear in the document at all, although we refer a little to learning Welsh and the section on Welsh Citizenship for All provides details our call to 'ensure that everyone, without exception', may engage in learning, experiencing and using Welsh meaningfully in their daily lives. (Jenkins, pers. comm., 2021)

Dyfodol i'r Gymraeg

This movement recognises the centrality of new speakers to the vitality and growth of Welsh. They assert that their manifesto 'Troi Dyhead yn Realiti' (Turning Aspiration into Reality) (Dyfodol i'r Iaith, 2020a) is very relevant and both encourages and supports new speakers.[77] This may be implied as there is no direct reference to new speakers in this or other of their documents. However, after citing several well-rehearsed actions they would like to see government initiate, they propose two reforms to the language regime. The first is the establishment of a new arm's length language authority. The second is the strengthening of the government's Welsh Language Division so that it can deliver Cymraeg 2050. Given recent prevarications and threats to downgrade the office, they would wish to see the guaranteeing of the Welsh Language Commissioner as an independent agency and a far greater incorporation of private sector considerations into the land use planning system.

Other Dyfodol documentation provides detailed recommendations on the role of Welsh in the workforce (Dyfodol i'r Iaith, 2020b). A serious handicap for those who wish to assess the use of Welsh in the workforce is the absence of accurate, consistent data, whether collected in the public or the private sector. Such data is essential, and a key recommendation made by Dyfodol would be a national level political directive to collect such evidence so as to assist in the planning of future needs and to establish a consistent provision of Welsh-medium services. However, greater specification of the expectations of consumers is not the answer as the supportive infrastructure to service such needs is a prime consideration. Investigation of the working language of local authorities produces a fragmented picture and one important step would be to encourage the use of Welsh as the dominant internal language of the four most Welsh-speaking authorities in the north and west, namely Gwynedd (which operates through Welsh), Ynys Môn, Ceredigion and Sir Gaerfyrddin. This would act as a catalyst for the extension of Welsh as a language of other agencies within public administration.

However, a note of caution must be observed for as Gruffydd contends:

> There is undoubted support within workplaces across Wales, particularly public sector, for staff to receive Welsh language training and the recent growth due to schemes such as *Work Welsh* is obviously to be welcomed. However, I am not yet convinced that the considerable investment of funding and staff time is leading to a strategic change within workplaces whereby a planned and demonstrable increase in the use of Welsh is being seen within the workplace. Consequently, it is not known to what extent this is aiding the local authorities listed above to move towards a Welsh language administration not to provide a fuller public service in Welsh. (Gruffydd, pers. comm., 2021)

---

[77] Answers and documents given by Ruth Richards, Chief Executive, 12 March 2021.

Conclusion

While there are undoubtedly elements who recognise that the needs of new speakers have to be better defined, there is also a reluctance to add yet another layer of policy initiative to a crowded agenda for action. Far better, it is argued, that new speakers be incorporated within mainstream language and educational policies and civil society activities. For the near future it is possible that a radical new dynamic will be constructed around something akin to the new speaker paradigm as the goal of creating more than a million speakers essentially rests on the production of non-traditional speakers, however they may be described. This need for radical and innovative policies was made even more acute by the release in December 2022 of the March 2021 Census of the Welsh language, conducted during the Covid 19 pandemic when education was severely disrupted for a long period (Welsh Government, 2022b). An estimated 538,300 residents aged three or older were reported as being able to speak Welsh, or 17.8 per cent of the population, a decrease of 23,700 people and 1.2 percentage points lower than the 19 per cent recorded in 2011. The biggest decline of 6 per cent was in the 5–15 age cohort, a blow to the education sector which has become the principal pillar of language revitalisation, following the atrophying of heartland communities and the stable, if low rates of intergenerational language transmission within households. In this respect the proposed recategorisation of schools from late 2022 onwards demonstrates the government's commitment to promote the teaching of Welsh, while its concern with well-being and future generations' welfare augurs well for a more holistic and supportive infrastructure within which additional initiatives may be launched.

4 Scotland: Cautious Consideration

Institutionally and economically Scotland has forged a distinct national identity operating as a separate country within the UK. It has an established set of national institutions, a distinguished history of achievement in all the major sciences and arts and has played a major role in the expansion of the British Empire and the UK's industrial growth. Scotland is characterised by a robust civil society and an engaging history of deliberative democracy. However, Gaelic in Scotland cannot be considered as the national language because of its demo-linguistic history and marginalisation since the fourteenth century and the persistence of the Highland/Lowland divide. Non-Gaelic-speaking Lowland Scots tend to feel that Gaelic had little to do with them. The language, unlike Welsh or Irish, was not part of a patrimony, lost, imagined or otherwise. This ideological divide has been exacerbated by three centuries of Whig history and historicism, and the acceptance of what some call a 'teutonist' ideology. Allied to this is a majoritarian perception, correct or otherwise, that much of Gaelic culture is imbued with anti-modernist perspectives. This allows them not only to disavow any responsibility for its fate but to distance themselves from the core values which it is claimed Gaelic culture espouses. Thus, rather than being seen as just a Scottish variant of Celtic language shift, it is more profitable to interpret this complex relationship between majority and minority as a form of ethnic redefinition.[1]

The restoration of a Scottish parliament did not occasion the same levels of commitment to the development of Gaelic as happened to Welsh in Wales. Until devolution, distinctly Scottish institutions, such as a separate legal system, the Presbyterian/Calvinist national church and the education system, with their attendant ideologies, had all been crucial in strengthening national identity. Scottish civil society is a far more developed construct than its Welsh or Northern Irish counterpart. But language does not figure as a central plank either of identity or of society. Thus, Gaelic and Scots are unlikely to achieve

---

[1] I owe this observation to Professor Robert Dunbar of Edinburgh University. Language issues have been, at best, a tiny footnote in Scottish devolution. Gaelic has episodically played a symbolic role in nationalist discourse, whereas institutions and ideologies have played the defining role in national self-definition.

salience in national politics. Neither language, for example, received any mention in the Scotland Act, 1998. There is some provision for Gaelic in the Standing Orders of the Scottish Parliament (Scots gets none) and there have been some titular concessions to Gaelic, as in signage at the parliament, the appointment of a Gaelic Officer and the occasional use of the language in a number of functions of national importance.[2] Since 2001 the recognition of Gaelic, alongside Welsh and Irish, in the Framework Convention and the European Charter for Regional or Minority Languages, has given it a distinct position within UK and international law.[3]

Gathering the Evidence

A similar approach to gathering evidence was undertaken in Scotland as for Wales and over the same period, including the same interview questions as recorded in the Appendix. Given the relatively precarious position of Gaelic it has been argued that the phenomenon of new speakers has not only been an ever-present feature within the community, but that its growth is a sign of vitality that Gaelic can attract more fluent speakers through formal education, marriage patterns and immersion within predominantly Gaelic-speaking communities. In consequence the reality of the new speaker construct has loomed larger here because the total number of residents who could read, write or understand Gaelic at around 87,056 (1.7 per cent of the population at the 2011 Census compared with 92,000, or 1.9 per cent, in 2001) is relatively small. Accordingly, new speakers have a disproportionate significance for language transmission, attraction and planning. Indeed, one might argue that they are an essential element of the language's survival. However, context is everything, for the situation of Gaelic remains perilous given the steady decline in the number of speakers throughout the twentieth century and the atrophying of the Gàidhealtachd (the conventional name for the predominantly Gaelic-speaking region), which continues apace. The nuances of Gaelic community use are described by McLeod (2020b) and in great detail in the Shawbost report (Mac an Tàilleir et al., 2010), which suggests that Gaelic there is at a tipping point but still capable of regeneration if remedial intervention strategies are adopted.[4]

Initial attempts to strengthen the language included the mobilisation of Gaelic pressure groups who sought to craft an agenda for action. This saw the introduction of immersion education in 1985, the passing of the

---

[2] In May 2002 Alec O' Henley, the first officer for Gaelic, courageously resigned his position in protest at the lack of progress on the language front. For the use of Gaelic in the Scottish parliament see www.parliament.scot/.
[3] Ratified by the UK 27 March 2001, in force 1 July 2001.
[4] An English summary is available at https://pureadmin.uhi.ac.uk/ws/portalfiles/portal/1582887/Munro_2011_The_state_of_Gaelic_in_Shawbost.pdf.

Broadcasting Act 1990 and the Broadcasting Act of 1996. However, the dawn of the new century heralded a change of gear and pace. I take the threshold base mark to be the 2001 Census as it is only since then that serious efforts at language revitalisation have shown any signs of success. In 2001, 58,969 Gaelic speakers aged 3 and over were recorded in Scotland, a mere 1.2 per cent of the national population (McLeod, 2016).[5] The General Register Office recorded 7,094 persons as being able to read or write Gaelic but not speak it, and a further 27,538 could understand Gaelic but not speak, read or write it (General Register Office for Scotland, 2005: Table 1).

A decade later the 2011 Census recorded 53, 375 people aged 3 and over able to speak Gaelic, 1.1 per cent of the population. The rate of decline had slowed during the decade 2001–11 as there was only a 2.2 per cent decline as opposed to 11.1 per cent in the decade 1991–2001. The age differentials reflect the influence of education. Dunmore (2019) notes that the Census showed growth, albeit of only 0.1 per cent, in the proportion of Gaelic speakers nationally under age 20, while the growth in numeric terms was actually 8.6 per cent for all speakers under 25.[6] The details are from 0.53 per cent to 0.70 per cent for 3–4-year-olds; from 0.91 per cent to 1.13 per cent for 5–11-year-olds; and from 1.04 per cent to 1.10 per cent for 12–17-year-olds. Some 41 per cent of Gaelic-speaking children aged 5 to 11 lived in households where all adults had some Gaelic language skills, 23 per cent lived in households where some (but not all) adults had some Gaelic language skills and 36 per cent lived in households where no adults had any Gaelic language skills (National Records of Scotland, 2015). These trends reflect the impact of Gaelic-medium school education, which grew steadily in the 1990s and early 2000s. However, the Gaelic-speaking population remains skewed to the older age groups while for people aged 65 and over the proportion fell from 1.8 per cent in 2001 to 1.5 per cent in 2011.

The 2011 Census reveals that 87,100 people aged 3 and over (1.7 per cent of the population) had some Gaelic language skills, while Figure 4.1 reveals their geographical distribution. Of these 32,400 (37 per cent) could understand, speak, read and write Gaelic; 57,600 (66 per cent) could speak Gaelic; 6,100

---

[5] McLeod (2016) notes the paucity of data for Gaelic speakers outside Scotland, especially as no question of Gaelic ability is included in the Census form used elsewhere in the UK. For information on Nova Scotia see Dunmore (2020). In March 2021 the NS government announced funding for the establishment of a Gaelic College Annexe in Mabou, Cape Breton, including a Gaelic-medium primary school.

[6] '57,602 people over the age of three were reported as being able to speak Gaelic, amounting to 1.1% of the total Scottish population (NROS 2013). The census showed marginal growth in the number of Gaelic speakers under the age of 20. Although the proportion of individuals in this group reporting oracy in Gaelic increased by just 0.1%, the actual increase in numbers of speakers under 25 amounted to 8.6% growth from the 2001 figure (NROS 2015: 9)' (Dunmore, 2019).

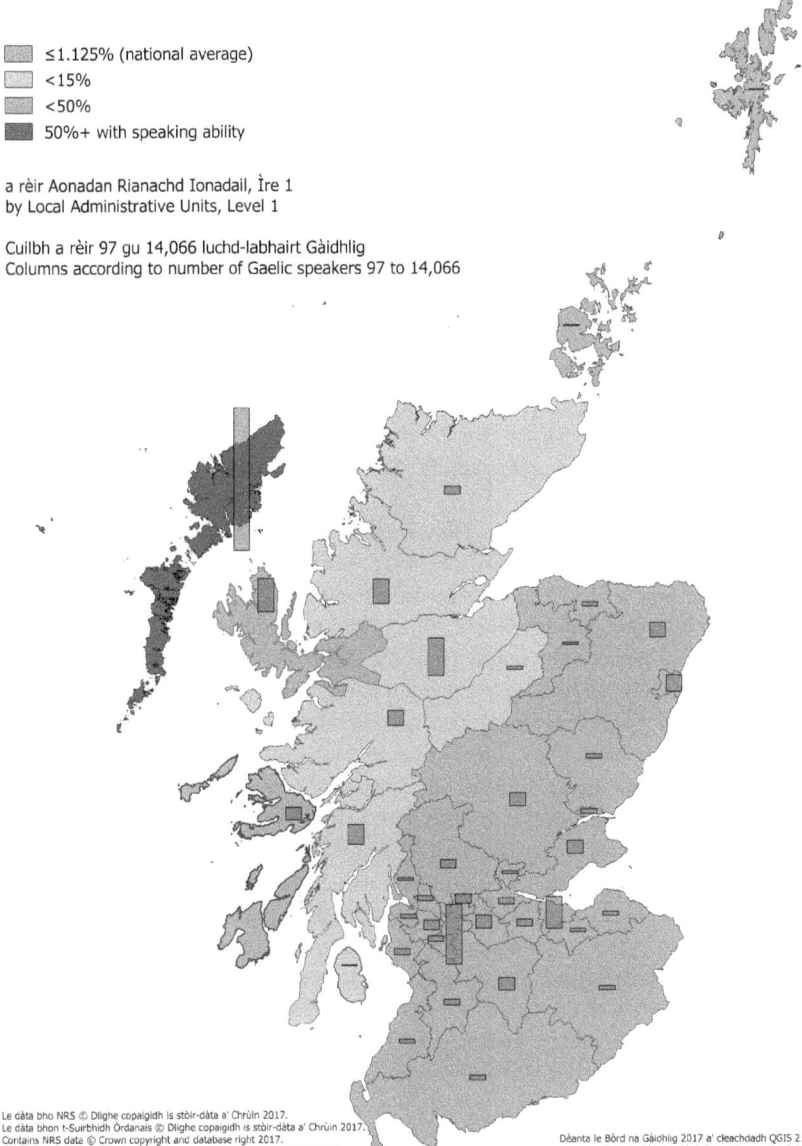

Figure 4.1 Number of Gaelic speakers in 2011 by local administrative units
(By permission of Bòrd na Gàidhlig)

(7 per cent) could read and/or write but not speak Gaelic; and 23,400 (27 per cent) were able to understand Gaelic, but not speak, read or write it (Scotland Census, Part 2, 2015). As identified in Figure 4.2 the local authority areas with the largest numbers of people with some Gaelic language ability were Highland, Eilean Siar and Glasgow City, which with 40 per cent contributed a significant number to the national total. The proportion with some Gaelic language skills was highest in Eilean Siar (61 per cent), Highland (7 per cent) and Argyll & Bute (6 per cent). Eilean Siar had the highest proportion of those that could understand, speak, read and write Gaelic at 50 per cent. Nationally, 25,000 people aged 3 and over (0.49 per cent of the population) reported using Gaelic at home in 2011.[7] Of people who were Gaelic speakers, 40 per cent reported using Gaelic at home. Of children aged 5 to 11 reported as using Gaelic at home, 61 per cent lived in households where all adults had some Gaelic language skills, 27 per cent lived in households where some adults had some Gaelic language skills and 12 per cent lived in households where no adults had any Gaelic language skills (Scotland's Census 2011: Gaelic report (part 2), 2015).[8]

The core speech area remains the Western Isles, where 61 per cent of the population in 2001 (15,723 out of 25,745) could speak Gaelic. McLeod (2020a) suggests that as the 2011 Census showed a decline to 52 per cent of the islands' population who could speak Gaelic, this would probably fall below 50 per cent in 2021. Total population numbers of the Western Isles fell by 41 per cent between 1911 and 2011 and are projected to fall a further 14 per cent by 2041.[9] The islands of Skye and Tiree also contain dense concentrations of Gaelic speakers, while the highest level of any mainland parish was recorded in Lochalsh (20.8 per cent). Other concentrations of speakers are recorded for the Highlands (5.4 per cent), in Argyll and Bute (4.0 per cent) and Inverness (4.9 per cent).

As a result of migration and language instruction through the schools, some 45 per cent of Gaelic speakers now live in the Lowlands, with significant concentrations in the larger urban areas, particularly the city of Glasgow with 5,878 such persons, who make up over 10.2 per cent of all of Scotland's Gaelic speakers, and greater Glasgow where over 11,000 speakers are located. The City of Edinburgh Council Area had 3,157 speakers at the 2011 Census, which represents 5.5 per cent of all Gaelic speakers.[10]

---

[7] McLeod advises that 'I think there is a lack of clarity concerning this metric. Many people having non-Gaelic-speaking partners may make little use of the language overall. But they may speak it regularly in other contexts. Also, how does someone living alone answer this question?' (McLeod, pers. comm., 2021).
[8] www.scotlandscensus.gov.uk/documents/analytical_reports/Report_part_2.pdf.
[9] www.thenational.scot/news/18200196.securing-gaelic-western-isles-beyond/.
[10] An overview of Gaelic speakers in Edinburgh by McLeod in 2005 is available at www.poileasaidh.celtscot.ed.ac.uk/aithisggaidhligdeURB.pdf.

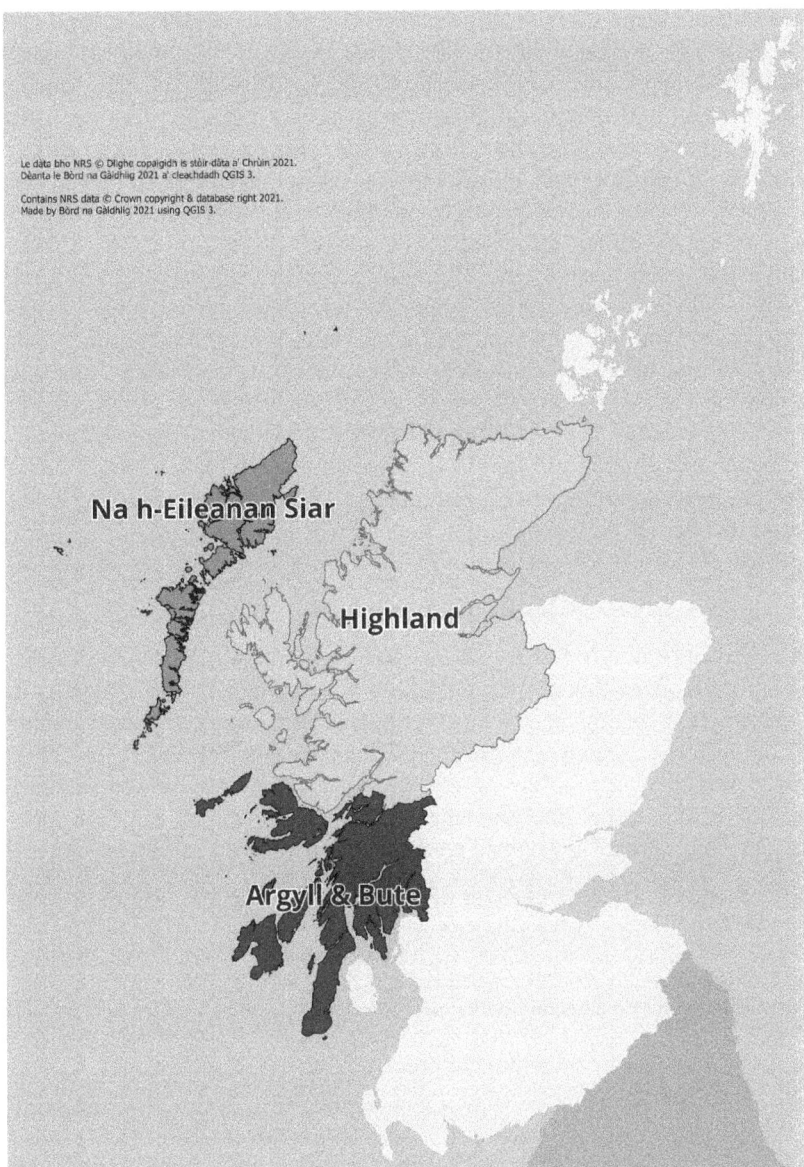

Figure 4.2 Local authority areas with indigenous Gaelic (By permission of Bòrd na Gàidhlig)

Household composition data from the 2011 Census suggest that language transmission is limited within the family, making it more essential that formal educational opportunities be made available. In 2011, at both the primary school stage (5–11 years) and the secondary school stage (12–17 years), the largest group of Gaelic speakers lived in households where no adult had any Gaelic skills (36.1 per cent at ages 5 to 11 and 39.3 per cent at ages 12 to 17). The 2011 Census records that where both male and female adults in a household had some Gaelic skills, 61.1 per cent of 5–11-year-olds in those households could speak Gaelic. Where all adults in the household had some Gaelic skills, the incidence of Gaelic-speaking ability among children was 14.6 per cent for children aged 0 to 2, 37.8 per cent for children aged 3 to 4, 48.6 per cent at ages 5 to 11 and 46.3 per cent at ages 12 to 17 (Gaelic Language Report Part 2, 2015).[11] In 2018, the census of pupils in Scotland showed 520 students in publicly funded schools had Gaelic as the main language at home, an increase of 5 per cent from 497 in 2014. During the same period, Gaelic-medium education grew from 3,583 pupils (5.3 per 1000) in 2014 to 4,343 pupils (6.3 per 1000).

The Legal and Strategic Framework

The legal and strategic framework for Gaelic promotion is relatively straightforward, although when seeking to identify direct responsibilities I found it to be a set of interlocking rather than overlapping relationships. The legal authority for current action stems from the Gaelic Language (Scotland) Act 2005, which declares Gaelic to be 'an official language of Scotland commanding equal respect with the English language'.[12] In launching the Act, Education Minister Peter Peacock, who had ministerial responsibility for Gaelic, said:

This is a momentous day for Gaelic as we open a new chapter in the language's history. We have come a long way since the dark days of 1616 when an Act of Parliament ruled that Gaelic should be 'abolishit and removit' from Scotland. Gaelic is a precious part of our history and our culture and the Gaelic Language Act will help to ensure it can also be a flourishing part of our country's future. This Act will create both the context and the

---

[11] In Eilean Siar, in 2011 the highest incidence of Gaelic speakers was for people in the 'Other Christian' (66.6 per cent) and 'Roman Catholic' (65.9 per cent) categories. The occupation category with the highest proportion of Gaelic speakers was 'weavers and knitters', at 14.2 per cent. 70.3 per cent of people who used Gaelic at home lived in Eilean Siar, Highland and Argyll & Bute. Two-fifths (40.2 per cent) of Gaelic speakers reported using Gaelic at home. This proportion decreased with the incidence of Gaelic speaking in the local community: whilst 79.7 per cent of Gaelic speakers used Gaelic at home in civil parishes where 50 per cent or more of the population spoke Gaelic, it was 22.1 per cent in civil parishes where 1 per cent or less of the population spoke Gaelic (Gaelic Language Report Part 2, 2015).

[12] For details on the impact of new speakers on selected minoritised language see Pujolar and O'Rourke (2019).

confidence for Gaelic to be passed on in families, promoted in schools and widely used in communities and workplaces. We already have growing numbers of young Gaelic speakers – thanks, largely, to the success and growing popularity of Gaelic medium education. Our challenge now is to nurture these youngsters and future generations ensuring they have continued opportunities to develop their language skills and, more importantly, to use them. That is what the Gaelic Language Act will do.[13]

This significant piece of legislation follows the UK's 2001 ratification of the European Charter for Regional or Minority Languages and designation of Gaelic under Part III thereof (Dunbar, 2003; 2006; McLeod, 2016). Under the 2005 Act, Bòrd na Gàidhlig, initially established in 2003, was placed on a statutory footing and given a range of specified powers and responsibilities, including the preparation of a National Gaelic Language Plan and guidance to education authorities with regard to Gaelic-medium education.[14] In following the Welsh model, the Bòrd may require any public body to prepare a Gaelic language plan, which reflects the operation of named organisations within designated geolinguistic areas. A key feature of the 2005 Act was that it would be Scotland-wide – despite earlier suggestions that it should only reach core 'Gaelic' areas. However, McLeod has cautioned that the omissions from the Act may be more significant than its actual provisions as follows:

- The phrase 'equal respect' as used in the preamble has no clearly recognised meaning in law and was chosen precisely to avoid any suggestion that Gaelic would have equal validity or parity of esteem with English, or that the Act might be construed as imposing a general duty to institutionalise Gaelic-English bilingualism. (In this respect the Act differs fundamentally from the Welsh Language Act 1993, which requires that Welsh and English are to be treated 'on a basis of equality').
- The National Gaelic Language Plan will not be legally enforceable, and there is a danger it will end up gathering dust on a shelf unless it is imbued with sufficient authority.
- The Act makes no requirements about the content of public bodies' language plans, and it is possible that some bodies may contemplate merely tokenistic schemes that do not involve the delivery of any Gaelic-medium services.
- Bòrd na Gàidhlig's powers to enforce compliance with Gaelic language plans are weak in comparison to those of comparable agencies or offices in other countries.
- There is nothing in the Act establishing rights to receive, or obligations to deliver, Gaelic education or to use Gaelic in the courts; indeed, the Act creates no language rights at all.
- Because it was enacted by the Scottish Parliament in Edinburgh rather than the Westminster Parliament in London, the Act covers Scottish public bodies only and does not extend to UK-wide bodies. As such, important authorities ranging from the

---

[13] Scottish Executive's website: www.scotland.gov.uk/News/Releases/2005/04/21162614.
[14] 'Technically this requirement was tightened by the Education (Scotland) Act 2016. The 2005 Act had stated that the Bòrd "may" issue such guidance. In 2016 this was changed to "must"' (McLeod, pers. comm., 2021). www.legislation.gov.uk/asp/2016/8/section/16/enacted.

Inland Revenue and the Department for Work and Pensions to the Post Office and Coast Guard will have no obligations under the Act. This makes it difficult to develop an integrated strategy for Gaelic development in the public sector and may lead to confusion and frustration for Gaelic speakers.
- The Act does not address the private sector at all; indeed, the possibility of imposing Gaelic-related obligations on private companies was never seriously contemplated. (McLeod, 2016, p. 7)

Despite these lacunae there remain a number of significant statutory requirements for advancing Gaelic policy and determining priorities. Thus, should the political will be sufficiently strong, the Scottish model has the basic tools to promote a reasonable revitalisation programme. The first of these political instruments is the government's overall strategy for Gaelic development, which, whilst not entirely comprehensive or compelling for some, does offer a political commitment and programme of action.[15] The second is the government's own Gaelic Language Plan prepared under the Gaelic Language (Scotland) Act 2005. Accordingly, a comprehensive set of domains have been identified within the Scottish Government Gaelic Language Plan 2015–2020 (Scottish Government, 2015) and programmes are currently being implemented. Thirdly there is the National Gaelic Language Plan, which in strict formal terms is developed, controlled, implemented and monitored by the Bòrd and not by the government. However, in reality the government does have a large role to play in the preparation of each National Plan. Section 2 of the Gaelic Language (Scotland) Act 2005 requires that Scottish ministers approve the plan, or require the Bòrd to change it, and therefore the government does, in effect, have ownership of the plan.

Bòrd na Gàidhlig (BnG) has statutory commitments and responsibilities to Scottish ministers in respect of Gaelic-medium education. BnG is expected to prepare and submit to the Scottish ministers guidance in relation to the provision of Gaelic education and the development of such provision. BnG's National Gaelic Education Strategy Steering Group (NGESSG) was tasked with providing strategic direction in regard to the aims of the National Gaelic Language Plan (NGLP) 2012–17 and again with the current NGLP for 2018–23.[16]

In addition to the production of the five-yearly NGLP, the Bòrd's remit requires it to oversee the creation of statutory Gaelic Language Plans (GLPs) by public bodies in which public authorities are required to set out the measures to be taken in respect of the promotion and provision of Gaelic services. While the 2005 Act allows public bodies to interpret the provisions of the Act according to their own

---

[15] This is independent of either the National Plan or the government's statutory Gaelic Language Plan.
[16] www.gaidhlig.scot/en/gaelic-language-plans/the-national-gaelic-language-plan/.

individual circumstances, but within the constraints of the statutory guidance, scholars have queried to what extent this latitude dents the effectiveness of GLPs, a tendency made more frustrating by the lack of rights and regulations to facilitate the usage of the language in public domains (McLeod, 2020b).

I undertook the first of several rounds of interviews regarding language policy and new speaker awareness with Bòrd na Gàidhlig's staff and Scottish Government civil servants in September 2015. The Bòrd argued that all its authority derived from the 2005 Gaelic Act which conferred on it a fair number of powers, but that the single most important lever was the Language Plan. GLP programmes were to be agreed with named authorities and implemented within a broader swathe of activities related to maintaining early years play groups, Gaelic-medium education, supporting community initiatives, promoting culture and the arts and advising the Scottish Government. Bòrd staff recognised that agreeing and implementing the Language Plans was a constant challenge for two reasons.[17] The first was the Bòrd's own capacity to fulfil its statutory obligations in respect of establishing the Language Plan regime. The second was the nature of representative democracy across the local authorities and for about half of all organisations with a democratic mandate/orientation who were required to prepare a plan. Within each unique discussion with named organisations, a specific dynamic had to be negotiated, framed by the guidelines and obligations of the requirements set out in the Act itself and also the statutory guidance to be followed. In practice the Bòrd had its own expectations which were not necessarily readily understood, let alone accepted, by the target organisations. Thus, a major challenge for the Bòrd was the management of expectations of all parties concerned. This was complicated by the fact that there was such a wide variation of attitudes and predispositions displayed by the organisations and as a consequence few, if any of the GLPs made explicit reference to advanced learners, let alone new speakers. Such a specific element was deemed to be a low priority when faced with the larger issue of making sure that the Language Plans themselves were fit for purpose.

The then current preoccupation was with the preparation of the NGLP and the Bòrd's input into the Education Bill as it passed through parliament. Concerns were expressed as to the budget constraints faced by the Bòrd in meeting all its responsibilities, especially in relation to supporting its many community partners in delivering all the agreed programmes.

When asked about the role of new speakers it was acknowledged that developing new speakers and influencing language choice during early parenthood were the two priorities currently being incorporated into the Bòrd's strategic thinking.[18] To that end the Bòrd had commissioned additional work

---

[17] Interview with Bòrd staff member concerned with Language Plans, 23 September 2015.
[18] Interview with Daibhidh Boag, the Bòrd's Director of Language Planning and Community, 23 September 2015.

to ascertain the patterns of language adoption and to recommend action. A real challenge is to influence parental support, not only for language transmission but also for placing their children in Gaelic-medium education. The main aim since 2015 has been to double the number of children entering primary 1 in Gaelic-medium primary schools from 400 in 2012 to around 600 in 2015 and up to 800 by 2017. This goal was not achieved: it rose from 548 in 2015 to 559 in 2018 and 653 in 2019–20. Such growth will be a significant boost to the numbers of new speakers over time, especially if the primary sector continues to grow. It was acknowledged that the Bòrd itself did not store data on the linguistic trajectory of learners and competent Gaelic speakers; rather it commissioned academic and commercial surveys on various aspects of their programmes to determine the effect of their interventions. This approach was partly because of the limited staff capacity within the Bòrd and partly because the new speaker concept per se had not been sufficiently grounded within the Bòrd's working culture to merit special attention, although its potential was clearly recognised. In fact, the lack of specialist capacity was a constant refrain voiced by most of the respondents. It influenced the degree to which the Bòrd's strategy could be diffused, it constrained the Bòrd's ability to implement ideas which derived from community initiatives, it limited its ability to maximise the potential of IT and social media developments and its ability to monitor and evaluate its own programmes and responsibilities. Additional staff would be welcomed to monitor the Language Plan's operation and to oversee its effectiveness.[19] The principal weakness of the system is that the Bòrd is too prescriptive in what is required of GLPs, which makes it difficult to assess some plans as not all public authorities have a statutory duty to carry out certain functions.

It is clear that the Bòrd believes that GLPs can contribute to the increased use of Gaelic and provided the following range of illustrations.

> Early years – we require local authorities to support and encourage early-years groups in their area.
>
> Education (schools) – local authorities are encouraged to expand Gaelic Language in the Primary School, Gaelic Medium Education, specific subjects through the medium of Gaelic, Gaelic learner education.
>
> Education (teachers) – with added provision, comes the need for extra resource
>
> Education (post school) we work with SQA, Scottish funding council, colleges, universities and encourage them to develop and expand Gaelic provisions
>
> Communities – each GLP is required to consider how they might support their local community i.e providing venues, financial support (grants) . . . .

---

[19] Interview with Bòrd staff member concerned with Language Plans, 23 September 2015.

Workplace – each GLP must include sections on language learning opportunities, awareness raising, opportunities to use the language, how staff with the language will be identified ...
Corpus – each GLP must contain a commitment to adhere to Gaelic orthographic conventions and placenames as per Ainmean-àite na h-Alba
Arts, media, heritage and tourism – each GLP is required to consider how they might support each area. (Bòrd na Gàidhlig representative, 23 September 2015)

Staff members provide advice to public organisations for policy content, examples of good practice from elsewhere, contacts with other stakeholders in the same situation, information about funding possibilities, ideas for joint projects, examples of projects underway or historical ones. Once the GLPs are in operation the Bòrd staff monitor their implementation, mainly through interrogating the annual monitoring report submitted by each public authority together with ancillary documents and statistics. The Bòrd seeks to maintain regular contact with each of the designated public authorities. However, there were no set criteria for this process in 2015 and Bòrd staff argued that a more detailed and strategic approach to this process would be an improvement, but that they simply did not have the resources to overcome that issue. Some eighteen months before the end of each plan, an independent assessment is carried out. The report usually includes recommendations – some of which are incorporated into the Bòrd's working practices if feasible. It is evident from the Bòrd's perspective that the GLPs are the primary instrument for achieving the aims of the NGLP: 'GLPs as a whole, cover every development area of the NGLP and without the statutory obligation on public authorities to develop and implement a GLP, there would not be as much, if any, Gaelic developments happening in each development area – especially education. However, not everybody agrees with / gets this' (Bòrd na Gàidhlig representative, 23 September 2015).

Education is the single most important formal domain for the transmission of the language and the creation of new speakers. The Bòrd works with others such as Comann nam Pàrant (CnP parents' organisation), which naturally does well in areas with a local Gaelic primary school. The Bòrd is involved with national level training courses and in lobbying for more funding for play leaders among the ninety or so early years groups. Significantly, many of those involved in the playgroups are themselves new speakers who improve their proficiency as their children go through the education system. Bòrd staff and inputs are heavily involved in the national committees and in the development of other initiatives such as Early Years, Core Alliance and the Stòrlann book translation service. A particular difficulty facing educational innovation is getting the best ideas into the mainstream and securing that local Language Plans, such as that which operates in the Western Isles, are integrated within the national strategy. Even convincing parents of the necessity of maintaining a linguistic transition from early years to primary school provision can be a struggle. This may be understandable in the anglicised urban areas such as Glasgow or Aberdeen, but harder to fathom in some of the Gàidhealtachd locales. A major challenge readily acknowledged by the Bòrd's educational officer is the fragmentation which characterises the system. Thus, a more integrated and robust infrastructure which could predict pupil numbers and see throughput from one level to another would be a major advance. Indeed, this sort of integrated forward planning is difficult enough when one has robust data and strong staff skills but is made more frustrating when neither obtain, which could be used as a partial explanation for any reticence shown towards taking on even more initiatives and responsibilities, both human and fiscal, as a result of embracing a new speaker initiative.

Working within existing structures causes some frustration as so much of the potential is not being realised. As McLeod et al. (2022b) argue, the most striking problem is the weakness of the plans adopted by key public bodies operating in areas of high Gaelic density, notably Comhairle nan Eilean Siar (CNES), the local authority for the Western Isles, and the Western Isles Health Board (Dunbar 2018). The council developed a bilingual policy shortly after its creation in the mid-1970s and consequently, under the statutory guidance on Gaelic Language Plans, Dunbar (2018) and McLeod et al. (2022b) believe it should be working towards developing a fully bilingual service provision and ethos. However, CNES has reported that although it had 1,300 employees with Gaelic language skills, only 167 were in posts in which Gaelic was an essential skill, mostly in education (Bòrd na Gàidhlig, 2021, p. 97). Both the lack of overt leadership on the part of the Council and the relatively weak communal pressure to use Gaelic in a wider set of domains do not bode well for its flourishing and offer a poor exemplar in comparison with Gwynedd County Council's policy and regulatory commitment.

Scottish Government staff responsible for Gaelic recognised that the new speaker phenomenon was an important element of future growth and were fully cognisant of the need to meet their requirements, albeit it within existing plans and programmes. To what extent this meant that the government was willing to act in any way differently from the main thrust of the Bòrd's activities was hard to determine. When asked what was most needed in the next five-year plan the respondents argued that a vision which appealed to normal people, rather than the professional language policy cadre, would go a long way in delivering realisable messages.

The government recognised that Gaelic needed to be infused with new energy and life so as to make it a living language in all contexts. Whether this was done through emphasising the contribution of mother tongue speakers in the Western Isles and Highlands or new speakers elsewhere in the land was not in dispute. The perilous nature of Gaelic rendered such distinctions as almost meaningless in policy terms, for 'we are all learners, whether mother tongue or new speaker'.[20] This is an important statement and explains in part why senior civil servants do not necessarily see the new speaker phenomenon as adding anything much to their understanding nor to their programme of action. However, it was well understood that the new cohort of young people not coming from Gaelic-fluent families was the new reality. As all were learners together it did not make much sense to divide people into silo categories, for the overall community of speakers was too small for such fine divisions to be used as a means of separating rather than uniting, notwithstanding the views of some that this was a misguided belief. It was conceded that new speakers represented a minority of learners and as a genuine expression of growth and accomplishment long-term policies should be developed to encourage them. Too many short-term expedient and instrumental measures had characterised Gaelic policy to date and those attempts at grafting best practice from other contexts, while fine in theory, just had not worked because too little investment had been expended in enabling them to flourish. Being realistic, with only some 1 per cent of the population speaking Gaelic, it was always going to be an uphill struggle.

Yet even now the respondents believed that changes to the instruments could achieve greater success. While the Gaelic Act created many new powers, they were not being implemented correctly. A case in point were the sixty or so Language Plans which represented a wish list of things which might be done in the service delivery system, rather than a more precise menu of the most important elements. One reform would be to simplify the instructions and regulations and reduce the over fifty pages of agreed guidance to some five critical pages of messages and instruction thereby transforming the document into a political expression of the intention to make long-lasting and meaningful changes. Allied to this there would need to be a more intensive and purposeful training of language officers as far too little knowledge of the workings of language policy and planning was in evidence within the public sector at large.

If senior civil servants believed they had a good grasp of what was needed, how was this perceived within civil society? One informed critic suggested that the sponsoring department had too much power and was too closely aligned to the Bòrd to act independently.[21] Protecting the minister seemed to be the key objective rather than challenging the direction and effectiveness of current Gaelic promotion policies. The informant reiterated a constant criticism from the civil society activists I interviewed that, despite expending some £52 million in targeted programmes, the government was not really interested in measuring the effectiveness of these programmes. In particular its neglect of

---

[20] Interview with Bòrd staff member concerned with Language Plans, 23 September 2015.
[21] Interview with Soillse representative, Inverness, 22 September 2015.

behavioural economics and outcome-based policy was a major weakness of the government's approach. Recourse to the mechanism of Gaelic Language Plans was not a sufficient defence of the Scottish model as the plans were 'worse than useless, they do not make a jot of difference' to the real use of Gaelic in society.[22] Where then should one look for meaningful initiatives, key instruments and sustainable opportunities to use Gaelic?

Economic and Regional Development Imperatives

The real driver of change, it is argued, is not the public sector but the economic development of Gaelic-speaking territories and clusters. It is here rather than in any campaign to support language rights that community efforts at lobbying should be directed. The fundamentals of economic diversification and employment generation were recognised by the Bòrd, the government and by civil society. Despite this consensus, all too often the language element was absent from regional planning proposals or capital investment projects, especially in the Highlands and Islands where energy and infrastructure initiatives could have significant effects on the language of the local school and associated community as so many workers and their families moved into the areas. On the positive side new employment opportunities in well-paid jobs could stem some of the long-term out-migration trends and introduce new sources of income, investment and infrastructural development, such as better internet connections and higher speed. Some of those from outwith the Highlands attracted to the new opportunities might also learn Gaelic.

Of course, this is a classic dilemma of regional planning: do you take work to the workers or encourage workers to move to more prosperous areas? The exploitation of the natural resources of the Highlands and Scottish waters, whether in terms of afforestation, hydro energy, the tidal generation of power or oil and gas exploration, requires an international workforce and rarely, if ever, do considerations regarding the safeguarding or use of Gaelic enter into contract negotiations.

However, with a new commitment to the reduction of carbon and a greater recognition of the salience of ecological thought and practice, some argue that there is a more ready understanding of the need to incorporate the Gaelic dimension into current energy and environmental plans for the Highlands and Islands. Holistic thought, ecological principles and government investment offer opportunities to reconfigure the nexus between land, language and environment.

Low Carbon Scotland declares that

---

[22] Interview with Soillse representative, Inverness, 22 September 2015.

the Scottish Government is updating its Climate Change Plan to reflect the increased ambition of the new targets set in the Climate Change (Emissions Reduction Targets) (Scotland) Act 2019. Actions outlined include:

- reducing greenhouse gas emissions through a Just Transition to a net-zero economy and society
- driving Scotland's adaptation to climate change
- supporting decarbonisation in the public sector
- engaging with business and industry on decarbonisation
- encouraging individuals to move towards low carbon living
- leading international action on climate change
- supporting communities to tackle climate change through the Climate Challenge Fund
- supporting developing countries to tackle climate change through the Climate Justice Fund
- preparing to participate in a UK Emission Trading Scheme (UK ETS) after leaving the EU ETS at the end of the EU Exit Transition Period. (Highlands and Islands Enterprise, 2020)

New thinking on how to make the best of the region's natural resources and peripheral location offers some degree of recalibrating the economic base in what is termed the circular economy.

Economic and regional development considerations have figured in past discussions on the fortunes of Gaelic, especially in relation to the media, arts and culture and is best represented by the work of Chalmers (2008) and Chalmers and Danson (2008; 2011). Their research suggested that it would be possible to ascribe the aggregate impacts of Gaelic arts and cultural activities on the Glasgow economy as being in the region of £3.55–4 million which supported almost 200 workers in professional and associated employment; they also found that approximately 113 full-time-equivalent posts existed in Glasgow where the ability to speak, read and write Gaelic was essential.

A study for the Highland and Islands Enterprise (HIE) revealed that Gaelic was seen as an asset by 60 per cent of businesses and 80 per cent of the community and being a key element of their activities, products or services often provided a unique asset such as enhancing the distinctiveness or uniqueness of products and services, enhancing perceptions of authenticity and provenance and increasing the appeal of products and services to target markets (Highland and Islands Enterprise, 2014). The research highlighted the interrelationship between Gaelic and economic and social developments. By using direct and indirect measures of value the authors calculated that the total of fifty-one businesses/enterprises which comprised their sample produced an estimated value for Gaelic to be around £5.6 million. Establishing a direct link between the field of economic development and linguistic renewal remains a challenge. Yet by applying similar measures and estimates beyond the core creative industries, tourism, food and drink sectors, Chalmers suggested that the 'potential value of Gaelic as an asset to the Scottish economy could safely and robustly be ascribed as being in the region of between £82 million and £149 million' (Chalmers, 2021). However, the relative dearth of informed analysis of the relationship between Gaelic and economic considerations is reflected in the fact that not a single chapter in a recent authoritative collection of insightful essays on Gaelic is devoted to the private sector or even a subset in terms of IT and AI (MacLeod and Smith-Christmas, 2018).

Recognising the salience of new speakers to language revitalisation efforts, the overwhelming majority of those interviewed within the Scottish civil service, the staff of Bòrd na Gàidhlig, academics and commentators viewed the encouragement and provision for the needs of new speakers to be a priority in policy terms. Increasingly they cite instrumental, employment reasons for developing language skills and as a consequence recognise that real value can be added to a person's life trajectory if they can but secure regular opportunities to use Gaelic in their work life.

Language Acquisition and Fluency

There is a keen awareness among decision makers and policy implementers that new speakers are critical if any future growth is to be sustained. However, informants suggested that as so little was known about the process by which people became new speakers it was difficult to base policies on concrete data and good evidence. This view was echoed by academics who suggested that there was little sociolinguistic profiling of new speakers, no mechanisms as to how they became new speakers and no independent measure of proficiency levels, such that any policy which addressed their needs would be operating in a vacuum.

One difficulty in the process of language acquisition is maintaining fluency throughout the life cycle and many people who experience the Gaelic *muda* as new speakers do so as adults, especially when they become parents. One organisation which helps parents realise their goal of becoming fluent is Comann nam Pàrant (CnP parents' organisation). It consists of a network of around thirty local groups across fourteen local authority areas, representing the interests of parents whose children are educated through Gaelic from preschool to secondary level. Each of the twenty-one parent and child early years support groups tend to be unique because of the local sociolinguistic situation. Although they have high-quality resources, the play leaders need help and, while training is available, typically the leaders are in post for a relatively short time. Bòrd na Gàidhlig offer educational grants for buildings, resources, equipment and so on, but it is argued that much more could be done to underwrite a robust infrastructure. As we saw in Wales this is a critical first step on the journey to becoming a new speaker and eventually a 'normalised' speaker of Gaelic and thus should be a priority issue for decision makers and funders.[23]

By definition, as the main aim of all CnP groups is 'to promote and support the establishment and maintenance of education through the medium of Gaelic', they have been the driving force in the development of Gaelic-medium education (GME) which first began in 1985. Today most of the children in GME come from homes where neither parent speaks Gaelic.[24] Thus it is fair to say that such students may be considered as new speakers as can a proportion of their parents.[25] Interestingly in some contexts, such as Edinburgh, a large proportion of the parents are in fact multilingual. Given the small size of Gaelic communities these speakers are an essential adjunct to the 'indigenous speakers' numbers. Yet specialists recognise that both simultaneous and sequential bilingualism remains a challenge for the younger cohorts, whilst a shortage of Gaelic caregivers also presents difficulties for the vitality of all-age communities.

A logical linguistic trajectory would suggest early socialisation in a parent and child group before moving on to Gaelic-medium primary school and depending on one's location to a form of immersion education in a Gaelic-medium high school. The statutory guidelines on Gaelic education prepared under Section 9 of the Gaelic Language (Scotland) Act 2005, which allow local authorities to provide such opportunities, are comprehensive and clearly outline the responsibility of the local authority and the expectations which parents may entertain about gaining access to Gaelic-medium education.[26] The Gaelic Specific Grant is offered under the Grants for Gaelic Language Education (Scotland) Regulations 1986. Through the scheme, funding is available to all Scottish education authorities for up to 75 per cent of the cost towards delivery of Gaelic education. The scheme of Gaelic Specific Grants covers all areas of Gaelic education from preschool, primary and secondary through to adult learning. Directly or indirectly the Scottish Government invests in the twenty-three education authorities, Stòrlann, STREAP[27] and the Gaelic Learners in the Primary School programme and as a consequence there exists a ready infrastructure which could be developed in time.

---

[23] www.gaidhlig.scot/.   [24] www.parant.org.uk/.
[25] Information from Margeidh Wentworth, CnP, Edinburgh, 8 September 2017.
[26] www.gaidhlig.scot/wp-content/uploads/2017/01/Statutory-Guidance-for-Gaelic-Education.pdf.
[27] STREAP is a one-year part-time programme delivered by Aberdeen University and Sabhal Mòr Ostaig for teachers who are already fluent in Gaelic. The course is fully funded by the Scottish Government and provides an opportunity for teachers to enhance their professional practice in the teaching of a subject or stage through the medium of Gaelic. It develops participants' Gaelic language skills, competence and confidence in classroom practice and critical reflection in a Gaelic medium context (Bòrd na Gàidhlig, 2017).

However, the reality is that so few adult new speakers have experienced such a path trajectory, either because of the recency of such provision or because of their location and personal experiences. A study on adult education opportunities by McLeod, MacCaluim and Pollock (2010) presented a series of recommendations to Bòrd na Gàidhlig which included the establishment of Gaelic for Adults centres and the provision of more intensive and diverse courses. This would certainly be a significant addition to the trusted breathing spaces within which speakers could interact and, following the Welsh model of Canolfannau Cymraeg, could be used as a central node in a local network of Gaelic language support, as a one-stop shop for Gaelic. Accordingly, ease of access and simple resource management techniques could enhance the service and consolidate what is on offer.

The Education (Scotland) Act 2016 legislated a process by which all local authorities are obliged to assess parental request for Gaelic-medium education, subject to 'reasonable demand' in the area. One difficulty was the precedent set by the denial in 2017 by the East Renfrewshire authority of parental request for such education on the grounds of insufficient demand. The decision was appealed in September 2017 and was seen as a litmus test for if local authorities can strike down apparently legitimate requests without sanction or recourse to the courts every time. It would seem that the influence and power of the Bòrd to intervene is severely limited.[28]

During interviews in October 2016, senior civil servants argued that many of the structures already in place facilitate the emergence of new speakers and encourage their participation within social, educational and media networks. It is evident that in both the world of Gaelic-oriented public affairs and scholarship a significant proportion of participants would describe themselves and be identified by others as new speakers and, for the most part, such individuals are heralded as doing sterling work in advancing the cause of the language in so many domains.

When asked about the relative absence of direct reference to new speakers in the National Gaelic Language Plan, 2018–2023, both senior government civil servants and staff of Bòrd na Gàidhlig were of the opinion that as the contribution was so obvious one did not need an additional descriptor to draw attention to their role and significance.[29] The existing interventions in terms of education, Language Plans, cultural subventions and broadcasting offered a sufficiently overarching framework for the use of Gaelic that to add to the responsibilities and expenditure an apparently superfluous concept, which the new speaker phenomenon represented, would be counterproductive and

---

[28] This issue was raised by Dunmore in correspondence and interview, September 2017.
[29] Interviews conducted with three Scottish Government civil servants, 4 October 2016 and with Bòrd na Gàidhlig staff, 6 October 2016.

ineffective. Some Bòrd staff also thought it would set up an institutionalised dichotomy between native speakers and new speakers, which they regarded as potentially damaging. Although their reticence was not expressed in terms of conflicting ideologies and discourses, it was evident that they considered launching an especial line of enquiry to promote new speakers specifically as something of a distraction. It was far better to consolidate and finesse the existing mechanisms as the Bòrd developed a wider capacity and stronger competence in evaluating and monitoring their activities to date, the most urgent of which was the implementation of the GLPs.

Between 17 February and 17 May 2017, a public consultation on the draft NGLP 2017–22 was undertaken as required under section 2 (3) of the Gaelic Language (Scotland) Act 2005.[30] It was requested by the Bòrd and in the light of the responses a revised draft of the NGLP was submitted to Scottish ministers for approval. As part of this consultation the Bòrd also held a series of information sessions about the NGLP in Stornoway, Inverness, Glasgow and Edinburgh. The analysis of responses was not released although several organisations, such as the Comann nam Pàrant (Dun Èideann), published their own responses in full on the web.[31]

Nevertheless, both government civil servants and Bòrd staff at interview were able to discuss some of the principal findings. The consultation questionnaire contained six questions and, of the 117 submitted responses, 78 were considered substantial. 61 per cent of the responses were in English and 39 per cent in Gaelic. 67 per cent of responses were submitted by organisations and 33 per cent by individuals. The geographic breakdown revealed that 92 per cent of responses (72 in number) were from Scotland, with others from Wales (2), USA (2), England (1) and New Zealand (1). What is interesting is that no responses were received from either Canada or Ireland, which is surprising given the long historical and current network activity supporting Gaelic culture in those two countries. Equally interesting is that not a single respondent made reference to the new speaker concept although most referred to learners of Gaelic.

The general response to the draft plan was positive, applauding its overall aims and aspirations. However, three broad criticisms were expressed. First, that there was too little substance to be able to ascertain how programmes and targets would be evaluated. Second, that as there was little reference to previous NGLPs it was hard to ascertain what was distinctive about the current draft, making it difficult to trace progress over time so that a more positive narrative on success could be crafted. Third, the draft plan conveyed the idea that each

---

[30] Please visit https://blogs.glowscotland.org.uk/ab/sali/files/2016/09/national-gaelic-language-plan2017-22-en.pdf.
[31] https://cnpduneideannblog.files.wordpress.com/2017/09/160517cnpde-national-glp.pdf.

subsection was a priority issue for the Bòrd whereas what was needed were fewer priorities thus ensuring that those that were foregrounded could be related to an increased use of Gaelic throughout the nation and the promotion of everyday use of Gaelic within traditional heartland communities. In terms of evaluation, respondents criticised the vague statements about progress, preferring a greater specification of realisable targets. This was particularly apposite in relation to intergenerational transmission and use of the language within the home and community.

At interview, the veracity of these responses was accepted. It was acknowledged that what was needed was a more robust good news story, so that a more encouraging narrative throughout the draft plan would send a strong strategic message. Greater provision of Gaelic-medium education was a must as was expansion of early years provision, HE/FE and adult learning. However, it was recognised that teacher training supply and competence together with in-service training and recruitment were severe barriers to the proposed expansion. How to navigate through these difficulties and remain positive was seen as being important, especially in relation to learning the language outside the formal education system and within the media generally. The Bòrd acknowledged that it needed to develop a more robust and engaging strategic approach.

Other concerns raised related to the overcoming of reluctant and negative assets and selling Gaelic language skills as prized resource, especially so as to grow the workforce who used Gaelic. If the Bòrd could construct a vision and situate the plan as a programme for the nation, not just for the Bòrd to fulfil its own statutory obligation, then respondents suggested that the Bòrd would occupy a more central, nodal position within a community of partners, rather than being perceived as essentially a grant distribution agency.

Responding to these criticisms Bòrd staff advised that many of the more acceptable ideas would be included within the submitted NGLP. They also indicated that they had employed a public relations specialist and had increased the language-planning expertise within Bòrd staff, not only to develop some of the themes identified within the consultative period but also to equip the Bòrd to better evaluate and monitor its interventions, thereby producing much-needed evidence to improve the implementation and operation of Bòrd programmes. It was recognised that a new period of evidence-based policy was in the offing, and that generating the data and evidence would now become a priority.

A fourth round of interviews with Bòrd na Gàidhlig staff in May 2018 indicated that the change of emphasis from the original guidance offered by the 2005 Act, which had produced a more rigorous approach to the requirements of GLPs, was also an important feature of their thinking going forward.[32]

---

[32] Interviews conducted in Inverness, 1–4 May 2018.

These changes included stronger guidance to public bodies on what was expected in the GLPs, together with a requirement that each successive iteration of a language plan should build on rather than dilute the previous plan's measures. Commenting on this change of approach, Dunbar advises that the Bòrd has lowered the threshold of service delivery requirements to take account of geolinguistic circumstances. He states:

the Bòrd has lowered the threshold for such an approach from areas with a majority of the population having Gaelic abilities to areas in which at least 20 per cent have such abilities ; as a practical matter, given that there are few communities outside the Outer Hebrides which have such percentages, these targets will not significantly increase the areas in which something approaching full bilingualism is expected, but they do ensure that areas with less than a majority of people with Gaelic abilities which could in the near future include several districts even in the Outer Hebrides, are covered by the strongest commitments. (Dunbar, 2019, p. 162).

The mainstream response of Bòrd staff to the question on what was a priority issue for them was to insist on the primacy of attending to the needs of the relatively fragile set of communities. How to maintain the vibrancy of traditional Gàidhealtachd communities with all their specific socio-economic needs was an abiding challenge, as had been repeated often within the consultative exercise. Demographic changes and migration patterns of the young, fecund and well-educated were challenges for all departments of government, but for the Bòrd especially the Gàidhealtachd communities represented more than a symbolic heartland. They were likened to a reservoir of culture, of language standards and innovation, of modes of interpreting the world from which the rest of the Gaelic-speaking community could draw inspiration, reference points and, most importantly of all, authenticity.

It was conceded that there remained many gaps in the support and provision for Gaelic adult learning but that improvements in the opportunities to use Gaelic in education, the economy, the media and the creative arts would reinforce that the commitment made by new speakers to skill acquisition would be valued and rewarded. It was readily accepted that the lack of opportunities to use the language and the progress made by some to integrate within communities was highly variable and dependent on well-established social networks, but that changes in social behaviour and advances in IT and communication patterns were creating opportunities which government could and should harness in partnership with civil society.

The head and staff of Bòrd na Gàidhlig reiterated that, as so many of their own people and those that they were involved with were new speakers, it made little sense to add an additional category for policy development, even though they were very interested in the phenomenon. In truth they argued that the concept of new speaker was so integral to Gaelic promotion that it had already been mainstreamed and normalised. The National Plan sought to promote simple messages for all, namely that a more positive attitude shift should be constructed, that greater opportunities to learn Gaelic should be created and that those who already knew Gaelic should use it more. This was to be achieved through the implementation of Gaelic Language Plans, even though it was recognised that they were only partially effective.

The GLPs remain an essential mechanism for the provision of Gaelic services and as such they are the subject of much debate in realising Bòrd na Gàidhlig's strategic policy aims. An analysis of the operation of the GLPs by Dunbar (2019) has indicated a range of difficulties in gathering data whereby a full evaluation can be undertaken. One fundamental feature is the design of the 2005 Act, which Dunbar argues incorporates rather weak measures for monitoring and enforcing the GLP mechanism. Even those measures which allow the Bòrd to report public authorities to the Scottish ministers for failing to implement their GLPs have not been exercised, such is the fragile nature of the co-dependency of all involved as the Bòrd does not wish to distance or stigmatise any public authority to the detriment of the overall goal of Gaelic promotion.

A further common response was that the initiatives had broadened the range of opportunities both to speak Gaelic and to use such skills in employment. Admittedly we are speaking about limited growth, but even so an increase in the bilingual nature of public services, including an implicit active offer of service and a more visible linguistic landscape within the public sector, all fed into the perception that Gaelic was an increasingly useful resource. The underpinning of such growth in awareness by the statutory guidelines of GLPs was heralded as an important step forward, However, many of the informants immediately qualified such statements by reference to the public's low levels of confidence in using Gaelic for official affairs. Commenting on this feature Birnie has put it thus: 'Individual speaker confidence and established linguistic norms would appear to be the main drivers for language use, rather than management initiatives which appear to merely raise the visibility of the language in the linguistic landscape rather than drive language use as intended by the language management documents' (Birnie, 2019, pp. 136–7). As such sentiments are a common feature of minoritised communities, such as the Basque and Welsh, how much more so must confidence levels be a barrier in Scotland where the proportion of new speakers and learners in the Gaelic-speaking population is so much higher.

The most important element in the creation of new speakers was family and friends, as the community and network ties were more intimate than public service delivery systems. Where the action points of the Language Plans came into their own was in reinforcing the need for opportunities to use the language and thereby strengthen the social interaction between Gaelic speakers.

The National Plan, it was argued, referred implicitly to the contribution of new speakers in each of the following seven sectors: initiatives targeting the use of Gaelic by young people; increasing the contribution Gaelic makes to the Scottish economy across different sectors; increasing the demand and provision for Gaelic education; developing Gaelic-medium workforce recruitment, retention, training and supply; Gaelic in the family; Gaelic Language Plans developed and implemented by public bodies; and promotion of the social, economic and cultural value of Gaelic (Bòrd na Gàidhlig, 2018).[33]

The New Speaker of Gaelic Experience

Academics and commentators interviewed argued that the role of new speakers, while crucial to the revitalisation efforts, were largely under-researched and taken for granted.[34] Little in detail was known of the precise stages through which advanced learners progressed to become new speakers. Professor McLeod suggested that there was no real sense of learners' proficiency level nor any mechanism by which one could ascertain how often and under what circumstance they spoke Gaelic.[35] Further, the term 'new speaker' tended to mean different things in different contexts and the absence of a stringent definition hampered comparative research into the phenomenon. Just as native speakers should not be considered an undifferentiated group, neither can new speakers be so treated, although it is tempting to suggest that, by concentrating on one feature only, namely competence in Gaelic, this learned skill and behaviour marks them out as a distinct group.

An investigation of new speakers in Glasgow and Edinburgh by McLeod, O'Rourke and Dunmore (2014) involved semi-structured interviews with twenty-three individuals and two focus group sessions involving an additional twelve people (seven in Edinburgh, five in Glasgow). This and other investigations revealed different interpretations, for some identified new speakers as those who were comfortable using Gaelic, others those who could conduct an interview, others those that could speak for forty-five minutes or so and yet others felt it related to the age of the individual. Several in the 2014 study felt that there was an obvious difference between people who are attending classes or engaged in other programmatic learning activities and those who have ceased such activities after reaching what

---

[33] I am grateful to Daibhidh Boag, Director of Language Planning and Community, for scheduling the eleven interviews which I conducted at Bòrd na Gàidhlig, Inverness, 1–4 May 2018.
[34] While I accept this observation, it is remarkable how much research has been undertaken on Gaelic speakers and is a testimony to the drive of the COST Network leaders based in Scottish universities. The principal academics interviewed several times during the period 2015–21 were I. Caimbeul, R. Dunbar, S. Dunmore, W. McLeod and B. O'Rourke.
[35] McLeod interview, Edinburgh University, 12 September 2018.

they consider to be an acceptable level of competence. The authors argue that:

> The commonly used term 'Gaelic learner' is partly to blame for this confusion. The shortcomings of the term 'learner' have been apparent for some time, leading some to search for alternative labels. The Gaelic organisation Clì (originally Comann an Luchdionnsachaidh, now Clì Gàidhlig) attempted to popularise the term Gàidheal Ùr, literally 'New Gael', in the early years of the 21st century, but this usage did not become widespread. The term 'new speaker' is as yet not well known among Gaelic speakers, whether 'new' or 'old', and its potential usefulness is compounded by the linguistic unwieldiness of the Gaelic equivalent, *neach/luchd-labhairt ùr(a) na Gàidhlig*. This was vividly demonstrated by one of the participants in this study, who struggled to articulate the phrase *luchd-labhairt ùra na Gàidhlig* and then made a mock gagging sound following her attempt to do so. An additional difficulty with the term 'new speaker' (as with 'new Gael') is the possibility of an unfortunate semantic contradistinction with what might implicitly be understood as 'old' speakers, with the accompanying suggestion that the 'new' is somehow more interesting or attractive than the 'old'. (McLeod, O'Rourke and Dunmore, 2014, p. 4)

Conscious that the 2014 study sample was small and largely derived from a friends and contacts network, it was evident that most participants had complex learning trajectories.

By far the most important inputs were university Gaelic degrees and long-term residential courses at Sabhal Mòr Ostaig. Fifteen participants (42%) had undergraduate "degrees, 15" in Celtic/Gaelic and another four had studied Gaelic to some extent at university as an outside subject. Fourteen participants (40%) had spent at least a year at Sabhal Mòr Ostaig (SMO) and another two had spent time at SMO on work placements, an input they described as being very important for the consolidation of their Gaelic skills. Others reported a learning path that involved evening classes of different kinds and short residential courses. Two who had learned Gaelic in the 1980s and 1990s reported informal conversation groups run by native speakers as playing an important role, and three who had learned Gaelic in recent years had taken Ùlpan classes. A few interviewees highlighted the importance of their informal or semi-formal social contacts with native speakers, at university and elsewhere, and several cited extensive input from Radio nan Gaidheal as playing an important role in their language learning. Two referred to the benefits of attending Gaelic church services and the related social interactions.

If time spent at Sabhal Mòr Ostaig is excluded, it is striking how few of the participants had ever spent time living in Gaelic-speaking areas. Only six had spent more than a month in such an environment, though one had spent several years working in the Western Isles. A few others reported visiting Gaelic-speaking areas relatively frequently, either as children or adults, although the nature of these contacts varied considerably.

Considered as a whole, it is remarkable how minor an input the school education was in the formation of these 'new speakers. Most obviously, the 31% who grew up outwith Scotland were not in a position to benefit from Gaelic teaching in Scottish schools, but it is striking how minor a role school education has played even for those educated in Scotland. Gaelic was simply not available to most of the participants when they were in school; this pattern reflects the very limited educational provision for Gaelic in most parts of Scotland, especially the Central Belt. (McLeod, O'Rourke and Dunmore, 2014, p. 10)[36]

The limited regular contact with Gaelic-speaking areas and relatively weak exposure to formal Gaelic-medium education that characterise this sample are factors which should figure prominently when discussing remedial interventions to boost the greater use of Gaelic. A further issue which concerned one of the authors was the middle-class bias, not only of the 2014 study sample but also of subsequent investigations where working-class learners were few and far between.[37]

A major feature limiting the development of competence was the lack of regular opportunities to interact in Gaelic. McLeod's several investigations revealed that few speakers had Gaelic-speaking partners and so nearly all domestic matters were discussed in English within the home. Seven of the twenty-three interviewees in the 2014 study were parents of children and all but one of them reported using Gaelic with their children consistently from the time of their birth. Rather more people in Glasgow than Edinburgh reported that they were able to use Gaelic a great deal in their professional and social lives, especially those who were self-employed and using Gaelic as their main medium of work. What is revealing is their views on learners and on native speakers. The label 'learner' could be viewed in a positive way as an expression of a lifelong trajectory seeking to master Gaelic even if, as was said, 'it doesn't matter how fluent you are, you're a learner'.

Some expressed a degree of impatience with the semantics of classifications or labels, perceiving it to be a distraction from normal communication. For others the obvious fact that they were learners evoked a patronising attitude among native speakers, which was not helpful but real nevertheless, and this stigma is a commonly reported feature in all the jurisdictions I studied. More generally there is a complaint that there are few opportunities for conversational practice in real-life situations. Those that exist offer a safe environment even if at times there is a tendency by some native speakers not to recognise the

---

[36] The authors contrast this with Ireland, 'where almost all new speakers of Irish acquired a good competence in the language as a result of mandatory Irish lessons at school, even if they then decided to improve their ability and, in some cases, make more active use of the language at a point subsequent to their leaving school' (McLeod, O'Rourke and Dunmore, 2014, p. 10).

[37] At interview, Edinburgh University, 12 September 2018. Dunmore advises that only four of the forty-six interviewees in his 2019 study could realistically be classed as new speakers, having had limited socialisation in Gaelic outwith school in childhood, but continuing to speak the language in adulthood. That 10 per cent figure was also more of less apparent in his quantitative survey (N=112) but care need to be taken due to the participant self-selection in purposive sample (Dunmore, pers. comm., 2021).

capacity of active learners who wished to participate fully within Gaelic networks. Indeed, one of the chief stumbling blocks was the reticence of some native speakers to fully engage with new speakers, a feature analysed previously by Armstrong (2013).[38] This is a widespread phenomenon reported in so many of the jurisdictions studied in this enquiry that it deserves special attention in future work.

The majority of participants in the 2014 study reported that native Gaelic speakers were willing to speak Gaelic with them. Some clearly had faced refusals to engage, and others were reticent to speak with native speakers even if everything that was being said was perfectly understood.[39] Several in the sample wanted to identify with native speakers, to imitate their accents, their register and, of course, their ease of conversation. They admired the naturalness and richness of native speakers. But others noted that they felt they had a different vocabulary and set of skills better suited to their own working environment in Glasgow or Edinburgh, and that, far from feeling any deficiency vis-à-vis native speakers, they felt a degree of empowerment. This is important to emphasise, for in Ireland, Wales and the BAC it is often the new speakers who have the better written and IT skills and can thus claim superior proficiency in the workplace. Together with changes which various transitional stages occasioned in identity construction, including a range of additional frustrations, ideological positions and linguistic practices of new speakers, it should be understood that for so many new speakers the new skills they have gained are a source of great pride, satisfaction and instrumental gain.

Typically, the academics recognised that both they and the participants in various samples made judgements on the slow rate of learner progression, the limitations of formal programmes for learning Gaelic and the relative lack of Gaelic usage even by those who had attended Gaelic-medium education. Dunmore (2014) suggests that few former GME pupils who did not come from Gaelic-speaking homes are now using their Gaelic frequently. One of the participants who had gone through Gaelic-medium education observed that she was the only person in her former primary school class who was now using Gaelic actively. The issue of education is a complex phenomenon for new speakers, as many in the 2014 sample felt that too much emphasis was placed on Gaelic-medium education in the schools, and that the approach of Bòrd na Gàidhlig and other policymakers was a matter of putting 'all the eggs in one basket', particularly in light of their observations about the quality of the Gaelic produced by children in Gaelic-medium education (see Dunmore, 2014). Several participants expressed the view that the learning of Gaelic by adults

---

[38] McLeod interview, Edinburgh University, 12 September 2018.
[39] Elements of discrimination and a lack of self-confidence are reported in all the cases I analysed, as they are common features for new speakers, especially in the earlier stages of their development as competent interlocutors.

did not receive sufficient attention from policymakers. One interviewee expressed the view that too much attention (and funding) was given to one-off projects, rather than ongoing initiatives that could have a greater long-term impact, while others argued that Bòrd na Gàidhlig allocated too much money to ineffective initiatives and did not put in place proper mechanisms to assess the effectiveness of particular strategies or policies.

When asked about the role of government intervention, a common response by the academics was that so many of the adult new speakers were individual isolates – for their partners and children rarely spoke Gaelic – so that indeed it was hard to plan for behavioural change given the low demographic weighting of Gaelic speakers within the nation. One way of overcoming this isolation, especially in metropolitan cores, would be to establish Gaelic language social centres which could also provide adult learning opportunities. In time the meagre provision of foundation courses available could be supplemented by a range of more advanced and tailor-made courses for different employment and leadership training purposes. But it was acknowledged that with low numbers in most urban areas the best option might be to initiate one or two such centres as a trial in the first instance. In some cases, McLeod felt that the situation had worsened over time, for he recognised that two decades ago learners could study up to twenty hours a week in fourteen further education colleges, whilst today the low level of provision has not kept pace with the needs of the sector. Some hope was provided by the Glasgow initiative providing better pathways for Gaelic within the Common European Framework of Reference. His recommendation was that the Scottish Government and selected local authorities should establish additional and special funding for adult and further education provision, and that this funding should be ringfenced and guaranteed for a significant period so that some momentum could be built up. It was noted that such funding was already made available for the acquisition of English within further education colleges by refugees and asylum seekers, and this precedent should be extended to the Gaelic learning context.

Another issue raised during my interviews was the lack of real integration of Gaelic educational and language policy issues within public policy considerations and debates. It was almost as if Gaelic affairs were treated as an addendum element rather than as integral to the government's policy community and this limited the majoritarian support for Gaelic learning and language transmission. Indeed, a regular refrain from commentators is to point to the superficial level of support which Gaelic receives as regards signposts and the linguistic landscape without there being much substance behind these initiatives.[40]

---

[40] Ian Jack, 'Saving a language is one thing, but I'm saddened by Scotland going Gaelic'. *Guardian*, 11 December 2010. www.theguardian.com/commentisfree/2010/dec/11/ian-jack-saddened-by-scotland-going-gaelic.

Criticisms were also made of the adequacy and quality of formal language plans and their inconsistent application. A clearer statement on Gaelic language rights would assist as would more detailed long-term planning documents and resource commitments by government. It was observed that few if any official enquiries had been made into the phenomenon of new speakers by government authorities. There was no generally understood mechanism as to how it was operating in a vacuum. Given that the figures were understandably low, it would not be a difficult operation to track and trace the interaction of new speakers in Scotland's towns and cities. But it was acknowledged that the term 'new speaker' did pose difficulties and it was emphasised that studies had variously defined a new speaker as one who could hold a conversation for around forty-five minutes, who could conduct an interview in Gaelic or who exuded confidence when engaged in a conversation.[41]

What was generally understood was that new speakers tended to be highly dependent on social media and digital social networks, rather than immediate face-to-face contacts, as so few such opportunities existed within twenty miles of Edinburgh and Glasgow. It was observed that much more was going on in the larger urban areas than in smaller peri-rural communities, which would stand in marked contrast to Wales, for example, where a whole range of locations would be involved. The lack of genuine, meaningful opportunities to interact and improve one's command of Gaelic was a severe impediment. When asked about the prevalence of new speakers within the traditional Gaelic-speaking areas, McLeod observed that it was not a recognised feature apart from the clusters which had grown up alongside Sleat as a result of the establishment of Sabhal Mòr Ostaig.

Given that a lack of opportunity to use one's Gaelic was a constant refrain, the academics were asked what improvements they would like to see. An obvious one for McLeod was the development of the adult learning agenda so that more challenging courses were provided. In 2010 the Bòrd had commissioned an investigation into adult learning, but most of the recommendations were not implemented (McLeod et al., 2010). Rather, the Bòrd invested in the Ùlpan courses devised by Deiseal Ltd which offered a structured learning pathway. After a few years it became evident that the provision was inadequate and the Bòrd withdrew funding following a review which highlighted problems in relation to course management and delivery, course impact, design and quality (MacLeod, Jones and Milligan-Dombrowski, 2015). The lead author of that report has subsequently commented that the safe learning environment of the Ùlpan classroom, with its emphasis on repetition of phrases and memorisation, contrasts with the everyday reality of using Gaelic in normal situations. Accordingly, it is advised that the successful completion of an Ùlpan course is

---

[41] McLeod interview, 12 September 2018.

no reliable predictor of proficiency or of the candidate becoming an active new speaker of Gaelic. For this to happen more intensive follow-on courses and exposure to Gaelic in adulthood is required (MacLeod, 2018).

University and summer school courses would also be very welcome so as to supplement any future Gaelic Language Centres that may be established. These developments would provide a skeletal framework for encouraging and improving Gaelic language skills, whereas what is on offer at present is a patchwork of fragmented opportunities with little to no logical progression in the linguistic trajectory of the competent learner.

The theme of lack of opportunities was endorsed by Professor Dunbar who argued that the tremendous improvements in Gaelic-medium education within Glasgow and Edinburgh had led many speakers to develop a real command of the language only for that enthusiasm to be muted by a lack of social networks in the post-school environment.[42] A prior difficulty was that many pupils who had attended Gaelic-medium primary schools did not choose to study Gaelic in those limited number of high schools where it was on offer. This lack of language transmission within the school system remained a challenge, especially for those pupils who perceived Gaelic as a subject only rather than a medium of social and economic interaction.

Given the steady decline of the Gàidhealtachd communities it was inevitable that the only real collective opportunity for Gaelic-speaking in such urban centres as Edinburgh, Glasgow, Inverness, Fort William and Oban was through the social networks where frequency, social density and quality of expression were important considerations even if they remained a challenge. One sign of vitality was the investment in the facilities of BBC Alba in Glasgow which demonstrated how workplace interaction could stimulate productivity and satisfaction within an important section of the national media. The difficulty was that there were few other illustrations of concentrated Gaelic-speaking clusters which could be cited. This was compounded in Dunbar's opinion by the decline of several pillars which historically had supported a Gaelic social network, such as churches, local and national cultural and sporting organisations and associations reflecting common ancestry, bonding and place-specific origins. Some were still viable, such as those which represented Skye or the Glasgow Lewis and Harris Association founded in 1887 which hold monthly meetings, dances and annual dinners and provide opportunities to socialise.

Asked whether the situation of Gaelic would have been different today had the new speaker and revivalist phenomenon been around in the 1960s and 1970s, Dunbar observed that it was all a matter of attitudes.[43] The world of

---

[42] Dunbar interview, 12 September 2018.
[43] I asked this question about Scotland based on the language campaigns in Wales which from c.1962–3 gathered momentum and led to a series of significant reforms. Dunbar interview, 12 September 2018.

urban Gaeldom in the sixties was still being fed by inward migration from the Highlands and Islands as a result of the modernisation of the Scottish economy and in consequence appeared to be flourishing. Traditional societies were thriving in Glasgow, Edinburgh and other urban locales, but the children of these migrants tended not to be taught the language at home and the absence of Gaelic-medium education compounded the problem. Thus, many opportunities were lost and even today it was claimed there are thousands of Gaels living in, for example, the Glasgow region who do not form part of any vibrant Gaelic-speaking community or network and they should not be excluded. True, some of them have placed their children or have seen their grandchildren being sent to Gaelic-medium schools, but the failure of intergenerational language transmission and the growth of rather negative attitudes towards the survival of Gaelic remain a real worry.

National language policies designed to mitigate the effects of decline must perforce reflect local geolinguistic situations as the fragmented nature of the speech community demands localised responses within an overall framework. Regional planning, rural development and infrastructure investment have created nodes where some consolidation of services and provision has been evident, as at Inverness and Sleat. This in turn creates employment opportunities for families and demand for Gaelic-medium education and offers a more vibrant socio-economic life within revivified or new networks.

Although in comparative international terms these variations seem miniscule, in Gaelic language policy terms they are significant and suggest some grounds for optimism that co-ordinated intervention can make a difference in mitigating an apparently inexorable decline.

The substantial growth of enrolments in Gaelic-medium primary and to a lesser extent secondary schools where some Gaelic-medium teaching is present has contributed greatly to the potential of new speakers becoming a major element of language revitalisation.

Whilst these numbers are encouraging, a concern among several of those interviewed was the quality of spoken Gaelic as a result of this increase in learners and new speakers.[44] Some argued that even the 'native' speakers were so influenced by the hegemony of English that the residual difference between native and new speakers was now diminishing among the younger age groups.

One feature of the Scottish context which stands in sharp contrast to Wales, the BAC and Catalonia is the lack of sustained grass-roots activism. True, there

---

[44] McLeod (2018) makes the point that in the past the new speaker concept has been examined using other terms such as 'non-native speaker', 'second-language speaker' and 'L2 speaker'. The employment of the term 'new speaker' is an attempt to move away from ideologically 'unhelpful' labels including 'native speaker' and 'nativeness'.

have been striking examples of individuals setting forth visions, plans and programmes for language revival and there have been successful arts, culture, folk and singer songwriters who have protested the neglect of Gaelic. In the main, however, Gaelic speakers have been quiescent and have not been overly militant in pressing their claims to insist on the right to use their language, even within the traditional heartlands. Had the Western Isles or Highlands Council continued its robust language policy similar to Gwynedd County Council from the 1970s onwards the situation would have been improved dramatically as far as the relevance and vitality of Gaelic was concerned. However, this initiative by Comhairle nan Eilean stagnated from the early 1980s onwards. Had it not, by the beginning of the twenty-first century, Gaelic might have been the default language of council business, a far greater number of employment opportunities would have been created and the council, in their interaction with other councils and central government, could have boosted the official use of Gaelic to a considerable extent.

Professor Dunbar observed that promoting Gaelic was not part of the mainstream political agenda. The SNP government did not see it as a priority as it was not a vote winner and had never figured strongly as part of any independence campaign. Even at the local level the issue of Gaelic signposts or any modicum of support for the language was often met with resistance. Negative attitudes were reinforced by the news media who ran far too many disparaging stories about the waste of public monies in support of Gaelic. One of the few ways to counteract the free licence to criticise Gaelic promotion was to make it more relevant for many people's lives, but this might involve the adoption of very strong policies by selected local authorities. However, even apparently comprehensive language plans, such as that adopted by NHS Eileanan Siar, are fraught with difficulty. The failure to implement agreed commitments in relation to face-to-face interaction, the training of medical professionals to communicate effectively in Gaelic, the virtual absence of the language on its websites and several other deficiencies makes it difficult for users to know what level of service to expect from the authority (Dunbar, 2018).

The conundrum is to know what to do about this state of affairs. The current consensus by all political parties who are mildly supportive of the promotion of Gaelic is that communities would fragment and numbers drop considerably if more compulsion were involved within selected local authority areas. And yet stronger language plans, implemented in a consistent manner with a full infrastructural back up, are the most likely means by which the additional opportunities so often called for could be established. This would not only give more resonance to the demands for Gaelic language use but would also improve the skill levels of local government officers and others charged with the delivery of language sensitive public services.

The Us and Them in Gaelic Perception

For non-Gaelic speaking Scots, the idea that a foreigner could learn Gaelic was often seen as remarkable. (McLeod and O'Rourke, 2017, p. 56)

For minority language speakers of Basque, Frisian, Irish and Welsh this is a familiar refrain, the more so if one introduces variables such as religion, skin colour and continent of origin, such as Asia or Africa, into the equation. Whilst the situation has changed over the past generation, the issue of to whom does the language belong and who belongs to the language was seen as unproblematic in times past. Birth and territory conferred fellowship, a membership not necessarily guaranteed by ancestry. A communal version of the distinction between *jus sanguinis* and *jus soli* played out in the minds of many who were suspicious of strangers, a common enough feature of predominantly rural societies in Europe but one which is increasingly obsolete as a consequence of urbanisation, industrialisation and globalisation.

So, what of foreigners who have learned Gaelic – what is their experience and how may they contribute to the impress of new speakers on language revitalisation? Work by McLeod and O'Rourke (2017) has identified a number of structural characteristics of a subset of Gaelic new speakers who were born outside the UK. The key findings were that unlike Scottish-born speakers none of the subset had any familial or emotive nationalist ties to the land, language and culture. None of the interviewees had learned Gaelic out of a desire to integrate into the local community, which according to the authors demonstrates the limited role of Gaelic even in the strongest Gaelic areas. This is a significant finding and one which should inform policymakers seeking to motivate more people to learn the language. It points to the relative difficulty of establishing just what is the community in question for, unlike the Welsh and Basque situation, there is not the density of speakers within which one could readily interact. Once again demography and numbers influence motivation and competence. Having learned Gaelic in a formal classroom situation, speakers complained that there were few opportunities available to develop their language and sociolinguistic skills, even if they had very positive interactions with Gaelic-speaking contacts. The possibility of sharing their language with a mentor was much appreciated, especially as less than half the interviewees had a partner who also spoke Gaelic fluently which was often compounded by the reticence of children to speak with them. A further difficulty was the absence of a wider family network who could use Gaelic.

Those from EU countries who had learned Gaelic found that the lack of learning resources in Gaelic compared with other languages they had learned was a real handicap. Those who had migrated from Ireland reported little or no difficulty in acquiring the basic structure of Gaelic and found much of the vocabulary familiar, although they did express difficulty in adjusting to the different phonology.

When I interviewed McLeod and O'Rourke individually, both authors emphasised the critical nature of understanding this subset, especially in relation to their decision to send their children to Gaelic-medium education where available or to work in a predominantly Gaelic environment.[45] The insights gained into their motivations and language transmission practices were invaluable and both authors advocated that more intensive ethnographic work should be undertaken on this small but significant subset of new speakers. However, it is quite difficult to suggest specific recommendations which focus exclusively on the contribution of this group but may yet bear fruit, as both the paradigm and the practice develop and embed themselves within the policy community.

A related issue is the degree to which adult learners who have attended Ùlpan courses have a successful learner pathway and continue on to become new speakers fully integrated within the socio-economic networks. MacLeod (2018) has sobering news about the effectiveness of such courses in producing fluent speakers. In part this is because of the limited nature of the largely foundational courses on offer and in part it reflects the tendency of learners to engage with other learners rather than native speakers outwith the safe environment of the classroom.[46] Greater investment in more advanced courses and more emphasis on the written skills required to connect with a virtual network of learners and users would help consolidate the foundations gained in the Ùlpan programme.

Thus, it would seem that for many new speakers from outwith the UK it is the actual process of learning the language which embodies their meaning-seeking experience. We should recognise that it is quite a different thing to use the language independently in non-educational domains; even more daunting is the recognition for them that they may be seen as saviours of the language, for so many reported that they felt constrained by what they could now do in relation to Gaelic (McLeod and O'Rourke, 2017, p. 55).

Fascinating research comparing and contrasting the experience of new speakers in Scotland and Nova Scotia by Stuart Dunmore reveals some of the intricacies involved in ascribing labels to learners who may not themselves fully accept such descriptors. His ethnographic research concluded that the new speaker concept, and all that it implied, had a far more positive acceptance in Nova Scotia:

The relative ease with which Nova Scotian new speakers of Gaelic appear to construct and negotiate their ethnolinguistic identities as Gaels thus stands in stark distinction to Scottish speakers' apparent disillusionment with the term. Whilst the evidence from

---

[45] McLeod interview, 12 September 2018; O'Rourke interview, 13 September 2018.
[46] In her study only 285 of the L2 learners sought to become fluent (MacLeod, 2018, p. 110).

Scotland I have discussed here tends to corroborate the view that essentialist conceptions envisaging a straightforward relationship between language and ethnolinguistic identity fail to adequately describe experiences of new speakers of minority languages, the evidence from Nova Scotia clearly challenges this hypothesis. (Dunmore, 2021c, p. 16)

At interview the author identified code-switching as a key feature of new speakers in both Scotland and Nova Scotia.[47] Interestingly for many in the Nova Scotia sample, Gaelic was their third language for they had been educated initially within French immersion schools. Elements of the school system in Nova Scotia do contribute to a sense of a Gaelic identity, but rarely is this manifested in the learning of the language. That is done as a result of individual volition and motivation and some of this is an attempt to capture a heritage which is currently being reproduced in largely non-linguistic ways, mainly through music, céilidh, storytelling, sport and pageantry.

The provincial Office of Gaelic Affairs (2018) has estimated that at least 230,000 people can claim descent from families who spoke Gaelic in times past. Even as late as 1880 Shaw (1977) has estimated that there were over 80,000 Gaelic speakers in the province. Dunmore believes that the few civil servants within the Office have a real sense of the need to promote the Gaelic heritage, but that is mainly conditioned by the tourism industry's requirements. There are plans to provide more courses in a few of the province's educational establishments such as Colaisde na Gàidhlig / The Gaelic College in St. Ann's[48] and at St Francis Xavier University among others. A recent Gaelic resource pack tracks the initiatives which the Office has funded.

Whilst the concept of new speakers does not figure greatly in official government documentation, nevertheless it is clear that the increased range of opportunities to engage in Gaelic-related affairs is a testimony to the government's increased awareness of Nova Scotia's distinct contribution to the Canadian multiculturalism vision. I append below an edited version of government action over the past twenty years. The range is very encouraging and suggests what a small, determined staff with a clear mandate and focus can achieve by harnessing community and government initiatives in a process of co-creation.

2001 Gaelic Cultural Studies 11 is offered to all students online.
2002 A report, Gaelic Nova Scotia: An Economic, Cultural and Social Impact Study, is published by the Nova Scotia Museum. Nova Scotia signs a Memorandum of Understanding with the Highland Council in Scotland. It highlights the Gaelic language, culture and kinship shared between the two regions. Cape Breton University begins an exchange programme with Sabhal Mòr Ostaig (SMO).

---

[47] Interview, Edinburgh University, 12 September 2018.　[48] https://gaeliccollege.edu/.

2003 The Department of Education offers Gaelic Studies 11 as one of the options for the mandatory Canadian history credit. A Gaelic cultural officer position is established in Nova Scotia along with funding to assist community-based language and cultural learning opportunities.

2004 The Gaelic Council of Nova Scotia presents the report Developing and Preserving Gaelic in Nova Scotia: Strategy for a Community-Based Initiative to the Minister of Tourism, Culture and Heritage. The Department of Education supports the development of the Gaelic Teachers' Resource Book and a new curriculum designed for grades 10, 11 and 12. Total Immersion Plus (TIP), a new way of teaching language to adults, is introduced from Scotland and shows early signs of success. The Department of Education supports the first week-long Summer Institute on Gaelic in Mabou, Inverness County.

2005 The Department of Education supports the development of an elementary to grade 9 Gaelic curriculum.

2006 The first Ministry of Gaelic Initiatives is established. The province establishes a boundary sign policy that includes Gaelic, Mi'kmaq and French along with English for the eastern districts of the province. Sruth nan Gàidheal Gael Stream, an interactive website, goes live. The website is an archive of songs, stories, anecdotes, prayers, customs and rhymes by native Nova Scotia Gaelic speakers. The first Oifis Iomairtean na Gàidhlig/The Office of Gaelic Affairs is established with locations in Halifax, Antigonish and Mabou. Sgoil Ghàidhlig an Àrd-Bhaile/The Gaelic Language Society of Halifax is established to offer Gaelic language and cultural programming in the Halifax area.

2007 The Department of Education establishes a Gaelic-language programme grant initiative for public schools. This results in an increase in the number of schools offering Gaelic-language instruction and Gaelic Studies 11.

2008 Comhairle na Gàidhlig and Oifis Iomairtean na Gàidhlig work together to develop a symbol to represent the Gaelic community of Nova Scotia. The symbol is officially recognised by the province. The first Gaelic academic conference is held outside of Scotland at St Francis Xavier University. Cainnt Mo Mhàthar/My Mother's Speech goes live on the Internet.

2009 The community-based mentorship programme that matches Gaelic learners with native Gaelic-speaking elders, Bun is Bàrr/Root and Branch, is created.

2012 The Scottish Government and Bòrd na Gàidhlig establish a Gaelic Language Bursary to support Nova Scotians learning Gaelic. The bursary also helps to promote greater awareness and understanding of Gaelic cultural expression. The Gaelic language and cultural expression

online resource An Drochaid Eadarainn/The Bridge Between Us is launched. It provides examples of Gaelic dialect and folklore from the Gaelic districts in Nova Scotia.
2013 Colaisde na Gàidhlig/The Gaelic College, initiates the youth mentorship program, Na Gaisgich Òga/The Young Heroes.
2015 The Department of Education and Early Childhood Development launches its Education Action Plan, which talks about including the languages, histories and cultures of Acadians, African Nova Scotians, Gaels and Mi'kmaq, in the grade primary to 12 curriculum.
2017 Nova Scotia's Culture Action Plan: Creativity and Community recognises Gaelic culture's role in shaping Nova Scotia's unique voice and character. This includes teaching the language, history and culture of Gaels in grades primary to 12 and strengthening the office of Gaelic Affairs. Mìos na Gàidhlig/Gaelic Awareness Month, is rebranded Mìos nan Gàidheal/Gaelic Nova Scotia Month. A Gaelic licence plate initiative featuring the symbol of the Gaels in Nova Scotia is launched. Sgioba nan Taoitearan/The GaB Instructors Team is established.
2018 Supporting Gaelic language and cultural initiatives, a Gaelic licence plate is made available for purchase at Access Nova Scotia. A mini-documentary on the Gaelic Affairs' mentorship programme Bun is Bàrr/Root and Branch is launched. Daltachas, an intermediate language mentorship programme, is developed and launched.
2019 A mini-documentary titled *Dòchas/Hope (Gaelic Youth in Nova Scotia)* is launched. Gaelic Nova Scotia: A Resource Guide is developed to raise awareness and help educators to teach Gaelic language, culture and history in Nova Scotia (Government of Nova Scotia, 2019).

Dunmore would argue that new speakers in Nova Scotia regard themselves as a central part of the local Gaelic community to a far greater degree than the Scottish-based interviewees, partly as a consequence of policymakers' and teachers' explicit objectives to inculcate that feeling in Nova Scotia, but perhaps also because the (native) community there is now so vanishingly small:

There's a sense of ethnocultural, almost apostolic succession in Nova Scotia, that new speakers are simply connecting with, learning and using 'their' language because it was spoken by one or more of their grandparents. For this reason, they wouldn't regard themselves as 'new' speakers, in spite of having made significant efforts since adolescence or early adulthood to learn Gaelic as an L2. (Dunmore, pers. comm., 2020)

In Edinburgh, of the 4,000 or so Gaelic speakers, 1,000 are considered to be native speakers, some of whom are keen to mentor younger speakers. However, Dunmore asserts that there is a growing rift between heartland and central belt perceptions and developments for, as the urban Gaels appear to believe that growth and innovation are working in their favour, the heartland Gaels believe they are becoming increasingly alienated from the wider drive to revitalise the language.[49] There is a certain irony in the mismatch between these perceptions as the new speakers often declare that they wish to become more like their Highlands and Islands 'brethren', modelling themselves on their register, accents and rich idiographic speech patterns.

The idea of 'the Gaelic community' (or the 'Gaels') is seemingly something more concrete, and current, and something that new speakers tend not to connect with in the same way as they do in Nova Scotia. The majority seem not to be motivated by ethnocultural heritage, and even for those with such heritage in the language, some can be quite 'squeamish' or hesitant about voicing it as a major motivator for learning or using Gaelic. (Dunmore, pers. comm., 2021)

One tantalising avenue for further research in order to unpack the motivational consideration is to determine to what extent the Gaelic dimension has been fully squared with discourses of civic nationalism and inclusiveness. For so much of the resistance to gaining fluency in Gaelic relates to the underlying ideologies within which both Gaelic and English are embedded, according to Professor O'Rourke.[50] The 'common sense' notion that English is sufficient and that Gaelic is superfluous is so deeply engrained in the popular consciousness that one has to be exceptional even to contemplate learning Gaelic. The same might be said, in her opinion, of Spanish vis-à-vis Galician, as we shall see in Chapter 7. A second feature of many new speakers is that, having gained fluency in Gaelic, they use the language a lot less than they had imagined when starting out as learners. Accordingly, a lack of momentum can diminish their competence and enthusiasm over time. There is no substitute for regular meaningful usage of a language. What surprises O'Rourke is that Gaelic civil society, especially its younger members, is far less militant than its Galician counterpart. Nevertheless, there is an untapped potential within civil society to promote a greater awareness of and fluency in Gaelic. Some of this potential could be unlocked by transferring good practice from Galicia or Catalonia, whereas many involved in Gaelic promotion seem to be fixated by developments in Ireland or Wales rather than elsewhere, Nova Scotian initiatives notwithstanding. A more worrying issue is the social-psychological challenge of changing behaviour in order to invoke a more positive response to Gaelic. This is a broad theme throughout the EU's minority language communities, but the abolition of the EU's Directorate General of Multilingualism and the lack of attention paid to minority language promotion within the reconfigured EU Directorate General of Education are really not encouraging signs for a more co-ordinated collective approach to minority language promotion.

[49] Interview, Edinburgh University, 12 September 2018.
[50] Interview, Edinburgh, 13 September 2018.

Scottish Government Summary

When questioned periodically between 2015 and 2021 about the specific attention the Scottish Government was paying to the new speaker phenomenon in Gaelic, a senior civil servant argued that, apart from the recognised areas in the north and west, effectively all speakers of Gaelic created in and through the school system and adult education are learners and many of them become competent speakers, so it made little sense to emphasise or create a different category called 'new speakers', especially as the numbers are so low. A request by me for information of changes in policy or programme initiatives asked if there was any fresh evidence within government documentation which mentioned specifically the potential of new speakers. If not, the department was asked to confirm that the orthodox thinking still prevailed. A senior Scottish Government civil servant confirmed that it remains the Scottish Government's wish to see an increase in the numbers of those learning, speaking and using Gaelic in Scotland. There are various strategies in place for this and without doubt new speakers are welcome and essential.[51] The Scottish Government recognises the need for a wide range of support to be in place for all Gaelic language speakers and Gaelic language learners. In the view of the civil service, good progress has been made in this area and a number of initiatives and projects are in place, but it was acknowledged that these were not enough. The current thinking is that there is a wish to put a varied programme of Gaelic language support in place to address the range of needs that are being identified. However, at present the system is not operating with a kind of support that was predominantly suitable for a distinct category of new speakers. Thus, while the category is acknowledged there are no specific policy initiatives as yet in place, although it is recognised that in time such a strong and varied programme of language support should be put in place. The civil servant's view is that people from different Gaelic language backgrounds and who had different routes to acquiring Gaelic could express similar needs for language support. For this reason, and at this stage, the government is not operating with a category of new speakers and a distinct approach to support for this category.

Approaching Death's Waiting-Room?

Gaelic is not yet just one heartbeat away from extinction, but its supporters share a crisis mentality. While twenty years ago each successive blow to the community was taken as a personal hurt and the emergence of each new speaker was considered a small triumph, by today such changes have become so much more normalised that it now seems fairly unremarkable. However,

---

[51] Correspondence from Scottish Government official, 7 April 2020.

new divisions and alternative perspectives dominate the current discussion regarding the vitality of heartland communities, official policy and the emergence of ideologically distinct subgroups.

Few studies provide a prognosis for the continued emasculation of the Gaelic-speaking community within official language-planning programmes. The most comprehensive is *The Gaelic Crisis in the Vernacular Community* produced by Ó Giollagáin et al. (2020), the essence of which has been distilled in Ó Giollagáin and Caimbeul (2021) and Ó Giollagáin (2021). For this University of the Highlands and Islands (UHI) research team, the inherent contradictions in the current approach to language planning and policy endanger the very survival of Gaelic communities they are ostensibly seeking to preserve.

The inadequate response to the Gaelic communities in crisis has its origins in four interrelated issues: the emphasis on the institutional status of Gaelic rather than on cultural and socio-economic development for Gaelic communities; the limitations of the 2005 Gaelic Act, as seen in the questionable relevance of poorly verified public authority Language Plans; the atomisation of Gaelic culture, whereby capable individuals benefit from the opportunities which the institutional promotion of Gaelic has provided; and the ideological acquiescence by key Gaelic power brokers in the sectoral provision of the Gaelic status quo. (Ó Giollagáin, 2021)

While the evidence is derived from Gaelic communities, the approaches to language minorities undergoing language shift are claimed to be more general. 'The ideological discourses informing much official LP are more of a constraint on formal processes to alleviate the social pressure towards LS than a benefit to the language minority .... This form of detrimental LP evades the vernacular demise of the language group by focusing on the vague aspirations for minority civic promotion, rather than on socio-economic capacity-building measures which could enhance the societal position of the minority' (Ó Giollagáin and Caimbeul, 2021, p. 187). Few would disagree with the call for more practical assistance and resource investment for struggling communities. What some have found contentious is the assertion that most Gaelic support agencies and plans are not fit for purpose. Both the Bòrd na Gàidhlig and Gaelic Language Plans are deemed unsatisfactory. The former because the Bòrd appears not to be fully engaged with the needs of the Gaelic community, preferring to focus on project-based interventions which favour well-placed clients rather than be a voice in and of the community. State bodies who serve the socio-economic development of the Gàidhealtachd are not integrated into language-planning frameworks, and as a consequence 'socio-economic modernisation and language promotion are strategically bifurcated' (Ó Giollagáin and Caimbeul, 2021, p. 191).

Gaelic Language Plans are ineffective according to investigations by Jones et al. (2016) and Dunbar (2018). Language promotion without communal language protection is deemed strategically flawed because it does not mitigate against 'the long-term assimilation of the Gaelic group into English-language cultural dominance and ... the incongruity of GLP collapsing in on its own contradictions' (Ó Giollagáin and Caimbeul, 2021, p. 201).

Given these structural inadequacies Ó Giollagáin et al. (2020) survey five reform options, the most radical of which is to reorientate language planning and the Gaelic Language Act 2005 towards a community-development model. Current legislation would be replaced by a Gaelic Language and Community Act which in train would establish two new organisations: Urras na Gàidhlig, which would replace the Bòrd with a vernacular-regeneration remit dedicated to the needs of the Highlands and Islands, while the Gaelic Language Commission would operate as an independent national language body for Gaelic development, setting the strategic agenda for key aspects of revitalisation.[52]

This analysis together with its proposed options for future language policy arrangements have evoked a very strong response from several leading Gaelic experts (McLeod, et al., 2022a). Their argument is that both the paper and the original IGRP report (Ó Giollagáin et al., 2020) sensationalised their findings so as to provoke an urgent response from both the media and policy community. However, the net result has been to provide more ammunition for opponents of Gaelic revitalisation efforts and more crucially could damage the prospects for language transmission. 'There is a clear risk that negative framing of this kind can demoralise speakers and lead to a self-fulfilling prophecy of language abandonment and non-transmission (see e.g., McEwan-Fujita 2006)' (McLeod, et al., 2022a, p. 85). It is claimed that three fundamental weaknesses characterise the research study. The first is its lack of conceptual clarity in relation to the composition and demographics of the Gaelic community and the second is its conscious decision to limit the study to a somewhat arbitrarily chosen subset of territories with high densities of Gaelic speakers, rather than to provide a more representative interpretation of Gaelic speakers' space. The authors do not justify their assertion that a predicted drop below 45 per cent density presages imminent collapse; arguably, the current levels of Gaelic use already demonstrate advanced language shift. The third weakness is an incomplete and misleading analysis of current Gaelic development policy and the failure to make a convincing case for the proposed community development-based trust, Urras na Gàidhlig, to replace so much of the existing institutional architecture which governs Gaelic language promotion and management of policy initiatives. A major source of division is the privileging of territorial heartland communities and the contention that they have been disadvantaged by a supposed policy bias in favour of other networks

---

[52] The idea of a Language Commission was one of the proposed recommendations both of the Welsh Language Board and of the Welsh Government (Williams, 2021a).

of Gaelic speakers elsewhere in Scotland. A concomitant implication is to reduce the worth of L2 and new speakers to revitalisation efforts. McLeod et al. (2022) are firmly of the opinion that attempts to strengthen relatively weak Gaelic networks, wherever they occur, all add purchase to revitalisation efforts, which are not helped by the fabrication of divisions based on the same ideological presumptions which have characterised Ó Giollagáin et al.'s earlier interpretations of the Irish case (Ó Giollagáin et al., 2007).

Ó Giollagáin's response is to argue that his opponents refuse to engage with reality for they represent the status quo position of Gaelic language promotion rather than support the prioritisation of language policy which would help the communities in crisis. He asserts that 'it is tragic for all those genuinely concerned about Gaelic protection and promotion that so many Gaelic academics devote so much of their time and energy to undermining the messengers. ... Rather than attempting to silence those who have voiced realistic concerns about the vernacular Gaelic crisis, it would be better if we could all devote our efforts to help those communities in crisis' (Ó Giollagáin, 2022).

This debate is reflective of the various discourses which derive from the 'beleaguered self' position we identified in the introduction. Disagreement and tension are to be expected in any sustained engagement, but a community divided within itself is hardy conducive to sound policy and practical outcomes. Nevertheless, Ó Giollagáin asserts that

as we know from conflict studies, admonishing conflicting sides/factions just to get along with each other is rather pointless, especially in the absence of a clinical appraisal of the relevant power dynamics in which the dispute has arisen in the first place, and without a sound awareness of how the various groups 'own' their part of the problem. What is at stake here is the imposition of a policy designed for another context on a community whose consent has not been sought. It is a problem of remote control, emanating from a disregard of core principles of community development. (Ó Giollagáin, pers. comm., 2022)

Conclusion

It is very evident that the new speaker phenomenon will constitute a larger proportion of the Gaelic-speaking population in the future. First because it is a significant element of growth in its own right and secondly because the western and northern reservoir of natural Gaelic speakers will continue to decline. An investigation by the James Hutton Institute (2018) into the Sparsely Populated Areas (SPA) of Scotland projected that the SPA would lose more than a quarter of its population by 2046, reducing from 137,540 in 2011 to an estimated 99,350 by 2046. The worst affected sub-regions are predicted to be the Western Isles, Argyll and Bute and the Southern Uplands which are forecast to lose more than 30 per cent of their 2011 population. The Northern Isles are forecast to decline by less than 20 per cent. The basic demographic reality is that the relatively small cohorts in the childbearing age group will likely lead to a spiral of decline, unless counterbalanced by substantial net in-migration.

Factors which need to be understood in order to determine whether increased migration should be recommended as a policy option include evolving settlement patterns which favour small towns and accessible rural areas at the expense of the SPA; changes in land-use patterns and their effects on the environment and ecology; the implications of increased personal mobility, developments in IT and communication patterns which can sustain lifestyles and economic activity in, and near, the SPA; the social and cultural implications of in-migration (James Hutton Institute, 2018). A more recent factor is the trend to relocate away from larger urban areas as an initial response to the Covid pandemic.

A difficult judgement is to determine to what extent the atrophying of 'natural Gaelic speaking communities' can be compensated for by the growth of new speakers, not only numerically but also in terms of the variables discussed in Chapter 1 in relation to the richness and variety of Gaelic, the perceived authenticity of the language and its associated culture and the degree to which Gaelic can ever become more than a reasonable second language spoken increasingly within urban settings.

While government civil servants and Bòrd na Gàidhlig staff argued that within current constraints a gradualist approach would bear fruit, civil society agencies and academics argued that, far from having been mainstreamed as integral to language revitalisation efforts, much more could be done to promote and integrate advanced learners and new speakers. The research evidence to date suggests that a significant proportion of the potential mass of new speakers was being lost due to the inability of the system to cater for their needs. In consequence far more attention should be paid to the provision of advanced Ùlpan courses, to the creation of new multipurpose Gaelic-medium social centres and to the creation of naturalistic contexts for new speakers. Timing is one of the ironic features of this development, for the elements are not mutually supportive. 'The problem is that the new speaker phenomenon has become prominent at the current juncture because "traditional" communities and intergenerational transmission are weakening so dramatically, a development that is anything but healthy' (McLeod, 2018, p. 89).

It is evident that the new speaker phenomenon has some potential to inform a wide range of government and civil society policies and programmes. The civil servants interviewed were cautiously optimistic about the role of new speakers but could not point to specific paragraphs within official documentation and programmes where this potential had already been signalled as policy. But they were generally adamant that, given the role of the statutory education system in producing new speakers, the system currently allowed for this growth in competent speakers to be nurtured.

Champions of the new speaker concept within academia express frustration that political decision makers and civil servants do not appear to grasp the operational potential of the phenomenon. While I sympathise with this stance, I would contend that the more convincing studies need to find their way into the political culture and mindset of public servants and private sector/civil society thinking alike, for the fine line between these sectors is becoming increasingly blurred. Hence the call for realisable, relevant recommendations, which will be explored in Chapter 8.

Conceptual frameworks of both governance and governmentality need better to account for these imbalances in public policy implementation, and greater attention to the ideological stance of both successive governments and the civil service may go some way towards providing an explanation.[53] In the next chapter we will turn our attention to the Irish experience.

---

[53] The role of public servants in implementing official language policy is a relatively neglected area, and the replication elsewhere of studies such as those conducted by Savoie (2013; 2015), which evaluate the relationship between Canadian politicians and public servants in the formulation and discharge of policy, would surely pay dividends. For elaboration see Williams and Walsh (2019).

5   Ireland: Tempered Acceptance

Introduction

In this chapter I draw out the strengths and inconsistencies of the Irish approach to language policy, highlight some best practice examples of promotion and engagement and report on the interviews I conducted with senior public servants, heads of government agencies, civil society organisations and academics. Particular attention is paid to the effectiveness of Foras na Gaeilge and An Chomhairle um Oideachais Gaeltachta agus Gaelscolaíochta (COGG) (The Council for Gaeltacht and Irish-Medium Education).

Ireland's first official language has been a source of much discussion within both national politics and comparative language planning. Overviews of the socio-political history of Irish are provided by Ó Huallacháin (1994), Crowley (2005) and Mac Giolla Chríost (2013) while the relationship between the language and economic development is examined in Walsh (2012). Few single country profiles have been produced; the best is *New Speakers of Irish in the Global Context*, where O'Rourke and Walsh (2020) offer an in-depth analysis of the national picture demonstrating how diverse a feature the new speaker phenomenon can be. The core of the volume is a very rich ethnographic analysis of ten individuals whose transition to becoming a new speaker of Irish have been faithfully recorded. This is reinforced by conversations with 100 informants which provides a wealth of evidence, insights and perceptions. In shunning any ideal-type categorisations the authors focus on the complex, messy, idiosyncratic, fragmented and often contradictory nature of the transition to becoming a new speaker of Irish.

An appealing feature is the inclusion of verbatim Irish speech so that we experience what becoming a new speaker of Irish feels like. There is an emphasis on experiential recall alongside the more conventional material relating to linguistic variation, dialect use, grammatical patterns and the influence of English on forms of speech, idioms and the like. The informants shared a great deal in common related to their self-perception of language ability, self-correction, motivation, identification with the struggle to promote Irish and above all a variable level of self-confidence when in the company of native Irish speakers.

Several of the complicated relationships which arise when adopting a new identity for individuals and the host speech community are given special attention: that between an Irish language identity and the adoption of a standard language or dialect; that of articulating their Irish language skills from the perspective of a primary English-speaking identity; and that which emerges from the intersection of linguistic and sexual identities.

In a critical overview of the Irish state's approach to language promotion O'Rourke and Walsh (2020) reveal that, despite crucial initiatives in education, the law and public administration, the long-term outcomes for the regular use of Irish remain idiosyncratic. What is revealing is that so many of the Irish-speaking networks, north and south, consist of new speakers produced largely by the statutory education system. Accordingly, rather than being seen as a useful addendum to the 'native speaker population' which is the conventional ideological trope, new speakers are themselves set to become an increasingly significant part of the Irish-speaking population and consequently deserve far greater attention than has hitherto been the case.

The State and Irish

Williams and Walsh (2019) argue that although the new Irish state in 1922 declared that Irish was to be maintained as the community language in the Gaeltacht, the officially recognised Irish-speaking districts, first designated in 1926 and subsequently modified, and revived elsewhere as the general means of communication, no Irish government has persistently adopted a vigorous approach to achieving those aims. At first glance this would seem to be an odd state of affairs for a sovereign county seeking to project its identity and distinctiveness. Irish is constitutionally both the 'national' and the 'first official' language of the state, and nearly all children are obliged to study it for an average of fourteen years at school.[1] However, the principal legislation governing the delivery of services, the Official Languages Act 2003 (OLA), is weak by international standards, and Irish speakers have very limited rights to such services even if they are located in the Gaeltacht (Walsh, 2017).[2]

---

[1] Seán Ó Cuirreáin advises that exemptions are granted for those with learning difficulties, those born abroad or those who spent significant time abroad during their formative years. The more liberal interpretation of these exemptions is a bone of contention at present (Ó Cuirreáin, pers. comm., 2021).

[2] Irish is mentioned in over 150 other pieces of legislation, revealing a complex and uneven framework of mostly limited or symbolic protection for the language with a notable restriction of language policy in recent decades.

The current policy initiative, the 20-Year Strategy for the Irish Language 2010–2030, has been weakened by subsequent government decisions to undermine or dilute various policy supports for Irish. The review process of the original Official Languages Act (Government of Ireland, 2010) has been torturously slow – it was first announced in 2011 and there has been ten years of delay, which is a damning indictment of the Irish government policy on Irish. It was only on 22 December 2021 that the president signed the 'Bill entitled an Act to amend and extend the Official Languages Act 2003; to amend the Juries Act 1976; and to provide for related matters'.

While the overt policy of the pre-eminence of Irish persists in a constitutional sense, reflected in aspects of public discourse, the de facto state policy continues to promote the overwhelming dominance of English and Irish is treated as a minority concern of lesser practical importance to the work of government. The problematic position of Irish as simultaneously national, first official and minority language has been discussed by authors in the fields of law and sociolinguistics (e.g., Ó Conaill, 2009; Nic Shuibhne, 1999; 2000; 2002; Ó Giollagáin, 2014; Walsh, 2015).[3] This makes Irish a relatively unusual case when compared to most official state languages as represented by members of the EU.

In most interpretations special attention is given to the role of the Gaeltacht both because it is the locus of the complex relationship between space, place, identity and the renewal of Irish and because it serves as a powerful reference point in the discourse and experience of new speakers. However, the primacy accorded to Irish speakers who derive from the Gaeltacht causes difficulties for many new speakers in terms of authenticity, ownership and legitimacy. More worryingly the analysis of the role of Irish in the education system and of the adequacy of the government's 20-Year Strategy for the Irish Language cast doubts on the capacity of the system to provide a robust framework for language reproduction in the coming years.

Liam Mac Mathúna has summarised the situation thus:

the general Irish attitude to the two languages is that English is essential for all, while having Irish in addition to English is (highly) desirable, but optional. On the positive side, the more Irish someone has the better. This facilitates two interesting phenomena: the gradual spread of whatever Irish terms / words are used within English in Ireland to the UK and US, e.g., *Taoiseach*, increasingly used by politicians and the media in the UK, and by e.g., Biden in the US. and the use of *cúpla focal* by both Queen Elizabeth ('*A Uachtaráin agus a chairde*') and President Obama ('*Is féidir linn*') both in 2011. Again, once one has English, Irish is a popular L2 in the States and elsewhere, cf. the

---

[3] The OLA has been interpreted as reflecting slippage from an ideology of a national language deserving robust promotion to one of a minority language merely tolerated on the margins (Walsh, 2015).

success of duolingo courses in that language, and the fact that approx. 10% of all digital usage of Irish is North American based. (Mac Mathúna, pers. comm., 2021)

How do the majority of citizens react to the role of Irish in society? One of the national narratives is to praise Irish as bestowing a unique culture and identity on the people, while simultaneously striving to avoid direct contact with it. The country has produced more than its fair share of criticism, contempt and scorn for the revival efforts, so much so that Cronin (2019) observes that guilt and confusion are the watchwords of contemporary approaches to language affairs.[4] He argues that by adopting an ecological perspective which values Irish as an integral element of life, one may escape from such fatalistic norms.

This sensation of being unsettled, of being in an uncertain, ambiguous space (the endless soul searching about Irish identity) can, of course, lead to resentful guilt or outright rejection. An ecological ethics based on appreciating, tolerating and accepting strangeness is, in many respects, a more realistic and more useful approach to Irish language learning for the majority population in Ireland than the older nationalist trope of sudden, effortless conversion. What is more, this necessary humility faced with the unfamiliar becomes an ecological virtue as we unlearn many of the prejudices we had about the environment and come to a new understanding of it through the uncanny, long-term perspective of the language. Irish forces us to look at our surroundings anew and it is precisely the need to be jolted out of our complacency which becomes a pressing necessity in the midst of a climate crisis. (Cronin, 2019, p. 57)

The atrophying of territory is a common concern among indigenous minority speakers and the vicissitudes of the Gaeltacht will figure prominently in our discussion. Supplementary means of social communication, such as the media, have played an increasingly important role in establishing and maintaining networked communities. The relevant services are TG4, the national Irish language television station, broadcasting with English subtitles and including many hours of English-only programming; RTÉ Raidió na Gaeltachta, an Irish language radio station focussed primarily on the Gaeltacht communities but broadcast throughout the island; and Raidió na Life, an Irish language community radio station, based in Dublin. Liam Mac Mathúna likens them to Benedict Anderson's 'imagined communities' as they play an important role in maintaining social cohesion (Mac Mathúna, pers. comm., 2021).

Be that as it may, one of the features of the Irish experience is that for many the language is seen far more as a symbol of identity than as a means of daily

---

[4] I am grateful to Professor M. Cronin of Trinity College, Dublin for sharing a copy of his 2019 volume and further insights with me in March 2021. Here is a sample of his powerful argument: 'It is in the context of the culture of extractivism, sacrifice zones and the liquefaction of nature through the creation of carbon markets, that a future role for the Irish language becomes manifest. If "language" is in there with "race" and "class" as a marker of peripherality and disadvantage, then struggles around language advocacy and translation rights become part of the broader ecological struggle' (Cronin, 2019, p. 20).

communication and this is the conundrum – how to convince people that the skills they have so assiduously acquired during formal education can be used in meaningful interactions thereafter.

Education

With the exception of those in the strongest Gaeltacht communities, education has come to replace the family and the community as the principal instrument for language production and the formation of new speakers. Accordingly, education has received the lion's share of attention as to how Irish can be produced and reproduced and there are excellent analyses of its strengths and weaknesses as a central pillar of Irish language policy and promotion (O Riagáin, 1997; 2008; Harris, 2006; 2008).

There remains a complex diversity in the linguistic background, proficiency and skill set of Gaeltacht pupils. Harris et al. (2006) found that there had been a significant drop between 1985 and 2002 in the standards of oral Irish among pupils in Gaeltacht primary schools. Mac Donnacha et al. (2005) found that a quarter of all pupils in Gaeltacht schools completed their primary schooling with only a fair mastery of the language and that approximately 10 per cent of pupils left primary school with little mastery of Irish.

Government acknowledgement of these trends formed the basis of the Policy on Gaeltacht Education, 2017–22, which has been implemented on a phased basis over its five-year term (Government of Ireland, 2016). It is recognised that the challenge facing Irish in education is daunting as over the past decade over two-thirds of Gaeltacht primary schools are 1–3 teacher schools and 79 per cent of schools are 1–4 teacher schools – significantly higher than the proportion of small schools in the state nationally. The average enrolment of the 132 primary schools in the Gaeltacht is 77. Eagraíocht na Scoileanna Gaeltachta reminds us that the smallest schools are situated in the Gaeltacht areas where Irish is more widely spoken and that these schools have the highest proportion of pupils whose first language is Irish.[5]

Similarly, the size of post-primary schools in Gaeltacht areas varies ranging from very small enrolment in Gaeltacht island schools (i.e., between 4 and 26 pupils) to much larger enrolment in some Gaeltacht towns, which may be between 450 and 500. The average enrolment of the twenty-six post-primary schools in the Gaeltacht is 207. If school size is one issue, the proficiency of the pupils is another. Currently there are 105 (of 131) schools partaking in the

---

[5] Eagraíocht na Scoileanna Gaeltachta (an organisation which promotes Irish medium teaching in the Gaeltacht) is no longer in operation and their role in relation to Gaeltacht schools was taken over by Gaeloideachas and Tuismitheoirí na Gaeltachta (a Gaeltacht parents' support organisation).

scheme (to achieve status as a Gaeltacht school) and 29 post-primary (of 31) (ni Ghréacháin, 2021).

Ní Mhóráin (2016) of COGG has suggested that one fundamental policy improvement would be to define what exactly is meant by a Gaeltacht school. Given that there are two new primary school curricula for juniors, there is some flexibility within the system to cope with the range of language skills displayed among the younger people of the Gaeltacht. Echoing a recurrent theme by several educationalists, Ní Mhóráin proposed an emphasis on immersion education without the use of English for the initial two years where the foundations of the Irish language could be taught and acquired.[6] English would easily be acquired at a later stage given its hegemonic position, and this has become the norm in line with the new Gaeltacht Education Policy which sets out a definition, based on schools succeeding in implementing the set criteria.

Allied to this there is a serious need for the professional development of Irish-medium teachers in Gaeltacht schools, providing language support for native speakers, dedicated opportunities for professional development for principals, a guide to encouraging parental support and participation and ensuring that the Irish curriculum is relevant to native speakers. All of these long-standing concerns have been identified in the details of the current Gaeltacht Education Policy.[7] Linking the fate of the language to parental awareness, support and their own linguistic development would be aided by the provision of a parental support resource pack, and guidance for those among the majority who have little Irish themselves would be advantageous, both to help parents manage some of the educational demands placed on their children and to encourage some of them to become new speakers of Irish. COGG offers regular advice to the Minister of Education, mainly in respect of the development of electronic resources, research and corpus development and the articulation of policies for the statutory education sector. There is a clear set of capacity issues which remain unresolved, showing that there has been a failure to implement these parts of the 20-Year Strategy for the Irish Language, even if other elements such as the 2016 Gaeltacht Education Policy have succeeded.

While second language speakers are set to grow, it is doubtful whether first language numbers will grow respectively even if the Gaeltacht remains the

---

[6] The fundamental reasoning here is that the acquisition of Irish by native speaking children should be given precedence and that not exposing them to English in those early crucial years of language acquisition would allow them to acquire good language acquisition norms in their first language before being exposed academically to the dominant language and its subordinating ideology.

[7] Ó Curreáin comments that it is ironic that the fifty-page document on teacher supply and demand published by the department in March 2021 doesn't mention the critical and challenging issue of teachers of Irish or teachers with Irish (Ó Curreáin, pers. comm., 2021).

mainstay. Mac Mathúna reminds us that there are also Irish-speaking families outside the Gaeltacht, some of which extend over three to four generations going back to the revival period at the beginning of the twentieth century. Their intergenerational transmission of Irish (or failure to pass on the language) would form an instructive object of study in its own right, with obvious significance for the long-term viability of new speakers as a group.

Outside the designated Gaeltacht regions, the local Irish-medium school is the principal pillar supporting the maintenance of an Irish-speaking network. In 1972 there were only eleven *Gaelscoileanna* at primary level and five at secondary level. By September 2020, there were 148 *Gaelscoileanna* at primary level attended by 44,857 students, and 44 post-primary, including *aonaid Ghaeilge* (Irish language units) attended by 11,196 students.[8] However, unlike the BAC, Catalonia and Wales, the proportion of pupils attending designated bilingual or immersions schools is low. Gaelscoileanna Teo was formed in 1973 while the existence of actual *Gaelscoileanna* precedes that organisation's establishment. They now account for 8 per cent of pupils at primary level and 4 per cent of pupils at post-primary level (ni Ghréacháin, 2021a).

The majority of pupils who attend all-Irish schools outside of Gaeltacht areas speak little or no Irish at home. The expectation of the primary language curriculum is that immersion pupils will achieve proficiency in Irish 'at a level appropriate to their abilities'. The aim is to achieve near native-like ability by the end of the school period, but Ó Duibhir (2018) believes that this sets a very high standard whose maintenance is not helped by the absence of non-educational opportunities to use Irish on a regular basis. Accordingly, many Irish learners do not transmit an accurate rendition of spoken, let alone written, Irish as they progress through life, unless of course they continue their secondary education through the medium of Irish. Granting language autonomy to advanced learners enables some to persevere despite their experience of constant error correction and feedback. But one might argue that this is a feature of native speaker learning also and should not be overemphasised. Indeed, O'Rourke and Walsh (2020) urge us to remember the difference between a 'learner', someone only learning Irish in an educational setting, and a 'new speaker', someone who makes social use of it in other non-institutional settings. By that yardstick, not all pupils in *Gaelscoileanna* would be new speakers as many do not use the language socially.

Gaeloideachas (formerly Gaelscoileanna Teo) is the lead organisation in the Irish-medium immersion education and preschool sector. It provides advice, assistance and support to people who wish to have their children educated

---

[8] I am grateful for detailed information received from Bláthnaid ni Ghréacháin of Gaeloideachas (pers. comm., 31 March, 26 May and 31 May 2021). For details, please see www.gaeloideachas.ie.

through the medium of Irish, as well as support services for those working in the sector.[9] The foundations for its engagements were set out in its Strategic Plan 2008–11, building on the Action Plan 2004–2007, which focussed on establishing and sustaining schools, and developing a social community outside the school context. This latter aim is a key feature of the new speaker concern to establish safe spaces within which they can interact with others (Gaelscoileanna, 2007). Its Strategic Plan 2018–2022 details the organisation's new role, which includes the provision of support services for Irish-medium schools in Gaeltacht areas together with a suite of new policies.[10]

Ní Ghréacháin (2016) of Gaeloideachas has asked in relation to education through Irish, who exactly is the system for? This is no simple rhetorical question. Clearly the aim and function of Gaeloideachas is to advocate for and facilitate the establishment and sustainability of Irish-medium schools. There is no doubting the growth of the sector since 1973, when parental and teachers' initiative established a separate Irish-medium sector, whose public perception is one of substantial growth and contented pupils. However, the perception may need to be modified as, although there was significant increase up to about a decade or so ago, recent growth has been stagnant with only a limited number of schools having been established. The key issue is unmet demand. Ní Ghréacháin explains that:

There is a very large oversubscription problem in many schools and the system and processes as set out by the Department of Education for new Irish-medium provision at primary level has been very poor. After much advocacy for a more equitable system to cater to the needs of those who wish for their children to be educated in Irish, a new system has been introduced that has improved the school establishment process. At post-primary level, the system is a hindrance to real provision, with so-called 'units' for immersion education being established in English-medium schools in place of independent, stand-alone immersion post-primary schools. We are developing the bones of a campaign at the moment, in collaboration with others, with the aim of facilitating legislation being enacted that will actually protect and provide for Irish-medium education. (Ní Ghréacháin, pers. comm., 2021)

Early Childhood Education and Care (ECEC) services are delivered outside the formal education system by a diverse range of private, community and voluntary interests and are described variously as crèches, nurseries, preschools, *naíonraí*, playgroups and daycare services. ECEC provision is primarily implemented by the Department of Children, Equality, Disability, Integration and Youth (DCEDIY) through the Early Childhood Care and Education programme (ECCE). The ECCE programme is a universal two-year preschool programme

---

[9] In 2016 Gaelscoileanna Teo changed its name to Gaeloideachas. See www.gaelscoileanna.ie/en/about/structure/.
[10] https://gaeloideachas.ie/about-gaeloideachas/what-we-do/plean-straiteiseach-gaeloideachas/; https://gaeloideachas.ie/wp-content/uploads/2019/12/Plean-Str%C3%A1it%C3%A9iseach-Gaeloideachas.pdf.

available to all children within the eligible age range (children who have turned 2 years and 8 months of age before 31 August, who will not turn 5 years and 6 months of age on or before 30 June of the programme year). It provides children with their first formal experience of early learning prior to commencing primary school. The programme is provided for three hours per day, five days per week over thirty-eight weeks per year and the programme year runs from September to June each year (Spáinneach, pers. comm., 2021).

Each year Gaeloideachas conducts a survey of *naíonraí* (playschools) outside Gaeltacht areas to build a profile of the sector and to inform the organisation's advocacy work and provision of supports and services. For the 2019–20 school year 180 *naíonraí* catered for 5,515 children across 283 sessions. Of the 5,515 children, 129 speak a home language that is neither English nor Irish, and 163 children have Special Educational Needs (SEN). Seventy-six of these *naíonraí* have waiting lists. Ninety-nine of them are co-located with Irish-medium primary schools. They employ 500 *naíonra* teachers, 103 of whom hold Teastas Eorpach na Gaeilge (TEG) qualifications in Irish language proficiency. Gaeloideachas recommends that the lead early years teacher in a *naíonra* should have a level B2[11] TEG qualification in Irish (or equivalent) and that assistant early years teachers should have a level B1 TEG qualification (or equivalent). This refers solely to the oral component of the qualification.[12]

In relation to immersion education by way of units, the 2021 Gaeloideachas AGM has called on the Department of Education:

> to define its policy for the development and operation of existing Irish-medium *Aonaid* and the criteria for their development to independent school status.
>
> This AGM calls on the Department of Education not to establish a new *Aonad* if full immersion education to Leaving Certificate level is not provided for in both policy and practice, and where it is not, to instead provide Irish-medium post-primary education through the establishment of independent schools or satellite schools under the management of Irish-medium post-primary schools until independent school status has been achieved. *Bord Stiúrtha Gaeloideachas.* (Ní Ghréacháin, pers. comm., 2021)

The organisation's brief has been described thus:

> Our role here is more in advocating for new provision and acting as a liaison between the Department and the community. Where school establishment was once a grassroots movement, facilitated by Gaeloideachas (or Gaelscoileanna at that time), that is all led by the Department now. They designate an area for establishment, identified by increased demographics, and we work with the community and respective patron bodies in generating interest for it being an Irish-medium school. This system is somewhat complex. We don't have an official role in maintaining professional development and standards – I would say it's more a case of provision of professional development opportunities on all matters

---

[11] www.teg.ie/_fileupload/syllabi-guides/B2_SG_cand_EN.pdf.
[12] www.teg.ie/_fileupload/syllabi-guides/B1_SG_cand_EN.pdf.

relating to immersion education and facilitating best-practice. (Ní Ghréacháin, pers. comm., 2021)[13]

The organisation is funded by Foras na Gaeilge to promote Irish-medium education and its responsibilities were broadened to Irish-medium schools in the Gaeltacht and *naíonraí* outside the Gaeltacht in 2013. It enjoys official status as an Education Partner of the Department of Education and is a member of the Early Years Consultation Forum, a body established by the Child and Family Agency (Tusla – the state's child and family agency).[14]

Yet to come back to the question of ownership and purpose, it is not at all evident that the state is doing as much as it could to sustain the Irish-medium school system, as was demonstrated in the detailed analysis presented in Ó Flatharta et al. (2014).

One of the concerns for the Irish-medium sector is the wide variation in teachers' competence in the language and teaching strategies applicable to the immersion education setting, pupils' skills and the overall awareness of the developmental needs of the sector. In 2016 the following were identified as critical issues for the Gaeltacht schools' sector: the variance in the linguistic profile of staff and students; accommodating various levels of competence throughout the whole system; and the position of native speakers and school enrolment policies that prioritise the need to keep student numbers up and the need to serve the community as a whole over linguistic priorities. Commenting five years on, ní Ghréacháin suggests that:

school enrolment is not as much an issue in the Gaeltacht as it is outwith. Outside the Gaeltacht, a new Admissions to School Bill was enacted which is very problematic and as of September 2020 primary schools are prohibited from giving priority to children from *naíonraí* (or any type of preschool, bar early intervention centres). This is also true for Gaeltacht schools but seeing as they are not generally oversubscribed as are schools outside the Gaeltacht it has no real and practical impact. It is a piece of legislation that seems to contravene the vision of the 20-Year Strategy. In the Gaeltacht now, and central to the policy, is the recognition of the importance of preschool immersion models and strategies are being developed to enhance that transition, while at the same time the legislation formally inhibits it. (Ní Ghréacháin, pers. comm., 2021)

One initiative outside of the Gaeltacht was the Language Support Scheme to support *naíonra* staff and non-teaching school staff members who wish to improve their Irish or to undertake the TEG, an accredited system linked to the Common European Framework of Reference for Languages. However, this scheme no longer exists;

---

[13] Occasional interviews with Gaeloideachas staff have been conducted since 2010 and I am grateful for their willingness to supply material and strategic plans.
[14] Walsh advises that 'Tusla is a made-up "Irish" word that is totally incorrect and ungrammatical!' (Walsh, pers. comm., 2021).

Instead we are running a pilot and offering free language development classes on line, tailored to needs of *naíonraí* teachers. The support and infrastructure of *naíonraí* is very poor in terms of continual professional development through Irish, language proficiency and quality control of Irish-medium settings. We are providing a very minimal service as the funds previously allocated to *Forbairt Naíonraí Teo.* to support *naíonraí* were never transferred to Gaeloideachas when *Forbairt Naíonraí Teo.* ceased to operate. We have been charged with providing support services to *naíonraí*, focussed on the implementation of the immersion model but with minimal resources. Other areas are neglected due to lack of appropriate funding. (Ní Ghréacháin, pers. comm., 2021)

With the influx of non-Irish speakers, the question arises to how best to protect the linguistic ethos of the Irish-medium Gaeltacht schools as they seek to integrate new arrivals into their classes. This is a feature of the new Gaeltacht Education Policy and time will tell how effective the new measures are.

Conventionally immersion education in Ireland does not use new speaker as an operational concept or policy goal for its L2 students. The central elements of immersion education are as follows:

L2 is the teaching medium; the curriculum is similar to the L1 curriculum; additive bilingualism is the objective; the contact with L2 is primarily restricted to the classroom and to the school environment in general; the staff is bilingual and fluent in Irish; children enter the system with the same level (restricted) in L2. (Gaelscoileanna, 2007)

With the aforementioned prohibition in school enrolment policies on giving priority to children from a *naíonra*, there is a danger that parents will believe that immersing a child in a *naíonra* prior to school is pointless if the child will not have an automatic right to continue her/his education through the medium of Irish. This would be a real loss to the language and to the child who would miss out on enjoying two years of early immersion, which offers a great linguistic advantage. There is a relatively new scheme, ECCE, which includes *naíonraí* which entitles all children to 2 years of free preschool (three hours a day) (ní Ghréacháin, pers. comm., 2021).

An abiding challenge is the recruitment of appropriate teachers from within the current stock which can be influenced by the decisions of the Teachers Redeployment Panel together with the willingness versus competence of individuals to teach in the Irish-medium school system. A report on this matter was laid before the Houses of the Oireachtas (Irish Parliament) in 2015, because the recommendations of an investigation by the first Coimisinéir Teanga (Irish Language Commissioner), Seán Ó Cuirreáin, had not been implemented. This was done in accordance with Section 26(5) of the Official Languages Act. It is the only time that his successor Rónán Ó Domhnaill made such a report to the Houses of the Oireachtas as Coimisinéir Teanga.[15]

---

[15] Rónán Ò Domhnaill, pers. comm., 31 March 2021. Please see www.coimisineir.ie/userfiles/files/ReporttotheHousesoftheOireachtasontheDepartmentofEducationandSkills2015.pdf.

Irish is a required qualification for all primary school teachers and an entrance requirement to obtain a place on an undergraduate primary teacher training course and as a consequence some Institutes of Education, such as that at Dublin City University, have a very healthy demand for Irish among their largely female student cohort.[16] However, beyond conventional teacher training provision there is no assurance of standard or quality at preschool level; neither is there a third-level qualification in early education specifically focussed on Irish-medium playschools. However, a recent BEd in primary education through Irish has been initiated at the Marino Institute of Education in Dublin[17] and programmes are available at St Mary's College in Belfast, and an MSc run by Coláiste Mhuire Gan Smál, in Limerick.[18]

A motion passed at the 2021 AGM of Gaeloideachas is instructive:

To address the lack of supply of primary teachers with a satisfactory standard of Irish, this AGM calls on the Teaching Council to require a TEG certificate at level B2 with merit (65% +) as a basic requirement for all who apply to register as a primary school teacher with the Council. Currently, as part of their entry requirements, all higher education institutions with the exception of Hibernia require a TEG certificate at level B1 (oral test with merit) for entry to the Professional Masters in Education (Primary) course. (Ní Ghréacháin, pers. comm., 2021)

What is astonishing, given the constitutional status of Irish and the long history of government promotion of Irish through education, is the situation whereby primary-level teacher training, save the course offered by Marino Institute of Education, does not prepare teachers for the Irish-medium education system.[19] The Department of Education argues that all such teachers are qualified to teach in either English-medium or Irish-medium schools! This was their argument in not differentiating between both sectors in their Teachers Redeployment Panels!

An insider's view is presented by Professor Mac Mathúna who spent a considerable period lecturing in Irish in St Patrick's College and a further ten years as Registrar there before moving to UCD:

My own interpretation of the situation/attitude is that following a gradual shift from Irish to English as the language of instruction in the 1960s in what were then known as Teacher Training Colleges, the period 1965–70 would have seen a steady rise in the number of student teachers who were ill-prepared for teaching through Irish. It may also be noted that there was considerable disillusionment with the ideals of the revival among the 1965–70 cohorts, who ironically would have had a good command of Irish. Primary

---

[16] Prof Pádraig Ó Duibhir, Deputy Dean, Institute of Education, DCU at interview, 10 April 2018.
[17] www.teachingcouncil.ie/en/teacher-education/initial-teacher-education/review-and-professional-accreditation-of-existing-programmes-of-ite/completed-reviews/completed-reviews.html.
[18] www.mie.ie/en/study_with_us/undergraduate_programmes/baitsileir_san_oideachas_tri_mhean_na_gaeilge/; www.stmarys-belfast.ac.uk/academic/education/ime_english.asp?cid=105671352943.
[19] For developments on this theme see https://tuairisc.ie/sceal-alice-in-wonderland-e-an-cur-chuige-i-leith-muinteoiri-do-scoileanna-lan-ghaeilge/.

school students' attitudes have been largely favourable since the mid-70s, notwithstanding increasing challenges with regard to their competence. It is worth noting with regard to redeployment, that the (theoretical) ability to assign/be assigned a teaching post anywhere in the State is valued both the Department of Education and primary teachers, who may wish to move location for family/personal reasons. (Mac Mathúna, pers. comm., 2021)

No extra qualification is required to teach in Irish at post-primary level, although one initial teacher education programme for second-level education is provided through the medium of Irish.[20] A further motion at the 2021 Gaeloideachas AGM highlights this need:

This AGM calls on the Department of Education to ensure that a higher education institution in the east of the country provides a full post-primary Professional Masters in Education course to meet the demand for and increase the supply of subject teachers for post-primary schools, currently being provided for by NUI Galway. (Ní Ghréacháin, pers. comm., 2021)

It is particularly difficult to recruit teachers with sufficient fluency and accuracy. Far from there being active efforts to attract suitable teachers to this sector what little incentives there were have been removed as a result of recent efforts to control overall state expenditure. Thus, the more favourable ratio of teachers to pupils in Irish-medium schools has been decreased and an allowance, formerly awarded for teaching through Irish, has been removed from new posts. Hence, there is the abiding difficulty in finding substitute teachers with an appropriate level of Irish, which compounds the deficiencies in provision of resources at all three levels (ní Ghréacháin, 2016). This remains a challenge for some post-primary schools which do not have the staff with the required subject knowledge to teach through Irish in an adequate manner.

Professor Pádraig Ó Duibhir advises that additional challenges remain, particularly the weakness of special educational needs provision, highlighted by a lack of tools and support in Irish. One curiosity is the management of dyslexia from which Irish has been exempt whereas provision is made in regard to the learning of English, French or German for some 15,000 students.[21] Professor Mac Mathúna responds that:

This is extraordinary. I was not aware of provision for French, German. Does this refer to native speakers of these languages? If so, one would expect Polish to be included.

---

[20] Ciara Ni Bhroin has advised that two courses are available through the medium for post-primary level – one in the south and one in the north of Ireland (Ni Bhroin, pers. comm., 2021). www.stmarys-belfast.ac.uk/academic/education/courses/pgce/pcgeirishmediumpostprimary.asp?cid=122174720514 and www.nuigalway.ie/courses/taught-postgraduate-courses/oideachas-irish.html.

[21] This exemption is available to students in English-medium schools only. 'The Circular and these Guidelines are for implementation in English-medium primary schools only' (May 2021). www.education.ie/en/Parents/Information/Irish-Exemption/exemptions-from-the-study-of-irish-guidelines-for-primary-schools.pdf. See here also www.education.ie/en/Parents/Information/Irish-Exemption/FAQs.html.

Perhaps it refers to second-level subject teaching? At any rate, the basic, underlying point is crucial. Unless a system can cater for all participants, including the weakest, it is doomed. If adequate Special Needs provision is not made for Irish, it is tantamount to labelling Irish an optional extra. (Mac Mathúna, pers. comm., 2021)

The criteria to receive a derogation from studying Irish due to dyslexia were changed recently and there has been an increase in the number of students receiving said derogation. While the exemption system has been changed in the last few years, insiders argue that this is the single biggest blow to the language in L2 schools as the rate of exemption is increasing. A second feature claimed is the tendency of some teachers not to encourage children from Irish-medium primary schools to pursue their education in Irish-medium secondary schools, especially those from poorer backgrounds. Ní Ghréacháin disagrees, arguing that limited post-primary provision inhibits the progression of students as does parental concern about how children will manage third-level courses in English. A wide subject choice reflecting the desires of their children will always be a priority for parents, and for parents of children in Irish-medium education consideration is given to the school's capacity to deliver said subjects to a high standard in Irish.

A third feature is the preponderance of Irish-medium pupils who pursue their university education through the medium of English. Thus, at each stage in the transition process the potential of the Irish-medium primary school is diluted.[22] Turning to new speakers, Ó Duibhir suggested that as native speakers tend to consider them as learners it is difficult for many to 'break through and develop confidence' unless, of course, they pursue further studies as adult learners.[23]

Two issues deserve further attention, namely phonology and competence. Phonology is the normal marker of a learner, advanced or otherwise, and a native speaker can quite readily identify a learner by the sound patterns and level of fluency. Phonological/phonemic accuracy and sentence rhythm are linked to regional dialects, which are increasingly problematic as a desired and/or realistic goal for L2 speakers. A proposal for a '*lárchanúint*' or central spoken standard has not gathered much momentum (Mac Mathúna, pers. comm., 2021). Variation is a fascinating feature of the new speaker development. Phonological variations in post-traditional radio presenters have been analysed by Moal, Ó Murchadha and Walsh (2018) and it is their contention that there is potential for such features to feed into both the enregisterment and iconisation process 'whereby linguistic features forms, and practices become imbued with social values and signification' (Moal et al., 2018, p. 191). The RíRá ar RnaG presenters may be characterised as outliers broadcasting to a post-traditional audience, but there is some ambivalence as to their salience

---

[22] Ibid.
[23] For details on Adult Learner examinations please visit www.teg.ie/english.167.html.

for the authors propose that pigeonholing within this genre could become a real possibility.[24] 'Ultimately, such an association could reproduce dominant overt language ideologies around linguistic variation within Irish, where traditional speech is valorised and post-traditional speech stigmatised' (Moal et al., 2018, p. 207).[25]

Competence is also a big issue. Many students have achieved TEG B2 level in assessments developed by the Language Centre at the National University of Ireland, Maynooth which is linked to the Common European Framework of Reference for Languages (Council of Europe, 2001). The test provides a benchmark, offering six levels in the system of certification for learners within and outside formal academic environments. The problem with such assessments is that they really do not tell one very much, especially if the formal instruction is not of the highest standard. Yet even so formal competence and daily use of mature Irish remains a conundrum. Ó Duibhir cautions that as only some 77,000 are daily speakers it is unwise to emphasise the differences between native and new speakers; one needs to be tolerant and accepting. His own research into immersion education reveals that the opportunities for new speakers to acquire a more native-like form are diminishing due to the decline in the numbers and proportion of native speakers (Ó Duibhir, 2018). One significant issue is the degree to which parents who went through immersion education are using their Irish at home with their children. The results would appear to be rather disappointing and impact on the broader issue of social use of Irish outside the classroom setting (Ó Duibhir, 2018).[26] Another challenge is the lack of sustainable social situations to use Irish in the wider community. While there are sporting clubs and occasional other recreational spaces, the government's priority is to invest in the educational system, and they would argue that they are responding to genuine parental pressure in this regard. But this type of top-down planning would need to be supplemented by a range of bottom-up communal initiatives, reminiscent of the 1970s and 1980s, which seem to have fallen away of late, according to Ó Duibhir.[27]

Several worrying trends for both L2 learners and L1 speakers were investigated by Hickey and Stenson (2016) who analysed the approach and preparedness of teachers in relation to their application of the 1999 Curriculum Guidelines. The guidelines advised teachers to build linguistic awareness via

---

[24] Walsh advises that 'this is a pop music programme provided by a youth station Raidió Rí-Rá (very much catering for new speakers) to national station RTÉ Raidió na Gaeltachta (RnaG), which is much more traditional in its linguistic output. In that sense, it is a complete outlier in the RnaG schedule' (Walsh, pers. comm., 2021).

[25] Also studied extensively by Noel Ó Murchadha; see www.tcd.ie/research/profiles/?profile=murchadn.

[26] Professor Pádraig Ó Duibhir, Deputy Dean, Institute of Education, DCU at interview, 10 April 2018.

[27] Prof. Pádraig Ó Duibhir, Deputy Dean, Institute of Education, DCU at interview 10 April 2018.

comparison of Irish and English spelling patterns, but most teachers interviewed indicated that they did not attempt this because they did not feel they had adequate preparation in how to do it. Consequently, literacy remained a challenge. Negativity towards Irish was also a big issue. This stemmed from three sources. First, the difficulty schools faced in managing a lack of family support for Irish and Irish homework, which may be directly tied to parents' negative experience of learning Irish themselves. Secondly, teachers thought that the negativity to Irish was more indirectly expressed, simply by parents demonstrating indifference to Irish as a less important subject. Thirdly, and more concerning, was the perception of a widespread decline in interest in teaching Irish among their teaching colleagues and among student teachers (Hickey and Stenson, 2016). In discussing the enlarged community of Irish speakers, they argue that

> digital literacy in Irish may be particularly important, and an educational system that focuses exclusively on oral skills is unduly limited for our changing world. We must prepare learners for the opportunities afforded by modern media in connecting widely distributed networks of minority language speakers. Literacy, including digital literacy, has an increasingly significant role to play in widening such access to Irish, a minority language that now has an international presence. (Hickey and Stenson, 2016, p. 16)

Curricular changes had the consequence of demoting Irish reading. This has downgraded the importance of literacy in the syllabus and has created problems for those studying Irish at third level. There is history here, most notably the ill-informed decision in 2006 by former Minister for Education Mary Hanafin to increase the number of marks awarded to the Leaving Certificate oral examination in Irish to 40 per cent of the total. All of this contributed to a perceived decline in the actual use of Irish where the skills and potential gained through statutory education were just not being realised in daily life.

These observations confirm a long-established trend assessed by Mac Gréil and Rhatigan (2009) whose report analysed attitude, competence and the use of Irish by 1,015 respondents in 2007–8. By replicating earlier studies from 1972–3 and 1988–9 they were able to determine time-series changes in significant domains pertaining to Irish. The most challenging finding was that only 22.7 per cent used Irish regularly, which was slightly less than half of the 47.2 per cent who claimed reasonable competence. They consequently urged consideration as how to translate competence into use.

In interpreting the growth of the school system between 1972 and 2022, the biggest lacuna is a lack of continuity between the primary and secondary levels within the minority sector. This has not only led to the diminution of Irish language skills of those who chose not to advance to Irish-medium secondary schools; it also weakens the case for a holistic representation of Irish, based on both need and demand. The current irony is that acute oversubscription of school places is a real issue. The Department of Education determines how demand is to be satisfied, and in many cases parental expectation is trumped by provision and expedience. The real need is for more well-disposed critical decision makers who are supportive of Irish-medium schools to animate innovative proposals raised by professional bodies and justified within the 20-Year Strategy for the Irish Language.

One such instance, again proposed by the 2021 Gaeloideachas AGM, is the call for an Irish-medium Education Policy, akin to the Gaeltacht Policy.

This AGM calls on the Department of Education to develop a National Policy for Irish-medium Education, as included in the programme for government and promised by the previous Minister and the Secretary General of the Department, and that this policy be core to the Department's action plan and Statement of Strategy to ensure a clear vision and programme of support for Irish-medium education. (Ní Ghréacháin, pers. comm., 2021)

Ní Ghréacháin suggests that it would be interesting to reference the demand as a percentage in contrast to the supply, for Kantar (2020) has shown that 49 per cent of respondents would choose a school in their area which teaches through the medium of Irish if available for their children. In the south 75 per cent of those asked agreed that pupils should have the right to continue with their Irish-medium education from primary school to secondary school (Kantar, 2020).[28]

The Department of Education has recently begun work on the initial stages of policy development for Irish-medium education, a move greatly welcomed by Gaeloideachas. The sad truth is that the provision of official support has all too often been weak and thus competence has varied widely within and between partner organisations.

But what of the products of non-Irish-medium schools? How do they contribute to the vitality of Irish? Mac Mathúna avers that:

Given that the predominant model of schooling, in some 90% of cases, is English-medium instruction with Irish taught essentially as a stand-alone subject, the importance of this sector should not be minimised. Despite of all the shortcomings in teacher competence the fact remains that primary-level teaching and the teaching of Irish as a subject at second level continue to attract a high proportion of dedicated and competent young people as teachers, who continue to be motivated by the ideals of the language revival movement. Of course, the fact that this situation has obtained for over 100 years since independence, and another twenty years prior to that, makes it difficult to maintain the effort among teachers and educationalists more generally. (Mac Mathúna, pers. comm., 2021)[29]

---

[28] Full report available at https://cnag.ie/images/NO2021_CEAS.pdf.
[29] 'At an anecdotal level, I might note that (1) one of the best final year BA groups of Irish students I had during forty years of teaching – all A and B+ students – was just before I retired from UCD

Irish Language Services

One of the principal complaints made by both native speakers and new speakers is the relative lack of opportunity to use Irish in meaningful ways with public bodies. A significant mechanism designed to enhance the use of Irish in public affairs was the language scheme initiative. By the end of 2006, forty-three schemes were in place, covering seventy-one public bodies. An analysis of these schemes categorised them into (a) national bodies without a specific Gaeltacht remit and (b) those with a specific link to the Gaeltacht. It found that the first category of schemes envisaged only very minimal provision of services, but that the second category at least had the potential to create employment for Irish speakers in the bodies in question. However, Walsh and McLeod (2008, p. 31) also identified a number of problems with the schemes related to (a) the competence of front-line staff in Irish, (b) an emphasis on written rather than oral communication, (c) recruitment of Irish-speaking staff and (d) stimulation of demand for services, failures which were to worsen during the subsequent years.

An analysis of the beliefs associated with the schemes ratified in 2007 uncovered a number of key ideological stances that were deemed to undermine their effectiveness in enhancing the delivery of services in Irish. There was widespread reliance on a training policy of teaching existing staff a minimal amount of Irish, rather than recruiting fully bilingual staff, despite the limitations of such an approach to serve fluent Irish speakers. Furthermore, the schemes revealed the belief that there was little public demand for Irish and that services would only be made available when requested rather than on the basis of the Canadian system of 'active offer'. An overarching ideology of the *cúpla focal* (the few words of Irish) was dominant if implicit in the schemes, meaning that for the public bodies concerned, a very limited service in Irish was deemed adequate to fulfil their statutory obligations. This is reflective of a widespread, if largely undocumented, ideology in Ireland that a tokenistic display of Irish will suffice in all cases, whereas those who had campaigned for the OLA wanted legislation that would guarantee a comprehensive level of state services in Irish. The Act was supposed to overcome such a limited position for Irish but through its reliance on minimalist language schemes, it has in fact institutionalised it (Walsh, 2012). The robustness of this ideology was detailed further by O'Rourke and Walsh (2020, p. 158) where evidence was presented that interviewees acknowledge that a few words was not enough and a proper conversation in the *ciorcail chomhrá* (conversation circles) was deemed essential even if the quality of the spoken Irish was often inconsistent.

in 2013; (2) of these only four had come through the Irish-medium system, the other eight came from the much-maligned mainstream system' (Mac Mathúna, pers. comm., 2021).

Currently the language scheme framework involves some 650 public bodies ranging from government departments to local authorities and semi-state companies covering many aspects of life. The legislative framework creates three categories of obligation: (a) direct obligations, covering a limited range of publications and correspondence with the public (Section 9 (2) and (3) and Section 10); (b) obligations based on ministerial regulations, related mostly to signage and oral announcements (Section 9 (1)); and (c) obligations based on language schemes, internal language plans outlining how public bodies will increase services in Irish (Sections 11 to 18). Each language scheme is agreed between the public body and the minister with responsibility for the Gaeltacht, and its implementation is monitored by An Coimisinéir Teanga. Every scheme lasts for three years and is supposed to be replaced by another scheme guaranteeing additional services in Irish, thereby ensuring a cumulative improvement in services over time.

A decade after the government's promised review, the implementation of a revised Official Languages Act remained at a crossroads. The legislation that civil society activists hoped would create a framework for the provision of state services in Irish has had only limited success. The Language Commissioner's annual reports indicate that there is greater awareness among public bodies of their direct obligations under the Act. However, over one-third of all complaints received in 2015 related to non-compliance with a provision of a language scheme. A second commentary on the Act, based on a detailed analysis of forty language schemes ratified in 2015 and 2016, concluded that the system was failing to achieve its stated objective. The Irish Language Commissioner, Rónán Ó Domhnaill found that there were significant delays – an average of three and a half years – between the time when a public body was requested by the minister to prepare a scheme and the date when the scheme came into effect, with delays as long as nine years in some cases. He identified a problem of 'regressive modifications of commitments' in subsequent language schemes: instead of enhancing services in Irish, only a small minority of the second and third language schemes agreed in 2015 and 2016 contained a significant improvement to services. In almost two-thirds of the schemes investigated, a commitment which was the subject of an investigation by the Commissioner was diluted or removed in a subsequent scheme, a situation described as 'extremely unsatisfactory' and confirmation of the 'dysfunctional nature of the system' (Coimisinéir Teanga, 2017, p. 6). It remains to be seen what will transpire from the implementation of the revised legislation, but it appears that there is now a consensus that language schemes are to be phased out.

Overall, the development of the OLA has been stymied by the failure of successive governments to see through the legislative process that would bring about a new Act. There is ample evidence of the low political prioritisation of Irish in the governmental agenda, ranging from weak implementation of the 20-Year Strategy for the Irish Language to the sluggish progress of the legislative review.

Following a general election on 8 February 2020, a new government took office on 27 June 2020 with Micheál Martin, the leader of Fianna Fáil, as Taoiseach and Leo Varadkar, the leader of Fine Gael, as Tánaiste. Norma Foley TD became the Minister for Education and Catherine Martin TD of the Green Party became the Minister for Tourism, Culture, Arts, Gaeltacht, Sport and Media.[30] This coalition government, comprised of Fianna Fáil, Fine Gael and the Green Party, has had to deal with three big challenges, namely the post-Brexit arrangements in Ireland's relationship with both the UK and the EU, the Covid-19 pandemic and the economic fluctuations which have been exacerbated by both political crises.

The dominant ideological backdrop remains that of a centre-right government with a neoliberal hue and without any strong interest in Irish beyond its limited referential function as a symbol of Irishness. This position, reflected in the widespread *cúpla focal* ideology, undermines policy initiatives which are aimed ostensibly at serving fluent Irish speakers in favour of those who wish to use a little Irish in order to satisfy a desire to mark their identity in a symbolic fashion.

The 2016 Census returns for Irish showed a decline, for the first time since 1946, in all key statistics about knowledge and use of the language. The most dramatic decline was recorded in the Gaeltacht, where the number of daily speakers outside education fell by 11 per cent from 23,175 or almost 24 per cent in 2011 to 20,586 or 21.4 per cent in 2016 (Central Statistics Office, 2017). It is not clear to what extent the decline can be attributed to the policy context, but the sluggish pace of implementation cannot be expected to yield positive demographic results. The Census figures are a stark reminder that the increase in numbers of Irish speakers over the past seventy years cannot be taken for granted.

The gap between the constitutional and legislative status of Irish and the failure of successive governments to fulfil more than the minimal requirements of statutory obligations should be a clear warning that, in contradistinction to many other aspects of public policy, minority language-specific enactments are more difficult to embed within the culture and machinery of the modern state, unless successive governments are fully committed to the political project.

Foras na Gaeilge

Foras na Gaeilge is the all-Ireland public body charged with the promotion of Irish. Established in 1999 it is the central agency whose planning remit and interventions cover corpus, status and acquisition language planning.

---

[30] Walsh has observed that Norma Foley is not fluent enough to do a media interview in Irish, but Catherine Martin is. There is no guarantee these days that even the Minister for the Gaeltacht will be a fluent speaker (Walsh, pers. comm., 2021).

Its position among European language planning agencies is unique as it is responsible to the North/South Ministerial Council (NSMC) which was established under the Belfast/Good Friday Agreement (1998), to develop consultation, co-operation and action on an all-Ireland basis.[31] The Language Body, consisting of two agencies, Foras na Gaeilge and Tha Boord o Ulster-Scotch, was one of six North/South Implementation Bodies, answerable through the Council both to the Oireachtas and the Northern Ireland Assembly.

Its Chief Executive, Seán Ó Coinn, is very mindful of the significance and needs of new speakers and the ultimate ambition is to normalise the use of Irish.[32] With headquarters in Dublin and Belfast, offices in five locations and fifty-eight staff, Foras na Gaeilge has developed into a key agency of the state. Its broad remit includes the following:

- Promotion of the Irish language.
- Facilitating and encouraging its use in speech and writing in public and private life in the Republic of Ireland and, in the context of Part III of the European Charter for Regional or Minority Languages, in Northern Ireland where there is appropriate demand.
- Advising both administrations, public bodies and other groups in the private and voluntary sectors.
- Undertaking supportive projects, and grant-aiding bodies and groups as considered necessary.
- Undertaking research, promotional campaigns, and public and media relations.
- Developing terminology and dictionaries.
- Supporting Irish-medium education and the teaching of Irish.[33]

Foras provides the funding for six Lead Organisations to take responsibility for carrying out development and progress in six major areas discussed below. Seán Ó Coinn advises that Foras na Gaeilge is seeking to develop a more business-like approach to language issues with a focus on intervention and best practice, evaluation and measurement of performance. Much of this shift in approach is driven by an awareness of the need to develop staff skills, the formation of cross-development teams and a determination to get the best out of its partner organisations. This change in emphasis from outputs to outcomes is reflective of changes in public sector ideology and practice throughout Ireland. Capacity building is accompanied by an ongoing effort at reorientation of the organisation's principal goal, which is to emphasise the centrality of strategic thinking and the development of corpus and status planning.

---

[31] Declaration of interest: I was part of the Good Friday process, attending meetings, preparing papers on language rights, equality and policy and subsequently advising and training civil servants of the Central Community Relations Unit, Northern Ireland Assembly, Belfast, from October 1998 onwards.
[32] Interviewed on a number of occasions, the most recent being 10 April 2018.
[33] www.forasnagaeilge.ie/about/about-foras-na-gaeilge/the-partnershop-forum/?lang=en.

Foras na Gaeilge would argue that it has had considerable impact across a range of activities as follows:
1. During the last fifteen years Foras na Gaeilge has been developing a suite of utilities to facilitate translation. These include:
   a. the Córas Creidiúnaithe d'Aistritheoirí (the translators' accreditation system) initiated in 2005, with over 220 accredited translators ensuring that the highest standards will prevail in the translation sector and will safeguard the reputation of good translators. A seal of accreditation is awarded to translators who reach a certain standard of excellence.
   b. www.aistear.ie, the main aim of which is to provide training and resources to translators, editors and all writers of Irish.
   c. Freagra – A Helpline for the Public Sector offers a service which provides advice to users of Irish addressing common difficulties with terminology and phrases. It is a central, identifiable contact point for all the community.
2. The community-development scheme Scéim Pobail Ghaeilge was initiated in 2005. Some twenty-two local Irish language groups are now funded to implement their work programmes and establish language-use networks. The scheme provides employment for up to twenty-two individuals as language development officers, but only on a four-day week basis despite the case being made for a five-day week. Five of these communities have also progressed to a more advanced stage of being considered as embryonic Irish Language Networks, which will become a focus of development as Irish language communities.
3. Foras na Gaeilge, in conjunction with Microsoft, developed an Irish language version of Windows XP and Office 2003 which has since been updated regularly.
4. Séideán Sí: this flagship primary schools' project, a joint project between Foras na Gaeilge and the Department of Education, entailed the publishing of a high standard literacy programme for Gaeltacht schools and Irish-medium schools for the eight years of primary school education. The project has now been extended to include a digital project to provide online electronic literacy resources.
5. The Irish–English Dictionary began its design and planning phase in July 2003. At the end of 2020, some 140,000 sense units, incorporated in 48,000 entries, were available on www.focloir.ie free to the public, with grammar files and a grammar wizard, pronunciation guidance sound-files, an app for mobile devices and a translation app for websites. In addition, online access to existing dictionaries was also available on a separate dictionary site. The online dictionary site had over 2.4 million unique

users in 2020. A printed concise English–Irish dictionary derived from the online dictionary was launched in 2020.
6. Foras na Gaeilge has also developed a National Terminology Database (www.tearma.ie). The online database is searchable in Irish and in English and has over 185,000 Irish language terms. It is primarily used by translators and interpreters and by university students. Development has been ongoing since 2004 and is now in Phase VII. The terminology database had 560,000 unique users in 2020. By 2021 around 185,000 bilingual entries were available in the database. A new website and editorial system were launched on 14 March 2019 based on Terminologue, an open-source platform developed by Gaois.
7. The Irish language Core-funded sector (nineteen organisations) has been reduced to six Lead Organisations that have responsibility for developing the Irish language across a range of strategic areas involving the development of Irish in the community. The new approach initiated in 2014 also entails a Partnership Forum for the six Lead Organisations, with Foras na Gaeilge the lead funding body, and a Community Language Forum to advise the Lead Organisations on priorities as indicated in Table 5.1.
8. Research by way of a major language survey conducted during 2013 which is the most inclusive report ever carried out into public attitudes, ability and use of Irish throughout the island.
9. The funding of an online news service, www.tuairisc.ie, which went live in October 2014. In the eight years since its inception 5.38 million people have visited the site and viewed 12.69 million pages of news content. Foras na Gaeilge also restructured its support for periodical publications to two priority publications: a lifestyle online publication, *Nós*, and a literary and current affair print publication, *Comhar*.

Table 5.1 *Lead Organisations by thematic responsibilities*

Lead Organisation	General area of work
Gaeloideachas	Irish-medium education/immersion education and Irish-medium preschool education
Gael Linn	Education in the English language sector and adult education, and opportunities for use for school pupils
Glór na nGael	Community and economic development
Oireachtas na Gaeilge	Opportunities which support the use of Irish and establishing networks for adults
Conradh na Gaeilge	Raising awareness, language protection and representation (on behalf of the language with state authorities)
Cumann na bhFiann	The development of opportunities for the use of Irish and networks for young people

10. Foras na Gaeilge serves the island through five offices – its main headquarters in Dublin, together with offices in Belfast, Gaoth Dobhair, the Ráth Chairn Gaeltacht in Co. Meath and a book-distribution warehouse in Co. Meath.
11. In 2016 Foras na Gaeilge created a portal website for the Irish language, www.gaeilge.ie, which is an online one-stop shop for information on the Irish language.
12. The Irish Language Community Scheme has been one of the more successful of Foras na Gaeilge's initiatives to support the development of Irish-speaking communities. Currently twenty-two communities are availing of funding to employ a development officer to implement a local language plan to develop language-use networks. Five of these communities have also progressed to a more advanced stage of being considered as embryonic Irish language networks, which will follow government-sanctioned seven-year language plans to become a focus of development as Irish Language Communities.
13. A suite of funding schemes includes funding for summer camps, youth activities, festivals, drama productions, Irish language publishers, literary activities and links with Gaelic speakers in Scotland.
14. Language planning has also begun in thirteen urban centres (Gaeltacht Service Towns) that serve Gaeltacht communities.
15. A scheme has been established to support the development of two community radio stations in Belfast and Dublin.[34]

While commending the Irish–English dictionary as a superb achievement, several of these Foras claims would be disputed by activists and commentators. Thus by 2021, eight years after the Gaeltacht Act came into effect, only one such Gaeltacht Services Town, Letterkenny, Co. Donegal, has formally begun the language-planning process. Foras is also criticised for not doing enough to support Irish language media and for losing a great deal of good will and support in the way it has handled the community partnership restructuring.

Community support is funded through its six Lead Organisations, including the encouragement of Irish in Gaelic Athletic Association clubs (GAA), music and dance activities and a wide and varied range of events and activities aimed at promoting the development of social language networks and language-use opportunities. Foras na Gaeilge has recognised that support to community groups needs to be more developmental and advisory so as to ensure a consistent level of performance among community-based groups and thereby offer more opportunities and spaces for speakers to interact.

However, it is also recognised that the capacity for the Lead Organisations to act has been curtailed over the recent period. Salary costs can in some cases be

---

[34] Source: Seán Ó Coinn, 7 November 2016; 1 April 2021.

as high as 80 per cent, leaving little room for innovative or speculative project development. This is compounded by a general understanding that renumeration levels for the Lead Organisations are at least a grade lower than their counterparts on equivalent civil service grades. Officers are animated when Foras refers to their high salary costs – for they are high in relation to the overall budget, but low in relation to what they should receive!

As a consequence, the new operative paradigm is networking, where both energy and costs are shared among a number of actors. Others would argue that the Community Language Forum, which forms part of the Partnership Forum, does not have the capacity to advise on priorities as it is a generic group of people with interest and expertise in Irish, who do not necessarily have an expertise in the required respective fields. For several of the six Lead Organisations the current structure is unsatisfactory. An evaluation of the new Lead Organisation Partnership Forum has been ongoing for several years – but it has failed to achieve the terms of reference.

One of the outcomes of the 20-Year Strategy for the Irish Language 2010–30 (Government of Ireland, 2010) was the Gaeltacht Act of 2012, which places the burden of community-planning activities on local voluntary groups and confers language-planning powers on Údarás na Gaeltachta in addition to its economic development role (O'Rourke and Walsh, 2020, p. 53). Significantly it also allows the minister to nominate a Gaeltacht area as a 'Language Planning District' and twenty-six were so nominated from 2014 to 2017. The Act also recognises the significance of other networks of new speakers outside the Gaeltacht and thus both Gaeltacht Service Towns and Irish Language Networks are now part of the language policy repertoire. As identified in Figure 5.1, this enlarges the designated locations within which language-related initiatives can be developed. In 2015 five areas were identified where local language planning would emerge: three in the Republic at Loughrea, Co. Galway, Ennis, Co. Clare and Clondalkin in Dublin; West Belfast and Carn Tóchair in Co. Derry were identified in Northern Ireland.

Ó Coinn stresses that the aim is to increase the capacity of these designated towns to provide Irish-medium services and Irish Language Networks where new speakers could avail themselves of the additional opportunities and spaces to make the maintenance of their language skills a worthwhile effort. Despite initial financial difficulties the period since 2017 has seen an increase in the resources expended on such initiatives, with increased Government investment in implementing language plans in the Gaeltacht language-planning regions, in the Gaeltacht Service Towns and in the Language Networks.

As part of Project Ireland 2040 (the government's National Development Plan) some €360m was allocated to rural regeneration. This included an Irish

Irish Language Services 179

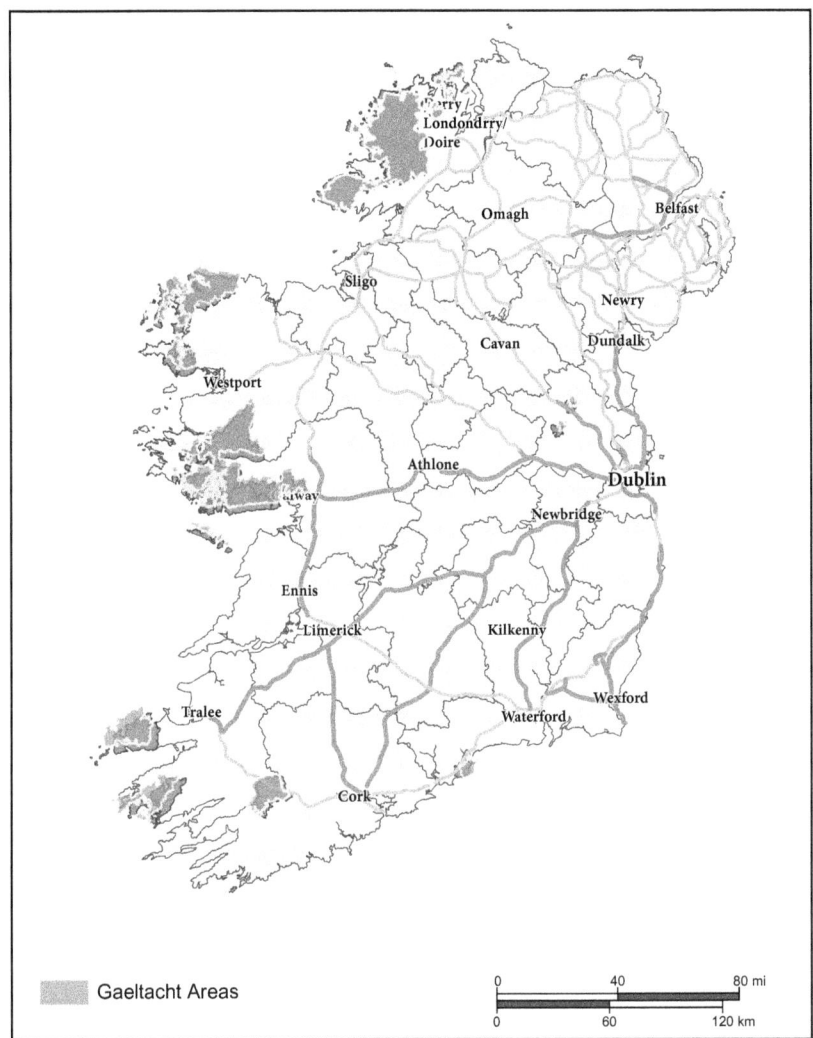

Figure 5.1 Gaeltacht areas in 2016 (By permission of Ordnance Survey Ireland)

language dimension, such as signs, linguistic landscape improvements, visitor centres and more support for small rural schools, cultural centres and the like. Public servants would advise that the period 2017 to today would seem to be a more optimistic political climate also for the promotion of Irish, especially in Northern Ireland, although academic criticism of the failings of the 20-Year

Strategy for the Irish Language 2010–2030 remain, especially in relation to its inconsistent and partial implementation.[35]

Social networks are the key to a vibrant future according to the Foras na Gaeilge CEO, especially in the light of an atrophying Gaeltacht and the decline in traditional community structures across the land. Interest groups will sustain the language in a way in which artificial, sporadic encouragements by official agencies will not. A second potential resource is the business community and the conviction that maintaining language skills could be an important economic asset. Foras na Gaeilge recognise that culture and education rather than commercial skills development has dominated their thinking since 1999 and now they are seeking to respond to interest from the business community which is using Irish in their messaging and activities. International corporations, such as the car maker Kia in Dublin, and other business organisations are using Irish when advertising goods and services on bilingual billboards and social network platforms are seen to be productive, as is offering a quality kitemark standards certification for best practice bilingual services.

However, Foras na Gaeilge is conscious that challenges remain, chief of which are:

1. To lead the Irish language community in taking ownership of the 20-Year Strategy for the Irish Language by:
    a. Taking forward the language-planning agenda at community level, to ensure that progress becomes self-sustaining with a long-term impact, with a focus on permanent institutions (Irish-medium crèches, childcare centres, Irish-medium schools, language safe spaces, small businesses providing Irish language workplaces) and networks (activity groups – walking groups, cycling groups, etc.). This will involve a focus on the current twenty-two communities, on a spectrum of development towards Network status.
    b. Ensuring the implementation of the government policy for education in the Gaeltacht and the development of a similar policy for Irish-medium education.
    c. Addressing the challenge of developing the teaching of Irish in English-medium schools, including developing CLIL (Content Language Integrated Learning), partial immersion and the initial training of primary school teachers with sufficiently well-developed language skills to meet the Irish language requirements of the primary school curriculum. It is currently accepted that much of the teaching in primary schools has been less than 'good' or 'very good'. This has been largely due to the issues of language competence among teachers.

---

[35] www.gov.ie/en/campaigns/09022006-project-ireland-2040/.

Irish Language Services 181

 d. Developing language centres (language safe spaces), which will require significant capital investment. Dublin, Cork and Galway are the main targets.
 e. Implementing a government digital strategy that will incorporate all aspects of twenty-first-century innovations, with particular focus on speech-recognition technology and automated translation.
2. To ensure preparation for the 2022 status as a fully recognised language of the EU.
3. The development of Irish–Irish and Irish–English online dictionaries will require the further development of an Irish language corpus, involving significant investment.
4. To develop partnerships approaches in what is a fragmented Irish-language support environment.
5. Creating a national awareness of the Irish language and its role in identity of the island.[36]

Of these, it is the Gaeltacht education reform which has attracted most interest. This is an important initiative, almost 100 years after the foundation of the state, and is the principal thrust of the Department of Education's intervention since 2018, in co-operation with COGG.[37]

Raising awareness among the wider community would seem to be an obvious tactic for Foras na Gaeilge, but it is recognised that the challenge remains closer to home within the public service as few other government departments turn to Foras na Gaeilge for advice and co-operation other than the department with responsibility for the Gaeltacht. Also, the lack of functional capacity of the civil service to operate in a bilingual fashion is a major impediment. Accordingly, Foras na Gaeilge embarked on a medium-term awareness strategy to streamline, simplify and forge messages which had more of an impact both within the various administrations and larger society. Emphasis is on social media, and together with their six Lead Organisations they have sought to make more of an impact on the general public in relation to the value and relevance of promoting Irish outside the statutory education system. The abiding challenge is to increase the use of Irish in as many socio-economic contexts as is possible so as to give real meaning to the worth of language reproduction in the future.

However, several commentators have criticised both the aims and the implementation of this community partnership restructuring. Many in the community sector would argue that the restructuring produced the opposite of the intended consequence, as this process was poorly handled and resulted in the loss of much institutional memory with the dissolution of organisations such as Comhdháil

---

[36] Source: Seán Ó Coinn, 7 November 2016 and 10 April 2018.
[37] www.gov.ie/en/organisation-information/852bb7-gaeltacht-education-policy-advisory-committee/.

Náisiúnta na Gaeilge (Ó Murchú, 2014). A further criticism is that Foras adopts an uncritical perspective on its own activities.[38] However, beyond Foras's own bureaucratic tendencies, it is recognised that politically they face a difficult situation, 'namely (1) being financed and governed jointly by two jurisdictions, (2) the frequent gaps when the Northern government is in abeyance or scarcely functioning, with most/many of the Unionist representatives being ideologically opposed to Irish. In fact, it could well be argued that these arrangements act as a break on positive initiatives south of the border, while being of a certain advantage in the North, given the weaker situation of Irish there' (Mac Mathúna, pers. comm., 2021).

An Chomhairle um Oideachais Gaeltachta agus Gaelscolaíochta (COGG)

COGG (The Council for Gaeltacht and Irish-Medium Education) was founded under the provisions of Article 31 of the Education Act of 1998 following a campaign led by Comhdháil Náisiúnta na Gaeilge, Gaelscoileanna and Eagraíocht na Scoileanna Gaeltachta to establish a structure to cater for the educational needs of Gaeltacht schools and of *Gaelscoileanna*. COGG's role relates to both primary and post-primary education. It provides advice to the Minister of Education and to the National Council for Curriculum and Assessment.[39] It has three functions:

- to co-ordinate the provision of teaching resources
- to support the provision of services to schools
- to fund research on the teaching of Irish.

At interview the CEO, Muireann Ní Mhóráin, advised that the biggest recent change to COGG's long-standing work in education was the ministerial decision that COGG should implement the 2016 Policy on Gaeltacht Education.[40] This required additional staff but it also promised an opportunity to influence both the determination and the implementation of policy as overseen by the dedicated unit within the Department of Education and Skills. One source of concern was the dearth of detailed work on the vitality of Irish in education and society, which, apart from the sterling efforts of scholars such as the late Peadar Ó Flatharta and Seosamh Mac Donnacha, was bereft of insights as to the patterns and trends of language transmission and use. COGG were able to fund doctoral research on Irish-medium education and as a result there is now a far greater understanding of the dynamics involved. Two decades ago, the challenge for COGG was the supply and content of appropriate textbooks for a new curriculum introduced in 1998. It failed

---

[38] The main findings from the Baker Tilly Report of the Foras's activities are instructive (https://tuairisc.ie, 13 April 2021).
[39] https://ncca.ie/en.
[40] Interview in COGG offices Dublin on 11 April 2018 and subsequent correspondence.

to commission teaching materials and as a consequence Gaeltacht schools threatened to go on strike. Subsequently supplying relevant textbooks for the Junior Cycle Irish has made a huge difference to the success of the teaching performance.

While COGG saw themselves having the greatest impact on schools and on parents, the latter needed to be constantly reminded of the benefits of bilingualism. COGG runs courses for teachers and prepares resources but direct contact with individual schools has reduced and it is even doubtful whether or not COGG had much influence on the discussions and policy formulation of the Department of Education and Skills as there is little interchange and dialogue, which is quite a statement given its status and that it is funded by the Department. Recently COGG's influencing capacity has increased since the establishment of the Education Policy Unit within the Department and the delegation of Gaeltacht Education Policy to COGG.

Despite providing briefing papers and undertaking background research, COGG see themselves as a convenient place for the Department of Education and Skills to 'park' issues and to 'dump' contentious Irish-related problems, so that government can say that they have consulted with specialist agencies in the field. One of these issues is the teaching of Irish in English-medium schools. While there is no integrated programme for teaching Irish in all types of schools, recent attempts to modernise the approaches have not made real progress and COGG is criticised while the issue of 'the Irish can is kicked down the road'. This is somewhat of an anomaly as the state's policy is to provide students with fourteen years of Irish with the aim of producing fluent speakers. However, COGG argues that so many difficulties abound within the system that expecting fluency for all is something of a chimera. Regular reports by the Chief Inspector for the Department of Education and Skills reveal that 33 per cent of primary school teachers do not have competence in Irish. A further 50 per cent of post-primary teachers who are meant to be qualified in Irish are not competent to teach it. Those who qualified outside Ireland are required to undertake the aptitude test, An Scrúdú le hAghaidh Cáilíochta sa Ghaeilge (SCG), as a means of acquiring the necessary qualification or experience an Adaptation Period (OCG – Oiriúnú le hAghaidh Cáilíochta sa Ghaeilge).[41]

---

[41] 'Teachers in national schools must be qualified to teach the range of subjects as outlined in the Primary School Curriculum – 1999 (Curaclam na Bunscoile) to children in all classes. The ability to speak Irish proficiently and to use Irish as the language of incidental communication in the classroom is a prerequisite for teaching Irish. Accordingly, teachers who obtained their teaching qualification outside the State and have a curriculum shortfall in Irish must make good this shortfall. Under the EU Recognition of Professional Qualifications (2005/36/EC) Regulations, 2008, as given effect in S.I. No 139 of 2008, teachers who have a curriculum shortfall in Irish have the choice to make up this shortfall, either by way of an Aptitude Test (SCG – An Scrúdú le hAghaidh Cáilíochta sa Ghaeilge) or an Adaptation Period (OCG – Oiriúnú le hAghaidh Cáilíochta sa Ghaeilge).' https://ilrweb.ie/wp-content/uploads/2020/08/SCG-GUIDE-compressed.pdf.

The Chief Inspector's Report of 2015 concluded that students' learning was found to be less than satisfactory in 24 per cent of Irish lessons in primary schools and 32 per cent of Irish lessons in post-primary schools. The lack of a comprehensive Irish language programme for English-medium primary schools and concerns about the Irish language competence of teachers in a small but significant number of classrooms were among the factors noted by the Chief Inspector.[42]

The Chief Inspector's Report of 2015 contained some fine rhetoric and welcome statistics, but little has happened subsequently to advance the cause of Irish teaching. Provision of Irish teacher training is fragmented, but there is a well-subscribed and successful four-year BEd qualification through Irish at Dublin City University (DCU) together with provision at Mary Immaculate College and a Professional Masters in Education through Irish at the University of Galway (formerly NUI Galway),[43] whilst the Marino Institute of Education declares that its 'courses are not taught exclusively through Irish but students are prepared and supported to undertake teaching placements in the Gaeltacht and/or in Gaelscoileanna'.[44] Despite this statement Irish-medium courses are in operation at MIE.[45]

In order to become a primary school teacher, students need to achieve a 60 per cent mark in Irish at Higher Level, but for many whilst at college their exposure to the language gets squeezed out so the consequence is that at a professional level teacher competence is a huge problem throughout the system.

Ní Mhóráin suggests that the Achilles heel of Irish-medium education is the supposition that many students would choose to sit their exams in English rather than Irish. One way of reducing this risk would be to reform the very strict syllabus set by the National Council for Curriculum and Assessment, which COGG advises. An additional difficulty is that the 40 per cent emphasis on the spoken word is not proficient, which is critical if new speakers are to be produced.

The CEO of COGG' has praise for An tÁisaonad at St Mary's University College, Belfast in the production of excellent Irish-medium resources which are used in the whole of the island. They also specialise in early learning materials and textbooks for the education system. Comhairle na Gaelscolaíochta was set up in 2000 by the Northern Ireland Department of Education and Skills to promote, facilitate and encourage Irish-medium

---

[42] M. Ní Mhóráin in interview at HQ, Dublin, 11 April 2018.
[43] www.nuigalway.ie/colleges-and-schools/arts-social-sciences-and-celtic-studies/education/initial-teacher-education-programmes/oideachas-irish.html; www.mic.ul.ie/faculty-of-education/programme/an-teastas-iarcheime-i-dteagasc-abharbhunaithe-tta-san.
[44] www.mie.ie/en/student_life/learning_through_irish.
[45] For example www.mie.ie/en/study_with_us/undergraduate_programmes/baitsileir_san_oideachas_tri_mhean_na_gaeilge/.

education and Irish-medium schools, and to do this in a planned, educationally efficient and cost-effective way. Its work includes:
1. assisting parents who wish to establish Irish-medium provision in their area;
2. planning for the creation of new Irish-medium schools;
3. promoting standards of good practice in Irish-medium education;
4. co-ordinating the activities of all those involved in Irish-medium education;
5. representing the Irish-medium education sector at all levels;
6. promoting Irish-medium education within the Northern Ireland Department of Education and Skills, the Education Authority, the Council for Catholic Maintained Schools, the Council for Curriculum, Examinations and Assessment and within other bodies;
7. providing advice, assistance and information in relation to Irish-medium education to those who need it and to groups seeking to establish Irish-medium schools and units.[46]

Specialist Services in Irish

Less successful has been the provision of Irish-medium specialist services which cover dyslexia, SEN and psychological issues. Ní Mhóráin avers that bilingualism is seen as a problem by many educationalist psychologists and as a consequence approaches to the development of literacy are varied, as was demonstrated in the COGG report on Special Educational Needs (COGG, 2010). Also, assessments through Irish, a lack of external educational professionals who can provide support services through Irish and resources remain a challenge. Hitherto SEN documents do not consider the production of new speakers as a pressing issue.

In contrast a recent study of SEN and Irish-medium schools by Barrett, Kinsella and Prendeville (2020) offers a more promising scenario. A review of the experiences of bilingual learners with SEN identified that they had fewer opportunities than their peers to learn in high-quality bilingual programmes and had been advised to be spoken to in the majority language only (Martínez-Álvarez, 2019). Whilst acknowledging that educating learners with SEN in an immersion education context is complex and potentially contentious, especially in relation to literacy difficulties, the authors provided policy recommendations on how to mitigate the more damaging effects of a lack of understanding of the SEN needs of Irish-medium pupils. They recommend that:

guidelines need to be developed in relation to the educational placement of such learners and effective additional support needs to be provided for learners presenting with SEN who are being educated in bilingual settings. Learners with literacy and language

---
[46] www.comhairle.org/english/about/about-us/.

difficulties in bilingual educational settings require support both in their dominant language and in the language of instruction, as first language proficiency emerged, both from the literature review and from the findings of this study, as a key predictor of success in bilingual education for SEN learners. (Barrett, Kinsella and Prendeville, 2020)

Three issues deserve attention. The first is that SEN bilingualism should be factored in when general resource allocation models are devised, and appropriate additional weighting given to Irish-medium schools. The second is the intensification of specific training for mainstream and SEN teachers within these schools and for external professionals who support them, including educational psychologists. The third is that both elements should be complemented by the training of parents in the language of instruction as lack of parental proficiency in the Irish language emerged in the study as a barrier to their children's participation in bilingual education.

Similar issues have been raised by Nic Aindriú (2021) who identifies challenges in terms of meeting the SEN of students in Irish immersion education, such as a lack of access to assessments through Irish, a lack of educational professionals (e.g., educational psychologists) providing their services through Irish and the need for more Irish language teaching resources (Andrews, 2019; Nic Aindriú, Ó Duibhir and Travers, 2021).[47]

Nic Aindriú suggests that:

> Teachers and parents also experienced challenges when educating these children through a L2. The challenges listed by these groups were in relation to parental concern, parental involvement, and opinions of educational professionals regarding the suitability of IM education for pupils with SEN. The additional supports that were listed by schools, pupils, and families that would enable them to overcome these challenges were the need for more Irish language academic resources, learning support through Irish, more education and training for teachers, the availability of external services and assessment materials through Irish. (Andrews, 2019)

The most frequently reported categories of SEN in these schools are (1) dyslexia, (2) autism spectrum disorder (ASD), (3) dyspraxia, (4) emotional and/or behavioural difficulties, (5) specific speech and language disorder (SSLD), (6) attention deficit hyperactivity disorder (ADHD), (7) assessed syndromes, and (8) mild general learning difficulties (GLD) (Barrett, William, and Prendeville, 2020; Nic Aindriú, Ó Duibhir and Travers, 2020).

Ní Ghréacháin advises that 'some parents and teachers have perceived that there are benefits for students with SEN when learning through Irish (Nic Aindriú, Ó Duibhir and Travers, 2021b). Benefits have been reported in

---

[47] Please see https://doi.org/10.1080/09500782.2021.1918707 and www.cogg.ie/wp-content/uploads/Additional-supports… -2.pdf. I am grateful to B. Ní Ghréacháin for these references as well as many other valuable observations on Irish-medium education (Ní Ghréacháin, pers. comm., 31 March and 28 May 2021).

terms of bilingualism, Irish language acquisition, academic benefits for post-primary school, high levels of self-esteem and self-confidence, and inclusive school cultures. In terms of investigating the personal experiences of these students, they have reported that they enjoy school, have access to a variety of inclusive pedagogies ... and have developed and maintained friendships in school' (Nic Aindriú, 2021).

Gaeloideachas has identified SEN services as a priority theme in recent years and are seeing progress in terms of

> enhanced recognition and awareness among state bodies charged with providing SEN services of the unique needs of the IME [Irish-medium education] sector; gradually, there is an acceptance that translation of materials does not equate to a tailored service for children with SEN in IME; there has been a big increase in research attention and funding to this area coupled with a greater provision of support materials – and we have had two very successful collaborations with 1) the Dyslexia Association of Ireland and 2) AsIam (autism support) in producing materials for the IME sector. There is a marked increase also in autism / special classes and all new school buildings will be required to incorporate a special class. Gaeloideachas runs training and seminars for teachers and parents on many SEN themes which are helping to raise awareness of the suitability of the sector for all children. (Ní Ghréacháin, 2021)[48]

It is argued that

> 'the National Educational Psychological Service' (NEPS) has expressed concern at the lack of assessment instruments available in Irish (NEPS, 2006). Cline (2000) and Deponio et al. (2000) indicate inappropriate assessment instruments have serious consequences, in that some children do not access early intervention programmes when they are necessary while others are incorrectly placed in special education [...] If the purpose of assessment is to gain an understanding of the student's strengths and weaknesses and to assess for intervention as opposed to diagnosis then criterion-referenced testing must take precedence. These assessment instruments also prevent the need to compare the achievements of bilingual students with monolingual students, as most standardised assessment instruments are normed on monolingual populations. (Ní Ghréacháin, 2021)[49]

The fundamental problem is that the Irish state has been over-reliant on a top-down, education-driven language revival. This is too great a burden for the education system to bear. It should have been accompanied by a far greater attempt to encourage socialisation in and through Irish, which may yet be encouraged by a renewed emphasis on usage. Significantly Gaeloideachas has developed interactive online resources for schools and their communities to promote the socialisation of Irish in the Irish-medium school/Gaeltacht school. This has been developed in recognition of the challenge Irish faces as a natural, organic choice of language between children in the IME setting, outside of formal learning.[50]

---

[48] Please see the website: https://gaeloideachas.ie/special-education/.
[49] www.cogg.ie/wp-content/uploads/an-tumoideachas-bua-no-dua.pdf.
[50] https://gaeloideachas.ie/beatha-teanga/.

Should this happen then Ní Mhóráin would feel more confident that a greater proportion of those who learn Irish will become active new speakers and thereby reinforce the faltering social networks and employment opportunities. Professional development would be an obvious target for language promotion, but even in those areas which have managed to establish an Irish qualification there has been a slippage in the past generation. Thus COGG is active in interventions in the field of Irish-medium professional training, as illustrated by its submission to the Legal Services Regulatory Authority Education on the education and training of legal practitioners.[51] In accordance with the Legal Practitioners (Irish Language) Act 2008, a high-quality course and qualification in the Irish language, covering both written and spoken language, was established and was to be made available to those wishing to undertake the course in order to enable themselves to operate through the medium of Irish in the courts.

However, in 2020 it had recourse to write to the Regulatory Authority advising that COGG:

recommends that the Irish-language courses and the awarding of this qualification be maintained in order to ensure that barristers and solicitors are available for those wishing to conduct their business through the medium of Irish. This would also provide recognition to those with a high standard of Irish acquired from the home or school and give them an opportunity to use the language professionally. *An Chomhairle um Oideachas Gaeltachta agus Gaelscolaíochta* also recommends that a policy be implemented in relation to the appointment of a sufficient number of Irish-speaking judges to the various courts. (COGG, 27 January 2020; Ní Mhóráin, pers. comm., 2020).

There is no lack of organisations to support Irish language activities, such as Conradh na Gaeilge and Gael Linn, but there is a need to provide greater opportunities for speakers to engage with Irish affairs, such as the successful Gaelchultúr-organised courses and events. Having been established in 2004 to promote Irish culture, including music, song and dance, Gaelchultúr also provides Irish language courses and learning resources, such as the e-learning website ranganna.com, which is aimed at those with an interest in Irish worldwide.

The New Speaker Experience

In my investigations it was evident that the new speaker term was interpreted in a number of ways. Professor Liam Mac Mathúna of DCU has suggested that 'new speakers of Irish' refers to people who speak Irish regularly but who were not raised with Irish in the Gaeltacht.[52] His view is that

---

[51] www.lsra.ie/wp-content/uploads/2020/11/ACOG-S33-Submission-AR2019-English.pdf.
[52] Ag tacú le 'nuachainteoirí': Ag tógáil Líonraí agus Pobal Gaeilge taobh amuigh den Ghaeltacht / Supporting 'new speakers': Building Irish Language Networks and Communities outside the Gaeltacht. Cruinniú geallsealbhóirí /Stakeholders' meeting, 14 October 2016, Trinity College, Dublin.

in Ireland the term is evidently intended to distinguish the Irish speakers in question from (1) those who acquire Irish as a first language via intergenerational transmission in the traditional Irish-speaking communities of the Gaeltacht, and (2) the unsatisfactory labelling of all other Irish speakers as 'learners'. However, its suitability and consequent usefulness as a term are weakened by the wide range of its application.

- Irish speakers from Gaeltacht areas, who did not speak the language in the family home
- a small number of first / second / third / fourth generation L1 speakers of Irish from elsewhere in the country, who were/are being brought up with Irish as their first language in families where e.g., the grandparents – be they Gaeltacht reared themselves or not – chose Irish as their household tongue as far back as the revival period (1900–1920)
- other regular speakers of Irish.

(Mac Mathúna, pers. comm., 2021)

The most authoritative statements on new speakers are contained in the *Research Report on New Speakers of Irish* (Walsh, O'Rourke and Rowland, 2015) and the *New Speakers of Irish in a Global Context* volume by O'Rourke and Walsh (2020). Together they provide a critical context by which to calibrate how decision makers and others perceive the utility of the new speaker category for policy formulation.

Typically, the new speaker of Irish acquires the language through bilingual or immersion education, or the acquisition occurs because of language reinforcement programmes or courses for adult learners, and the following structural characteristics may be noted:

The majority of new speakers acquire Irish outside of the home, usually in the education system. There are some speakers who have active competence in Irish because it was spoken to them at home, or because both English and Irish were spoken to them, but Irish was not the language of the community in their vicinity i.e., people raised with Irish outside the Gaeltacht (traditional Irish-speaking districts). Other new speakers come from a Gaeltacht background, i.e. they heard Irish spoken traditionally by relatives or neighbours, but Irish was not spoken to them at home. New speakers often acquire Irish to a high level of competence i.e., level B2 or higher of the Common European Framework of Reference for Languages. Although many new speakers use Irish regularly during their life, the sociolinguistic context may restrict that usage. An integral part of the concept is the efforts new speakers make to increase the range of uses in which they speak Irish outside of educational contexts. (Walsh, O'Rourke and Rowland, 2015)[53]

The investigation reveals that new speakers of Irish are from a variety of sociolinguistic backgrounds, in terms of both family upbringing and experience of the education system. Many attended English-medium schools, but several report that they had inspirational Irish teachers. New speakers report defining changes towards the use of Irish at various points in their lives, for instance

---

[53] See www.cost.eu/COST_Actions/isch/Actions/IS1306 and www.nspk.org.uk/.

because of Gaeltacht visits or while attending university. Depending on their competence and dedication, new speakers use Irish in different ways. Some depend on conversation groups to speak Irish occasionally, but others use Irish as the family language with their children. The Gaeltacht is important to the new speakers, but their opinions regarding how important or authoritative the traditional dialects spoken there vary. Some new speakers believe that they do not have the same degree of ownership of Irish as Gaeltacht communities. The new speakers also have varying opinions about the government's language policy for Irish. Some demand language rights emphatically, while others prefer to expend their efforts on speaking Irish socially (Walsh, O'Rourke and Rowland, 2015).[54]

A specific feature for comparative analysis is the Irish concern with categorising Gaeltacht and non-Gaeltacht speakers. There may be valid historical and sociolinguistic justifications for the persistence of this differentiation, but for new speakers the marker by which they are often judged is the competence of native speakers within the Gaeltacht rather than their contemporaries in largely urban settings. Warnings of the collapse and disappearance of the Gaeltacht communities by experts such as Dr Brian Ó Curnáin, Professor Conchúr Ó Giollagáin and others make it even more difficult for new speakers to avail themselves of the advantages of inhabiting (even for a short time) predominantly Irish-speaking communities, let alone having a template on offer by which they may calibrate their idiomatic and natural use of the language.[55]

Others are of the view that such warnings are exaggerated, for Seán Ó Cuirreáin argues that 'The collapse or disappearance hasn't been to such an extent or such speed over the past 10–20 years that there is no Gaeltacht left for new speakers to take advantage of. We're still here! Should it arise it would obviously make it more difficult then for new speakers' (Ó Cuirreáin, pers. comm., 2021).

However, it is worth asking to what extent the official Gaeltacht designation assists in the implementation of economic and regional development and community co-creation. The Gaeltacht areas (Figure 5.2) by 2016 reveal a fragmented pattern which intuitively militates against co-ordinated action, despite the efforts of government departments, other state agencies, such as Foras and Údarás na Gaeltachta, and community organisations. An abiding concern is to what extent Gaeltacht and non-Gaeltacht areas are pitched the one against the other in terms of public investment, political capital, inspiration for learners and new speakers. Would new, more radical ideologies and discourses salve or exacerbate such historical divisions? Can language

---

[54] See www.cost.eu/COST_Actions/isch/Actions/IS1306 and www.nspk.org.uk/.
[55] www.irishtimes.com/topics/topics-7.1213540?article=true&tag_person=Brian+O+Curnain; www.cogg.ie/wp-content/uploads/Linguistic-Study-of-the-Use-of-Irish-in-the-Gaeltacht.pdf.

The New Speaker Experience   191

officials develop more holistic, seamless policies which attest to the continuum of experiences one may gain from such a diverse range of locales wherever one is resident?

In seeking to integrate the findings of their work into national strategies the Walsh, O'Rourke and Rowland report reminds us that the 20-Year Strategy for

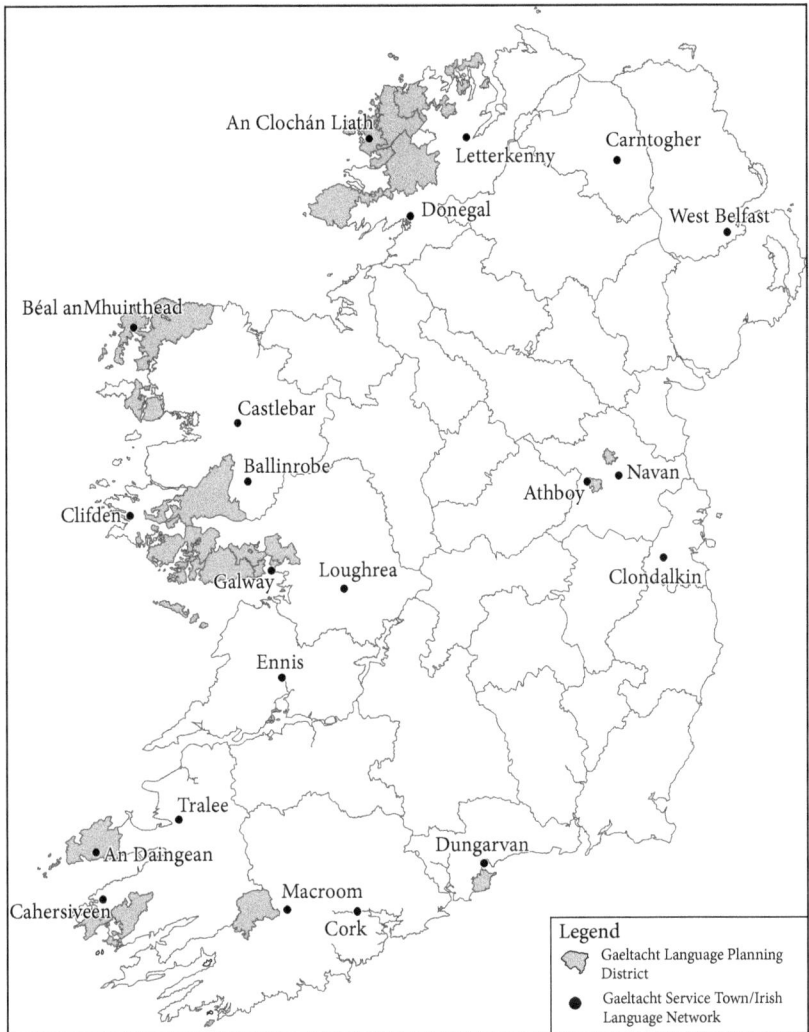

Figure 5.2 Gaeltacht Language Planning Districts and Service Towns (By permission of John Walsh, University of Galway)

the Irish Language states that the 'objective of Government policy in relation to Irish is to increase on an incremental basis the use and knowledge of Irish as a community language. Specifically, the Government's aim is to ensure that as many citizens as possible are bilingual in both Irish and English. It is an integral component of the Government's Irish language policy that close attention be given to its place in the Gaeltacht, particularly in light of research which indicates that the language's viability as a household and community language in the Gaeltacht is under threat.'

The aim of Government policy is also to:

- increase the number of families throughout the country who use Irish as the daily language of communication.
- provide linguistic support for the Gaeltacht as an Irish-speaking community and to recognise the issues which arise in areas where Irish is the household and community language.
- ensure that in public discourse and in public services the use of Irish or English will be, as far as practical, a choice for the citizen to make and that over time more and more people throughout the State will choose to do their business in Irish; and
- ensure that Irish becomes more visible in our society, both as a spoken language by our citizens and also in areas such as signage and literature. (Government of Ireland, 2010, p. 3).

In seeking to highlight the specific requirements of new speakers within this overarching strategy, the report recommends that the Irish language policy and planning system:

- Support the creation of more language 'safe spaces' where Irish can be spoken socially. Such spaces should cater for a variety of levels and backgrounds from those with limited competence to speakers closer to the expert category.
- Strengthen the existing network of '*ciorcail chomhrá*' [conversation circles] and create a wide variety of new social spaces for Irish in cities and towns. Such spaces should range from physical Irish language centres to Irish language activities in other places not normally associated with the language.
- Action the 'resource centres' for Irish in the main cities as advocated in the 20-Year Strategy (Government of Ireland, 2010, p. 25).
- Inform potential new speakers about how to integrate themselves into existing Irish-speaking networks. Ongoing curricular reform of Irish at second and third level should include pedagogical material for students offering them guidance about how to join such networks.
- Action the educational proposals in the 20-Year Strategy such as part-immersion and significant reform of teacher training which have the potential to produce larger numbers of new speakers (Government of Ireland, 2010, pp. 23–36).

- Seek to reduce new speakers' social anxiety about speaking Irish and boost levels of confidence in their ability to communicate effectively with Gaeltacht speakers. Policy initiatives should emphasise the fact that becoming an Irish speaker does not necessarily mean adopting a traditional variety and that other competent speakers could act as role models for potential new speakers.
- Improve awareness among both new and Gaeltacht speakers alike of different types of speakers including traditional speakers and the various profiles of new speakers which obtain.
- Reconceptualise what it means to be an Irish speaker in the twenty-first century, through messages imparted via the school curricula and media representations.
- Initiate a series of properly funded awareness, broadcast and social media campaigns as has happened in other minority language contexts such as Catalonia (see for instance Plataforma per la Llengua 2010) so as to highlight the personal accounts of new speakers of Irish which could be used to inspire potential new speakers.[56]
- Increase the government's financial support for local language-planning initiatives in the Gaeltacht as mandated in the Gaeltacht Act 2012.
- Take cognisance of the experience and requirements of new speakers when designing and implementing the 'Irish-language networks' outside the Gaeltacht.

(modified from Walsh, O'Rourke and Rowland, 2015)

Thus, a good number of recommendations exist in the system, but how well diffused are they and are the stakeholders ready and willing to implement them?

When these proposals were discussed with senior civil and public servants, the response was that, while nominally sound, the real difficulty with such recommendations was in their implementation, the allocation of support measures to different agencies and the evaluation of outcomes as a result of such interventions. These are all credible reactions by public servants who have to make difficult policy and resource decisions and one of the challenges for new speaker advocates is to provide robust arguments and to detail both short- and long-term actions by which such measures are to be put in place.

Some have championed the role of IT and AI in providing bilingual and multilingual services, while others argue that there is a dearth of formal settings (e.g., negotiating state services) where Irish can now be used. The situation would have been better in the past, when one physically entered an office and face-to-face contact required a competent Irish speaker to deliver the service. It

---

[56] It was observed that the absence of such high-profile campaigns is a major weakness in Irish language policy at present.

is acknowledged that phone contact was more problematic, while the switch from talking by phone to emails has moved the goalposts and the greater use of IT in the future may herald a new dawn of language equality but actually reduce the need for a large number of competent bilinguals to operate a system.

Testing the Waters: The Stakeholders' Perspective

How well established is the new speaker phenomenon and how do those responsible for promoting Irish perceive its utility as an operational concept? To ascertain the views and current practice of stakeholders a meeting was convened in Dublin on 14 October 2016. It was intended to provide a state-of-the-art overview as to where official bodies and civil society representatives believed they were headed in relation to the promotion of Irish and to ascertain to what extent the new speaker phenomenon would figure in their thinking and plans. Accordingly, this was the first opportunity for an open discussion with groups that are promoting Irish outside the Gaeltacht and who work for the most part with new speakers of Irish, but who were not raised with Irish in the Gaeltacht.[57]

The New Speakers Network invited representatives of Irish Language Networks and groups interested in applying for status as Gaeltacht Service Towns to discuss the challenges and opportunities associated with this initiative. As reported in Walsh and O'Rourke (2016) representatives of Foras na Gaeilge and Údarás na Gaeltachta were present to explain the background to the Networks and Gaeltacht Service Towns and to share experience of language planning in the Gaeltacht. This was a prescient move as there has subsequently been poor integration between Scéim Phobail Gaeilge and the new Irish Language Networks, which remains the subject of a dispute between the Networks and Foras na Gaeilge. Representatives of Glór na nGael and An Droichead in Belfast also addressed the meeting, as did I to reflect on the Welsh and Irish experiences from a comparative perspective.[58]

A lack of a shared consensus as to how to deal with new speakers prompted many in the meeting to welcome engagement with language planning bodies and to begin to formulate recommendations as to how they could put Irish language networks in place. 'A reason for accepting the invitation to participate in the workshop was that as language officers, they were dealing with these questions in their everyday roles. The participants at the workshop all saw

---

[57] Ag tacú le 'nuachainteoirí': Ag tógáil Líonraí agus Pobal Gaeilge taobh amuigh den Ghaeltacht / Supporting 'new speakers': Building Irish Language Networks and Communities outside the Gaeltacht. Cruinniú geallsealbhóirí /Stakeholders' meeting. 14 October 2016, Trinity College, Dublin.

[58] Cruinniú geallsealbhóirí/Stakeholders' meeting, 14 October 2016, Coláiste na Tríonóide/ Trinity College, Dublin.

themselves as having central roles in putting in place a strategy on how to set up a network in their local areas' (Walsh and O'Rourke, 2018b).

Clearly many salient challenges emerged and may be enumerated as follows:
- a lack of confidence among speakers in the community as well as low levels of competence in Irish
- the low presence of Irish in many of the communities where they were working
- the lack of physical spaces in which learners would feel comfortable and able to express their needs
- difficulties in getting younger age-groups involved and catering specifically for their needs (Walsh and O'Rourke, 2018b)

This is a remarkable situation given the long history of civil society involvement with Irish language promotion and learning. It is as if the momentum has bypassed the needs of advanced learners and new speakers within the strategic planning considerations.

Given these challenges, the notion of establishing a range of Irish language networks was enthusiastically endorsed. It was seen as a mechanism by which the language could be brought back to the people and as a means of encouraging its broader use. New opportunities for using Irish in sport, music and cultural activities were much needed. The Irish Language Network initiative was also considered as a way of providing learning opportunities for children whose parents were supportive of the language and were actively seeking provision for their children. In sum, the participants saw the initiative as a way of rethinking what spaces can be identified or created to facilitate those within the communities to hear Irish and to speak it. Clearly then Irish speakers would benefit from such developments, but was there a particular set of ideas as to how new speakers might be drawn into such initiatives, and should there be additional or supplementary opportunities targeted at their needs? In short was the new speaker concept generally understood and could it be used as a means of informing fresh policy initiatives?

Of the fourteen representatives, twelve said they were familiar with the concept of 'new speaker'. For some it was useful because it was seen to give recognition to learners and people who had taken up the language. Others said it was useful because it was easier to understand and a clearer term than '*Gaeilgeoir*' (literally 'Irish speaker' but a term that can carry other often conflicting meanings) or 'L2' as examined by O'Rourke and Walsh (2018). They saw it as conferring a better status on Irish speakers outside of the Gaeltacht (Walsh and O'Rourke, 2018b). It could also be counted as a more positive appellation, useful in boosting the confidence levels of the communities in question.

Others expressed concern that introducing yet another operative term might lead to further divisions as it might exacerbate the split between Gaeltacht and non-Gaeltacht speakers, which had long bedevilled some language activist interventions. The origins of the split go back to the foundation of the state where Gaeltacht residents were put on a pedestal as the authentic representation of Gaeldom, even if so many others throughout the country were equally proficient speakers and discerningly representative of Irish culture, economic practice, political fortitude and ideological commitment. A follow up illustrative comment expressing disquiet runs thus:

> I have to admit, I don't feel I can identify with the term new-speaker, even though I am a 'learner' of Irish, as opposed to a native speaker. I have committed my life to the language in my career and as the language of our home. I do think it could be divisive or misleading as a term but perhaps there are different titles/categories of speaker under that umbrella term that I'm not aware of and that would fit the range of contexts more aptly. (Ní Ghréacháin, pers. comm., 2021)

Another representative considered it relatively useful as long as it was not overused and not rendered meaningless, as has happened to the term globalisation. This sentiment was repeated often in the discussions and interviews carried out as part of my research project and it would appear that for some the vagueness of the new speaker concept was a stumbling block which obfuscated programmes targeted essentially at learners. It was also seen by some as a diversion which took attention away from the relative failure of government engagement in Irish language promotion.

One of the salient features of the stakeholder discussion was the realisation that so few professionals knew what their colleagues were achieving in detail as regards meeting the needs of advanced learners and new speakers. This became clear in reaction to a series of presentations by government bodies and civil society agencies which indicated the extent to which recent initiatives were seeking to mitigate the lack of robust social networks, the absence of language safe places and the neglect of the more marginalised elements of the Irish-speaking community.

Dr Gearóid Trimble of Foras na Gaeilge described the initiatives his organisation undertook in in relation to increasing the number of Irish speakers, in particular the designation of Gaeltacht Service Towns (towns of strategic importance for language planning either near or within the Gaeltacht), the establishment of Irish Language Networks and the rollout of countywide language plans in counties containing a Gaeltacht area. Five Irish Language Networks have been selected under the Gaeltacht Act and twenty-two Irish Language Community Schemes are already funded by Foras na Gaeilge (Walsh and O'Rourke, 2016).

Máire Ní Mhainnín of Údarás na Gaeltachta spoke about her organisation's experience of language planning in the Gaeltacht, which had focussed on preserving and supporting those communities that speak Irish as the community language. It was accepted that less attention had been devoted to the significant numbers of people in the Gaeltacht who do not speak Irish or who are learning it, namely the potential new speakers. There has been a campaign to create more accessible learning activities to help such people integrate into existing language communities. However, the language planning process highlights several challenges, including its high dependency on volunteers and the need to convert sympathetic non-daily users in the Gaeltacht to daily users. There is also the issue of mastering proficiency in Irish; traditionally learners were treated with a degree of impatience and annoyance. How this behaviour could be modified was deemed to be urgent as it represented a significant barrier to the integration of new speakers in Gaeltacht areas.

There followed brief presentations by representatives of the five Irish Language Networks that have been designated under the Gaeltacht Act 2012. Eoghan Mac Cormaic spoke on behalf of Gaeilge Locha Riach (Co. Galway). Initially it was established in 1999 to co-ordinate a campaign for the establishment of a Gaelscoil in the town. The area was Irish speaking until the early twentieth century and there were relics of Irish in local speech and many older residents had been educated through Irish. Forty shops took part in a scheme to promote Irish and erected signage if staff were able to speak the language. In 2001 they employed their first Development Officer and achieved funding under the Scéim Pobail Ghaeilge (Irish-Language Community Scheme) of Foras na Gaeilge. This funding continued until 2016 but was then discontinued. They have produced bilingual newsletters, initiated other local activities and expanded their space to open a library. Without continued funding these new facilities were deemed to be at risk and the community basis for sustaining an Irish Language Network would wither away.

Dónall Ó Loingsigh spoke on behalf of An Clár as Gaeilge (Ennis, Co. Clare). He pointed out that their involvement in the Language Network initiative stemmed from the town's success in the Glór na nGael competition as well as the strong reputation for the use of the Irish language in the town. The workload was large, so it was decided to set up permanent administration centre with a full-time employee. The key tenets linked to the role were to:
1. Enhance the status of Irish in the county and to make sure that local authorities were able to provide services in Irish as well as making the public aware of such services.
2. Encourage Irish speakers to use the language more frequently and to increase take-up in the use of Irish for public services.

3. Focus on young people to generate enthusiasm for Irish and take Irish out of the classroom.
4. Increase the visibility of the language, particularly in the town of Ennis, through a proper policy of public signage.
5. Develop the use of Irish in the private sector, such as the promotion of shopping in Irish in Ennis.

Brian Ó Gaibhín spoke on behalf of Muintir Chrónáin, Clondalkin in west Dublin. Due to local *Gaelscoileanna* a new generation of Irish speakers had been created, but the challenge was to create opportunities for them to use Irish on a daily basis both in and out of a school environment. In the 1980s a committee was formed to promote Irish and an Irish language centre, Áras Chrónáin, was set up in the heart of the village. Muintir Chrónáin have representation on various organisations and councils such as South Dublin Chamber of Commerce, sporting groups and youth groups. Continuity of efforts is very important, but their biggest challenge is funding. Nevertheless, the establishment of a 'language safe space' and a 'one-stop shop' for the promotion of Irish in the local community was an important step forward and one which could be imitated elsewhere in non-Gaeltacht locales.

Feargal Mac Ionnrachtaigh and Piaras Mac Alasdair addressed the meeting on behalf of Forbairt Feirste in west Belfast. Forbairt Feirste is located within two of the five poorest wards in Northern Ireland. Irish language initiatives have been active in the area since the 1960s and there has been much grassroots activity without any support from the state until recently. There has been an exponential rise in the social use Irish in social, sporting and youth clubs, but less focus on the sociolinguistic dynamics. Various capital projects in Belfast have included the west of the city but there is a need to work out how to maximise the sociolinguistic benefit of such projects as there has been an absence of language planning to date. Forbairt Feirste sought to develop a language action plan but it was claimed that there was no funding available from Foras na Gaeilge to drive it forward. Once again, we are presented with the old conundrum: opportunities are being created, funding is limited, outputs are monitored but outcomes in the form of linguistic switching to Irish are neither planned for nor evaluated on a regular basis. Since 2016 funding has been agreed and the current discussion is about how exactly it is to be allocated.

Liam Ó Flannagáin spoke on behalf of the Carn Tóchair project in Co. Derry. Faced with socio-economic deprivation in the 1990s the community came together and decided to use the Irish language as the main driver of development. They don't use the term 'new speakers' as the break in the chain of transmission is very small. These are not entirely new communities of Irish speakers as the Census of 1901 shows that many people's grandparents were themselves native speakers. Therefore, this is a former Gaeltacht area that is on its way back. They identified Irish-medium education as the tool to create vibrant populations of new speakers. Former pupils of the local school came back to teach there and to work in the community, leading to greater community cohesion. They purchased the local post office business as a community enterprise and opened a bookshop and library service. They also strongly emphasise sustainability in their community development efforts, have developed an organic farm and promote Irish language cultural tourism in the area. This appears to be an excellent example where ecological thinking, sustainable development and Irish language promotion are working hand in hand.

Frainc Mac Cionnaith of Glór na nGael spoke about the language-planning issues that have come to the fore as a result of the continued process of language shift. Glór na nGael is the lead national organisation tasked with promoting Irish as the family language. However, despite their myriad activities it was argued that the details of their role in the language-planning process have not been made entirely clear. Currently the organisation's work involves a new scheme, Teanga Tí, to support the use of Irish in Gaelscoil communities. The scheme provides funding of up to €900 per school to support the organisation of events for participating families. In 2016 Glór na nGael published a national strategy to support the Irish language as a family language, *Towards a Strategic Plan for Irish as a Family Language*.[59]

Pól Deeds, director of An Droichead Irish language centre in South Belfast, argued that their experience is typical: a small group of parents wanted to develop a Gaelscoil and then realised that it would take more to develop an Irish-speaking community. An Droichead developed significantly with the assistance of multiple funders but there was a danger of mission drift due to the variety of funding sources. By 2013 they were concerned that many of their strategic goals did not relate strongly enough to the Irish language, so the goals were overhauled to reflect the core aim which was community building work and outreach.

There followed a presentation in which I outlined the comparative lessons to be gleaned from the Welsh and Irish experiences. In advance of the meeting, I had circulated the following discussion questions related to potential Irish developments:

1. Is there a sufficiently proven 'community involvement and engagement' element in the formulation and implementation of Irish language policy?
2. What would it take to turn the recent initiative on Irish Language Networks into self-sustaining nodes of Irish language vitality?
3. How does one maximise the opportunities for, and involvement of new speakers in a wide variety of sociolinguistic networks?

---

[59] www.glornangael.ie/wp-content/uploads/2016/10/An-Strait%C3%A9is-Teaghlach.pdf.

4. What types of locations in practical terms would constitute the language 'safe spaces' for new speakers of Irish as recommended in Walsh et al. (2015)?
5. How is it possible to guarantee more attention to outcome-based behavioural change when the structural tendency for organisations is to focus on administrative and institutional processes?

Several of the participants took the opportunity to reflect on these questions; for example, Mac Cionnaith commented that some groups fully understand the integration of community, business and language development but warned that 'the potential benefits of the projects are often flying under the radar of the business community'. To better realise these initiatives, it was necessary to develop strong leadership skills to animate the Irish Language Networks; to encourage broad support across the community as such networks needed full community buy-in and, of course, all agreed that greater investment on the part of government was essential to the long-term success of these ventures. Currently too little finance was awarded to create realistic and viable plans. A further issue was the fragmentation inherent in the system as there would appear to be little sharing of good practice across different networks. A third issue was the dynamic nature of the communities which language officers sought to serve and shape.[60]

Participants discussed ideas to take several initiatives forward. These included taking stock of who can speak Irish in their community, what are their needs, what is being doing already, who identifies as a new speaker and why, etc. Most agreed that the onus was on the community sector to impress upon Foras na Gaeilge what should be delivered on the ground and called for community groups to come together and present their needs. It was decided that Oireachtas na Gaeilge provided a good opportunity to share best practice and thoughts on where to go from here and Foras na Gaeilge spoke of organising other information events which would bring Irish Language Networks together to discuss planning and to share good practice.

Two strong recommendations emerged during the meeting, namely that:
- the language be presented to people in a way that makes sense to them so that they could see Irish as something that is embedded in their own lives and surroundings; and
- funding and support be advocated for in support of Irish language networks in Northern Ireland.

Suggestions for further developments included planning for an event where people could meet and speak to new speakers of Irish and listen to their stories

---

[60] 'This was seen as not something specific to the Irish context but was also the case in Wales and in other minority language communities across Europe. Prof. Williams pointed out that in Wales there is no is longer a Welsh speaking community, but instead we have Welsh speakers within communities' (Walsh and O'Rourke, 2017).

and to the challenges they may have. Other suggestions were to guarantee more time for reflection, discussion and formulation of new avenues for action. The organisers recognised that the new speakers featured in these discussions were significant examples of people who have converted support for Irish into an actual use of it. A recurring theme in the data relates to the difficulties involved in making that transition. Thus, it was recommended that:

- policy measures be developed to support people who wish to move beyond being learners of Irish to becoming active new speakers
- existing new speakers be offered additional supports in their efforts to increase their competence in Irish and their use of it
- additional research be undertaken on the various profiles and trajectories of new speakers of Irish from a comparative perspective (Walsh and O' Rourke, 2018b)

It is recognised that the number of people who make the transition to becoming new speakers is quite small so that further research is required to understand the ideologies and identities of these speakers and their potential role in the future development of Irish. Very little is known about the larger group of potential new speakers who appear to have the will to speak Irish but have not yet undergone a *muda*.

What we do know about *muda* is largely the result of work by Walsh and O' Rourke (2014) and Puigdevall, Walsh, Amorrortu and Ortega (2018). These researchers have identified seven types of *muda* transition, which reflect different stages in a life cycle, where individuals adopt more Irish into their linguistic repertoire and/or report 'becoming' new speakers of Irish: namely (1) primary/secondary school *muda*; (2) Gaelscoil *muda*; (3) Gaeltacht *muda*; (4) university *muda*; (5) family *muda*; (6) work *muda*; and (7) retirement *muda*. Insights into each of these types were gleaned from a sample of fifty participants who were asked to describe what happens when a *muda* takes place. Some report tension between learners and native speakers, some relish passing as a native speaker and others celebrate their command of regular use of Irish even if that means a less traditional variety. We will illustrate each in turn. G1 criticised other weaker learners for not attempting to imitate Gaeltacht speech:

G1: I don't like the way that learners treat native speakers sometimes // em some of them people who are líofa lofa [fluent but highly inaccurate] as they say, complain that people aren't willing to talk to them in Irish and, eh I would understand why the native speakers wouldn't be willing to suffer them because I suppose they are tired of dealing with people like them em.

I: What do you mean líofa lofa?

G1: Eh I suppose people who are interested in the language and, but perhaps don't have enough interest to learn it correctly, em and they often try to show off how much Irish they have but em despite the fact that they have so little really, people who aren't too thoughtful I suppose about the language but em that's one group. (G1, male, 28, interview)

Others cited the satisfaction of being thought of as a native speaker:

People sometimes thought I was a native speaker and always if I'm asked a question directly, no I'm not a native speaker, I don't know if anyone from [the area where he learned Irish] thinks I'm a native speaker but people from other places [do] and perhaps that gives you more freedom if people think you're a native speaker, that you // can do you what you like with it. (J3, male, 27, interview)

While others aspired to emulate a Gaeltacht speaker, others took pride in asserting their 'Dublin Irish':

so sin é you know I am not from the Gaeltacht you know, I was never living there, I have Dublin Irish, so that's it you know. (B1, female, 40s, interview)

The authors observe that, in contrast to Catalan, 'mudes may be less dramatic and more incremental, reflecting the language's relatively weak sociolinguistic presence. In other words, speakers may refer to a number of mudes during their lives, each representing a cumulative improvement in their ability in Irish' (Walsh and O'Rourke, 2014, p. 6). A second insight is the strong relationship between experiencing the *muda* journey and the significance of education, particularly in relation to Irish as a core school subject and for many a university period of increased linguistic awareness. The role of the Gaeltacht is relatively unique as a touchstone, in comparison to Y Fro Gymraeg in Wales, for example, for while new speakers

hold the traditional speech of the Gaeltacht in high esteem ... there is tension between this overt ideology and practice, due to variations in the extent to which even highly competent new speakers adhere to traditional Gaeltacht norms. Less competent speakers report less exposure or contact with the Gaeltacht and a traditional Gaeltacht variety, but aspirations to becoming a 'better' speaker and an 'expert speaker' are also linked to acquisition of Gaeltacht varieties. (Walsh and O'Rourke, 2014, p. 7)

More recent observations on the experience of *muda* has been presented in O'Rourke and Walsh (2020), but the essentials are the same with additional information on the intersection of linguistic and sexual identities, the production of linguistic resources and a recognition that diversity now characterises the community of practice of Irish speakers.

Looking beyond conventional social interaction, increasing attention is being paid to the application of AI and IT to create new opportunities to use Irish. While the digital divide between English and Irish is well recognised, there are encouraging examples of how IT and digital applications have widened the practical use of Irish in many situations. Speech and braille applications are now becoming more widespread and Professor Ailbhe Ní Chasaide of the Phonetics and Speech Laboratory (CLCS), Trinity College, Dublin argues that the synthesis systems developed under the ABAIR project hold out great promise for the further development of machine-assisted learning and communication.[61] Cabóigín I developed an Ulster voice, while Cabógaí II developed a Connaught voice (Ráth Chairn) and a voice for Munster Irish (Dingle Peninsula). A digital plan for the Irish language, which would improve its online presence, includes a new Irish language section on RTÉ Player and a new RTÉ Irish language app for children. This initiative, funded by the Department of Culture, Heritage and the Gaeltacht,[62] was welcomed by the community and was seen as a means of breathing new life into the 20-Year Strategy for the Irish Language.[63]

Irish Language Schemes and Regulatory Compliance

We saw in the previous chapter that Bórd na Gaidhlig officers considered the language plans as a powerful instrument through which new opportunities could be created for speakers to engage in meaningful and often formal activities. The same might be said of the Irish language schemes, for they have transformed the linguistic landscape of public administration, despite the weaknesses identified above. Concerning the implementation of language rights as opposed to statutory responsibilities, Williams and Walsh (2019) have detailed the limited requirements related to the language competence of public bodies serving the Gaeltacht, but only as part of Irish language schemes (Section 13 (2)), and they observe there is no obligation on the state to make Irish its primary language when dealing with Gaeltacht residents. It is evident that only a limited number of unambiguous rights are conferred on Irish speakers in relation to the use of Irish in the Oireachtas and the courts (Sections 6 and 8), and for the most part the success of the legislation is dependent on the extent to which public bodies comply with their obligations. Regulating the observance of the suite of rights is the function of the Language Commissioner, an independent office which was established as a result of the passage of the 2003 Official Language Act. An Coimisinéir Teanga (Oifig Choimisinéir na dTeangacha Oifigiúla) discharges regulatory functions monitoring compliance and providing an ombudsman and advisory service on rights and obligations. The promotional remit falls to Foras na Gaeilge.

---

[61] Presentation to the Language Revitalization conference held at Cambridge University, 2 July 2019. Cabóigín I's goal was to develop a full-fledged Text-to-Speech synthesis system for Irish and was funded by Foras na Gaeilge. It built on foundational research done in the WISPR (Welsh and Irish Speech Processing Resources) project funded by the European Union under the INTERREG IIIA programme. The research was conducted in cooperation with Bangor University, Dublin City University, University College Dublin and the Linguistics Institute of Ireland.
[62] www.abair.tcd.ie/en/background/.
[63] www.irishtimes.com/news/ireland/irish-news/government-launch-new-action-plan-for-irish-language-1.3548174.

The Commissioner's functions, powers and investigative processes are described in Part 4 of the Act. Section 21 outlines the Commissioner's six functions, which are: (a) to monitor how public bodies comply with the Act, (b) to take all measures within his or her authority to ensure compliance by public bodies; (c) to investigate complaints related to failures by public bodies to comply with the Act; (d) to provide advice or assistance to the public regarding their rights under the Act; (e) to provide advice or assistance to public bodies regarding their obligations under the Act; and (f) to investigate complaints related to failures by public bodies to comply with any other enactment regarding the status or use of an official language. Walsh has detailed how more than 150 pieces of legislation, other than the Official Languages Act, are covered by sub-section (f), a small number of which have far-reaching implications for language policy in fields such as education and broadcasting (Walsh, 2017). The time devoted to the advisory and compliance functions is roughly equal, although a stronger emphasis in recent years on the duties of public bodies (under Article 21 (e)) has led to an increase in the number of cases where advice is offered (Ó Domhnaill, pers. comm., 2016).

The powers of the Commissioner are outlined in Section 22 which stipulates that he or she may require that any person possessing information or records relevant to one of the Commissioner's functions appear before him or her, and that such a person must comply. Anyone who fails to do so or 'who hinders or obstructs the Commissioner in the performance of his or her functions shall be guilty of an offence and shall be liable on summary conviction to a fine not exceeding €2,000 or to imprisonment for a term not exceeding 6 months or both' (Section 22 (4)).

The Commissioner has some latitude to take the initiative in investigative proceedings and while this has not yet been exercised it is the Commissioner's view that periodically public bodies need to be reminded of this power (Ó Domhnaill, pers. comm., 2016).

Following an investigation into a complaint that a public body has failed to comply with the Act, the Commissioner in accordance with Section 26 will issue to the public body, the Minister and, if relevant, the complainant a written report and recommendations as appropriate. Failure to implement the recommendations may be reported to the Houses of the Oireachtas, as has happened on several occasions. Appeals may be made by any party to such investigations, under Section 28, but this has happened only once in over 100 investigations: an appeal by the Revenue Commissioners which the High Court rejected. Section 30 allows the Commissioner to publish reports on any investigation or other function and two such reports have emerged one regarding the weaknesses of the Act (2011) and the other a detailed analysis of Irish language schemes (2017) (Williams and Walsh, 2019).

The communitarian utopianism which Michael Cronin identifies in so much of the writing on Irish needs to be tempered by the forging of creative scenarios which are credible (Cronin, 2005, p. 57). In relation to new speaker needs several concrete policy proposals are in circulation which we shall consider in Chapter 9. The most critical relate to encouraging the transition process to support people who wish to move beyond being learners of Irish to becoming active new speakers. Such measures have been identified in the research report by Walsh, O'Rourke and Rowland (2015) and could include:

- The creation of more 'safe spaces' where Irish can be spoken socially. Such spaces should cater for a variety of levels and backgrounds from those with limited competence to speakers closer to the expert category. This would entail strengthening the existing network of *ciorcail chomhrá* [conversation circles] and creating a wide variety of new social spaces for Irish in cities and towns. Such spaces should range from physical Irish-language centres to Irish language activities in other places not normally associated with the language. The 20-Year Strategy refers to the need to develop 'resource centres' for Irish in the main cities (Government of Ireland 2010: 25) but at the time of writing no obvious progress had been made in that regard.
- Potential new speakers need to be informed about how to integrate themselves into existing Irish-speaking networks. Ongoing curricular reform of Irish at second and third level should include pedagogical material for students offering them guidance about how to join such networks.
- Educational proposals in the 20-Year Strategy, such as part-immersion and significant reform of teacher training, also have the potential to produce larger numbers of new speakers (Government of Ireland 2010: 23–36) but, while progress has been slow, significant developments have taken place in the areas of initial and post-graduate teacher education, and primary and post-primary curricula. Marino Institute of Education now offers a Bachelor in Education for Irish-medium Primary Education and Mary Immaculate College (University of Limerick) offers an Masters in Irish-medium and Gaeltacht Education.

The report illustrates how many new speakers suffer social anxiety about speaking Irish and have low levels of confidence in their ability to communicate effectively with Gaeltacht speakers. Policy initiatives should emphasise the fact that becoming an Irish speaker does not necessarily mean adopting a traditional variety and that other competent speakers could act as role models for potential new speakers.

- More awareness needs to be developed among both new and Gaeltacht speakers alike of different types of speakers including traditional speakers and the various profiles of new speakers outlined in the introduction to this report. This could be addressed in the school curricula and through broader media representations of what it means to be an Irish speaker in the 21st Century. Personal accounts of new speakers of Irish could be used to inspire potential new speakers. This could be done through properly funded awareness, broadcast and social media campaigns as has happened in other minority language contexts such as Catalonia (see for instance Plataforma per la Llengua 2010).

The absence of such high-profile campaigns is a major weakness in Irish language policy at present.
- New speakers clearly value the role of the Gaeltacht in providing social opportunities to learn, practice or improve their Irish and many of them believe the Gaeltacht is necessary for the future of Irish. The support offered to Gaeltacht communities to engage in language planning under the Gaeltacht Act 2012 is clearly inadequate. The government needs to greatly increase financial support for local language planning initiatives in the Gaeltacht far beyond the current paltry allocation.
- The Gaeltacht Act also pledges to recognise 'Irish-language networks' outside the Gaeltacht, many of which comprise new speakers similar to those featured in this report. It is crucial to consider the experiences and requirements of such new speakers when developing these Irish language networks. (Walsh, O'Rourke and Rowland, 2015)

The authors recognise that these recommendations form only a part of the policy portfolio as the number of people who make the transition to becoming new speakers is small while several new speakers achieve their aims sometimes in the face of significant obstacles. They recommend that additional research is required to understand the ideologies and identities of these speakers and their potential role in the development of Irish. O'Rourke and Walsh (2020) repeat the argument for the establishment of safe breathing spaces and harmonising authentic spaces to enable new speakers to represent themselves without let or hindrance and thereby boost their skills and confidence levels in cementing elements of social cohesion in society. Some may argue that the use of the term 'safe spaces' is too defensive in tone and implication, as if new speakers have to be protected rather than encouraged to be 'out there'. However, the analysis throughout underscores an element of anxiety which seems to pervade so many of the new speakers' interactions. Key policy recommendations related to the strengthening of Irish-medium networks and a telling reminder that the primacy of the Gaeltacht in the national discourse should not obfuscate the need for policy intervention and the allocation of additional resources, together with infrastructure development wherever Irish is spoken, provide an element of pragmatism sorely needed by current official discourse related to new speakers.

However, little is known about a larger group of potential new speakers who appear to have the will to speak Irish but have not yet undergone a *muda*. Some members of that group may even have relatively high levels of competence but lack the opportunity or the confidence to become new speakers. Much more research would be required to understand why this is the case and what can be done to resolve it (Walsh, O'Rourke and Rowland, 2015).

Educationalists and academics argued that the current teaching of Irish, especially at post-secondary level, was witnessing a substantial growth in numbers and that recruitment for teacher training was strong.[64] As a consequence,

---

[64] Interviews conducted with Ciarán Mac Murchaidh, Fiontar and educational colleagues at Dublin City University, 11–13 March 2018.

they saw great potential in harnessing educational programmes to strengthen the transitional phase for advanced learners becoming active new speakers. They did not shy away from the fact that many of the new speakers were limited in their capacities, registers and competence compared with native speakers. They also expressed some concern that so many of these new speakers undergoing teacher training, for example, at Dublin City University, would represent their form of Irish when engaged in the classroom and as a consequence child would pattern themselves on these new speakers rather than on the conventional teacher profile, many of whom were native speakers. This disquiet was countered by others who argued that Ireland had long experienced a mixture of teacher repertoires, styles and competences and the current situation was not a cause for alarm or disquiet. Quite the opposite, in fact, for they recognised that if Irish was to flourish it was only from the pool of advanced learners and new speakers that new growth, dynamism and innovation would come. My judgement is that there is a great deal of good will and practice regarding new speakers among civil society agencies but that for a variety of reasons, whether ideological, administrative or financial, the government departments are reticent to incorporate these practices as part of their official programmes and strategies. There is almost no discussion of new speakers of Irish among established politicians. This may well change during the medium term as it becomes better recognised that new speakers constitute a significant resource for the long-term vitality of the Irish-speaking community.

Official Languages (Amendment) Bill 2019

The Official Languages (Amendment) Bill 2019 passed all stages in Dáil Éireann (the Irish Parliament) on 6 October 2021 and moved for debate in November to Seanad Éireann (the Senate). The amending of the Official Languages Act 2003 was signalled in 2011, when the then Minister of State with responsibility for the Gaeltacht and Irish language issues announced a review of the act. The dominant narrative at the time was to reduce the obligations on state or public bodies to provide services in Irish.[65] However, a public consultation exercise which was dominated by Irish language activists suggested that the legislation should be strengthened rather than weakened. Despite overwhelming support for stronger legislation this was not reflected in the 'heads of a bill' which were produced. The amending legislation was presented as a Bill to the House of the Oireachtas (Parliament) on 11 December 2019. It progressed through parliament, reaching Committee Stage for section-by-section consideration on 8 October 2020. An extensive debate ensued with well over 300 amendments to the government's Bill tabled

---

[65] I am grateful to Seán Ó Cuirreáin for his advice on aspects of the Act's revision (Ó Cuirreáin, pers. comm., 2021).

primarily by opposition members. The debate lasted over twenty-five hours, in blocks of two hours due to Covid-19 restrictions, over a number of months. Many of the amendments were ruled out of order by the Bills Office for procedural reasons or rejected by the Minister of State responsible for Gaeltacht and Irish language issues.

The Minister of State, however, undertook to consider some of the proposed amendments before bringing the Bill back to Parliament for consideration at the Report Stage. The Minister tabled forty-nine new amendments to his own bill when the debate resumed on 6 October 2021, most of which were based on opposition amendments from the earlier committee stage debate. The opposition tabled a further 314 amendments. In a short debate limited to three hours the Minister's amendments were accepted and the opposition's rejected.

On 15 December 2021 the Official Languages (Amendment) Bill 2019 passed through Dáil Éireann (Houses of the Oireachtas, 2021).[66] As anticipated, the main provisions include increasing the number of Irish speakers recruited to the public service, such that by 2030, 20 per cent of new recruits will be Irish speakers; that state services will be provided through the medium of Irish in the Gaeltacht; and that all public offices located in a Gaeltacht area will operate through the medium of Irish. An Irish Language Services Advisory Committee has been established and will publish a National Plan for the provision of public services through the medium of Irish. The committee is dominated by civil and public servants but includes one representative from the Gaeltacht and one representative of Irish speakers from outside the Gaeltacht.

The legislation will terminate one of the main features of the Official Languages Act 2003 – namely, the language scheme system whereby public bodies were required to produce and implement language plans as to how they would increase their services through Irish over a period of time. Schemes will be replaced by a new language standards approach based on the Welsh model (Williams, 2013a; 2021b). The new legislation gives little detail on how the standards system will function but enables the Minister to create the standards by means of regulations.

All public bodies will be required to have 20 per cent of their advertising in Irish and 5 per cent of their advertising must be placed in Irish language media, defined as media whose content is at least 50 per cent in Irish. Public bodies will also require marketing material to be issued bilingually or in Irish and must reply in Irish on social media channels to queries in that language.

---

[66] 'The enactment of this Bill comes at a historic time in the life of the Irish language as the derogation on the use of Irish in the European Union institutions will end on 1 January 2022 – giving the language the same status in the Union as major European languages.' www.gov.ie/en/press-release/b82ac-historic-day-as-the-official-languages-bill-is-ready-for-enactment-by-the-president-of-ireland/.

The ability of public bodies to utilise the *síneadh fada* – the length accent on vowels in Irish similar to the French *accent aigu*, the acute accent – in names and addresses in databases and IT systems, long a bone of contention, is also addressed in the new legislation. The provision allows for the Minister to make regulations which will prescribe public bodies who will be required to make provisions for the use of the *síneadh fada*. No timescale is given or any indication in law as to how public bodies will be identified and prescribed for this purpose.

Other provisions will introduce the requirement for the use of Irish or bilingual logos by public bodies, and all new state agencies created after the commencement of the new legislation will have their names in Irish. Forms generally used by public bodies must in future be provide in Irish or bilingually in line with regulations to be made by the Minister.

Catherine Martin TD, Minister for Tourism, Culture, Arts, Gaeltacht, Sport and Media, stated that the passage of the Official Languages Bill was a historic day and the Minister of State Jack Chambers declared that 'a strong foundation has been laid to demonstrate real leadership in preserving the language for future generations' (Government of Ireland, 2021).

I asked Seán Ó Cuirreáin, the first Irish Language Commissioner, for his views on the amendments to the Act. He replied that:

There is no doubt but that the amending legislation strengthens the original 2003 Act and is a welcome sign that the current Government recognises the need for a change of approach which saw the language marginalised in many areas of the public sector. An example of this would be the attitude of the Health Service Executive – the largest public sector body in Ireland with a staff of over 100,000 – to disregard the Irish language during every stage of the Covid pandemic to all intents and purposes and communicate exclusively through English even in the Gaeltacht with only some very minor exceptions.

One of the most important amendments is the requirement to recruit a significant number of Irish speakers to the public service (20 per cent of new recruits by 2030), which if fully implemented could be seen as a 'game changer'. The requirement is not limited to the civil service (currently about 40,000 people) but to the much wider public sector (well over 300,000 people in around 600 public bodies). If this initiative were to succeed it would have a twinfold advantage in increasing those able to provide service through Irish and also encouraging students to focus on Irish in their education in order to increase their chances of appointment to public service positions.

It could be argued that requiring all public bodies, including those with little or no interaction with the public in general or with Irish speakers in particular, to employ a significant percentage of Irish speakers may lead to some 'push-back' when the legislation takes effect. The major challenge will be to find Irish speakers for these new positions. A commitment by An Garda Síochána (the police service) to reserve 10 per cent of recruitment places for fluent Irish speakers has failed to attract the numbers required, with only a handful of fluent speakers appointed in intakes of over 600 recruits at a time in recent years. The job of finding Irish speakers at a time when recruiting English speakers can prove difficult in some sectors may prove a challenge to the legislation unless the National Plan to be developed can find ways of addressing this matter.

The critical issues in relation to the amended legislation will centre on how the responsible department – the Department of Tourism, Culture, Arts, Gaeltacht, Sport and Media – will roll out and manage the many elements of the legislation which have been left to the creation of regulations by statutory instrument. The language standards system which will replace the language schemes has to be designed and implemented. It was a failure by that department (Gaeltacht) to manage the language schemes system which led to its effective collapse, with long delays in agreeing new schemes with public bodies and the rolling back of commitments made in previous schemes. Unless the new language standards system is straightforward, well communicated and carefully managed, there may be cause for concern in relation to the new system.

Overall, there is no doubt that the amended legislation is a step forward and it has the potential to make significant improvements. Creating legislation is not always the difficult task – implementing it is. The old Irish proverb '*Beart de réir briathair*' springs to mind. It might be translated as 'Actions to meet the promises or the Biblical quote "By their deeds you will know them"' (Ó Cuirreáin, pers. comm., 2021).

Conclusion

The passage of new legislation may indeed herald a new phase of the state's involvement in the promotion and protection of Irish and impact on a trend identified by John Walsh as 'the retreat of the State under the guise of partnership' (Walsh, 2021). His judgement is that the governance of the Irish language has been weakened by the partial transfer of responsibility to outside sources.

In a compelling discussion on language and ecology Cronin (2019) argues that

> The future lies with languages that can maximise diversity, alter human interaction with the non-human and reveal ways of being that are connected to the specificities of place but are open to the world. Irish is one of those languages of the future. The genuine pragmatists are those who look to the language for resources to build an alternative future, not the monolingual fantasists who would condemn us to an intolerable past in the name of an unsustainable future. (Cronin, 2019, p. 19)

This reasoning taps into the synergy which some language activists and environmentalists have forged over the past generation, myself included (Williams, 1991; 2002). Such holistic thought and practice are limited in government circles as the silo approach of departmental responsibility tends to inhibit overarching interventions. I titled this chapter as one of tempered acceptance of new speakers on behalf of many agencies, but Cronin warns that 'dismissive indifference' may be a more accurate future prospect: 'If many Irish speakers did indeed die during the wars of conquest at the end of a gun, they have experienced a second death at the end of the pen of dismissive indifference.' Unless a more holistic and radical reconceptualisation of Irish is adopted 'there is no future, only monocultures of extinction' (Cronin, 2019, p. 72).

This need not be the anticipated future as so many pin their hopes on new speakers strengthening the base of Irish vitality but developing new communities of practice remains a challenge. The solutions are rooted within Irish society, but some degree of best practice transfer may be gleaned from other contexts so let us turn our attention to how these issues are managed in the BAC and Navarre.

6 The Basque Autonomous Community and Navarre: Enthusiastic Endorsement

Introduction

In this and the next chapter I survey the extent to which policymakers and implementers are aware of the needs of new speakers within four constituent jurisdictions of the Spanish state and comment on the salience which this awareness has for the redesign and implementation of official language policy and planning.[1]

In the past decade new speaker research in the BAC, Navarre, Catalonia and Galicia has been energetic and fruitful. Three prominent tropes have characterised these efforts, namely the effectiveness of pedagogical advances, the experiences and emotions of those who have transitioned to become new speakers and the attempts to integrate immigrants and refugees into society. The dominant approach has used ethnographic methodologies to gain an understanding of people's views, attitudes and behaviours to illumine the patterns of change witnessed. The single best collection of interpretations is *Neohablantes de lenguas minorizada en el Estado español* (Ramallo, Amorrortu and Puigdevall, 2019). Readers who wish to get inside the new speaker experience are advised to consult the works of Joan Pujolar, Maite Puigdevall, Fernando Ramallo, Bernadette O'Rourke, Jone Goirigolzarri, Estibaliz Amorrortu and Ane Ortega.

With some 572 million speakers, of whom some 472 million are considered to be native speakers, Spanish is truly a powerful, global language. In terms of native speakers, it is the second most spoken language, after Chinese. Catalan can muster some 9.1 million speakers and in total some 11 million claim to understand the language, mainly in Catalonia, Andorra and parts of Valencia, the Balearic Islands, Sardinia and southwest France. Estimates on the number of Galician speakers range between 3 and 4 million in Galicia, parts of Asturias and Castilla y León. Within the BAC population of 2,237,309 some 737,000 are able to speak and 415,000 able to understand Basque, while the proportion of

---

[1] Clearly policymakers are active at different levels in the socio-political hierarchy and civil society organisations are also tasked with determining and implementing elements of language policy.

Basque speakers is 34 per cent (speakers) and 19 per cent (passive speakers). The population of Navarre is 650,000, with some 83,850 able to speak and 66,950 able to understand Basque while the proportion of speakers is 12.9 per cent (speakers) and 10.3 per cent (passive speakers).[2]

At the heart of contemporary debates around identity and sovereignty there lies the intractable dilemma of appeals to legality and legitimacy by majoritarian and minority political forces. The abiding tensions between the constituent autonomous nations and the one and indivisible Spanish state colour relations not only between the political core and the autonomous territories but also between factions within the BAC, Navarre, Catalonia and Galicia. Inevitably questions about language policy and the construction of civil identity reflect such tensions. But it would be salutary to reflect on Kathryn Woolard's advice that the shifting ideologies of linguistic authority impacted by political and demographic changes render the situation both fluid and complicated. She writes:

less than one-third of the population of Catalonia now speaks Catalan as its first language. In contrast, about 55 per cent of the adult population are first language speakers of Castilian ... (IDESCAT 2013). Most of these Castilian speakers are working-class immigrants themselves or the children and grandchildren of such immigrants from other parts of Spain. In short, the autochthonous and Catalan-speaking population of Catalonia is demographically outweighed by Castilian speakers with roots in the rest of Spain, complicating any easy Romanticist assumption of a fiercely motivating pride in Catalan language and cultural heritage. (Woolard, 2016, pp. 3–4)

Madrid's reaction to demands for autonomous sovereignty are well known and frequently reported as the defence of the status quo which operates in the interests of all Spanish citizens. 'The approach of the Spanish Government gives preference to a formal reading of the Constitution and democratic legitimacy in Parliament over the demands presented by the autonomous community ... regarding self-determination' (Gagnon and Sanjaume-Calvet, 2017, p. 284).

Despite the standing of the 1982 Law of Normalisation, which applies in all three territories – known as the Llei de normalització lingüística del català, Euskararen normalizazio legea and Lei de Normalización – from the standpoint of the dominant Spanish political and ideological discourse, recent Catalan language policy is considered to be an expression of illiberal nationalism and an attack on the inalienable rights of Castilian speakers, wherever they happen to live within the state's territory. By contrast Catalan apologists would argue

---

[2] www.irekia.euskadi.eus/uploads/attachments/9954/VI_INK_SOZLG-EH_eus.pdf?1499236557. Different estimates suggest that there are 1.8 million speakers, of which 1.2 million are fluent, see https://en.eustat.eus/elementos/ele0014700/ti_poblacion-de-la-ca-de-euskadi-por-ambitos-territoriales-lengua-materna-y-lengua-hablada-en-casa-2016/tbl0014754_i.html.

that they are at the forefront of progressive European thinking, being open, welcoming, inclusive, diverse and supportive of all who reside in their territory. The key instrument for achieving social cohesion is the Catalan language. Accordingly, language policy is viewed as an essential means of realising the opportunities available to all within the framework of the Catalan project, initiated by Jordi Pujol when he became the first president of Catalonia following the restoration of democratic elections in 1980.

Similar tensions have characterised Basque–Madrid relations, except in this case the use of violence as an instrument of political force has overshadowed the more routine negotiations and compromises between various political actors.[3] Language revitalisation within the Basque Country has been both impressive and far-reaching for two reasons. First because of the lower threshold base from which it started, such was the severity of structural oppression witnessed during the dictatorship. However, as Rodríguez (2021) observes, the discourse of challenges has been influenced by fragmentation in the Basque Country, resulting in a lack of political consensus as the territory is divided into two nation states and three administrative units.

Secondly, language revitalisation has been impressive because of the intensity of political commitment shown by successive governments and social movements, albeit that it has been episodic and has not followed a linear logical development. The championing of language and educational policy is an intensely political affair, and the ideological grounding and discursive framing of Basque promotion is a process of construction and negotiation, not simply an appeal to the inherent best interests of the population. The revitalisation of Basque accompanied the standardisation of the language which sought to provide literacy for native speakers and to secure access to the minority language for those who did not know it Rodríguez (2021).

The Basque Autonomous Community

At the beginning of the twentieth century Basque national identity was strongly linked to racial ancestry, a unique language and a striving for political autonomy. Elements of a more precise definition of Basque political ambition were honed after the establishment of the Basque National Party in 1917 when the language was seen as a key to group survival, but it was not necessarily a political priority. Its preservation was considered as a unifying link between all the Basque people in Spain and France, but its significance was more symbolic than was its employment as a communicative vehicle

---

[3] I am refraining from discussing the use of violence as a social movement tactic and political weapon, although it is a significant element. For details, see Garmendia, 1980; Linz, 1986; and Wieviorka, 1997.

per se.[4] The situation changed markedly under the suppression by the Franco regime when support for the language became the defining means of expressing anti-Fascist opposition to authoritarian rule. However, it was not necessarily the only mobilising force as solidarity in the name of the working class, proletarian internationalism and antagonism to organised religion, to rampant capitalism and to the state's use of organised violence were also significant in the opposition movement, as was exemplified in the various testimonies and statements of the Burgos Trials, 3–9 December 1970, among other episodes.

"To speak Basque is a revolutionary act"[5]

In order to understand the duality of the Basque approach to their language one may, following the Ararteko, Manuel Lezertua, distinguish between primordialist and constructivist perspectives. He argues that it has been difficult to find consensus on what being Basque really means. For primordialists the essence of Basque identity has been the occupancy of a defined homeland by kindred spirits, tied together by blood, soil and struggle to an ancestral cause – group survival against the odds. For constructivists, reframing the role of Basque in an increasingly multilingual society is the over-riding goal. For too long, Lezertua (2016) argues, the Basque people viewed their language as a symbol of their uniqueness, rather than as a communicative vehicle and a means of earning a living. In today's more pragmatic times, creating and absorbing new speakers from a constructivist perspective is not seen as a weakening or a dilution of the purity of the Basque heritage but rather as the injection of new lifeblood and a means of opening up Basque culture and civil society to wider global influences.[6] The republic of genes is gradually yielding to the open society of identification.

Following the death of General Franco in 1975, the establishment of Spain's seventeen Autonomous Communities was codified in the 1978 Spanish Constitution. The current BAC population of 2,237,309 represents an admixture of indigenous people plus generations of immigrants from different parts of Spain and from Spanish-speaking countries, especially within Latin America.[7] A long period of decline in the number and proportion of Basque speakers from an estimated 70 per cent in 1800 to 21.9 per cent in 1981 prompted a widespread language revitalisation movement, spearheaded by a renewed commitment by the Basque Autonomous Government to intervene

---

[4] Rodríguez adds that 'there is an interesting paradox here. Sabino Arana, the founder of PNV and Basque nationalism believed in each province having its own standard. He himself was not a linguist, of course' (Rodríguez, pers. comm., 2021).
[5] See Jean-Paul Sartre's introduction to Halimi (1971) and for discussion see Conversi (1997).
[6] The Ararteko is the Basque ombudsman; see www.theioi.org/ioi-members/europe/spain/ararteko-ombudsman-for-the-basque-country.
[7] www.statista.com/statistics/445549/population-of-spain-by-autonomous-community/.

so as to bring about language reversal. This ambition was a key part of the legal and institutional reforms ushered in by the Basque Statute of Autonomy 1979, and the Basic Law of 1982 which sought to mainstream the recognition and use of the official languages and the subsequent sectoral development of the Basque language, principally within public administration, education and parts of private sector (Baztarrika, 2019). The Basic Law applied to all three territories and should be contextualised by the primacy given to Spanish under Article 3 of the Constitution which, although it allows the officiality of Euskera, Catalan and Galician to be implemented in their statutes, still subordinates them to the dominance of Spanish. This is formulated in the declaration that: 'Article 3 1. Castilian is the official Spanish language of the State. All Spaniards have the duty to know it and the right to use it. 2. The other Spanish languages shall also be official in the respective Autonomous Communities in accordance with their Statutes. 3. The wealth of the different language modalities of Spain is a cultural heritage which shall be the object of special respect and protection'.[8]

The constitutional basis of Basque self-government is the Statute of Autonomy of 1979. It established a new actor and jurisdiction, the BAC, comprised of three historic territories, namely Gipuzkoa, Araba and Bizkaia, while Nafarroa constituted a separate autonomous region. In both the BAC and Navarre, the Basque language has official status, and the population has the right to know and use the Basque language, but not the duty, while for Castilian a stronger official injunction obtains, for the Constitution insists that all Spanish citizens have the duty of knowing it and the right of using it.[9]

Allied to this political autonomy is fiscal control, what is known as the 'Economic Agreement'. This gives the BAC and its institutions autonomy to collect and administer public taxation depending on their own budgets and on agreements signed with the central Spanish administration. Such measures allow for a fair degree of latitude in differentiating Basque priorities from other parts of the state and have resulted in an innovative economic investment strategy, whereby the economy has been transformed from one reliant on mining, shipbuilding and heavy industry, à la South Wales and Central Scotland, to one which specialises in IT, high-tech manufacturing in clusters of companies, technology institutes and research centres. Typically, such clusters specialise in machine tools, white goods such as refrigerators and washing machines, aeronautics, automation, transport and logistics, and environmental industries. Just after the turn of the century this had resulted in the establishment of ten applied technology centres, thirteen research and

---

[8] Spanish Constitution, 1978, www.boe.es/legislacion/documentos/ConstitucionINGLES.pdf.
[9] http://batzarirekiak.bngipuzkoa.org/down/Estatuto_de_Autonomia_para_el_Pais_Vasco_1979.pdf.

development centres, four research laboratories, two public research organisations and three technology parks.

Co-operation is the leitmotif of such developments, but unlike other examples of local initiatives, such as the industrial strategy developed for the Gaeltacht in Ireland, these do not attract grant-dependent operations in need of government support but rather genuine entrepreneurial companies, such as Eroski and Iberdrola, well able to compete on an international stage.

A second consideration is the emphasis on the social and welfare side of economic investment and the co-creation of significant institutions designed both to lessen inequality and to add purchase to the instrumental use of the Basque language. The most famous is the Mondragon Cooperative Enterprises, founded in 1956 by five former students of José María Arizmendiarrieta, a priest inspired by Catholic and socialist ideals. The co-operative spirit was very evident in the development of the multi-site Mondragon University, which since 1997 has also proved invaluable to the professional development of a skilled workforce, many of them fluent in Basque and anticipating using their skills and training in a range of industries from engineering to business management, gastronomy and applied social services.

Other agencies, such as Euskal Irrati Telebista (EITB – Basque Radio and Television) and Osakidetza (the Basque health-care service with 26.500 workers)[10] together with the Ertzaintza (the autonomous community police force with more than 7,000 officers) have witnessed an increased knowledge of Basque through the Basqueisation plans for training and service which they have implemented lately.[11] However, Jone Goirigolzarri Garaizar suggests that even if the knowledge of Basque among the Ertzaintza has increased considerably it still has a long way to go. In 2017, 51 per cent of police officers did not meet the Basque linguistic requirements which had been established by law (Goirigolzarri Garaizar, pers. comm., 2021). When allied with the increased opportunities available within public administration, such initiatives give a real choice to young Basque speakers to deploy their talents in a worthwhile range of employment positions.

The original Basque language strategy was based on a socio-historic diagnosis undertaken by the Royal Academy of the Basque Language and published as *El libro blanco del euskara* (1977). Strategically significant statistical diagnosis of levels of knowledge and use of Basque within the population were undertaken by the EKB agency. The Basque government, through its Ministry of Culture, established a Basque Language Advisory Board (Euskara Aholku Batzordea), comprised of well-known experts, which thereafter became the principal architect of Basque language planning and set the policy agenda for the next generation. The Basque language-planning approach is

---

[10] www.osakidetza.euskadi.eus/portada/.
[11] I owe this and other observations to Jasone Aldekoa and Durk Gorter.

characterised by systematic evidence-based analysis which every five years undertakes a comprehensive sociolinguistic survey that results in a series of mapped representations of the different measures of vitality.[12] Accordingly place-specific interventions can be targeted to influence patterns of language change and use.

The foundation for the Basque approach is laid out in the *Plan general de promoción del uso del euskera* (1999). This is a wide-ranging and articulate statement of intent, which covers many themes and policy fields that subsequent strategic documents reiterate.[13] Of particular note is the extensive reference made to the need to build up expertise, knowledge, capacity and the diffusion of corpus planning for Basque. This reflects a long concern with language standardisation and codification which began as early as the 1600s with Lazarraga. The current strategy gives expression to these long-cherished aims. Both the *Plan general de promoción del uso del euskera* (Eusko Jaurlaritza, 2003) and the *Criterios para la normalización del uso del euskera en las administraciones públicas* (Eusko Jaurlaritza, 2007) also adhere to elements of a policy cycle. In the case of the 2007/8 document there is a visual model of the key elements that constitute the various segments of the plan which were to be realised beyond 2012 (p. 34). The official documentation makes a great play of positioning the Basque vision for language promotion squarely within the professional discourse on language planning (pp. 9–14). Indeed, in its use of a wide-ranging technical vocabulary and its constant referencing of indicators and criteria by which the policy goals might be evaluated, the Basque model evinces a highly professional and self-conscious approach to language policy implementation. This is especially so as the vision statement and the rhetoric are accompanied by sound strategic goals and methodological frameworks whereby *euskararen normalizazioa*, also called *euskaldunization,* demonstrate how the 'normalización' of Basque is to be achieved, specifically within public administration.

One curiosity in the law 10/1982, which was published in a bilingual format, is that the name of the law is different in Basque and in Spanish.[14] In Spanish it is the Basic Law for the Normalisation of the Use of the Basque Language, while in Basque it is the Basic Law for the Regulation of the Use of

---

[12] www.euskara.euskadi.net/r59-734/en/.

[13] Eusko Jaurlaritza, Kultura Saila, *Euskara Biziberritzeko Plan Nagusia*. Vitoria-Gasteiz: Eusko Jaurlaritzaren Argitalpen Zerbitzu Nagusia, 1999.

[14] Jasone Aldekoa (2021) has provided the original text as follows:

1955	1955
Azaroaren 24ko 10/1982 oinarrizko LEGEA, Euskeraren erabilpena arauzkotzezkoa	LEY 10/1982, de 24 de Noviembre, básica de normalización del uso del Euskera

Her advice is that the term 'normalisation' in Spanish derives from Mediterranean sociolinguistics, especially Vicent Aracil whose influence has been important in Catalan-speaking countries, but in the 1990s the term was replaced by Anglo-Germanic sociolinguistic concepts in the Basque Country.

the Basque Language. However, in both it is the use of the Basque language which prevails.

The main themes of Basque language strategy may be gleaned from the Basque Language Advisory Board's *Basis for a Language Policy for the Early 21st Century: Towards a Renewed Agreement* (Basque Government, 2009). This wide-ranging document was prepared by the Sub-Ministry for Language Policy in order to meet its public commitment for the period 2005–9. It derives from an extensive consultation which had four aims: (1) to debate language policy without prejudice or limits; (2) to promote the participation of all possible sectors in the debate; (3) to locate the references required to continue with the work of revitalising the Basque language; (4) to contribute to a social consensus, which is vital in revitalising the fortunes of a minority language. This wealth of evidence has been useful both in informing the ongoing reversing language shift strategy and in increasing the public's awareness for the need for consensus-building in dealing both with Basque language promotion and how best to make the language available or accessible to the increasing number of immigrants into society. Since 2009 subsequent documents have made more reference to the need to cater for new speakers and immigrants so as to boost social cohesion. This remains a consistent theme, for the support for Basque as an integrative factor remained constant even when government ideology and programmes changed, such as during the period 2009–12 when the PSE-EE ruled.

The Basque model of language revitalisation is sometimes represented as one of logical, linear growth since the death of Franco and one to be emulated elsewhere in Europe due to its persistence and success. But this linear continuity narrative is far from smooth as internal ideological and party-political differences remain and have forged an epiphenomenal trajectory for language promotion. In their detailed analysis of party-political approaches to language rights and management, Goirigolzarri-Garaizar and Landabidea Urresti (2020) demonstrate how parliamentary parties have engaged with the language question, adopting quite distinct positions regarding various fundamental issues such as the Normalisation of the Use of Euskara in 1982, the legal text that regulates the linguistic system in the BAC and its revitalisation process; the public management of bilingualism; the requirement for civil servants to demonstrate varying competences in Basque; the gradual extension of language rights; and the normalisation of Basque within the economy and other spheres of social interaction. The four prominent parties, namely the Euzko Alderdi Jeltzalea–Partido Nacionalista Vasco (Basque Nationalist Party, EAJ–PNV), the Ezker Abertzalea (Abertzale Left – literally Patriotic Left – Ezker Abertzalea), the Euskadiko Alderdi Popularra–Partido Popular del País Vasco (Popular Party, PP) and the PSE–EE (Partido Socialista de Euskadi–Euskadiko Ezkerra) which is part of the Spanish Social Party (PSOE) have each developed quite distinctive stances which reflect both their origins and ideological disposition towards the relationship between the BAC and the Spanish state. In the current legislature Vox (a right-wing party) is represented in the parliament with one member among seventy-five.

Unsurprisingly it is the EAJ–PNV which has through its periods in office been most responsible for developing and enhancing the linguistic system in the BAC. It is also explicitly in favour of developing the capacity of the language community through the promotion of new speakers and their subsequent integration into active speaker networks.

The Ezker Abertzalea has defended the idea that all Basque citizens should know Basque and has proposed that the equal status of Basque with Spanish and French be secured throughout the whole Basque Country. This prospect was aided when on 8 April 2021, the proposal by Paul Molac that protects access to public education in minoritised languages in France was approved. Rodríguez (pers. comm., 2021) believes that this is a historic moment for Basque which may lead the way to further revitalisation opportunities as envisioned by the Ezker Abertzalea.

Clearly this would require a more radical and thoroughgoing normalisation of the language than that currently conceived of by any government. The PSE–EE is also in favour of the normalisation of the Basque language, but its routine position is quite conservative.

In marked contrast the PP has consistently adopted a more intransigent approach which, although recognising the identity value of Basque language and the bilingual character of the territory, does not wish to extend the use of the language. Goirigolzarri Garaizar and Landabidea Urresti (2020) argue that the PP policy is to maintain 'the non-recognition of its instrumental-communicative functions beyond the "natural" community of Basque speakers'. We await a detailed analysis of the socialist PSOE approach to language policy.

The decline of Basque speakers, down from 70 per cent of population in 1800 to 21.9 per cent in 1981, is often attributed to political repression. Gorter advises that one should be careful not to attribute the diminution of Basque to the repressive measures instituted under Franco, for the decline started long before, even if it was accelerated by his dictatorial regime (Gorter, pers. comm., 2021). During the nineteenth century in some regions the extended family and community were no longer able to reproduce the language adequately. In Navarre a number of variables influenced transmission rates, such as the distance to the capital Pamplona, the attitude of the local priest, the rate of industrialisation and gender differences. On the other hand, in Basque-speaking villages and towns, families and community are still perfectly capable of transmitting the language within a vibrant context (Gorter, pers. comm., 2021).

The Production of New Speakers

The BAC displays an impressive and urgent understanding of the need to incorporate new speakers into mainstream linguistic, educational and community affairs. A number of relatively well-established programmes exists by which governments seek to incorporate new speakers. The demographic weight of new speakers, both as competent learners and relatively recent migrants, makes it imperative that such programmes work, for there is a fear that if they do not then the vitality of the indigenous Basque-speaking population will be reduced.

The early signs of this forty-year involvement are that the current proportion of Basque speakers stands at 41 per cent of the population.[15] Figures 6.1 and 6.2 identify the numerical and proportional representation of Basque speakers in 2016.

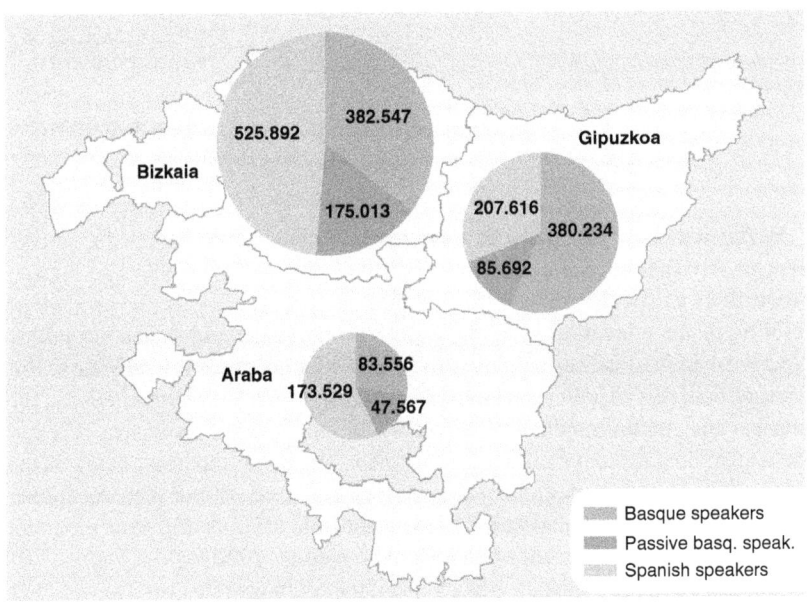

Figure 6.1 Numerical representation of Basque speakers in BAC, 2016
Source: *EUSTAT.BiztanleriarenetaEtxebizitzenEstatistika*

---

[15] Gorter advises a note of caution as there are different estimates and proportions in circulation derived from both sociolinguistic surveys and census data. 'Basque speakers' is also an ambiguous category when 'passive speakers' (those who understand but cannot speak) are included in the estimates (Gorter, 2021, pers. comm.).

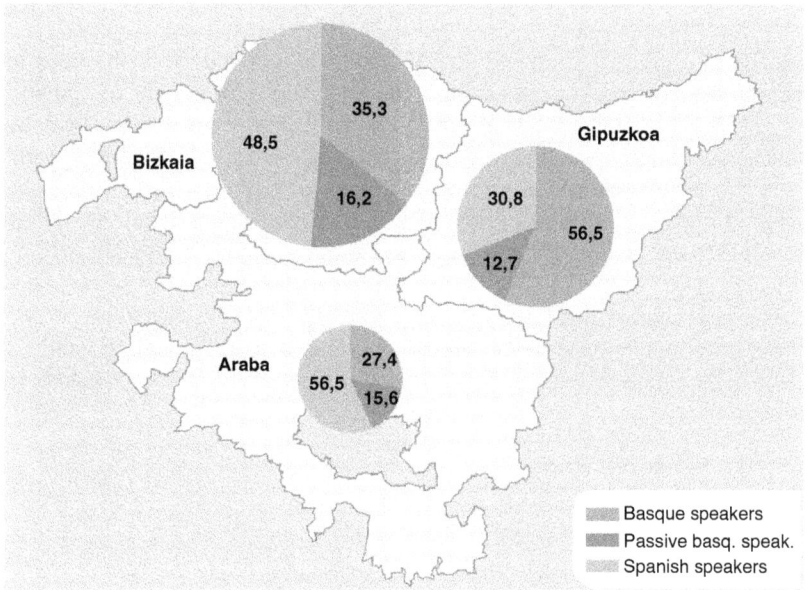

Figure 6.2 Proportional representation of Basque speakers in BAC, 2016
Source: *EUSTAT.Biztanleriareneta Etxebizitzen Estatistika*

Baztarrika (2019) suggests that various initiatives have produced a current total of 416,000 speakers and some 73,000 'passive' speakers. The highest proportions of speakers are in the younger age groups, largely the product of reforms in the education system. Thus, both language and education policy have worked in close collaboration to bring about language revitalisation. But because both sets of policies respond to different implementation schedules, the impact and measurements of success do not always coincide. Clearly the educational system continues to be one of the most important bases of the Basque language reversing language shift (RLS) process, but the educational system, as Aldekoa emphasises, is also responsible for pursuing other essential and ethical social objectives (Aldekoa, pers. comm., 2020).

The growth of the Basque education system demonstrates how society has embraced the integral use of Basque from kindergarten to higher education. A generation ago some 15 per cent of children and students were enrolled in Basque-medium schools; now there are 80 per cent plus in both the Euskal Eskola Publikoa (public education system) and within the *ikastolas* which are a type of semi-private school financed mostly by public funds, what are called '*escuelas concertadas*'. The Law on the Normalisation of the Basque Language (1982) ensured the possibility of using either Basque or Spanish as the language of instruction whilst maintaining that both Castilian and Basque were compulsory. The Bilingualism Decree of 1983 established three school models which have been the subject of a great deal of investigation and discussion. They are:

> Model A schools, in which Basque is offered as a second language. Currently only some 3 per cent of enrolments of 3-year-olds are in Model A schools, the result of a massive swing in parental choice away from Spanish-medium schools.
>
> Model B schools in which both Spanish and Basque are offered as a subject and are used as languages of instruction for approximately 50 per cent of the curriculum.
>
> Model D schools in which Basque is used as a language of instruction and in which Spanish is taught as a subject for four to five hours per week. Model D was 'originally created as a language maintenance program for native speakers of Basque' (Cenoz, 2008, p. 16). The popularity of the D Model and of the use of Basque as a language of instruction has increased, necessitating a huge investment by successive governments and educational authorities in teacher training, educational resources and assessment bodies.

When the three school models were established, approximately 20 per cent of the pupils received Basque-medium teaching (Zalbide and Cenoz, 2008, p. 10). In the school year 2008–9, 8.8 per cent of all pupils at the level of primary education attended a Model A school, whereas 29.96 per cent were enrolled in Model B and 60.47 per cent in Model D schools (Cenoz, 2008, p. 17). At secondary school level, 19.08 per cent attended a Model A school, 27.54 per cent a Model B school and 52.64 per cent a Model D school, while Gorter (pers. comm., 2021) advises that the B Model is not very successful. The percentage which Model B schools represent has remained steady at about 20 per cent and intriguingly A streams can become B and B streams can become D, meaning that one can have both B and D within the same school centre.

In 2011 Darquennes (2011) suggested that the popularity of Model D schools would continue to increase in the years to come and his prognostication has proved valid. He argued that the success of Model D schools (and one could add the Model B schools) meant that Basque-speaking pupils now had the institutional basis to improve their knowledge of Basque and the schools effectively socialised many students who had no knowledge of Basque when they entered school. But he advised that one should not overestimate the effects of the rise of the population in Model D schools on the future of Basque. 'Even though they are quite happy with the positive evolution in Model D schools, Basque language planning officials as well as Basque academics point out that not just the number of pupils is important. One also needs to carefully look at the sort of Basque competences the pupils develop at school. And one has to find out in how far the increase of the popularity of Model D also leads to maintaining or increasing the use of Basque in society' (Darquennes, 2013). Prescient advice indeed, which by now fully occupies the minds of planners and educators alike.

Jasone Aldekoa, following Pauli Dávila (2003), would attribute the success of the Basque models to additional reasons. The same school year in which the Basque education models were implemented (1982–3), more than 20 per cent of the students opted for a B or D Model, and from then on, the demand for Basque models has been increasing year after year. However, three other reasons may be given for such growth. The first is that the system has increased access thereby facilitating greater choice for families; the second is the greater acceptance of bilingual education as a legitimate pathway; the third is that the continuous *euskaldunization,* training, improvement and innovation of the teaching staff who taught in Basque, has inspired greater confidence among parents. In other words, opportunity, dissemination and continuous improvement have had a significant influence on the evolution of Basque studies (Aldekoa, pers. comm., 2021).

The transformation in the relative change in parental choice for schools type is revealed in the contrast between the figures for 1983–4 and 2017–18 as indicated in Table 6.1.

In consequence it is the education system that is the principal means by which new Basque speakers are produced and sustained. The conventional pillars of language transmission, the extended family and the community, are no longer able to perform these tasks in such an effective manner. This is a common experience for linguistic minorities throughout western Europe and has been accompanied by fears of territorial shrinkage, atrophy and communal fragmentation. It is as if the baton of language transmission has been passed from informal, but grounded, conduits of reproduction to more formal agencies, sanctioned and funded by the local state.

Table 6.1 *Proportionate change in school attendance by type*

School type	1983–4	2017–18
A	77%	13%
B	8.1%	24.3%
D	14.2%	62.7%

Source: Baztarrika (2019)

By combining information from at least five reliable data sources, it is possible to demonstrate the sustained growth in the number of Basque speakers. The five data sources are:
1. The VI. Sociolinguistic Survey of 2016.
2. The enrolment figures in Basque streams for compulsory education and for higher education.
3. The results obtained in Basque competence assessments by pupils of 4th primary and 2nd secondary in the biannual Diagnostic Assessments (developed and corrected by ISEI-IVEI Basque Institute for Research and Evaluation in Education). This is a censual test, done by all students (N> 40.000) of the BAC for these age groups and educational levels. These official tests follow the criteria of the CEFR – the Common European Framework of Reference for Languages, Learning, Teaching, Assessment.
4. The figures on Basque language use in the school context, obtained biannually by the ARRUE project.
5. The figures on Basque language street use as measured by the Basque Sociolinguistic Cluster. (Aldekoa, pers. comm., 2020)

Arrue uses the ISEI-IVEI data which demonstrates that, while students have proficiency, the actual use of the language, even in the classroom, is much less and there is a characteristic decline from primary to secondary, which is true also of Ireland, Wales, Scotland and other European cases. The data on the use of Basque in the street shows little increase which is a concern and must temper any claim of an ever-increasing growth and vibrancy in relation to language dynamics.

There are varying degrees of success in attainment rates and assessment levels between secondary school and higher education levels. Aldekoa has identified five elements which help interpret the situation. The dominant one is that when educational reforms are implemented the students clearly benefit from such interventions, an improvement which is carried through to progression into higher education. A second element is the interplay between fundamental structural reforms in the school community and the more episodic, dynamic interventions which can influence the effectiveness of the language planning framework. The third element is that the number of dropouts from a Basque stream to a non-Basque stream is insignificant during compulsory education and baccalaureate. The fourth element is the throughput into Basque-medium education at university. The fifth element is that the availability of vocational training studies in Basque is increasing thanks to the Basque language plan as developed by the Vice-Ministry of Vocational Training (Aldekoa, pers. comm., 2020). Gorter suggests that vocational training remains a challenge as it has been neglected until recently and thus Basque is used a lot less in secondary schools for professional training than in pre-university schools (Gorter, pers. comm., 2021).

Given the changing demographic profile of society there is an extra impetus to deal with the impact of migrants and to socialise more people into a set of Basque-medium social networks. Understandably a great deal of attention is now paid in the formulation of curriculum development, educational pedagogy, adult education classes and university education, as to how to best encourage new speakers to accelerate their learning and contribute to the socio-economic success of the Basque Country. By definition, given their preponderance, some would claim that it is new speakers who constitute the vast majority of Basque students, and as a result all mainstream policies necessarily incorporate their interests as a matter of routine deliberation and implementation. However, there is some dissent as to whether or not one can sustain such claims. Gorter asks: 'if 50% of these students come from Spanish-speaking homes, but have started all of their education in Basque from age 2 or 3, can they be considered "new speakers"? Again, many children now entering the system are descendants of students that have gone through the system when it grew in the 1990s. Perhaps their parents could be characterised as new speakers, but are their children still new speakers?' (Gorter, pers. comm., 2021). The same observation applies to the children of students from English-speaking homes in Wales who received their education in the Welsh-medium schools of the seventies, eighties and nineties.

Notwithstanding these qualifications the Basque case represents a good template by which best practice principles can be identified and calibrated in relation to a variety of strategies aimed at producing and nourishing new speakers. Some best practice elements have been identified by Aldekoa from which it can be deduced that:

- The language-planning developed by the Department of Education of the BAC has been satisfactory, and this has allowed the department to offer the citizens in the educational domain those services legally established.
- RLS processes should be carried out following scientific models; in other words, following the process of diagnosis-implementation-evaluation and adapted (= tailor made) in each case to the specific organisation or institution in question. Experiences should be planned with extreme good judgment and in a rational way, because the means, resources and availability of the linguistic community are limited.[16]
- In line with those principles, it is recognised that the Ulibarri Program, to promote the oral and written use of Basque within the school community members, has had

---

[16] Aldekoa, is conscious of the relevance of J. A. Fishman's claims:

RLS is a difficult and risky operation and requires a very fine sense of balance, an extremely delicate sense of boundary definition, of functional analysis (as to shared functions and exclusively dominated functions) and a constant recognition of priorities, such that the right thing to do is the right thing only if it is done at the right time and in the right sequence with other things. Such a combination of delicacy and stubbornness, of sensitivity and of priorities, is extremely difficult to achieve (Fishman, 2001: 8). (Aldekoa, pers. comm., 2020)

a positive impact on the school arena. Each school designs and implements its own 4-year Ulibarri project following the diagnostic-implementation-evaluation process. It is understood that an interval of 8–10 years which is equivalent to 2 strategic projects of 4 years each plus one or two additional years is required to produce statistically significant results of increased use of the Basque language by the members of the school community. (Aldekoa, pers. comm., 2021)

The Ulibarri programme has provided examples of good practices in other domains also. One highly relevant illustration is the relationship between vocational education centres and local companies designed so as to spread the linguistic competence acquired in school to the workplace context and to facilitate the use of Euskara in labour and professional relations. This has been achieved with the corresponding help and co-ordination between the Vice-Ministry of Linguistic Policy and the Vice-Ministry of Professional Training. A second illustration is the collaboration among students–teachers–parents–local authorities to promote the oral and written use of Basque, based on a knowledge of Basque traditions, sports, biodiversity, gender and cultural heritage. The commitment to establishing a firm foundation for the grounding of Basque as a community language is evidenced in the more than ten years of sustained participation of 100 per cent of schools and local authorities within selected areas, involving some 90 per cent of students, 60 per cent of teachers and 33 per cent of students–teachers–parents in a collective effort to deepen the roots of Basque-medium education.

A third illustration is the close collaboration in many areas between local schools and town halls to promote Basque language and culture. Cultural creativity, heritage and cultural context/domains combine to promote the use of the minority language, together with social cohesion and group identification. This has been a mainstay of Basque community efforts for more than twenty-five years and local initiatives are assisted by the active co-ordination between the Vice-Ministry of Linguistic Policy and the Vice-Ministry of Education (Aldekoa, 2012). A further initiative is the *Berbalagun* (talking friends) development established for well over twenty years. For experts and policy implementers, such as Jasone Aldekoa, these collective experiences are vital for three reasons. First, they offer a way to foster language-embedded cultural identity. Several studies demonstrate the interdependence between language, culture and community when planning RLS efforts, because language shift and cultural shift go hand in hand (Lee and McLaughlin, 2001).

Secondly, such experiences demonstrate the means of achieving some degree of sustained informal community organisation; it is a way to strengthen the *Gemeinschaft*, to recognise the anthropological and ethnocultural knowledge and experience of volunteers and to provide social support to students, adolescents or families in the chain of linguistic and cultural transmission (Subirats, 2002; Azurmendi et al., 1998). Thirdly, such experiences derive

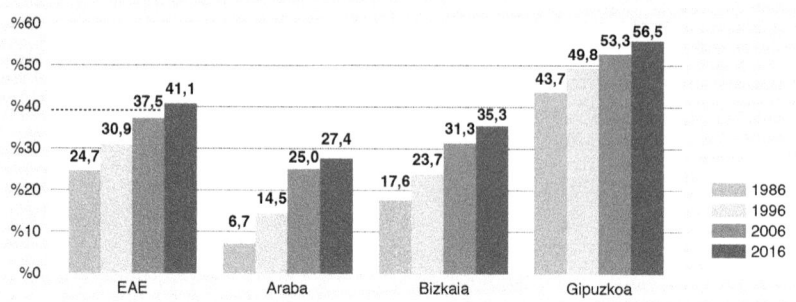

Figure 6.3 Evolution of Basque speakers in BAC, 1986–2016
Source: *EUSTAT.Biztanleriareneta Etxebizitzen Estatistika*

from bottom-up informal proposals that, after having gained significant acceptance in the community, are partially promoted by businesses alongside formal support systems – municipalities, schools and voluntary and private cultural groups. The diffusion of such experiences has been proven to have an impact in the promotion of the Basque language use and in the consumption of Basque culture such as books, internet, television and radio (Aldekoa, 2012).

There is no doubting that transformation of the use of Basque within the educational system from the kindergarten through to higher and further education has been profound. It has involved wholescale changes in teaching methods and materials, the retraining of the teaching profession and additional recruitment of competent Basque speakers, administrators, IT specialists, etc. The evolution of Basque speakers since the early reforms in 1986 up until 2016 (Figure 6.3) demonstrates the profound nature of these structural changes, which one would assume are irreversible.

However, this is not inevitable and as is sometimes said 'the past has a past also', meaning that much of this work has been undertaken within an atmosphere of considerable uncertainty and, for some, opposition to the new trajectory, especially as they were not convinced that such reforms would be permanent and were thus likely to be overturned by successive governments. Consequently, this social transformation, spearheaded by the education sector, reveals a number of underlying trends which cause some concerns for practitioners and policymakers.

It is now recognised that the formal assessment of various skills and competencies exhibited by the current generation of scholars does not match the expectations of either professionals or parents. Different reasons are offered for this perception of a decline in standards; some relate to the quality of Basque employed by members of the teaching staff, some to the challenges faced while teaching specialist subjects in Basque for the first time, some to the relative dearth of specialist teaching materials and resources in Basque compared with Spanish, some to the reticence of many students and their families to being subjected to this radical, experimental transformation in educational philosophy and praxis.

Put boldly, within the overall language revitalisation programme, the school has its limits. A slight majority (56 per cent) of pupils learn Basque as a second language, often within an extra-school environment which is not conducive to reinforcing the daily use of Basque. Many schools are distant, both geographically and socially, from the habitual patterns which constitute the 'normal' socialisation processes of many students and thus the only domain within which Basque has resonance is the educational sector. Students report that the opportunities to use Basque outside of the classroom setting are limited,

Accordingly, there are early-warning signals that the spectacular growth to date is being questioned by both supporters and opponents alike. Were the concerns limited to opponents alone, protagonists could legitimately dismiss them as ideologically and political motivated, rather than based on empirical evidence. In 2008 when the educational policy was fully established, if not fully operational, opponents such as Susana Marqués, of the Platform for the Freedom of Linguistic Choice, claimed that schools teaching Spanish had become ghettoes hampered by lack of funding because the authorities were keen to promote Basque at the expense of all else. She argued that the Basque authorities wanted schools to have a high level of Basque in order to receive generous local funding: 'The only way to do this was total immersion in the language. In 20 years of this policy, they still have not managed to get bilingualism here. It is not the language of the street. And 70 per cent of companies here never use Basque.' Marqués's group had appealed to Spain's ombudsman, Enrique Múgica, arguing that their rights were being denied. Patxi Baztarrika, deputy head of linguistic politics for the Basque government, responded that: 'Spanish is present and should be. To say that Basque poses any threat to it is ridiculous.'[17]

However, the fact that advocates of the Basque reforms are also expressing concerns as to the direction and pace of change is a matter of real disquiet and needs to be addressed. The policy imperative for decision makers and senior public servants is how to manage the expected backlash if and when it occurs. Of course, there will always be elements in society who will make political capital concerning the promotion of Basque and will appeal to all Spanish political and social interest groups to reinforce their presumed rights within the Spanish state. This is a normal, if not always peaceful, reaction witnessed in so many instances of reversing language shift in Europe. The former supplicants

---

[17] www.theguardian.com/world/2008/may/04/spain.

are now deemed to be intrusive antagonistic upstarts who threaten to overturn the established hegemonic order. But the Spanish state has been marked by its aggressive stance towards national minorities throughout the twentieth century which continues until today – witness the determined harassment of Catalan demands for greater recognition through democratic means.

Some teacher trainers argue for better training methods, others for differentiated classroom practices to account for diversity of home languages and argue that it is unfair to expect L2 to match L1 competences in a short space of time.[18] The levels of language competence in Basque obtained by the 4th primary and 2nd secondary students in the biannual Diagnostic Assessment tests are lower than the authorities would have anticipated, especially if the parameters established by the European Commission (i.e., greater then 15 per cent in the initial level of competence) are taken into account.

Results from 2019 show that:

4th primary mean results: N= 20.797
- 37 per cent of pupils in the initial level interval of the competence in Basque;
- but only 8.4 per cent of pupils are in the initial interval in both official languages;
- only 4.9 per cent of the pupils are in the initial interval when we consider the three languages of schooling (Basque, Spanish & English);
- Only 3.95 per cent of the students are enrolled in an A stream where they are taught through the medium of Spanish/English and learn Basque as a subject (four hours per week);
- 63 per cent of the students have an intermediate or high level of competence in Basque although only 17.14 per cent have Basque as their family language.

The corresponding 2019 data for the 2nd secondary mean results: N= 20.621 are:
- 45.3 per cent of pupils in the initial level interval of the competence in Basque;
- but only 10.8 per cent of pupils are in the initial interval in both official languages;
- only 5 per cent of the pupils are in the initial interval when we consider the three languages of schooling (Basque, Spanish and English);
- only 6.04 per cent of the students are enrolled in an A stream where they are taught through the medium of Spanish/English and learn Basque as a subject (four hours per week);
- 54.7 per cent of the students have an intermediate or high level of competence in Basque although only 10.18 per cent have Basque as their family language.[19] (Aldekoa, pers. comm., 2020)

---

[18] Interviews conducted with J. Goirigolzarri Garaizar and A. Ortega at Lasarte, 17 May 2018.
[19] In answer to my questions Aldekoa concludes that 'those results are dependent on many variables that shed light on which areas of improvement to develop from the educational

The 40 per cent difference between Basque home language proportions and those who achieve competence as a result of formal education suggests how significant the contribution of new speakers is to the mass of the Basque-speaking population going forward. However, when speculating about the policy implications of expanding the proportion of Basque speakers in society and their consequent ability to sustain trends in language reproduction, Aldekoa comments:

Have we hit the ceiling? Can we expect 100% of the students to know and speak Basque 100% of the time in all socio-functional domains? Joshua Fishman (2001) clearly states that when it comes to a minority language, it is essential to continue with revitalization efforts if we want to reverse the language shift. By this I do not mean that minority language loyalists are subject to the punishment of Sisyphus. Absolutely not! Evaluations and figures show our progress. However, it is obvious that as, among others, Josiane Hammers (2007)[20] pointed out, there are bilingual and multilingual individuals, but the language-communities, despite having monolingual, bilingual, and multilingual members, use one language or another for the different socio-functional domains. Therefore, I believe that it is necessary to constantly evaluate the results of plans and programs to promote the knowledge/use of the minority language and look for areas of improvement, as well as rethink language planning in light of social and political changes. (Aldekoa, pers. comm., 2020)

Some educationalists put their faith in the development of translanguaging as an effective method both for the development of metalinguistic awareness and for the greater use of Basque in society as a regular act. Cenoz and Gorter have demonstrated that through careful planning, the gradual introduction of two or more languages in the classroom setting and a recognition that the social context and repertoire of the students is vital, it is possible to empower pupils to increase their competence, develop a stronger self-esteem and recognise that, within a multilingual context, different languages may be used for different purposes without being 'unfaithful' to the school's medium of instruction. The original Welsh model of translanguaging as *trawsieithu*, as developed by educationalists in Bangor University, relied on alternating the two languages (Williams, 1994; Lewis, Jones and Baker, 2012). But this innovative method had to contend with the protection of the minority language and a relatively strict separation of Welsh and English as was employed in bilingual classroom design. Hard boundaries in a bilingual setting were the norm. By contrast, pedagogical translanguaging recognises that languages are separate entities but that their boundaries are soft and as a consequence adopts a less rigid approach to the traditional ideologies of language

---

point of view, and those are the areas/elements of improvement proposed by the Direction of Innovation of the Department of Education we work on for' (Aldekoa, pers. comm., 2020).

[20] Eusko Jaurlaritza, Hezkuntza, Unibertsitate eta Ikerketa Saila. *Análisis de la educación bilingüe*. Vitoria-Gasteiz: Eusko Jaurlaritzaren Argitalpen Zerbitzua, 2007.

separation. Allied to this is a greater awareness of the need to develop students' awareness about the way languages are used in natural communication. Thus, Cenoz and Gorter (2021) argue that pedagogical translanguaging implies a focus on multilingualism based on the concept of the multilingual speaker, the whole linguistic repertoire and the social context. Trialling of this pedagogical approach in the school system where Basque, Spanish and English are taught suggests that both pupils and teachers recognise the advantages of translanguaging and report greater confidence in learning languages, improved self-esteem for Basque speakers and a greater appreciation of the structures of the three languages being taught.[21]

However, this innovative approach must overcome certain prejudices and concerns. The first is that teachers who have been weaned on the ideology of protecting the minority language, and consequently adopting a strict separation between Basque, Spanish and English, have expressed resistance to the concept of soft boundaries implied by translanguaging. Secondly, championing the multilingual identity when it is difficult enough to stabilise a bilingual identity remains a challenge. Cenoz and Gorter (2021) argue that with the gradual introduction of such methods within carefully planned lessons, some of these prejudices can be reduced.

There remains the question of how to stimulate spontaneous and regular use of Basque in society. One suggestion is to create breathing spaces for minority language speakers, a concept we reviewed earlier in this volume. Cenoz and Gorter (2021) envisage a triangular framework whose virtues include translanguaging spaces, breathing spaces and the protection of the minority language. This concern with space is an adaptation of the earlier work of Williams (1981), Fishman (1991) and Cummins (2014), with a new special emphasis on translanguaging spaces as befits the emergence of the multilingual identity as a more common reality. Breathing spaces, created outside the confines of the classroom, should help promote a more regular, default use of Basque. The advantage of the concept is that it is not prescriptive and could be formulated to meet the exigencies of any local, particular circumstance. However, much greater thought would have to be given as to what counts as breathing space in minority language contexts and to how one would evaluate such interventions in terms of their success. Are such spaces to be developed in early childhood and, as Estibaliz Amorrortu and her team have proposed, PAR (Participatory Action Research), to foster the transformation of individuals in adopting the minoritised language?[22] Or are they essentially 'safe breathing spaces' divorced from the education system directed at adult learners and speakers in the form of social centres?

---

[21] As reported by Cenoz and Gorter (2021) in the update of their research results.
[22] www.culturanavarra.es/es/fontes-linguae-vasconum-50-urte.

A further challenge raised by several of the interviews undertaken was that there is evidence that the non-Basque element of the resident population may grow increasingly resentful of the current revitalisation programme. Accordingly, increased appeals to 'outside authorities' to redress the balance in favour of Spanish have been made. These have taken the form of appeals to the Spanish state and its ombudsman, to international agencies and to professional bodies concerned with education. Jasone Aldekoa was asked how real a challenge this was, and if it could influence the rate and pace of change in favour of the normalisation of Basque. Her view was that given the political and educational changes in recent times it is difficult to foresee the future, but factors such as the high enrolment figures of students in Basque streams, the good results obtained in the non-Basque official language and in the foreign language suggest that overall the system is working well. Public opinion tends to support the promotional efforts and in the sociolinguistic survey of 2016, 65 per cent of inhabitants over the age of sixteen were in favour of promoting the use of Basque, a further 25.8 per cent were neither in favour nor against, and only 9.3 per cent were against. 'I consider that the status-planning in our RLS process, and especially the educational language-policy, presents ethical and legal principles that have allowed us to reach the point in which we are in a very peaceful way and always based on agreements, which, in turn, shields the process of promoting the knowledge/use of Basque (Bergara, 1996; Urrutia, 2005)' (Aldekoa, pers. comm., 2020).[23]

A timely illustration of solidarity during the Covid-19 episode of 2020–2 has been the community-fostering reaction of many people during the lockdown period. Reinforcing the messages derived from the Internet and Basque TV, films, videos and social media generally, Basque volunteers have arranged to interact with pupils from non-Basque family backgrounds so that they have the opportunity to use the language orally.[24] This action was initiated because for thousands of students the dominant place to practise their Basque was in school, an opportunity which was vastly diminished under the Covid-19 restrictions. This is a spontaneous version of the long-established Catalan Voluntariat per la Llengua discussed in the next chapter.

In addition, there is a related concern that despite the enormous investment in educational provision and the corresponding increase in the requirement to demonstrate Basque language skills in sectors of the economy, the actual usage of Basque in so many socio-economic contexts remains disappointing, even taking

---

[23] 'Besides, as you very well know, because you have also been involved in such processes, the Vice-ministry of language politics and the Ministry of Education appeal to "outside authorities", as you put it, (Spanish, European, International) to guide us in the evaluation and improvement processes of our Basque language promotion plans and programs. (i.e., the analysis of bilingual education, developed in 2006, published in 2007)' (Aldekoa, pers. comm., 2020).

[24] A good illustration would be https://jalgihadimundura.blogspot.com/.

into account the more recent emphasis on vocational training within the system. It was assumed that increasing the total number of speakers through the education system, the Basque for Adults programme, numerous well-evidenced government initiatives and the social mobilisation of actors would readily transfer into social usage outside education, given the sheer weight of numbers and socio-economic transformation of the workforce, requiring increased skills in Basque.

The Basque for Adults, HABE system in particular was seen as a motor for language revitalisation. According to sociolinguistics experts, almost a third of the 275,000 new speakers in the country have learned Basque outside the school system constituting 90,000 people who have studied in *euskaltegis*.[25] Comprised of 103 centres, with approximately 1,320 and 35,527 students in 2019–20, it is estimated that the sector produces some 4,500 new speakers per annum.[26] To this we should add the 'alternative system' of AEK as the biggest 'private' or bottom-up provider.[27]

The Basque system is very good at producing sociolinguistic surveys and at monitoring and evaluating successive interventionists programmes within many domains. What is unclear is the extent to which these new speakers put into operative effect the skill set that they have so assiduously acquired. This has prompted a fresh round of initiatives by both government and civil society to reinforce patterns of language choice in favour of Basque. Increasing Basque language use is a major challenge for it has been proven that a numerical growth in speakers does not automatically produce increased use, neither does a favourable set of attitudes towards the language ensure its increased use.

The Euskaraldia *Initiative*

Basque society has a strong tradition of innovation and initiatives, and the government language policy team is a dynamic and technically sophisticated unit.[28] It has sought to ally itself with the community so as to unite bottom-up

---

[25] www.berria.eus/paperekoa/1981/002/001/2021-03-28/euskaltegiak-motor-berrien-bila.htm.

[26] www.habe.euskadi.eus/s23-edukiak/es/contenidos/informacion/habe_estatistika/es_def/index.shtml.

[27] In answering the question how Wales could benefit from the HABE experience, Helen Prosser, the Strategic Director of the National Centre for Learning Welsh, said on 16 October 2018 that 'there were several differences, but the most obvious was the intensity of the learning. Most people learning Basque study for around nine hours per week, while hundreds study on a full-time basis over an extended period. At a minimum, the language is taught to adults for four hours each week. Back home, most of our learners tend to learn for two hours per week. However, the Centre is keen to encourage its learners to increase the number of learning hours each week, so that they can learn the language more quickly – one way we're doing this is by offering combination courses, which combine two hours of classroom learning with two hours of online learning each week.' Source: https://learnwelsh.cymru/news/a-visit-to-the-basque-country/.

[28] Patxi Baztarrika, discussion with former Deputy Minister for Language Policy, Autonomous Government of the Basque Country, in Cardiff, 29 September 2019.

and top-down language revitalisation strategies in a series of programmes designed to boost the use of Basque writ large. At successive interviews between 2012 and 2019 government language specialist were convinced that by seeking to actively intervene in the social and economic conversations and interactions so as to favour Basque, a determined adherence to the principle of beginning all interactions with Basque statements might prompt a shift in favour of the language in the future. The most significant initiative has been the establishment of Udaltop, which is an annual gathering of language officers, social activists and government officials who seek to diffuse innovative practices. The Udaltop meeting in Lasarte, May 2018, sought to embed the social use of Basque through the Euskaraldia initiative, which was run in combination with 316 local committees.[29] The aims of the Euskarak 365 Egun dynamic were:

- To change language habits and encourage the taking of steps in order that as many people as possible start to make greater use of the Basque language.
- To prompt action among local agents who work in favour of the Basque language in order for them to facilitate new language practices and energize the Basque-speaking community.
- To encourage all kinds of organisations to take protective steps making it possible to live in the Basque language and minimising obstacles in this respect.
- To succeed, once the initiative has been completed, in maintaining the progress made and the relations established in the Basque language.[30]

The initiative organised 'Euskaraldia: 11 Days in Euskera', from 23 November to 3 December 2018 (International Day of the Basque Language) and established it as a biannual event with the second held in 2020. During this period adult speakers were encouraged to use Euskera in their daily relations with the aim of breaking the inertia and promoting more robust linguistic practices in Euskera. The citizens become *ahobizi* (an active mouth) and *belarriprest* (an attentive ear). The *ahobizi* are those who will speak in Euskera with anyone who understands and carry an identifying pin demonstrating their linguistic affiliation and readiness to initiate a conversation in Basque during these eleven days. *Belarriprest* are those who understand Euskera and who welcome others to talk to them in Euskera (even though they are not obliged to speak in

---

[29] Declaration of interest as I was the Plenary Speaker at the Euskaraldia initiative launch in Lasarte on 17 May 2018, suggesting proven best practice interventions for language use and revitalisation. Joxean Amundarain and Estibaliz Alkorta Barragán were extremely helpful in sharing professional information on language policy initiatives and arranging contacts to be interviewed for this project.

[30] For details, please see www.udaltop.eus/documents/192363/1177782/Proposamen+berria+hiz kuntza-ohiturak+eta+gizarte+aktibazioa+lantzeko_.pdf/18d62314-4f28-4b2a-b70f-c009e59f7466.

Euskera). The *belarriprest* also carried an identifying pin during these eleven days.

The medium-term aim was to establish new patterns of sociolinguistic relations and to boost the confidence of new speakers, so that with patterned repetition more robust norms for the social use of Basque would be established and rooted in new domains. Initial evaluations suggest that this initiative has been successful and has led to other initiatives designed to strengthen the communal and transactional use of Basque outside the educational settings of school and college. Government investigations of the Euskaraldia outcomes together with social investigative research by specialist organisations, such as Soziolinguistika Klusterra, now offer a diagnosis, a methodology for evaluation and further ideas for improvement related to *arrue* (analysis), *berbekin* (spoken competence) and *aldahitz* (promoting language switching) which feature new speakers as an essential element of the remedial actions. National and local government officials who were interviewed were fully supportive of such actions and indeed in the case of the national government initiated and funded many of them directly so as to influence the outcomes.

The Basque government commissioned an evaluation of the merits of the Euskaraldia initiative. The approach involved a three-stage questionnaire documenting the before and after experience of Euskaraldia participants from twenty municipalities, together with an interpretation of what prompted any changes that were identified. The first questionnaire was undertaken prior to starting Euskaraldia on 23 November 2018. The second questionnaire was administered soon after finishing Euskaraldia after 3 December 2018, while the third questionnaire was completed three months after finishing Euskaraldia in March 2019.

Professor Pello Jauregi and Uxoa Anduaga (2019) have produced a very comprehensive analysis of the initiative, which reports on the high level of participation achieved as 225,154 people were enrolled; accordingly, this is one of the most representative of samples concerned with mass survey work on Basque. The *ahobizi* were committed to the practice of speaking Basque with everyone who understood it, as well as making the first contact in Basque with strangers. The *belarriprest* were more reluctant to ask Basque speakers to address them in Basque, because they considered it forced behaviour in most cases. However, the Euskaraldia initiative did lead to a significant change in the linguistic use of the participants during the eleven days of the trial. Even three months later the evaluators identified a lasting sustained change in language behaviour, but whether or not these are permanent structural and behavioural changes is an open debate. Many of the participants felt that the exercise was too short to have a lasting effect and for them to internalise the new patterns of sociolinguistic interaction. Accordingly, the second initiative in November–December 2020 lasted an additional two weeks and was considered a success.

The most important changes were detected among those who had lower levels of language skills in Basque, in those who were not so used to speaking Basque and in those who lived in sociolinguistic zones where Basque was spoken less.[31] This is a progressive sign if social cohesion and the relevance and utility of Basque are to be encouraged. For those at the other end of the competence spectrum – that is, those who had a clear tendency to speak Basque and those who lived in sociolinguistic zones where Basque was more widely spoken – no major changes were recorded.

In rank order of social impact, the changes brought about by Euskaraldia were greatest for the passive *euskalduns belarriprest*, then the active *euskaldun belarriprest* and finally the *euskaldun ahobizi*. The report suggests that the greatest success was Euskaraldia's prompting of the *belarriprest* to speak Basque in a spontaneous way. Although the *euskaldun ahobizi* category was the most numerous in *Euskaral,* data show the value of other options: (a) those who, despite have a few limitations when speaking Basque, were confident enough to opt for the role of *ahobizi* (passive *euskaldun ahobizi*); (b) those who, despite not experiencing any problems in speaking Basque, opted for the role of *belarriprest* (*euskaldun belarriprest*); and (c) those who, despite having clear difficulties in speaking Basque, nevertheless chose the role of *belarriprest* (passive *euskaldun belarriprest*).

In broader sociolinguistic terms there are clear identifiable strengths demonstrated by the analysis. It was evident that mutual support and encouragement featured prominently in the group nature of the exercise; watching and imitating others' behaviour was an integral feature as was the degree of respect demonstrated throughout the initiative. The large degree of institutional co-operation and networking was identified as an important support element enabling the initiative to be diffused and implemented in so many locations. The cumulative impact was to restore the current vitality of the Basque language to a prominent position within collective social discourse. It was confirmed that bilingual conversations, while common enough, were an important trigger to switch to using Basque, although it was also recognised that for many changing language patterns with others with whom long-established rules of engagement and language behaviour had been established proved difficult. A common statement was that it seemed unnatural to now speak Basque with someone with whom one had habitually spoken Spanish (or French). A similar comment was that having detailed their language habits over

---

[31] Sociolinguistic zones are a way of classifying the towns, villages and cities of the Basque Country, taking into account the proportion of people who can speak and understand Basque. Four sociolinguistic zones are identified. The first zone is made up of the municipalities in which less than 20 per cent of people can speak Basque; in the second, the proportion is between 20 and 50 per cent; in the third, 50–80 per cent; and in the fourth, above 80 per cent. Twenty municipalities were included in the final survey (Jauregi and Anduaga, 2019).

the time of the initiative, many people had come to recognise that they actually spoke far less Basque in real terms than they had imagined.

The survey results revealed weaknesses that would need to be addressed in future strategic thinking and policy initiatives. A dominant complaint was the lack of real possibility of using Basque in far too many institutional settings, where in principle it was not only allowed but encouraged. The social reality was often far removed from that which official discourse suggested. A second weakness was the lack of commitment demonstrated by many native Basque speakers to using their language in as many domains as was possible, thereby reducing the purchase of the language in social interaction. A third weakness was the practice of switching back to Spanish having established that the other interlocutors could understand Basque, because the content of the conversation rendered both understanding and the effective discharge of the interchange more efficient in the hegemonic language. This is a feature shared by so many minority language speech communities in western Europe, and for the most part Irish, Frisian, Swedish-Finnish and Welsh speakers are so attuned to this type of language switching that they do not perceive it to be a problem. In fact, for many people official transactions are more 'efficient' in the state language.

Jauregi and Anduaga (2019) recommend that future strategies be devoted to encouraging the *belarriprest* to attract interlocutors to the Basque language from diverse elements of society. One of the strengths of the Euskaraldia was the use of a highly visible badge denoting involvement in the initiative. Many people, especially the *ahobizi,* felt very supported in speaking Basque with everyone who understood it, particularly when addressing other people who were wearing the badge – what the authors term the 'social pact mechanism'. The second was a trigger mechanism whereby those who persistently used Basque prompted others to respond to them in Basque, which is termed the 'linguistic symmetry mechanism'. Both mechanisms were mutually supportive and generated a great deal of positive behaviour within new social domains.

One of the virtues of the Euskaraldia was its transformative ability to create new, safe and vibrant social spaces. In summarising the generative power for social change, the report concludes that:

Those who wished to speak Basque have felt socially legitimised to do it in a natural way. Many others have seen a good opportunity to get out of their comfort zone and start processes of change. Many people who had difficulty speaking Basque have felt encouraged to do so, leaving their embarrassment and fears behind. Finally, the possibility of being able to use Spanish or French (without hindering communication in Basque) has been a powerful self-regulating tool for many people who had difficulties speaking Basque to get involved in using Basque without holding back their progress. *Euskaraldia* has given many of the participants a more realistic perspective on linguistic practices. There is a perception that a movement to create awareness of the linguistic reality has taken place. Many participants have realised that they spoke Basque less than they thought. This has been an incentive for many of them to try and improve their linguistic behaviour. Many others have seen that attitudes that did not seem so difficult to them before *Euskaraldia* are more complicated than they believed (adapting the way of expressing oneself when speaking to people who have linguistic difficulties, maintaining bilingual conversations, etc.). Nevertheless, this more realistic perspective has not hindered an improvement in linguistic behaviour. Many people feel they have become more aware in a positive way, realising that there are many more people who understand and speak Basque than they thought. Therefore, *Euskaraldia* has fulfilled an important function in terms of a lot of people made a realistic sociolinguistic analysis of themselves and their immediate environment, and most cases this realism has been an incentive to speak Basque. (Jauregi and Anduaga, 2019, pp. 61–4)

From 20 November to 4 December 2020 the second version of Euskaraldia took place, hampered in part by the Covid-19 restrictions. This included an innovation which is in tune with several of the recommendations gathered during this investigation. Participants were encouraged to create *arigunes*, that is, safe spaces for the use of Basque (Goirigolzarri Garaizar, pers. comm., 2021).[32] This is potentially a very promising initiative for it creates a group synergy which reinforces individual motivation. The slogan was 'More, with more participants and more days' which reflects some of the criticisms voiced during the first survey responses.[33] Other issues noted which are a challenge for subsequent initiatives include:

the attitude of speaking Basque with people who have difficulty understanding and speaking Basque has not spread; there is still a major gap for speakers to express themselves in Basque naturally in communicative situations in which they should adapt their way of speaking towards registers that are easier or more comprehensible; maintaining long bilingual conversations; this practice has not taken root yet in the behaviours of the participants, although some progress has been made; when inviting or asking an interlocutor to speak Basque, many participants felt quite uncomfortable, particularly many who played the role of *belarriprest*. All these behaviours tend towards the use of Spanish or French in current sociolinguistic practice and culture, and this was the case for many participants in *Euskaraldia*. Although some progress has been made, there is still a long way to go in that direction. And it is a necessary path to follow; it is where the challenge of relations between *euskalduns* and passive *euskalduns* lies, and that challenge is precisely one of the key factors in the revitalisation of Basque. (Jauregi and Anduaga, 2019, p. 63)

The evidence on the experience of new speakers in seeking to adjust and engage with the mainstream Basque networks demonstrates that this is not an unalloyed success. The work of Ortega and colleagues reveals that there is a 'a hierarchy in the case of Basque, where we find a continuum of emic categories of Basque speakers, going from least authentic to most authentic, equivalent to

---

[32] See www.etxepare.eus/en/registrations-are-open-for-euskaraldia-2020.
[33] See the website https://euskaraldia.eus/.

"new Basque speaker", "Basque speaker" and "native Basque speaker"' (Ortega et al., 2014; 2015). They argue that the key to this on-the-ground classification is mode of acquisition, degree of use and variety of use.[34] It is suggested that only those who acquire Basque through intergenerational transmission can ever count as fully authentic and fully legitimate Basque speakers. However, Rodríguez argues that it is 'more complicated and less static than this. While it is true that higher legitimacy and authenticity is afforded to those who have learned the language at home, which can be indexed through the variety one speaks (local variety) two key processes helped new speakers in achieving more legitimacy: 1) extending their network to Basque-speaking people 2) adopting a regional variety' (Rodríguez, pers. comm., 2021).

Accordingly, designations such as 'new Basque speaker' and 'Basque speaker' are both categories of people who learned outside this mode of acquisition. Ortega suggests that what differentiates them is the degree with which 'Basque speakers' use the language in more settings and have a greater variety of use. A second basis for differentiation is that 'new Basque speakers' speak standard Basque, while 'Basque speakers' speak a geographically marked dialect. Rodríguez argues that 'it is the *euskaldunzaharra* "native speaker" category that is associated with speaking a regional variety. Those who claim to be *euskaldun* (Basque speaker) achieve a greater sense of legitimacy (more so than new speakers), by means of 1) using the language 2) adopting a regional variety (even if it is not fully comprehensive)' (pers. comm., 2021). Identification and rootedness within a local community was also a consideration as the researchers found that 'one new speaker interviewed longed "to speak a Basque that is from somewhere"' (Ortega et al., 2017, p. 55). Some, such as Gorter, would disagree: 'This I would dispute. Standard Basque or Batua is largely based on the Gipuzkoan dialect, so what do they speak? It is a view from Biscay, and it is in my humble opinion usually quite exaggerated because it is used as a basis for distinction. A few other words, a few other sounds and that makes it more or less authentic. The "dialect continuum" of Basque is linguistically rather narrow, people from the far ends can understand each other (with a little effort)' (Gorter, pers. comm., 2021). Perhaps it is also more generally related to the idea, strong in Basque society, that you are from a place, an ancestral place of origin of the family (Gorter, pers. comm., 2021). Having a marked accent, a distinctive form of pronunciation and a general feeling of 'yet to be fully integrated' is a general phenomenon for new speakers, frequently observed in other contexts.[35]

Politicians and policymakers recognise that the main challenge is how to secure Basque as a second language and grow the numbers of new speakers so

---

[34] See Ortega et al. (2017).
[35] Rodríguez observes that not all new speakers want to sound like a native speaker (Rodríguez, pers. comm., 2021). See Nance et al. (2016) on the Scottish Gaelic case.

that they can sustain such growth in a cumulative fashion. Paxi Baztarrika and his colleagues would argue that the vitality of Basque is at stake and that governments and agencies need to act quickly and decisively if the imbalance regarding the hegemony of Spanish is not to become a chronic problem. While he recognises that political leadership and official intervention are essential, he also recognises that such involvement does not necessarily guarantee success within formal and informal contexts (Baztarrika, 2019). A new campaign and discourse would need to be initiated by the authorities and civil society which emphasised elements such as attraction, perception, incentive and values pertaining to Basque language acquisition and use.

When asked whether or not society wholeheartedly welcomes the phenomenon of the Basque new speaker, most of my informants provided a very positive answer. Granted, some had reservations about the phenomenon, but the general line was that the Basque new speaker idea has never been an issue in the Basque Country. The lived experience of the informants suggested that there was a great deal of gratitude extended towards new speakers for identifying with the language. In general conversation, new speakers were often thanked or applauded for their choices and willingness to use Basque. There have been local ceremonies in many places where new Basque speakers, writers, TV presenters and actors have been publicly congratulated and rewarded for their efforts to become new Basque speakers. Immigrants who have become new Basque speakers were celebrated in the many ceremonies, functions and actions, in villages, towns, cities or valleys, designed to encourage and thank immigrants and to create a sense of social solidarity regardless of place of birth, race or ethnic origin. These expressions of support have been reinforced by national TV programmes which recognise the effort and achievements of new Basque speakers all over the BAC. In public events universities have recognised non-Basque native graduates, who have subsequently carried out their work in Basque, due to the significance they have and the multiplier effect they produce.

Many more initiatives which stress social cohesion through language operate at different levels. While institutions are keen to emphasise that the languages of immigrants are taken into account, such immigrants should be aware that Basque is being normalised and they have a role in that process.[36] Each of these various expressions of gratitude generate a collective feeling of shared destiny which animates the more formal legal provision that Basque is to be considered as an element for social integration and cohesion.

---

[36] For example: www.gipuzkoa.eus/eu/web/hizkuntzaberdintasuna/gipuzkoakohizkuntzak/harrera-protokoloa.

As stated in the preliminary section of Law 10/1982 passed on 24 November, on the standardisation of the use of Basque:

> The intention is to recognize the Basque language as the most viable and objective sign of our community and an instrument of the full integration of the individual in it through knowledge and use of the language. The character of the Basque language as the mother tongue of the Basque people and as an official language together with Spanish should not, under any circumstances, impair the rights of those citizens who for different reasons cannot make use of it, in accordance with that which is expressly laid down in number 3 of article 6 of the Statute of Autonomy of the Basque Country. (Basque Autonomous Community, 1982)

Government officials would suggest that agreement, co-operation and social cohesion have been the cornerstones of Basque language policy (Bergara, 1996; Urrutia, 2005). The Basque government, following the Basque Advisory Council, declared in its 2009 policy statement *Euskara 21: Bases for Language Policy at the Outset of the 21st Century: Towards a Renewed Covenant* that social cohesion and the inclusion of new speakers were priority areas, as illustrated in the following policy recommendations:

> 9. To make communication standards in Basque richer and more flexible as a way of encouraging expressiveness among new speakers, shifting from considering formal correctness as the sole criteria for assessment to assessing standards of communication and expression.
> 11. To make Basque attractive and raise its profile: Basque contains a multitude of worlds and there is room within it for the worlds of those who come to the language. The world of Basque is more plural than the image that we currently give would suggest, and we must make it more plural still, so that it becomes as plural as society itself.
> 12. To enhance the image of Basque by clearly disseminating cultural and communication-related achievements on the one hand and giving practical expression as part of our discourse to the idea that Basque is an essential component of social cohesion in the Basque Country.
> 14. To permanently encourage and strengthen broad-based agreements on matters of language policy with a view to achieving a renewed covenant in which the revitalisation of Basque is closely linked to social cohesion. (Basque Government, 2009)

Such statements, emphasising both social cohesion and the contribution of new speakers, are relatively rare in comparative European official language strategies. Many other cases make passing reference to both, but do not detail such elements as a priority for government language policy. In that sense the Basque Country may be considered as a pioneer in detailing and safeguarding the interests of new speakers.

Generally speaking, it would be good to know why those for whom Basque is a second language reach a good level of Basque and perhaps more importantly what triggers them to start using it as their regular language. This would involve extensive work in sociolinguistics, determining the relevant psycholinguistic factors, analysing ideology and linguistic representations, and so on. While we have some studies, which detail new speaker behaviour within university settings (Goirigolzarri, Amorrortu and Ortega, 2019), cyberspace and sporting activities, little detailed evidence exists to allow one to predict what preconditioning factors would trigger the transition into being a new speaker, notwithstanding that Spanish would always be a powerful part of their linguistic repertoire. Such information is vital if purposive innovative policy is to be initiated.

Paxi Baztarrika (2019) has made an important distinction between the identity and use value of Basque. For far too long many were able to rest content with a strong identity value and entrusted the socialisation and reproduction efforts of learning the language to the statutory education system. Civil society activists now feel it is time to go back to basics, to invoke the co-operation of the family and the community to supplement and give meaning to the skills so assiduously acquired through the education system. They argue that 'with respect to the family, we believe that the time has come for it to take action. Steps must be taken by the Administration and by the school in order to ensure that, in the near future, the transmission of Basque will take place, to the greatest possible extent, from within the family itself. Why, in the case of many speakers, for whom Basque is the second language, do they not choose Basque as the language spoken in the home? What can we do to change that situation?' (Baztarrika, 2019).

Their answer would involve a three-pronged attack on the incipient tendency to shift responsibility for the language's future to official agencies. Empowerment is the watchword of this new infusion of self-help. Thus, each committed speaker should actively encourage new speakers as a matter of course: 'I have often witnessed myself how the native Basques (old and young; literate and illiterate) have welcomed and thanked the new Basque speaker for his/her approach and willingness to use the Basque language' (Baztarrika, 2019).[37] Secondly, the tendency for some communities to honour and celebrate new speakers in public displays of appreciation should be extended and become an integral feature of festivals, carnivals and fetes, together with award ceremonies in literature, the arts, sport and theatre. Thirdly, the consideration of Basque as an element for social integration and cohesion, as stated in the preliminary section of Law 10/1982 on the standardisation of the use of Basque, should be extended to explicitly include the contribution of new speakers.

---

[37] 'During the lockdown, Basque native volunteers help pupils to interact weekly, this implies a positive attitude and disposition to help those who are on their way to becoming new speakers' (Baztarrika, 2019).

Interim Conclusion

The BAC approach is one of the few cases in Europe of an official language policy explicitly recognising the importance of addressing the needs of new speakers thereby strengthening social cohesion. Consequently, it is not surprising that the dominant attitude displayed is an enthusiastic endorsement of measures to enhance the position of new speakers as an integral element of language revitalisation.

We saw that one intervention to increase the confidence and social use of new speakers was the Euskaraldia programme. Another issue which has animated many is the question of creating safe or breathing spaces. In their influential overview of the Basque language from 1981 to 2011, Iñaki Martinez de Luna, Xabier Erize and Mikel Zalbide (2016) ask a fundamental question which is common to all the jurisdictions analysed in this volume. How do we carve out a safe space for the lesser-used language so that it is not always penetrated by speakers of the hegemonic language? The answer they propose is a new, well-designed compartmentalisation framework for a geolinguistic division of space. Here is their reasoning:

> How are we to structure this shared use in terms that do not lead to the gradual loss and eventual disappearance of the weaker language? It is known that, outside of code switching (or the use of humorous or affectionate expressions, which are very common in bilingual contexts such as ours), the use of two or more linguistic codes to convey verbal interaction in a single usage environment is a clearly dispensable social behaviour: a mere redundancy, incapable of preserving the intergenerational continuity of the weaker language community. If two or more languages must coexist in a long-lasting way in the same place, each one needs its own undisputed space for use. The social (and not just individual) configuration of stable bilingualism is, therefore, in our case, a sine qua non. So, it is necessary to define criteria for compartmentalisation that allow Basque speakers the broadest possible range of interaction in Basque, cementing its position in a framework where the hegemonic language has an active, not transitional, presence. A new compartmentalisation framework, that adjusts to our sociolinguistic conditions in the present and the foreseeable future, needs to be formulated, discussed, agreed and implemented. (Martinez de Luna et al., 2016)

The authors do not propose a physical separation of language spaces; rather they advocate a functional, parallel set of spaces for Spanish and Basque wherever feasible. This is so that Basque can have a chance to breathe within its own homeland.

> In technical terms, a new diglossia system must be drafted (Zalbide, 2011). The places where this project is most viable are the Basque breathing spaces: they do not accommodate the largest number of active Basque speakers, but they largely retain Basque i.e., the same speakers, topics and communicative strategies. It is not necessarily a geographical area (that would have a great potential for stabilisation and as such is highly desirable, but the possibility is very weak in our case and as such barely applies). That space can be (and, in our case, often must be) sociofunctional. (Martinez de Luna et al., 2016)

It will be fascinating to see how such spaces are to be realised in the medium term and to what extent their presence does indeed fulfil some of the requirements prescribed for new speaker engagement and self-confidence.[38]

In summary, it may be said that the Basque jurisdiction is fully aware of the significance of encouraging new speakers, devising programmes to meet their needs and keen to adopt other best practice features from cognate contexts in Europe, for they recognise that increasing Basque language use remains a major challenge.

Navarre Situation

Navarre is a transitional context for while the Basque language is official and BAC policies apply to the north of Navarre, where a traditional Basque-speaking population still exists, they do not apply to the entire Autonomous Community. Accordingly, this interpretation relates largely to the situation in the northern portions of the community. In this diglossic situation the degree to which Basque is spoken depends on the prevailing social structural characteristics or on the linguistic competence and environment of the interlocutors. Geolinguistically the different zones of Navarre, as established by the Law of Basque (1986), determine the local possibilities and there is a clear north–south divide, with many residents in the southern district being opposed to the use of Basque.[39] However, in the north its usage has increased, resulting in a social and linguistic situation which is not so different from large parts of Gipuzkoa in the BAC.

The new speaker concept is neither as well established nor as fully endorsed in Navarre language policy as it is in the BAC, but things are changing, as we shall see below.

The education system prior to entering university offers three different linguistic models:

A Model: teaching in Spanish with just a subject in Basque.

---

[38] Gorter observes that 'It came to my mind that the concept *Euskaldun berry* existed long before the concept "new speaker" (similar to Galicia), but in Friesland we never made the distinction this clearly. Why is that?' (Gorter, pers. comm., 2021).

[39] Professor Nekane Oros Bretón gives a personal testimony as follows: 'In my particular case, in Pamplona, I can speak Basque with the persons I know that have this attitude or the competence to speak it: in the University, at the market, in some bars, with some of my friends, in my family with my son and daughter (but not with my brothers because they are contrary to the language, even if it was our family language in the generation before Franquism), at my hairdresser´s . . . I would say that I choose the services knowing if they speak Basque or not and this is a plus for me and Basque speaking people like me who have the same feeling. In the case of my students, they all speak in Basque at the University. It´s true that sometimes, when they finish their studies, they don´t speak the language. The explanation can be the fact of having acquired the language as an academic one. But it´s also true that they do it if the service they are going to use provides the possibility to do it' (Oros Bretón, pers. comm., 2020).

D Model (immersion in Basque): teaching in Basque with just a subject in Spanish.

G Model: teaching entirely in Spanish.

In the 2018–19 academic year, among the students enrolled in early childhood and primary education in Navarre, 27.3 per cent were enrolled in Model D schools, 19.9 per cent in Model A schools and 52.8 per cent in Model G schools (Government of Navarre, 2020).

Given the reforms of the Navarre education system, which have produced significant numbers of new Basque speakers, it would seem likely that the phenomenon could become a significant element of language management in the medium term. One difficulty is language progression as there are significant breaks between key threshold levels at each stage. It would seem that parents and students may be content to attend Basque-medium primary and junior secondary schools but may be tempted to switch to using Spanish for senior school and for higher and further education studies. This is a common enough phenomenon for, when the parents of such children in other European contexts are anxious to assist their children in preparing for formal examinations, they are tempted to place them in mainstream education and/or enrol them for pre-university examinations in the majoritarian state language.

Paula Kasares of the Public University of Navarra advises that parents can choose from one of the three school types available (Kasares, pers. comm., 2021). The Regional Law 18/1986 on Euskera has been modified on several occasions, most significantly by the:

– *Ley Foral 4/2015 de 24 de febrero, de modificación parcial de la Ley Foral 18/1986.*

– *Ley Foral 9/2017 por la que se modifica el título y el articulado de la Ley Foral 18/1986.*

These two changes have been included as a consequence of the variability of the sociolinguistic situation of the community (one town has passed from the Mixed Zone to the Basque zone while no fewer than forty-three towns have transferred from the non-Basque-speaking area to the Mixed Zone) and are closely related to the linguistic models in public education (Oros Bretón, pers. comm., 2021).

These models are present in both the public and private schools. The latter are financed by public funds, but are managed by private institutions, most of them religious; but they also include the *ikastolas* schools which started teaching in Basque during the Francoist period and continue to this day, The private education sector (*educación concertada*) caters for 41 per cent of the students in Navarre. Most of the private schools remain religious foundations and teach in Model G, while the density and social influence of Model D *ikastolas* is proportionally lower, mainly in the southern part of Navarre.

In-migrant residents usually choose education in Spanish either in a private school or in a public one. Few such students study in Basque, but the ones who do so usually do not have problems in coping with social integration within the Basque-speaking community. Hitherto there is very little research on this specific field.

The relationship between home language use and school educational medium may be discerned from the survey by the Department of Education undertaken in February 2019. This revealed that when asked about the language spoken at home when all family members are together, among all the students of 4th primary education (9–10 years old) and 2nd secondary education cohorts (13–14 years old), 51.2 per cent of the pupils of Model D schools of 4th grade of primary education and 54.1 per cent of the pupils of the Model D of 2nd year of compulsory secondary education replied that they never spoke Basque. Accordingly, for a large number of younger pupils, Basque is very much a language of schooling with variable degrees of usage outside the school system depending on the context. The same is true of many parts of the BAC where the social use of the language is very low as described by Ortega et al. (2016, pp. 239–56).[40]

Professor Nekane Oros Bretón advises that, in relation to higher education, students who have studied in Basque immersion programmes (Model D) can continue their studies in Basque for degree courses, mainly within education, agriculture and medical care, at either the Public University of Navarre (UPNA) or the University of the Basque Country (UPV). Of course, they can also continue in Spanish in other universities throughout the state, even if few choose that option. Normally they do not have academic or linguistic difficulties in undertaking such degrees in either Basque or Spanish, even if they have completed all their previous studies in Basque. The initial evaluation exam for students arriving at the UPNA university (*Evau*) is taken in Basque for such students and the academic results are similar whether they have studied in Basque or Spanish. Understandably Navarre is a diglossic community and most students lead their lives through Spanish even if they study in Basque.[41]

A pressing issue for civil activists and policy evaluators is the extent to which the children of migrant/immigrant residents manage to master the Basque language and integrate well into the Basque-speaking community. The situation varies from zone to zone. In the regions where Basque has great social vitality, children from migrant families are schooled in Basque

---

[40] https://blogs.deusto.es/euskalgaiak/wp-content/uploads/sites/42/2016/11/Nuevos-hablantes-de-euskera-DIG.pdf.

[41] Professor Nekane Oros Bretón adds that 'I teach a subject in Spanish to students who have accomplished all their studies in Basque and have similar problems, for instance in orthography, lexicon, competence in metalinguistic analysis or grammar that the ones who have done it in Spanish' (Oros Bretón, pers. comm., 2020).

and are linguistically integrated into the Basque-speaking community. In areas where Basque is not known by the majority of the population and where the language does not enjoy official status, children from migrant families tend not to study in Basque and do not therefore learn the Basque language.

For both the BAC and Navarre many people have commented that the skills acquired through formal education in Basque are not necessarily translated into actual usage in those domains where this is possible. Educational specialists such as Paula Kasares acknowledge that for younger generations of new Basque speakers to integrate the language into their daily lives is an ongoing challenge in the BAC, Navarre and the French Basque Country. To do this, opportunities for social use have to be expanded and it is in this area where efforts are being made: expanding areas of extracurricular use, in the field of leisure, free time and in new technologies. Some experiences show that if opportunities are presented, the use of Basque grows. However, as Gorter observes, the role of Spanish in society, locally and at large needs to be constantly kept in mind. It is not just a matter of Basque but of the contact, competition and conflict with Spanish and to a lesser degree with English (Gorter, pers. comm., 2021).

A related issue is that some educationalists and language policy planners expect a negative reaction on two fronts. First, that the levels of competence in Basque-medium teaching are not as high as was expected several years ago; and second, that the non-Basque element of the resident population may grow increasingly resentful of current educational programmes and appeal to state authorities to redress the balance in favour of Spanish. When asked how real this was and if it could influence the rate and pace of change in favour of the normalisation of Basque, respondents replied that they shared these fears. It was acknowledged that the level of competence of children who are schooled in Basque, but do not have a Basque-speaking family or social environment, does not allow them to use Basque comfortably, fluently and spontaneously. Gorter avers that 'one has to wonder why this is so ... after 16 years (2–18) in a system that is 70% through Basque ... (25 hours per week, minus 4 hours of Spanish and 3 hours of English, so roughly 18/25=0.72)' (Gorter, pers. comm., 2021). One way of mitigating this frustration is to offer extracurricular activities, so as to complement and enrich school learning.

Specialists such as Professor Bretón believe that a relative lack of competence is a phenomenon which is taking place not just in Basque but also in Spanish, and the younger generations know English a lot better than their parents. She argues that this is a result of use of the Internet and new technologies, which effectively means that students read less and are not as competent in writing long assignments as the previous generation. However, they are certainly engaged in reading material on social media outlets, reflecting a global trend not specific to the Basque case.

On the other hand, part of the non-Basque-speaking population that does not have a favourable attitude towards the promotion of Basque interprets any progress in the social equality of both languages as threatening to its position and readily opposes such initiatives. In Navarre this is very much a political issue because the conservative UPN party and the PP (now Navarra Suma) are more antagonistic towards Basque in Navarre than is the PP in the BAC. This is not a recent phenomenon, and such opposition may intensify as a result of the emergence of Vox, the new right-wing party which has one seat in BAC, none in Navarre (Gorter, pers. comm., 2021). The rise of Vox displays an especially belligerent attitude towards other languages while they defend the use of Spanish only. In Navarre this has been a long-standing attitude held by both the majority and the political classes such that what has been achieved in terms of bilingual education has been really difficult. Nevertheless, owing to the great amount of work already undertaken and consolidated, such reforms are unlikely to be undone because they are approved by a significant portion of the population.

Above all, the advance in the administrative use of Basque and its requirement for access to some jobs in the Administration is usually problematic. There is a common trope in the discourse regarding the imposition of Basque which is used systematically by the dissatisfied sector of the population and is very reminiscent of the public complaints one receives regarding the use of Gaelic in Scotland and of Irish in Ireland.

The Basque language in Navarre has not been 'normalised' in the way it has been accomplished in the BAC. In Navarre, the political majority until 2015 had been opposed to the normalisation of the Basque language. From 2015 to 2019 the government was in favour of the language. The Partido Socialista de Navarra (PSN), a part of PSOE, which forms the current government, traditionally tolerated the status quo as regards the language, but more recently its stance has shifted, in part being moderated by more pro-Basque parties. This has been reflected in the Second Strategic Plan (2020–7) for the Basque Language, which is a continuation of the First Strategic Plan (2016–19) carried out by the previous pro-Basque government of Geroa Bai. Critically, new speakers of Basque are one of the six strategic aims of both plans and as a consequence reflect the growing acceptance of the term within official language policies.[42] The six policy areas are: (1) social use of Basque; (2) new Basque speakers; (3) Basque in public services; (4) the prestige and attractiveness of Basque; (5) Basque as an economic engine; (6) Basque in the capital (Government of Navarre, 2020). To date, little detail is available on

---

[42] See https://euskarabidea.es/castellano/planes-estrategicos/ii-plan-estrategico-del-euskera-2020-2027. I thank Jone Goirigolzarri Garaizar for bringing this to my attention. Private correspondence, 11 April 2021.

how the concern with new speakers is to be implemented, but the very fact that it has been identified as a strategic area is a significant development.

What then can we say about society's attitude towards the phenomenon of the Basque new speaker? Is it to be welcomed or are there real concerns regarding this phenomenon? Specialists argue that they are not really concerned about a backlash or lack of support for new speakers. The new speakers who are produced either by the public and private education route or as an adult Basque learner are made welcome. It is true that Basque new speakers (*euskaldun berriak*) are not always valued by a more linguistically conservative element of the population who, in seeking to maintain linguistic purity, have complained about the lack of grammatical accuracy, dialect infelicities and accents. This was more of an issue in the 1980s; now it is a small rearguard action. However, complaints about the quality of the language remain and are a more general feature of the debate regarding the health of Basque. A more pressing case has been made recently to end the dichotomy of *euskaldun berriak* and *euskaldun zaharrak* and adopt the single term *euskaldun* for everybody.

For the most part new speakers are welcomed, appreciated and considered to be a vital source of future vitality. Rodríguez observes that 'at an institutional level, they are supported, but like in any society, they are still regarded as "less authentic" which speaks to hegemonic native speaker ideologies. The fact that new initiatives are invested in bringing cohesion speaks to the fact that the Basque-speaking population is somehow fragmented as well' (Rodríguez, pers. comm., 2021).

At a micro level, as families interact one can observe a great deal of variation, even within the same family. For example, parents can be indifferent towards the Basque language but, when their offspring mature to become parents, they in turn often decide to enrol their children within the bilingual education system. In this manner the language is increasingly able to permeate throughout society.

The phenomenon of new Basque speakers is, in general, socially well received. Adult learning, such as the courses at *euskaltegi*, is seen, along with children's education in the language, as the basis for the social recovery of Basque. Gorter advises that adult learning also offers a 'second opportunity for many who went to A or B Model schools (chosen by their parents) and now want (or need) to learn Basque, because of their children, extended family, friends or work' (Gorter, pers. comm., 2021). Clearly more needs to be known about how *euskaltegis* progress and what they feel about their reception by the native speakers.

It has historically been a sector driven by social initiatives, accompanied by great dynamism and a fair degree of commitment. It produces speakers who often report that they are well satisfied with their courses and can thereby contribute to the social cohesion of the Basque-speaking community.

The popular activities related to the cohesion of the Basque-speaking community and the practice of the Basque language, such as 'Euskaraldia: 11 days in Euskera' or 'Korrika', also include Navarre. In this context, Bretón asserts that there is a great feeling of shared identity through language in both the BAC and Navarre (Oros Bretón, pers. comm., 2021). Of critical value is the degree of support offered by the BAC Administration which has a significant impact on the language policy programme and an equally important if more diffuse impact in Navarre, primarily related to educational provision and practice. The medium-term impact of both can be measured through evaluation studies and, while education is central, there is no doubt that guaranteeing linguistic transmission within the family is the key to supporting the extension of the use of Basque to a wider array of socio-economic domains.

One identifiable lacuna in the policy realm is the relationship between traditional speakers and new speakers. Rodríguez has averred that:

Something that no policy maker addresses is the need for non-new-speakers to better embrace new speakers, and to remove the biases that they exist towards them. That is, we need to educate traditional speakers and foster linguistic diversity and variation as a natural source of linguistic practice – 'contact features do not ruin the language' 'Standard Basque is a SPOKEN variety too!' – We have the term *euskalki* (that is often just referred to traditional varieties). Even most Basque linguists treat standard Basque as this 'created Standard' when in fact, it is a *EUSKALKI* as well. Maybe this is something that more localized policies could address? (Rodríguez, pers. comm., 2021)

Conclusion

The analysis of the BAC and Navarre suggests that the new speaker phenomenon has been widely accepted and endorsed by governing parties, especially the EAJ–PNV, and by civil society organisations. New blood and younger generations of speakers are welcomed as a boost to the total number of speakers and an expansion of the ethnolinguistic base of the population. A particular welcome is given to the progeny of migrants from other parts of Spain and from other parts of Europe, especially Romania, together with South America and Africa; their acquisition of Basque is seen as aiding social cohesion and boosting the long-term vitality of the language.

In theory the positive investment from the government in education and social initiatives favours the realisation of the language rights of all citizens allowing a great measure of linguistic freedom to opt for one's own language of use. The reality, however, is far less positive as commentators have observed that the language rights of citizens are systematically violated.[43]

---

[43] See www.behatokia.eus/EN/ (Goirigolzarri Garaizar, pers. comm., 2021).

When governments have adopted a moderate affirmative action policy for Basque it is evident that a great deal of adjustment has had to take place, especially within the education and training sectors. The big issue facing language promoters is the relatively low level of active use of the language relative to its successful acquisition by those who are proficient but not necessarily inclined to use it as a chosen language of regular interaction. The last decade has witnessed a significant period of additional investment both of purpose and energy in the Basque revitalisation process and Basque language policy and planning. Key informants, such as Goirigolzarri Garaizar, underline this disjuncture between acquisition of knowledge and social use in the following commentary:

Since the revitalisation process of Basque began, the level of knowledge has greatly increased, particularly in the under 25-year-olds, thanks to formal education. However, its social use has seen very little increase. Consequently, there is quite a widespread consensus that the strategy of linguistic revitalisation focused on language acquisition has reached a ceiling, at least in the Basque Autonomous Community. That is why the present challenge of the language policy is to foster what has been termed in Basque Sociolinguistics an 'activation' of those who can speak the language but have not taken the step to use it in their everyday life. Therefore, over the last decade, Basque civil society organisations and public authorities have launched many different initiatives aimed to encourage speakers' use of Basque; one good example being *Euskaraldia*. Besides, a fruitful joint reflection period has taken place among different agents in order to think about the future strategy of the revitalisation of Basque. (Goirigolzarri Garaizar, pers. comm., 2021)[44]

---

[44] This activation process has materialised in fruitful workshops and documents, such as 'Eta hemendik aurrera zer?/And from now on what?' (Hizkuntza Politika Sailburuordetza/Vice Council of Language Policy, 2016), www.euskadi.eus/web01-a2aznscp/es/k75aWebPublicacion esWar/k75aObtenerPublicacionDigitalServlet?R01HNoPortal=true&N_LIBR=051906&N_EDI C=0001&C_IDIOM=es&FORMATO=.pdf; 'Berrikasi eta berrikusi/Review and relearn' (Euskaltzaileen Topagunea, 2015), www.erabili.eus/zer_berri/muinetik/dokumentuak/2015/Berr ikasiEtaBerrikusi.pdf; 'Berrindartu eta jauzi/Strengthen and jump' (Euskaltzaleen Topagunea, 2020), https://topagunea.eus/wp-content/uploads/2018/12/TopaBerri67_orrika.pdf; 'Azken 30 urtetako bilakaera soziolinguistikoa (1981–2011)/Sociolinguistic evolution of the last 30 years (1981–2011)' (Soziolinguistika Klusterra/Sociolinguistic Cluster, 2016), www.euskadi.eus/we b01-s2ing/es/contenidos/informacion/bibl_digital/es_documen/adjuntos/Euskararen_Bilakaera_ Soziolinguistikoa_eus.pdf; 'Euskararen Etorkizuneko Eszenarioak Elkarrekin Eraikitzen/ Collectively building scenarios for the future of Basque' (Eusko Ikaskuntza – Basque Studies Society, 2017–19), www.eusko-ikaskuntza.eus/es/proyectos/euskararen-etorkizuneko-eszenarioak-elkarrekin-eraikitzen/pr-4/; 'Elefantea ikusi/Discover the elephant' (an initiative of Patxi Saez with the collaboration of Euskaltzaindia – Academy of the Basque Language, 2016), www.noticiasdegipuzkoa.eus/actualidad/sociedad/2016/02/13/euskaltzaindia-liderara-nueva-est-rategia-fomento/424548.html; 'Euskararen biziberritzea: marko, diskurtso eta praktika berriak birpentsatzen/The revitalization of Basque: rethinking new frameworks, speeches and practices' (an initiative of Jone Goirigolzarri Garaizar, Ibon Manterola and Xabier Landabidea with the collaboration of Udako Euskal Unibertsitatea – the Summer Basque University, 2017), www .ueu.eus/denda/ikusi/euskararen_biziberritzea__marko__diskurtso_eta_praktika_berriak_birpent satzen. Source: Goirigolzarri Garaizar, pers. comm., 11April 2021.

Two key initiatives, the Euskaraldia programme and the various attempts at establishing safe social spaces, offer some degree of optimism that hitherto difficult barriers can be overcome. An interesting addition to Euskaraldia 2020 were the *arigune* practising spaces. They supplemented the *arnasguneak* (breathing spaces) that existed already in municipalities where over 80 per cent of the population speaks Basque.[45] These *arnasguneak* have become very important to lead the recuperation and maintenance of the language and apply also to socio-functional areas, called *arnasgune funtzionalak*, which have a more varied application incorporating a workgroup, an interest group or a service provision.[46]

The acid test of the utility of Basque is in its instrumental capacity to enable one to earn a living in a bilingual economy, as is the case in a large part of the public sector where Basque is often a requirement, and it is becoming increasingly so in large parts of the private sector also.

In comparative terms it is unquestionable that Basque language promoters have actively welcomed and endorsed the new speaker phenomenon and other parts of Europe would do well to examine Basque best practice. Be that as it may, new speakers still face many challenges, particularly in finding spaces where Basque could be used. Despite sure signs of success, Basque policy will doubtless continue to address new challenges in a globalised linguistic market.

---

[45] See https://euskaraldia.eus/es/arigunes/; www.euskadi.eus/evaluacion-del-impacto-linguistico/web01-a2lingu/es/.

[46] I am grateful to Beñat Egues Cuesta, Joxean Amundarain Iturrioz and colleagues within the Gipuzkoako Hizkuntza Berdintasuneko Zuzendaritza Nagusia for this and many other observations related to official Basque policy.

7 Catalonia and Galicia: Unalloyed Support?

Catalonia

One thorny structural issue which underpins the freedom of action available to the Catalan authorities is the tension between and the proper respective weight given to the decisions of the Catalan government and those of the Spanish government and the Constitutional and Supreme Court rulings. Such considerations hang over Catalan affairs like a dark shadow, made all the more pernicious by the difficult relationship that has existed periodically between Madrid and Barcelona. A simple illustration will suffice: when the English industrialist William Morris wanted to build a factory in Catalonia, King Alfonso III insisted it had to be in Guadalajara, near Madrid. Accordingly, no factory was built.[1] This fractured relationship has been aggravated since the outbreak of the Spanish Civil War and the subsequent repression of Catalan rights under Franco's dictatorship. The subjective ethnolinguistic vitality of autochthonous Catalans is relatively high as they display a determination to forge society in their own image, rather than be a pale reflection of a majoritarian Spanish society which they deem to be inimical to true Catalan values, more given to negotiate solutions to problems – in the commercial tradition – than to try and defeat the opponent.

Of the jurisdictions investigated herein it is the Catalan case which provides the most comprehensive and effective framework for the development of learners and the integration of new speakers. In part this is because the Catalan language is in a strong position as the original language of the nation and in consequence investment in education, resource expenditure and the mainstreaming of language promotional initiatives are interpreted as part of the public good of society.[2]

---

[1] I owe this and other observations to the late Miquel Strubell who has been able to critique Catalan language policy from a position of authority having been the head of the Servei de Normalització Lingüística of the Generalitat de Catalunya (Government of Catalonia) and head of the Direcció General de Política Lingüística, the Institut de Sociolingüística Catalana, before becoming a professor at UOC until his retirement in 2014.

[2] Those who count only 'native speakers' say that only around 30 per cent fall within this category. https://llengua.gencat.cat/web/.content/documents/publicacions/publicacions_en_linia/arxius/eul p2018-opuscle.pdf. I am grateful to Professor Joan Pujolar (personal correspondence, 4 March 2021)

A feature of Catalan life for several generations is that many migrants, largely from other parts of Spain, have been integrated, as have their descendants, and although during the time of their absorption they would not have been termed new speakers of Catalan, that in effect is what they became. Boix-Fuster and Paradis (2019) have interpreted new speakers' ideologies and trajectories in bilingual families and, while it is very evident that 'both processes of acquisition and loss of the Catalan language occur in inter generational language transmission', nevertheless,

> most of these catalanized new speakers display a deep symbolic identification with the Catalan language. They have a strong predisposition to be part of the community, they do not want to confine in monolingualism, they want to incorporate 'catalanitat' as a dimension which allows them to open up to the country, to its people, to the social networks, to the trade unions, to the parties, etc. Catalan speakers, generally considered to have higher social status, have become a reference group for these new speakers. (Boix-Fuster and Paradis, 2019, p. 217)

For such families Spanish will still be prevalent, in line with its demographic dominance in society. However, 'new aspects are open for research: for example, the children's perspective, the evolution of both linguistic socialization and family language policy in the long run, and the comparison between declared principles and actual practices by means of ethnographic fieldwork' (Boix-Fuster and Paradis, 2019, p. 219).

The other reason is a settled socio-political will that social cohesion depends on the production of optimum facilities to allow in-migrants, immigrants and refugees to 'fit in' and 'benefit' from full participation in society. This does not mean that there are not quite a few flash points and tensions when it comes to housing allocation, the perceived higher rates of unemployment and dependence of newer arrivals who are sub-sections of the population. By far the greater part arrive via Barajas airport in Madrid from South America, or legally from other countries both in the EU and elsewhere (particularly China, Pakistan and India). There is a small but growing phenomenon of 'refugees' who arrive on small boats and rafts, originally from sub-Saharan Africa but increasingly from the Middle East.

An intriguing question is why Catalonia has been characterised by such a strong rate of in-migration in recent times. Strubell has offered an answer based on the previous large in-migration from Spain in the period 1955–75 and even more acutely before, when Catalonia experienced an extremely low birth rate among native Catalans in 1935 (Vandellós, 1935) followed by a substantial exodus in 1939 (Strubell, pers. comm., 2021).[3] It is argued that general

---

and Professor Xavier Lamuela (personal correspondence, 18 August 2021) for valuable observations. Supplementary sources and discussions include: https://llengua.gencat.cat/en/direccio_general_politica_linguistica/index.html, Solé (1996) and Vernet et al. (2003).

[3] See https://publicacions.iec.cat/repository/pdf/00000173/00000091.pdf.

demographic factors, particularly the age pyramid, in Spain induce large scale in-migration where immigrants expect to learn Spanish and integrate.[4] The Catalan age pyramid and relatively low birth rate also induce migration, but here such migrants tend to be under pressure to learn Spanish rather than Catalan.[5] Adherence to Catalan together with political leanings can be explained in part by the resident's family origins. Less straightforward are any claims that familial background can predict support for independence, but such claims are made often within political discourse.[6] The rootedness of the population may be measured by what percentage of the population has one, two, three, four or no grandparents born in the territory in each Autonomous Community. At one end of the graph, Andalusia has 77 per cent and Galicia 76 per cent of residents with four grandparents born in that territory, whereas Catalonia has 20 per cent, while Madrid has only 9 per cent.[7]

Indigenous and migrant population cohorts may exacerbate both linguistic and political affiliations, but we should be careful not to interpret such divisions as fixed and immutable for their offspring who have been socialised within Catalonia. Such inter-group difficulties will always be present, but what characterises Catalonia is the institutional response to managing the issues of social cohesion and immigrant adjustment, which are seen as having positive benefits both for the recipients and the wider society at large. Accordingly, discussions and programmes for the support of new speakers are more generic and less tangential to mainstream educational and language policies.

Underlying civil society's drive to promote the interests of Catalan learners and new speakers is a moral imperative which is both profound and compelling. 'Everyone who lives and works in Catalonia is Catalan' is the integrative motto of different Catalanist parties. Many Catalans actively support new speakers for a variety of reasons, principally the respect for the individual and to demonstrate the open, welcoming nature of Catalan integration. Of course, there are instrumental reasons also at play (Dalmazzone, 1999). These range from a desire to maximise the speaker's participation in and contribution to the economy, to the democratic impulse to make social cohesion as robust a feature of collective life as is possible. Others are more wary of the impact of new speakers per se and display rather negative attitudes as they believe that the quality of Catalan will deteriorate (Boix, pers. comm., 2021). This purist ideology is found in many contexts but is quite prevalent in Catalonia.

But there is a long-term strategy influencing individual choices also and that is the realisation that if learners and new speakers are not encouraged

---

[4] See www.populationpyramid.net/spain/2021/.
[5] See https://geografiabatxillerat.wordpress.com/2014/11/10/dinamica-de-la-poblacio-catalana/.
[6] See www.vilaweb.cat/noticies/existeix-una-generacio-de-l1-o/.
[7] See www.naciodigital.cat/noticia/191545/vuit-cognoms-autoctons-catalunya-madrid-mes-dificil-enlloc.

along their life trajectory to feel embedded and valued within the Catalan sociolinguistic networks, then inevitably the default position for such people will be to further bolster the role and dominance of Spanish in so many formal and non-formal situations. It is the main concern. Internal meetings between the different government departments acknowledge this. It is acknowledged that immersion schools work in terms of language production and knowledge, but time-series analyses show that the trend is downwards in terms of language use outside education.

The adage that languages in contact are very often languages in competition runs true here in so many ways. Catalan may be a language widely spoken by its citizens,[8] but its people display a set of minoritised characteristics, not surprising given the hegemonic role of Spanish within the kingdom and the episodic impulses of oppression, denial and conflict directed against the Catalan territories by the central state. At first sight there is something incoherent about the persistence of this mindset. Government statements make great claims that the Catalan population is a substantial demographic mass of around 7.5 million residents of the total 10 million who speak a variety of Catalan within Spain, notably in the Valencia Country and the Balearic Islands. But this claim needs to be tempered by the realisation that approximately 1.245 million are (first generation) foreigners (Strubell, pers. comm., 2021).[9] Were they to be an independent state, they would rank both demographically and economically within the higher echelons of EU states, and thus could function effectively as an autonomous polity after some initial bedding-in difficulties were overcome. They have what economists call brand recognition and are respected both for the high quality of their products and their creative design flair. Indeed, in comparative terms they have a very high quality of life coupled with impressive educational standards, good services and infrastructure.[10]

And yet there is a deep consciousness of not being allowed to be completely free and at one with themselves, for the shadow of the Caudillo and his successors still permeates so much of popular consciousness and animates the grievances which political parties and movements list as characterising the dysfunctional relationship between Madrid and Barcelona. This is best illustrated by the fact that some members of the former government of Catalonia were imprisoned in 2017; another nine, including former regional vice-president Oriol Junqueras, were in 2019 sentenced to between nine and thirteen years in prison for sedition and misuse of public funds. They were pardoned and released from prison on 24 June 2021, but a ban on the politicians holding public office remains in place. Carles Puigdemont, the 130th President of Catalonia from 2016 to 2017, is in exile and currently resides in Belgium.

---

[8] See www.idescat.cat/indicadors/?id=anuals&n=10364.
[9] www.idescat.cat/indicadors/?id=anuals&n=10332.   [10] Catalan is also official in Andorra.

Legislation and Language Policy

The principal agency for government language policy is the Secretaria de Política Lingüística de la Generalitat de Catalunya.[11] It is an innovative and well-regarded agency.[12] The basis of Catalan language policy has been well established and is enshrined in Act No. 1 of 7 January 1998, on linguistic policy, together with the Organic Act 6/2006, dated 19 June, reforming the Statute of Autonomy of Catalonia. In terms of language, Article 6 specifies the following:

> Article 6. Catalonia's own language and official languages 1. Catalonia's own language is Catalan.[13] As such, Catalan is the language of normal and preferential use in Public Administration bodies and in the public media of Catalonia and is also the language of normal use for teaching and learning in the education system. 2. Catalan is the official language of Catalonia, together with Castilian, the official language of the Spanish State. All persons have the right to use the two official languages and citizens of Catalonia have the right and the duty to know them. The public authorities of Catalonia shall establish the necessary measures to enable the exercise of these rights and the fulfilment of this duty. In keeping with the provisions of Article 32, there shall be no discrimination on the basis of use of either of the two languages. 3. The Generalitat and the State shall undertake the necessary measures to obtain official status for Catalan within the European Union and its presence and use in international organisations and in international treaties of cultural or linguistic content. 4. The Generalitat shall promote communication and cooperation with the other communities and territories that share a linguistic heritage with Catalonia. To this end, the Generalitat and the State may, as appropriate, sign agreements, treaties, and other collaboration instruments for the promotion and external dissemination of Catalan. 5. The Occitan language, known as Aranese in Aran, is Aran's own language and is official in Catalonia, as established by this Estatut and by the acts of linguistic normalisation.[14]

However, this Statute was modified by the ruling of the Constitutional Court on the 28 June 2010, which investigated a challenge of unconstitutionality no. 8045–2006 brought against several provisions of the Organic Act 6/2006. In terms of language, it should be noted that the ruling declares the phrase 'and preferred' in section 1 of article 6 of the Act to be unconstitutional. Furthermore, the court ruling submits article 5 (language in relation to historic rights), article 6.2 (official languages), article 33.5 (relations between citizens and national constitutional and legal bodies), article 34 (language rights of

---

[11] https://llengua.gencat.cat/en/direccio_general_politica_linguistica/index.html.

[12] I am grateful for the unstinting support I have received for many years from senior civil servants of the Secretaria de Política Lingüística which was formerly the Direcció General de Política Lingüística de la Generalitat de Catalunya.

[13] Lamuela advises that a grammatical term, *pròpia* ('own'), has become a juridical one with the approximate meaning of 'territorial language'. It seems correct to assume that, if it had been possible, the expression 'national language' would have been chosen (Lamuela, pers. comm., 2021).

[14] Statute of Autonomy, 2006, www.parlament.cat/document/cataleg/150259.pdf.

consumers and users), article 35.1 and 2 (education) and article 50.5 (language of internal procedures, communications and notifications) to its own interpretation. On a positive note, such pronouncements recognised the citizen's right to have Catalan available as per the Organic Act; on a negative note, the ruling did declare the phrase 'and preferred' in section 1 of article 6 of the Act to be unconstitutional. A separate advance was the recognition of Catalan sign language as a legitimate means of communication (Pons, 2019; Pons, 2020).[15]

One abiding concern within Catalonia is the gap between official claims and lived reality. The public discourse on Catalan persistently claims that Catalan is a majority language. However, analysis of the latest sociolinguistic data reports that Catalan is still a minority language in its own territory in terms of initial language, identification language and 'habitual' or everyday language (Generalitat de Catalunya, 2019). Thus we need to be conscious that in political terms Catalan is portrayed as a majoritarian language, while in sociolinguistic terms it is increasingly a minority language.

Added to the linguistic complexity is the social class element of many predominantly Spanish-speaking neighbourhoods, especially in Barcelona, which do not necessarily espouse or support the normalisation programme. Indeed, their opposition to the advance of Catalan can take myriad forms but underlying much of the frustration is the dual resentment stemming from a perceived under-investment in largely working-class suburbs and opposition to the current calls for full independence. Loyalty to the one and indivisible Spanish state can take many forms, but one is the presumption that Catalan should not supersede Spanish as the default language of social interaction. New speakers are part of this heady mix of social solidarity, collective representation and the struggle for language-related equality and justice.

Demography and Language Trends

In 2020 Catalan residents constituted some 16 per cent of the population of the Spanish state, which stood at 46,937,060.[16] At the beginning of the century Catalonia's population was 6,261,999 rising to 7,539,618 by 2011 and 7,722,203 by 2020, a growth rate of 13.39 per cent. A critical period of demographic change was the period 2000–2020 where foreign-born migrants rose from 181,590 to 1,185,852, representing 15.7 per cent of the population. Catalonia also records internal migrants from the rest of Spain which in 2019 numbered 52,379.[17]

---

[15] For articles on language law since the Statutes of Autonomy of Catalonia and the Basque Country of 1979, see Pons (2019), http://84.88.27.115/index.php/rld/article/view/10.2436-rld.i72.2019.3391/n72-pons-ca.pdf.

[16] Statistical Institute of Catalonia, www.idescat.cat/pub/?id=aec&n=245&lang=en.

[17] For the number of Spanish nationals born outside Catalonia please consult idescat at www.idescat.cat/tema/migra?lang=en.

In 2011 the population's linguistic ability was as follows: those who could understand Catalan, 6,949,344; those who could speak it, 5,345,484; those able to read it 5,750,348; and those able to write in Catalan, 4,069,219. Those unable to understand Catalan stood at 356,728 which was 4.8 per cent of the total population. Table 7.1 indicates the proportionate changes in various language indicators between 2013 and 2018.[18]

There is also a clear disjuncture between the number of those who can speak Catalan and use it very often (Table 7.2).

Not only has language identification and use changed but so also has the origin of the Catalan population, as revealed in Table 7.3 and Figure 7.1.

It is evident from Figure 7.1 that while the non-Catalan Spanish origin of migrants has changed from 34.4 per cent in 1981 to 16 per cent in 2020, the foreign-born population has grown from 1.5 per cent in 1981 to constitute 20.4 per cent of the current population by 2020.

This significant change in the composition of the population has thrown up several challenges and socio-economic tensions and placed a great strain on the public services. Thus, for Catalan language strategists, the way such immigrants

Table 7.1 *First language, language of identification and usual language, percentages 2013–18*

	First language, 2013–18 (%)	Language of identification, 2013–18 (%)	Usual language, 2013–18 (%)
Catalan	31.0–31.5	36.4–36.3	36.3–36.1
Catalan and Spanish	2.4–2.8	7.0–6.9	6.8–7.4
Spanish	55.1–52.7	47.6–46.6	50.7–48.6
Other languages	10.1–10.8	8.0–8.1	4.7–4.4
Other combinations	0.1–10.00	0.5–1.5	1.2–3.0

Source: Direcció General de Política Lingüística and Institut d'Estadística de Catalunya (2019)

Table 7.2 *Those who declare that they can speak Catalan in 2018*

	Use it				
Can speak Catalan	Never	Little	Fairly often	Quite often	Much
81.2%	23.6%	24.9%	15.5%	17.6%	18.5%

Source: DGPL and Idescat (2019)

[18] https://llengua.gencat.cat/ca/serveis/dades_i_estudis/poblacio/Enquesta-EULP/Enquesta-dusos-lingueistics-de-la-poblacio-2018.

Table: 7.3 *Total and foreign population series, 2000–11, Catalonia*

	(1) Population	Foreign population			
		total	% of (1)	abs. var.	% var.
2011	7.539.618	1.185.852	15,73	−12.686	−1,06
2010	7.512.381	1.198.538	15,95	9.259	0,78
2009	7.475.420	1.189.279	15,91	85.489	7,75
2008	7.364.078	1.103.790	14,99	131.283	13,50
2007	7.210.508	972.507	13,49	58.750	6,43
2006	7.134.697	913.757	12,81	114.853	14,38
2005	6.995.206	798.904	11,42	156.058	24,28
2004	6.813.319	642.846	9,44	99.838	18,39
2003	6.704.146	543.008	8,10	160.988	42,14
2002	6.506.440	382.020	5,87	124.700	48,46
2001	6.361.365	257.320	4,05	75.730	41,70
2000	6.261.999	181.590	2,90		

Source: Idescat, based on census data as supplied to the author by DGPL on 18 May 2012

are integrated into mainstream society is an urgent and politically sensitive matter, the more so given the numbers involved and the fact that both Castilian and Catalan are potential recruiting grounds for new speakers. Apart from those who derive from Latin America, migrants to Catalonia have the double task of learning both host languages if they are to be well integrated into civil society and many express frustration; having come to Spain, they see the requirement to learn two official languages as a further encumbrance. This integration maxim is redolent in well-intentioned policy documents which insist that one needs both languages, but there are many areas in Catalonia where Catalan is practically non-existent.

A major analysis of the situation is contained in the 2010, 2016 and 2019 Language Policy Reports concerning the Catalan language (Generalitat de Catalunya, 2011; 2017a; 2020).[19] The 2010 Report recorded in statistical terms that Catalan has pulling power, for Catalan communities win speakers in the intergenerational language transmission processes. Successive analyses of intergenerational language transmission show that Catalan continues to make appreciable gains and that this progress is still taking place in almost all sectors of society. Consequently, the 2010 Report argued that Catalan society is dynamic, and the vast majority of citizens are committed to its language. The 2016 Language Policy Report (Generalitat de Catalunya, 2017a) indicates that people born outside Catalonia account for 35 per cent of the population. Some 94 per cent of people aged 15 and over understand

---

[19] https://llengua.gencat.cat/ca/direccio_general_politica_linguistica/informe_de_politica_lin guistica/.

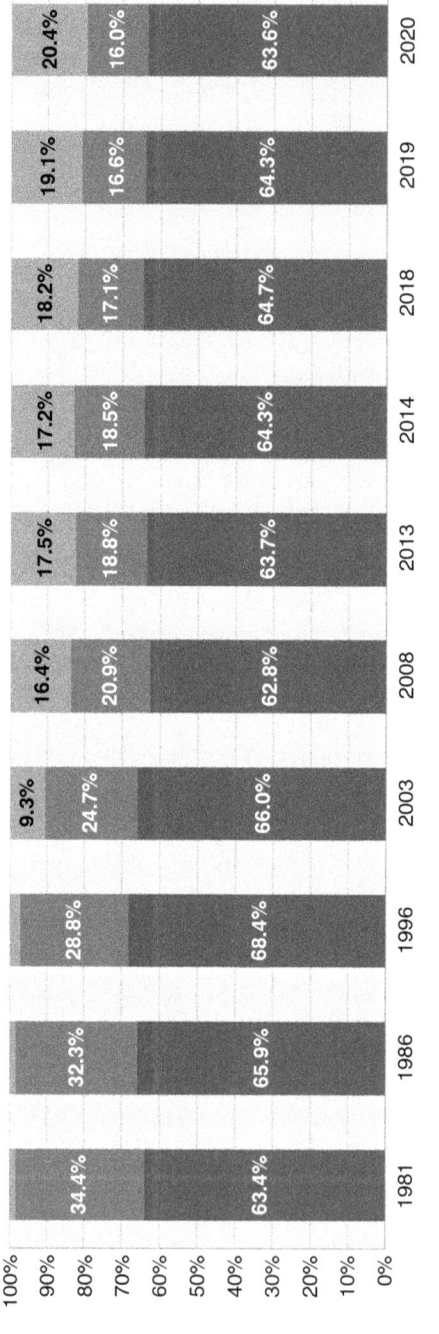

Figure 7.1 Place of birth of population, 1981–2020
Source: Idescat (2022)

Catalan and 80 per cent can speak it. Some 73 per cent of people use Catalan on social media and messaging apps. However, sociolinguists advise that there is a decreasing use of Catalan in secondary education compared with primary levels while Catalan is not much used on digital platforms (Boix, pers. comm., 2021). Government reports have been criticised for offering a very positive gloss on the language situation and many academics I interviewed offered a more cautious view of the reality both of linguistic competence and more incisively of patterns of language use.

The political system has adopted as its main language strategy a guarantee that all citizens will have access to knowledge of Catalan and the possibility of full language integration. To this end the language is used in compulsory education and is the official language at university and in post-secondary education. The growth in international migration is reflected in the proportion of students of foreign origin within statutory education, as revealed in Figure 7.2.

Most lower-secondary education students have a high or medium-high level in Catalan, Spanish and English while French is taken by only 0.5 per cent of the pupils. Catalan is the language in all regional schools, with Spanish being taught for fewer hours per week, although schools may add specific subjects in Spanish if they

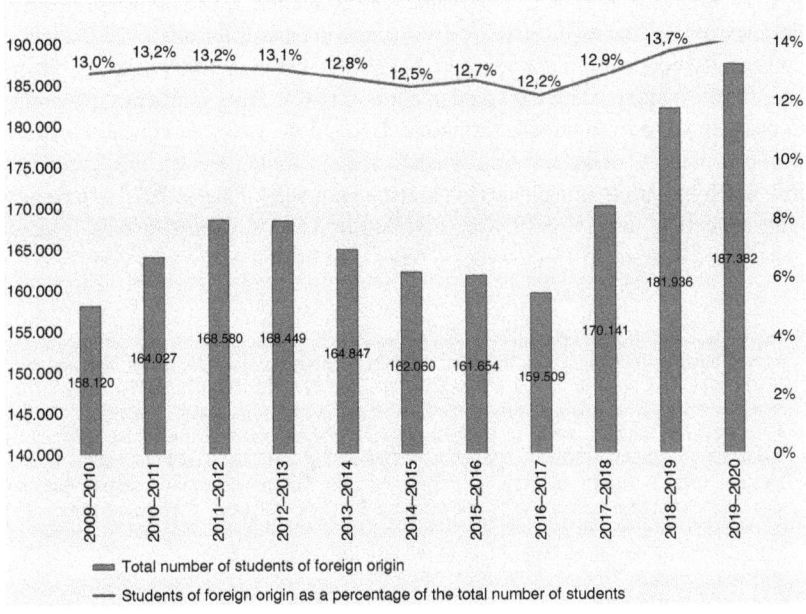

Figure 7.2 Students of foreign origin within statutory education, 2009–20
Source: Department of Education (2021)

feel that children need more exposure.[20] In reality Spanish is much more present, making it difficult to assess the precise mix of language of instruction. Many of the informants I questioned argued that current reality differed quite considerably from what was officially declared, citing the many reports from teachers and parents confirming that Spanish is used more often than is officially recognised.

A ruling of 20 December 2020 imposes 25 per cent of Spanish as a vehicular language and accordingly the Catalan government has launched a legal challenge which is part of an ongoing struggle to assert control.[21] These rights and obligations are monitored and investigated by the Oficina de Garanties Lingüístiques (the Office for Language Rights), which seeks to ensure compliance with the current language legislation. Established in 1984, the Sindic de Greuges de Catalunya (the Catalan ombudsman) investigates complaints made against agencies and institutions within public administration, ranging from the Catalan Generalitat (government) to local councils, provincial governments or county councils. The office is charged with supervising private companies that provide services of public interest, such as electricity, telephony, water, gas and the post. The ombudsman, Rafael Ribó, is elected by a qualified majority vote in parliament and his role is guaranteed to be politically independent. Language complaints form a small but significant element of the office's workload.[22]

The average use of Catalan in university degree courses is 75.5 per cent and in masters programmes it is 55.7 per cent. The education sector demonstrates the vibrancy of the language. In 2016, 696 reception classes hosted 8,923 students. Community education plans reached 341,858 students in 1,005 schools. There were 5,921 students studying Catalan courses at Catalan universities, of whom 73 per cent were from outside Catalonia. Beyond the statutory education sector there are many Catalan for Adults courses and training for specific groups is provided by a variety of agencies in almost all domains. Thus in 2017 in terms of adult education some 76,939 were enrolled in 3,541 Language Normalisation Consortium courses in 159 towns, up 5 per cent from the previous year.[23]

---

[20] There has been virulent opposition to the government's language policy. An anti-nationalist party, Ciutadans (Citizens), was launched in 2006 to oppose 'linguistic politics' in Catalonia. The PP argue that Spanish suffers in Catalonia; for example Carina Mejías, spokeswoman of the opposition right-wing Popular Party in the Catalan parliament, argued that 'fifty per cent of the population of Catalonia are from Spanish-speaking origins, and it is impossible to study in Spanish in private schools or in state schools'. Dismissing such claims as a fabrication, Bernat Joan, a Catalan Euro-MP and expert on linguistics, said: 'This protest would only be legitimate if students did not have adequate Spanish teaching. This is not the case.' Such expressions could be multiplied a thousand-fold and they have increased following the referendum episode of 2017 and the subsequent jailing of several political leaders in 2019.
[21] www.lavanguardia.com/politica/20201217/6130515/tsjc-impone-25-clases-castellano-plena-polemica-ley-celaa.html.
[22] www.sindic.cat/en/page.asp?id=1.
[23] For additional details see The Language Policy of Catalonia, Department of Culture (2017); https://llengua.gencat.cat/web/.content/documents/informepl/arxius/IPL2017_en.pdf.

The Catalan system offers a comprehensive range of language learning technologies. Corpus planning initiatives have included the full range of standard resources required when normalising a language and Catalonia is a world leader in the development of IT and increasingly AI within the media and communication industries. The government has been developing language technology tools such as Parla.cat, which in 2016 had 253,262 users and attracts some 40,000 new users every year. These users can take advantage of the interactive tool, Dictation online and the constant production of other new learning tools and apps. Other resources include facilities for improving the quality of Catalan used, principally Termcat, the Catalan Terminological Centre, which has 619,000 terminological entries online;[24] Optimot which deals with language questions and enquires regarding inconsistencies, and in 2017 received more than 15.8 million enquiries; Automatic translators, which in 2017 contained 68 million words for translation and received 460, 000 enquiries.

Other forms of support include the awarding of a Certificate of Catalan, which in 2017 were issued to 15,223 residents. Universities receive financial support to promote Catalan either for research projects or to produce specialist materials, volumes and technical manuals. Direct government institutional support is provided for the Institute of Catalan Studies and the Institut Ramon Lull which specialises in the promotion of Catalan studies abroad.

The Catalan system is acutely conscious that it needs to encourage the social cohesion of the c.35 per cent of the population born outside of Catalonia. This is done primarily through formal education and the principal instrument for socialising immigrants is the Language Consortium (CPNL), which in 2017 provided 242 language courses for 5,291 students in immigrant associations. In addition, a further 4,744 activities were hosted for 172,881 participants through the CPNL Language and Cohesion Programme.

The main concerns now are that even if students learn Catalan in compulsory education, they hardly use it and turn to Spanish. Trends in terms of language use are going down. This is a source of concern among language planners within the Education Department and the Secretariat for Language Policy.

By 2018 the numbers who identified as Catalan speakers (*Llengua inicial*) stood at 2,010,400 while those who identified as Spanish speakers was 3,366,000 (Generalitat de Catalunya, 2019b, p. 15). Other differences may be expressed in terms of proportions, thus for those recorded as *Llengua inicial* it is 31.5 per cent Catalan and 52.7 per cent Spanish; *Llengua d'identificació*, 36.3 per cent Catalan and 46.6 per cent Spanish; *Llengua habitual* 36.1 per cent Catalan and 48.6 per cent Spanish (Generalitat de Catalunya, 2019b, p. 16).

---

[24] www.termcat.cat/.

In 1986 the proportion of those born in the rest of Spain was 40.3 per cent and abroad just 1.9 per cent. In 2018 the proportion born in the rest of Spain fell to 19.9 per cent while for those born abroad it rose to 20.2 per cent (Generalitat de Catalunya, 2019b, p. 5). The five most common source areas for migrants in 2018 were Morocco at 211,192 (19.6 per cent of the total foreign population); Romania, 89,177 (8.3 per cent); China, 59,380 (5.5 per cent); Italy 55,823 (5.2 per cent); and Pakistan, 45,125 (4.2 per cent). The best represented of traditional source countries of origin from Central and South America were Honduras, 33,728 (3.1 per cent), and Bolivia, 30,095 (2.8 per cent) while Argentina recorded 19,192 (1.8 per cent) and the Dominican Republic 18,620 (1.7 per cent of the total foreign-born of 1,079,207) (Generalitat de Catalunya, 2019b, p. 9). Not surprisingly the proportion of those who tend to habitually use a language other than Catalan or Spanish has increased from 4.4 per cent in 2003 to 10.3 per cent in 2018 (Generalitat de Catalunya, 2019b, p. 17).

How do the authorities deal with this new and growing reality of pluralism? Given the strong desire to make immigrants feel that they have equal opportunities to progress over time, civil society activists and local authorities have introduced Voluntariat per la Llengua (VxL, the Language Volunteers programme), which we will examine below. This is an exemplary illustration of language intervention best practice and has been adopted in several other European contexts. The VxL programme provides not only language use practice and linguistic pattern reinforcement but also friendship, access to local social networks and most critically supportive advice on how to navigate one's way through the bureaucratic and institutional support agencies when searching for accommodation, employment, educational options and basic social rights. This is an important vehicle for the reduction of tensions which inevitably accompany the fear some immigrants and refugees may feel as they accommodate to a new social order.

Added to this one could cite language integration plans for adults and children (reception classrooms) and once a basic fluency has been achieved there are additional online resources which can be accessed as supplementary backup, such as Intercat.[25]

A critical goal of successive governments has been the fostering of the social use of Catalan in all sectors and giving support for the development of services and content in Catalan. To this end Catalan is the language used by the Catalan Civil Service and Catalan must be present in all the government's interdepartmental plans and in its dealings with the public. Thus, developing and offering language services for the public has been a major commitment since 1978 and is reflected in the provision of both face-to-face engagements and in the IT developments of Parla.cat and Optimot, to cite just two initiatives.

---

[25] www.intercat.cat/en/.

The use of Catalan in the commercial sector reflects its relevance as for many using Catalan is a normal business practice reflecting an obvious local demand in Catalan. It is harder to claim that there is a universal demand (Idescat, 2019, pp. 30–4), which is why the linguistic NGO Plataforma per la Llengua very often reminds militants of the scarcity of the use of Catalan in commercial affairs and urges them to boost its significance in this domain (Boix, pers. comm., 2021).

The presence of Catalan within products is one of the precepts included in what is called social responsibility. Thus, in theory companies are requested to label goods in Catalan, including essential information on all their mass-market products distributed in Catalonia. However, this maxim is not always upheld. Rather than take things for granted, government sources are keen to point out that commercial organisations and corporations are 'supporting Catalan' and it is used by a significant number within the media, including the main ICT operators. Catalan is also promoted in films, social media and popular music.

The Secretariat for Language Policy promotes the use of Catalan in the socio-economic sphere through different projects, namely Emmarca't and Ofercat. Emmarca't is aimed at promoting the use of Catalan in major brands through marketing strategies, specifically within the main stores within a given municipality. One hundred and twenty local stores have been selected for this initial phase and actions related to the promotion of Catalan in signs and panels, telephone customer service, publicity or social media have been developed (NPLD, 2019). Situated within a strong entrepreneurial culture, small, often family-owned businesses have been a core element in the economy, reflected in the number of establishments (92,711 in 2018). However, two factors have changed this pattern of ownership: first, a decline in the number of such businesses over a decade (in 2018 there were 6,700 fewer than in 2008); secondly, a significant increase in the foreign-born population has resulted in the reduction of the use of Catalan within such businesses, down from 51 per cent in 2003 to 39 per cent in 2013. In 2018 long-standing Ofercat data collection was harnessed to establish Ofercat plans designed to reverse such trends and increase the presence and use of Catalan in businesses. Interventionist support would appear essential to stabilise an apparently declining use of the language in key sectors.

Such nuanced claims of support bespeak a continued exceptionalism which dates from an earlier period, for official sources and informants recognise the necessity of reminding the populace that Catalan has been normalised. Interviewees insist that the reality is that it is far from being normalised.

But in that case one wonders why such promotional efforts are made continuously by representatives who are expert at devising innovative advertising and marketing campaigns. It is as if a type of institutionalised fragility is at play.[26]

---

[26] Pujolar advises that each innovation brings a new challenge. It took a long time for Catalan to be available on Windows computers (although it is ever-present in open software thanks to myriads

This commercial social responsibility reflects the political responsibility shouldered by government and, despite occasional and predictable instances of fragmentation and deep division as to the details of policy, the general trajectory is by now well established. The Catalan language support structure reveals a complex system which works as an integrated network adopting a holistic approach.

The Government Structure for Language Policy

The government structure for language policy is comprised of the following elements:
1. Government bodies with language powers
   1.1. Secretariat for Language Policy
   1.2. Language Policy Technical Commission and Language Policy Technical Network
   1.3. Generalitat Centre in Perpignan
   1.4. Place Names Commission
   1.5. Catalan Consumer Agency
2. Other bodies which take part in the government's language policy.
   2.1. Consortium for Language Normalisation
   2.2. TERMCAT
   2.3. Ramon Llull Institute
   2.4. Institut d'Estudis Catalans (Catalan Academy)
   2.5. Social Council of the Catalan Language
   2.6. Catalan Audio-visual Council.

The Secretaria/Direcció General de Política Lingüística[27]

For over a generation I have been interpreting the operation of the Secretaria de Política Lingüística (SPL)/Direcció General de Política Lingüística (DGPL) of the Government of Catalunya and have been encouraging other nations and territories to adopt several of its principles and best practices (Williams, 1993; 2007a; 2007b; 2008; 2013a).

Information and insights as to the working of Catalan language policy, including observations on the need to cater for new speakers, have been gleaned from regular interviews with senior civil servants between September 2011 and September 2021.[28]

---

of volunteers); not so long in smartphones. Availability of Catalan in cinema has contracted substantially and is almost non-existent in the new streaming providers. Alexa, Siri and Google Home do not work in Catalan (Pujolar, pers. comm., 2020).

[27] https://llengua.gencat.cat/en/el-catala/organismes/organismes-de-politica-lingueistica/.
[28] Interviews conducted on 13 March 2018 at the DGPL, Carrer del Portal de Santa Madrona, Barcelona involved Marta Xirinachs i Codina, Subdirectora general de Política Lingüística,

The March 2018 meeting discussed the challenges facing those responsible for language policy and planning. It was emphasised that political reporting was vital to the relevance and legitimacy of the DGPL, and this was undertaken through an annual report presented to the Catalan parliament via the Social Council of the Catalan Language. The political representatives approve, or not, the general direction of the DGPL and may specify additional emphases which the policy formulators need to take on board. By September 2021 the biggest change had been the influence of social media in both increasing awareness of challenges and focussing on specific instances of government failing or reticence to invest in new domains such as films, audio-visual and videogames.

The SPL staff do not see themselves as activists but as career bureaucrats who follow the government's mandate and guidelines. Clearly the Director is very conscious that he is under great pressure to change the system and mode of operation so as to produce real sociolinguistic change. He is particularly concerned with negative trends in the use of Catalan within the health service, which has seen a substantial decrease in its capacity to function in Catalan as a result of three factors. The first is the tremendous demographic change which has introduced a far more diverse multilingual workforce and clientele. The second is the loss of skilled medics who emigrate to the USA, UK and Germany. The third is the inability of the Catalan health system to insist that new employees, from places such as Portugal, commit to learning Catalan as a requirement of their employment. To counter these deleterious trends in health and other sectors stronger measures and nudge theory initiatives need to be put in place so as to restore Catalan to a strong position in the workplace, social networks and community interaction. Accordingly, the short-term challenge for the SPL is to understand how the dynamic system is changing, make a diagnosis and develop a new strategy with action plans for specific sectors.[29]

The strongest pillar of the SPL is the permanent constructive popular support which it receives from citizens. This is particularly significant considering the recent demographic changes which have witnessed an increase to 35 per cent of the population born outside the country. There has been a corresponding increase in the respect demonstrated both to the acquisition of Catalan and to the place of birth of many of its new speakers. A shift in emphasis from a primordialist to an instrumental view of Catalan as a vehicular language within a multicultural society has aided this transition, as explored in Woolard (2016) and Woolard and Frekko (2013).

The overarching policy goal is to increase and deepen social cohesion. The Statute of Autonomy 2006 provides a comprehensive overview of the

Deputy Director and Vicent Climent-Ferrando, Technical Adviser to the Deputy Director. They were interviewed again on 23 September 2021 while discussions with the Director, D. F. Xavier Vila, were held on 23 and 27 September 2021.

[29] Xavier Vila interview, 27 September 2021.

governing principles, rights, obligations and conventions by which the Catalan people are to be governed. It requires that school pupils should not be separated based on their language.[30] As they progress to the world of work, individuals are guaranteed their right to exercise their skills in both official languages as the public fully support the idea that all should be competent in both Catalan and Spanish. An important part of language policy is that the public administration and service delivery systems should respect the right of individuals to opt for either Catalan or Spanish when interacting with national and local government. However, there is an emphasis on making Catalan the preferred language of work for public servants, while central government offices in Catalonia are widely criticised for not accepting the use of Catalan.

With respect to new speakers as an element within language policy, in 2021 SPL representatives repeated their 2018 conviction that neither the term nor the need to pay particular attention to this category is evidenced in any official documentation. When asked if this was because of conceptual redundancy or political convention, the officials suggested that the term was not sufficiently explicit to work as an operational instrument of policy. It was either too vague or too broad to encompass the range of experiences, from pupils from non-Catalan-speaking homes learning Catalan at a young age in school to adults born abroad learning Catalan through evening classes. The official discourse adhered to time-honoured categories such as Catalan speakers (L1 and L2 individuals) and non-Catalan speakers, although Lamuela advises that the descriptor of L2 speaker is problematic as many Catalan L2 speakers have acquired the language very early in life and have a better knowledge of it than most native speakers (Lamuela, pers. comm., 2021).

As such categories were readily understood both in government circles and among the general population there was no urgency or specific justification for adding an additional concept such as new speaker to the official discourse.

---

[30] 'Article 21. Rights and obligations in the field of education 1. Each individual has the right to a high-quality education and to equality of access. The Generalitat shall establish a model of education in the public interest that guarantees these rights. 2. In accordance with the principles established in Article 37.4, parents are guaranteed the right of their children to receive moral and religious education in accord with their convictions in State schools, in which the education is non-religious. 3. Private schools may be supported with public funds in accordance with the provisions of the law, in order to guarantee the rights to equal access and to a high-quality education. 4. Education is free at all compulsory stages and at other levels as may be established by law. 5. Each individual has the right to occupational and continuous training, under the terms established by law. 6. Each individual has the right to receive, under the terms and conditions which may be established by law, public assistance to meet his or her educational needs, and equal access to higher levels of education, in accordance with his or her economic resources, aptitudes and preferences. 7. Individuals with special educational needs have the right to receive the necessary support to gain access to the educational system, in accordance with the provisions of the law. 8. The members of the educational community have the right to participate in school and university affairs under the terms established by law' (www.parlament.cat/document/cataleg/150259.pdf).

However, it was recognised that recent research on the new speaker concept in Catalonia has thrown up interesting ideas which one day might be incorporated into official thinking.

In May 2021 a new government was formed comprised of the Esquerra Republicana (ERC) and Together for Catalonia (JxCat). Having played down the language issue when in opposition so as to broaden the base of their parties, the new government declared its commitment to making Catalan a core policy issue during its mandate. To that end the long-standing social debate regarding the role of Catalan as a unifying force was revitalised with a series of principles which underly current programmes, namely that:

1. Catalan is the language of all people and should be known by all.
2. Catalan is a language for all purposes.
3. Catalonia is comprised of a single people where the language should be understood by all.

In truth this is a restatement of the original post-Franco social consensus which clearly has not come to pass and thus a new consensus, named the National Agreement, is being constructed. Central to this was the decision to steer the SPL in a new direction with the appointment of Xavier Vila as Director in July 2021. Prior to his appointment it is argued that the DGPL, under Ester Franquesa, was essentially concerned with the delivery of services and the development of language-related technical improvements, such as the strengthening of Termcat. For a long time, the strategic vision was excessively linguistic and had too little to commend in terms of social/political aspects and popular usage. Now, however, the goal is to influence behavioural change so as to increase the use of Catalan through a series of interventions. Initially this requires a thorough analysis and diagnosis of the weaknesses in the system and then the formulation of short-term and medium-term interventions. Xavier Vila argues that for far too long the government assumed that once individuals had gained competence in Catalan they would automatically participate in the many social networks and use Catalan increasingly in employment. Recent data suggests that this is just not happening; consequently what is required is a change of mindset, an attempt to recapture the dynamism of the early eighties when attempts to normalise the language emphasised the need to exercise language rights.[31] Vila is concerned that, while budgets may be limited, there is an acute need to construct a plan which will address the many challenges faced by Catalan in an increasingly diverse demographic context where the workplace, the social networks and the community do not effectively reinforce the sociolinguistic integration of new residents, let alone new speakers.

---

[31] Xavier Vila interview, 27 September 2021.

How then might government draw attention to the needs of recent arrivals or to those who have experienced a *muda* in their deliberations and programmes?[32] The answer given by civil servants was that Catalonia has a long tradition of dealing with migrants as 'newcomers in our midst'. It would therefore be unwise to emphasise the non-Catalan origins of such people. Indeed, there has been a strong push towards positive discrimination and investing heavily in educational initiatives to enable those born abroad, constituting some 65 per cent of those now enrolled in adult education classes, to integrate. Figure 7.3 identifies the number of registrations on CPNL courses in 2017–20.

The 65 per cent figure is high because the conventional migration flow into Catalonia from the rest of Spain has declined steadily since its peak in the 1960s as demonstrated by Figure 7.1. While Spanish still plays a pivotal role in social cohesion the government is conscious that migrants from abroad do not integrate as well as did Spanish 'internal migrants' in times past.

One illustration of this phenomenon will suffice. Maria Sabaté-Dalmau (2020) has demonstrated how the Pakistani diaspora living in Barcelona invest in Spanish rather than Catalan as the 'integration' language, despite being categorised as 'deficient' users of it.

They present themselves as 'native' speakers of Urdu, which indexes modern 'Muslimness' and 'Pakistaniness', while Punjabi users, associated with the 'yokels', are silenced. English is ambivalently taken-up as an intra-group sign of educational status and political power and as an anti-Muslim 'coloniser' language. Overall, these stratifying sociolinguistic behaviours reveal how Pakistanis' home/host multilingual resources get re-ideologised through linguistic hierarchisations which foster the maintenance of majority languages only, dismissing minority language speakers, in unchartered transnational contexts where these are already 'delanguaged'. (Sabaté-Dalmau, 2021)

This is a common enough phenomenon and one of the long-term challenges for the Catalan authorities and civil society is to attract such migrants to the Catalan speech community.

The principal instrument for improving this situation is the Catalan adult education system, which has had a great deal of success in facilitating the language transition process. In the first phase of language learning the adult students are presented with idioms and pictorial representations of key ideas, concepts and facts with the accompanying Catalan term. Initially for those who did not know either Catalan or Spanish, English was used to introduce the classes until the students had a basic grasp of Catalan. Now under a new strategy French and Arabic are also used. The one exception is in dealing with migrants from Chinese-speaking territories where tutors are sought who can communicate effectively with the new arrivals in one of their own languages of wider communication.

---

[32] *Muda* comes from the Latin *muta* from the verb *mutare*.

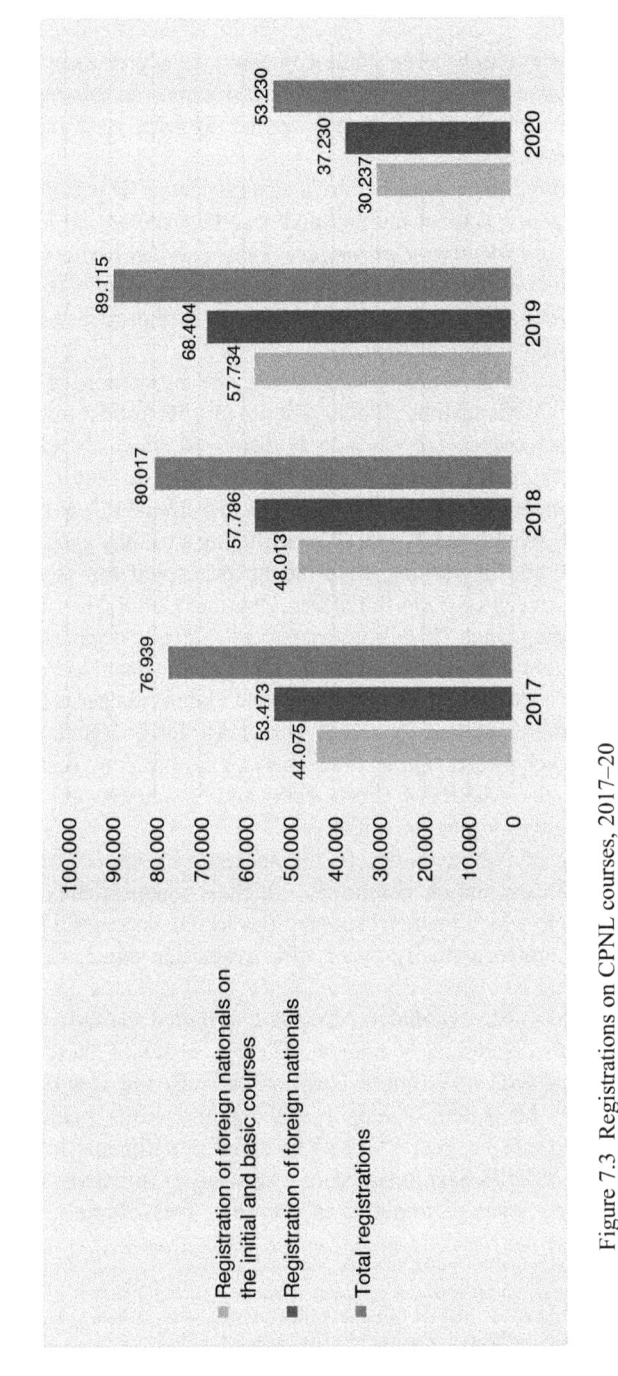

Figure 7.3 Registrations on CPNL courses, 2017–20
Source: Consorci per a la Normalització Lingüística (2022)

One precondition in comparable systems would be an official recognition of the candidate's right to receive adult education as a precursor to entering society. The Catalan system is very flexible and mature in this regard, but to become naturalised as a Spaniard, the central Spanish state requires only Spanish (Boix, pers. comm., 2021).

No one is required to be identified by their passport or ID permit. All that is needed is a telephone contact number and an NIE (*Número de Identidad de Extranjero*/*número d'identitat d'estranger*). This is so that barriers to learning Catalan in as short a time as possible are removed. A certificate of skills in Spanish and Catalan, the *arrelament* certificate, must be produced so as to 'put down roots' in society as a resident.

While the SPL leads on language issues, the promotion of Catalan is a transversal policy mandating all departments of government to be involved in the effort to achieve social cohesion as discussed above. In addition, it is recognised that in such a strong society the 189 civil society organisations involved in language and cultural promotion have a crucial role to play, both in implementing the overall social goal of constructing a healthy and vital context for the language and in pushing government to account for its actions and adopting progressive grass-roots initiatives. Òmnium Cultural has not accepted government funding since 2010, but it remains the largest organisation by far. CAL (Coordinadora d'Associacions per la Llengua Catalana/Associations for the Catalan Language) was a mainstay, while the Plataforma per la Llengua has become much more evident in recent years. All three organisations have comprehensive websites detailing their campaigns, projects, opinion pieces and news while the XERREM (Let's Talk) and Voluntariat per la Llengua agencies constitute best practice initiatives.[33]

The awarding of public money to the successful competitive tenders is undertaken by an evaluation committee which is independent of the SPL, while the degree to which financial subventions lead to successful behavioural outcomes is calibrated annually by an SPL evaluation panel. Critics would argue that funding has been very scarce since 2008 and as a consequence it would appear that SPL external funding is distributed via agreements with actors in a more discretionary manner. Clearly many of these successful organisations deal with newcomers, language learners and new speakers and it is assumed that this pattern of support will obtain over the medium term.

However, there are no guarantees as financial curtailments following the monetary crisis of 2008 have resulted in a slowing of initiatives and a more carefully managed approach to public expenditure. This, officials claim, is the

---

[33] Please see www.omnium.cat/en/ www.cal.cat/contacte/ www.plataforma-llengua.cat/. The evolution can be traced at https://llengua.gencat.cat/ca/serveis/dades_i_estudis/monsocioeconomic/oferta/ofercat_1_descripcio/. The latest is for 2019.

biggest challenge over the coming decade and the response is to adopt a more fine-grained approach to promoting Catalan. The first such action was to launch a marketing exercise, the Emmarca't Project, part of a broader framework of Brand CAT, whereby a communication strategy has been put in place to strengthen the identification with Catalan values. The programme is rolled out sector by sector and currently 408 brands are participants in the scheme. The role of the Catalan language is not made explicit and there is certainly no desire to foreground the role of the DGPL. The approach is more subtle, and typically Catalan, in being very sophisticated and anticipating how the public will respond to such messaging. The initiative covers content production, webpages, client services, advertising and marketing material. There is more than 80 per cent popular support for the initiative to make Catalan more integral to commercial and economic life. Analysis of the changes is undertaken through survey evaluations of four features, namely (1) awareness of the BrandCat initiative; (2) how information is communicated to the public, a type of linguistic landscape measure; (3) the quality of the oral customer service provision; (4) reactions to whether the customer is addressed initially in Spanish or Catalan.[34] Regular measurement of the linguistic landscape in the main shopping streets of selected localities reports on the degree to which this transformation is working and is reported upon in the official Language Policy Reports, such as those published for 2016 and 2017 (Generalitat de Catalunya, 2017a; 2018). Exceptions to this obligation include international brands such as Zara and Women's Secret. In several cases Catalan is superior or dominant, for as the customer enters the premises the greeting would tend to be in Catalan, the employees would tend to have a high knowledge of the language and thus the whole programme is designed as a catalyst for behavioural change and the reinforcement of Catalan as the default language of exchange. Nevertheless, other sources identify a less positive element of engagement (Idescat, 2019, p. 33).

However, the public financing of such programmes is subject to the abrogation of periodic budgets, as happened between September and December 2017 when the Spanish Economy Minister froze the Catalan budget. This meant that Generalitat Departments could neither spend monies nor prepare budget lines and as a consequence many initiatives proposed by the DGPL were placed in abeyance.

Recently there have been challenges to this approach by the decisions of the Spanish courts which have ruled against aspects of the programme. This is part and parcel of a broader restriction on Catalan initiatives, as witnessed in the detention and imprisonment of those involved in the independence referendum, the Constitutional Court's ruling against Catalonia's foreign action plan and

---

[34] A further measure is whether the owner's address is recorded in Catalan or not.

engagement with the EU on 30 October 2019[35] and the Supreme Court confirmation on 28 September 2020 that Catalan president Quim Torra be removed from office as he was declared guilty of disobedience for displaying signs in solidarity with the imprisoned pro-independence leaders on public buildings (as called for, incidentally, by a UN working group and international organisations such as Amnesty).[36] Such acts are part and parcel of a broader ideological stance taken by the Spanish state whose treatment of the Catalan demands 'follows the imperial logic of modern constitutionalism that excludes the politics of recognition' (Gagnon and Sanjaume-Calvet, 2017, p. 284).

In summary the official line is that government planners are aware of the potential of the new speaker concept and of the work undertaken by Catalan scholars. The social reality underpinning the concept is well understood and is utilised in different ways within the various policies of the government and indeed has been so used for several decades thus far. There is no intent to introduce the new speaker concept as an important element within official strategies, review documents or general statements, although this may change in time. No one within official circles really believes that a higher proportion of new speakers will dilute the Catalan language, or in some way posit a threat to the 'authenticity' of Catalan, even though some elements within society make great capital about this 'foreign influence' – this was believed to be a political tactic, not a substantive issue. However, this is changing as there are 'increasing warning bells', the latest being the concerns raised by a grouping of sociolinguists regarding the future of the language.[37] Their primary concern is that the gains made in integrating newcomers and cementing social cohesion could be put at risk by the long-standing dispute between the Catalan authorities and the Spanish state. This is most evident in the control of the public purse by Madrid and the decisions of various Spanish courts which overturn or declare illegal previous actions by the Generalitat. Sociolinguists advise that the risk of triggering conflict according to ethnolinguistic lines persists, mainly because the media are controlled by Madrid-based sources and because of the persistence of group polarisation and a relative lack of social cohesion (Boix, pers. comm., 2021).

The current government seeks to make the promotion and use of Catalan a central part of their programme whereby the consensus on the National Agreement is to be channelled into specific SPL initiatives. Senior civil

---

[35] www.catalannews.com/politics/item/spain-s-constitutional-court-suspends-catalan-foreign-action-plan-and-relations-with-the-eu.

[36] The court upheld a previous verdict banning the Catalan head of government from holding public office for 18 months – the second time in three years that a Catalan president has been sacked. www.catalannews.com/politics/item/catalan-president-to-be-ousted-as-spanish-court-upholds-disobedience-verdict-2.

[37] www.vilaweb.cat/etiqueta/el-futur-del-catala/.

servants advise that four initiatives will be pursued in the medium term, namely (1) conduct an evaluation of the use of Catalan in the work place, which would also require all government departments to assess how their inputs influence language choice in the economy and commercial life; (2) collect new forms of data which emphasise language use not just language skills; (3) develop detailed plans to implement the new emphasis on language use; (4) support the needs of the education system, particularly in relation to the provision of well-qualified Catalan teachers. It is acknowledged that teacher training was taken for granted and assumed to have been normalised. Now it is recognised that this is not the case and there is a dire need to guarantee a plentiful supply of competent Catalan language teachers, which is most readily allied to a new emphasis on lifelong training.[38]

In such circumstances the civil servants I interviewed would prefer to consolidate what they have already established as social practice rather than introduce a new element, such as the new speaker phenomenon, into the governance discourse and strategy. We shall see below to what extent this reticence is shared by other policy formulators and actors at the provincial and civil society level.

Voluntariat per la Llengua   The Voluntariat per la Llengua (VxL) programme is an excellent example of how both residents and migrants who are learners of Catalan might become more proficient and confident in their dealings with the complexity of adjusting to a new social order. The VxL programme is designed to encourage Catalan language learners to both improve their use of the language and to socially cohere by teaming up with a local volunteer and spend time together as a pair in a socially constructive manner. The programme, established in 2003, is sponsored by the SPL and managed by the Consortium for Language Normalisation. Since its inauguration over 150,000 couples have been created.[39] The annual number of language pairs has grown from 9,437 in 2008 to 11,425 in 2019, totalling 11,634 participants comprised of 7,268 learners and 4,366 volunteers. Of the pairs, 96 per cent were organised by the Consortium for Language Normalisation and a further 4 per cent were organised by non-governmental organisations working in partnership with the Consorci. The work of VxL has been widely diffused and is active in 210 locations throughout Catalonia (Generalitat de Catalunya, 2017a). This reach is made possible by the extensive support network to facilitate meetings between language pairs as demonstrated by the 4,307 agreements that the Consortium signed in 2016 with 683 organisations which provide activities and venues to practise Catalan and with 3,624 partner establishments involved in the programme. A further 1,855 single activities

---

[38] SPL interview, 22 September 2021.   [39] www.vxl.cat/virtual.

such as reading, going to the cinema, sporting fixtures and food shopping involved 70,286 participants. The most populous age bracket for forming pairs is that aged 50–65 followed by the 18–29 age bracket. For those within statutory education a further 363 new language pairs were formed in seven primary schools and eighteen secondary schools. Beyond the normal community engagements, the VxL is operative within specific sectors of the economy and workforce as follows: justice, business, sport, healthcare, education, religious diversity and disability, which together in 2016 saw the establishment of 2,339 language pairs (23.35 per cent of the total).

The geographical origin of the new learners is reflective of the migration pattern in the past two decades. In 2016 the most populous source areas of language learners were South America at 1,018 (39 per cent); North Africa, 464 (18 per cent); the EU, 450 (17 per cent); Central America, Mexico and the Caribbean, 272 (10 per cent); non-EU Europe, 143 (6 per cent); Asia, 138 (5 per cent); rest of Africa, 116 (4 per cent); USA and Canada, 24 (1 per cent); and Oceania at one participant (Generalitat de Catalunya, 2017a).[40]

A second means of teaching the language and improving one's skills is the XERREM programme. In March 2018 interviews were conducted with those responsible for promoting the integration of migrants, language learners and the development of new speakers in the province of Girona.[41]

Girona Illustration

The SPL is the principal strategic agency implementing government language policy and promotion efforts. It is the main co-ordinating body within each of the nation's four provinces. I have chosen Girona as it is the province with the highest proportion of Catalan speakers and represents best practice as regards innovative planning for new speakers. Established in December 1988 the CNL is the main co-ordinating body for the promotion of Catalan within the community.[42] Its authority comes from a government mandate which it implements through twenty-two centres and a network of partner organisations. In the province of Girona there were initially 120 member organisations, which after the 2009 financial crisis was reduced to 66 members with a corresponding loss of employees and related activities. The SPL managers I interviewed feel an acute sense of being handicapped as the resources devoted to the public

---

[40] For an update on the 2019 data, see https://llengua.gencat.cat/web/.content/documents/infor mepl/arxius/IPL-2019.pdf, p. 79.
[41] The interviews were conducted in Girona on 19 March 2018 and the informants were Montserrat Mas of the DGPL, Montse Deulofeu of the Voluntariat per la Llengua and Agnès Llagostera of the Coordinació Ensenyament CNL Girona. The interview was facilitated by Dr Puigdevall i Serralvo, UOC who participated in the discussion.
[42] www.cpnl.cat/xarxa/cnlterresebre/vxl/.

administration of the territory have been reduced. In consequence they believe that their effectiveness has been harmed and for the first time since its establishment the directives of the SPL and the implementation efforts of the Consorci would appear to be faltering. Accordingly, a reduction in capacity to deliver innovative programmes would appear to be the prime challenge facing language policy agencies throughout Catalonia. This is a doubly difficult issue for it occurs precisely when there is a more activist, 'militant' tendency growing within Catalan society to defend the gains made to date and to improve the efficacy of language interventions, especially in relation to the progress made by migrants, refugees and 'others in our midst'.

The three areas of responsibility which the SPL sponsored network advances are: (1) consolidating language domains, especially varieties of educational experiences and outcomes; (2) language promotion in society and the economy; (3) the extension of the VxL programme. Underpinning these activities there is an occasional evaluation and assessment element which feeds back into both provincial and national policy refinement. While it is recognised that evaluation is a significant part of the language policy and planning system, it is also acknowledged that currently a lack of trained personnel is a major impediment to maintaining high standards of regular time-series evaluation of the programmes.

One of the strengths of the Catalan approach is the ability to integrate the work of independent institutions, such as universities, into the collective work of the Consorci. Currently thirteen such institutions operate in tandem, under the co-ordinating umbrella of the Consorci in diverse fields, such as tackling the needs of immigrants and refugees and promoting Catalan in the domains of business and justice. More than 200,000 people participate each year in the socio-cultural activities promoted by the Consortium and their collective impact is a major source of pride for organisers and activists alike. For learners based abroad the system is run in parallel with the Institut Ramon Llull.[43]

In terms of advanced leaners and new speakers, adult learner provision for Girona stabilises at around seven to eight thousand learners at any one time. In the period 2007–10 the system could cope with a maximum of fifteen thousand students. The courses are online and delivered through the parla.cat portal which enables one either to learn Catalan exclusively online, which is free, or through discussions with a tutor, for which a moderate fee is required.[44] Teaching methods tend to be a mixture of blended learning while the majority of students prefer face-to-face teaching in a conventional classroom setting. When companies enrol their employees on the courses, they can negotiate a package deal as can elements of the public sector, such as the professional

---

[43] www.llull.cat/english/quisom/quisom.cfm.
[44] www.parla.cat/pres_catalaenlinia/AppPHP/login/index.php?lang=en.

colleges which train personnel in public administration. Operating throughout Catalonia with a wide variety of course available, the parla.cat system can handle the requirements of all levels of learners. Some 65 per cent of learners are immigrants, mainly from Latin America and North Africa, together with Europeans, particularly Ukrainians and Romanians. The Honduran diaspora is more numerous in Girona than anywhere else in the world, as females are employed to take care of elderly residents and in time, once established, are joined by their children and extended families. Whilst valuing the social service they provide it is acknowledged that by working such long hours, they often have little time to attend the formal classes provided. Accordingly, the success of the programme can be very varied.

Tutors and instructors are invariably university graduates with a high proficiency in Catalan and for many of the native-born Catalan students, especially those aged 60 and over, the courses offer a chance to improve their skills. This is significant as the older age group did not receive formal Catalan instruction under the Franco regime and may therefore feel that some of their skills are lacking. They come through the parla.cat system so as to improve their competence and confidence. Specifically, they wish to improve their vocabulary, accent, register, literacy and so on, and become more effective communicators either in the workplace or more often within the family, especially with the nurturing of grandchildren.

One feature which is different from that of adult learners in Scotland and Wales is that hardly any of the former students become tutors. Allied to this is a second difference relating to the term new speaker which is perhaps more reflective of deeper structural and socio-political commitments and tendencies. When asked how resonant the new speaker term was both as a construct and as a shorthand phrase, the programme managers in Girona stated that they did not use the term at a professional level. They were clearly cognisant of the work done by Catalan scholars on the new speaker linguistic turn but did not appropriate the term for their own purposes in teaching and supporting advanced adult learners. Whilst acknowledging that there were two distinct features to the new speaker phenomenon, namely the different range of experiences and competence described by the term and the linguistic diversity of the mix of languages displayed by such speakers, they nevertheless shunned the term. People were either described as Catalan or non-Catalans, speakers or non-speakers. There had been earlier attempts in the 1980s to capture the experiences and reactions of migrants to Catalonia by adopting the term New Catalans or alternatively *els altres catalans* as depicted in the book by Valencian-born Catalan author Francesc Candel Tortajada, from a Spanish-speaking area, Rincón de Ademuz, in C. Racó d'Ademús.[45]

---

[45] Paco Candel's 1964 book *Els Altres Catalans* focussed on the experiences of Spanish-speaking migrants who were arriving in Barcelona mainly from Andalucía. The Valencian Country

When asked whether the interviewees thought the new speaker term might be more widely used in some ten years' time, they thought not. They based this on the previous attempts to promote the descriptor 'learners of Catalan' but argued that the general public and the teaching profession preferred not to distinguish between learners and non-learners. The intriguing follow-up question is how then they distinguish between different types or categories of speakers. The answer was that in Catalan society there is a great deal of latitude and flexibility. One common view is that people become Catalan speakers the moment they decide to use the language in earnest and such actions are warmly applauded by the local population, even if they themselves are not fluent in Catalan. This is because there has been an attitudinal shift in the past generation which prizes social cohesion and language support. A romantic gloss on varying degrees of social acceptance was put forward by those interviewed, all Catalan speakers, who claimed that regardless of skin colour, accent or place of origin, new Catalan speakers were largely encouraged and welcomed into the speech community, a courtesy which was not necessarily extended to people who only spoke Spanish. Lamuela observes, 'But there are strong in-group norms for the use of Catalan: if you are black, even if born in Catalonia and perfectly fluent in Catalan, you are systematically addressed in Spanish!' (Lamuela, pers. comm., 2021).

Older native Catalan speakers have problems with orthography and prescriptive grammar and vocabulary, but not with accent. Clearly there are strong linguistic ideologies at play here. These have been shaped in part by the major government and civil society campaigns directed at the promotion of Catalan rather than Spanish among the population, and although one can trace significant evidence of success, the differential power and attraction exerted by the two languages remains a challenge for Catalan language activists and government alike.

One consideration raised by a number of those interviewed at national and provincial level was the over-reliance on statistics to bolster an argument for normalisation and programme success. A representative comment would be:

My main criticism is that the Language Policy is too linguistic and too little social/human. They often speak in quantitative terms (headlines on the number of speakers that enrol in Catalan Courses; headlines on number of immigrants attending the so-called Welcome Classes (*aules d'acollida*). But this does not mean that they use the language, or they are willing to use it and to make the 'muda'. They are not New Speakers at all. (Public official, 2021)

A further criticism is the manner in which new residents, on achieving their formal certification, the 'Catalan language certificate' (only forty-five hours),

---

includes territories that have always been Spanish speaking, although people there usually understand or learn Catalan as a second language. Candel was born in one of these areas.

rarely went on to use the language in social situations. This is line with the recent sociolinguistic data which suggests that 60 per cent of the non-Catalan speakers in the metropolitan area of Barcelona – 5 million people residing in the area – have no interest in learning Catalan, whereas 37 per cent of that population do.

The principal reason why so many subscribe to the initial free course is that a 2014 law requires such action in order to quality for a mandatory integration certificate which measures knowledge of society and Catalan to qualify for residence but not work. In time this will facilitate the application for nationality. However, officials are acutely conscious of the irony that the mandatory requirement enforces such action in the full knowledge that the overwhelming majority of applicants will not use Catalan to a great extent in future.[46] Accordingly, there is a great deal of concern that analysis needs to unpack what really is happening in terms of the social impact of language policy and programmes.

In comparable European situations there has been a tendency to denigrate the quality of the language learned and thus it is intriguing to enquire whether there is a robust purist element in the Catalan reaction to the learner phenomenon. Interviewees argued that the opposite was the case as acceptance of shades of quality of the Catalan spoken was now a common feature of most interactions, though there continues to be a widespread complaint that many Catalan speakers switch to Spanish if they perceive that their interlocutor is not an L1 speaker (native). Fundamentally it was claimed that the broad acceptance reflected a strong degree of mutual respect and empathy, although it was recognised that there remained some prejudice against adult learners, especially if it was thought that they were learning the language for instrumental reasons only and not assimilating into Catalan culture and norms. Above and beyond the specifics of the individual choices, interventionist programmes still have to grapple with the overwhelming social norms which guide language choice in interethnic encounters and work in favour of Spanish, as detailed by Woolard (2016).

This complexity is a result of the significant change in the clientele of the adult learner sector. Given the racial, geographical and class origins of the learners now any new speaker accent is welcomed, and several fundamental features of Catalan speech are changing apace. A good example is the degree of tolerance shown to the use of voiced s and voiceless s and to the tendency to fail in producing vowel reduction in unstressed syllable, as examined in Ortega-Llebaria, Vanrell and Prietp (2010). Lamuela adds that very bad Catalan has become common (also for native speakers), but the perception of an accent or

---

[46] Observation by Clement, interview 23 September 2021.

any other foreign trait such as skin colour triggers the use of Spanish (Lamuela, pers. comm., 2021).

Another feature is more social and was illustrated by the reaction of many students from Latin America who acknowledged that having moved to Catalonia they were faced by the realities of living in a bilingual/multicultural society, where speaking Spanish was not sufficient for their needs. One way of tracking such adjustments was the use of learner diaries, encouraged by the CNL in Girona. These revealed that many students, particularly those from the Maghreb and China, found the characteristics of the language to be confusing and strange. By interpreting the comments and perceptions as recorded by students, the Catalan teachers could identify difficulties in syntax, vocabulary and grammar, and accordingly improve their technique and lesson content and planning.

An intriguing issue is how one enters the world of Catalan learning. I asked my interviewees to imagine that if I were recently arrived from Taiwan, with no previous contact or family in Girona, how would I go about seeking help in learning Catalan in a formal setting? The instinctive answer is that friends and acquaintances recommend the recent arrival to contact the CNL. A second route is to be referred to the CNL by the authorities once one has registered with the municipal government. For Catalan learners with children of school age there is a possibility for parents and children to be taught in CNL co-ordinated programmes. A common feature is for school parent–teacher associations to organise such classes for learners and to diffuse CNL information for potential new learners within the school catchment area. A longer-term strategy is to attain citizenship, and although this is a 'painful process' a prior step is to declare oneself as being 'rooted in society' while demonstrating some competence in Catalan as evidence of a desire to become a permanent resident.

Evaluation and assessment of the CNL programmes have been undertaken through periodic surveys. The project ÈLIA (Estratègies de Llengua i Aprenentatge) has as its objective to innovate in Catalan teaching methods for adults and adapt them to present social circumstances. In 2017, as a first phase of its work, it undertook a survey to measure the perceptions of 3,500 students and former students of the CPNL and Parla.cat. while a second survey of 3,000 adults was undertaken to gauge the general public's views on the performance of the government in this domain.

A more routine source of feedback is the questionnaires distributed to each cohort of learners registered on their programmes. However, it was acknowledged that both types of surveys, while yielding interesting information, do not really capture the essence of the learners' experience which is to measure how successful the students have been in managing their learning process and to what extent they feel they have put their language skills to use in a variety of contexts. Consequently, longer-term, post-programme investigations are to be encouraged at regular intervals to see how the target population navigate their pathway through their additional opportunities to use Catalan. These in turn are contextualised through the *Enquesta d'usos lingüístics a la població*, which is a survey undertaken every five years to assess the general sociolinguistic situation.

One informal way of judging the progress of learners is through the feedback received from partners in the VxL programme.[47] This mentoring programme has received a great deal of praise for the way in which it seeks to integrate new residents into society through their informal partnering with competent Catalan speakers. Typically, the partners would interact for up to thirty hours and in addition to the day-to-day experience of practising the language within a 'safe confine', the partners can assist the learners in resolving practical issues, such as help with official documentation, advice on visiting the doctor and so on. One danger in such involvement is that the host partners can become unofficial social workers and carry the burdens of the newcomers, but that is one of the side effects of welcoming 'strangers in our midst'. Shouldering responsibilities is an integral part of the social contract entered. Once the arranged meetings have expired many couples continue to meet on a regular basis and through this the new resident is introduced to a much wider range of contacts than would be possible only in a formal classroom setting.

This self-generating impulse is very much in keeping with the Catalan civil approach to language promotion. Thus, while the SPL's strategies do not set targets, they do create a context and provide resources which animate and legitimise innovation from within the ranks of social activists. Of course, the interviewees in Girona did acknowledge that demand always outstrips supply, and they also bemoaned the lack of time available for the technical staff to achieve all they were required to do. Nevertheless, they were confident that their collective efforts not only made a material difference to the lives of the new residents but also that they were fulfilling an important part of the Catalan language strategy. This was especially so as they felt empowered to undertake localised initiatives and not just follow a national, top-down set of instructions. Being grounded in the realities of society and having started in one location, Cornellà de Llobregat, which has a significant proportion of immigrants in its population, the interviewees believed that their services were meeting real local needs and strengthening the national position of Catalan by helping to produce more integrated residents.

Structurally the partner organisations have regular communications with the DGPL/SPL and organise annual meetings, together with more frequent sectoral meetings, usually online. Subject-specific working groups improve the quality of the services available and allow for new, innovative practices to be diffused

---

[47] www.cpnl.cat/xarxa/cnlterresebre/VxL/.

throughout the system. Characteristically over 90 per cent of those involved throughout this sector, both as managers and tutors, are women.

One may conclude this illustration by saying that formal adult education classes, allied with the VxL programme, are making significant differences to the sociolinguistic vitality of Catalan and to lessening the social tensions and distances between the settled community and the newly arrived migrants, refugees and asylum seekers.

Academic Interpretations

Scholars working in the field of language learning and social cohesion make use of the new speaker paradigm but do not overburden the concept in their interpretations. Having followed their pioneering work it was decided to interview two of the most influential scholars, Dr Joan Pujolar and Dr Maite Puigdevall i Serralvo, so as to gain insights into the traction which the concept and its utility might have within Catalan discourse and policy.[48] Both individuals have been very influential within the COST New Speakers Network.[49]

They suggested that while the public had adopted a defensive reaction towards the new speaker phenomenon, their academic colleagues within the New Speakers Network had carved out an identifiable field of enquiry which had great potential. The underlying challenge was whether the concept had sufficient purchase to sustain the theoretical advances and practical implementation the early studies had promised. Their view was that less energy should be expended on searching for a precise definition of the concept and more on the types of new questions that approaching linguistic change and language contact from the perspective of the new speaker could generate. An early attempt at defining the concept sought 'to describe individuals with little or no home or community exposure to a minority language but who instead acquire it through immersion or bilingual educational programs, revitalization projects or as adult language learners' (O'Rourke, Pujolar and Ramallo, 2015).

Given that the concept had little social currency in Catalonia they argued that they had used the new speaker paradigm less and less in professional publications, whilst not deviating from their desire to track and trace the impact of the phenomenon. Consequently, the real virtue of the new speaker approach was to create a meeting point between different disciplines and to pursue new questions which had previously not been emphasised. The most important question

---

[48] They were interviewed at UOC, Barcelona on 23 March 2018, and in Girona on 24 September 2021.

[49] Dr Pujolar was the joint coordinator of the network together with Professor Bernie O'Rourke, while Dr Puigdevall was joint leader with Dr John Walsh of the Working Group on 'Speakerness: Subjectivities, Trajectories and Socialisation.'

related to multilingualism and how language learning and confidence-building were nurtured outside of the formal classroom setting.

Their view was that language specialists had already been active in researching aspects of minority language rights, promotion, governance and public service provision. However, they had been less involved in a range of psychological and social psychological issues which would affect applied linguistic studies. Accordingly, how people engage with each other and create new identities, forge new skills and repertoires, and adopt social norms was a fascinating, if under-researched, area so far as new speakers, migrants, refugees and asylum seekers were concerned. It was recognised that some of these issues had lain outside mainstream academic concerns, because they were contentious, too political or not fashionable, but they were pressing nevertheless if the overall goal was to strengthen the social cohesion of society.

The New Speakers Network had created space for a new generation of scholars to tackle epistemological and methodological issues and to be trained in an interdisciplinary fashion. The overwhelming majority of such scholars were female early career researchers who were engaged in new and interesting fields of enquiry. In seeking to train such scholars Pujolar and Puigdevall favoured going beyond the conventional interview and observational techniques by seeking to interpret the processes of social interaction. They argued that this offered a more dynamic and long-term perspective. The favoured methodology was intense ethnographic research, describing and interpreting real-world interactions in detail. Few of the younger scholars were concerned with the policy implications of their work, preferring to build up a body of evidence as to what went on over time when residents and migrants sought to acquire additional languages. Of particular concern were the emotional aspects of navigating a trajectory of acquiring an additional language in educational and social contexts, such as was found in the work of Pastor and María (2018) and Walsh (2019).

Considerations of language appropriation, legitimacy and the construction of a social persona in and through a new language were the focus of their research at the Universitat Oberta de Catalunya (UOC). Tracking the various stages which characterised this process of transition was vital and one paradigm they proposed caught the imagination of their fellow researchers. This was the '*muda*' concept, defined in their influential position paper as the transition in specific biographical junctures (Pujolar and Puigdevall, 2015). *Mudes* is the Catalan term for variations in social performance, such as dressing up for an event or changing one's appearance generally (Pujolar and Gonzàlez, 2013). Their analysis is based on a combination of quantitative data from the 2003 *Enquesta d'usos lingüístics* and a qualitative study conducted in 2008 and 2009 that included twenty-four interviews and fifteen focus groups covering a total of 102 people under 35 years old, of different sexes and linguistic, educational, social and residential backgrounds (Gonzàlez et al., 2009; Pujolar, Gonzàlez and Martinez, 2010). An important element of their approach is the assertion that by tracking changes in language behaviour over time, demonstrating how linguistic practices may evolve and change throughout the life cycle of individuals, they are able to provide a more nuanced view of the linguistic ideologies that underpin linguistic practices. A particular concern is to counter the view that seeks to reduce these practices to their base instincts so as to construct a defence for ethnolinguistic belonging, reinforcing the 'we' against the 'other' in society. Dynamism was what they hoped to capture as was explained: 'Indeed, by focusing on how individuals become new speakers, we turn these phenomena into processes characterised by change, movement and maturation rather than staticity and placeness' (Pujolar and Puigdevall, 2015, p. 168).

Mudes were moments within daily routines that involved a change of settings, activities in which and participants with whom individuals engaged in a relatively intensive and routine fashion.[50] The *muda* opened up a range of new options and forced subjects to construct the social, spatial and situational categories that bear on the decisions to use one language rather than another. Thus, their research questions were: 'How did new speakers go about constructing these categories? Did they create new ones, or did they borrow the categories available around them?' (Pujolar and Puigdevall, 2015, p. 172).

Earlier work by Gonzàlez et al. (2009) had identified six junctures during which *mudes* took place and the following percentages relate to the observations in the Pujolar and Puigdevall sample: (a) in primary school (23.7 per cent of Castilian speakers and 10.8 per cent of Catalan speakers; (b) in high school (16.9 per cent and 2.7 per cent); (c) at university (13.6 per cent and 16.2 per cent); (d) when getting one's first job (50.8 per cent and 40.5 per cent); (e) when establishing a new family (20.3 per cent and 13.5 per cent); and (f) when becoming a parent (45.8 per cent and 5.4 per cent).

While most studies of the *muda* transformation process have involved analysing participants' memories, experiences and perceptions, including techniques such as the keeping of individual diaries, a supplementary approach is to observe and interpret what happens to participants when interacting in new social situations. Patiño-Santos's (2019) study of language mixing by a group of secondary students of migrant origins in Barcelona has suggested that once the linguistic *muda* has taken place, new speakers are able to integrate the new language into their linguistic repertoires. In their sample secondary school within a working-class neighbourhood, it is evident that Catalan is the language

---

[50] They explain that 'at these moments, it is important to understand that individuals did not suddenly substitute the language(s) they had been using up to then: the new language usually came from meeting new people and the new social spaces and activities. However, the new spaces of language choice also queried the existing ones' (Pujolar and Puigdevall, 2015, p. 172).

of instruction while Spanish is the language of social relations. Such language mixing by both students and teachers alike becomes the established norm.

This does not necessarily mean that the new language is the default linguistic resource in their daily activities or that such students can master linguistic skills to the same level as in other languages in their repertoires (Pujolar and Gonzàlez, 2013). However, it has been demonstrated that such language-mixing practices can be presented as a continuum and that interactions can establish a third space within which identities can be nurtured and extensive language mixing sanctioned (Bhabha, 1994).

The research by Pujolar, Puigdevall and Patiño-Santos provides insights into how new speakers of Catalan navigate these junctures and should be of value in triggering similar investigations in other European contexts. Perhaps the most important lesson for the current analysis is that their findings assert the 'messiness' of interaction. They argue that 'as social subjects invest in specific linguistic capitals that are marked by the struggles over access to symbolic and material resources, they inevitably accompany their positions with emotional investments that also draw upon the discourses and ideologies that partake in these struggles' (Pujolar and Puigdevall, 2015, p. 186).[51]

They also argue that their findings have implications for the ways in which linguistic minority communities have been constructed in nationalist discourses and for the language policies that have traditionally drawn upon these discourses to promote the language of these communities, or to promote assimilation by the dominant language.

Language revitalisation has historically privileged the significance of using the language as a form of embodying national identity, even in the face of ongoing language shift due to economic or other factors – that have, in turn, been treated as spurious, discordant, or even as false consciousness. This ideology has been complemented with the notions of linguistic purity and of language as cultural inheritance that has privileged the focus on the reproduction of the community of native speakers, and this while other out-group speakers could be easily ignored. Catalonia, as Pujolar (2007) showed, was one such context where the experiences of new speakers of Catalan were silenced. This is no longer tenable. The future of Catalan, as arguably for many other minority languages, lies in the ambivalences and contentions encountered and confronted by non-native speakers. (Pujolar and Puigdevall, 2015, p. 186)

Their views on this tendency were elaborated at interviews when they explained that language appropriation is a process whereby individuals and groups draw on language to construct social personae. Claims are made on the basis of the resultant categorisation; some are beneficial and allow for social integration, but some are negative and enable the host, control group to exclude

---

[51] 'Thus, an exclusively 'instrumental' investment into speaking Catalan appears as a theoretical oxymoron only possible for those who believe languages to be neutral cognitive resources. This is not how Catalans, or any other group, live languages.' (Pujolar and Puigdevall, 2015, p. 186).

certain people. They argue that such practices have been sidelined and ignored by sociolinguistics and deserve to be highlighted as part of a broader understanding of ways of socialising in different languages. The three critical elements of this new approach are the analysis of language appropriation, life trajectories and time-series assessment of the processes. One of the ways such processes could be applied would be through the induction and training of the VxL volunteers to make them more aware of the experiential nature of their involvement adding real meaning to the lives of their partners. Another would be by influencing language policy and planning at different levels to take into consideration the wide range of learner experience in their programme targets and outcome goals. A third conduit would be the media, but here a note of caution entered as the media tended to sensationalise the language question in Catalonia and did not always adopt a nuanced approach to the needs of migrants, refugees and asylum seekers as they sought to become competent in Catalan. Strubell suggests that there is plenty of evidence that the main NGOs involved in the initial reception of such migrants use almost exclusively Spanish, thus sending a very negative message about the importance of Catalan (Strubell, pers. comm., 2021).

Further applied work is necessary to make policy initiatives more integral to Catalan society. Pujolar and Puigdevall reason that traditional sociolinguistic dichotomies such as power and solidarity, us and them, and integrative versus instrumental motivations for language acquisition need to be revisited. It was argued that the new speakers as social subjects invest in specific linguistic capitals that are marked by struggles over access to symbolic and material resources. Consequently, their positions are charged with emotional investments that also draw upon the discourses and ideologies that partake in these struggles. Thus, there is an a priori need to understand these discourses and ideologies if sound policy outcomes are to be achieved (Pujolar and Puigdevall, 2015).

Emili Boix argues that the current reality is not represented within the official discourse and government interpretations. It would seem that far from ensuring greater social cohesion there is an increased polarisation between Catalan speakers and residents of Spanish and migrant origin, which has been exacerbated by the whole independence issue. The Catalan government has been keen, since the recovery of democracy, to stress that knowledge and understanding of Catalan, rather than its use, is the prime political objective. This is because it is fearful that the detailed reporting of current use will show a steady decline and thus render its claims of effective language promotion rather suspect.[52] Increasingly it is argued that Catalan youth, even in the more predominantly Catalan-speaking regions, are switching to Spanish and are less concerned with insisting on their language rights, as did the previous

---

[52] Boix interview, 21 September 2021.

generation. For today's youngsters in a normalised context the use of Catalan, Spanish and English are an expression of their social repertoire rather than intuitively related to any sense of national identity and language loyalty. This trend is confirmed by Xavier Vila who argues that demographic trends and globalisation have created a generation of bilingual and multilingual residents who gravitate towards Spanish in many domains.[53]

Initiatives to Promote Catalan

One great advantage of the media was its search for novel ways to promote Catalan at home and abroad. Opportunities were given to new speakers to express themselves and a very good illustration of this is the TV3 series *Katalonski* which documents the lives of mostly 'new speakers' of Catalan living abroad who maintained the use of the language and their connection with Catalonia. The first episode, screened on 5 April 2018, featured the Icelandic musician Halldor Mar, a resident of Catalonia, who composed and played the programme's signature tune, while subsequent programmes travelled to several countries including Canada to discover the Catalan new speakers, as the aim was to investigate those 'who live beyond the borders, but speak their language all over the world.'[54] *Katalonski* is a co-production between TV3, Broadcaster Audiovisual Services and La Lupa Productions, with the support and collaboration of the SPL in the Department of Culture, the Institut Ramon Llull and the Department of Institutional and Exterior Affairs and Relations and Transparency.[55] The inaugural presentation of *Katalonski* was opened by Manuel Forcano, the then director of the Institut Ramon Llull, who explained what the Institut does abroad to promote the learning of Catalan.

We want Catalan to be at the leading universities of the world. We promote the Catalan language all over the world. There are over 6000 students, and the institute procures and promotes the programmes specialising in the learning of Catalan. 'Katalonski' is a TV programme that will provide a showcase for our work. Now Catalan is already a mid-level language in Europe, the 88th most widely spoken in the world. And it has public media that are leaders in the country. The programme presents, through personal stories, the life and role of Catalan in a globalised world.[56]

---

[53] Vila interview, 27 September 2021.
[54] On 12 March 2018, at the Institut Ramon Llull, the launch of *Katalonski* was attended by Vicent Sanchis, director of TV3; Manuel Forcano, director of the Institut Ramon Llull; Ester Franquesa, director general of the Catalan Government Language Policy; Oriol Gispert, director of the programme; Valentí Roda, executive producer of the programme; and Halldor Mar, presenter of *Katalonski*: a reflection of the significance of this type of outreach.
[55] https://london.llull.cat/offices/london/actualitat_detall.cfm?id=35331&url=presentation-of-tv3-programme-katalonski.html.
[56] Vicent Sanchis emphasised that 'languages are won and lost through prestige and use. And here we are always at a disadvantage because we don't believe we are important. But there are people

Oriol Gisbert added:

> We are always thinking up stories and, if there are 150 centres in the world where you can study Catalan, we thought it could be interesting to find out about their history. So, we started to explore, and it was unbelievable. What's more, there was a great deal of interest, because we received over 500 requests to take part. Indeed, those people who have learned Catalan were glad to be acknowledged by the public television and to be given a space, because they feel legitimated. They are also grateful for the work of the Catalan public media because they reach the whole world. Many of them have taken an interest in Catalan thanks to internet and to seeing a programme.[57]

Pujolar and Puigdevall believe that such initiatives not only promote Catalan but also provide a showcase for new speakers, many of whom have learned online via Parla.cat, and such TV series encourage others who live in Catalonia to follow suit. It helps that in many neighbourhoods Catalan is the majority default language, so learners and new speakers are more likely to integrate well. Yet even here issues of correctness and quality of language are frequent bones of contention. While in school the students are encouraged not to switch from Catalan to Spanish, in the community claims are often made that new speakers of Catalan are diluting the language, a reflection of purist ideology. Critics, both personally and online, refer to misuse of clitic pronouns, poor grammar, 'bad' accents, disregard for the conventions and so on. Lamuela observes that: 'In fact, very bad Catalan is in use, but the blame is to be put first on the social subordination to Spanish and then on the general conception of language norms and variation, the education system and the media' (Lamuela, pers. comm., 2021). The guardians of the language, those who oppose several of the more recent trends within society, view the migrants and some new speakers as spoiling the 'pure line' of Catalan descent, forgetting that so many of their fellow native Catalans had migrated to the country in earlier times from other regions and further abroad. Thus, just below the surface there is a constant question of legitimacy, of membership, of who really counts and for many appropriating Catalan and speaking it to a high level of competence is not a sufficient guarantee of acceptance. Even within the ranks of the VxL, whose host members are keen to promote sport, museum visits, cultural celebrations, poetry festivals and the like to taste the richness of popular culture, there is a need to remember that there are class and financial assumptions at work which do not necessarily allow their learner partners, especially recent migrants, to participate fully and avail

---

living outside Catalonia, who learn Catalan, and that is what we see in "Katalonski". And it shows it in a very interesting way, in television format, talking about many things that happen in the city where they live, why they have learned Catalan, how it has changed their lives'; https://london.llull.cat/offices/london/actualitat_detall.cfm?id=35331&url=presentation-of-tv3-programme-katalonski.html.

[57] www.llull.cat/espanyol/actualitat/actualitat_premsa_detall.cfm?id=35301&url=presentacion-del-programa-_katalonski_.html.

themselves of much that is on offer. During the Covid-19 pandemic period the VxL developed a wide range of virtual platforms, TV and video resources, blogs and remotely accessible materials which are available online.[58]

Clearly it is hard to generalise about 2.4 million new speakers, some 35 per cent of the population, especially as there are clear categories of speakers, ranging from the children of previous migrants now in full-time education to the most recent asylum seekers and refugees. Those from among a migrant community who have become public figures are celebrated and used as mentors to encourage others, TV personalities, MPs, sportspeople and novelists such as Najat El Hachmi who at the age of eight emigrated to Vic from Morocco and has written about her experiences in her first book in 2004, *Jo també sóc catalana* [*I Also Am Catalan*], about how she and her family integrated into Catalan society.[59]

An additional way in which to diffuse this new approach to language behaviour is to target the political parties so that they adopt some of the measures advocated by new speaker research in their discourse and platforms. However, the academics interviewed were wary of being identified with any political party or ideological leaning as the whole thrust of their research was to uncover new and complex means of understanding the dynamics of social change and offering credible interpretations of future patterns of interaction between the myriad demographic and sociolinguistic groupings in Catalunya.

Language policy is an expression of political will. The full implementation of language policy is an expression of political commitment. While insisting on their professional impartiality the senior civil servants and public officials interviewed were acutely conscious that things had changed since the independence referendum of 1 October 2017. The discourse both for and against the movement for greater autonomy had grown sharper and political interest groups opposed to Catalanisation were more virulent and outspoken, claiming that their loyalty to the Spanish state outweighed the demands of the independentists. Public servants were acutely aware that the Catalan language could be perceived as an instrument of politicisation and that parties opposed to the official language policy actively encouraged this perception. Indeed, as with many other nineteenth-century nationalist ideologies in Europe, Catalan nationalism was infused with language-related concerns and ambitions. While they may have insisted that their responsibility was to serve one single people, public servants nevertheless recognised that for two generations at least there were elements in

---

[58] www.VxLl.cat/virtual.
[59] Najat El Hachmi (born in Morocco on 2 July 1979) is a Moroccan-Spanish writer. She holds a degree in Arabic Studies from the University of Barcelona. She is the author of a personal essay on her bicultural identity, (2004), prior to a series of novels, the first of which earned her the 2008 Ramon Llull Prize, the 2009 Prix Ulysse, and was a finalist for the 2009 Prix Méditerranée Étranger; the last one won the Nadal Prize for a Spanish novel in 2021.

society who argued that the insistence on the increased use of Catalan in schools and public administration was anti-democratic. Most notable were political groups, like Ciudadanos, which by their messages and actions encouraged language conflict. For example, it was claimed that the rights of Spanish people who happened to reside in Catalonia were being subjugated to a minority's usurpation of their position and they in turn perceived themselves to be second-class citizens. The challenge for public servants was to meet such claims with equanimity and evidence. In their dealings with clients, seeking to explain and implement language policy, it was imperative that the arguments put forth were both legitimate and consensus-building. Attracting advanced learners and new speakers was part of the challenge of bolstering both the language and social cohesion; the two policy aims went hand in hand. Strubell argues that from the early 1980s, a social pact was preached: Catalan speakers will continue to learn Spanish, but Spanish speakers (almost all descendants of in-migrants, or in-migrants themselves) were asked to do the same and learn Catalan in order to achieve a society in which knowledge of both (official) languages would be generalised. This has remained a cornerstone of Catalonia's language-in-education policy (Strubell, pers. comm., 2021). Accordingly, public servants recognised that they had a mission-destiny orientation which was rooted in their conception of democratic participation, the integration of migrants and the defence of Catalan values and identity.

Galicia

No Spanish interpretation would be complete without a brief excursion into the Galician experience, which is especially significant as it was the early work on *neofalantes* which inspired so many subsequent investigations in Europe. No interviews were conducted with government officials although discussions and interviews were conducted with leading researchers specialising on Galician new speakers.[60] In comparing the Galician and Catalan situation Lamuela advises that in the former new speakers are mainly Galicians that have undergone language shift and in the latter they are newcomers or the descendants of newcomers (Lamuela, pers. comm., 2021). This fact raises interesting identity issues which we shall explore.

Galicia has a population of 2,772,533 inhabitants, with a population density of 93.4 inhabitants/km^2. The native language is Galician, whilst Galician and Spanish are the community's two official languages (Xunta da Galicia, 2010). The older a person is, the more likely they are to speak Galician, as less than 30 per cent of the under-25 age group have acquired Galician as their first

---

[60] Covid-19 restrictions put paid to the planned interview schedule in Galicia.

language, which compares with 65 per cent in the over-50 age group (O'Rourke and Ramallo, 2015, p. 149).

Political culture is the key to language policy. In Euskadi and Catalonia, the main political parties who tend to rule are predominantly regionalist/nationalist parties. In Galicia it is the state-wide People's Party (PP) which rules. In the 12 July 2020 election Alberto Nunez Feijoo, president of Galicia's regional government, won a fourth term as his PP claimed forty-one seats in the seventy-five-seat assembly.

Attempts to transmit the language through schooling only took off from the 1980s onwards when standard Galician was introduced and subsequently it has moved closer to its Portuguese roots. In part this is an attempt to distance Galego from Spanish and provide an authentic vocabulary and terminology, a move which favours being re-integrated into the Portuguese sphere reflecting a long-held ideological undercurrent. Lamuela clarifies that this is different from a current trend that seeks effective integration of a Galician norm into the Portuguese language (compared with the Brazilian norm) (Lamuela, pers. comm., 2021).

However, there is a persistent controversy around this with some arguing that standardising the language moved it further away from its Portuguese roots with criticism of the Xunta for aligning it more closely with Spanish (Dayan-Fernandez and O'Rourke, 2020).

The effect of greater prominence in the statutory education system has produced a new generation of Galician speakers who technically have a very formal command of the language, together with a far greater sociolinguistic awareness. However, as we saw in relation to Basque there has been a chequered increase in the use of the language. Thus 'while almost ninety percent of those under twenty-five say they can speak Galician "well", only forty five percent report active use of the language. This figure drops to twenty percent amongst young people living in urban contexts' (O'Rourke and Ramallo, 2015, p. 149). Language policy has increased the symbolic and economic value of the language, but it has not brought about a reversal of language shift, even if it has triggered a partial process of majority language displacement.

A significant theme of early work on Galician is the native speaker–*neofalante* dichotomy (O'Rourke and Ramallo, 2011). The life history trajectories of new speakers and the distinct critical life junctures or *mudes* stages of transition were examined, including a synthesis of the reasons given for the various stages of development.[61] One of the significant reasons why someone can become a fully competent *neofalante* (literally 'neo speaker'), so much so that it displaces Spanish in many domains, is the closeness in linguistic terms between Galician and Spanish. O'Rourke (pers. comm., 2021) observes that the linguistic proximity between the two languages was frequently used to justify classifications of

---

[61] At interview in Edinburgh, 13 September 2018. See also O'Rourke and Ramallo (2013).

Galician as a dialect of Castilian, rather than as a language in its own right. The historical subordination of Galician had led to what Kloss (1967) refers to as 'dialectalization', defined as a politically motivated process which occurs when enough structural similarity exists between a dominant and a subordinate language to classify the latter variety as a substandard dialect (O'Rourke and Ramallo, 2013, p. 289).

In many rural areas this transition could be sustained, but on entering a cosmopolitan urban context the hegemony of Spanish would be reasserted. As with most bilingual educational and social settings there is a constant interchange between both languages. Typically, the hegemonic language exercises its attraction as a more powerful and comprehensive force. Understandably tensions arise both as to the formal nature of the educational process and as to a perception that one's preferred language is somehow at a disadvantage under the established arrangements.

In Galicia, at least half of teaching must be in the regional tongue. Gloria Lago, a founder of Bilingual Galicia, said: 'The children ask to be taught in Spanish and this is not allowed because the law prevents it. When the bell goes, they start speaking their own language.' This group attracted the attention of the media, and saw a controversial 2007 proposed amendment to the imposition of Galician on those members of the population who prefer to use Spanish and therefore an infringement of their linguistic rights (O'Rourke, 2011, p. 87). However, Marisol López, Galician head of linguistic policies, insisted: 'Children study in two languages. If we don't discriminate positively in favour of Galician, Spanish will dominate' (Keeley, 2008).

Younger elements of the population were found to be more militant and robust advocates of promoting Galician at all times, driving forward the language revitalisation efforts. Even so it is very evident that the *neofalantes* do not speak like their grandparents, neither are their social profiles and usage similar. Their search for purity, for expunging their speech from Spanish words and phrases, whilst ideologically motivated, does not in practice hold up as their normal speech pattern is so full of Spanish words and idioms, which is not at all surprising given the relative histories of the two languages and the impact of the Spanish state throughout its territory. A distinctive trend nevertheless is an acutely conscious attempt by *neofalantes* to keep out Spanish influences whereas the native speakers' patterns are heavily infused by such influences.

Any attempt to number the *neofalantes* population is difficult for there are at least three variants. O'Rourke estimates that it may be around 2 per cent of the population, a figure which relates only to those who were Spanish speakers but switched almost exclusively to Galician for most purposes.[62] Lamuela avers

---

[62] Interview in Edinburgh, 13 September 2018. Because of its peripheral location and low industrialisation rate, Galicia did not experience the considerable immigration of Spanish

that this seems too different from the previous data about those under 25: 45 per cent report active use of the language – 30 per cent have Galician as their first language = at least 15 per cent are active new speakers. Then there is a larger group of 'potential new speakers' who are disposed to using the language, but do not sometimes because of lack of opportunities and other reasons. Thirdly there would be another group of 'bilinguals' who report using Galician as much as Spanish.

This immediately raises the question as to how feasible it is for the authorities to plan programmes and policies specifically for *neofalantes* as a distinct subset of all Galician speakers. In that respect the *neofalantes*, although superficially similar to other minority experiences of new speaker emergence such as Gaelic new speakers, would appear to be far too numerically weak to uphold a language revitalisation effort. Besides which, native Galician speakers are proportionately far stronger than would be their putative equivalents elsewhere, such as Gaels in Scotland. Thus, in Galician *neofalantes* tends to be used to refer to a very specific minority group – often language activists who have almost exclusively switched to Galician; in other jurisdictions 'new speakers' denote a much broader group to include those who are bilinguals or who use the *cúpla focal* as in the Irish case (O'Rourke and Pujolar, 2013).

Intergenerational transmission of a language at home has been recognised as a *sine qua non* of language reproduction and a cardinal feature of language policy. However, O'Rourke and Nandi (2019) argue that new speakers bring complexity to this paradigm and prompt questions about their role as parents and as potential agents of sociolinguistic change in the process of language revitalisation (O'Rourke and Pujolar, 2013). It is observed that through their individual as well as collective linguistic practices, new speaker parents have the potential to generate visible and invisible language planning by influencing their children's language learning and creating future generations of speakers. By analysing the ideologies and discourses of the *neofalantes* who are brought up speaking Spanish but make a conscious decision to adopt Galician language practices and in some contexts adopt an almost exclusively Galician language repertoire, the authors are able to identify the internal tensions and nuances occasioned by such a transition or *mudes* (O'Rourke and Ramallo, 2013).[63]

Neofalantes are to a large extent the product of official language revitalisation policies, but in becoming active new speakers they are also engaging in a reflective process which questions existing power structures. The abiding, if ironic, consequence is that in seeking to establish safe spaces for their children, free from the hegemony of Spanish, parents have struggled with recognising

---

workers as did the urban nodes of the Basque Country and Catalonia. Neither did it see high levels of immigration from Latin America; in fact, the region has long been a net exporter of young and well-educated migrants.

[63] For a detailed exposition of the *mudes* concept see Puigdevall et al., 2018.

the plurality of identities in Galician society and the translingual practices that this produced and with setting up clear-cut boundaries to 'protect' what they see as a threatened language and culture.

For some the Galician field data reinforces a common dualism whereby mixed or plural identities are validated, but in practice the construction of boundaries so as to defend these threatened identities almost inevitably reproduces the power relations derived from monolingual ideologies which previously produced long-established oppression and suppression (Woolard, 1998). However, Lamuela disagrees with such a prognosis, arguing that 'power relations exist mainly in facts (number of speakers, state policies, economic relations, domination configurations in language use . . .) and ideologies just reflect, justify and reinforce these facts. A monolingual ideology of a subordinate language is misguided, but it is necessary to ensure some spaces of monolingual use to get both an efficient language for all uses and the confidence necessary to use it regularly' (Lamuela, pers. comm., 2021).

There is a rich irony in all this where perception becomes reality and structures the options available in language choice matters. If this is true, it is a very telling observation, and the question remains: how do actors escape from this impasse?

Neofalantes tend to be better educated than native speakers, often having been 'radicalised' at university, and now may be required by their position as civil servants, local government and health administrators or teachers to gain fluency in Galician. They espouse views which suggest that their language transition is part and parcel of an attempt to improve the quality of life of their society and are keenly aware of their contribution in seeing restorative justice to the position of Galician, which for so long suffered discrimination at the hands of the Spanish state. The *neofalantes* have a very public role in the society; consequently many non-Galician speakers often tend to express negative views of their actions and condemn their radicalism. The public may also be intimidated by any suggestion that as they are not fluent in Galician they are not 'really' Galician, a phenomenon often found elsewhere in Europe.

One sphere in which this tension is manifested is in the planning of new educational facilities and in the growth of Galician in the school system. The education system is regulated by the Organic Law of Education 2/2006 of 3 May 2006, which came into effect in the 2007–8 school year. Officially the education system is presented as a bilingual model, but too often Galego ends up being taught as a subject only rather than as a medium for a full range of disciplines, depending on the school and location (reminiscent of most schools in Wales prior to the Education Reform Act 1988). A substantial proportion of parents are concerned that their children come home speaking Spanish only and appear to be less competent in Galego than anticipated. Several attempts to initiate a more robust presence for Galego have resulted in the establishment of a series of private schools, mainly in rural areas, a movement which has not been supported by government as it goes against the official policy.

The early gains made in locations such as Santiago, where parental groups persuaded the local authority to improve provision for Galician, were thwarted when the 2009 election returned the Partido Popular de Galicia to its semi-permanent position of government. It had long maintained a lukewarm language policy stance and sought to dilute the former elements of a bilingual provision by modernising its system to embrace a trilingual provision, including English.[64]

However, independent research suggests that this reform has had a negative impact on Galego. In an examination of primary teachers' experience of plurilingual education, Conde Moure (2019) found that 'teachers' perceptions of the policy respond mainly to personal linguistic ideologies'. Their experiences with the policy's implementation process are heavily influenced by school habitat and education model.

Of great interest is the finding that it is the 'linguistic domination dynamics the plurilingual policy reinforces' which has a 'detrimental effect that its "aseptic" distribution of the vehicular use of each language might have for the region's minority language'. The thesis suggests first that a reformulation of the concept of 'plurilingualism' is needed based on notions of linguistic complementarity and sociolinguistic considerations, and secondly that the programmes would be much improved were the teachers to be more directly involved in the policy's decision-making process. These are interesting results for some fear that over time the prestige of two vehicular languages, such as Spanish and English, might relegate Galician to a very marginal position and be supplanted by a more formal bilingual education based on the two hegemonic tongues.

O'Rourke and Ramallo contend that the government's approach to the language question reflects an ideological position that seeks to maintain the linguistic and social status quo. 'In doing so it aimed to reassure the dominant (albeit numerically smaller) Spanish-seeking sectors that their existing positions of power would remain unchanged. This approach, which was a consequence of neo-liberal principles, promoted (although implicitly) the idea of "harmonious" bilingualism, and more recently "friendly" (cordial) bilingualism, that is the non-conflictive co-existence of Castilian and Galician within the community' (O'Rourke and Ramallo, 2015, p. 153).

The most authoritative account of the transition to becoming a *neofalante* is that offered by Moralejo Silva and Ramallo (2019) where they use

---

[64] Other developments include a parent-led grass-roots group in Santiago who founded immersion schools in Galician, building on the *ikastola* model in the Basque Country (O'Rourke, 2018a; 2018b). The grass-roots movement Semente is also active in primary education initiatives.

ethnographic investigations to demonstrate both the motivations and the contexts which can induce people to change their behavioural identity. A university experience seemed to be pivotal in the lives of many that they sampled as they became both socialised and radicalised into accepting the values inherent in the *muda* process. By analysing the resultant linguistic trajectory, the authors can make informed predictions about the possible future vitality of *neofalantes* as a contributing element to the continued revitalisation of Galego, with all its contradictions and possibilities. Detailed ethnographic accounts by O'Rourke (2011) confirm this in the experience of Alexandra who was a university student in Vigo and transitioning to becoming a *neofalante* in 2004 and follow-up encounters with her in 2012 almost ten years later as reported in O'Rourke (2018a, pp. 408 and 412) which confirmed subsequent transitional phases.

Several scholars have suggested that the reasons given by *neofalantes* for changing their sociolinguistic behaviour were deeply embedded in a collective consciousness to preserve the Galician language and a reaction to perceived social and political injustices (O' Rourke, 2018b). Indeed, the fervour and determination to act is reminiscent of environmental and feminist groups, but unlike these movements the *neofalantes* temper their strong feelings of responsibility with elements of guilt for not having used the language in a more proactive manner. Feeling ashamed for not utilising their linguistic skills in the past drove many to be more determined than ever to switch from Spanish to Galician whenever they could. By so doing they would relieve some of the inherent tensions and dissonance occasioned by balancing two languages within a single persona. This despite the full knowledge that for many of them pursuing their activities in Galician might create frustration, challenges and a greater degree of personal involvement in the language struggle. Many reported an element of difficulty involved in the transition process, a period of stigmatisation which was only resolved when they became fully competent speakers and a situation which ultimately gave rise to considerable satisfaction for having crossed the bridge to community acceptance.

It is evident that IT, AI and multimedia developments impact so much on everyday life and can be reasonably be expected to influence both language learning and language use to a greater degree in the future. Accordingly, the work of Padín (2019) offers interesting insights into the differences between the linguistic practice of *neofalantes* online and offline. It is observed that there is a much stronger tendency to adopt standardised communication forms online which may please some purists and disappoint others as they would celebrate the idiomatic and idiosyncratic expressions in any language. Of equal interest is the way in which the linguistic *mudes* can operate in cyberspace. Most of the material investigated relates to very specific linguistic forms and patterns of speech rather than social interaction or behavioural change. Nevertheless, in terms of the *neofalantes*' influence on linguistic norms and on how they may in time also influence the speech patterns of native speakers as they increasingly engage with the growing online opportunities, the work is very telling. It also has resonance for many other lesser-used languages such as Frisian, Gaelic and Welsh.

The government's reaction to the growth in *neofalantes* is to treat it as a potential which has yet to be harnessed. Part of the difficulty is the perception that promoting Galician is equated with adopting a nationalist political stance or supporting one of the nationalist parties such as the Bloque Nacionalista Galego. Galician is claimed to be heavily laden with nationalist ideology and values whilst in contrast, Spanish, ironically enough, is deemed to be value-neutral and apolitical. Respondents do not necessarily accept any accusation that the Spanish state has acted in an imperial fashion or has treated Galicia as an internal colony. Indeed, quite the opposite case may be made as many would celebrate Galician-born heroes of the Spanish Empire, overseas territories and diaspora population.[65] Muniain (2018) and Monteagudo and Muniain (2020) report on the Galician community of Buenos Aires and its attempts to establish new speaker networks within a complex environment which evidences a range of attitudes both towards the recovery of the language and the Spanish state.

The close relationship between the promotion of a minority language and incipient nationalism is a common enough phenomenon throughout western Europe. The nineteenth and twentieth centuries witnessed the episodic ebb and flow of linguistic nationalism which saw the emergence of independent nation states such as Estonia, Finland and the Czech Republic, due in large part to the identification of a national language as both the reason for, and justification of, a strong political movement, often in acute opposition to a foreign overlord (Williams, 1985; 1994). Today one need only think of the close relationship between Plaid Cymru and the defence of Welsh or Sinn Féin and the struggle for a greater recognition of Irish language rights in Northern Ireland to understand the perception.

Be that as it may, official responses to the call for greater specification of the needs of *neofalantes* have been lukewarm. As with other jurisdictions, language planning initiatives could be used to promote the well-being and self-confidence of the *neofalantes* elements within the broader Galician revitalisation efforts and one obvious first step, as advocated by local associations, would be the establishment of designated centres in urban locales where people could pursue a range of activities, confident that the *lingua propia* in such spaces would be Galician and all participants, regardless of their proficiency, would be welcomed, nurtured and respected therein. Should this be deemed too exclusionary for support by the

---

[65] Galicia has produced political leaders, such as Franco, born 1892 in El Ferrol, and Fidel Castro, born in Birán, Cuba in 1926, together with his brother Raúl Castro, born in 1931, whose father Ángel María Bautista Castro y Argiz was born in Láncara, and went to Cuba as a Spanish soldier during the War of Independence. He returned to Cuba in 1906 and became a wealthy landowner.

public purse, then such centres could be multipurpose and host environmental groups, feminist meetings and adult learning classes, all elements which would conduce to a strengthening of community solidarity. They could also lead to a strengthening of conventional Galician pursuits such as traditional dancing or *regueifa* singing, forms of cultural association which add so much to the meaning-seeking urges of the *neofalantes* as well as the mother-tongue Galicians. Whilst much of the public manifestation of traditional culture has been male-oriented, including the choral singing tradition, a new emphasis on equality and the role of women has been a prominent feature of the Galician revival.

A critical area for development is the role of Galego in integrating into mainstream global social relations. Media specialists have argued that minority languages need to maximise the potential of specialist media opportunities as a defence strategy, else they will become increasingly redundant in the digital economy. The adaptation of newspapers designed for mobile phones could be a net boon for minority languages, yet most of this development has happened in Asia. Cunliffe (2019a) argues that despite their potential role in supporting and revitalising minority languages, minority language app markets remain practically unstudied. Further such markets face obvious challenges due to their small absolute size (in terms of consumers, developers and apps) and their small relative size compared with the majority language app market.

As dominant corporations determine both access to and content within significant platforms such as Facebook, WhatsApp, YouTube and the like, it is imperative that lesser-used languages keep pace with IT advances. Typically, the public think of such platforms as devices for personal social interaction and entertainment, but increasingly governments, regulatory authorities and service utility companies either require or induce customers to connect with them via the Internet.

Salgado advises that there are over 500 languages online; Google alone hosted 380 languages in 2018 and in 2020 was able to translate 108 languages. The power of such corporations is beginning to be challenged, witnessed by the February 2021 tensions between Australia and Facebook. This stems from a piece of legislation – the News Media Bargaining Code which was intended to force companies like Facebook to compensate news outlets and publishers for stories that they host or share on their platforms and news feeds. Facebook has argued that in some jurisdictions such as the UK it pays selected new sources for its material. In submission to the Australian Senate inquiry Sir Tim Berners-Lee said he had been deeply concerned about the social media giant's failure to curb abuse and the spread of disinformation. However, if the move to force companies to pay for certain links spread around the world, it could make the Internet as we know it unworkable. He advocated the principle of net neutrality – that all traffic should be treated equally and flow freely rather than being taxed or slowed down according to its nature, and this trumps all other concerns.[66]

If net neutrality is a universal feature, then payment for net access and software products is a more localised affair. The question arises of who pays for a minority language community's access to internet developments. We saw in relation to Ireland that Foras secured deals with Microsoft and the like to develop services in Irish, as did the Basque Government for Basque. By contrast the Welsh Language Board initiated a co-operative venture whereby it offered to produce Welsh versions of Microsoft products in exchange for access to platforms, products and licences. What of future more wide-ranging products and protocols? Is there a point beyond which it is simply not affordable for some languages to be permanently represented in a wide range of domains? And if so with what consequences for the future use of such languages?

The focus on new speakers has thrown up several new challenges to both practitioners and policymakers alike. As most of the issues are intimately connected it is hard to prioritise key insights, but one which has attracted a great deal of attention is how power is wielded and to what end in contact situations. Following Bourdieu (1991) a fresh approach as to how power is embedded in social relations has been constructed. New speaker research seeks to identify 'how individuals and groups are coerced into language acquisition, language loss, and patterns of language use by powerful external forces that control the processes of language policymaking' (Tollefson, 2015b, p. 141). A very good illustration of this is the reaction of the pro-Spanish section of the Galician population to the 2007 proposal that half of the school subjects be taught in Galician. Their opposition turned on a perceived denial of their basic linguistic rights as Spanish subjects, their concern for future employment in the linguistic market and fears of potential shifts in the balance of power which they perceived as less favourable to them (Álvarez-Cáccamo, 2011). O'Rourke and Nandi's (2019) discussion of this opposition could equally well be applied to the educational reforms in Catalonia and the Basque Country, with one notable exception: the ambiguity which characterises the implementation of policy in Galicia has evolved into a far more robust statement of normalisation in Euskadi and Catalonia. The consequence is that both these language regimes face all the attendant problems of managing a successful educational system which places great strains on teacher training and resource development to equip a school population to be competent in at least three languages, that of the host nation, the Spanish state and English.

Soler and Darquennes (2019b) argue that new speaker research illumines how power operates in structures of domination or conflict, and how human

---

[66] www.bbc.co.uk/news/technology-56120281.

agency plays a role in co-constructing such frameworks. By detailing processes of resistance or adaptation to given language regimes, new speaker research fruitfully adds to what Pakir (1994) has called 'invisible language planning', or augments Baldauf's (1993) notion of 'unplanned language planning'. But what do such statements mean in reality? Clearly the ethnographic interpretation of speaker engagement offers a sympathetic, not to say uncritical construction of what is at stake for the new speaker and established speaker alike in terms of social acceptance, legitimacy, group norms and civic action. But as many of the observed interactions vary so much it is hard to quantify, let alone generalise, from the results obtained. Also, despite the lip service paid to power relations, few of the new speaker case studies deconstruct what is going on in detail and with what consequences for the sharing and maintenance of power differentials. It clearly also makes a difference as to who is involved in the interchange, experience and process of identity transformation.

To illustrate, there is a huge difference in the potential of an Irish-born non-Irish speaker becoming a competent new Irish speaker, with all that entails for future civic engagement, in comparison with a Chinese migrant to Frankfurt seeking to accommodate as a new speaker of German. This is not to say that comparative fieldwork is problematic; merely that one should guard against reading over from some situations to a more general set of principles and practices which can be applied in any multilingual context. When experiences and events turn out to be less propitious than expected for the new speaker, it is too easy to castigate the host society and its attendant expectations, norms and values as exercising its power to resist the accommodation of new speakers. To concentrate attention thus is to absolve or ignore the agency of the new speaker him or herself and as a consequence only a partial interpretation is given and received.

A second claim is that it is relatively rare to find examples which include micro, meso and macro level interpretations of new speakers operating in distinct jurisdictions or contexts. This will surely change as both the concept and the outcomes related to policy initiatives embed themselves in the social practice. However, the results of academic analyses need to be summarised and transposed as realisable interpretations and practical recommendations which policymakers can evaluate and incorporate into their professional work, as few will be willing or able to seek out specialist academic journals for evidence. Thus, it is incumbent on those who seek to advance the interests of new speakers to also provide policy-oriented briefings to decision makers and the policy community.

For minority languages that have undergone successful revitalisation and (re-)entered the public sphere, we often see a competing set of values of legitimacy, linked to education, standardisation and economically instrumental use. For example, McLeod and O'Rourke (2015) showed that 'authentic' Gaelic continues to be the locus of legitimacy, but some new speakers point to the value of the new Gaelic forms introduced into professional Gaelic, and some of them deny that one needs a local accent.

Conclusion

In broad terms public administration in the Basque Country, Navarre, Catalonia and Galicia follow Spanish state-wide norms and structures. In comparative European terms conventionally the Spanish approach to policymaking does not favour public consultation, regular evidence-based reforms or anticipating the impact of policy on sections of the population. Thus, unlike Sweden, the UK, the Netherlands or Finland, Spain tends to harness ideas and good practice initiatives from within its own bureaucracies. In 2018 a European Commission report on public administration characterised the Spanish experience as being inherently conservative and fragmented. Having described the main contours of policy formation and implementation, it commented that:

> Unsurprisingly, Spain scores low in the use of 'societal consultation' and of 'evidence-based policy' making since there is no connection between policy-making and general schemes of consultation or more specific consultation with external experts from consultancy firms, think tanks or the academia. (Sources: Bertelsmann Stiftung, World Bank). Occasionally, some ministries may create expert groups for a specific topic although those sessions are similar to 'talking shops' and are not backed by research ... The ministerial websites have a point of access to the opinion of the public, but each ministry is deploying its own distinctive approach and it is unclear how the ministerial authorities are using this feedback from citizens. At the same time, policy advice comes mostly from within the bureaucracy. At the request of political appointees and policy advisers, reports are produced but the use of quantitative data and forecast is restricted to a few policy areas. (European Commission, 2018)

In recent years the Spanish Executive has made significant changes to encourage consistency and establish a more cohesive framework for policy formation and implementation. 'A law on administrative procedures (39/2015) passed in 2015 makes compulsory "smart regulation" and "better regulation", which entails, when drafting a piece of regulation, the assessment of budgetary consequences, environmental impact, gender concerns, and potential impact on people with disabilities. This suggests that systematic planning and search for evidence will be needed before drafting a law' (European Commission, 2018). Accordingly, current Spanish practice is more in line with European norms, save for the greater politicised element of many public sector appointments.

By contrast in the field of language policy both the Basque Country and Catalonia have a very fine tradition of evidence gathering, public consultation, the garnering of expert evidence from academics and specialist agencies, such as Euskaltzaindia, Soziolinguistika Klusterra, the Institute for Catalan Studies and CIEMEN (Centre Internacional Escarré per a les Minories Ètniques i les Nacions).[67] Given the centrality of language and human rights to both country's political projects, there has also been a superabundance of academic and professional conferences devoted to a wide variety of themes and challenges related to linguistic justice, group equality, the arts and creative industries, literature and poetry, the use of IT and AI in language teaching and public service provision, the political implications of revivalist ideologies and practice and perhaps most significantly of all the recovery of submerged memories, and the restoration of democratic practices enhancing national dignity.

Chapters 6 and 7 have compared the new speaker experience in four nations and autonomous regions of Spain. While civil society activists and some government and third sector agencies were enthusiastic about the phenomenon, higher-level policymakers were less convinced by any arguments in support of adding a new category to their programmes of action. However, this does not suggest that the experiences of learners of official languages are in any way marginal or that once learned the target languages are not used extensively. Quite the opposite case can be made, for in all four locations the advanced learning of official languages by non-native speakers has been a major feature of the education system and of social integration. It is just that there is a more muted formal enthusiasm for the term and by and large policymakers are not convinced that by adding a new phenomenon to their retinue of policy goals they will make any appreciable gains. In this sense we must distinguish between the phenomenon of new speaker and its appellation or formal terminological naming. From my point of view the justification for the tempered consideration of the term and its implications is an important heuristic lesson and a valuable contribution to the overall analysis and set of arguments examined herein.

---

[67] Fewer such agencies exist in Navarra where the Academy of the Basque Language is the consultative institution for linguistic standards.

8   The Policy Community and Recommendations on New Speakers

The Policy Community

The aim of this chapter is to suggest ways by which the results of new speaker research could be framed within generic and specific recommendations for policymakers. The new speaker evidence base was sparse a decade ago and accordingly I welcome the work of the COST New Speakers project for it has generated a great deal of fresh data and evidence and enriched our understanding of the new speaker experience. We may now ask the question, à la Lenin (1901) following Nikolay Gavrilovich Chernyshevsky (1863), what is to be done?

The salience of the evidence undertaken both by the New Speakers Network and others will be enhanced if members of the policy community are made aware of the needs of new speakers and can be influenced by the force of key recommendations. I have argued that without knowing the predisposition of decision makers in government and civil society to act so as to strengthen the needs and requirements of new speakers, well-formulated recommendations would not gain much purchase and could be seen as being one step removed from the policy landscape they seek to influence.[1]

The policy community is an admixture of interests, resource allocation imperatives and competing political ideologies, often articulated by strong personalities.[2] For organisations, agencies and government departments concerned with language maintenance or revitalisation, there is a clear understanding that the contribution of 'native or indigenous speakers' is vital as a source of legitimacy, authenticity and creativity in reproducing both language and its associated culture(s).[3] However, our evidence suggests that they are less certain as to how to categorise or operationalise programmes which seek to acknowledge

---

[1] I am grateful to Professor B. O' Rourke for encouraging me to prepare the original paper on policy recommendations which appeared as Williams (2019b).

[2] Policy is inherently deeply political; its full implementation tends to be an admixture of expediency and pragmatism as exercised by departmental heads and deputy ministers, hence the views of both politicians and senior civil servants were investigated in this project.

[3] This analysis is primarily concerned with instances of minority language revitalisation although Catalan and Canadian data relates to localised majorities.

the salience and contribution of new speakers as distinct from the conventionally termed L2 learners.[4] The reticence in some jurisdictions to advance specific new speaker interventions and programmes is compounded by the general climate of decision-making in an age of uncertainty.

In recent years, a new wave of language policy studies has emerged within the framework of ethnographic and discursive approaches (Blommaert et al., 2009; Hult, 2010; Johnson, 2009; 2013; McCarty, 2011; Johnson and Ricento, 2013; Halonen, Ihalainen and Saarinen, 2015; Barakos and Unger, 2016). These are claimed to supplement the classical language policy and planning theories (e.g., Cooper, 1989; Kaplan and Baldauf, 1997; Shohamy, 2006; Spolsky, 2004; 2009). From such a perspective, the key idea is that language policy is a multi-layered phenomenon, something that agents constantly recreate through their complex discursive interaction (Barakos and Unger, 2016).

Spotti and Kroon (2019) observe that local solutions are needed for local challenges, but that these might end up playing a role as local inputs for informing top-down language policy developments. I take such observations to be a part of the normal working of policy, for pragmatic processes filter both up and down the chain of command and influence. This was true in the case of the individual Welsh Mentrau Iaith attempts to nurture new speakers from within the host and immigrant communities, because examples of best practice were then incorporated into the national network of Mentrau Iaith Cymru activities and within official strategies of the Welsh government. Similar localised developments were observed in Catalonia with the Voluntariat VxL initiative and in the BAC with the Euskaraldia programme (Puigdevall, 2022).

Language policy framers may be conscious of the impact which new speakers will have on their target populations, but what is relatively absent from the contemporary research is a demonstrable direct reference to the significance of new speakers within official language and educational strategies. Now this may be because of the recency of the phenomenon or because senior civil servants are not fully convinced of the cogency of the concept as an operational mechanism.[5] Accordingly there is scope to examine the range of indirect references to new speakers as an element in official language policy. But the difficulty is in knowing precisely what this might look like and how adequate it would be to convince one of any previous attention having been paid to new speakers. Thus, a certain caution needs to be introduced against the tendency to exaggerate the pertinence of new speakers for public policy formulation.

---

[4] There was no a priori expectation that there would be a comprehensive interpretation of the requirements and roles of new speakers in language policy development expressed by those official representatives interviewed.

[5] This is a feature worth re-examining in c. five to ten years' time in a range of European contexts so as to gauge the result of the COST Network initiative's impact on official language strategies.

Over and above the new speaker particularities there is a deeper question concerning policy formulation for minority language speakers. It stems from the fact that new paradoxes emerged which policymakers in the eighties and nineties did not anticipate. Rodríguez observes that, in the Basque Country,

the idea was to create more bilinguals and the assumption is that when you create new speakers, they are going to automatically speak the language. Another assumption was the idea of transmission in Fishman's terms (that was the goal in the Basque case). And again, we have not seen it play out as expected. The Basque case (as many others in Europe) has shown that the heterogeneity in new speakerhood is a product of sociohistoricity of that language interacting with policy making practices, but this heterogeneity has also challenged assumptions that those in the eighties made and new anxieties to be addressed, especially in a globalised linguistic market. To me, some of the questions I see as important are how can new policymakers address the needs of ANY speaker of a minority language (or future speakers of such languages) taking into account the heterogenous complexities that they entail?' (Rodríguez, pers. comm., 2021)

This is an important reminder that the culture of public administration, institutional memory, modes of framing policy and determining interventions are all crucial determinants of the process of language planning.

Here it is necessary to reinforce the salience of the key questions which animated this investigation.

Key Questions

- What particular aspects does the new speaker phenomenon illuminate more clearly than other related concepts?
- What are the ideas and beliefs of different sorts of actors about new speakers in a given setting?
- How can the new speaker concept inform language policy scholarship and practice?
- How do different jurisdictions interpret the role and potential contribution of new speakers to the vitality of the target language population(s)?
- How is the governance of any programme targeted at new speaker promotion and satisfaction to be managed?
- What policy outcomes can be identified in terms of inequalities and social stratification affecting new speakers more directly?

Clearly, while emphasising the novelty of the new speaker paradigm care should be taken not to underplay the fundamental needs of native speakers, because some of the tensions that have arisen within new speakers cannot be understood fully without considering 'traditional' speakers and the relationships between the two (Rodríguez, pers. comm., 2021).

Having sought evidence to answer these questions a variety of responses may be given to each depending upon which jurisdiction is under review.

A general observation is that the new speaker phenomenon is still relatively novel and may not be as integral as expected or as easy to incorporate into mainstream language and educational policy. In order to justify greater attention being paid to these current developments it is fair to ask just what would count as a successful new speaker policy and why? What sort of evidence would be required to help formulate policy? Would we be able to recognise it as a distinct element of language planning interventions? How would we measure it?

There is no normative expectation that stand-alone new speaker policies should be developed as this would create further diversification within the language communities. However, it would appear desirable that future policy-makers should pay more attention to new speaker needs within more holistic frameworks.

Furthermore, it is more likely a priori that rather than have a fully comprehensive and specific new speaker policy, most government interventions would contain elements of support for new speaker needs within more established educational, linguistic or social programmes of action. Determining on what basis such elements are conceived and actioned is likely to be a difficult task.

However, interventions per se are a difficult concept for many officials as there may be inherently awkward or uncomfortable political implications involved. Some elements in society may be favoured and others simultaneously disadvantaged compared with the *status quo ante*. This is a clear thread in the majority–minority relations as practised by states which respect cultural pluralism. Attacks on the notion of freedom and the fear engendered by a possible threat to one's standing as a member of the majority can induce a negative overreaction.

Then again there is the temporal element involved in evaluation, so we perforce need to ask over what time frame would we seek to measure the impact of any recommendation? Many who work within the policy community acknowledge that they require sufficient evidence to inform their decisions and perhaps modify their programmes but need also to temper such evidence with other considerations, such as the financial implications involved, the alternative pressing policy demands and the political feasibility of adopting more robust interventions in favour of the issue under review.

Here we may ask a most profound question: does it make any sense at all to separate out the new speaker dimension from generic language policy and planning programmes? This is especially true in situations such as for Basque, Gaelic, Frisian and Welsh, where an increasing proportion of fluent speakers are produced by the statutory education system rather than the hearth, home and community.

However, it probably doesn't make sense in settings where existing language policies or broader social and educational policies already take new speaker profiles into account, without referencing the new speaker label. In other contexts, it might suffice to fine-tune existing language policies instead of aiming for new or additional policies that explicitly take the new speaker dimension into account.

There are many ways in which governments can intervene without making a fetish of the new speaker category. Thus, the answer very much depends on the context-specific language ecologies, the existing policy traditions, the terminology used by policymakers, the weight policy formulators give to certain labels, their take on academia, as a result of their training and exposure to recent scholarship.[6]

The Response of the Policy Community

Interviews and document analysis were undertaken with the policy community in the following jurisdictions: the BAC, Canada, Catalonia, Finland, Galicia, Ireland, Navarre, Scotland and Wales.[7] Here we need only be reminded of the most important finding which is that while innovative interventions were practised in the BAC, Navarre and Catalonia, for the most part there was little intuitive agreement as to the salience of embedding new speaker concerns within language and education policies throughout most other jurisdictions. There was little consensus, some confusion and only an occasional thorough-going professional commitment to the concept and its implementation.

When the issue of policy reform in favour of considering the needs of new speakers was introduced at interview, two dominant reactions were registered. Either the contribution of new speakers was considered to be vital to the future health of the language and the social cohesion of society, as in the BAC and Catalonia, or the policy formulators insisted that such needs were already catered for in well-established programmes, and in consequence there was no great urgency to adapt existing priorities to take account of such needs. Few senior policy advisers enthusiastically endorsed a fresh approach to new speakers as if it were a novel, urgent and sustainable policy item. Some argued that in time consideration might be given to enlarging the scope of current programmes in relation to education and community integration, but this was in most cases couched in terms of a larger integration approach to migrants, whether or not they had identified as new speakers. Social cohesion and a reduction in group tension was the motivating factor here rather than language promotion per se. This position has both resonance and political pragmatism, for as Rodríguez remarks, 'this could be a way "to unmark" the

---

[6] These reasons were suggested by Jeroen Darquennes (pers. comm., 2021).
[7] Because of Covid-19 restrictions in 2019–21 some of the planned face-to-face interviews were conducted either by Zoom or as email correspondence.

minoritized language and make it more "anonymous" in Woolard's terms. In fact, this was her hypothesis in 2008, in that the future of Catalan resided in its anonymity as a national language and this included non-Spanish immigrants' (Rodríguez, pers. comm., 2021).

Canadian enquiries revealed that the new speaker concept was neither readily used nor considered to be particularly useful for language or education policy formulation. As a largely immigrant country with generations of New Canadians becoming full participants in society, it was obvious that a great deal of energy and investment had already been put into second or third language learning of both official languages. Immigrants who had become competent in one or both official languages were in fact new speakers of French or English from a European perspective. Accordingly, even if the term 'new speaker' is not used in common currency, the reality which the phenomenon portrays is a major feature of Canadian state formation and social identity. If one focusses on indigenous language revitalisation programmes the participants may in fact be new speakers of subordinated languages whilst not necessarily adopting the new speaker framework. Oftentimes, instead, they follow heritage speaker ideals, given the strong relationship between language, race/ethnicity and territoriality in the North American context (Rodríguez, pers. comm., 2021).

When Federal Canadian ministers or former ministers were interviewed their standard line was that once in office, they operationalised the broad parameters of policy as established by their predecessors, particularly under Stéphane Dion, President of the Privy Council and Minister of Intergovernmental Affairs. In launching the five-year Action Plan, on 12 March 2003, Dion highlighted the plan's aim to enable Canada to take full advantage of its linguistic duality, where people's language skills were one of the keys to competitive success both at home and abroad. The Dion inheritance was strengthened if it was felt that the former administration had diluted the contours of official language strategy, as had happened in Canada under the Harper government. When in opposition, interim Liberal leader Bob Rae appointed Dion as the Liberal Critic for Intergovernmental Affairs and spokesperson for La Francophonie. At interview Dion did not see the relevance of the new speaker paradigm but did reinforce the centrality of linguistic dualism for Canadian federation.[8] His speeches and statement set the tone for the reform of the Official Language Strategies when the Liberals came to power following the November 2015 elections. On 4 November 2015, Dion was appointed Minister of Foreign Affairs in Justin Trudeau's cabinet and, although not directly responsible for federal language policy, he along with several others is credited with making the French–English dualism a significant feature once more of federal politics.

---

[8] Stephane Dion, Canadian parliament, Ottawa, 27 May 2014.

Leading senators Serge Joyal[9] and Claudette Tardif[10] while fully committed to linguistic dualism did not see the relevance of the new speaker concept for Canadian public policy and were wary of adding yet another possible distraction to an already crowded and often conflictual discourse.

Senior officials in Canadian Heritage were asked how the Dion plan worked out in practice.[11] They argued that under the Dion plan 2003–8, twelve departments were given funding for linguistic duality, an additional $750,000,000 for new programmes., but such funding had been cut in the intervening ten years of three Conservative administrations under Harper. The Dion plan, they argued, had a vision which was missing from the Language Roadmaps. Before the Liberals lost power to the Conservatives in 2006, they amended the Official Languages Act to make Part 8 and Part 7 subject to legal recourses; parliament added a section that Canadian Heritage must take positive measures to foster this aim, and this included the possibility of a court challenge if federal departments did not take such measures as this would be a violation of the Official Languages Act. This in turn increased the salience of the Commissioner of Official Languages operating under Part 7 in 2005. Federal departments now understood that linguistic duality was a serious business. After the Conservatives gained power the Dion plan for 2003–8 was evaluated and many of its good ideas were confirmed as adding to the vitality of the official language communities, but really it was hard to measure the effect of the policy.

Interviews conducted with Canadian federal civil servants in May 2015 and November 2018 revealed that the new speaker paradigm had yet to make an impact within official circles.[12] None of those interviewed were aware of the new speaker concept, nor of its related data sets and case studies. However, they did express an interest in learning more and argued that an increased comparative European–Canadian perspective on such issues would doubtless yield fruitful policy developments.

By contrast throughout all European jurisdictions surveyed most civil society policymakers, academics and commentators approached were strongly of the opinion that specific, tailor-made policy initiatives were needed to reflect better the contribution of new speakers whether as competent learners or migrants seeking to integrate. The argument was that fragile minority language communities were going to be increasingly reliant on attracting fresh members

---

[9] Serge Joyal, Canadian parliament, 29 May 2014.
[10] Claudette Tardif, Canadian parliament, 3 June 2014.
[11] Y. Déry and Christine Lessard, Canadian Heritage, Ottawa, 28 May 2015.
[12] Mark Tremblay and colleagues, Treasury Board, Government of Canada, Ottawa, 29 May 2015. Carsten Quell and colleagues at the Centre of Excellence on Official Languages, Treasury Board, Government of Canada, Ottawa, 2 November 2018; Sylvie Painchaud and her federal and provincial colleagues interviewed at the Annual Meeting of the Canadian Federal and Provincial Ministers Responsible for Francophone Affairs, Montreal, 7 and 8 November 2018.

who, by their enthusiasm, diversity and commitment, were likely to provide much-needed support to struggling communities and networks. In addition, the presence of a more diverse socio-cultural speaker component was lauded both as a positive sign and as an affirmation of the open, welcoming nature of the minority language community. Accordingly, the community itself could benefit from a sense of positive feedback as to its own magnanimous approach to incorporating new blood.

No one believed that this fresh source of energy could compensate for the atrophying of heartland territories on the balance sheet of minority language accounting, but many believed that in the absence of heartland revivals, attracting and sustaining new speakers was the most realistic prospect for growth. Concerns were raised as to the quality of the language used by new speakers, how authentic or pure it tended to be and whether or not it became a primarily instrumental means of earning a living and of communicating, rather than an expression of a meaning-seeking identity closely tied to a dependent culture and world-view. Be that as it may, the prospect of both an infusion of new speakers and a greater use of IT and AI augured well if only the potential of both trends could be harnessed.

The downside was a realisation that for many new speakers, being isolates in a complex, multi-layered, multilingual context, and the persistent negative reactions on behalf of some native speakers could lead not only to frustration but also to disenchantment. The more so as many new speakers did not necessarily embrace or endorse the associated cultural practices of native speakers in some societies, either because such practices were considered too closely related to a peri-rural habitat, as in Gaelic traditional culture, or too politicised, as in Basque nationalism. This resulted in fewer non-educational opportunities to socialise with others, a break in a steep upward trajectory which had led them to becoming new speakers in the first place. This lack of a continuum, of a series of set-aside or safe breathing spaces, was a major impediment to their continued progress, confidence and satisfaction in expressing themselves in and through their adopted language. Identifying such spaces will doubtless become a key element of future policy considerations. And this is a major point of realisation that the new speaker perspective is relational as is, of course, the minority/majority (language) concept.

The broad human concerns in the experiences we have been describing are not necessarily to be understood as precluding attachment to the state majoritarian language, such as English, Spanish, French or any other tongue – quite the opposite. Indeed, for the most part it is from that language environment that many minority new speakers spring, and it is through instruction in one of those languages that they learned their now prized minority language. It is also through such a hegemonic language that many of the new speakers earn their living, socialise, derive pleasure and enjoyment in social and sporting realms.

So, in that respect they have an additional diglossic arrangement of their time and activities. This adaptation may be justified by a second sociolinguistic consideration, namely the desire to 'pass' as legitimate members of more than one host community, the default one of their birth or rearing and the chosen one(s) of circumstances, volition and preference. Neither is this sort of arrangement confined only to two languages, for many of the new speakers are, on investigation, actually multilingual. This is most evident for migrants, refugees and asylum seekers, but it also often revealed in others' family history of intermarriage, geographical displacement as a result of warfare or the economic imperative which drives the search for betterment in a new country.

The degree of volition in a migrant's trajectory is a significant element. One of the more promising international movements which provides a great deal of information and context for understanding the scale and dynamism of forced international migration is the Responsibility to Protect (R2P) movement established by the UN at its World Summit in 2005. This reflects the international political commitment to halt mass atrocity crimes whose four key concerns are to prevent genocide, war crimes, ethnic cleansing and crimes against humanity. It is based on three pillars, the first of which declares that 'every state has the Responsibility to Protect its populations from four mass atrocity crimes: genocide, war crimes, crimes against humanity and ethnic cleansing'; pillar two emphasises that 'the wider international community has the responsibility to encourage and assist individual states in meeting that responsibility', and the third declares that 'if a state is manifestly failing to protect its populations, the international community must be prepared to take appropriate collective action, in a timely and decisive manner and in accordance with the UN Charter'.[13]

It is conventional for advanced industrial societies to consider R2P as an external commitment, protecting target populations from mass atrocities in contexts such as Kenya, 2007–8; Ivory Coast, 2011; Libya, 2011; Central African Republic, 2013; or the ongoing turmoil in Syria, Burundi, Yemen and Afghanistan. But as the Centre for Geopolitics at Cambridge University has suggested, recent events have shown that Europe itself might also be vulnerable to pressures leading to the four R2P crimes and raise concern as to how European states can better protect their own vulnerable populations.[14]

In seeking to move beyond the controversial notion of the *droit d'ingérence* of the 1990s, the R2P norm sought to recast their involvement in terms of responsibility and protection rather than of the right to intervene. As a consequence, there is a great deal of animated discussion and empirical fieldwork which investigates not only the military and security implications of conflict

---

[13] www.un.org/en/genocideprevention/about-responsibility-to-protect.shtml.
[14] www.cfg.polis.cam.ac.uk/events/r2p-europe-pillar-i-challenges.

management but increasingly a concern with the plight of displaced persons, refugees and asylum seekers. From our perspective the interesting issue is, how do these displaced people navigate into the mainstream of their new host society? One of the determining features of their success, but by no means a well-understood variable, is their ability to learn a new language and fit in to a new culture. For new speakers in such situations, it would appear that the simultaneous learning of a state language and, for a significant number, one of the state's minority languages, is a double burden. Superficially that may be true, but beyond the often negative banner headlines, there are genuine success stories where asylum seekers have rejoiced in their ability to learn the language of the local host community and more encouraging still have engaged in the promotion of that minority language to convince many of the indigenous people to follow suit.[15]

Thus, inherent in the learning trajectory of many new speakers there are deep emotional stirrings and disturbances which should not be undervalued. Several of those interviewed for the New Speakers Network relayed their family history and their longing to restore the broken lineage of a lost inheritance by reacquiring an additional language as their own. This was a strong feature of the Celtic language communities and also of Basque. An important resource which captured such experiences was curated by Deirdre MacKenna for the New Speakers Network. This collection consists of a series of cultural tools to enable people to explore the dynamics involved in becoming a new speaker of a language in the context of a multilingual Europe. The aim is to bring to the attention of influence formers the merit of considering new speaker needs and interests.[16] The resource-rich collection has a range of items which could be used by advocacy groups to inform decision makers of their recommendations and increase awareness of the diverse range of experiences, profiles and situations covered by the term new speaker. This collection includes a range of films, edited in different ways to suit audience preferences and situations, including art exhibitions, public sector meetings and general Internet-based awareness raising. Most useful is the 'New Speaker Guide', a booklet explaining the concept and including quotes from new speakers about their experiences. This is complemented by a series of posters which foreground key statements made by participants so as to convey the messages in a more arresting and succinct manner. Finally, the resource contains an archive of significant statements made by the participants about their transitional experiences into becoming new speakers. This initiative represents good practice and may be readily imitated within other language communities to create a resource

---

[15] www.theguardian.com/uk-news/2020/mar/06/i-was-lucky-the-asylum-seeker-campaigning-for-others-to-learn-welsh.
[16] www.nspk.org.uk/the-new-speaker-studio.html.

capable of enriching a campaign or programme of interaction with policy formulators.

An under-researched element is the cost involved in the new speaker trajectory. For the individual, pre or post either a single *muda,* or a series of *mudes,* there are varying financial costs involved in acquiring a new language, such as travel expenses and fees to attend adult education classes. In some jurisdictions the costs of attending formal language classes are either subsidised by the local authority or the teaching establishment or else one's employer may contribute towards the costs if deemed a necessary or desirable element of employment. A more difficult cost to evaluate and attend to are the emotional considerations involved within any identity transition process. Clearly there are identifiable satisfactory emotional turns as one becomes more and more competent in an additional language and the opportunities afforded thereby to work and socialise. Ciriza (2019) has investigated the complications of new speakerhood, especially the difficulties of bringing about a parental *muda.* 'Such *mudas* are traversed by competing ideologies of language and language socialization. In disrupting monolingual ideologies, participatory approaches which aim at increasing the symbolic value of the language clash with the attitudes of speakers who view these *mudas* as inconsequential for achieving normalization' (Ciriza, 2019). Other ethnographic studies also describe the negative turns, as native speakers deride or shun the efforts which advanced learners make or question their right to belong to the in-group. Notwithstanding the positive public rhetoric advanced, members of minority language communities are not necessarily more magnanimous than hegemonic language speakers when it comes to addressing issues of race, faith, religious mores or the accommodation needs of refuge or asylum seekers, no matter how much they profess they want to belong to society by learning Basque, Catalan or Welsh.

We acknowledge that there are other types of frustration which derive from the lack of an automatic transmission of the 'new' language within the family, perhaps as a result of the partner's reticence or the absence of high school provision for the children's continued education within the target language. Given the idiosyncratic nature of human volition there is no guarantee that the offspring will appreciate the advantages of learning the new language as has the parent or vice versa. In fact, given that this lack of intergenerational language transmission is a well-established feature of native speaking families, why would one expect greater success with the family groupings of new speakers? It would be a signal service to ascertain whether and to what extent the new speaker phenomenon is an individual enterprise or one which prompts whole family acquisition and with what costs and benefits. And, if one supplements the families' contribution, we may ask to what extent new speakers with all their different profiles and geographical backgrounds can be considered to form a 'social group' or a 'subgroup' of a 'historical minority speech community'.[17]

The intensely personal nature of the relationship for the first generation of new speakers in a family may in fact be repeated in successive generations' journeys of rediscovery whose inner force propels adherence and identification. At its apogee this is the story of the recovery of modern Hebrew as described by Zuckermann (2020). While I accept that this is a special case because of the tragic history of suffering and the geostrategic considerations surrounding the establishment of the state of Israel, nevertheless at a much smaller scale the factors which conduce to a whole people's sacrifice to possess a language, having occupied a space, can be likened to the individual's struggle to come to terms with a new language.[18] We do not need a historical doctrine of The Land, of Eretz Israel, a promise from antiquity or a marked theological tradition to contextualise and provide a supportive infrastructure in our search for a new speaker justification (Davies, 1982). But we do need a back story to support the continued efforts of such speakers, else they will feel betrayed and bereft. That is why in each jurisdiction studied, the role of civil society is crucial in the effort to convict the new speakers of the worth of their investment in time, energy and emotion in coming to grips with the new language, either as an entry to a new set of relationships or a certificate of skills and competence in seeking employment and additional ways of communicating.

This need for infrastructural support, which is both personal and meaningful, has been demonstrated most forcibly by the Voluntariat per la Llengua experience in Catalonia, an initiative which did not derive from a think tank or a civil service role-playing scenario. Rather it was born from the necessity of dealing with 'strangers in our midst' by sensitive and responsive civil society members. Only later, once they had demonstrated their worth, did they attract government support and funding. But this latter development is crucial for it is through the largesse or foresight of government that good ideas and best practice can be replicated and diffused through the system, as demonstrated so effectively by the adoption of the Voluntariat per la Llengua by the Catalan Government. A similar pathway from community initiative to government support can be traced for the Mentrau Iaith and Canolfannau Cymraeg in Wales.

However, it was also evident that among those interviewed there was some frustration with the new speaker paradigm, for it failed to differentiate

---

[17] Jeroen Darquennes, following Erik Allardt (1981), suggests that these are usually defined on the basis of a number of criteria such as lineage, language and culture, self-categorisation and social organisation (Darquennes, pers. comm., 2021).

[18] Rodríguez observes that 'this success exists, but we know little about it (of course, it is not even close to the Hebrew case). In fact, scholars on new speakers are starting to ask how do native speakers of standard varieties (who presumably learned it at home through new speaker parents) situate themselves?' (Rodríguez, pers. comm., 2021).

adequately between different trajectories followed by new speakers, whether as students from non-native language homes who had learned the target language within statutory education, as adult learners or as migrants/refugees predisposed to learning the target language so as to cope with and be absorbed into parts of the minority host community.

Others argued that the new speaker concept was a sop, a form of deceit to cover over several long-standing and well-established weaknesses in the education system which had failed to produce competent L2 speakers and users in sufficient quantities to justify the time, resources and efforts in promoting the target language within certain jurisdictions. They further argued that the concept and its accompanying rationale, literature and advocacy was an as yet unproven case. In consequence, they were not minded to embrace this new dimension of policy and curriculum reform until such time as realistic, measurable and significant advantages could be demonstrated. This is an important line of reasoning and as it is held by influential decision makers within the policy community across several jurisdictions, is worth giving serious consideration to by those who advocate a more holistic approach to the incorporation of new speaker needs into the system.

An additional concern raised by some public servants was that many who advocated robust recommendations regarding new speakers were limited in their operational knowledge and pragmatic understanding as to how policy formulation and implementation worked. Advocates assumed that there was a single point of entry for their proposals, whereas in fact there were many such entry points and not all were concerned primarily with matters linguistic.

It may be asked whether the responses of senior civil servants are completely reliable. While I have no doubt that the public servants I dealt with by interview or correspondence were sincere in their answers, there remains the possibility that they did not fully acknowledge their reticence or inability to service the needs of new speakers in their policy formulation.[19]

Clearly the senior civil servants I interviewed were under no obligation to attend any of my meetings; they could simply have delegated the affair to junior colleagues or have refused permission outright. Why therefore am I fairly confident that the answers they gave were accurate and sincere? There are three reasons which revolve around the issue of trust. I have been engaged in analysing aspects of minority language promotion and regulation for fifty years. For the most part this engagement has been as a critical academic with a dual mission. The most significant is to translate good practice from one

---

[19] I base this on the fact that I have known and co-operated with many of those interviewed for a long period, either as a result of previous research investigations or in my dealings with them as a member of the Welsh Language Board or international agencies such as the European Bureau for Lesser Used Languages and the Network for the Promotion of Language Diversity.

jurisdiction to another based on evidence and proven success and has involved a great deal of engagement with successive cohorts of government officials in Europe and Canada. The second is something close to an iconoclastic mission to expose the weaknesses and hypocrisy of official statements, a feature reflected in my use of the conceit of the Mask of Piety which animated an earlier volume (Williams, 2013a). The third reason is that as a member of the Welsh Language Board between 2000 and 2012 and subsequently as an adviser to the Welsh Government involved with policy, I have had opportunities to engage with many of the civil servants in the UK, Ireland and other parts of the EU in an official capacity. It is my conviction that colleagues would recognise that I was grappling with the same issues as were they and seeking better solutions to the challenges which we all faced collectively. In other words, I feel that I know them and can trust their responses.[20]

Part of the aim of the investigation was to understand the challenges from the perspective of the policy formulator. Thus, when interviewing senior public servants about their policy support for speakers and new speakers it was salutary to recall the sound advice from the UK government.

1. Diagnose the difficulties, the underlying problem.
2. Treat the sources as well as the symptom, do not suppress it.
3. Hold on to your principles, stay sane, stay legal, do not let the antagonists drive you off the intellectual high ground.
4. Self-delusion, both individual and collective, is the enemy of progress.
5. Balance between reason and unreason, between the intellect and emotion.
6. Do not allow the activists to dictate the agenda for there needs to be a conscious buy-in from many sections in civil society, the majority, who after all are both the electorate and tax funders of any strategy.
7. Despite short term setbacks stick to the strategy if it is valid.
8. Statutory duty as civil servants to give the best advice. But the UK Civil Service Act gives one an obligation to share the confidence of the Minister.
9. The duty of a UK Civil Servant is as follows:

As a civil servant, you are appointed on merit on the basis of fair and open competition and are expected to carry out your role with dedication and a commitment to the Civil Service and its core values: integrity, honesty, objectivity and impartiality. In this code:

- 'integrity' is putting the obligations of public service above your own personal interests
- 'honesty' is being truthful and open
- 'objectivity' is basing your advice and decisions on rigorous analysis of the evidence

---

[20] An additional reason, no less true in the UK, Ireland, the Basque Country and Catalonia, is that some of the key informants whom I interviewed were either supervised by me at PhD level or were examined by me for a higher degree and have remained friends and colleagues subsequently. It is my contention that they would have been open with me and sympathised with the aim of getting to grips with how official policy was reacting to the new speaker phenomenon.

- 'impartiality' is acting solely according to the merits of the case and serving equally well governments of different political persuasions

These core values support good government and ensure the achievement of the highest possible standards in all that the Civil Service does. This in turn helps the Civil Service to gain and retain the respect of ministers, Parliament, the public and its customers. (Constitutional Reform and Governance Act; UK Government, 2010)

It may be argued that due to the liminality of the new speaker phenomenon there is no direct one-to-one correspondence between the needs of new speakers and any government intervention and programme. Although such observations are not without force, they are of subsidiary importance for this is to misread the challenge, as any additional emphasis on creating a supportive infrastructure should lead to increased social cohesion and integration. Different strategies are needed when considering new speakers as a category as opposed to the requirements of individuals. Thus, at an aggregate level any intervention in support of the target language, such as in increased statutory educational provision or adult education, ineluctably allows advanced learners and new speakers to cohere better with their cohort peers. Similarly, support for social centres, such as the Canolfannau Cymraeg, creates spaces for interaction, instruction, leisure, the pursuit of hobbies or collective pastimes such as drama, choral singing and creative writing. Resourcing programmes such as the Voluntariat per la Llengua allow civil activists and local authorities to assist individuals to enter the early stages of the trajectory which leads to them possibly becoming new speakers and certainly better-informed residents and participants within the host society. Accordingly, there are many ways in which governments at local and national level can intervene without making a fetish of the new speaker category.

International Networks and Agencies

Political and economic organisations such as the EU have been largely silent on the challenges posed by the emergent varieties of new speakers, at least in a minority language context. Both the EU and the UN have been prominent in the promotion of majoritarian state languages, claiming that the learning of such languages readily helps the sharing of information and the free movement of capital and labour. Socialisation and educational experiences also testify to the salience of the international perspective on multilingualism. The Erasmus Scheme is cited as an excellent way of deepening attachment to a nominal European citizenship with its emphasis on operating through non-mother-tongue communications, enhancing both the learning and use of additional languages. On a more specific scale the promotion of state languages also allows migrants and refuges to fit in and access the full range of public services so as to improve their conditions of living and keep them safe.

The New Speaker project has shared its findings with the EU's Directorate of Education, but much more can and should be done to influence decision makers. A critical, consistent response by international civil servants is that if public money is to be invested in learning languages, then it should be languages of wider communication with a clear geostrategic or commercial potential that should be supported. They have in mind Arabic, Japanese and a version of Chinese and from a commercial, military, resource extraction and management perspective this is a readily understandable position. Once again, however, minority languages are placed at a disadvantage by being located on the wrong end of a so-called modern–traditional continuum of linguistic relevance. Such equivocation, far from being eroded from the public discourse, seems to have gained new momentum of late as calls for learning a variant of Chinese or another Asian language have further marginalised the instrumental relevance of smaller minority languages within a crowded curriculum and the ideological mindset of so many politicians in advanced liberal democracies. The normalcy of powerful state languages, deeply engrained in our subconscious as well as in everyday reality, has such powerful resonance that it becomes an integral part of common sense as identified by Gramsci's concern with subaltern consciousness in hegemonic processes (Gramsci, 2011). In so many cases any attempt at introducing a far greater role for minority languages is deemed deviant rather than an expression of a localised public good, such is the power of majoritarian ideology and practice.

For non-governmental associations such as FUEN (Federal Union of European Nationalities), the NDLP (Network to Promote Linguistic Diversity), ELEN (European Language Equality Network) and the International Association of Language Commissioners, the emphasis has been on boosting access through statutory education, consciousness raising for civil servants and the greater specification of language duties, obligations and rights. Advocates of new speaker recognition suggest that it is through investment in the opportunities afforded by the formal education system for both students and adult learners that competent learners will transition to become new speakers. Once fully trained and confident, then the question is raised, how do such speakers gain access to social networks established and maintained by mother tongue speakers? Historically the onus has been on the individual aspiring to be fully accepted as a 'one of us'. But increasingly it is being recognised that much of the rate and quality of acceptance depends on the predisposition and behaviour of the host community to welcome such speakers into their midst. Consequently, a great deal of attention needs to be focussed on how local majorities react to newcomers and new speakers, and recommendations targeted to the majority population as well as to the specific subgroups need to be put in place.

When considering the policy implications there is a need to identify and influence the range of stakeholders and agencies that would benefit from learning from and adopting some of my recommendations and those which derive from the COST Network. Here I present some generic recommendations but recognise that most recommendations will be specific to individual jurisdictions and contexts. It should also be emphasised that the policies need to be deliverable and framed in such a way that they fit in with the established political culture.

The salience of this observation can be supported by the advice given by a senior civil servant to earlier challenges, namely the implementation of the language policy aspects of the Good Friday Agreement, 1998, and the European Charter for Regional or Minority Languages, 1992. Dr Edward Rooney was the Under-Secretary at the Northern Ireland Department of Culture, Arts and Leisure and he advised the following five considerations when implementing language policy:

Clarity of Purpose

While the spirit of support for language policy development emerges strongly from the relevant paragraphs of the Agreement, virtually every sentence contains at least one ambiguous or qualifying term which could be the subject of debate as to its precise meaning. Consider the following instances:

- Take resolute action to promote the language
- *Facilitate and encourage* the use of the language in public and private life where there is *appropriate demand*
- *Seek to* remove, *where possible*, restrictions which would discourage or work against the maintenance of development of the language
- *Make provision* for liaising with the Irish language community, representing their views to public authorities and investigating complaints.

Shared Vision and Goals

It helps the process of policy development and implementation if there is at least a basic consensus around vision and goals ... my impression is that it is the differences rather than consensus that are most evident in the area of language policy. This can be said both in relation to attitudes and approaches to language development across Government Departments as well as in the interaction between them and within different language groups. The shared vision and goals may be there, but if they are, they struggle to surface.

Evidence of Success and Impact

It is difficult to overstate the importance of producing evidence of the effectiveness of action to promote language policy development. This will require the gathering of robust data, identification of good practice and evidence to support the contribution of language policy to the wider community. And while it is a term that many baulk at, it also involves establishing value for money for this action.

Realism

There is a need for realism about resource availability and about the speed of implementation of language policy. With respect to resource availability, it is worth remembering that the honeymoon period for language funding is likely to be short lived, especially in a situation where there is intense competition for scarce resources. Regarding speed of implementation ... it is important to be realistic about what can be achieved within particular timescales. (Rooney, 2001, pp. 59–60)

Realism and pragmatism are the watchwords of policy implementation and accordingly most of the recommendations I advance here are realisable within existing frameworks and official language or educational strategies. A distinction is made below between different policy domains such as education, official language use, language use in the private sphere and so on; but the underlying rationale is to achieve a holistic/transversal approach that links different policy domains, including ones that some would perhaps not automatically relate to language policy, such as healthcare, well-being, commerce, the economy and IT/AI.

What is in contention is the determination to adopt such recommendations as part of the political calculus which underpins policy choices.

Generic Recommendations

Clearly the vast experience of new speakers of hegemonic languages, such as English and Spanish, is available and should be harnessed to promote best practice and to warn against those strategies which have produced a poor experience, as exemplars for the minority language communities which concern us.

Recommendations which pertain to minority language communities are almost always mediated through one of the majority languages and indeed in most west European contexts the majority of parliamentarians and government members are not fluent in the respective minority language. Accordingly, appealing to the public good rather than to a special interest perspective would seem to be a prudent line of persuasion.

It is imperative that recommendations are framed in such a way that they are both readily understandable and suitable for action by decision makers at several levels within the policy community.

There is a need for studies to describe and evidence best practice principles and processes of new speaker engagement and then seek to apply these findings to various jurisdictions when suitably modified.

- Develop standardised statements in support of the plurality of new speaker needs in language, educational and work domains. Differentiation and variation should not be occluded in promoting a one-size-fits-all new speaker programme of interventions and support.
- Develop and test the efficacy of the ideas and methodologies associated with translanguaging so as to maximise the linguistic repertoire of students who inhabit an increasingly multilingual and highly mobile universe.

- Develop specific profiles of the new speaker subgroups currently amalgamated under the new speaker paradigm: namely, non-native speakers who have learned the target language at school; adult learners who have embraced the target language for whatever reason; and migrants/refugees who have learned the target language as a result of their new circumstances.
- Consider integrating some of the concerns of refugees and asylum seekers with the broader set of international considerations such as the Responsibility to Protect project, for herein lies the origin of their path trajectory and movement from conflict-ridden contexts to 'safe havens' and a set of fresh opportunities and challenges to reconfigure their life experiences in a new context.
- Develop accurate assessments of the various stages in the transition process of becoming new speakers so that should the authorities wish to promote this process they would know at which trigger points to intervene and offer support.

Despite significant exceptions calling for a more plural and diverse language promotion discourse, the dominance of the nationalistic monoglossic discourses renders it difficult to navigate a path for new speakers in many contexts. As a consequence, robust narratives pertaining to social inclusivity need to be constructed and diffused within policy making circles.[21]

In so many jurisdictions the creation of additional safe spaces or breathing spaces and the establishment of designated centres in urban locales has been a constant concern. In such locations people could pursue a range of activities, confident that the *lengua propria* used would be their chosen language and all participants, regardless of their proficiency, would be welcomed, nurtured and respected therein.

A most effective way to harness the potential for new speakers to engage with the host community would be through the development of multi-agency resources centres with a social outreach remit. Thus, consideration needs to be given how such sociolinguistic spaces can be developed, sustained and evaluated to gauge if they are fit for purpose.

Given that most new speakers operate in a triangular sociolinguistic environment, it would be prudent to construct syncretic interpretations of their experiences as they navigate simultaneously both through majoritarian and lesser-used language pathways.

---

[21] Puigdevall et al. argue that 'Attention to new speakers also provides a necessary balance to dominant ideologies based on nativeness, authenticity and monolingualism that often obscures the social conditions that enable or hamper people's participation in specific language communities. Thus, it is paramount in order to change the framing of language policies and to move away from traditional nationalist monoglossic discourses towards a less prescriptive promotion of the language that allows new speakers to gain access more easily to boost their integration into their respective communities' Puigdevall et al. (2018, p. 455).

Innovative methods need to be developed whereby value may be added to the commitment and experience of new speakers as they navigate into the mainstream of the target language community so that their initial enthusiasm is not dented by disappointment and frustration, and they are thereby lost to the vitality of the target group.

Language intervention policies should bear in mind that language reproduction and cultural reproduction are not the same phenomenon. Consequently, the current instrumental emphasis on language skills development should be tempered by a leavening of cultural infusion so as to add greater meaning to the group identification process.

Develop standardised statements in support of new speaker needs in language and educational domains.

Describe and evidence best practice principles and processes of new speaker engagement and apply to various jurisdictions when suitably modified.

Empower some within the migrant community to become more active stakeholders in shaping language policy.

Inform and empower new speaker representatives about their input in influencing the dialogue and potential policy changes regarding the role of new speakers in public policy determination. Hitherto there has been a tendency to speak on behalf of new speakers as if they were objects, constituting a dependent category and in consequence there are too few robust examples of new speakers becoming active voices in the construction of their own narratives. Additional opportunities and pathways need to be constructed so that new speakers may be the authors and representatives of their own destiny as far as that is possible.

However, the practical involvement of migrant representatives can pose a challenge as by continuing to view them as supplicants rather than as actors in the process, their agency is weakened. Another practical difficulty is to gauge how representative any migrant delegate(s) might be of the whole migrant experience of learning a lesser-used language, whose constituents could range from birth origins in Latin America, North Africa or Asia. But even if this were to be achieved there would remain the issue of influencing the predominant approach adopted by civil servants as framers of language and educational policies as to what such policies are meant to achieve and their implicit assumptions regarding both the role and the salience of migrant new speakers in civic integration ideologies and practice.

Specific Recommendations

For each jurisdiction I have chosen to highlight only a few context-specific recommendations. Naturally, many of them will apply elsewhere, but those that are suggested have been derived from the fieldwork and interview data recorded in each location together with some cross-referencing of good practice identified throughout the study.

In the Basque Autonomous Community there is a need to strengthen the role of new speakers as a genuine element of language revitalisation and to reduce the ideological gap between native and new speakers.[22] A key aspect in bridging this gap is to treat standard Basque as a modern spoken variety (and emphasise its differences from the formal written form) – that is, standard Basque is a variety that new speakers claim as 'their own' and the way they speak is a way to show that 'they belong'. One way to do this is to teach 'spoken Batua' in schools as part of the linguistic diversity curriculum.[23]

There is a need to capitalise on the current potential of new speakers for fear of losing the contribution of many to the overall vitality of the language revitalisation efforts.

It is recommended that integrated programmes of increasing the societal use of Basque, such as Euskaraldia, be strengthened and repeated on a regular basis so that new and enduring patterns of language interaction may be secured.

It is also recommended that the nascent safe spaces idea be realised so that a variety of breathing spaces can be established and monitored regularly to see how effective they are in achieving the required outcomes of behavioural change.

In Navarre the following key recommendations should be advanced:

Strengthen the practice of intergenerational language transmission, especially within historically mixed language marriage situations.

Extend the number of predominantly Basque-medium schools and ensure progression from primary, through secondary to university and college level instruction in Basque.

Initiate and then accelerate the partnerships between civil society and government along the lines of the BAC Euskaraldia intervention.

Create one-stop shops and safe spaces for meaningful interaction in and through Basque.

Enhance and develop the school-based initiatives based on sporting activities. Emphasising fun and action in and through Basque would add so much more enjoyment and meaning to language use and reduce somewhat the element of moral duty which is such a part of the conventional approach to maintaining a threatened language.

---

[22] In the BAC this assumes that there is a settled acceptance of what constitutes a native speaker. Many of my informants advised that care has to be taken in determining when a child/student is considered a native speaker.

[23] Rodríguez argues that 'linguists and traditional speakers need to embrace this variation as well' (Rodríguez, pers. comm., 2021).

The incorporation of the new speaker paradigm into the latest language strategy demonstrates awareness but needs to be accompanied by a thorough time-series evaluation programme to monitor the implementation of policy interventions.

In Catalonia the work of academics has suggested a rethink of the manner in which new speakers are conceived within official planning circles. An a priori need is to understand the discourses and ideologies which influence new speaker choices and behaviour if sound policy outcomes are to be achieved.

It is recommended that the excellent Voluntariat per la Llengua programme be extended. Three further modifications may enhance its impact. The first is to use the programme's underlying principles and modus operandi to engage more with small group, not just individual, interaction. By so doing the practical advantages of learning and using Catalan in context may be enriched by a stronger element of shared experience, both with other new speakers and a wider range of native speakers.

The second is that the induction and training of the VxL volunteers should include some concise background material on the analysis of language appropriation, life trajectories and time-series assessment so as to make them more aware of the experiential nature of their involvement adding real meaning to the lives of their partners.

The third element is to share abroad the tactics, methods and success stories so that those in other contexts can adopt a variant of the VxL programme in a more systematic rather than an hoc manner as is currently the case.

It is recommended that the idea of safe, encouraging linguistic spaces be developed by the authorities and civil society so as to provide a reinforcement for the other programmes designed to integrate immigrant new speakers into society.

It is recommended that the Consorci undertake long-term, post-programme investigations at regular intervals to see how the target population navigate their pathway through any additional opportunities to use Catalan.

In Galicia it would be desirable to see the establishment of designated centres in urban locales where people could pursue a range of activities, confident that the *lengua propria* in such spaces would be Galician and that all participants, regardless of their proficiency, would be welcomed, nurtured and respected.

It is recommended that in order to improve the support for Galego, teachers be more fully involved in both the educational and social aspects of the language policy decision-making process.

It is recommended that new programmes be established which are designed to encourage new speakers to integrate themselves better into existing Galician-speaking networks.

In Ireland, where detailed investigations have been undertaken, several recommendations on new speakers are in the public domain. These include:

Undertake research to understand the ideologies and identities of new speakers and their potential role in the future development of Irish.

Develop policy measures to support people who wish to move beyond being learners of Irish to becoming active new speakers.

Inform potential new speakers about how to integrate themselves into existing Irish-speaking networks. This is seen as largely the responsibility of civil society and the many Irish support agencies, which although often funded by central government are not a direct reflection of official language policy.

The creation of designated language centres which could serve as 'safe spaces' for the native and new speaker to mingle and thus develop the competence and confidence of the new speakers in as many communities as it is feasible.

To which we would add further recommendations:

Implement the educational proposals in the 20-Year Irish Language Strategy, such as part-immersion and significant reform of teacher training, to boost the potential to produce larger numbers of new speakers.[24]

Inform new speakers about how to integrate themselves better into existing Irish-speaking networks.

As some new speakers suffer some social anxiety about speaking Irish and have low levels of confidence in their ability to communicate effectively with speakers in the Gaeltacht, it is recommended that policy initiatives should emphasise the fact that becoming an Irish speaker does not necessarily mean adopting a traditional variety and that other competent speakers could act as role models for potential new speakers.

Mount a highly visible campaign to increase awareness of the diverse profile of new speakers so that negative stereotypes and 'traditional' interpretations are countered.

Initiate a high-profile campaign to reflect and represent the diversity of people who are Irish speakers so that conventional stereotypes may be ameliorated somewhat. This should be linked to the renewed promotion of the Gaeltacht and its language plans for revitalisation so that Irish language networks would be doubly strengthened as interaction with the Gaeltacht is a two-way process.

Improve the opportunities provided by Gaeltacht communities to engage in language planning under the Gaeltacht Act 2012 so as to boost the social opportunities to learn, practise or improve Irish.

---

[24] Please see Government of Ireland 2010, pp. 23–36 and visit www.chg.gov.ie/app/uploads/2015/07/20-Year-Strategy-English-version.pdf.

An ambitious vision for the Irish language ECEC workforce and the provision of services for children should be articulated and the workforce should be supported to realise it.

While the 5-year implementation plan for First 5, 2018–2022 includes some actions to support this work, they are not sufficient to significantly develop the capacity of the workforce to support quality improvement or to guarantee the sustainability of provision for children. A far more robust and ambitious set of actions should be agreed and funded for the coming years.[25]

Irish-medium ECEC provision should be foundational to the Policy on Irish-medium Education that is currently being developed by the Department of Education and Skills.[26]

The measures to support Irish-medium ECEC provision in Gaeltacht areas as outlined in the Policy on Gaeltacht Education 2017–22[27] should be further strengthened in the next iteration of the policy.

Care should be taken when implementing the amended Official Languages Act to ensure that the state delivers on its support for Irish-medium and Gaeltacht ECEC services.

In Scotland it is recommended that in order for the potential of new speakers to contribute more effectively to language revitalisation efforts there is a need for the greater specification of the legal rights of speakers, a greater satisfaction of their expectations when faced with the frustration of not receiving the services which are advertised as theirs by statutory obligation and delivered through Language Plans and a deeper sense that Gaelic policy is an integral part of public policy writ large.

It is recommended that remedial policies be advanced to halt the atrophying Gàidhealtachd communities. This would involve a greater fusion of regional development, housing, local government and sustainable development initiatives with sociolinguistic considerations.

Language impact assessment requirements should accompany environmental impact assessments by statute whenever significant land use change or capital intensive projects are being considered in Gaelic-sensitive designated areas.

It is recommended that strengthening existing policy structures and adopting such structures more effectively offers a better approach to strengthening Gaelic than an over-reliance on a set of policies based on ideologies which

---

[25] www.gov.ie/en/publication/26b2ce-first-5-implementation-plan-2019-2021/.
[26] www.education.ie/en/Press-Events/Press-Releases/2019-press-releases/PR19-12-30.html.
[27] www.education.ie/en/Publications/Policy-Reports/Policy-on-Gaeltacht-Education-2017-2022.pdf.

privilege the Gàidhealtachd as the natural or superior locale for Gaelic language reproduction.

Much of the criticism of Gaelic Language Plans relates to their implementation rather than to their design. Accordingly, the potential of the existing policy framework has not been fully exploited and Gaelic language plans should be strengthened considerably before any serious consideration is given to their abandonment and replacement by a system of language standards.

It is recommended that official language planning pay attention to putting more cultural elements into the language learning experience as it is believed that culture and language are becoming increasingly divorced the one from the other. The prevailing experience of new speakers is increasingly instrumental, well able to develop skills but less likely to identify with the full range of Gaelic culture.

A campaign to increase awareness of the diverse profile of new speakers, especially those who reside in metropolitan locales, would be beneficial in countering negative stereotypes and 'traditional' interpretations.

It is recommended that additional opportunities be provided for social interaction through the establishment of trial Gaelic language social centres in promising locations throughout Scotland, not just in historically significant locales.

Increased investment and better training for Gaelic-medium playschool leaders and assistants would secure a more robust platform for launching a successful linguistic trajectory.

An emphasis on formal education has led to a partial neglect of the need to reinforce the home and community domain so as to encourage the parents of children in Gaelic-medium education to develop a greater understanding of support features such as BBC Alba, social media and the like and in time to develop their own competence, thus reinforcing regular use of the language outwith the classroom setting. It would also lead to an inverted language transmission process whereby children become the instigators and resource for adult language learning.

It is recommended that greater resources be channelled in and through Comunn na Gàidhlig so as to strengthen its capacity for generating community initiatives.

Holistic government efforts should be directed at achieving a more widespread level of competence in Gaelic in the expectation that a proportion of such learners will become fluent new speakers. This relates to threshold levels of language acquisition and a greater effort is thus required to provide a platform for language stability once moderate thresholds have been established.

In consequence far more attention should be paid to the provision of advanced Ùlpan courses, to the creation of new multipurpose Gaelic-medium social centres and to the creation of naturalistic contexts for new speakers.

It is recommended that new speaker best practice and sound initiatives be shared with agencies and organisations in Nova Scotia.

Most significantly, profiling for the purpose of finding terms or descriptors that new speakers can identify with would be a step forward.

In Wales it is recommended that periodic time-series reviews be undertaken of the manner in which new speakers will contribute to the strategic aim of producing a target of one million Welsh speakers by 2050. This would include a sophisticated range of evidence-based indicators to adjudge how far down the process the various policy interventions and measures have reached.

Given that it is the statutory education system which is charged with producing additional speakers it is imperative that the 2022 school reorganisation reforms, including the designation of Dual Language Schools, be specified in law within a proposed new Education Act as soon as is feasible.

In similar manner many of the draft new curriculum reforms regarding Welsh both as a subject and as a language of instruction in a wider range of subjects should be implemented as a matter of urgency.

The debate surrounding Welsh as a first or second language and the nomenclature associated with the notion of a range of language skills along a continuum needs to be defined, clarified and incorporated into current practice so as to mitigate against confusion, obfuscation and refusal to implement the thinking behind the new discourse of language skills and performance.

Accordingly, it would also be prudent to secure the rights and stability of educational policies which guarantee the permanence of Welsh as a first language, a *lengua propria*, so that a co-equality of Welsh and English is maintained rather than fudged in compromise reforms.

It is recommended that current educational reforms which seek to erode the long-established division between first and second language learners, together with any official certification of skills acquisition at whatever level, does not overwhelm or exaggerate the capacity of new speakers to perform a comprehensive set of functions. The management of expectations is a critical part of the evaluation of how successful current educational programmes are in producing advanced learners and new speakers.

It is evident that an increased proportion of the active Welsh speakers in the future will be new speakers. In consequence it may be advisable for the Welsh Government, having chosen not to use second language speakers as an operational description, to adopt a variant of new speaker ideology/descriptor so as to identify a subsection of the population, who will also need targeted programmes beyond the educational sector to reinforce their role within a variety of sociolinguistic and economic networks.

The co-equality of Welsh and English is an established feature of national government and public administration. In time this co-equality principle could be extended to other legislative domains such as town and country planning, regional development, anti-poverty, quality of life and housing regulations.

It is recognised that in some cases a more thoroughgoing specification of a suite of language rights may cause some concern, and even a reversal of current practice if not managed sensitively. However, reform of the legislative system so as to identify and regulate citizens' Welsh language rights would go a long way to clarifying just what the current regulatory system is meant to uphold in law, not just by fiat in relation to administrative ordinances.

The incorporation of sociolinguistic considerations into mainstream government acts and measures, such as happens in the Well-Being of Future Generations (Wales) Act 2015, should be emulated in future statutory measures designed to alleviate poverty, improve access to affordable housing and protect the culturally sensitive nature of the Welsh heritage and linguistic landscape.

The Technical Advice note TAN 20, which informs planning and the Welsh language, should be strengthened so as to deal with major capital intensive proposals, such as nuclear power and urban infrastructural developments, and be supported by a far more rigorous and binding linguistic impact assessment framework which matches the impact of the current environmental impact assessment processes.

It is recommended that the Welsh Government constantly update its expectations as to what non-governmental agencies and civil society can contribute to achieving the strategic target of one million speakers, a significant proportion of whom would be new speakers.

Interventionist initiatives derived from nudge theory and behavioural change should be encouraged to a greater extent. This would seek to challenge historically structured language preferences and incorporate sophisticated AI and IT programs so as to influence the design architecture of language choice when customers are engaging with official and private sector administrative tasks.

Similarly, a greater utilisation of strategies for behavioural change derived from social psychology, applied economics and marketing should be deployed to boost the confidence levels of Welsh speakers in managing difficult interaction, especially if these decisions are accompanied by more subtle indirect techniques of persuasion and behaviour changing impulses.

It is a moot point whether or not stricter language protection enforcement measures should be applied or limited to specific geographical zones or sociolinguistic conditions.

Concluding Observations

There is a case for arguing that the dynamic reality of multilingualism is in advance of policy in the field of language planning and that over the medium term much more discussion of new speakers will appear in official government strategies, as has already happened in the Navarre context. Paradoxically, it was the initial goal of most language policies to create more speakers. In that respect, they have undoubtedly succeeded. What has been downplayed (or assumed) is the heterogeneity that they have created (Rodríguez, pers. comm., 2021).

For those who support increasing awareness of the requirements of new speakers it seems that a radical rethink of language policy is in order, leading Joan Pujolar, Maite Puigdevall and Bernadette O' Rourke to suggest placing new speakers more centrally within a more inclusive conceptualisation of speakers writ large and a more realistic interpretation of contemporary multilingualism.

The narratives crafted will doubtless influence the degree to which any recommendations are adopted. Policymakers have a critical role to play as 'narrative entrepreneurs', that is, those who tap in to the 'wisdom in crowds' approach and recast their policies to reflect better the exigencies of the situation.

For some decision makers and policy implementers, positive rhetoric, substantive discourse and symbols are inspiring and can overcome the inherently exasperating nature of statutory regulations, requirements and obligations which dull the focus of their ambitions to showcase their support for new speakers. Most policy is discussed far away from the public gaze. Even elected politicians do not control the policy process in toto, for it is neither a cycle nor a linear stage, but all too often a set of outputs and outcomes which can be fully recognised only after the fact, when the impact of the policy is subject to critical evaluation. The arrival of a new minister or the replacement of a senior civil servant can change markedly the stated aims and timescale of a policy. Furthermore, what counts as the chosen policy trajectory can be interpreted differently by various sections within a government department who may have alternative evidence-based initiatives to pursue in order to influence understanding of the options available. Thus, multiple streams conduce to the actual policy which is put in place.

We recognise that local administrative leadership is often just as important as national/state political leadership, thus recalcitrant managers in fields such as education, healthcare, employment and housing provision can slow down reform while purposive managers can implement recommendations with conviction, resulting in a strategy, an action plan and demonstrable results. For such agencies it is outcomes rather than outputs which matter for they are essentially concerned with behavioural change in addition to the attainment of targets.

Mutual respect is the essential value for any organisation involved in integration and social cohesion: respect for new residents, citizens, for institutions, for public servants and for politicians. Yet ultimately respect is so often culture-bound that it is nigh on impossible to manufacture, so a more pressing virtue would be to seek mutual accommodation as a more realisable goal in the first period of co-creative programmes for social cohesion. Being allowed to become a member of an existing set of networks is no mean feat and we are acutely aware that not all advanced learners and new speakers are treated equally. The prejudices of the majoritarian society do not wither away merely because one is a member of a minority group!

In all interventions, appropriate resource investment and infrastructural development are essential if there is to be a financial guarantee of the political, human right and policy agreements. Pronouncing co-equality of treatment without the capacity to deliver the attendant programmes is a surefire way of prolonging or reigniting grievance-based opposition. It is also the most acid test of the commitment of the authorities to demonstrating in fact what their rhetoric and strategies promise.

Most critically, policy recommendations need to be framed in such a way that public servants can understand and implement them. Thus, following periods of reform, intervention and consensus building, we need to be able to evaluate the real behavioural, political and socio-economic changes brought about by promotional and integration measures, both to reassure interested parties and to contribute to best practice principles.

Regular evaluation of programmes and outcomes is critical, over the medium and the long term, to allow judicious assessments and improvements and also because continued frustration can damage the enthusiasm of new speakers, redefine long-standing issues as current crucial priorities and allow for fractured memories to be reactivated by pressing, instrumental factors.

The narratives reproduced by both official reports and independent scholars, writing some time after the initiation of policies and programmes, may seem at variance with the recollections, perceptions and memories of the participants involved. This is because there is a tendency to rationalise, to sanitise and to impose trajectories upon a context which may undervalue the emotional, conflictual and irrational bases for behaviour. For members of minority language communities, the discourse surrounding new speakers tends to be positive and reflects well on their efforts to be welcoming and supportive. The reality for many new speakers, especially those who derive from an immigrant or refugee background, may be very different. Accordingly, greater attention should be paid to the testimony of the new speakers themselves. Apart from a limited number of ethnographic accounts, it may be that in many jurisdictions we have to wait a generation before a full and frank interpretation of the first generation's experience is recorded and absorbed into the thinking of policymakers and civil society activists. In the BAC, Galicia and Catalonia a second generation is already available from which one may draw lessons and advance evidence-based policies.

Should many of these recommendations not be acted upon, then there may be a steady impoverishment of the new speaker concept, but the reality which the paradigm seeks to capture is destined to grow and mutate so other formulations will need to be created in order to manage and harness the dynamism which this phenomenon represents. For, at root, advocates of the needs of new speakers and of their place in language promotion are change-makers. They would argue that they are on the right side of history and in consequence are destined to have a significant impact on the formulation and implementation of minority language policy.

9   Conclusion: Contemporary Challenges

The task of this chapter is to assess the analytical and normative claims made for the new speaker phenomenon. Accordingly, does the evidence gathered from documentary analysis and interviews undertaken indicate that the policy community is not only cognisant of but also operationalising the implications of the new speaker challenge?

A second consideration is whether the new speaker phenomenon is fulfilling the normative promises which its proponents have claimed for it. Or is it proving to be a slippery and unstable concept, apparently attractive but hard to implement in any programmatic way?

The evidence suggests that the new speaker phenomenon captures a new reality, a different way of approaching multilingualism and a promising way for minority language communities to augment their numbers by welcoming individuals and groups from non-traditional source areas. This is always done within the context of a competing set of claims, attractions and pressures from hegemonic languages. But rather than conceive of this process as a binary zero-sum situation, it is more profitable and realistic to conceive of it as a necessary set of practices to be negotiated and overcome if one is to be a successful new speaker of a minority language. It is recognised that many learners initially approach the educational task of comprehending an additional language through a majoritarian language such as French, English or Spanish. To underplay the utility of these global trends for some spurious ideological gain is folly. Furthermore, it is far more likely that new speakers, whether indigenous or migrant, will earn a living predominantly through the majority language and further enrich their lives through using the minority language when opportunities arise, so the real merit of this reality is the acquisition of further communication skills and to a certain extent the empowerment of the individual to exercise choice and add value to their new experiences.

Two features influence the 'free choice' of new speakers. One is the subordination of the minority language, even if it is not always conscious. The other is the tendency for native speakers to make the choice for new speakers and migrants as they determine that skin colour, appearance and other characteristics may necessitate being addressed in the hegemonic language. Thus, a young girl of Moroccan origin in Barcelona would be automatically addressed in Spanish rather than Catalan.

The full impact of the new speaker phenomenon on language strategy is less clear. For the most part the civil servants interviewed were conscious of the need to plan for new speaker growth, but the more active adoption of innovative strategies tended to happen at the regional and local level and only once they had been demonstrated to be effective did they percolate up to the higher levels of policy formulation.

Three reasons were given by national-level policy formulators for any reticence they may have. The first was to argue that the needs of new speakers were well catered for in existing programmes and designs, and such interventions were not perceived or identified as new speaker components. The second was that the definition of new speaker was too broad and thus did not transfer very well into policy outputs and outcomes whose effects could not be readily measured. The third was the additional costs involved in spreading the policy purview too wide and consequently opening up the responsible departments to unwieldy financial obligations. When pressed, civil servants were unable to calculate the full cost of adopting more integrative measures for new speaker needs. This was especially pertinent in the light of budget freezes which were reported in several jurisdictions, most notably in Catalonia where whole departmental budgets were frozen and in Wales where there had been a block on the appointment of civil servants and by implication a restriction on additional interventions.

For civil society organisers it was recognised that many individuals, particularly migrants, refugees and asylum seekers, had borne substantial emotional and financial costs as they transitioned to become more active members of society. There is an increasing body of work which identifies such costs, mainly from an experiential rather than a financial perspective (Bermingham and Higham, 2018; Higham, 2020).

The challenging part for advocates of new speaker needs is how to access and influence the considerations and formulations of policy by politicians and public servants. I would submit that this requires a three-pronged strategy. The first is the accumulation and diffusion of data, evidence and arguments which are likely to inform the public discourse in fields such as education, language planning, migrant adjustment and social cohesion. The second is the preparation of policy-oriented documents which demonstrate both the need and the demand for the inclusion of aspects of the new speaker phenomenon within government programmes and action. The third is direct interaction with individual public servants and government agencies and periodic involvement in official reviews, workshops and parliamentary committees gathering evidence so as to highlight the relevance of the issues under review.

For those who represent new speaker interests such participation leads to trust and confidence building; it may also empower them to develop skills in advocacy and organising, and lead to rewarding feelings that what they undertake adds value to the policy process. Without that final stage the civic enthusiasm and academic research engendered will remain a distant consideration for decision makers. On occasion, such as when there is an environmental or refugee adjustment crisis, or a failure to deal with a major episode of social unrest by a portion of the population, such as happened under Black Lives Matter, calls are made for greater integration, tolerance, mutual respect and understanding.

Beyond these episodic pressures, innovators are redefining the relationship between citizens and the state. I have argued that several critical issues, which influence the current relationship between the citizen and the state, need careful scrutiny (Williams, 2008; 2013a). The first is the logic of the neoliberal discourse, which avers that the contemporary state is an enabling agency, which by seeking to minimise citizen dependency on the state apparatus releases the full potential of its citizenry. This is done by shifting a range of social responsibilities from the welfare state back to the realm of civil society. Nominally this shift is about the empowerment and strengthening of the capacity of para-public and voluntary agencies to deliver services formally provided by the state. But as Marquand (2004) has demonstrated, all too often this leads to a diminution of the quality and frequency of services and to the disenfranchisement of the poorer, marginal sections of society.

The second issue is the related notion of community empowerment and language planning intervention. I have argued that

instilling a sense of ownership within communities which have been ravaged by successive waves of deindustrialization, social fragmentation and economic collapse is a huge challenge ... the key question is to what extent such a challenge can, or should, be met by organizing around the issue of language decline and revitalization. Apart from the disingenuous nature of government policy, shifting responsibility, without releasing sufficient resources to maintain community development, there is also the question of structural tension and mutual suspicion between the state and civil society and between fractions within society. These arise when questions of ownership of a social process are engaged and challenged, especially when languages in contact are also languages in competition. (Williams, 2000, p. 222)

Empowerment is an attractive notion but all too often such initiatives turn out to be illusory or transitory or both.

The third issue is the discourse of language management/planning within which many of the contradictions of the neoliberal perspectives have become embedded. In order to strengthen the role of advocates and innovators, new approaches to determining language policy and planning need to be entertained.

Conclusion: Contemporary Challenges 339

One promising approach is people power, defined as activity that enables citizens to help one another, create social connections and take collective action to shape change – which is often undervalued by public services. Several significant ways in which people may engage with decision makers so as to influence their policies are contained in a report by Nesta (Old and Bibby, 2020):

Aligning strategic aims. Why is a people-powered approach in this context valuable to your overall strategy? In which ways can people powered methods be used in alignment with your organisational strategy? How will the value generated by these methods contribute to your strategic outcome goals?

Choosing the right type of people power. Which form(s) of people power is best suited for the activity? Who will benefit from your people-powered activities (e.g., individuals, community, institutions, wider society)? How can you design a service that involves people in its development, thus creating specific types of value?

Using existing evidence. How can you increase the confidence level that using people power will generate the outcomes you're aiming for? Is there previous evidence of people-powered approaches in a similar context having the desired effect?

Generating new evidence. How can you measure this type of value at the population level? How can you articulate and evidence a range of different types of value generated by the people-powered approach? (Old and Bibby, 2020, p. 41)

When allied with more established approaches such as deliberative democracy (Held, 2006), people power can offer a genuine means forward. We have been primarily concerned with how decision makers in regional and national positions of authority react to the new speaker challenge, but there are multiple other loci for influence as discussed by Saward (2003):

- In specially constructed micro-forums ... where a small representative sample of people debate and, in some cases, vote on issues (deliberative polls, citizens' juries etc);
- Within political parties.
- In national and other parliaments.
- In supra-national committee networks such as those in the governing structures of the European Union.
- Within private or voluntary associations.
- Within courts; or
- Within a diverse 'public' sphere of 'protected enclaves' or 'subaltern counter publics', in other words, oppressed groups in society. (Saward, 2003, pp. 123–4)

Such opportunities for localised decision-making may go some way to ameliorating the banal tendency to repudiate authority claiming that it is too distant, too inconsistent and too reflective of the tyranny of the majority. It may also assuage the paralysing conscience of inaction which many within minority communities display as they reflect on centuries of historical oppression and discrimination, having absorbed the mindset of the conquered. Accordingly, they often approach the modern state and its agencies more as supplicants than as fully empowered citizens. They have limited expectations and often limited ambitions for their own development as a permanent minority within a multicultural polity. When the established powers address their needs, they often do so within a context which offers false peace for, rather than examining difficult issues together, the powers that be tend to close down options by arguing that this is what the constitution declares, or previous legislation permits, rather than recognising that previous enactments reflect conditions which have now passed and that new conditions demand contemporary solutions to an officially sanctioned impasse. The remnants of such ideologies still haunt contemporary Spain, for despite establishing autonomous governments and legalising the use of Basque or Catalan in many domains, the centralist practices of Madrid, qua the Spanish state and its Supreme Court decisions, stifle the logical maturation of such restorative measures.

Even within minority communities we are aware of the damage which often high-minded, if sincere, people can inflict on the hopes and aspirations of new speakers, especially those from significantly different cultural backgrounds, by insisting that in order to be accepted they have to obey not only the linguistic norms but also the socio-cultural values and practices of the indigenous group. It is as if hybridity is recognised as a half-truth, but to be truly accepted major portions of the indigenous culture have to be absorbed alongside the language skills.

We also need to consider the structural character of the host society and the increasing effects of globalisation of the contours of democracy. Language issues are directly related to questions of citizenship, education, socialisation and participation, especially in the public sphere. We have seen that in progressive systems, such as the BAC and Catalonia, where the incorporation of new speakers is viewed as a means of advancing social cohesion and seen as a public good. Professional realism characterises this approach to managing the increasingly diverse resident population needs. Other jurisdictions are turning towards more rigid language-testing regimes as a way of controlling both the quantity and the skills levels of potential in-migrants. There is also tremendous pressure on institutions within the EU to simplify and harmonise the range of services offered within a particular suite of languages. I have examined how post-sovereign interaction in the Europeanisation of public affairs renders formal language planning increasingly difficult (Williams, 2013b). This is because the post-Enlightenment notions of inclusive citizenship are breaking down in the face of market segmentation and apparent consumer empowerment. This leads to a tension between commonality and fragmentation, between the basic needs of state socialisation, including communicative competence in state-designated languages, and the reality of individual choices and the community-orientation of many interest groups. A major concern is access to public services by marginalised groups. But as Marquand has cautioned, 'the barriers that once protected the public domain from the market and private domains grew up piecemeal, but it does not follow that they can be renewed in the same manner. In the twenty-first century, the inexplicit, half-conscious incrementalism of the late nineteenth century is unlikely to be enough' (Marquand, 2004, p. 148).

To reduce this malaise, one needs to establish a firm defence for the appropriate role of identity groups in society. This involves recognising that individuals may be transformed during their lifetime and that categories of birth and ancestry may not always fully define the subject. Our discussions of the *muda* process are evidence of this because individuals may choose to join identity groups for a variety of reasons, some of which are:

- To publicly express what they consider an important aspect of their identity.
- To conserve their culture, which they identify with the group.
- To gain more material (and other) goods for themselves and their group (whether justified or not).
- To fight in a group for or against discrimination and other injustices.
- To receive mutual support from others who share some part of their social identity; and
- To express and act upon ethical commitments that they share with a group.
  (Gutman, 2003, p. 210)

Systems of governance have to balance both the legitimate demands of the identity groups and the expectations of the majority that they will not necessarily be disadvantaged by the recognition of alternative claims in a liberal democracy. 'Citizens who are concerned about democratic justice need to distinguish the better from the worse while recognizing that the aims of abolishing identity groups or elevating them above basic individual rights would threaten the very cause of democratic justice that they wish to be defending' (Gutman, 2003, p. 211).

One bulwark for the defence of justice is the legal system. We are conscious that while in Canada the courts are a major bastion for the protection and the promotion of official language minorities, in the UK, Ireland and Spain the legal system is a relatively underdeveloped instrument for the articulation of language rights and services (Williams, 2003; 2006; 2013b). Indeed, in some cases court decisions may work to disavow previously recognised privileges, rights, duties and obligations. Yet, however under-developed, language-related legislation remains a *sine qua non* for the establishment of a binding commitment by the state to honour the putative rights of speakers of officially recognised languages. It is also the basis by which the growth of people power and deliberative democracy is enabled.

We recognise that one cannot legislate for a more robust culture or a deep sense of empathy towards the other, but one can through the norms and conventions of legally sanctioned ordinances create the conditions of possibility to encourage the search for roots, for a safe anchorage, for pathways and structures to enable everyday life to be fulfilling. This is the essence of the Catalan approach to the conferment of the *arrelament* certificate, enabling newcomers to settle down and place firm foundations within their adopted society.

We recognise that because technology is driving towards English and other hegemonic languages, the digital divide between majority and minority languages will widen. Yet as we saw in relation to Basque, Catalan and Irish, innovative projects which seek to improve literacy, service provision, the media and GIS geolinguistic mapping are harnessing the potential of IT and the digital economy. This in turn is dependent on a wider trend, namely building digital knowledge in government so as to capture and hone the utility of large data sets into integrated systems. Providing bilingual or multilingual services will be greatly enhanced should such generic developments be seen as an aid to meeting the needs of minority language speakers.

The new speaker paradigm and associated activity have generated a great deal of innovative and rewarding case study material in a variety of European contexts. The COST New Speakers Action Network has also encouraged comparative work drawing in a relatively large number of young scholars to look afresh at issues of language learning, inter-group accommodation, the utility value of both hegemonic and lesser-used languages in social and commercial contexts and the ever-present concern with anxiety and low levels of confidence exhibited by new speakers in the early stages of their transition to fluency. Some of the interpretations have been ambiguous, but there are few simple truths for complex issues.

Above all the new speaker initiative has sought to shift attention from linguistics to speakers in an attempt to move the object of study from language and linguistic science to people in an increasingly multilingual context. By focussing on the social discourse of speaking a range of languages, the hope is that the transitions which characterise a dynamic society will be explicated, recorded and used to improve the lives of residents. It is also claimed that the new speaker perspective enables more realistic discussions of how other salient issues such as social class, inequality and demographic change impact on language trends and discourses, thereby lessening the tendency to make automatic connections between language and place, ancestry, bloodlines and the like.[1]

Future research is likely to go beyond the predominant ethnographic approach and incorporate a range of methodologies from linguistics, the social sciences and social psychology. Three issues deserve attention. The first is the parallel cross-fertilisation of evidence and best practice from new speaker experiences within hegemonic and lesser-used languages together with the additional hurdles faced by those who simultaneously grapple with a new hegemonic and lesser-used language, such as learning English and Irish in tandem, which must surely be a daunting prospect for migrants and refugees alike. The second is to analyse how and to what extent members of the host community either welcome or frustrate the attempts by new speakers to be fully accepted as co-equal members, and with what consequences for the perseverance of new speakers. The third is to distil the essence of this new wave of research into practical policy proposals in a range of domains so that outcome-based programmes and actions can be initiated by political authorities who are charged with improving the opportunities and realisation of those who wish to move beyond being learners into being active new speakers and full participants in their chosen milieu.

If new speakers are viewed as an important element within the sociolinguistic vitality of minority communities, then it is imperative that both consciousness raising and best practice be diffused throughout the appropriate international organisations such as the Network for the Promotion of Language Diversity, the Federal Union of European Nationalities, the International Association of Language Commissioners, let alone state-to-state collaborative partnerships such as the British–Irish Council, the Nordic Council and the major international players such as the European Union, Council of Europe and United Nations.

However, we recognise that influencing such amorphous complex organisations is one of the great challenges of the culture of modernity. Citizen demands for change have to be enframed in particular ways which are dictated by the practice of atomism and instrumentalism. There are points of resistance, of disconnect and of protest, but in the main they threaten to be quietened and subsumed with the passage of time. But each seed, each railing against the inequity of current injustices, can cumulatively change the climate of opinion and feed into the next generation's prevailing paradigms. This is what I envisage will happen with the role of new speakers in buttressing several of the minority language communities we

---

[1] Sentiments expressed by Joan Pujolar, Maite Puigdevall and Xavier Lamuela, interviewed in Girona, 24 September 2021.

have been discussing. By taking the initiative and setting some of the agenda, new speaker advocates will be more purposive not reactive and with an ensemble of ideas, methods and arguments seek to make their presence felt in a more sustainable manner. The new speaker challenge may yet influence language and educational policies in profound ways, but in so doing will also bring forth fresh challenges which have less to do with the practice of language use and communication and much more to do with the dynamic contours of a changing culture and the deeper, always evolving, questions of identity and belonging.

Appendix 1.1

The following core questions were used in the interviews conducted and were supplemented by jurisdiction-specific questions to elicit local details.

Questions on New Speakers and Language Policy
Colin Williams, Cardiff and Cambridge University
williamsch@cardiff.ac.uk

These questions are intended for framers of language policy, together with those who implement or critique aspects of policy. Following standard conventions, language y in this context refers to the non-hegemonic language of the state/political unit.

1. Could I start by asking you to identify the main opportunities and challenges which relate to your official language policy?
2. I am interested in how new speakers are handled within your policy and in your experience of language matters, so are you familiar with the term/concept new speaker? If so, how did you come to know this term (have you read any publications, been involved in the COST NS network in some way, etc.)?
3. What does the label/idea convey to you? (How useful or not do you find the term cf. other ways of describing / labelling different kinds of language speakers?)
4. The conventional usage divides the term into two: a) local people who have learned language y and are comfortable in using it for most aspects of their life; or b) migrants who over time have developed a comptence in language y. Are either or both of these uses familiar in your context?
5. Does the concept of the new speaker figure in your official language and educational policies?
6. If so, please give details and references to this usage. If not, how are different kinds of speakers referred to (native speakers, first language/second language speakers, y learners, etc.)?
7. What sorts of references are made to new speakers in your policy discourse?

8. Are these considerations well established or relatively new?
9. Is there any conscious attempt made to give prominence to new speakers in your policies?
10. What form does this take? Give examples if possible, please.
11. How effective are such initatives in reaching some of the goals of language policy?
12. If not very effective, do you believe that more attention should be given to the needs/interests of new speakers in policy terms?
13. How would this extra input be designed and implemented?
14. In your experience are there different types of profiles within the new speaker category and do different policies apply accordingly to such types?
15. Either in your view or that of other elements in society, do any of these developments pose a threat to the quality or authenticity of language y? How and why?
16. Could I ask you to provide some comments on what difference it makes now that language y is spoken by a larger number of new speakers and spoken by many migrants also – are there any downsides to these developments?
17. Which actors need to be convinced if new speakers are to be a more significant part of language policy?
18. Have your government departments/authorities made any investigations in whole or in part to the promises and challenges which relate to the contribution of new speakers to the vitality of language y?
19. If few of the above are a significant part of your current policies, do you have any plans to develop policies which attend to the needs of new speakers?
20. How do local speakers perceive the new speakers? Can you illustrate, please?
21. Do you have an opinion on how other institutions or organisations handle the issues which are prompted by new speakers and their concerns?
22. Any further comments, documents or insights you might like to share with me now or in the future.
23. Thank you for this interview and for signing the permission request form.

Appendix 1.2 Interview/Permission Request Form

Language Policy and New Speakers

Thank you for agreeing to allow me to use material from interviews and data collection in relation to this project. Only I will see the original data and it will be stored on my own computer and nowhere else as this is an individual project being undertaken by myself in my own name and not as part of a wider survey.

It is anticipated that a Final Report/volume will be forthcoming in 2022.

Interview Consent

1. Professor Williams has described the research project to me and I understand what the research is about and why it is being undertaken.
2. I agree to the recording of the interview on the basis that it is being conducted on a confidential basis for the purpose of supporting an independent academic research project.
3. I agree to the use of anonymous quotes from the interview in the research project report and in related publications. However, if I consent, I may be named in the acknowledgement and end note sections of the proposed manuscript(s) which will be produced from this project.
4. I understand that for the purposes of cost and time, the interviewer does not intend to transcribe my interview in full and is not obliged to present a transcribed copy to me. I can, however, request an audio copy of my interview. The interview will be stored on the researcher's own laptop.

   Name of interviewee ....
   Date of Permission ... Interview conducted on
   With thanks to you in advance for your ready co-operation.
   Colin H Williams ....
williamsch@cardiff.ac.uk

Bibliography

Acierno. S. and Baquero Cruz, J. (2005). The Order of the Spanish Constitutional Court on the proposal to convert the Basque Country into a freely associated community: Keeping hands off constitutional politics. *International Journal of Constitutional Law*, 3, 94, 687–95.

Aldekoa, J. (2012). Ekina baragarria da! Ba dozak hamabost urte normalkuntza proiektuak martxan direla. *Bat soziolinguistika aldizkaria*, 82, 149–73.

Alexander, N. (2011). Review of J. Orman, *Language Policy and Nation-Building in Post-Apartheid South Africa*. *Journal of Multilingual and Multicultural Development*, 32, 6, 593–5.

Allardt, E. (1981). Ethnic mobilization and minority resources. *Zeitschrift Für Soziologie*, 10, 4, Oktober, S. 427–37.

Allardt, E. (1992). Qu'est-ce qu'une minorité linguistique? in Giordan, H., ed., *Les minorités en Europe: Droits linguistiques et Droits de l'Homme*. Paris: Kime, pp. 45–54.

Álvarez-Cáccamo, C. (2011). Contra o capitalismo linguístico: Perante a crise da língua na Galiza. *Agália, Revista de Estudos na Cultura*, 104, 2, 11–28.

Andrews, S. (2019). *The Additional Supports Required by Pupils with Special Educational Needs in Irish Medium Schools*. [Dublin]: An Chomhairle um Oideachas Gaeltachta agus Gaelscolaíochta. www.cogg.ie/wp-content/uploads/Additional-supports-2.pdf.

Ardrey, R. (1966). *The Territorial Imperative*. New York: Atheneum.

Armstrong, T. C. (2013). 'Why won't you speak to me in Gaelic?': Authenticity, integration and the Heritage Language Learning Project. *Journal of Language, Identity, and Education*, 12, 340–56.

Augustyniak, A. and Higham, G. (2019). Contesting sub-state integration policies: Migrant new speakers as stakeholders in language regimes. *Language Policy*, 18, 4, 513–53.

Azurmendi, M-J. and Martinez de Luna, I., eds. (2007). *The Case of Basque: Past, Present and Future*. Andoain: Soziolonguistica Klusterra.

Azurmendi, M-J., Bourhis, R. Y., Ros, M. and García, I. (1998). Identidad etnolingüística y construcción de la ciudadanía en las Comunidades Autónomas bilingües de España. *Revista de Psicología Social*, 13, 3, 559–89.

Baldauf, R. B. Jr (1993). Unplanned language policy and language planning. *Annual Review of Applied Linguistics*, 14, 82–9.

Baldauf, R. B. Jr (2006). Rearticulating the case for micro language planning in a language ecology context. *Current Issues in Language Planning*, 7, 2, 147–70.

Barakos, E. (2012). Language policy and planning in urban professional settings: Bilingualism in Cardiff businesses. *Current Issues in Language Planning*, 13, 3, 167–86.

Barakos, E. (2016). Language policy and governmentality in businesses in Wales: A continuum of empowerment and regulation. *Multilingua, Journal of Cross-Cultural and Interlanguage Communication*, 35, 4, 361–91.

Barakos, E. (2018). The nexus of language policy, ideology and practice in businesses in Wales, in Nekvapil, J. and Sherman, T., eds., *English in Business and Commerce: Interactions and Policies*. Berlin: Mouton de Gruyter, pp. 73–95.

Barakos, E. and Unger, J. (2016). *Discursive Approaches to Language Policy*. Basingstoke: Palgrave Macmillan.

Barrett, M., Kinsella, W. and Prendeville, P. (2020). Special educational needs in bilingual primary schools in the Republic of Ireland. *Irish Educational Studies*, 39, 3, 273–95.

Basque Autonomous Community (1982). *Law for the Normalization of Basque. Ley 10/ 1982*, BOPV 16-12-1982. https://bit.ly/3Amgnzm.

Basque Government (2009). *Euskara 21: Bases for Language Policy at the Outset of the 21st Century: Towards a Renewed Covenant*. Vitoria-Gasteiz: Basque Government.

Basque Government (2013). *Talking Pupils: The Arrue Project 2011*. Vitoria-Gasteiz: Department of Education, Language Policy and Culture of the Basque Government and the Sociolinguistics Cluster.

Bastardas-Boada, A. (1989). Language extension in linguistic normalization processes: General patterns and the Catalan experience. *Catalan Review*, 111, 1, 59–84.

Bastardas-Boada, A. (1994). Language management: An eco-dynamic perspective from/on the case of Spain. Paper presented at the XIII World Congress of Sociology, Bielefeld, Germany.

Bastardas-Boada, A. Boix-Fuster, E. and Torrens-Guerrini, R. M., eds. (2019). *Family Multilingualism in Medium-Sized Language Communities*. Berlin: Peter Lang.

Baztarrika, P. (2019). The contemporary situation in the Basque Country. Panel talk presented at the Gwlad, Gwlad 'Promoting Minority Languages: Evaluating the Work of Regional Governments' forum, Senedd Cymru, Cardiff, 28 September.

BBC News (2021). GCSEs: New subjects launched as part of overhaul in Wales, 14 October. www.bbc.co.uk/news/uk-wales-58898196.

Bechhofer, F. and McCrone, D. (2014). What makes a Gael? Identity, language and ancestry in the Scottish Gàidhealtachd. *Identities: Global Studies in Culture and Power*, 21, 113–33.

Bellin, W. (1994). Caring professions and Welsh speakers: A perspective from Language and Social Psychology, in Williams, R. H., Williams, H. and Davies, E., eds., *Social Work and the Welsh Language*. Cardiff: University of Wales Press, pp. 75–121.

Bellin, W. and Thomas, R. (1996). Caregivers, community and transmission of the Welsh language, in Stephens, J., ed., *Teod, Teanga, Tafod: Language Acquisition in Preschool Children in Brittany, Ireland, Scotland and Wales*. Cardiff: University of Wales Institute, pp. 60–4.

Bennett Institute for Public Policy (2020). A new public policy institute for the age of disruption, https://bit.ly/3duPj8e.

Bergara, A. (1996). *Hezkuntza- eta Hizkuntza-eskubideak indarreko lege-araubidean*. Vitoria-Gasteiz: Arartekoa.

Bermingham, N. (2018). Double new speakers? Language ideologies of immigrant students in Galicia, in Smith-Christmas, C., Ó Murchadha, N., Hornsby, M. and Moriarty, M., eds., *New Speakers of Minority Languages: Linguistic Ideologies and Practices*. London: Palgrave Macmillan, pp. 111–30.

Bermingham, N. and Higham, G. (2018). Immigrants as new speakers in Galicia and Wales: Issues of integration, belonging and legitimacy. *Journal of Multilingual and Multicultural Development*, 39, 5, 394–406.

Bhabha, H. K. (1994). *The Location of Culture*. London: Routledge.

Biagini, E. and Mulhall, D., eds. (2016). *The Shaping of Modern Ireland: A Centenary Assessment*. Sallins: Irish Academic Press.

Birnie, I. (2018). Gaelic language use in public domains, in MacLeod, M. and Smith-Christmas, C. (eds.), *Gaelic in Contemporary Scotland*. Edinburgh: Edinburgh University Press, pp. 128–40.

Blommaert, J., Kelly-Holmes, H., Lane, P., Leppänen, S., Moriarty, M., Pietikäinen, S. and Piirainen-Marsh, A. (2009). Media, multilingualism, and language policing: An introduction. *Language Policy*, 8, 3, 203–7.

Boix-Fuster, E. and Paradis, A. (2019). New speakers' ideologies and trajectories in bilingual families in Catalonia, in Bastardas-Boada, A. Boix-Fuster, E. and Torrens-Guerrini, R. M., eds., *Family Multilingualism in Medium-Sized Language Communities*. Berlin: Peter Lang, pp. 193–222.

Bòrd na Gàidhlig (2006). *First National Plan for Gaelic 2007–12*. Inverness: Bòrd na Gàidhlig.

Bòrd na Gàidhlig (2011). *The National Gaelic Language Plan 2013–17*. Inverness: Bòrd na Gàidhlig.

Bòrd na Gàidhlig (2017). *Statutory Guidance of Gaelic Education*. Inverness: Bòrd na Gàidhlig. https://bit.ly/3duPj8e.

Bòrd na Gàidhlig (2018). *National Gaelic Language Plan, 2018–2023*. Inverness: Bòrd na Gàidhlig.

Bòrd na Gàidhlig (2021). *Annual Report on Implementation of Gaelic Language Plans*. Inverness: Bòrd na Gàidhlig.

Bourdieu, P. (1991). *Language and Symbolic Power*. Cambridge: Polity Press.

Bretxa, V., Comajoan-Colomé, L. and Xavier Vila, F. (2017). *Les veus del professorat: L'ensenyament i la gestió de les llengües a secundària*. Barcelona: Horsori.

Brooks, S. (2019). @Seimonbrooks. Twitter Page.

Bufon, M. Malloy, T. H. and Williams, C. H., eds. (2021). *Societies and Spaces in Contact: Between Convergence and Divergence*. Berlin: Peter Lang.

Caglitutuncigil, T. (2018). Between myth and reality: Language classrooms in Spanish and Catalan social integration programs. *Journal of Multilingual and Multicultural Development*, 39, 5, 431–44.

Cairney, P. (2012). *Understanding Public Policy*. Basingstoke: Palgrave.

Cairney, P. (2016). *The Politics of Evidence-Based Policy Making*. Basingstoke: Palgrave Macmillan.

Campbell, C. (2000). Menter Cwm Gwendraeth: A case study in community language planning, in Williams, C. H. (ed.), *Language Revitalization*. Cardiff: University of Wales Press, pp. 247–91.

Canagarajah, S. (2006). Ethnographic methods in language policy, in Ricento, T. (ed.), *An Introduction to Language Policy: Theory and Method*. Oxford: Wiley Blackwell, pp. 153–69.

Candel Tortajada, F. (1964). *Els altres Catalans*. Barcelona: Llibres a l'Abast/Grup 62.

Cardiff University (2014). *A Review of the Work of Mentrau Iaith, Language Action Plans and the Aman Tawe Language Promotion Scheme*. Cardiff: Cardiff University. http://gov.wales/topics/welshlanguage/publications/review-of-mentrau-iaith/?lang=en.

Cardinal, L. and Williams, C. H. (2020). Bridging the gap between the politics of recognition and the politics of language service delivery in Ontario and Wales, *Treatises and Documents*, 84, 5–31.

Cassels-Johnson, D. (2013). *Language Policy*. Basingstoke: Palgrave Macmillan.

Cenoz, J. (2008) Achievements and challenges in bilingual and multilingual education in the Basque Country. *AILA Review*, 22, 13–30.

Cenoz, J. and Gorter, D. (2014). Focus on multilingualism as an approach in educational contexts, in Blackledge, A. and Creese, A. , eds., *Heteroglossia As Practice and Pedagogy*. Dordrecht: Springer, pp. 239–54.

Cenoz, J. and Gorter, D. (2017). Minority languages and sustainable translanguaging: Threat or opportunity? *Journal of Multilingual and Multicultural Development*, 38, 901–12.

Cenoz, J. and Gorter, D. (2020). Teaching English through pedagogical translanguaging. *World Englishes*, 39, 300–11. https://onlinelibrary.wiley.com/doi/epdf/10.1111/weng.12462.

Central Statistics Office (2017). *Census 2016 Report. Profile Ten Education, Skills and the Irish Language*. Dublin: Central Statistics Office.

Chalmers, D. (2008). The promotion of arts and culture as a tool of economic regeneration: An opportunity or a threat to minority language development. The Case of Gaelic in Scotland, in Pertot, S., Priestly, T. M. S. and Williams, C. H., eds., *Rights, Promotion and Integration Issues for Minority Languages in Europe*. Basingstoke: Palgrave Macmillan, pp. 141–164.

Chalmers, D. (2021). *Gaelic As an Economic Asset: A Thirty-Year Journey*. Glasgow: Glasgow Caledonian University.

Chalmers, D. and Danson, M. (2008). *The Economic Impact of Gaelic Arts and Culture within Glasgow*, Glasgow: Glasgow City Council.

Chalmers, D. and Danson, M. (2011). The role of arts and culture in economic regeneration: Gaelic in Glasgow, in Lorentzen, A. and van Heur, B., eds., *Cultural Political Economy of Small Cities*. Abingdon: Routledge.

Chernyshevsky, N. G. (1863/1989). *What Is to Be Done?* Ithaca, NY: Cornell University Press.

Ciriza del Puy., M. (2019). Towards a parental *muda* for new Basque speakers: Assessing emotional factors and language ideologies. *Journal of Sociolinguistics*, 23, 4, 367–85.

Clément, R. and Foucher, P. (2014). *Fifty Years of Official Bilingualism*. Ottawa: Invenire.

COGG (2010). *Special Education Needs in Irish Medium Schools: All-Island Research on the Support and Training Needs of the Sector*. Dublin: An Chomhairle um Oideachas Gaeltachta agus Gaelscolaíochta, POBAL.

Coimisinéir Teanga (2017). *Annual Report*. An Spidéal: An Coimisinéir Teanga.
Collette, E. and Le Coz, C. (2018). *After the Storm: Learning from the EU Response to the Migration Crisis*. Brussels: Migration Policy Institute Europe. www.migrationpolicy.org/research/after-storm-learning-eu-response-migration-crisis.
Conde Moure, D. (2019). Plurilingual education in diglossic contexts: Primary school teachers' voices on the Galician plurilingual education policy. Master's Thesis, University of Oslo.
Conversi, D. (1997). *The Basque, the Catalans and Spain*. Reno: The University of Nevada Press.
Cooper, R. L. (1989). *Language Planning and Social Change*. Cambridge: Cambridge University Press.
Costa, J., De Korne, H. and Lane, P. (2017). Standardising minority languages: Reinventing peripheral languages in the 21st century? In Lane, P, Costa, J. and De Korne, H. eds., *Standardizing Minority Languages: Competing Ideologies of Authority and Authenticity in the Global Periphery*. Abingdon: Routledge, pp. 1–23
COST New Speakers (2017). Recent language initiatives, COST New Speakers Network. www.nspk.org.uk/images/TCD_Stakeholders_Final_Report.pdf.
COST New Speakers (2018). *From 'New Speaker' to 'Speaker' in a Multilingual Europe: Outcomes and Reflections from COST Action IS1306 on New Speakers*. COST New Speakers Network. Edinburgh: Herriot Watt University.
Council of Europe (2001). *Common European Framework of Reference for Languages*. Strasbourg: Council of Europe.
Council of Europe (2020). *Language Tests*. Strasbourg: Council of Europe. www.coe.int/en/web/lang-migrants/language-tests.
Crameri, K. (2000). *Language, the Novelist and National Identity in Post-Franco Catalonia*. Oxford: University of Oxford/Legenda.
Cronin, M. (2005). *Irish in the New Century*. Dublin: Cois Life.
Cronin, M. (2019). *Irish and Ecology*. Dublin: Foilseacháin Ábhair Spioradálta.
Crowley, T. (2005). *Wars of Words: The Politics of Language in Ireland 1537–2004*. Oxford: Oxford University Press.
Crystal, D. (2003). *English As a Global Language*. 2nd ed. Cambridge: Cambridge University Press.
Crystal, D. (2019). *The Cambridge Encyclopaedia of the English Language*. 3rd ed. Cambridge: Cambridge University Press.
Cummins, J. (2014) To what extent are Canadian second language policies evidence-based? Reflections on the intersections of research and policy. *Frontiers in Psychology*, 7, 1–358.
Cunliffe D. (2019a). Minority languages and the social media, in Hogan-Brun, G. and O'Rourke, B., eds., *The Palgrave Handbook of Minority Languages and Communities*. Basingstoke: Palgrave Macmillan, pp. 451–80.
Cunliffe, D. (2019b). The market for Welsh language mobile applications: A developers' perspective. *Telematics and Informatics*, 36, March, 12–16.
Cuvelier. P. et al. (2010). *Multilingualism from Below*. Pretoria: Van Schaik Publishers.
Cymdeithas yr Iaith (2020). *Mwy na Miliwn*. Aberystwyth: Cymdeithas yr Iaith Gymraeg.
Dalmazzone, S. (1999). Economics of language: A network externalities approach, in Breton, A. A., ed., *Exploring the Economics of Language*. Ottawa: Canadian

Heritage, pp. 33–44. https://documents.pub/document/breton-albert-ed-exploring-the-economics-of-language.html.
Darquennes, J. (2011). Minorities, language politics and language planning in Europe, in Kortmann, B. and van der Auwera, J. (eds.), *The Languages and Linguistics of Europe*. New York: de Gruyter, pp. 547–60.
Darquennes, J. (2013). Language use at school in the BAC: The Arrue project as a source of inspiration for minority language acquisition planning in Europe, in Basque Government, in *Talking Pupils: The Arrue Project 2011*. Vitoria-Gasteiz: Department of Education, Basque Government.
Davies, A. (2007). *An Introduction to Applied Linguistics: From Practice to Theory*. Edinburgh: Edinburgh University Press.
Davies, P. and Pila, J. eds. (2015). *The Jurisprudence of Lord Hoffman*. London: Bloomsbury.
Davies, W. D. (1982). *The Territorial Dimension of Judaism*. Oakland: University of California Press.
Dávila, P. (2003). Introducción, in Dávila, P., ed., *Enseñanza y educación en el País Vasco contemporáneo*. Donostia: Erein, pp. 9–12.
Dayan-Fernandez, A. and O'Rourke, B. (2020). Galician-Portuguese and the politics of language in contemporary Galicia, in Strani, K., ed., *Multilingualism and Politics*. London: Palgrave Macmillan, pp. 231–60.
Del Percio, A., and Van Hoof, S. (2017). Enterprising migrants: Language, education and the politics of activation, in Flubacher, M and Del Percio, A., eds., *Language, Education, and Neoliberalism*. Bristol: Multilingual Matters, pp. 140–62.
Dewaele, J. M. (2017). Why the dichotomy 'L1 versus LX user' is better than 'native versus non-native speaker.' *Applied Linguistics*. DOI: https://doi.org/10.1093/applin/amw055.
Dion, S. (2003). Why Immersion has a Prominent Place in the Action Plan for Official Languages. Notes for an address by the Honourable Stéphane Dion, President of the Privy Council and Minister of Intergovernmental Affairs. New Brunswick: Canadian Parents for French.
Direcció General de Política Lingüística and Institut d'Estadística de Catalunya (2019). *Els usos lingüístics de la població de Catalunya: Resultats de l'Enquesta d'usos lingüístics de la població 2018*. Barcelona: Generalitat de Catalunya.
Djillali, A. et al. (2017). The management of critical illness-related corticosteroid insufficiency (CIRCI) in critically ill patients. *Critical Care Medicine and Intensive Care Medicine*. December, 45, 12, pp. 2078–88.
Duchêne, A. and Heller, M. eds. (2007). *Discourses of Endangerment Ideology and Interest in the Defence of Languages*. London: Continuum.
Duchêne, A. and Heller, M., eds. (2012). *Language in Late Capitalism: Pride and Profit*. Abingdon: Routledge.
Dunbar, R. (2003). The ratification by the United Kingdom of the European Charter for Regional or Minority Languages. Mercator linguistic rights and legislation, working paper no. 10. Ciemen. https://eric.ed.gov/?id=ED479896.
Dunbar, R. (2006). Is there a duty to legislate for linguistic minorities? *Journal of Law and Society*, 33, 1, 181–98.
Dunbar, R. (2018). Organisational language planning: Gaelic Language Plans in the public sector, in MacLeod, M. and Smith-Christmas, C. eds., *Gaelic in Contemporary Scotland*. Edinburgh: Edinburgh University Press, pp. 156–72.

Dunbar, R. (2019). An Coimisinéir Teanga and Comisiynydd y Gymraeg: The challenges of a changing legislative environment, in Amon, H. and James, E. (eds.), *Constitutional Pioneers: Language Commissioners and the Protection of Official, Minority and Indigenous Languages*. Montreal: Éditions Yves Blais, pp. 101–24.

Dunmore, S. (2014). Bilingual life after school? Language use, ideologies and attitudes among Gaelic-medium educated adults. Unpublished PhD thesis, Edinburgh University.

Dunmore, S. (2016). *Gàidheil, Goill agus Coimhearsnachd na Gàidhlig: Ideòlasan cànain inbhich a fhuair foghlam tro mheadhan na Gàidhlig* [Gaels, Lowlanders and the Gaelic Community: Language ideologies among adults who received Gaelic-medium education], Rannsachadh na Gàidhlig 8. Edinburgh: Dunedin Academic Press.

Dunmore, S. (2017). Immersion education outcomes and the Gaelic community: Identities and language ideologies among Gaelic-medium educated adults in Scotland. *Journal of Multilingual and Multicultural Development*, 38, 726–41. DOI: http://dx.doi.org/10.1080/01434632.2016.1249875.

Dunmore, S. (2018a). When school is over and done with: Linguistic practices and socio-demographic profiles of Gaelic-medium educated adults, in MacLeod, M. and Smith-Christmas, C. (eds.), *Gaelic in Contemporary Scotland: The Revitalisation of an Endangered Language*. Edinburgh: Edinburgh University Press, pp. 62–78.

Dunmore, S. (2018b). New Gaelic Speakers, new Gaels? Language ideologies and ethnolinguistic continuity among Gaelic-medium educated adults, in Smith-Christmas et al. (eds.), *New Speakers of Minority Languages: Linguistic Practice and Ideology*. Basingstoke: Palgrave, pp. 23–44.

Dunmore, S. (2018c). Bilingual life after school? Opportunity, choice and ideology among former Gaelic-medium students. *Transactions of the Gaelic Society of Inverness*, LXVIII, 287–316.

Dunmore, S. (2019). *Language Revitalisation in Gaelic Scotland: Linguistic Practice and Ideology*. Edinburgh: Edinburgh University Press.

Dunmore, S. (2020). Language policy and prospects: Metalinguistic discourses on social disruption and language maintenance in a transatlantic, minority community. *Language and Communication*, 76, 69–78.

Dunmore S. (2021a). Emic and essentialist perspectives on Gaelic heritage: New speakers, language policy and cultural identity in Nova Scotia and Scotland. *Language in Society*, 50, 259–81.

Dunmore, S. (2021b). Review: 'Minority languages, national languages, and official language policies', by Lane-Mercier, G., Merkle, D. and Koustas, J. (eds). *British Journal of Canadian Studies*, 27, 2, 130–1.

Dunmore S. (2021c) Transatlantic context for Gaelic language revitalisation. *Studia Celtica Posnaniensia*, 5, 1, 1–20.

Dyfodol i'r Iaith (2020a). *Troi Dyhead yn Realiti*. Caerfyrddin: Dyfodol i'r Iaith.

Dyfodol i'r Iaith (2020b). *Y Gymraeg yn y gweithle a gweithleoedd Cymraeg*. Caerfyrddin: Dyfodol i'r Iaith.

Eaves, S., Jones, G., Jones, K., Jones, M. P and Williams, C. H. (2017). *Cyrraedd y miliwn/Reaching the million*. National Assembly for Wales, A. M. Policy Paper prepared by Iaith. Castell Newydd Emlyn: Iaith.

El Hachmi, N. (2010). *Jo també sóc catalana*, Barcelona: labutxaca.
Estonian Language Foundation (2011). *Development Plan of the Estonian Language, 2011–2017*. Tallinn: Estonian Language Foundation.
Estyn (2017). *The Annual Report of Her Majesty's Chief Inspector of Education and Training in Wales 2016–2017*. Cardiff: Estyn.
European Commission (2018). *Public Administration Characteristics and Performance in EU28 Spain*. Brussels: European Commission.
Euskaltzaindia (1977). *El libro blanco del euskara*. Bilbao: Euskaltzaindia, Real Academia de la Lengua Vasca.
Euskararen Aholku Batzordea (2009). *Basis for a Language Policy for the Early 21st Century: Towards a Renewed Agreement*. Vitoria-Gasteiz: Euskararen Aholku Batzordea [Basque Language Advisory Board].
Eusko Jaurlaritza (1990a). *Euskal Irakaskuntza 1979–80/1989–90*. Vitoria-Gasteiz: Eusko Jaurlaritzaren Argitalpen Zerbitzu Nagusia.
Eusko Jaurlaritza (1990b). *Euskal Eskola Publikoaren Lehen Kongresua 1–2*. Vitoria-Gasteiz: Eusko Jaurlaritzaren Argitalpen Zerbitzu Nagusia.
Eusko Jaurlaritza (1999). *Plan General de Promoción del Uso del Euskera*. Vitoria-Gasteiz: Eusko Jaurlaritzaren Argitalpen Zerbitzu Nagusia.
Eusko Jaurlaritza (2003). *Plan General de Promoción del Uso del Euskera: 2003–2006*. Vitoria-Gasteiz: Gobierno Vasco.
Eusko Jaurlaritza (2005). *Euskararen B2 maila derrigorrezko irakaskuntzaren amaieran (DBH-4)*. Vitoria-Gasteiz: Eusko Jaurlaritzaren Argitalpen Zerbitzu Nagusia.
Eusko Jaurlaritza (2007). *Criterios para la normalización del uso del euskera en las administraciones públicas*. Vitoria-Gasteiz: Gobierno Vasco.
Eusko Jaurlaritza (2008). *Fourth Sociolinguistic Survey 2006*. Vitoria-Gasteiz: Eusko Jaurlaritzaren Argitalpen Zerbitzu Nagusia.
Eusko Jaurlaritza (2010). *Ebaluazio diagnostikoa 2010. Txosten exekutiboa*. www.isei-ivei.net/.
Evans, Rh. (2008). *Gwynfor Evans: Portrait of a Patriot*. Talybont: Y Lolfa.
Evas, J., Morris, J. and Whitmarsh, L. (2017). *Ymchwil i'r amodau sydd yn dylanwadu ar arferion teuluoedd mewn perthynas â throsglwyddo a defnyddio'r Gymraeg/ Research into conditions influencing Welsh language transmission and use in families*. Cardiff: Welsh Government.
Extra, G., and Spotti, M. (2009). Testing regimes for newcomers to the Netherlands, in Extra, G., Spotti, M. and Van Avermaet, P., eds., *Language Testing, Migration and Citizenship: Cross-National Perspectives on Integration Regimes*. London: Continuum, pp. 125–47.
FCFA (La Fédération des Commautés Francophones et Acadiennes du Canada] (2011). Notes pour une allocution de la présidente de la FCFA, Marie- France Kenny. Au Comité permanent des langues officielles de la Chambre des communes dans le cadre de l'étude sur l'évaluation de la Feuille de route : amélioration des programmes et de la prestation des services Ottawa, 24 novembre. Ottawa: Parlement du Canada.
Fernández Barrera, A. (2015). Bilingual commodification in La Mancha: From language policies to classroom practices. *Procedia – Social and Behavioural Sciences*, 212, 80–4.
Fiontar (2009). *20-Year Strategy for the Irish Language*. Dublin: Fiontar.

Fishman, J. A., ed. (1976). *Advances in the Sociology of Language. Volume 1. Basic Concepts, Theories and Problems: Alternative Approaches*. The Hague: Mouton

Fishman, J. A. (1991). *Reversing Language Shift: Theoretical and Empirical Foundations of Assistance to Threatened Languages*. Clevedon: Multilingual Matters.

Gaelscoileanna (2007). *Strategic Plan*. Dublin: Gaelscoileanna.

Gaelscoileanna Teo (2017). *Strategic Plan 2008–2011*. Dublin: Gaelscoileanna Teo.

Gagnon, A.-G. and Sanjaume-Calvet, M. (2017). Clash of legitimacies in Catalonia and Spain: The imperial logic of modern constitutionalism versus multinational federalism, in Kraus, P. A. and Vergès Gifra, J., eds., *The Catalan Process: Sovereignty, Self-Determination and Democracy in the 21st Century*. Barcelona: Institut d'Éstudies de l'Autogovern, pp. 275–99.

Gardbaum, S. (2013). *The New Commonwealth Model of Constitutionalism*. Cambridge: Cambridge University Press.

Gardner, N. (1989). Language Planning in the Autonomous Community of the Basque Country, 1975–1989. Nant Gwrtheyrn, Wales, 10–12, November.

Garmendia, J. M. (1980). *Historia de E.T.A*. San Sebastian: Haranburu, 2 vols.

Garrido, M. R. (2018). Voluntary work, transnational mobility and language learning in a social movement. *Language and Intercultural Communication*, 18, 4, 451–63.

Garrido Sardà, M. R. (2019). Language socialisation and *muda*: The case of two transnational migrants in Emmaus Barcelona. *International Journal of the Sociology of Language*, 257, 137–63.

Gathercole, V. C. M. et al. (2007). *Language Transmission in Bilingual Families in Wales*. Cardiff: Welsh Language Board.

Gazzola, M. (2014). *The Evaluation of Language Regimes*. Amsterdam: John Benjamins.

Generalitat de Catalunya (1995). *Pla general de normalització lingüística*. Barcelona: Generalitat de Catalunya.

Generalitat de Catalunya (2011). *Language Policy Report 2010*. Barcelona: Catalan Ministry of Culture.

Generalitat de Catalunya (2017a). *Language Policy Report 2016*. Barcelona: Catalan Ministry of Culture.

Generalitat de Catalunya (2017b). *The Language Policy of Catalonia*. Barcelona: Departament de Cultura/Politica Lingüística.

Generalitat de Catalunya (2018). *Language Policy Report 2017*. Barcelona: Catalan Ministry of Culture.

Generalitat de Catalunya (2019a). *Language Policy Report 2018*. Barcelona: Catalan Ministry of Culture.

Generalitat de Catalunya (2019b). *EULP 2018 Enquesta d'usos lingüístics de la población*. Barcelona: Institut d'Estadística de Catalunya.

Generalitat de Catalunya (2020). *Language Policy Report 2019*. Barcelona: Catalan Ministry of Culture.

General Register for Scotland (2005). *General Register Office for Scotland Annual Report*, 151st Edition. Edinburgh: General Register Office for Scotland.

Glór na nGael (2016). *Towards a Strategic Plan for Irish As a Family Language*. Dublin: Glór na nGael.

Goirigolzarri Garaizar, J. (2017a). Zergaitik dira garrantzitsuak hiztun berrientzat euskal hedabideak XXI. mendean? [Why are Basque media important for new speakers in the 21st century?]. 'Euskal hedabideak itun bila' [Basque media in search of alliances], Euskaltzaindia, Bilbao, 22 February.
Goirigolzarri Garaizar, J. (2017b). *Hizkuntzak eta alderdi politikoak: diskurtso linguistikoak Euskal Autonomia Erkidegoan*. Vitoria-Gasteiz: Eusko Jaurlaritza.
Goirigolzarri Garaizar, J. and Landabidea Urresti, X. (2020). Conflicting discourses on language rights in the Basque Autonomous Community. *Language Policy*, 19, 4, 502–25.
Goirigolzarri, J. Amorrortu, E. and Ortega, A. (2019). Activación lingüística de jóvenes neohablantes de Euskera en la Universidad, in Ramallo, F. Amorrortu, E. and Puigdevall, M., eds., *Neohablantes de lenguas minorizadas en el Estado español*. Madrid: Iberoamericana, pp. 23–46.
Gonzàlez, I., Pujolar, J., Font, A. and Martínez, R. (2009). *Entre la identitat i el pragmatisme lingüístic. Usos i percepcions lingüístiques dels joves catalans a principis de segle [Between linguistic identity and pragmatism. Linguistic usages and perceptions of Catalan youth at the beginning of the century]*. Generalitat de Catalunya, Direcció General de Política Lingüística.
González González, M., ed. (2011). *Mapa Sociolingüístico de Galicia 2004*. Vol. III: *Actitudes Lingüísticas en Galicia*. A Coruña: Real Academia Galega.
Gorter, D., and Cenoz, J. (2017). Language education policy and multilingual assessment. *Language and Education*, 31, 231–48.
Gorter, D., Zenotz, V. and Cenoz, J., eds. (2014). *Minority Languages and Multilingual Education: Bridging the Local and the Global*. New York: Springer Dordrecht Heidelberg.
Government of the Basque Country (1979). *Statute of Autonomy of the Basque Country of 1979*. Vitoria-Gasteiz: Government of the Basque Country. www.basquecountry.eus/t 32448/en/contenidos/informacion/estatuto_guernica/en_455/adjuntos/estatu_i.pdf.
Government of Ireland (2002). *Commission for the Gaeltacht 2002*. Dublin: Government of Ireland.
Government of Ireland (2010). *20-Year Strategy for the Irish Language*. Dublin: Department of Tourism, Arts, Culture, Gaeltacht, Sport and Media.
Government of Ireland (2016). *Policy on Gaeltacht Education, 2017–22*. Dublin: Department of Education.
Government of Ireland (2021). Historic day as the Official Languages Bill is ready for enactment by the President of Ireland. Press Release, 15 December. Dublin: Government of Ireland.
Government of Navarre (2020). *Strategic Plan for Basque (2020–2027)*. Pamplona: Euskarabidea.
Government of Nova Scotia (2019). *Gaelic Nova Scotia: A Resource Guide*. Halifax: Government of Nova Scotia.
Gramsci, A. (2011). *Prison Notebooks*. New York: Columbia University Press.
Grin, F. (1994). Combining immigrant and autochthonous language rights: A territorial approach to multilingualism, in Skutnabb-Kangas, T. and Phillipson, R., eds., *Linguistic Human Rights*. Berlin: De Gruyter, pp. 31–48.
Grin, F. (2003). *Language Policy Evaluation and the European Charter for Regional or Minority Languages*. New York: Palgrave.

Gruffudd, H. (2014). Cymunedau Hyfyw. LSW Eisteddfod lecture, Llanelli.
Gruffudd, H. and Morris, S. (2012). *Canolfannau Cymraeg and Social Networks of Adult Learners of Welsh: Efforts to Reverse Language Shift in Comparatively Non-Welsh-Speaking Communities*. Swansea: Academi Hywel Teifi.
Gutman, A. (2003). *Identity in Democracy*. Princeton, NJ: Princeton University Press.
Halimi, G. (1971). *Le procès de Burgos*. Paris: Gallimard.
Halonen, M., Ihalainen, P. and Saarinen, T., eds. (2015). *Language Policies in Finland and Sweden: Interdisciplinary and Multi-sited Comparisons*. Bristol: Multilingual Matters.
Harcourt Publishing (2016). *Harcourt Dictionary of the English Language*. Boston, MA: Houghton Mifflin Harcourt.
Harris, J. (2006). *Irish in Primary Schools: Long Term National Trends in Achievement*. Dublin: Department of Education and Science.
Harris, J. (2008). Irish in the Education System, in Nic Pháidín, C. and Ó Cearnaigh, S., eds., *A New View of the Irish Language*. Dublin: Cois Life, pp. 178–90.
Harris, J., Forde, P., Archer, P., Nic Fhearails, S. and O'Gorman, M. (2006). *Irish in Primary Schools*. Dublin: Department of Education and Science.
Harrison, G. et al. (1981). *Bilingual Mothers in Wales and the Language of Their Children*. Cardiff: University of Wales Press.
Held, D. (2006). *Models of Democracy*. Cambridge: Polity.
Hernandez. F. X. (2007). *The History of Catalonia*. Barelcona: Rafael Dalmau, Editori.
Hickey, T. N. and Stenson, M. (2016). One step forward and two steps back in teaching an endangered language? Revisiting L2 reading in Irish. *Language, Culture and Curriculum*, 29, 3, 302–18.
Higham, G. (2020). *Creu Dinasyddiaeth i Gymru: Mewnfudo Rhyngwladol a'r Gymraeg*. Caerdydd: Gwasg Prifysgol Cymru.
Highlands and Islands Enterprise (2014). *Economic and Social Value of Gaelic as an Asset*. Inverness: HIE.
Highlands and Islands Enterprise (2020). *Low Carbon Scotland*. Inverness: HIE. www.hie.co.uk/support/browse-all-support-services/low-carbon-scotland/.
Hornsby M. (2016a). Lemko linguistic identity: Contested pluralities. *Language Documentation and Conservation in Europe*, 9, 13–25.
Hornsby M. (2016b). Varieties of variation in a very small place revisited: Some considerations from Wilamowice, in Olko, J., Wicherkiewicz, T. and Borges, R., eds., *Integral Strategies for Language Revitalization*. Warsaw: University of Warsaw, pp. 81–90.
Hornsby M. (2016c). Du shtetl à la ville: à la recherche d'un yiddish (presque) perdu. *Droit et Cultures: Les langues autochtones dans la cité*, 72, 2, 227–40.
Hornsby, M. and Rosiak, K. (2016). Motivational factors in the acquisition of Welsh in Poland. *Studia Celtica Posnaniensia*, 1, 57–72.
Hornberger, N., and Johnson, D. (2007). Slicing the onion ethnographically: Layers and spaces in multilingual language education policy and practice. *TESOL Quarterly*, 41, 3, 509–32.
Houses of the Oireachtas (2021). *Official Languages (Amendment) Bill, 2019 (Bill 104 of 2019)*. Dublin: Houses of the Oireachtas.
Hult, F. (2010). Analysis of language policy discourses across the scales of space and time. *International Journal of the Sociology of Language*, 202, 7–24.

Idescat (2019). *Report on the Use of the Catalan Language in Commerce*. Barcelona: Idescat. www.idescat.cat/?lang=en.

Irujo Ametzaga, X. and Urrutia Libarona, I. (2009). *A Legal History of the Basque Language (1789–2009)*. Donostia: Eusko Ikaskuntza.

James Hutton Institute (2018). *Demographic change in the sparsely populated areas of Scotland (1991–2046)*. Aberdeen: The James Hutton Institute.

Jauregi, P. and Anduaga, U. (2019). Euskaraldia: An analysis of the results. Territory of the Basque Language 2018–2019. https://soziolinguistika.eus/en/argitalpenak/euskaraldia-i-an-analysis-of-the-results-territory-of-the-basque-language-2018-2019/.

Joan i Mari, B. (2009). Language policies and strategies promoted by the Language Policy Secretariat of the Catalan Government. Presentation to the NPLD Language Planning Seminar Dublin, December.

Johnson, D. C. (2009). Ethnography of language policy. *Language Policy*, 8, 2, 139–59.

Johnson, D. C. (2013). Language Policy? in *Language Policy*. London: Palgrave Macmillan, pp. 3–25.

Johnson, D. and Ricento, T. (2013). Conceptual and theoretical perspectives in language planning and policy: Situating the ethnography of language policy. *International Journal of the Sociology of Language*, 219, 7–21.

Jones, K., Williams, C. H., Dunmore, S., McLeod, W. and. Dunbar, R. (2016). *Assessment of the National Gaelic Language Plan 2012–17*. Inverness: Bòrd na Gàidhlig.

Jones, M. C. (2002). *Jersey Norman French: A Linguistic Study of an Obsolescent Dialect*. Oxford: Wiley-Blackwell.

Jones, M. C. (2018). Does language loss follow a principled structural path? Evidence from Jersey Norman French. *Journal of French Language Studies*, 28, 3, 399–429.

Jones, Rh. (2021). The geography of minority language use, in Lewis, H. and McLeod, W., eds., *Language Revitalisation and Social Transformation*. London: Palgrave Macmillan, pp. 37–65.

Kantar (2020). *Céard é an Scéal? Public Opinions on the Irish Language 2020 Annual Analysis 6*. Dublin: Conradh na Gaeilge and Foras na Gaeilge.

Kaplan, R. B. and Baldauf, R. B. (1997). *Language Planning from Practice to Theory*. Clevedon: Multilingual Matters.

Keating, M. (2018). The Basque Statute of Autonomy. Centre on Constitutional Change. Edinburgh University, 19 October. www.centreonconstitutionalchange.ac.uk/opinions/basque-statute-autonomy.

Keeley, G. (2008). Spanish speakers fight to save their language as regions have their say. *Guardian*, 4 May. www.theguardian.com/world/2008/may/04/spain.

Kloss, H. (1967) 'Abstand Languages' and 'Ausbau Languages'. *Anthropological Linguistics*, 9, 7, 29–41.

Kourdi, J. (2009). *Business Strategy*. London: The Economist.

Kraft, K. (2019). Language policies and linguistic competence: New speakers in the Norwegian construction industry. *Language Policy*, 18, 4, 573–91.

Kramsch, C. and Whiteside, A. (2008). Language ecology in multilingual settings: Towards a theory of symbolic competence. *Applied Linguistics*, 29, 4, 645–71.

Kurvers, J. J. H. and Spotti, M. (2015). The shifting landscape of Dutch integration policy, in Simpson, J. and Whiteside, A., eds., *Adult Learning, Education and Immigration: Challenging Agendas in Policy and Practice*. Abingdon: Routledge, pp. 173–86.

Lane, P. and Räisänen, A.-K. (2019). Heritage language policies: The case of Kven in Norway, in Seals, C. A. and Shaw, S., eds., *Heritage Language Policies around the World*. London: Routledge.

Lane, P., Costa, J. and De Korne, H., eds. (2017). *Standardizing Minority Languages: Competing Ideologies of Authority and Authenticity in the Global Periphery*. Abingdon: Routledge.

Lanttom, H. (2018). New Basques and code-switching: Purist tendencies, social pressures, in Smith-Christmas, C., Ó Murchadha, N., Hornsby, M. and Moriarty, M., eds., *New Speakers of Minority Languages: Linguistic Ideologies and Practices*. London: Palgrave Macmillan, pp. 165–84.

Lee, T. S. and McLaughlin, D. (2001). Reversing Navajo Language Shift, revisited, in Fishman, J. A., ed., *Can Threatened Languages Be Saved?* Clevedon: Multilingual Matters, pp. 1–22.

Lenin, V.I. (1901). *What Is to Be Done?* Translated by Fineberg, J. and Hanna, G., Marxists Internet Archive. www.marxists.org/archive/lenin/works/1901/witbd/.

Leonet, O., Cenoz, J. and Gorter, D. (2017). Challenging minority language isolation: Translanguaging in a trilingual school in the Basque Country. *Journal of Language, Identity and Education*, 16, 216–27.

Lewis, H. and McLeod, W., eds. (2021). *Language Revitalisation and Social Transformation*. London: Palgrave Macmillan.

Lewis, G., Jones, B. and Baker, C. (2012). Translanguaging: Developing its conceptualisation and contextualisation. *Educational Research and Evaluation*, 18, 7, 655–70.

Lezertua, M. (2016). Language and Identity in the Basque Country, Presentation to the International Association of Language Commissioners, 8 March 2016, Galway.

Linz, J. (1986). *Conflicto en Euskadi*. Madrid: Espalso Calpa.

Lourido, G. and Evans, B. (2019). The effects of language dominance switch in bilinguals: Galician new speakers' speech production and perception. *Bilingualism: Language and Cognition*, 22, 3, 637–54.

Mac an Tàilleir, I., Rothach, G. and Armstrong, T. C. (2010). *Baraíl agus Comas Cànain: Aithisg rannsachaidh airson Bòrd na Gàidhlig*. Sleat: Sabhal Mòr Ostaig.

MacCaluim, A. (2007). *Reversing Language Shift: The Social Identity and Role of Scottish Gaelic Learners*. Belfast: Cló Ollscoil na Banríona.

McCarty, T., ed. (2011). *Ethnography and Language Policy*. New York: Routledge.

McCarty, T. (2015). Ethnography in language planning and policy research, in Hul, F. and Johnson, D., eds., *Research Methods in Language Policy and Planning: A Practical Guide*. Oxford: Wiley Blackwell, pp. 81–93.

Mac Cormaic, A. (2016). *Modes of Politicization in the Irish Civil Service*. Basingstoke: Palgrave Macmillan.

Mac Donnacha, S., Ní Chualáin, F., Ní Shéaghdha, A. and Ní Mhainín, T. (2005). *Staid Reatha na Scoileanna Gaeltachta 2004 (Baseline Study of Gaeltacht Schools)*. Baile Átha Cliath: An Chomhairle um Oideachas Gaeltachta agus Gaelscolaíochta. www.cogg.ie/wp-content/uploads/Achoimre-Staid-Reatha-na-Scoileanna-Gaeltachta-2004.pdf.

McEwan-Fujita, E. (2006). 'Gaelic doomed as speakers die out'? The public discourse of Gaelic language death in Scotland, in McLeod W., ed., *Revitalising Gaelic in Scotland*. Edinburgh: Dunedin Academic Press, pp. 279–93.

McEwan-Fujita, E. (2010). Ideology, affect and socialization in language shift and revitalization: The experiences of adults learning Gaelic in the Western Isles of Scotland. *Language in Society*, 39, 27–64.

Mac Giolla Chríost, D. (2013). *The Irish Language in Ireland from Goídel to Globalisation*. Abingdon: Routledge.

Mac Giolla Chríost, D. (2016). *The Welsh Language Commissioner: Roles, Methods and Relationships*. Cardiff: University of Wales Press.

Mac Giolla Chríost, D., Carlin, P. and Williams, C. H. (2016). Translating y Cofnod: Translation policy and the official status of the Welsh language in Wales. *Translation Studies*, 9, 2, 212–27.

Mac Gréil, M. and Rhatigan, F. (2009). *The Irish Language and the Irish People*. Maynooth: Department of Sociology, NUI Maynooth.

MacLeod, M. (2018). Learning Gaelic in adulthood: Second language learning in minority language contexts, in MacLeod, M. and Smith-Christmas, C., eds., *Gaelic in Contemporary Scotland*. Edinburgh: Edinburgh University Press, pp. 94–113.

MacLeod, M. and Smith-Christmas, C., eds. (2018). *Gaelic in Contemporary Scotland*. Edinburgh: Edinburgh University Press.

MacLeod, M., Jones, K. and Milligan-Dombrowski, L. (2015). *Delivery of Gaelic to Adults through Ulpan*. Inverness: Bòrd na Gàidhlig.

McLeod, W. (2016). Gaelic in contemporary Scotland: Contradictions, challenges and strategies, in Day, D., Rewi, P. and Higgins, R., eds., *The Journeys of Besieged Languages*. Newcastle: Cambridge Scholars, pp. 249–72.

McLeod, W. (2018). New speakers of Gaelic: A historical and policy perspective, in MacLeod, M. and Smith-Christmas, C., eds., *Gaelic in Contemporary Scotland*. Edinburgh: Edinburgh University Press, pp. 79–93.

McLeod, W. (2020a). Securing Gaelic in the Western Isles and beyond. *The National*, 31, January. www.thenational.scot/news/18200196.securing-gaelic-western-isles-beyond/.

McLeod, W. (2020b). *Gaelic in Scotland*. Edinburgh: Edinburgh University Press.

McLeod, W. and O'Rourke, B. (2015). 'New speakers' of Gaelic: Perceptions of linguistic authenticity and appropriateness. *Applied Linguistics Review*, 6, 2, 151–72.

McLeod, W. and O'Rourke, B. (2017). *New Speakers of Gaelic from Outside the UK*. Edinburgh: Soillse.

McLeod, W., MacCaluim, A. and Pollock, I. (2010). *Adult Gaelic Learning in Scotland: Opportunities, Motivations and Challenges: A Research Report for Bòrd na Gàidhlig*. Edinburgh: Celtic and Scottish Studies, Edinburgh University.

McLeod, W., O'Rourke, B. and Dunmore, S. (2014). *'New Speakers' of Gaelic in Edinburgh and Glasgow*. Project Report. Edinburgh: Soillse.

McLeod, W., Dunbar, R., Jones, K. and Walsh, J., eds. (2022a). *Language, Policy and Territory: A Festschrift for Colin H. Williams*. London: Palgrave Macmillan.

McLeod, W., Dunbar, R., Macleod, M., O'Rourke, B., Dunmore, S., Armstrong, T. C. and Munro, G. (2022b). Against exclusionary Gaelic language policy: A response to Ó Giollagáin and Caimbeul. *Scottish Affairs*, 31, 1, 84–103.

Marquand, D. (2004). *Decline of the Public*. Cambridge: Polity Press.

Martín Rojo, L. and Rodríguez, L. R. (2016). Muda lingüística y movilidad social. Trayectorias de jóvenes migrantes hacia la universidad. *Discurso y Sociedad*, 10, 1, 100–33.

Martínez-Álvarez, P. (2019). Dis/ability labels and emergent bilingual children: Current research and new possibilities to grow as bilingual and biliterate learners. *Race, Ethnicity and Education*, 22, 2, 174–93.

Martinez de Luna, I., Erize, X. and Zalbide, M. (2016). *Euskararen bilakaera Soziolinguistikoa (1981–2011)*. Andoain: Soziolinguistika Klusterra.

Massias, J.-P., Urrutia, I. and Irujo, X., eds. (2015). *Droits Culturels et Démocratisation/ Cultural Rights and Democratisation*, Clermont-Ferrand: Institut Universitaire Varenne: Collection 'Kultura'.

Mertz, E. (1989). Sociolinguistic creativity: Cape Breton Gaelic's linguistic 'tip', in Dorian, N. C., ed., *Investigating Obsolescence: Studies in Language Contraction and Death*. Cambridge: Cambridge University Press, pp. 103–16.

Moal, S. Ó Murchadha, N. P. and Walsh, J. (2018). New speakers and language in the media: Design in Breton and Irish broadcast media, in Smith-Christmas, C., Ó Murchadha, N., Hornsby, M. and Moriarty, M., eds., *New Speakers of Minority Languages. Linguistic Ideologies and Practices*. London: Palgrave Macmillan, pp. 189–210.

Monteagudo, H. and Muniain, F. R. (2020). Language and migration: The sociolinguistic and glottopolitical dynamics of the Galician community in Buenos Aires from the nineteenth century to the present day. *Journal of Multilingual and Multicultural Development*, 41, 1, 97–107.

Moralejo Silva, R. and Ramallo, F. (2019). Las condiciones del (pre).beofalantismo y el processo de conversion lingüistica en Galicia, in Ramallo, F., Amorrortu, E. and Puigdevall, M., eds., *Neohablantes de lenguas minorizadas en el Estado español*. Madrid: Iberoamericana, pp. 165–84.

Morgan, K. O. (1995). *Modern Wales*. Cardiff: The University of Wales Press.

Morgan, P. (2000). The Gael is dead; Long live the Gaelic: The changing relationship between native and learner Gaelic users, in McCoy. G. with Scott. M., eds., *Aithne na nGael/Gaelic Identities*. Belfast: Institute of Irish Studies, Queen's University Belfast/Ultach Trust, pp. 126–32.

Morgan, Rh. (2013). School reorganisation: A lesson in how not to do it. The case of Canton, Cardiff West, in Thomas, H. S. and Williams, C. H., eds., *Parents, Personalities and Powers: Welsh-Medium Schools in South-East Wales*. Cardiff: University of Wales Press, pp. 242–52.

Moriarty, M. (2015). *Globalizing Language Policy and Planning: An Irish Language Perspective*. Basingstoke: Palgrave Macmillan.

Mosaic (2017). Our work with refugees. *Mosaic*, www.mosaicbc.org/about/.

Mudiad Meithrin (2020). Winter Newsletter. Aberystwyth: Mudiad Meithrin.

Mullor, J. S. and Torres Pérez, A. (2019). The Constitution of Spain: The challenges for the constitutional order under European and global governance, in Albi, A. and Bardutzky, S., eds., *National Constitutions in European and Global Governance: Democracy, Rights, the Rule of Law*. The Hague: T. M. C. Asser, pp. 543–90.

Muniain. F. R. (2018). Lengua, Identidad y Política lingüística familiar en a comunidad gallega de Buenos Aires, in Patzelt, C. et al., *Migrationsbedingte Sprachkontakte in der Romania des 21. JH*. Berlin: Peter Lang, pp. 295–322.

Nance, C., McLeod, W. O'Rourke, B. and Dunmore, S. (2016). Identity, accent aim, and motivation in second language users: New Scottish Gaelic speakers' use of phonetic

variation. *Journal of Sociolinguistics*, 20, 164–91. https://onlinelibrary.wiley.com/doi/abs/10.1111/josl.12173.
National Assembly for Wales (2019). *Supporting and Promoting the Welsh Language*. Cardiff: Culture, Welsh Language and Communications Committee.
National Records of Scotland (2015). *Scotland's Census 2011: Gaelic report (part 1)*. Edinburgh: National Records of Scotland.
Newcombe, L. (2002). Second Language Acquisition and Adult Learners of Welsh. Unpublished PhD, University of Wales.
Newcombe, L. (2016). *Speak Welsh Outside the Class: You Can Do It!* Talybont: Y Lolfa
Newman, J. H. (1852/2015). *The Idea of a University*. London: Eterna Press.
Nic Aindriú, S. (2021). The reasons why parents choose to transfer students with special educational needs from Irish immersion education. *Language and Education*, 36, 1, 59–73. DOI: https://doi.org/10.1080/09500782.2021.1918707.
Nic Aindriú, S., Ó Duibhir, P. and Travers, J. (2020). The prevalence and types of special educational needs in Irish immersion primary schools in the Republic of Ireland. *European Journal of Special Needs Education*, 35, 5, 603–19.
Nic Aindriú, S., Ó Duibhir, P. and Travers, J. (2021). A survey of assessment and additional teaching support in Irish immersion education. *Languages*, 6, 62, 1–20.
Nic Shuibhne, N. (1999). Ascertaining a linguistic minority: Ireland as a case study. In Fottrell, D. and Bowring, B. (eds.), *Minority and Group Rights in the New Millennium*. Leiden: Martinus Nijhoff, pp. 87–110.
Nic Shuibhne, N. (2000). Rethinking Irish language policy: A legal perspective. *Contemporary Issues in Irish Law and Society*, 3, 36–53.
Nic Shuibhne, N. (2002). *EC Law and Minority Language Policy: Culture, Citizenship and Fundamental Rights*. The Hague: Kluwer.
Ní Ghréacháin, B. (2016). Education outside the Gaeltacht. Presentation at the IALC conference on Language Rights, Galway.
Ní Ghréacháin, B. (2021). *Irish-Medium Early Years Services outside Gaeltacht Areas*. Dublin: Gaeloideachas.
Ní Mhóráin, M. (2016). Education in the Gaeltacht. Presentation at the IALC conference on Language Rights, Galway.
NPLD (Network to Promote Linguistic Diversity) (2019). *Activating the Social Use of Minority Languages*. Brussels: NPLD Focus Report No. 5.
Oakes, L. and Peled, Y. (2018). *Normative Language Policy: Ethics, Politics, Principles*. Cambridge: Cambridge University Press.
Observatorio da Cultura Galega. (2011). *A(s). lingua(s). a debate. Inquerito sobre opinións, actitudes e expectativas da sociedade galega*. Santiago de Compostela: Consello da Cultura Galega.
Ó Conaill, S. (2009). The Irish Language and the Irish Legal System: 1922 to present. Unpublished PhD thesis, Cardiff University.
O'Connell, E., Walsh, J. and Denvir, G., eds. (2008). *TG4@10: Deich mBliana de TG4/ Ten Years of TG4*. Indreabhán: Cló Iar-Chonnachta.
Ó Duibhir. P. (2018). *Immersion Education: Lessons from a Minority Language Context*. Bristol: Multilingual Matters.
Ó Flatharta, P., Sandberg, S. and Williams, C. H. (2014). *From Act to Action: Implementing Language Legislation in Finland, Ireland and Wales*. Dublin: Dublin City University.

Ó Flatharta, P., Nic Pháidín, C., Lo Bianco, J., Grin, F. and Williams, C. H. (2009). *A Twenty-Year Irish Language Strategy*. Dublin: Fiontar, Dublin City University.

Ó Giollagáin, C. (2014). From revivalist to undertaker? New developments in official policies and attitudes towards 'first language'. *Language Policy and Language Planning*, 38, 2, 101–27.

Ó Giollagáin, C. (2021). Gaelic crisis requires more than cultural promotion. *The Herald*, 22 May.

Ó Giollagáin, C. (2022) Reality of the Gaelic crisis needs addressed. *West Highland Free Press*, 21 January.

Ó Giollagáin, C. and Caimbeul, I. (2021). Moving beyond asocial minority-language policy. *Scottish Affairs*, 30, 2, 178–211.

Ó Giollagáin, C. and Mac Donnacha, S. (2008). The Gaeltacht today, in Nic Pháidín, C. and Ó Cearnaigh, S., eds., *A New View of the Irish Language*. Dublin: Cois Life Teoranta, pp. 108–20.

Ó Giollagáin, C. et al. (2007). *Comprehensive Linguistic Study of the Use of Irish in the Gaeltacht: Principal Findings and Recommendations*. Dublin: The Department of Community, Rural and Gaeltacht Affairs.

Ó Giollagáin, C. et al. (2020). *The Gaelic Crisis in the Vernacular Community: A Comprehensive Sociolinguistic Survey of Scottish Gaelic*. Aberdeen: Aberdeen University Press.

Ó hIfearnáin, T. and Walsh, J. eds. (2018). *An Meon Folaithe: Idé-eolaíochtaí agus iompar lucht labhartha na Gaeilge*. Dublin: Cois Life.

Ó Huallacháin, C. (1994). *The Irish and Irish*. Dublin: Assisi Press.

Old, R. and Bibby, W. (2020). *The Value of People Power*. London: Nesta. https://media.nesta.org.uk/documents/The_value_of_people_power_-_FINAL.pdf.

Ó Murchú, H. (2014). *More Facts About Irish*. Dublin: European Bureau for Lesser Used Languages.

Ó Riagáin, P. (1997). *Language Policy and Social Reproduction: Ireland, 1893–1993*. Oxford: Clarendon Press.

O Riagáin, P. (2008). Irish-language policy 1922–2007: Balancing maintenance and revival, in Nic Pháidín, C. and Ó Cearnaigh, S., eds., *A New View of the Irish Language*. Dublin: Cois Life, pp. 55–65.

O'Rourke, B. (2011). *Galician and Irish in European Contexts. Attitudes towards Weak and Strong Minority Languages*. Basingstoke: Palgrave Macmillan.

O'Rourke, B. (2014). The Galician language in the twenty-first century, in Miguélez-Carballeira, H., ed., *A Companion to Galician Culture*. Woodbridge: Tamesis, pp. 73–92.

O'Rourke, B. (2018a). Carving out breathing spaces for Galician: New speakers' investment in monolingual practices, in Jaspers, J. and Madsen, L. M., eds., *Critical Perspectives on Linguistic Fixity and Fluidity: Languagised Lives*. Abingdon: Routledge.

O'Rourke, B. (2018b). Just use it! Linguistic conversion and identities of resistance amongst Galician new speakers. *Journal of Multilingual and Multicultural Development*, 39, 5, 407–18.

O'Rourke, B. and Nandi, A. (2019). New speaker parents as grassroots policy makers in contemporary Galicia: Ideologies, management and practices. *Language Policy*, 18, 4, 493–511.

O'Rourke, B. and Pujolar, J. (2013). From native speakers to 'New speakers': Problematizing nativeness in language revitalization contexts. *Histoire Épistémologie Langage*, 35, 2, 47–67.
O'Rourke, B. and Pujolar, J. (2015). New speakers and processes of new speakerness across time and space. *Applied Linguistics Review*, 6, 2, 145–50.
O'Rourke, B. and Ramallo, F. (2011). The native-non-native dichotomy in minority language contexts: Comparisons between Irish and Galician. *Language Problems and Language Planning*, 35, 2, 139–59.
O'Rourke, B. and Ramallo, F. (2013). Competing ideologies of linguistic authority amongst new speakers in contemporary Galicia. *Language in Society*. 42, 3, 287–305.
O'Rourke, B. and Ramallo, F. (2015). *Neofalantes* as an active minority: Understanding language practices and motivations for change amongst new speakers of Galician. *International Journal for the Sociology of Language*, 231, 147–65.
O'Rourke, B. and Ramallo, F. (2018). Identities and new speakers of minority languages: A focus on Galician, in Smith-Christmas, C., Ó Murchadha, N., Hornsby, M. and Moriarty, M., eds., *New Speakers of Minority Languages: Linguistic Ideologies and Practices*. London: Palgrave Macmillan, pp. 91–106.
O'Rourke, B. and Walsh, J. (2018). Introduction: Comparing 'new speakers' across language contexts: Mobility and motivations. *Journal of Multilingual and Multicultural Development*, 39, 5, 377–81.
O'Rourke, B. and Walsh, J. (2020). *New Speakers of Irish in the Global Context: New Revival?* New York: Routledge.
O'Rourke, B., Pujolar, J. and Ramallo, F. (2015). New speakers of minority languages: The challenging opportunity. *International Journal for the Sociology of Language*, 231, 1–20.
O'Rourke, B., Pujolar, J. and Walsh, J. (2017). Language education and new speakers of minority languages, in McCarty, T., ed., *Encyclopaedia of Language and Education*. 3rd ed. New York: Springer, pp. 1–12.
O'Rourke, B., Soler, J. and Darquennes, J. (2018). New speakers and language policy, in Tollefson, J. and Pérez-Milans, M., eds., *The Oxford Handbook of Language Policy*. Oxford: Oxford University Press, pp. 610–32.
Oroz, N. and Sotés Ruiz, P. (2008). Bilingual education in Navarre: Achievements and challenges. *Language, Culture and Curriculum*, 21, 1, 21–38.
Ortega, A., Amorrortu, E., Goirigolzarri, J. and Urla, J. (2016). *Euskal hiztun berriak: esperientziak, jarrerak eta identitateak*. Bilbao: University of Deusto and Bizkailab.
Ortega, A., Amorrortu, E., Goirigolzarri, J. and Urla, J. (2017). *Nuevos hablantes de euskera: experiencias, actitudes e identidades*. https://blogs.deusto.es/euskalgaiak/wp-content/uploads/2016/11/Euskal-hiztun-berriak-2016-Deustuko-Unibertsitatea.pdf.
Ortega, A., Urla, J., Amorrortu, E., Goirigolzarri, J. and Uranga, B. (2014). Nous parlants de basc: identitat i legitimitat. *Digithum*, 16, 6–7.
Ortega, A., Urla, J., Amorrortu, E., Goirigolzarri, J. and Uranga, B. (2015). Linguistic identity among new speakers of Basque. *International Journal of the Sociology of Language*, 231, 85–105.
Ortega-Llebaria, M., Vanrell, M. del Mar and Prieto, P. (2010). Catalan speakers' perception of word stress in unaccented contexts. *Journal of the Acoustic Society of America*, 127, 1, 462–71.

Padín, P. (2019). Neofalantes online, in Ramallo, F., Amorrortu, E. and Puigdevall, M., eds., *Neohablantes de lenguas minorizadas en el Estado español*. Madrid: Iberoamericana, pp. 147–64.

Pakir, A. (2009). English as a lingua franca: Analyzing research frameworks in international English, world Englishes, and ELF. *World Englishes*, 28, 2, 224–35.

Parlamento Vasco (2010). *Lenguas Minoritaria en la Administración*. Vitoria-Gasteiz: Parlamento Vasco.

Pastor, R. and María, A. (2018). Understanding bilingualism in Castilla-La Mancha: Emotional and moral stance taking in parental narratives. *Revista Española de Lingüística Aplicada/Spanish Journal of Applied Linguistics*, 31, 2, 578–604.

Patiño-Santos, A. (2018). 'No-one told me it would all be in Catalan!' Narratives and language ideologies in the Latin American community at school. *International Journal of Sociology of Language*, 250, 59–86.

Patiño-Santos, A. (2019). When language mixing is the norm: Documenting post-muda language choice in a state school in Barcelona. *International Journal of the Sociology of Language*, 257, 109–35.

Pavlenko, A. (2018). Superdiversity and why it isn't, in Breidach, S, Küster, L. and Schmenk, B. (eds.), *Sloganizations in Language Education Discourse*. Bristol: Multilingual Matters, pp. 142–68.

Peled, Y. (2018). Language barriers and epistemic injustice in healthcare settings. *Bioethics*, 32, 6, 360–7.

Peled, Y. and Bonotti, M. (2019). Sound reasoning: Why accent bias matters for democratic theory. *The Journal of Politics*, 81, 2, 411–25.

Pilar Perea, M. and Boix-Fuster, E., eds. (2020). *Llengua i dialectes: esperances per al català, el gallec i el basc*. Barcelona: Les Edicions de la Universitat de Barcelona.

Pons, E. (2019). 40 anys de legislació lingüística: balanç i reptes de future. *Revista de Llengua i Dret*, 72, 1–4.

Pons, E. (2020). Language law and language policies, in Argenter, J. and Ludtke, J., eds., *Manual of Catalan Linguistics*, 25. Berlin: De Gruyter, pp. 649–68.

Pradilla, M. A. (2011). *La Catalanofonia*: A community in search of linguistic normality, in Strubell, M. and Boix-Fuster, E., eds., *Democratic Policies for Language Revitalization: The Case of Catalan*. Basingstoke: Palgrave, pp. 17–56.

Puigdevall, M. (2014). Els nous parlants de llengües minoritàries: pertinences i legitimitats. *Digithum*, 16, 3–5.

Puigdevall, M. (2022) Voluntariat per la Llengua: Building social cohesion through language. In McLeod, W., Dunbar, R., Jones, K. and Walsh, J. (eds.), *Language, Policy and Territory*. London: Palgrave Macmillan, pp. 365–85.

Puigdevall, M. and Walsh, J. (2017). Speakerness: Subjectivities, Trajectories, Spaces. WG 8 Report (Period of Phase 2: April 2015 to September 2016). COST New Speakers Network.

Puigdevall, M., Colombo, A. and Pujolar, J. (2019). Espacios de adopción del catalán, una aproximación etnográfica a las mudas lingüísticas en Cataluña, in Ramallo, F., Amorrtu, E. and Puigdevall, M., eds., *Neohablantes de lenguas minorizadas en el Estado español*. Madrid: Iberoamericana, pp. 111–30.

Puigdevall, M. Pujolar, J. and Colombo, A. (2021) Linguistic safe spaces and stepping stones: Rethinking mudes to Catalan through the lens of space. *Journal of Multilingual and Multicultural Development*, 43, 1, 21–31.

Puigdevall, M., Walsh, J., Amorrortu, E. and Ortega, A. (2018). 'I'll be one of them': Linguistic *mudes* and new speakers in three minority language contexts. *Journal of Multilingual and Multicultural Development*, 39, 5, 445–57.
Pujolar, J. (2020a). Nous parlants: llengua i subjectivitat. *Treballs de Sociolingüística Catalana*, 30, 17–38.
Pujolar, J. (2020b). Migration in Catalonia: Language and diversity in the global era, in Argenter, J. and Ludtke, J., eds., *Manual of Catalan Linguistics*. Berlin: De Gruyter, pp. 723–38.
Pujolar, J. (2021). New speakers: New linguistic subjects, in Slavkov, N., ed., *The Changing Face of the 'Native Speaker': Perspectives from Multilingualism and Globalization*. Berlin: De Gruyter, pp. 71–103.
Pujolar, J., and Gonzàlez, I. (2013). Linguistic 'mudes' and the de-ethnicization of language choice in Catalonia. *International Journal of Bilingual Education and Bilingualism*, 16, 2, 138–52.
Pujolar, J. and O'Rourke, B., eds. (2019). *From New Speaker to Speaker: Outcomes, reflections and policy recommendations from COST Action IS1306 on New Speakers in a Multilingual Europe: Opportunities and Challenges*. Castell Newydd Emlyn: IAITH.
Pujolar, J. and O'Rourke, B. (2022). Theorizing the speaker and speakerness in applied linguistics. *Journal of Applied Linguistics and Professional Practice*, 16, 2, 207–31.
Pujolar, J. and Puigdevall, M. (2015). Linguistic mudes: How to become a new speaker in Catalonia. *International Journal of the Sociology of Language*, 231, 167–87.
Pujolar, J., Gonzàlez, I. and Martinez, R. (2010). Les mudes lingüístiques dels joves catalans [The linguistic 'mudes' of Catalan youth]. *Llengua i ús: revista tècnica de política lingüística*, 48, 65–75.
Querol Puig, E. and Strubell i Trueta, M., eds. (2009). *Llengua i reivindicacions nacionals a Catalunya*. Barcelona: Edtiorial UOC.
Ramallo, F. (2012). El gallego en la familia: entre la producción y la reproducción. *Caplletra*, 53, 167–91.
Ramallo, F. and O'Rourke, B. (2013). Competing ideologies of linguistic authority amongst new speakers in contemporary Galicia. *Language in Society*, 42, 3, 287–305.
Ramallo, F., Amorrortu, E. and Puigdevall, M. eds. (2019). *Neohablantes de lenguas minorizadas en el Estado español*. Madrid: Iberoamericana.
Recalde, F. M. (2000). Le parcours socioculturel du galician. Du Moyen Âge au XXe siècle. *Lengas*, 47, 11–38.
Relaño Pastor, A. M. (2017). Bilingual education and neoliberal CLIL practices, in Tollefson, J. W. and Pérez-Milans, M., eds., *The Oxford Handbook of Language Policy and Planning*. Oxford: Oxford University Press, pp. 505–25.
Reniu, M. (1995). El pla general de normalització lingüística: un projecte per a Tothom, *Revista de Llengua i Dret*, 23, Juliol. http://vlex.com/vid/pla-normalitzacio-projecte-per-tothom-77633053.
Richards, S. (2011). Demanding Theresa May's head on a plate solves nothing. *Independent*, 10 November.
Rodríguez, I. (2021). The role of social meaning in contact-induced variation among new speakers of Basque. *Journal of Sociolinguistics*, 25, 4, 533–56.
Rodríguez-Ordóñez, I. (2020). New speakers of Basque: A Basque-Spanish contact approach, in Lourdes Oñederra, M. and Igartua, I., eds., *Linguistic Minorities in Europe Online*. Berlin: De Gruyter.

Roger, G. and De Bres, J. (2017). Langues de France et Charte européenne des langues régionales et minoritaires: inventaire critique des arguments anti-ratification (2014–2015). *Sociolinguistic Studies*, 11, 1, 131–52.

Rooney, E. (2001). Language policy implementation: A DCAL's civil servant perspective, in Kirk, J.M. and Ó Baoill, D., eds., *Linguistic Politics*. Belfast: Cló Ollscoil na Banríona, pp. 55–60.

Sabaté-Dalmau, M. (2021). Hidden language 'battles' in the diaspora: Linguistic identities and ideologies towards home and host languages among Pakistanis in Barcelona. *Journal of Asian Pacific Communication*, 31, 2, 213–35.

Sabaté-Dalmau, M., Garrido, M. R. and Codó, E. (2017). Language-mediated services for migrants: Monolingualist institutional regimes and translinguistic user practices, in Canagarajah, S., ed., *The Routledge Handbook of Migration and Language*. London: Routledge, pp. 558–76.

Sainz, M., Perez, K. and Alonso, I. (2013). A look from several angles of language use in pupils: Reflections and forward-looking considerations, in Basque Government (ed.), *Talking Pupils: The Arrue Project 2011*. Vitoria-Gasteiz: Department of Education, Language Policy and Culture, pp. 291–9.

Sandberg, S., Ó Flatharta, P. and Williams, C. H. (2014). *From Act to Action: Implementing Language Legislation in Finland, Ireland and Wales*. Dublin: Fiontar, Dublin City University.

Savoie, D. J. (2013). *Whatever Happened to the Music Teacher?* Montreal: McGill–Queen's University Press.

Savoie, D. J. (2015). *What Is Government Good At? A Canadian Answer*. Montreal:

Saward, M. (2003). *Democracy*. Cambridge: Cambridge University Press.

Scottish Government (2015) *The Scottish Government Gaelic Language Plan: 2015–2020*. Edinburgh: Scottish Government.

Shaw, J. (1977). Bithidh iad a' moladh na Gàidhlig, ach 'sann anns a' Bheurla. *West Highland Free Press*, 23 September.

Shohamy, E. (2006). *Language Policy: Hidden Agendas and New Approaches*. Abingdon: Routledge.

Sierra, J. and Olaziregi, I. (1989). EIFE 2: Influence of factors on the learning of Basque. Eusko Jaurlaritzaren Argitalpen Zerbitzu Nagusia, Gasteiz.

Sierra, J. and Olaziregi, I. (1991). EIFE 3: Influence of factors on the learning of Basque. Eusko Jaurlaritzaren Argitalpen Zerbitzu Nagusia, Gasteiz.

Smith-Christmas, C. and Ó Murchadha, N. (2018). Reflections on new speaker research and future trajectories, in Smith-Christmas, C., Ó Murchadha, N., Hornsby, M. and Moriarty, M., eds., *New Speakers of Minority Languages: Linguistic Ideologies and Practices*. London: Palgrave Macmillan, pp. 283–8.

Solé, J. R. (1996). El concepte de llengua pròpia en el dret i en la normalització de l'idioma a Catalunya. *Revista de Llengua i Dret*, 26, 95–120.

Soler, J. and Darquennes, J. (2019a). Language policy and 'new speakers': An introduction to the thematic issue. *Language Policy*, 18, 4, 467–73.

Soler J. and Darquennes, J. (2019b). 'New speakers' and language policy research: Thematic and theoretical contributions to the field. *Language Policy*, 18, 4, 475–91.

Soler, J. and Marten, H. F. (2019). Resistance and adaptation for new speakers in educational institutions: Two tales from Estonia. *Language Policy*, 18, 4, 553–72.

Spolsky, B. (2004). *Language Policy*. Cambridge: Cambridge University Press.
Spolsky, B. (2009). *Language Management*. Cambridge: Cambridge University Press.
Spotti, M., Kroon, S. and Li, J. (2019). New speakers of new and old languages: An investigation into the gap between language practices and language policy. *Language Policy*, 18, 4, 535–51.
Strubell, M. (1997). How to preserve and strengthen minority languages: A Catherine wheel model. *IATEFL Newsletter*, Slovenian branch, 7–9.
Strubell, M. and Boix-Fuster, E., eds. (2011). *Democratic Policies for Language Revitalization: The Case of Catalan*. Basingstoke: Palgrave.
StatsWales (2021). *Number of pupils in primary, middle and secondary school classes by local authority and Welsh category*. Cardiff: Welsh Government.
Subirats, J., ed. (2002). *Gobierno local y educación. La importancia del territorio y la comunidad en el papel de la escuela*. Barcelona: Ariel.
Taylor, C. (1991). *The Malaise of Modernity*. Concord: Anansi.
Taylor, C. (2016). *The Language Animal: The Full Shape of the Human Linguistic Capacity*. Boston, MA: Belknap Press.
Thaler, R. and Sunstein, C. (2008). *Nudge: Improving Decisions About Health, Wealth and Happiness*. New Haven, CT: Yale University Press.
Thomas, H. S. (2010). *Brwydr i Baradwys?* Caerdydd: Gwasg Prifysgol Cymru.
Thomas, H. S. and Williams, C. H., eds. (2013). *Parents, Personalities and Power: Welsh-medium schools in South-East Wales*. Cardiff: University of Wales Press.
Tollefson, J. W. (2015). Language education policy in late modernity: Insights from situated approaches – commentary. *Language Policy*, 14, 2, 183–9.
Tollefson, J. W. (2015b). Historical-structural analysis, in Hult, F. and Johnson, D., eds., *Research Methods in Language Policy and Planning: A Practical Guide*. Malden, MA: Wiley, pp. 140–51.
UK Government (2004). *Strategy Survival Guide*. Cabinet Office. London: HMSO. https://odi.org/documents/1087/7270.pdf.
UK Government (2010). Constitutional Reform and Governance Act 2010. London: HMSO. www.legislation.gov.uk/ukpga/2010/25/contents.
Urla, J. (2012). *Reclaiming Basque: Language, Nation and Cultural Activism*. Reno, NV: University of Nevada Press.
Urla, J., Amorrortu, E., Ortega, A. and Goirigolzarri, J. (2017) Basque standardization and the new speaker: Political praxis and the shifting dynamics of authority and value, in. Lane, P. M. J. and Costa, J (eds)., *Standardizing Minority Languages: Competing Ideologies of Authority and Authenticity in the Global Periphery*. London: Routledge, pp. 24–46.
Urla, J., Amorrortu, E., Ortega, A., Goirigolzarri, J. and Uranga, B. (2016). Authenticity and linguistic variety among new speakers of Basque, in Ferreir, V. and Bouda, B., eds., *Language Documentation and Conservation in Europe*. Honolulu, HI: University of Hawai'i Press, pp. 1–12.
Urrutia, I. (2005). *Derechos lingüísticos y Euskera en el sistema educativo*. Iruña: LETE argitaletxea.
Vandellós, J. A. (1935). *Catalunya, poble decadent*. Barcelona: Biblioteca Catalana d'Autors Independents.
Vernet, J., Pons, E., Pou, A., Solé, J. R. and Pla, A. M. (2003). *Dret lingüístic*. Valls: Cossetània Edicions.

Walsh, J. (2002). *Díchoimisiúnú Teanga: Coimisiún na Gaeltachta 1926*. Dublin: Cois Life.
Walsh, J. (2012). *Contests and Contexts: The Irish Language and Ireland's Socio-Economic Development*. Bern: Peter Lang.
Walsh, J. (2015). Nuachainteoirí Gaeilge – in Éirinn agus thar lear, in de Mórdha, M., ed., *Ceiliúradh an Bhlascaoid 18: Saibhreas agus Dán na Teanga*. Dublin: Coiscéim, pp. 49–63.
Walsh, J. (2017). Enactments concerning the Irish language, 1922–2016. *Dublin University Law Journal*, 39, 2, 449–66.
Walsh, J. (2019). The role of emotions and positionality in the trajectories of 'new speakers' of Irish. *International Journal of Bilingualism*, 23, 1, 221–35.
Walsh, J. (2021). The governance of Irish in the neoliberal age: The retreat of the state under the guise of partnership, in Lewis, H. and McLeod, W. (eds.), *Language Revitalisation and Social Transformation*. Basingstoke: Palgrave Macmillan, pp. 311–42.
Walsh, J. and McLeod, W. (2008). An overcoat wrapped around an invisible man? Language legislation and language revitalisation in Ireland. *Language Policy*, 7, 21–46.
Walsh, J. and Ní Dhúda, L. (2015). 'New speakers' of Irish in the United States: Practices and motivations. *Applied Linguistics Review*, 6, 2, 173–92.
Walsh, J. and Ó Muircheartaigh, P., eds. (2016). *Ag Siúl an Bhealaigh Mhóir: Aistí in ómós don Ollamh Nollaig Mac Congáil*. Dublin: Leabhair Comhar.
Walsh, J. and O'Rourke, B. (2014). Becoming a new speaker of Irish: Linguistic mudes throughout the life cycle. *Digithum*, 16, 67–74.
Walsh, J. and O'Rourke, B. (2015). *Mudes* teangeolaíocha agus nuachainteoirí na Gaeilge. *Comhar Taighde* (1). www.comhartaighde.com/eagrain/1/walsh-orourke/.
Walsh, J. and O'Rourke, B. (2016). *Ag tacú le 'nuachainteoirí': Ag tógáil Líonraí agus Pobal Gaeilge taobh amuigh den Ghaeltacht*. www.nspk.org.uk/images/TCD_Stakeholders_Final_Report.pdf.
Walsh, J. and O'Rourke, B. (2018a). Comparing 'new speakers' across language contexts: Mobility and motivations. *Journal of Multilingual and Multicultural Development*, 39, 5, 377–81.
Walsh, J. and O'Rourke, B. (2018b). *Supporting 'New Speakers': Building Irish Language Networks and Communities outside the Gaeltacht*. Edinburgh: COST New Speakers Network.
Walsh, J., O'Rourke, B. and Rowland, H. (2015). *Research Report on New Speakers of Irish*. Dublin: Foras na Gaeilge. www.forasnagaeilge.ie/wp-content/uploads/2015/10/New-speakers-of-Irish-report.pdf.
Webber, M. M. (1963). Order in diversity: Community without propinquity, in Wingo, L., ed., *Cities and Space: The Future Use of Urban Land*. Baltimore, MD: Johns Hopkins Press, pp. 23–56.
Webber, M. M. (1964). The urban place and the nonplace urban realm, in Webber, M. M., Dyckman, J. W., Foley, D. L., Guttenberg, A. Z., Wheaton, W. L. C. and Bauer Wurster, C., eds., *Metropolitan Area: Explorations into Urban Structure*. Philadelphia: University of Pennsylvania Press, pp. 79–153.
Weinrich, U. (1968). *Languages in Contact: Findings and Problems*. The Hague: Mouton.

Welsh Assembly Government (2003). *Iaith Pawb*. Cardiff: Welsh Assembly Government.
Welsh Government (2010). *Welsh-Medium Education Strategy (WMES)*. Cardiff: Welsh Government.
Welsh Government (2011). *A Living Language: A Language for Living*. Cardiff: Welsh Government.
Welsh Government (2013a). *Welsh Language Households and Transmission*. Cardiff: Welsh Government.
Welsh Government (2013b) *Written Statement – One Language for All: A Review of Welsh Second Language at Key Stages 3 and 4*. Cardiff: Welsh Government.
Welsh Government (2014a). *Policy Statement on the Welsh Language, A Living Language: A Language for Living – Moving Forward*. Cardiff: Welsh Government. https://gov.wales/welsh-language-strategy-2012-2017-moving-forward.
Welsh Government (2014b). *Teaching Tomorrow's Teachers: Final Report Prepared by Prof. J. Furlong*. Cardiff: Government of Wales.
Welsh Government (2014c). *Review of Welsh Second Language at Key Stages 3 and 4: Final Report of Task Group Chaired by Prof. S. Davies*. Cardiff: Welsh Government.
Welsh Government (2014d). *Response to Mentrau Iaith Report*. Cardiff: Welsh Government. http://gov.wales/topics/welshlanguage/publications/response-to-the-review-of-mentrau-iaith-and-aman-tawereport/?lang=en.
Welsh Government (2015a). *Successful Futures: The Donaldson Report*. Cardiff: Welsh Government.
Welsh Government (2015b). *More Than Just Words. Delivering the Active Offer Information Pack*. Cardiff: Welsh Government. https://socialcare.wales/cms_assets/file-uploads/150928activeoffersocialservicesen.pdf.
Welsh Government (2016). *Language, Work and Bilingual Services: Report of the Working Group on the Welsh Language and Local Government*. Cardiff: Welsh Government.
Welsh Government (2017a). *Written Statement – Summary Report of Responses to the Call for Evidence: Preparing for a Welsh Language Bill/ Summary of Responses*. 18 July. Cardiff: Welsh Government.
Welsh Government (2017b). *Written Statement – A White Paper on Proposals for a New Welsh Language Bill*. 19 July. Cardiff: Welsh Government.
Welsh Government (2017c). *White Paper Consultation Document. Striking the Right Balance: Proposals for a Welsh Language Bill*. 9 August. Cardiff: Welsh Government.
Welsh Government (2017d). *Cymraeg 2050: A Million Welsh Speakers*. Draft Consultative Document. Cardiff: Welsh Government. www.assembly.wales/laid%20documents/gen-ld11108/gen-ld11108-e.pdf.
Welsh Government (2017e). *Cymraeg 2050: A Million Welsh Speakers*. Cardiff: Welsh Government. https://gov.wales/sites/default/files/publications/2018-12/cymraeg-2050-welsh-language-strategy.pdf.
Welsh Government (2017f). *Welsh in Education Action Plan 2017–2021*. Cardiff: Welsh Government.
Welsh Government (2020a). *National Policy on Welsh Language Transmission and Use in Families*. Cardiff: Government of Wales.

Welsh Government (2020b). *Welsh Language Technology Action Plan: Progress Report 2020*. Cardiff: Welsh Government .

Welsh Government (2021). *Evaluation of the Welsh Language Sabbatical Scheme for Education Practitioners: Summary*. Cardiff: Welsh Government.

Welsh Government (2022a). *Guidance on School Categories According to Welsh-Medium Provision*. Cardiff: Welsh Government.

Welsh Government (2022b) *Welsh Language in Wales (Census 2021)*. Cardiff: Welsh Government.

Welsh Language Board (2010). *Annual Review 2009–2010*. Cardiff: The Welsh Language Board.

Welsh Language Commission (2021). *The Position of the Welsh Language 2016–20: Welsh Language Commissioner's 5-year Report*. Cardiff: Welsh Language Commission.

Wieviorka, M. (1997). ETA and Basque Political Violence, in Apter, D. E. (ed.), *The Legitimization of Violence*. London: Macmillan, pp. 292–349.

Williams, C. H. (1980). Language contact and language change in Wales, 1901–1971: A study in historical geolinguistics. *The Welsh History Review*, 10, 2, 207–38.

Williams, C. H. (1981). On culture space. *Etudes Celtiques*, 18, 273–96.

Williams, C. H. (1985). Conceived in bondage: Called unto liberty. *Progress in Human Geography*, 9, 3, 42–57.

Williams, C. H. (1991). Language planning and social change: Ecological speculations, in Marshall, D., ed., *Focus on Language Planning: Essays in Honour of Joshua A. Fishman*. Amsterdam: John Benjamins, pp. 53–74.

Williams, C. H. (1993). The European Community's lesser used languages. *Rivista Geografica Italiana*, 100, 2, 531–64.

Williams, C. H. (1994). *Called Unto Liberty: On Language and Nationalism*. Clevedon: Multilingual Matters.

Williams, C. H. (1996). Citizenship and minority cultures: Virile participants or dependent supplicants? in Lapierre, A. Smart, P. and Savard, P., eds., *Language, Culture and Values in Canada at the Dawn of the 21st Century*. Ottawa: Carleton University Press, pp. 155–84.

Williams, C. H., ed. (2000). *Language Revitalization: Policy and Planning in Wales*. Cardiff: University of Wales Press.

Williams, C. H. (2002). Geolinguistic representation, in Boudreau, A., Dubois, L., Maurais, J. and McConnel, G., eds., *L'Écologie des Langues: Mélanges William Mackey. Ecology of Languages: Homage to William Mackey*. Paris: L'Harmattan, pp. 211–36.

Williams, C. H. (2003). Language policy and planning issues in multicultural societies, in Larrivée, P. (ed.), *Linguistic Conflict and Language Laws: Understanding the Quebec Question*. London: Palgrave Macmillan, pp. 1–57.

Williams, C. H. (2004). Iaith Pawb: The doctrine of plenary inclusion. *Contemporary Wales*, 17, Summer, 1–27.

Williams, C. H. (2006). The role of para–governmental institutions in language planning. *Supreme Court Law Review*, 31, 61–83. Reprinted in Braën, F. and Le Bouthillier, Y. (eds.), *Language, Constitutionalism and Minorities/Langues, constitutionliasme et minorities*. Markham, ON: LexisNexis Butterworths, pp. 139–59.

Williams, C. H. (2007a). Els drets linguistics com a factor d'inclusió social. *Europa de les Naciones*, 62, 12–22.
Williams, C. H. (2007b). Applicar el mârqueting al gal-lès en un context ambivalent. *Noves SL: Revista de Sociolingüística*, Autumn–Winter, 1–13.
Williams, C. H. (2008). *Linguistic Minorities in Democratic Context*. Basingstoke: Palgrave Macmillan.
Williams, C. H. (2009). Foras na Gaeilge and Bwrdd yr Iaith Gymraeg: Yoked but not yet shackled. *Irish Studies Review*, 17, 1, 55–88.
Williams, C. H. (2010). Linguistic diversity and legislative Regimes, in Basque Parliament, *Lenguas Minoritaria en la Administración*. Vitoria-Gasteiz: Parlamento Vasco, pp. 23–50.
Williams, C. H. (2013a). *Minority Language Promotion, Protection and Regulation: The Mask of Piety*. Basingstoke: Palgrave Macmillan.
Williams, C. H. (2013b). Perfidious hope: The legislative turn in official language regimes. *Journal of Regional and Federal Studies*, 23, 1, 101–22.
Williams, C. H. (2013c). Reflections: Rapporteur's Presentation. International Conference on Language Rights, Dublin: Irish Language Commissioner, Fiontar and Cardiff University, 23–4 May.
Williams, C. H. (2014). The lightening veil: Language revitalization in Wales. *AREA, Review of Education*, 38, 1, 265–95.
Williams, C. H. (2015a). Cultural rights and democratization: Legislative devolution and the enactment of the official status of Welsh in Wales, in Urrutia, I., Massias, J.-P. and Irujo, X., eds., *Droits Culturels et Démocratisation/Cultural Rights and Democratisation*. Clermont-Ferrand: Institut Universitaire Varenne: Collection 'Kultura', pp. 183–203.
Williams, C. H. (2015b). New Perspectives and Challenges on Protecting Language Rights: Promoting Linguistic Pluralism. Rapporteur's Address to the Annual Conference of the International Association of Language Commissioners, University of Ottawa, 22 May 2015. http://languagecommissioners.org/documents/May_2015_IALC_Conference_report.pdf.
Williams, C. H. (2016). Recent Language Initiatives. COST New Speakers Network. www.nspk.org.uk/images/TCD_Stakeholders_Final_Report.pdf.
Williams, C. H. (2017a). *Whither Language Rights and Language Commissioners in the Mosaic of Mutual Influence?* Cardiff: International Association of Language Commissioners. www.languagecommissioners.org/research_corner/publications/whither_language_rights_and_commissioners_in_the_mosaic_of_mutual_influence.pdf.
Williams, C. H. (2017b). Policy review: Wake me up in 2050! Formulating language policy in Wales. *Languages, Society & Policy*. DOI: https://doi.org/10.17863/CAM.9802.
Williams, C. H. (2018). Assailed but not yet daunted, in MacLeod, M. and Smith-Christmas, C., eds., *Gaelic in Contemporary Scotland: The Revitalisation of an Endangered Language*. Edinburgh: Edinburgh University Press, pp. xiii–xv.
Williams, C. H. (2019a). Creative ambiguity in the service of language policy and new speakers. *Language Policy*, 18, 4, 593–608.
Williams, C. H. (2019b). The policy community and recommendations on new speakers, in O' Rourke, B. and Pujolar, J., eds., *From New Speaker to Speaker: Outcomes, Reflections and Policy Recommendations from COST Action IS1306 on*

New Speakers in a Multilingual Europe: Opportunities and Challenges. Castell Newydd Emlyn, Wales: IAITH, pp. 28–56.

Williams, C. H. (2021a). Forging hope in the company of cynics, in Lewis, H. and McLeod, W., eds., *Language Revitalisation and Social Transformation.* London: Palgrave Macmillan, pp. 363–80.

Williams, C. H. (2021b). Minority language revitalisation: European conundrums, in Boucher, D., ed., *Language, Culture and Colonialism.* Capetown: HRS Press.

Williams, C. H. (2021c). On the side of angels: Dignity and virtue in minority–majority relations, in Bufon, M., Malloy, T. and Williams, C. H, eds., *Societies and Cultures in Contact: Between Convergence and Divergence.* Bern: Peter Lang, pp. 35–65.

Williams, C.H. and Walsh, J. (2019). Minority language governance and regulation, in Hogan-Brun, G. and O' Rourke, B., eds., *Handbook on Minority Languages and Communities.* Basingstoke: Palgrave Macmillan, pp. 101–30.

Willliams, C. H., Dell'Aquila, V., Soler Carbonell, J. and Puigdevall i Serralvo, M. (2015). *La política lingüística a altres estats multilingües del Món.* Barcelona: UOC.

Williams, C. H., Evas, J., Mac Giolla Chriost, D., Williams, C.H. and Chwmni Sbectrwm (2014). *Adolygiad o Waith y Mentrau Iaith, Y Cynlluniau Gweithredu Iaith a Chynllun Hybu'r Gymraeg Aman Tawe / A Review of the Work of Mentrau Iaith, Language Action Plans and the Aman Tawe Language Promotion Scheme.* Caerdydd/Cardiff: Llywodraeth Cymru/Welsh Government.

Woolard, K. A. (1989). *Double Talk. Bilingualism and the Politics of Ethnicity in Catalonia.* Stanford, CA: Stanford University Press.

Woolard, K. A. (1998). Introduction: Language ideology as a field of inquiry, in Schieffelin, B. B., Woolard, K. A. and Kroskrity, P. V., eds., *Language Ideologies: Practice and Theory.* Oxford: Oxford University Press, pp. 3–47.

Woolard, K. A. (2008). Language and identity choice in Catalonia: The interplay of contrasting ideologies of linguistic authority, in Süselbeck, K., Mühlschlegel, U. and Masson, P., eds., *Lengua, nación e identidad: La regulación del plurilingüismo en España y América Latina.* Frankfurt am Main: Vervuert, pp. 303–23.

Woolard, K. A. (2016). *Singular and Plural: Ideologies of Linguistic Authority in 21st Century Catalonia.* Oxford: Oxford University Press.

Woolard, K. A. and Frekko, S. (2013). Catalan in the twenty-first century: Romantic publics and cosmopolitan communities. *International Journal of Bilingual Education and Bilingualism*, 16, 2, 129–37.

Xunta de Galicia (no date). Guide to the Education System in Galician. www.edu.xunta.es/ftpserver/portal/DXC/diversidade/educacion_guia_ingles.pdf.

Xunta de Galicia (2004). *Plan general de normalización lingüística.* Santiago: Xunta de Galicia.

Xunta de Galicia (2008). *Plan xeral de normalización da lingua galega.* Santiago: Xunta de Galicia.

Xunta de Galicia (2010). *INFORMACIÓN ESTADÍSTICA, Año 2010.* Santiago: Xunta de Galicia.

Zalbide, M. (1987). Basque Language Loyalism at the Beginning of the Century: Strengths and Failings. Donostia Second World Basque Conference, 30 August to 4 September.

Zalbide, M. (2000). Irakas-sistemaren hizkuntz normalkuntza: Nondik norakoaren ebaluazio- saio bat. *Eleria*, 5, 45–61.

Zalbide, M. (2007). *Proposanem metodologikoa*. Donostia: Euskaltzaindia.

Zalbide, M. and Cenoz, J. (2008) Bilingual education in the Basque Autonomous Community: Achievements and challenges. *Language, Culture and Curriculum*, 21, 5–20.

Zenker, O. (2013). *Irish/ness Is All Around As: Language Revivalism and the Culture of Ethnic Identity in Northern Ireland*. New York: Berghahn Books.

Zuckermann, G. (2020). *Revivalistics: From the Genesis of Israeli to Language Reclamation in Australia and Beyond*. New York: Oxford University Press.

Index

20-Year Strategy for the Irish Language
    2010–2030, 156
active offer of service, 74
adult learners, 1
ahobizi, 235
AI
    Artifical Intelligence, 50
Aldekoa, Jasone, 224
An Chomhairle um Oideachais Gaeltachta agus
    Gaelscolaíochta (COGG), 154, 188
An Garda Síochána, 210
Andorra, 212
Araba, 216
Arabic, 272
Ararteko,
    Basque Commissioner, 215
Argentina, 2
Argyll & Bute, 114
Arizmendiarrieta, José María, 217
Asturias, 212
asylum seekers, 32
Augustyaniak, Anna and Higham,
    Gwennan, 105
Australia, 2
authenticity, 16

BAC
    Basque Autonomous Community, 9, 212–245
Balearic Islands, 257
BAME, 28
Basque, 2
Basque Advisory Council, 242
Basque Bilingualism Decree of 1983, 223
Basque education, 222
Basque Government
    Vice-Ministry of Education, 227
    Vice-Ministry of Linguistic Policy, 227
    Vice-Ministry of Professional Training, 227
Basque National Party, 214
Basque Political Parties, 219
Basque-medium teaching, 223

BBC Alba, 330
belarriprest, 235
Belfast/Good Friday Agreement, 174
Bennett Institute, 13
    Cambridge University, 13
Berlin, Isaiah, 2
Bizkaia, 216
Black Lives Matter, 338
Boix, Emili, 289
Bonotti, Matteo and Peled, Yael, 48
Bòrd na Gàidhlig, 117, 118
boundaries, 8
breathing spaces, 128, 232
    Basque society, 232
British Empire, 110
British imperialism, 68
British-Irish Council, 93, 343
Broadcasting Acts, Scotland
    1990 and 1996, 112
Brooks, Simon, 66
bureaucracy, 304
Burgos Trial, 215

Caimbeul, Iain, 149
CAL (Coordinadora d'Associacions per la
    Llengua Catalana), 274
Cambridge University, 13
Canada, 2
    Action Plan, 12
    Official Language Strategies.
    Roadmap for Canada's Linguistic Duality,
    2008–2013
Canada Heritage, 312
Canolfannau Cymraeg, 38, 79, 317
capitalism, 215
Cardiff, 33
Cardiff University, 71
    Sabbatical Scheme, 102
Cardinal, Linda and Williams, Colin. H., 34
Castilian language, 261
Catalan, 2
    language skills and abilities, 260

Catalan for Adults, 264
  Girona, 264
Catalan Health System, 269
Catalan Language Consortium (CPNL),
  213, 265
Catalan language policy, 213
Catalan Ombudsman, 264
Catalan Parliament, 269
Catalan sociolinguistic networks, 257
Catalan teaching, 283
Catalonia, 9
  low birth rate, 255
Cenoz, Jasone, 38
Cenoz, Jasone and Gorter, Durk, 232
Census of Catalonia 2016, 27
Census, Welsh Language, 54
Census in Wales 2016, 83
Centre for Geopolitics
  Cambridge University, 314
Centre Internacional Escarré per a les Minories Ètniques i les Nacions, 305
Channel Islands, 9
childhood, 3
children, 25
Children's Rights Impact Assessment, 92
Chile, 69
China
  Catalan residents born in China, 19
Chinese-speaking territories, 272
CIEMEN, 305
City of Edinburgh Council Area, 114
Civil Service
  Ireland, 178
  UK, 320
  Wales, 90
civil society
  Basque, 326
  Catalonia, 27
  Wales, 96
Clì Gàidhlig, 134
Climate Change
  Wales, 15
Climate Change (Emissions Reduction Targets) (Scotland) Act 2019., 125
Climate Change Plan
  Scotland, 125
Coast Guard
  UK, 118
code switching, 244
COGG (An Chomhairle um Oideachas Gaeltachta agus Gaelscolaíochta), 159
Coimisinéir Teanga, 164
Columbia, 19
Comann nam Pàrant, 121
Comhairle na Gaelscolaíochta, 184

Comhairle na Gàidhlig, 145
Comhairle nan Eilean Siar, 122
Common European Framework of Reference for Languages (CEFR), 45, 163
community development, 37, 77, 151
community language planning
  Wales, 75
community socialisation, 54
Comunn na Gàidhlig, 190, 330
Congo, 19
Connaught voice, 203
Conradh na Gaeilge, 176, 180, 188
Consorci per a la Normalització Lingüística, x, 277, 279, 327
Constitutional Reform and Governance Act 2010., 320
Cornwall, 9
corpus planning
  Basque, 218
COST New Speakers Network, 6, 7, 31, 285
Council of Europe
  European Language Portfolio, 45
Covid-19 pandemic, 14
Cronin, Michael A., 211
Crystal, David, 22
cultural identity, 227
cultural pluralism, 309
Cunliffe, Daniel, 40
curriculum design, 42
curriculum development, 4
curriculum, national, 61
CYDAG, 58
Cylch Meithrin, 72
Cymdeithas yr Iaith Gymraeg, 60, 107
Cymraeg 2050, 58, 59, 65, 69, 73–98, 108
  Welsh Language Strategy, 58
Cymuned, 58
Cymwysterau Cymru, 66
Czech Republic, 300

Dáil Éireann, 207
Darquennes, Jeroen, 223
Davies, Alun, 84
Davies, Gwenllian Lansdown, 74
Davies, Lowri, 102
Davies, W. D., 24
DCU (Dublin City University), 188
decarbonisation, 125
democracy
  deliberative, 110
  science, 13
democracy,
  Spanish transition, 2
demographic change, 131
demographic transitions, 29

Department of Culture
  Catalonia, 290
Department of Culture, Heritage and the
  Gaeltacht, 203
development, 294
devolution
  Wales, 87
DGPL, 269–275, 285
diaspora
  Honduran, 280
dictatorship
  Franco, 214
dictionaries, 174
digital space, 34
diglossia
  Basque, 244
dignity, 32
Dion, Stéphane, 311
Directorate General of Multilingualism
  European Union, 147
disadvantage, 295
discourse, official, 6
discourse, policy, 26
discourse, public, 8
discrimination, 258
divergence, political, 2
Donegal, County, 177
Drakeford, Mark
  First Minister of Wales, 97
Dublin, 87
Dublin City University, 165
Dunbar, Robert, 87, 110, 117, 122, 131–149
Dunmore, Stuart, 112
Dutch language, 39
Dyfodol i'r Gymraeg, 108
Dyfodol i'r Iaith, 72
Dyslexia Association of Ireland, 187

EAJ–PNV
  Basque political party, 219
Early Childhood Education and Care, 161
ECEC
  Ireland, 329
ecologists, 49
Edinburgh, 117
Education (Scotland) Act 2016, 128
Egypt, 19
Eilean Siar Council, 114
El Hachmi, Najat, 292
ELEN, 321
ÈLIA (Estratègies de Llengua
  i Aprenentatge), 283
e–literacy, 44
Emmarca't, 267
emotions, 212

employment, 39
endangered languages, 94
English in Canada, 2, 311
English, language, 100
entrepreneurial companies, 217
environment, 8
environment, home, 5
environmentalists, 211
equality, 43
Equality Impact Assessment, 92
Erasmus Scheme, 320
Eretz Israel, 317
Eroski, 217
Ertzaintza,
  BAC police force, 217
Esquerra Republicana (ERC), 271
Estonia, 300
Estonian Language Foundation, 11
Ethnic communities, 68
ethnocultural, 146
ethnography, 26
ethnolinguistic, 21
EU Directorate of Education, 321
EU (European Union), 258, 320
European Bureau for Lesser Used
  Languages, 93
European Charter for Regional or Minority
  Languages, 111
European Commission, 230
European Parliament, 94
Euskadi, 105
Euskal Irrati Telebista –(EITB), 217
euskaldunzaharra
  Basque native speaker, 240
Euskara 21. Bases for Language Policy, 242
Euskaraldia initiative, 234
Euskaraldia: 11 days in Euskera, 27
Evans, Gwynfor, 60

faith and religion, 41
Finland, 9, 300
First Strategic Plan (2016–2019)
  Basque Autonomous Community, 249
Foras na Gaeilge, 154, 173, 194–198, 200–203
Franco
  General Francisco Franco Bahamonde, 2
French in Canada, 311
FUEN, 321

Gael Linn, 188
Gaelchultúr, 188
Gaelic, 5
Gaelic Crisis in the Vernacular
  Community, 149
Gaelic in Scotland, 110

Index 379

Gaelic language, 26
Gaelic Language (Scotland) Act 2005, 116
Gaelic Language Plans, 118, 132–133, 149, 330
Gaelic Medium Education (GME), 118
Gaelic speaking territories, 124
Gaeloideachas, 160, 187
Gaelscoileanna, 160
Gaeltacht communities, 157
Gaeltacht education, 181
Gaeltacht Education Policy, 159
Gaeltacht schools, 158, 159, 163, 164
Gaeltacht Service Towns, 194
Gàidhealtachd, 111
Gàidhealtachd communities, 139
Galicia, 9, 18, 293
Galicia Organic Law of Education 2/2006, 297
General Register Office
    Scottish Statistics, 112
geolinguistic areas, 117
geolinguistic circumstances, 131
geolinguistic contexts, 75
Geolinguistics, 23
Germany, 269
Gipuzkoa, 216
Gipuzkoan dialect, 240
Girona, 278
Glasgow City, 114
global pandemic, 1
globalisation, 14
Goirigolzarri Garaizar, Jone, 217
Gorter, Durk, 220
governance, 18
Government of Ireland
    Department of Education, 165
Government of Wales Act 1998, 60
Green Party
    Ireland, 173
Gruffudd, Heini, 38
Gruffydd, Ifor, 66
Gutman, Amy, 341
Gwynedd County Council, 122

Harper, Stephen, 12
heartland, 14
Hebrew, 317
hegemonic languages, 4
hegemonic states, 39
Henrician Acts of Union 1536 and 1542, 53
Heritage Speakers, 311
hierarchy, 15
Higham, Gwennan, 19
Highland, 114
Highland Council, 114, 141
holistic thought and practice, 211
Houses of the Oireachtas, 164

housing, 34
housing regulations, 332
hybridity, 2

Iaith Fyw: Iaith Byw, 96
    Welsh Language Strategy, 91
Iaith Gwaith (Working Welsh), 69
Iaith Pawb, 96
Iberdrola, 217
ikastolas, 33
immersion education in Ireland, 164
immigrants
    Canada, 311
    Catalonia, 213
immigration policy
    The Netherlands, 45
Indigenous people, 315
    Basque Autonomous Community, 215
industrialisation
    Scotland, 142
Inland Revenue
    UK, 118
Institut Ramon Llull, 265, 279
Institute for Catalan Studies, 305
intergenerational language transmission, 69, 261
intermarriage, 314
internal colonialism, 19
International Association of Language
    Commissioners, 321
Inverness, 114
Ireland, 2
    Official Languages Act 2003 (OLA), 155
Ireland, 9
Irish government, 155
Irish language networks, 178
Irish language, 86
Irish-medium education, 161, 165–167,
    170–176, 180–187, 199, 307, 318, 329
Irish Language Services, 171
Isle of Man, 9
Israel, 317
Itxaso Rodríguez-Ordóñez, 333

Jaffe, Alexandra, 22
Japanese
    language, 321
Jones, Carwyn, 89
    First Minister of Wales, 97
Jones, Kathryn, viii
Jones, Meirion P, 55
Joyal, Serge, 312
Judaism, 24

Kasares, Paula, 246
Key Research Questions, 7

380   Index

L2 learners, 16, 67, 146, 164–168, 186, 195, 230, 270, 307, 318
land use planning system, 108
language acquisition, 69
　Basque, 241
language development, 322
language learners, viii
language legislation, 58
　Catalan, 264
language management, 15
language planning, 5
　Ireland, 199
language planning processes, viii
language revitalisation, 86, 214
　Wales, 58
language rights
　Catalonia, 289
　Northern Ireland, 300
language shift
　Galicia, 294
language skills, 12
　Wales, 58
language transmission, 316
Law of Normalization, 1982, 213
Lenin, Vladimir I., 306
Lessard, Christine, 312
lesser –used languages, 49
LGBTQI, 71
Liberal Party of Canada, 311
linguistic ecology, 49
linguistic equality, 48
linguistic justice, 48
literacy
　Basque, 214
　Wales, 68
local government, 34
local regulations, 28
Los Angeles, 2
Low Carbon Scotland, 124

Mac Donnacha, Joe, 158
Mac Giolla Chriost, Diarmait, 87, 154
MacKenna, Deirdre, 315
Madrid, 2
Marquand, David, 77, 341
Mary Immaculate College, 184
McLeod, Wilson, 18, 21, 44, 112–114, 117–122, 128, 133–140, 143–152, 171, 224
McLeod, Wilson and O'Rourke, Bernadette, 18
Mentrau Iaith, 75–79, 95, 307, 317
methodology, 8
methodology, evaluation
　Basque, 236
Microsoft

　Ireland, 175
　Wales, 302
Middle East, 255
migrants, viii
migrants in Wales
　refugees, asylum seekers, 105
Miles, Jeremy, 69
minority language, 69
minority language communities, 1
Mondragon Cooperative Enterprises, 217
Morgan, Eluned, 93
Morgan, William, 53
Morris, Steven, 38
mother tongue, 5
muda
　Irish, 206
mudes, 8, 287
Mudiad Meithrin, 72–77
multilingualism, 29
Munster Irish, 203
mutual respect, 41

National Assembly
　Wales, 60
national curriculum,
　Wales, 60
National Eisteddfod, 54, 80
National Gaelic Language Plan, 117
Navarre, 9, 216, 245
Navarre Regional Law 18/1986 on Euskera, 246
NDLP, 321
neofalante, 20, 294
Nesta: The Innovation Foundation, 13
Netherlands, the, 44
Network for the Promotion of Linguistic Diversity (NPLD), 93
New Canadians, 311
New Englishes, 5
new speaker, 1
New Zealand, 20, 129
Ni Bhroin, Ciara, 166
non-Catalan speaking homes, 270
Nordic Council, 343
Northern Ireland, 300
Northern Ireland Assembly, 174
Nova Scotia, 143
　Office of Gaelic Affairs, 144
NPLD (Network for the Promotion of Language Diversity), 93
nuclear power, 332
Nudge theory, 11

Ó Cuirreáin, Seán, 190, 207
Ó Domhnaill, Rónán, 172

Ó Flatharta, Peadar, 163
Ó Giollagáin, Conchúr, 149
Ó Giollagáin, Conchúr and Caimbeul, Iain, 149
O' Rourke, Bernadette, 1, 4, 6, 16–19, 201, 299, 306, 333
O'Rourke, Bernadette and Pujolar, Joan, 4
O'Rourke, Bernadette and Walsh, John, 1
Occitan language, 258
Ofercat, 267
Office of the Commissioner of Official Languages
  Canada, ix
Official Language Policies, 1
Official Language Strategies, 9
Official Languages (Amendment) Bill, 2019
  Ireland, 207
Official Languages Act, 1969, 312
  Canada, 511–15
Official Languages Act, 2003
  Ireland, 203
Òmnium Cultural, 274
on–line teaching, 4
Optimot
  Catalan language enquiries, 265
Ortega. Ana, 239
Osakidetza,
  Basque Health Service, 217
Outer Hebrides, 131
out-migration
  Wales, 100

Pamplona, 220
Parla Cat, 279
Partido Socialista de Navarra (PSN), 249
Patagonia, 75
People's Party (PP), 294
peripherality, 157
Plaid Cymru, 59, 300
Plan General de Promoción del Uso del Euskera, 218
Policy Community, 306
policy environment, 8
Policy on Gaeltacht Education, 2017–2022, 158
policy recommendations, 3, 325
Polish, 166
political assimilation, 53
political autonomy, 214
Popinjays, 31
Portugal, 69, 269
Post Office
  UK, 118
Previn, Andre, 2
Project Ireland 2040, 178
PSE–EE
  Basque political party, 219
public services, 28
Public University of Navarra, 246
Puigdemont, Carles, 257
Puigdevall i Serralvo, Maite, 4, 19, 21, 35, 72, 201, 212, 278–290, 333
Pujolar, Joan, 4, 8, 16, 21, 35, 72, 116, 212, 254–268, 285, 297, 333
Pujolar, Joan and Puigdevall, Maite, 8, 35
Pujolar, Joan and O'Rourke, Bernadette, 16

racial linguistics, 1
radicalism, 297
Rae, Bob, 311
Ramallo, Fernando, 212
refugees, viii
regional development, 125
Regulatory Impact Assessment, 92
Relationships and Sexuality Education, 68
Religious Education, 68
Responsibility to Protect (R2P), 314
Roman Catholicism, 116
Rooney, Edward, 322
Royal Academy of the Basque Language, 217
RTÉ Raidió na Gaeltachta (RnaG), 157, 167

Sabhal Mòr Ostaig, 134
safe spaces, 24, 37
Sardinia, 212
Saward, Michael, 339
Scale and hierarchy, 37
Scéim Phobail Gaeilge, 194
school environment, 198
Scotland, 9
Scotland Act, 1998, 111
Scotland's Census 2011, 112
Scottish Government
  Gaelic Language Policy, 148
Scottish Government Language Plan 2015–2020, 118
Scottish Parliament, 110, 117
second language acquisition, 20
Second Strategic Plan (2020–2027), Basque Autonomous Community, 249
Secretaria de Política Lingüística de la Generalitat de Catalunya, 258, 268–285
self-perception, 23
Sianel Pedwar Cymru (S4 C), 58
Sindic de Greuges de Catalunya, 264
Sinn Fein, 300
Skye and Tiree, 114
slavery, 68
social cohesion, 20
social media, 120

social networking, 39
Soillse, 123
Soler, Joseph and Darquennes, Jeroen, 4
Soziolinguistika Klusterra, 236
Spanish Civil War, 2, 254
Spanish Constitutional Court, 275
Spanish Courts, 275
Spanish language, 254
Spanish government, 254
Sparsely Populated Areas of Scotland, 151
Special Educational Needs, 185
SPL, 269
Spolsky, Bernard, 307
stakeholders, 10
Statute of Autonomy of Catalonia, 258
statutory education system, 1
Strategic Plan, 2008–11
  Ireland, 161
Strubell, Michael, 289
Sweden, 69

Tardif, Claudette, 312
Taylor, Charles, 22, 29
teaching methodology
  Wales, 61
Teastas Eorpach na Gaeilge, 163
Technical Advice Note (TAN), 332
Termcat, the Catalan Terminological
  Centre, 265
territory, 24
TG4 television channel, 157
Tha Boord o Ulster-Scotch, 174
Tilburg, 41
Together for Catalonia (JxCat), 271
translanguaging, 1
translanguaging spaces, 232
translation, 53
Tremblay, Mark, 312
Trudeau, Justin, 311
TV3 Katalonski, 290

Udaltop, 235
Údarás na Gaeltachta, 178, 197
UK Emission Trading Scheme (UK ETS), 125
UK government, 90
Ulster voice, 203
UN (United Nations), 320, 343
Universitat Oberta de Catalunya, UOC, 286
University of Barcelona, 292
University of the Basque Country, 247
University of the Highlands and Islands
  (UHI), 149

USA, 2
Urdd Gobaith Cymru, 76

Valencia, 257
vocabulary, 37
Voluntariat per la Llengua, 9, 104, 266, 277
voluntary sector, 174

Wales, 2, 9
  new curriculum, 68
Walsh, John, 1, 19, 21, 85–88, 153–160,
  167–178, 189–93, 197–203, 204, 221
warfare, 314
Webber, Melvin, 23
Welsh, 5
Welsh for Adults
  Dysgu Cymraeg, 60
Welsh Government, 87
Welsh Government's Well-Being of Future
  Generations (Wales) Act 2015, 15
Welsh in Education Strategic Plans, 62
Welsh Language (Wales) Measure 2011,
  59, 100
Welsh Language Act 1993, 117
Welsh Language Act 1967, 60
Welsh Language Board, 55, 80, 87
Welsh Language Commissioner, 59
Welsh Language Division, 72
Welsh Language Impact Assessment, 92
Welsh Language Rights Day, 69
Welsh Language Standards, 59
Welsh Language Strategy, 82
Welsh Office, 60
Welsh Refugee Council, 106
Welsh speaking community, 55
Welsh-medium / bilingual education in
  Wales, 64
Western Isles, 114
Western Isles Health Board, 122
Westminster Parliament, 117
Williams, Colin H. and Walsh, John, 205
Woolard, Kathryn, 22
workplace, 46

XERREM, 274
Xunta de Galicia, 11

Y Fro Gymraeg (Welsh Heartland), 202
Ysgolion Cymraeg, 33

Zalbide, Mikel, 244
Zalbide, Mikel and Cenoz, Jasone, 223

For EU product safety concerns, contact us at Calle de José Abascal, 56–1°,
28003 Madrid, Spain or eugpsr@cambridge.org.

www.ingramcontent.com/pod-product-compliance
Ingram Content Group UK Ltd.
Pitfield, Milton Keynes, MK11 3LW, UK
UKHW040056310825
462435UK00019B/406